The Ultimate Instant Pot Cookbook

1001 Easy, Healthy and Flavorful Recipes For Every Model of
Instant Pot And for both Beginners and Advanced Users

Gloria S. Saul

Table of Content

Chapter 7 Fish and Seafood 50

Chapter 8 Pork, Beef, and Lamb 69

Chapter 9 Poultry 95

Chapter 10 Soups, Stews, and Chilies 115

Chapter 11 Appetizers and Sides .137

Chapter 1: The Basics of the Instant Pot

Daily Usage and Maintenance for the Instant Pot

1. First unplug the device and let it cool down before cleaning it.

2. The dishwasher can be used for cleaning the inner pot, lid, steam rack, and sealing ring. The cooker base should not be placed in the dishwasher.

3. Use a damp cloth for cleaning the outer part of the Instant Pot.

4. Use non-abrasive scrubbers for cleaning every part.

5. Use vinegar to clean any stains on the bottom of the inner pot. Let the vinegar sit for a few minutes and wipe with a damp sponge before rinsing off.

6. Check for any food debris in the float valve or release valve. Debris will prevent the Instant Pot from allowing pressure cooking.

7. Clean the anti-block shield from underneath the lid after every use of the device. Use warm water with dish soap and clean off any food splatters.

8. The silicone sealing rings should be allowed to dry before inserting it back into the lid. Check for any damage to the sealing ring before using it. The ring is essential for the device to function properly and should immediately be replaced if there is any damage. Make sure it is secured in place before you cook anything in the Instant Pot.

9. The condensation collector can be cleaned periodically. Hand wash it and let it dry before replacing back inside the Instant Pot.

Functions of the Instant Pot

The Instant Pot has many functions and it is very easy to use. Just use the instruction manual to get a hang of the different symbols on the pot. The following are some of the different functions the Instant Pot can perform:

- Pressure cook
- Steam
- Slow cook
- Warm
- Bake
- Sterilize
- Sauté or sear

You can use different functions to cook many different kinds of delicious keto meals for you and your family.

Pressure/Steam Releases

Pressure-cooking is a great way to prepare many dishes. It helps in retaining nutrition in the food since the cooking time is reduced. The longer you cook, the more nutrition is lost from the food. Pressure-cooking also helps to retain vitamin C and B in the food. It also helps in killing pathogens. Food may often contain some bacteria or other microorganisms that can harm your health. Pressure-cooking helps in getting rid of these. Food is also cooked in a lot less time as compared to some other types of cooking. It makes food a lot more flavorful as well since it infuses the food with flavor under pressure. Pressure-cooking is a great way to meal prep too.

Chapter 2 Instant Pot Cooking Pantry List

You are now ready to get started with the cooking process! As you prepare to enjoy all of the benefits of your Instant Pot, keep these tips and tricks in mind. It is a wonderfully simple appliance to use once you get the hang of it. You will appreciate its convenience and ease as you experiment with different recipes and cuisines. When stocking your pantry, consider the following staple items to keep on hand. They will benefit you in many dishes, allowing you to create wonderful and flavorful meals.

Broth Concentrates/Bone Broth/Bouillon Cubes

One of the main uses of these ingredients is to create flavorful soups, broths, and sauces. Any great soup or stew needs to have a flavorful base. The ingredients you add to it become secondary. You can keep a variety of these products in your pantry, as they do not expire very quickly if they are unopened. Keep in mind that you can also use them to flavor foods that are not liquid-based, such as rice, pasta, potatoes, and meats.

Curry Paste

Using curry paste while you cook is sure to give any food a burst of flavor. You can add it to soups for a quick boost of seasoning in your meal. Its most common use, however, is in curries and stews. You don't have to stick to these traditional uses, though. Add it to noodles, salad dressings, and seafood—it makes a nice flavorful addition to nearly any meal.

Dried Fruits and Vegetables

Because your Instant Pot relies on steam to cook your food, using dried fruits and vegetables is a smart decision. You can keep them in stock in your pantry without worrying about them going bad. The steam heats them perfectly, providing you with tender ingredients that add a flavorful addition to your meals. Sometimes, using fresh fruits and veggies is less favorable because they might get soggy or mushy while cooking in the steam.

Grains and Beans

Not only do they taste great, but grains and beans are great for you. When you are making anything that needs a little bit more nutritional value, adding some grains or beans will prove to be beneficial. There are countless varieties of each one, so you can choose some of your favorites to always keep stocked up in your pantry. Grains and beans are so great because they do not just belong to one type of cuisine. They are universal ingredients.

Tomato Paste

Generally used to thicken and enrich tomato sauces, tomato paste can also be used to flavor other semi-liquid meals, such as stews and soups. Because the flavor is not very strong, tomato paste is suitable for many different dishes. It is meant to elevate the flavors of your meal, even if you are not creating an Italian classic. You will see that tomato paste will become a staple item as you work with your Instant Pot more.

Worcestershire Sauce

This is a very flavorful sauce that is unknowingly used in many of your favorite meals. It is added to Caesar salad dressing, cocktail sauce, and many barbeque sauces. Keeping it handy will give you the option to add a necessary boost of flavor to your dishes. It doesn't take much because it is so potent, so you shouldn't have to purchase a new bottle very frequently.

Cornstarch

A thickening agent, cornstarch is a very useful ingredient when you are using an Instant Pot to cook. Whether you are making a soup, gravy, custard, or other semi-liquid meal, you can always add cornstarch for extra thickness. It is sometimes preferred over flour because it creates a flavorless and translucent option for your meals. Many Instant Pot recipes will call for cornstarch, so it is best to always keep some in your pantry just in case.

Cream Cheese

Cream cheese makes a nice addition to many dishes. It provides a creamy and delicious flavor that gives comfort food its feeling. You can even add it to your scrambled eggs, polenta, and mac and cheese. There are no rules when it comes to how you'd like to use cream cheese. Anything that needs to be a little more flavorful and creamy will benefit from its addition to the recipe.

Garlic

Not only is garlic very flavorful, but it is also healthy for your heart. Almost any recipe that you make can benefit from the addition of one or two cloves of garlic. When you let it cook for a prolonged period of time, the flavors come out boldly. Adding garlic to your dishes will give them a nice touch and add to their wonderful flavors. It even brings out the natural flavors of the other ingredients you use.

Lemons and Limes

Two zesty fruits, and they both make great additions to your dishes. Whether you use slices of lemons and limes to compliment your meals, or you extract their juices or zest, both of them come in handy while cooking savory and sweet foods. For a quick way to add flavor to your Instant Pot creation, make sure that you always have some in your house.

Below you will find a list of recommended staples to stock your pantry with, but please, don't buy it if you know you won't use it. Change the list to go with recipes that you like to cook often.

- Variety of herbs and spices
- Cooking pastes
- Broth/Bouillon
- Flour
- Cornstarch
- Baking powder
- Sesame seeds
- Sugar (or a sugar substitute)
- Sauces and condiments
- Apple cider vinegar
- Balsamic vinegar
- Vinegar
- Cooking wine
- Olive oil
- Sesame oil
- Vegetable or canola oil
- Coconut milk
- Heavy cream (Half-and-half if you prefer)
- Butter
- Spreadable Cheese
- Cream Cheese
- Cheese

Chapter 3 Complimentary Kitchen Utensils

If you plan on immersing yourself into Instant Pot cooking completely, you may need to kit your kitchen out a bit more. Recipes will usually tell you when you need a specific tool you may not already have in your kitchen. So, again, there's no need to rush out and buy all the utensils you can think of.

Instant Pots are supposed to make your life easier, not cause stress because you blew your budget on a set of specialized spoons. I do suggest you invest in some silicone or wooden utensils. They will prolong the shiny, new look of your inner pot, whereas metal instruments will cause unsightly scratch marks.

Still, I will list some implements that I recommend you get if you think they'll add value to the cooking process.

- Silicone, heat-resistant mitts to protect your hands.

- Extra inner pot. This is especially helpful if you are one to meal prep over weekends. You can cover the one inner pot and place it in the fridge, while you make something else in the other.

- Extra silicone rings. As mentioned earlier in this book, silicone rings absorb the odor of strong foods. Although there are ways to get rid of the smell, I prefer having a different ring for savory, seafood, and sweet dishes. These rings also need replacing, and I find that having one on hand is much better than frantically rushing out to get a new one.

- Kitchen thermometers come in handy if you want to see if the meat is cooked, but it is essential if you plan on using your Instant Pot to make yogurt and sweets like caramel or fudge.

- An immersion blender to remove any lumps from sauces and gravies or to puree fruits and vegetables. Using this small handheld appliance is quick and clean compared to a countertop blender.

- Bowls, pans, and dishes small enough to fit inside your cooker if you plan on cooking pot-in-pot.

- A steamer basket to steam veggies.

- Fat separator. A vital tool if you're trying to cut back on your fat consumption. Since pressure cooking tends to extract a lot of fat from meats, you may want to strain the fat from homemade broths and other cooking liquid.

Don't forget about measuring cups and spoons, strainers, potato mashers, handheld mixers, food processors, and enough bowls to mix in. But I am sure you already have all these; they are common-place in most kitchens.

Chapter 4 Ultimate Tips to Instant Pot Success

Using an Instant Pot is relatively straightforward, but there are some things to consider to ensure your success.

Water Is Essential

It's the steam released from the liquid that creates the pressure since it has nowhere to escape. Without liquid, your cooker won't come to pressure. One cup of fluid makes pressurization possible.

Deglaze as You Sauté

When you sauté food, there will inevitably be some parts that stick to the bottom of the inner pot. You don't want this food to burn when the pot comes to pressure later, so add a little water or oil and scrape any bits off with a silicone or wooden spoon.

You Always Need the Inner Pot!

Don't attempt to add ingredients to the cooker when the inner pot is not placed inside. Not only will you waste a lot of good ingredients, but you'll also damage your Instant Pot.

A Stovetop Is Not a Safe Place for the Cooker

Create space to place your Instant Pot that is not on top of another heat source. Accidents happen, and you may switch on the burner by mistake and ruin your pot completely.

Safety Tips

Furthermore, there are some safety tips you need to keep in mind:

- Check that the inner pot and heating plate are both clean and dry.
- Check the lid for any stuck food particles. Pay extra attention to the float valve, exhaust valve, and anti-block shield.
- Check the sealing ring is secure.
- Check the steam release valve is set to 'Sealing.'
- Make sure not to overfill the Instant Pot. At no time should the contents in the pot surpass the three-quarter mark. If you're cooking starchy foods, the halfway mark is ideal.
- Be careful when you release the steam.
- Unplug the multicooker when not in use.
- No part of the pot that contains electrical components should be submerged in water.

FAQ

"I have a six-quart pot. Can I cook six quarts of food in it?"

Interestingly, the maximum amount of food you can cook in a six-quart pot is four quarts. You must account for room for the water at the bottom of the pot. As well, some foods expand after they have been cooked, such as grains and rice.

"Why is my pot taking so long to come to pressure?"

Ensure that your valve has not been mistakenly turned to its "open" position. If you notice that there is no pressure building up, then it is probably escaping somehow. Make sure the lid is sealed properly.

"How do I adjust the cooking time and pressure setting?"

You can use the + and - buttons to adjust your cooking time. If you are using a preset button, this will set the appropriate time automatically. To adjust your pressure setting, select the Manual button.

"Is it okay to fill my pot above the max line, to the brim?"

No, if you fill your Instant Pot too much, this can clog its venting knob. It is best to keep your levels to the fill line to avoid any accidental overflow or clogs. Your food also won't be able to cook properly if the pot is too full.

"Can I cook frozen meat directly in the Instant Pot?"

Yes, you can safely cook frozen meat in your Instant Pot. Unlike a traditional pressure cooker, the Instant Pot cooks your food quickly, preventing it from staying at a dangerous temperature for too long.

"My Instant Pot won't seal. What's the matter?"

Make sure to check that you have the silicone seal ring installed correctly. If it is not properly in place, your pot will not want to close or seal properly. This will also prevent pressure and steam from building inside.

"Why can't I open my Instant Pot?"

It is probably in its locked position. Take a look at the indicators. Remember, you must turn your pot's lid clockwise to open and unlock the pot. The indicator should read "Open."

"Can I cook in the Instant Pot without the stainless steel pot liner?"

It is not recommended, as you can break or damage your pot. If you accidentally pour something into your pot without the liner in place, unplug the pot as soon as you notice. Dry it off as much as you can, and let it air dry until all the moisture is gone.

"How do I know when the natural pressure release is complete?"

Pay attention to your float valve. When the natural pressure release is complete, your float valve will drop, and your lid will unlock and open.

"What does releasing the pressure for X amount of time do in a recipe?"

The timing of your pressure release matters for different recipes because your food is still cooking when it is pressurized. This slow method of cooking makes your food more soft or tender, depending on what you are making.

"My Instant Pot releases steam when it comes to pressure. Is this normal?"

Yes, this is normal. You might even hear a hissing noise while this is happening. As long as your pot is completely sealed and you have enough liquid in the pot, you can allow it to steam and hiss while it cooks. The steam should be coming from the float valve or steam release area. If you notice that it is coming out of the sides of your pot, your seal ring is probably installed incorrectly.

Chapter 5 Breakfasts

Breakfast Chicken Pizza

Prep time: 15 minutes | Cook time: 20 minutes | Serves 4 to 5

2 tablespoons avocado oil
1 pound (454 g) ground chicken
¼ cup water
½ teaspoon crushed red pepper
½ teaspoon freshly ground black pepper
½ teaspoon dried parsley

½ teaspoon kosher salt
½ teaspoon dried basil
1 (14-ounce / 397-g) can unsweetened crushed tomatoes, drained
1 cup shredded Cheddar cheese
2 to 4 slices bacon, cooked and finely cut

Press the Sauté button on the Instant Pot and melt the avocado oil. Add the ground chicken to the pot and sauté for 5 minutes, or until browned. Pour in the water. Push the chicken down with a spatula to form a flat, even layer, covering the bottom of the pot. In a small bowl, stir together the red pepper, black pepper, parsley, salt and basil. Spread the tomatoes over the chicken. Add a layer of cheese and then the bacon. Top with the spice and herb mixture. Lock the lid. Select the Manual mode and set the cooking time for 15 minutes on High Pressure. Once the timer goes off, perform a natural pressure release for 10 minutes, then release any remaining pressure. Carefully open the lid. Remove the pizza with a spatula. Serve hot.

Tofu and Spinach Tortillas

Prep time: 5 minutes | Cook time: 27 minutes | Serves 4

2 teaspoons extra virgin olive oil, divided
½ yellow onion, diced
2 cups water
½ cup dry black beans, rinsed
1 chipotle pepper in adobo sauce
½ teaspoon garlic powder
¾ teaspoon sea salt, plus more to taste
1 teaspoon adobo sauce

8 ounce (225g) extra-firm tofu, drained
Pinch of ground turmeric
8 small corn tortillas, warmed in the microwave or lightly charred in a skillet
1 cup baby spinach
1 avocado, sliced
1 cup pico de gallo
2 radishes, thinly sliced
1 cup fresh cilantro

Select Sauté (Medium), and heat 1 teaspoon oil (optional), in the inner pot until hot. (Otherwise, you can dry sauté in the hot pot or add a bit of water in the bottom of the pot.) Add the onion and sauté until softened and golden, 3 to 5 minutes. Press Cancel. Add 2 cups water, beans, chipotle pepper, and garlic powder. Lock the lid and ensure the steam release valve is set to the sealing position. Select Pressure Cook (High), and set the cook time for 27 minutes. Once the cook time is complete, allow the pressure to release naturally for 10 minutes, then quick release any remaining pressure. Carefully remove the lid. Stir in the salt, and remove and discard the chipotle pepper. Transfer to a medium bowl. Add the adobo sauce ¼ teaspoon at a time to add heat to taste, if desired. Rinse out the inner pot and place back into the Instant Pot. Select Sauté (High), and heat the remaining 1 teaspoon oil. Pat the tofu with paper towels to soak up as much water as possible. Crumble the tofu into the pot with the hot oil. Season with turmeric and salt. Sauté until hot, about 2 minutes. Drain the beans and add them into the tofu scramble, or keep them separate. Press Cancel. To assemble the dish, place the warm tortillas on plates. Top with a few spinach leaves and the bean and tofu scramble, avocado, pico de gallo, radish, and cilantro. Enjoy immediately.

Baked Cauliflower and Chicken

Prep time: 10 minutes | Cook time: 15 minutes | Serves 4

4 eggs, beaten
1 cup shredded cauliflower
1 tablespoon Italian seasonings
½ teaspoon salt

½ cup ground chicken
¼ cup shredded Cheddar cheese
1 cup water

In a bowl, stir together the beaten eggs, shredded cauliflower, Italian seasonings and salt. Pour the mixture into four ramekins. Add the ground chicken to the ramekins and top with the Cheddar cheese. Pour the water and insert the trivet in the Instant Pot. Put the ramekins on the trivet. Set the lid in place. Select the Manual mode and set the cooking time for 15 minutes on High Pressure. When the timer goes off, do a quick pressure release. Carefully open the lid. Serve immediately.

Pancake Bites

Prep time: 5 minutes | Cook time: 20 minutes | Serves 7

2 eggs
1 cup almond flour
⅔ cup Swerve
¼ cup full-fat coconut milk

1 tablespoon butter, softened
½ teaspoon kosher salt
¼ teaspoon baking soda
1 cup water

Pour the water and insert the trivet in the Instant Pot. In a large bowl, stir together the remaining ingredients. Transfer the mixture into two well-greased egg bites molds. Using a sling, place the molds onto the trivet. Stack two egg bites molds on top of each other. Cover loosely with aluminum foil. Lock the lid. Select the Manual mode and set the cooking time for 20 minutes on High Pressure. Once the timer goes off, perform a natural pressure release for 10 minutes, then release any remaining pressure. Carefully open the lid. Remove the molds from the pot. Let cool for 5 minutes before serving.

Egg and Avocado Toast

Prep time: 7 minutes | Cook time: 3 minutes | Serves 1

½ cup water
1 egg
1 slice whole-wheat or multigrain bread

½ very ripe avocado
1 teaspoon freshly squeezed lemon juice
Dash kosher salt

Place a rack in the Instant Pot. Add the water to the Instant Pot and place the egg, in its shell, on the rack. Lock on the lid and set the timer for 3 minutes at High Pressure. While the egg cooks, toast the bread in a toaster or toaster oven. Using a spoon, scrape the avocado flesh into a small bowl. Add the lemon juice and salt and mash the avocado with the spoon until it is a creamy spread, but with a few chunks still remaining. When the Instant Pot timer goes off, quick release the pressure, open the Instant Pot, and remove the egg with a pair of tongs or a slotted spoon. Rinse it under cool water until just cool enough to handle. Peel the egg. Spread the avocado mixture on the toasted bread. Place the egg on top of the avocado, and cut it in half. The yolk will be runny; let it spill out of the white onto the avocado. Serve immediately.

Bacon and Kale Frittatas

Prep time: 10 minutes | Cook time: 20 minutes | Serves 4

6 eggs, beaten
4 slices bacon, finely cut, cooked
1 cup chopped kale
2 tablespoons coconut oil
½ teaspoon full-fat coconut milk
½ teaspoon dried parsley
½ teaspoon dried cilantro
½ teaspoon dried basil
½ teaspoon chili powder
½ teaspoon kosher salt
½ teaspoon freshly ground black pepper
1 cup water

Pour the water and insert the trivet in the Instant Pot. In a large bowl, stir together the remaining ingredients. Divide the mixture evenly among four well-greased ramekins. Make sure to leave room on top of each for possible expansion during cooking. Place all the ramekins on the trivet. Lock the lid. Select the Manual mode and set the cooking time for 20 minutes on High Pressure. Once the timer goes off, perform a natural pressure release for 10 minutes, then release any remaining pressure. Carefully open the lid. Remove the ramekins from the pot and let cool for 5 to 10 minutes. Serve warm.

Walnut Pumpkin Cake

Prep time: 5 minutes | Cook time: 40 minutes | Serves 5 to 6

Base:
3 eggs
1 cup almond flour
¾ cup chopped walnuts
½ cup organic pumpkin purée
¼ cup heavy whipping cream
Topping:
¼ cup heavy whipping cream
½ cup Swerve
2 tablespoons butter, softened
½ teaspoon ground cinnamon
½ teaspoon ground nutmeg
½ teaspoon baking powder
½ teaspoon salt

½ cup unsweetened coconut flakes

Pour 1 cup water and insert the trivet in the Instant Pot. Using an electric mixer, combine all the ingredients for the cake. Mix thoroughly. Transfer the mixture into a well-greased baking pan. Place the pan onto the trivet and cover loosely with aluminum foil. Lock the lid. Select the Manual mode and set the cooking time for 40 minutes on High Pressure. Meanwhile, in a large bowl, whisk together all the ingredients for the topping. Once the timer goes off, perform a natural pressure release for 10 minutes, then release any remaining pressure. Carefully open the lid. Remove the pan from the pot. Sprinkle the topping mixture evenly over the cake. Let cool for 5 minutes before serving.

Turkey, Bacon, and Spinach Breakfast Casserole

Prep time: 10 minutes | Cook time: 10 minutes | Serves 4 to 5

2 tablespoons coconut oil
1 pound (454 g) ground turkey
3 slices bacon, cooked and crumbled
1 cup chopped bell peppers
½ cup chopped spinach
½ cup heavy cream
¼ cup shredded full-fat
Cheddar cheese
1 teaspoon dried oregano
½ teaspoon crushed red pepper
½ teaspoon kosher salt
½ teaspoon freshly ground black pepper

Press the Sauté button on the Instant Pot and melt the coconut oil. Add the turkey to the pot and sauté for 5 minutes. Stir in the remaining ingredients and continue to cook for 5 minutes, or until the turkey is browned and cooked all the way through. Transfer the dish to plates and serve immediately.

Tomato and Cheddar Egg Bake

Prep time: 5 minutes | Cook time: 20 minutes | Serves 4

2 tablespoons coconut oil
6 eggs
1 (14-ounce / 397-g) can sugar-free crushed tomatoes
1 cup shredded full-fat Cheddar cheese
½ teaspoon dried cilantro
½ teaspoon chili powder
½ jalapeño, finely chopped
½ teaspoon kosher salt
½ teaspoon freshly ground black pepper
½ cup water

Pour the water and insert the trivet in the Instant Pot. In a large bowl, stir together the remaining ingredients. Transfer the mixture into a well-greased baking pan and cover loosely with aluminum foil. Using a sling, place the pan on top of the trivet. Lock the lid. Select the Manual mode and set the cooking time for 20 minutes on High Pressure. Once the timer goes off, perform a natural pressure release for 10 minutes, then release any remaining pressure. Carefully open the lid. Transfer the dish to a plate and serve.

Coconut and Pumpkin Seed Porridge

Prep time: 5 minutes | Cook time: 5 minutes | Serves 4

½ cup chopped almonds
4 tablespoons shredded unsweetened coconut
2 tablespoons flaxseed
2 tablespoons pumpkin seeds
1 teaspoon ground cinnamon
½ teaspoon grated nutmeg
¼ teaspoon ground cloves
Himalayan salt, to taste
1 cup boiling water

Add all the ingredients to the Instant Pot and stir to combine. Set the lid in place. Select the Manual mode and set the cooking time for 5 minutes on High Pressure. When the timer goes off, do a quick pressure release. Carefully open the lid. Serve immediately.

Chicken Sausage and Kale Egg Muffins

Prep time: 5 minutes | Cook time: 9 to 10 minutes | Serves 2

3 teaspoons avocado oil, divided
4 ounces (113 g) fully cooked chicken sausage, diced
4 small kale leaves, finely chopped
½ teaspoon kosher salt,
divided
½ teaspoon ground black pepper, divided
4 large eggs
¼ cup heavy whipping cream
1 cup water

Grease the bottom and insides of four silicone muffin cups with 1 teaspoon of the avocado oil. Press the Sauté button on the Instant Pot and heat the remaining 2 teaspoons of the avocado oil. Add the sausage to the pot and sauté for 2 minutes. Add the chopped kale and ¼ teaspoon of the salt and black pepper. Sauté for 2 to 3 minutes, or until the kale is wilted. Meanwhile, in a medium bowl, lightly whisk together the eggs, cream and the remaining ¼ teaspoon of the salt and pepper. Divide the kale and sausage mixture among the four muffin cups. Pour the egg mixture evenly over the kale and sausage and stir lightly with a fork. Loosely cover the cups with foil. Pour the water and insert the trivet in the Instant Pot. Put the muffin cups on the trivet. Lock the lid. Select the Manual mode and set the cooking time for 5 minutes on High Pressure. Once the timer goes off, perform a natural pressure release for 10 minutes, then release any remaining pressure. Carefully open the lid. Remove the muffins from the Instant Pot. Serve hot.

Strawberry Mug Cakes

Prep time: 5 minutes | Cook time: 20 minutes | Serves 3 to 4

2 eggs
⅔ cup almond flour
½ cup Swerve
1 tablespoon butter, softened
1 teaspoon vanilla extract

1 teaspoon smooth almond butter
4 strawberries, hulled and chopped

In a large bowl, stir together all the ingredients. Pour the mixture evenly into mugs, filling each about halfway. Cover each loosely with aluminum foil. Pour 1 cup water and insert the trivet in the Instant Pot. Put the mugs on the trivet. Lock the lid. Select the Manual mode and set the cooking time for 20 minutes on High Pressure. Once the timer goes off, perform a natural pressure release for 10 minutes, then release any remaining pressure. Carefully open the lid. Transfer the mugs to a cooling rack. Let cool completely before serving.

Mediterranean Eggs

Prep time: 5 minutes | Cook time: 1 minute | Serves 2 to 4

2 tablespoons coconut oil
1 (14-ounce / 397-g) can roasted sugar-free tomatoes
1 garlic clove, minced
2 cups shredded full-fat Cheddar cheese
½ teaspoon ground cayenne pepper

½ teaspoon ground cumin
½ teaspoon dried oregano
½ teaspoon dried cilantro
½ teaspoon kosher salt
½ teaspoon freshly ground black pepper
6 eggs

Press the Sauté button on the Instant Pot and melt the coconut oil. Stir in the remaining ingredients, except for the eggs, to the pot. Carefully crack the eggs into the mixture, maintaining the yolks. Make sure they are spaced evenly apart. Set the lid in place. Select the Manual mode and set the cooking time for 1 minute on High Pressure. When the timer goes off, do a quick pressure release. Carefully open the lid. Serve warm.

Creamy Beef and Cabbage Bowl

Prep time: 10 minutes | Cook time: 7 minutes | Serves 4

1 tablespoon avocado oil
1 pound (454 g) ground beef
1 clove garlic, minced
½ teaspoon sea salt
½ teaspoon ground black pepper
½ teaspoon ground turmeric

¼ teaspoon ground cinnamon
¼ teaspoon ground coriander
¼ cup almond butter
½ cup full-fat coconut milk
1 small head green cabbage, shredded

Press the Sauté button on the Instant Pot and heat the oil. Crumble in the ground beef and cook for 3 minutes, breaking up the meat with a wooden spoon or meat chopper. Stir in the garlic, salt, black pepper, turmeric, cinnamon, and coriander. Add the almond butter and coconut milk. Stir constantly until the almond butter melts and mixes with the coconut milk. Layer the cabbage on top of the meat mixture but do not stir. Set the lid in place. Select the Manual mode and set the cooking time for 4 minutes on High Pressure. When the timer goes off, do a quick pressure release. Carefully open the lid. Stir the meat mixture. Taste and adjust the salt and black pepper, and add more red pepper flakes if desired. Use a slotted spoon to transfer the mixture to a serving bowl. Serve hot.

Bell Pepper and Ham Frittata

Prep time: 10 minutes | Cook time: 40 minutes | Serves 2

2 tablespoons avocado oil, divided
¼ cup chopped onion
¼ cup chopped green bell pepper
¼ cup chopped red bell pepper
½ pound (227 g) cooked ham, cubed
6 large eggs

½ cup heavy whipping cream
½ teaspoon sea salt
¼ teaspoon ground black pepper
¼ teaspoon dried basil
¼ teaspoon dried parsley
¼ teaspoon red pepper flakes
1 cup water

Grease a baking pan with 2 teaspoons of the avocado oil. Press the Sauté button on the Instant Pot and heat the remaining 1⅓ tablespoons of the avocado oil. Add the onion and bell peppers to the pot and sauté for 3 minutes, or until tender. Add the ham and continue to sauté for 2 minutes. Transfer the ham and onion mixture to a bowl. Clean the pot. In a medium bowl, whisk together the eggs, cream, salt, black pepper, basil, parsley and pepper flakes. Pour the mixture into the prepared baking pan. Stir in the ham and onion mixture. Cover the pan with foil. Pour the water and insert the trivet in the Instant Pot. Put the pan on the trivet. Lock the lid. Select the Manual mode and set the cooking time for 35 minutes on High Pressure. Once the timer goes off, perform a natural pressure release for 10 minutes, then release any remaining pressure. Carefully open the lid. Remove the baking pan from the pot. Serve hot.

Kale and Bacon Quiche

Prep time: 10 minutes | Cook time: 20 minutes | Serves 4 to 5

6 eggs
6 slices bacon, cooked and finely chopped
¼ small onion, thinly sliced
½ cup shredded full-fat Cheddar cheese
½ cup Ricotta cheese
½ cup chopped kale

¼ cup full-fat coconut milk
2 tablespoons coconut oil
½ teaspoon dried basil
½ teaspoon dried parsley
½ teaspoon kosher salt
½ teaspoon freshly ground black pepper

Add all the ingredients to a baking pan and stir to combine. Pour 1 cup water and insert the trivet in the Instant Pot. Put the pan on the trivet. Cover with aluminium foil. Lock the lid. Select the Manual mode and set the cooking time for 20 minutes on High Pressure. Once the timer goes off, perform a natural pressure release for 10 minutes, then release any remaining pressure. Carefully open the lid. Serve immediately.

Paprika Cauliflower Hash

Prep time: 5 minutes | Cook time: 10 minutes | Serves 4

2 tablespoons grass-fed butter, softened
1 pound (454 g) cauliflower, chopped into small pieces
½ teaspoon garlic

½ teaspoon fresh paprika
½ teaspoon kosher salt
½ teaspoon freshly ground black pepper

Press the Sauté button on the Instant Pot and melt the butter. Place the cauliflower into the Instant Pot, along with the garlic, paprika, salt, and pepper. Keep stirring until the cauliflower hash is completely cooked. Divide the cauliflower hash among fours bowls and serve.

Ham and Broccoli Frittata

Prep time: 10 minutes | Cook time: 20 minutes | Serves 4

1 cup sliced bell peppers
8 ounces (227 g) ham, cubed
2 cups frozen broccoli florets
4 eggs
1 cup heavy cream

1 cup grated Cheddar cheese
1 teaspoon salt
2 teaspoons freshly ground
black pepper

Arrange the pepper slices in a greased pan. Place the cubed ham on top. Cover with the frozen broccoli. In a bowl, whisk together the remaining ingredients. Pour the egg mixture over the vegetables and ham. Cover the pan with aluminum foil. Pour 2 cups water and insert the trivet in the Instant Pot. Put the pan on the trivet. Lock the lid. Select the Manual mode and set the cooking time for 20 minutes on High Pressure. Once the timer goes off, perform a natural pressure release for 10 minutes, then release any remaining pressure. Carefully open the lid. Carefully remove the pan from the pot and remove the foil. Let the frittata sit for 5 to 10 minutes before transferring the frittata onto the plate. Serve warm.

Mushroom and Cheddar Egg Cups

Prep time: 10 minutes | Cook time: 7 to 8 minutes | Serves 4

4 eggs, beaten
1 cup diced mushrooms
½ cup grated sharp Cheddar
cheese
¼ cup heavy cream

1 teaspoon salt
1 teaspoon freshly ground
black pepper
2 tablespoons chopped fresh
cilantro

In a medium bowl, stir together all the ingredients. Divide the mixture among four glass jars. Place the lids on top of the jars, but do not tighten. Pour 2 cups water and insert the trivet in the Instant Pot. Place the egg jars on the trivet. Set the lid in place. Select the Manual mode and set the cooking time for 5 minutes on High Pressure. When the timer goes off, do a quick pressure release. Carefully open the lid. Remove the jars from the pot and remove the lids from the jars. Serve warm.

Chorizo and Egg Lettuce Tacos

Prep time: 5 minutes | Cook time: 12 minutes | Serves 6

2 tablespoons avocado oil
1½ pounds (680 g) fresh
chorizo
¾ cup sour cream

½ cup chicken broth
6 large eggs, washed
6 large lettuce leaves

Press the Sauté button on the Instant Pot and heat the oil. Crumble in the chorizo. Sauté for 2 minutes, breaking up the meat with a wooden spoon or meat chopper. Stir in the sour cream and broth. Place a long-legged metal trivet directly on top of the sausage mixture. Place the eggs on the trivet. Set the lid in place. Select the Pressure Cook mode and set the cooking time for 10 minutes on High Pressure. Meanwhile, fill a medium bowl with ice water for the eggs. When the timer goes off, do a quick pressure release. Carefully open the lid. Use tongs or a large spoon to transfer the eggs immediately to the ice bath. Stir the chorizo mixture and allow it to rest in the Instant Pot on Keep Warm. When the eggs are cool enough to handle, peel and slice them. To serve, use a slotted spoon to spoon the chorizo into lettuce leaves.

Cauliflower Mac and Cheese

Prep time: 5 minutes | Cook time: 8 to 10 minutes | Serves 4

2 cups cauliflower, cut into
florets
2 tablespoons cream cheese,
at room temperature
½ cup heavy cream

½ cup grated sharp Cheddar
cheese
1 teaspoon salt
1 teaspoon freshly ground
black pepper

In a blender, place the cauliflower florets and pulse until puréed. In a heatproof bowl, mix the cauliflower along with the remaining ingredients. Cover the bowl with aluminum foil. Pour 2 cups water and insert the trivet in the Instant Pot. Put the bowl on the trivet. Lock the lid. Select the Manual mode and set the cooking time for 5 minutes on High Pressure. Once the timer goes off, perform a natural pressure release for 10 minutes, then release any remaining pressure. Carefully open the lid. Place the cooked cauliflower in a broiler and broil for 3 to 5 minutes, or until the cheese is browned and bubbling. Serve immediately.

Egg and Chorizo Lettuce Tacos

Prep time: 5 minutes | Cook time: 12 minutes | Serves 6

2 tablespoons avocado oil
1½ pounds (680 g) fresh
chorizo
¾ cup sour cream

½ cup chicken broth
6 large eggs, washed
6 large lettuce leaves

Press the Sauté button on the Instant Pot and heat the oil. Crumble in the chorizo. Sauté for 2 minutes, breaking up the meat with a wooden spoon or meat chopper. Stir in the sour cream and broth. Place a long-legged metal trivet directly on top of the sausage mixture. Place the eggs on the trivet. Set the lid in place. Select the Manual mode and set the cooking time for 10 minutes on High Pressure. Meanwhile, fill a medium bowl with ice water for the eggs. When the timer goes off, do a quick pressure release. Carefully open the lid. Use tongs or a large spoon to transfer the eggs immediately to the ice bath. Stir the chorizo mixture and allow it to rest in the Instant Pot on Keep Warm. When the eggs are cool enough to handle, peel and slice them. To serve, use a slotted spoon to spoon the chorizo into lettuce leaves.

Coconut and Hemp Heart Porridge

Prep time: 5 minutes | Cook time: 4 minutes | Serves 3

¼ cup unsweetened shredded
coconut
½ cup hemp hearts
3 large eggs
⅓ cup water
1 (13.5-ounce / 383-g) can full-

fat coconut milk
½ teaspoon vanilla extract
1½ teaspoons pumpkin pie
spice
¼ teaspoon sea salt

Set the Instant Pot to Sauté mode. Add the coconut and hemp to the dry pot insert and cook, stirring frequently, until lightly browned and the hemp starts to smell nutty, 3 minutes. Meanwhile, in a blender, combine the eggs, water, coconut milk, vanilla, pumpkin pie spice, and salt. Pour the egg mixture into the pot and stir. Lock the lid. Select the Manual mode and set the cooking time for 1 minute on High Pressure. Once the timer goes off, perform a natural pressure release for 5 minutes, then release any remaining pressure. Carefully open the lid. Give the porridge a good stir. Spoon the porridge into individual serving bowls.

Broccoli and Bacon Frittata

Prep time: 5 minutes | Cook time: 19 minutes | Serves 2

2 teaspoons avocado oil
4 slices bacon
2 cups chopped broccoli
½ teaspoon sea salt
¼ teaspoon ground black pepper

4 large eggs
¼ cup heavy whipping cream
¼ teaspoon ground cumin
¾ cup crumbled Feta cheese
1 cup water

Use the avocado oil to grease a baking dish that fits inside your Instant Pot. Set the Instant Pot to Sauté mode. When hot, add the bacon and cook, flipping occasionally, until the bacon is crispy. Remove to a plate. Add the broccoli to the pot and season with ¼ teaspoon of the salt and ⅛ teaspoon of the pepper. Sauté for 3 minutes, then transfer the broccoli to a small bowl. In a medium bowl, lightly beat together the eggs, cream, cumin, and the remaining ¼ teaspoon salt and ⅛ teaspoon pepper. Crumble the bacon and stir it into the eggs, along with half the feta cheese. Pour the egg mixture into the prepared baking dish. Quickly stir in the broccoli. Sprinkle with the remaining feta cheese. Cover with a metal or silicone lid, or use foil. Wipe out the Instant Pot if desired. Pour in the water and place the trivet inside. Arrange the sling over it so the two ends stick up like handles, then lower the baking dish onto the sling and the trivet. Lock the lid. Select the Manual mode and set the cooking time for 16 minutes on High Pressure. Once the timer goes off, perform a natural pressure release for 5 minutes, then release any remaining pressure. Carefully open the lid. Use the sling to carefully remove the hot baking dish. Serve hot or at room temperature.

Sausage and Swiss Chard Stuffed Mushrooms

Prep time: 10 minutes | Cook time: 15 to 16 minutes | Serves 2

12 large white mushrooms, washed, stems removed and reserved
1 tablespoon avocado oil
¼ teaspoon kosher salt
¼ teaspoon ground black pepper
1 tablespoon butter

6 ounces (170 g) sugar-free bulk pork breakfast sausage
1 clove garlic, minced
¼ cup full-fat coconut milk
1 cup finely chopped Swiss chard
1 cup water

Finely chop the mushroom stems and set aside. Place the mushroom caps stemmed side down in a medium bowl and pour the avocado oil over them. Season with the salt and pepper. Toss gently to coat the mushrooms with oil without breaking them. Set the Instant Pot to Sauté mode and melt the butter. When it is melted, crumble in the sausage and add the chopped mushroom stems. Sauté, stirring occasionally, until only a little pink remains in the pork, 3 to 4 minutes. Add the garlic and sauté until the pork is cooked through. Deglaze the pot with the coconut milk, scraping the bottom with a wooden spoon to loosen any browned bits. Stir in the chopped chard and cook just until they are wilted. Transfer the pork to a bowl. Taste and adjust the salt and pepper. Wipe or wash out the pot insert. Stuff the pork mixture into the mushrooms. Place the mushrooms stem side up in two stackable stainless steel insert pans, 6 mushrooms per pan. Stack and secure the lid on the pans. Pour the water into the Instant Pot and lower the stacked pans into the pot. Set the lid in place. Select the Steam mode and set the cooking time for 12 minutes on High Pressure. When the timer goes off, do a quick pressure release. Carefully open the lid. Transfer the pan from the pot. Open the insert pans and transfer the mushrooms to serving plates. Serve warm.

Cauliflower and Blueberry Rice Pudding

Prep time: 5 minutes | Cook time: 3 minutes | Serves 4

2 tablespoons coconut oil
4 cups raw cauliflower rice
1 cup unsweetened almond milk

2 scoops vanilla-flavored protein powder
¼ teaspoon sea salt
½ cup blueberries

Press the Sauté button on the Instant Pot and heat the oil. Add the cauliflower rice and stir to coat it with the cacao butter. Add the almond milk, protein powder, salt and blueberries and stir very well to combine. Lock the lid. Select the Manual mode and set the cooking time for 3 minutes on High Pressure. Once the timer goes off, perform a natural pressure release for 5 minutes, then release any remaining pressure. Carefully open the lid. Stir the pudding. Spoon the pudding into individual bowls and allow it to cool for a few minutes. Serve warm or at room temperature.

Almond and Blueberry Cereal

Prep time: 5 minutes | Cook time: 2 minutes | Serves 4

⅓ cup crushed roasted almonds
¼ cup almond flour
¼ cup unsalted butter, softened
¼ cup vanilla-flavored egg

white protein powder
2 tablespoons Swerve
1 teaspoon blueberry extract
1 teaspoon ground cinnamon

Add all the ingredients to the Instant Pot and stir to combine. Lock the lid, select the Manual mode and set the cooking time for 2 minutes on High Pressure. When the timer goes off, do a natural pressure release for 10 minutes, then release any remaining pressure. Open the lid. Stir well and pour the mixture onto a sheet lined with parchment paper to cool. It will be crispy when completely cool. Serve the cereal in bowls.

Spinach and Mushroom Frittata

Prep time: 5 minutes | Cook time: 30 minutes | Serves 6

1 cup sliced fresh mushrooms
1 cup fresh baby spinach leaves
6 large eggs
¼ cup heavy cream
1 teaspoon sea salt

½ teaspoon ground black pepper
½ cup shredded Monterey Jack cheese
½ avocado, sliced
Cooking spray

Spray a soufflé dish with cooking spray. Arrange the mushrooms and spinach leaves in the bottom of the dish. Set aside. In a large bowl, combine the eggs, heavy cream, sea salt, and black pepper. Mix well to combine. Gently pour the egg mixture over the mushrooms and spinach. Add 1½ cups water to the bottom of the inner pot. Place the soufflé dish on the trivet and grasp the trivet handles to lower the trivet and dish into the pot. Lock the lid. Select the Manual mode and set the cooking time for 30 minutes on High Pressure. Once the timer goes off, perform a natural pressure release for 10 minutes, then release any remaining pressure. Carefully open the lid. Sprinkle the Jack cheese over top of the frittata. Replace the lid and allow the residual heat to melt the cheese for 5 minutes. Open the lid and carefully grasp the trivet handles to lift the trivet and dish out of the pot. Transfer the frittata to a serving platter, cut into 6 equal-sized wedges, and top with the sliced avocado. Serve warm.

Breakfast Sardine Green Salad

Prep time: 10 minutes | Cook time: 14 to 15 minutes | Serves 2

2 large eggs
1 cup water
1 tablespoon avocado oil
4 slices bacon, cut into small pieces
2 tablespoons minced shallots
1 tablespoon apple cider vinegar
1 (4.4-ounce / 125-g) can oil-

packed sardines
¼ cup fresh parsley leaves
4 cups chopped romaine lettuce
2 cups baby spinach, torn into smaller pieces
¼ teaspoon ground black pepper
1 medium avocado, sliced

Pour the water into the Instant Pot. Place the trivet inside and place the eggs on top. Set the lid in place. Select the Manual mode and set the cooking time for 10 minutes on High Pressure. Meanwhile, prepare a bowl with ice water to cool the eggs. When the timer goes off, do a quick pressure release. Carefully open the lid. Use tongs to transfer the eggs to the ice bath. When cool, peel and slice the eggs. Carefully pour the water out of the Instant Pot and wipe it dry. Set the Instant Pot to Sauté mode and heat the avocado oil. Add the bacon and cook for 3 minutes. Add the shallots and cook until the bacon is crispy, another 1 to 2 minutes. Press Cancel. Deglaze the pot with the vinegar, scraping the bottom with a wooden spoon to loosen any browned bits. Use a fork to break up the sardines and add them, along with their oil, to the pot. Stir in the parsley. Place the lettuce, spinach, and pepper in the pot and mix well to coat the greens with the oil. Divide the mixture between two large serving bowls, scraping any remaining dressing from the pot. Top each salad with half the sliced avocado and 1 sliced egg. Crack some black pepper over the top and serve immediately.

Spinach and Bacon Bake

Prep time: 5 minutes | Cook time: 9 minutes | Serves 4

2 tablespoons unsalted butter, divided
½ cup diced bacon
⅓ cup finely diced shallots
⅓ cup chopped spinach, leaves only
Pinch of sea salt

Pinch of black pepper
½ cup water
¼ cup heavy whipping cream
8 large eggs
1 tablespoon chopped fresh chives, for garnish

Set the Instant Pot on the Sauté mode and melt 1 tablespoon of the butter. Add the bacon to the pot and sauté for about 4 minutes, or until crispy. Using a slotted spoon, transfer the bacon bits to a bowl and set aside. Add the remaining 1 tablespoon of the butter and shallots to the pot and sauté for about 2 minutes, or until tender. Add the spinach leaves and sauté for 1 minute, or until wilted. Season with sea salt and black pepper and stir. Transfer the spinach to a separate bowl and set aside. Drain the oil from the pot into a bowl. Pour in the water and put the trivet inside. With a paper towel, coat four ramekins with the bacon grease. In each ramekin, place 1 tablespoon of the heavy whipping cream, reserved bacon bits and sautéed spinach. Crack two eggs without breaking the yolks in each ramekin. Cover the ramekins with aluminum foil. Place two ramekins on the trivet and stack the other two on top. Lock the lid. Select the Manual mode and set the cooking time for 2 minutes at Low Pressure. When the timer goes off, use a natural pressure release for 5 minutes, then release any remaining pressure. Carefully open the lid. Carefully take out the ramekins and serve garnished with the chives.

Chicken and Tomato Pizza

Prep time: 15 minutes | Cook time: 20 minutes | Serves 4 to 5

2 tablespoons avocado oil
1 pound (454 g) ground chicken
¼ cup water
½ teaspoon crushed red pepper
½ teaspoon freshly ground black pepper
½ teaspoon dried parsley

½ teaspoon kosher salt
½ teaspoon dried basil
1 (14-ounce / 397-g) can unsweetened crushed tomatoes, drained
1 cup shredded Cheddar cheese
2 to 4 slices bacon, cooked and finely cut

Press the Sauté button on the Instant Pot and melt the avocado oil. Add the ground chicken to the pot and sauté for 5 minutes, or until browned. Pour in the water. Push the chicken down with a spatula to form a flat, even layer, covering the bottom of the pot. In a small bowl, stir together the red pepper, black pepper, parsley, salt and basil. Spread the tomatoes over the chicken. Add a layer of cheese and then the bacon. Top with the spice and herb mixture. Lock the lid. Select the Pressure Cook mode and set the cooking time for 15 minutes on High Pressure. Once the timer goes off, perform a natural pressure release for 10 minutes, then release any remaining pressure. Carefully open the lid. Remove the pizza with a spatula. Serve hot.

Ham and Cheddar Egg Bake

Prep time: 5 minutes | Cook time: 5 minutes | Serves 2

4 large eggs, beaten
4 slices ham, diced
½ cup shredded Cheddar cheese

½ cup heavy cream
½ teaspoon sea salt
Pinch ground black pepper

Grease two ramekins. In a large bowl, whisk together all the ingredients. Divide the egg mixture equally between the ramekins. Set a trivet in the Instant Pot and pour in 1 cup water. Place the ramekins on the trivet. Lock the lid. Select the Manual mode and set the cooking time for 5 minutes on High Pressure. When the timer goes off, perform a quick pressure release. Carefully open the lid. Remove the ramekins from the Instant Pot. Serve immediately.

Nut Granola

Prep time: 5 minutes | Cook time: 2 hours 30 minutes | Serves 10

1 cup raw almonds
1 cup pumpkin seeds
1 cup raw walnuts
1 cup raw cashews
1 tablespoon coconut oil

¼ cup unsweetened coconut chips
1 teaspoon sea salt
1 teaspoon cinnamon

In a large bowl, stir together the almonds, pumpkin seeds, walnuts, cashews and coconut oil. Make sure all the nuts are coated with the coconut oil. Place the nut mixture in the Instant Pot and cover the pot with a paper towel. Lock the lid. Select the Slow Cook mode and set the cooking time for 1 hour on More. When the timer goes off, stir the nuts. Set the timer for another hour. Again, when the timer goes off, stir the nut mixture and add the coconut chips. Set the timer for another 30 minutes. The cashews should become a nice golden color. When the timer goes off, transfer the nut mixture to a baking pan to cool and sprinkle with the sea salt and cinnamon. Serve.

Almond and Mixed Berry Porridge

Prep time: 5 minutes | Cook time: 2 minutes | Serves 4

8 tablespoons unsalted and shelled raw sunflower seeds
10 tablespoons almond flour
4 tablespoons golden flaxseed meal
2½ tablespoons butter, melted
2⅓ cups water
1 cup unsweetened almond

milk
½ teaspoon vanilla extract
½ teaspoon ground cinnamon
4 teaspoons erythritol-oligosaccharide granular sweetener blend
2 cups mixed berries

Add the sunflower seeds to a small food processor or blender. Pulse until a flour-like texture is achieved. In a medium bowl, combine the sunflower meal, almond flour, and flaxseed meal. Mix until well combined. Add the melted butter to the pot and then add the almond-flaxseed mixture and water. Stir until well combined. Set the lid in place. Select the Manual mode and set the cooking time for 2 minutes on High Pressure. When the timer goes off, do a quick pressure release. Carefully open the lid. Stir in the almond milk and vanilla extract. Spoon the porridge into serving bowls. Top each serving with ⅛ teaspoon cinnamon, 1 teaspoon sweetener, and ½ cup of the berries. Serve warm.

Creamy Pumpkin Pudding

Prep time: 5 minutes | Cook time: 5 minutes | Serves 4

2 large eggs
4 ounces (113 g) cream cheese, softened
1 cup pumpkin purée

½ cup Swerve
¼ cup heavy cream
1 teaspoon pumpkin pie spice
1 teaspoon ground cinnamon

Place all the ingredients in a blender and pulse until smooth. Divide the purée among four ramekins. Set a trivet in the Instant Pot and pour in 1 cup water. Use a foil sling to lower the ramekins onto the trivet. Close and secure the lid. Select the Manual mode and set the cooking time for 5 minutes at High Pressure. Once cooking is complete, do a quick pressure release. Carefully open the lid. Lift the ramekins out of the Instant Pot using the foil sling. Serve warm or chilled.

Bacon and Cheddar Egg Cups

Prep time: 5 minutes | Cook time: 7 minutes | Serves 4

6 large eggs
2 strips cooked bacon, sliced in ¼-inch wide pieces
½ cup Cheddar cheese, divided

¼ teaspoon sea salt
¼ teaspoon black pepper
1 cup water
1 tablespoon chopped fresh flat leaf parsley

In a small bowl, beat the eggs. Stir in the cooked bacon, ¼ cup of the cheese, sea salt and pepper. Divide the egg mixture equally among four ramekins and loosely cover with aluminum foil. Pour the water and place the trivet in the Instant Pot. Place two ramekins on the trivet and stack the other two on the top. Lock the lid. Select the Manual mode and set the cooking time for 7 minutes at High Pressure. When the timer goes off, use a natural pressure release for 10 minutes, then release any remaining pressure. Carefully open the lid. Top each ramekin with the remaining ¼ cup of the cheese. Lock the lid and melt the cheese for 2 minutes. Garnish with the chopped parsley and serve immediately.

Egg Pepper Cups with Mayo-Dijon Sauce

Prep time: 5 minutes | Cook time: 3 minutes | Serves 8

4 large eggs
4 medium bell peppers, tops
Sauce:
¼ cup mayonnaise
1 teaspoon Dijon mustard
½ teaspoon lemon juice
½ teaspoon white vinegar

and seeds removed
6 baby arugula leaves

¼ teaspoon fine grind sea salt
⅛ teaspoon ground black pepper
¼ teaspoon ground turmeric

Place the trivet in the inner pot and add 1 cup water to the bottom of the pot. Make the sauce by combining the mayonnaise, Dijon mustard, lemon juice, vinegar, sea salt, black pepper, and turmeric in a small bowl. Whisk until blended. Cover and refrigerate. Carefully crack 1 egg into each bell pepper cup, making sure to keep the yolk intact, and cover the top of each pepper with a small square of aluminum foil. Place the covered peppers on the trivet. Lock the lid. Select the Manual mode and set the cooking time for 3 minutes on High Pressure. Once the timer goes off, perform a natural pressure release for 2 minutes, then release any remaining pressure. Carefully open the lid. Transfer the peppers to a serving platter. Remove the foil and top each pepper with 1 tablespoon of the sauce, and then garnish with the arugula leaves. Serve hot.

Coffee Cake

Prep time: 10 minutes | Cook time: 45 minutes | Serves 8

Cake:
2 cups almond flour
1 cup granulated erythritol
1 teaspoon baking powder
Pinch of salt
2 eggs
½ cup sour cream
4 tablespoons butter, melted
Icing:
2 ounces (56 g) cream cheese, softened
1 cup powdered erythritol

2 teaspoons vanilla extract
2 tablespoons brown sugar substitute
1½ teaspoons ground cinnamon
Cooking spray
½ cup water

1 tablespoon heavy cream
½ teaspoon vanilla extract

In the bowl of a stand mixer, combine the almond flour, granulated erythritol, baking powder and salt. Mix until no lumps remain. Add the eggs, sour cream, butter and vanilla to the mixer bowl and mix until well combined. In a separate bowl, mix together the brown sugar substitute and cinnamon. Spritz the baking pan with cooking spray. Pour in the cake batter and use a knife to make sure it is level around the pan. Sprinkle the cinnamon mixture on top. Cover the pan tightly with aluminum foil. Pour the water and insert the trivet in the Instant Pot. Put the pan on the trivet. Set the lid in place. Select the Pressure Cook mode and set the cooking time for 45 minutes on High Pressure. When the timer goes off, do a quick pressure release. Carefully open the lid. Remove the cake from the pot and remove the foil. Blot off any moisture on top of the cake with a paper towel, if necessary. Let rest in the pan for 5 minutes. Meanwhile, make the icing: In a small bowl, use a mixer to whip the cream cheese until it is light and fluffy. Slowly fold in the powdered erythritol and mix until well combined. Add the heavy cream and vanilla extract and mix until thoroughly combined. When the cake is cooled, transfer it to a platter and drizzle the icing all over.

Cauliflower, Nut, and Seed Porridge

Prep time: 40 minutes | Cook time: 5 minutes | Serves 4

2½ cups water, divided
½ cup raw cashews
½ cup almond slivers
¼ cup raw pumpkin seeds
Topping:
¼ cup hemp seeds
¼ cup chia seeds

¼ head cauliflower, chopped
Sea salt, to taste
¼ cup heavy whipping cream

1 tablespoon cinnamon

In a small bowl, add 2 cups of the water, the cashews, almonds and pumpkin seeds. Soak for 30 minutes. Drain the water and set aside. Reserve a few nuts and pumpkin seeds in a separate bowl to be used as garnish. Pour the remaining ½ cup of the water into the Instant Pot and add the soaked nuts mixture, cauliflower and sea salt. Lock the lid. Select the Manual mode and set the cooking time for 5 minutes at High Pressure. When the timer goes off, use a natural pressure release for 10 minutes, then release any remaining pressure. Carefully open the lid. Transfer the cauliflower and nuts mixture to a food processor, add the heavy cream and pulse until smooth. Season with a pinch of sea salt. Garnish with the reserved nuts, pumpkin seeds, hemp seeds and chia seeds and sprinkle with the cinnamon. Serve immediately.

Chocolate and Pecan Fat Bombs

Prep time: 5 minutes | Cook time: 5 minutes | Serves 5 to 6

2 tablespoons salted grass-fed butter, softened
1 cup raw coconut butter
1 cup sugar-free chocolate

chips
½ cup chopped pecans, or more to taste

Press the Sauté button on the Instant Pot and melt the butter. Fold in the coconut butter, chocolate chips, and pecans and stir until the mixture is smooth. Transfer the mixture to a silicone mini-muffin mold and freeze until firm. Remove from the muffin mold and serve chilled.

Herbed Broccoli and Cheese Egg Cups

Prep time: 10 minutes | Cook time: 6 minutes | Serves 4

7 large eggs, divided
1½ cups half-and-half
3 tablespoons shredded Swiss cheese
1 teaspoon minced fresh basil
2 teaspoons minced fresh parsley

¼ teaspoon salt
⅛ teaspoon cayenne pepper
Cooking spray
1½ cups frozen broccoli florets, thawed
1 cup water

Spritz four ramekins with cooking spray and set aside. Beat together three eggs with the half-and-half, cheese, basil, parsley, salt, and cayenne pepper in a large bowl until well incorporated. Pour the egg mixture evenly into the greased ramekins. Divide the broccoli florets among the ramekins and top each with one remaining egg. Add the water and trivet to the Instant Pot, then place the ramekins on top of the trivet. Cover them loosely with foil. Lock the lid. Select the Steam mode and set the cooking time for 6 minutes at High Pressure. Once cooking is complete, do a quick pressure release. Carefully open the lid. Allow to cool for 5 minutes before removing and serving.

Pumpkin Cake

Prep time: 10 minutes | Cook time: 30 minutes | Serves 8

Streusel Topping:
¼ cup Swerve
¼ cup almond flour
2 tablespoons coconut oil or
Cake:
2 large eggs, beaten
2 cups almond flour
1 cup pumpkin purée
¾ cup Swerve
Glaze:
½ cup Swerve
3 tablespoons unsweetened almond milk

unsalted butter, softened
½ teaspoon ground cinnamon

2 teaspoons pumpkin pie spice
2 teaspoons vanilla extract
½ teaspoon fine sea salt

Set a trivet in the Instant Pot and pour in 1 cup water. Line a baking pan with parchment paper. In a small bowl, whisk together all the ingredients for the streusel topping with a fork. In a medium-sized bowl, stir together all the ingredients for the cake until thoroughly combined. Scoop half of the batter into the prepared baking pan and sprinkle half of the streusel topping on top. Repeat with the remaining batter and topping. Place the baking pan on the trivet in the Instant Pot. Lock the lid, select the Manual mode and set the cooking time for 30 minutes on High Pressure. Meanwhile, whisk together the Swerve and almond milk in a small bowl until it reaches a runny consistency. When the timer goes off, do a natural pressure release for 10 minutes, then release any remaining pressure. Open the lid. Remove the baking pan from the pot. Let cool in the pan for 10 minutes. Transfer the cake onto a plate and peel off the parchment paper. Transfer the cake onto a serving platter. Spoon the glaze over the top of the cake. Serve immediately.

German Berry Pancake

Prep time: 5 minutes | Cook time: 1 hour 30 minutes | Serves 6

4 large eggs
½ cup unsweetened almond milk
½ teaspoon lemon juice
1 teaspoon vanilla extract
1 cup almond flour
¼ cup erythritol and oligosaccharide-blend granular

sweetener
½ teaspoon baking powder
¼ teaspoon ground sea salt
3 tablespoons melted butter, divided
2 tablespoons no-sugar-added berry jam

In a large bowl, combine the eggs, almond milk, lemon juice, and vanilla extract. Whisk to combine. Set aside. In a medium bowl, combine the almond flour, sweetener, baking powder, and sea salt. Mix well. Add the wet ingredients to the dry ingredients and mix until the batter is well combined and no lumps remain. Coat the bottom of the inner pot with 1 tablespoon of the melted butter and then add the batter. Set the lid in place. Select the Slow Cook mode and set the cooking time for 1 hour 30 minutes on High Pressure. When the cook time is complete, open the lid and insert a toothpick into the center of the pancake to check for doneness. (The toothpick should come out clean.) Remove the inner pot from the base. Using a spatula, carefully loosen the edges of the pancake from the sides of the pot and transfer the pancake to a large plate. Use the spatula to flip the pancake over so the browned side is facing up. Slice into 6 equal-sized wedges. Drizzle 1 teaspoon of the melted butter over each wedge and then top each serving with 1 teaspoon of the berry jam. Serve warm.

Mushroom and Bacon Quiche Lorraine

Prep time: 10 minutes | Cook time: 37 minutes | Serves 4

4 strips bacon, chopped
2 cups sliced button mushrooms
½ cup diced onions
8 large eggs
1½ cups shredded Swiss cheese

1 cup unsweetened almond milk
¼ cup sliced green onions
½ teaspoon sea salt
¼ teaspoon ground black pepper
2 tablespoons coconut flour

Press the Sauté button on the Instant Pot and add the bacon. Sauté for 4 minutes, or until crisp. Transfer the bacon to a plate lined with paper towel to drain, leaving the drippings in the pot. Add the mushrooms and diced onions to the pot and sauté for 3 minutes, or until the onions are tender. Remove the mixture from the pot to a large bowl. Wipe the Instant Pot clean. Set a trivet in the Instant Pot and pour in 1 cup water. In a medium bowl, stir together the eggs, cheese, almond milk, green onions, salt and pepper. Pour the egg mixture into the bowl with the mushrooms and onions. Stir to combine. Fold in the coconut flour. Pour the mixture into a greased round casserole dish. Spread the cooked bacon onto top. Place the casserole dish onto the trivet in the Instant Pot. Lock the lid, select the Manual mode and set the cooking time for 30 minutes on High Pressure. When the timer goes off, do a natural pressure release for 15 minutes, then release any remaining pressure. Open the lid. Remove the casserole dish from the Instant Pot. Let cool for 15 to 30 minutes before cutting into 4 pieces. Serve immediately.

Pumpkin Balls

Prep time: 5 minutes | Cook time: 5 minutes | Serves 5 to 6

2 tablespoons salted grass-fed butter, softened
2 cups sugar-free chocolate chips
½ cup organic pumpkin purée, or more to taste

¾ cup raw coconut butter
⅓ cup Swerve, or more to taste
2 teaspoons shredded coconut (optional)
⅛ teaspoon ground cinnamon

Press the Sauté button on the Instant Pot and melt the butter. Fold in the chocolate chips, pumpkin purée, coconut butter, Swerve, coconut (if desired), and cinnamon and stir until melted. Transfer the mixture to a silicone mini-muffin mold and freeze until firm. Serve chilled.

Lemony Applesauce

Prep time: 10 minutes | Cook time: 3 minutes | Makes 5 cups

7 medium apples (about 3 pounds / 1.4 kg), peeled and cored
½ cup water

½ cup sugar
1 tablespoon lemon juice
¼ teaspoon vanilla extract

Slice each apple into 8 wedges on your cutting board, then slice each wedge crosswise in half. Add the apples to the Instant Pot along with the remaining ingredients. Stir well. Secure the lid. Select the Manual mode and set the cooking time for 3 minutes at High Pressure. Once cooking is complete, do a natural pressure release for 10 minutes, then release any remaining pressure. Carefully open the lid. Blend the mixture with an immersion blender until your desired consistency is achieved. Serve warm.

Eggs In Purgatory

Prep time: 15 minutes | Cook time: 24 minutes | Serves 4

2 (14½-ounce / 411-g) cans fire-roasted diced tomatoes, undrained
½ cup water
1 medium onion, chopped
2 garlic cloves, minced
2 tablespoons canola oil
2 teaspoons smoked paprika
½ teaspoon red pepper flakes
½ teaspoon sugar

¼ cup tomato paste
4 large eggs
¼ cup shredded Monterey Jack cheese
2 tablespoons minced fresh parsley
1 (18-ounce / 510-g) tube polenta, sliced and warmed (optional)

Place the tomatoes, water, onion, garlic, oil, paprika, red pepper flakes, and sugar into the Instant Pot and stir to combine. Secure the lid. Select the Pressure Cook mode and set the cooking time for 4 minutes at High Pressure. Once cooking is complete, do a quick pressure release. Carefully open the lid. Set the Instant Pot to Sauté and stir in the tomato paste. Let it simmer for about 10 minutes, stirring occasionally, or until the mixture is slightly thickened. With the back of a spoon, make 4 wells in the sauce and crack an egg into each. Scatter with the shredded cheese. Cover (do not lock the lid) and allow to simmer for 8 to 10 minutes, or until the egg whites are completely set. Sprinkle the parsley on top and serve with the polenta slices, if desired.

Walnut and Pecan Granola

Prep time: 10 minutes | Cook time: 2 minutes | Serves 12

2 cups chopped raw pecans
1¾ cups vanilla-flavored egg white protein powder
1¼ cups unsalted butter, softened
1 cup sunflower seeds

½ cup chopped raw walnuts
½ cup slivered almonds
½ cup sesame seeds
½ cup Swerve
1 teaspoon ground cinnamon
½ teaspoon sea salt

Add all the ingredients to the Instant Pot and stir to combine. Lock the lid, select the Manual mode and set the cooking time for 2 minutes on High Pressure. When the timer goes off, do a natural pressure release for 10 minutes, then release any remaining pressure. Open the lid. Stir well and pour the granola onto a sheet of parchment paper to cool. It will become crispy when completely cool. Serve the granola in bowls.

Apple Smoothie

Prep time: 10 minutes | Cook time: 3 minutes | Makes 5 cups

7 medium apples (about 3 pounds / 1.4 kg), peeled and cored
½ cup water
½ cup sugar
1 tablespoon lemon juice
¼ teaspoon vanilla extract

Slice each apple into 8 wedges on your cutting board, then slice each wedge crosswise in half. Add the apples to the Instant Pot along with the remaining ingredients. Stir well. Secure the lid. Select the Pressure Cook mode and set the cooking time for 3 minutes at High Pressure. Once cooking is complete, do a natural pressure release for 10 minutes, then release any remaining pressure. Carefully open the lid. Blend the mixture with an immersion blender until your desired consistency is achieved. Serve warm.

Pumpkin and Walnut Cake

Prep time: 5 minutes | Cook time: 40 minutes | Serves 5 to 6

Base:

3 eggs	2 tablespoons butter, softened
1 cup almond flour	½ teaspoon ground cinnamon
¾ cup chopped walnuts	½ teaspoon ground nutmeg
½ cup organic pumpkin purée	½ teaspoon baking powder
¼ cup heavy whipping cream	½ teaspoon salt

Topping:

¼ cup heavy whipping cream	½ cup unsweetened coconut
½ cup Swerve	flakes

Pour 1 cup water and insert the trivet in the Instant Pot. Using an electric mixer, combine all the ingredients for the cake. Mix thoroughly. Transfer the mixture into a well-greased baking pan. Place the pan onto the trivet and cover loosely with aluminum foil. Lock the lid. Select the Pressure Cook mode and set the cooking time for 40 minutes on High Pressure. Meanwhile, in a large bowl, whisk together all the ingredients for the topping. Once the timer goes off, perform a natural pressure release for 10 minutes, then release any remaining pressure. Carefully open the lid. Remove the pan from the pot. Sprinkle the topping mixture evenly over the cake. Let cool for 5 minutes before serving.

Broccoli and Ham Frittata

Prep time: 10 minutes | Cook time: 20 minutes | Serves 4

1 cup sliced bell peppers	1 cup grated Cheddar cheese
8 ounces (227 g) ham, cubed	1 teaspoon salt
2 cups frozen broccoli florets	2 teaspoons freshly ground
4 eggs	black pepper
1 cup heavy cream	

Arrange the pepper slices in a greased pan. Place the cubed ham on top. Cover with the frozen broccoli. In a bowl, whisk together the remaining ingredients. Pour the egg mixture over the vegetables and ham. Cover the pan with aluminum foil. Pour 2 cups water and insert the trivet in the Instant Pot. Put the pan on the trivet. Lock the lid. Select the Pressure Cook mode and set the cooking time for 20 minutes on High Pressure. Once the timer goes off, perform a natural pressure release for 10 minutes, then release any remaining pressure. Carefully open the lid. Carefully remove the pan from the pot and remove the foil. Let the frittata sit for 5 to 10 minutes before transferring the frittata onto the plate. Serve warm.

Apple Butter

Prep time: 15 minutes | Cook time: 3 minutes | Makes 5 cups

4 pounds (1.8 kg) large apples,	¼ teaspoon ground cloves
cored and quartered	¼ teaspoon ground allspice
¾ to 1 cup sugar	¼ teaspoon ground nutmeg
¼ cup water	¼ cup creamy peanut butter
3 teaspoons ground cinnamon	

Combine all the ingredients except the butter in the Instant Pot. Secure the lid. Select the Manual mode and set the cooking time for 3 minutes at High Pressure. Once cooking is complete, do a natural pressure release for 5 minutes, then release any remaining pressure. Carefully open the lid. Blend the mixture with an immersion blender. Add the peanut butter and whisk until smooth. Let the mixture cool to room temperature. Serve immediately.

Kale and Sausage Egg Muffins

Prep time: 5 minutes | Cook time: 9 to 10 minutes | Serves 2

3 teaspoons avocado oil,	divided
divided	½ teaspoon ground black
4 ounces (113 g) fully cooked	pepper, divided
chicken sausage, diced	4 large eggs
4 small kale leaves, finely	¼ cup heavy whipping cream
chopped	1 cup water
½ teaspoon kosher salt,	

Grease the bottom and insides of four silicone muffin cups with 1 teaspoon of the avocado oil. Press the Sauté button on the Instant Pot and heat the remaining 2 teaspoons of the avocado oil. Add the sausage to the pot and sauté for 2 minutes. Add the chopped kale and ¼ teaspoon of the salt and black pepper. Sauté for 2 to 3 minutes, or until the kale is wilted. Meanwhile, in a medium bowl, lightly whisk together the eggs, cream and the remaining ¼ teaspoon of the salt and pepper. Divide the kale and sausage mixture among the four muffin cups. Pour the egg mixture evenly over the kale and sausage and stir lightly with a fork. Loosely cover the cups with foil. Pour the water and insert the trivet in the Instant Pot. Put the muffin cups on the trivet. Lock the lid. Select the Pressure Cook mode and set the cooking time for 5 minutes on High Pressure. Once the timer goes off, perform a natural pressure release for 10 minutes, then release any remaining pressure. Carefully open the lid. Remove the muffins from the Instant Pot. Serve hot.

Chicken Congee

Prep time: 5 minutes | Cook time: 5 minutes | Serves 4

1 pound (454 g) chicken	2 tablespoons grass-fed butter,
breasts, cooked and shredded	softened
4 cups grass-fed bone broth	½ teaspoon garlic
1 cup chopped cauliflower	½ teaspoon dried parsley
¼ small onion, thinly sliced	2 bay leaves

Combine all the ingredients in the Instant Pot. Secure the lid. Select the Manual mode and set the cooking time for 5 minutes at High Pressure. Once cooking is complete, do a quick pressure release. Carefully open the lid. Ladle into bowls and serve warm.

Muesli Stuffed Apples

Prep time: 10 minutes | Cook time: 3 minutes | Serves 2

⅓ cup water
2 large unpeeled organic apples, cored and tops removed

Filling:

½ cup coconut muesli	2 teaspoons packed brown
2 tablespoons butter, cubed	sugar
½ teaspoon ground cinnamon	

Pour the water into the Instant Pot and set aside. Mix together all the ingredients for the filling in a bowl, mashing gently with a fork until incorporated. Stuff each apple evenly with the muesli mixture, then arrange them in the Instant Pot. Lock the lid. Select the Pressure Cook mode and set the cooking time for 3 minutes at Low Pressure, depending on how large the apples are. Once cooking is complete, do a natural pressure release for 10 minutes, then release any remaining pressure. Carefully open the lid. Let the apples cool for 5 minutes and serve.

Bell Pepper and Ham Frittata

Prep time: 10 minutes | Cook time: 40 minutes | Serves 2

2 tablespoons avocado oil, divided
¼ cup chopped onion
¼ cup chopped green bell pepper
¼ cup chopped red bell pepper
½ pound (227 g) cooked ham, cubed
6 large eggs
½ cup heavy whipping cream
½ teaspoon sea salt
¼ teaspoon ground black pepper
¼ teaspoon dried basil
¼ teaspoon dried parsley
¼ teaspoon red pepper flakes
1 cup water

Grease a baking pan with 2 teaspoons of the avocado oil. Press the Sauté button on the Instant Pot and heat the remaining 1⅓ tablespoons of the avocado oil. Add the onion and bell peppers to the pot and sauté for 3 minutes, or until tender. Add the ham and continue to sauté for 2 minutes. Transfer the ham and onion mixture to a bowl. Clean the pot. In a medium bowl, whisk together the eggs, cream, salt, black pepper, basil, parsley and pepper flakes. Pour the mixture into the prepared baking pan. Stir in the ham and onion mixture. Cover the pan with foil. Pour the water and insert the trivet in the Instant Pot. Put the pan on the trivet. Lock the lid. Select the Pressure Cook mode and set the cooking time for 35 minutes on High Pressure. Once the timer goes off, perform a natural pressure release for 10 minutes, then release any remaining pressure. Carefully open the lid. Remove the baking pan from the pot. Serve hot.

Buckwheat Groat Bowls

Prep time: 5 minutes | Cook time: 1 minute | Serves 6

2 cups buckwheat groats, soaked for at least 20 minutes, drained, and rinsed
3 cups water
¼ cup pure maple syrup
1 teaspoon ground cinnamon
¼ teaspoon fine sea salt
1 teaspoon vanilla extract
Chopped or sliced fresh fruit, for serving (optional)

In the Instant Pot, combine the buckwheat groats, water, maple syrup, cinnamon, salt, and vanilla. Lock the lid. Select the Pressure Cook mode and set the cooking time for 1 minute at High Pressure. Once cooking is complete, do a natural pressure release for 10 minutes, then release any remaining pressure. Carefully open the lid and stir well. Serve chilled or warm with the fresh fruits, if desired.

Avocado and Bacon Burger

Prep time: 5 minutes | Cook time: 10 minutes | Serves 2

2 tablespoons coconut oil
2 eggs, lightly beaten
3 slices no-sugar-added bacon
½ cup shredded full-fat Cheddar cheese
½ teaspoon kosher salt
½ teaspoon freshly ground black pepper
1 cup shredded lettuce
1 avocado, halved and pitted
2 tablespoons sesame seeds

Press the Sauté button on the Instant Pot and melt the coconut oil. Fold in the beaten eggs, bacon, cheese, salt, and pepper and stir thoroughly and continuously. When cooked, remove the egg mixture from the pot to a bowl. Assemble the burger: Place an avocado half on a clean work surface and top with the egg mixture and shredded lettuce, and finish with the other half of the avocado. Scatter the sesame seeds on top and serve immediately.

Cinnamon Oatmeal

Prep time: 5 minutes | Cook time: 14 minutes | Serves 2

½ cup steel-cut oats
1½ cups water
¼ cup maple syrup, plus additional as needed
2 tablespoons packed brown sugar
¼ teaspoon ground cinnamon
Pinch kosher salt, plus additional as needed
1 tablespoon unsalted butter

Press the Sauté button on the Instant Pot. Add the steel-cut oats and toast for about 2 minutes, stirring occasionally. Add the water, ¼ cup of maple syrup, brown sugar, cinnamon, and pinch salt to the Instant Pot and stir well. Lock the lid. Select the Pressure Cook mode and set the cooking time for 12 minutes at High Pressure. Once cooking is complete, do a natural pressure release for 10 minutes, then release any remaining pressure. Carefully open the lid. Stir the oatmeal and taste, adding additional maple syrup or salt as needed. Let the oatmeal sit for 10 minutes. When ready, add the butter and stir well. Ladle into bowls and serve immediately.

Pecan and Cauliflower Breakfast Bowl

Prep time: 5 minutes | Cook time: 5 minutes | Serves 2

½ cup full-fat coconut milk
⅓ cup riced cauliflower
¼ cup Swerve, or more to taste
2 tablespoons grass-fed butter
½ cup heavy whipping cream
½ cup chopped pecans

Mix together all the ingredients except the heavy whipping cream and pecans in the Instant Pot and stir to combine. Secure the lid. Select the Pressure Cook mode and set the cooking time for 5 minutes at High Pressure. Once cooking is complete, do a natural pressure release for 10 minutes, then release any remaining pressure. Carefully open the lid. Stir in the heavy whipping cream and pecans and serve.

Cabbage and Beef Breakfast Bowl

Prep time: 10 minutes | Cook time: 7 minutes | Serves 4

1 tablespoon avocado oil
1 pound (454 g) ground beef
1 clove garlic, minced
½ teaspoon sea salt
½ teaspoon ground black pepper
½ teaspoon ground turmeric
¼ teaspoon ground cinnamon
¼ teaspoon ground coriander
¼ cup almond butter
½ cup full-fat coconut milk
1 small head green cabbage, shredded

Press the Sauté button on the Instant Pot and heat the oil. Crumble in the ground beef and cook for 3 minutes, breaking up the meat with a wooden spoon or meat chopper. Stir in the garlic, salt, black pepper, turmeric, cinnamon, and coriander. Add the almond butter and coconut milk. Stir constantly until the almond butter melts and mixes with the coconut milk. Layer the cabbage on top of the meat mixture but do not stir. Set the lid in place. Select the Pressure Cook mode and set the cooking time for 4 minutes on High Pressure. When the timer goes off, do a quick pressure release. Carefully open the lid. Stir the meat mixture. Taste and adjust the salt and black pepper, and add more red pepper flakes if desired. Use a slotted spoon to transfer the mixture to a serving bowl. Serve hot.

Bacon and Broccoli Frittata

Prep time: 5 minutes | Cook time: 19 minutes | Serves 2

2 teaspoons avocado oil	4 large eggs
4 slices bacon	¼ cup heavy whipping cream
2 cups chopped broccoli	¼ teaspoon ground cumin
½ teaspoon sea salt	¾ cup crumbled Feta cheese
¼ teaspoon ground black pepper	1 cup water

Use the avocado oil to grease a baking dish that fits inside your Instant Pot. Set the Instant Pot to Sauté mode. When hot, add the bacon and cook, flipping occasionally, until the bacon is crispy. Remove to a plate. Add the broccoli to the pot and season with ¼ teaspoon of the salt and ⅛ teaspoon of the pepper. Sauté for 3 minutes, then transfer the broccoli to a small bowl. In a medium bowl, lightly beat together the eggs, cream, cumin, and the remaining ¼ teaspoon salt and ⅛ teaspoon pepper. Crumble the bacon and stir it into the eggs, along with half the feta cheese. Pour the egg mixture into the prepared baking dish. Quickly stir in the broccoli. Sprinkle with the remaining feta cheese. Cover with a metal or silicone lid, or use foil. Wipe out the Instant Pot if desired. Pour in the water and place the trivet inside. Arrange the sling over it so the two ends stick up like handles, then lower the baking dish onto the sling and the trivet. Lock the lid. Select the Pressure Cook mode and set the cooking time for 16 minutes on High Pressure. Once the timer goes off, perform a natural pressure release for 5 minutes, then release any remaining pressure. Carefully open the lid. Use the sling to carefully remove the hot baking dish. Serve hot or at room temperature.

Sardine and Bacon Green Salad

Prep time: 10 minutes | Cook time: 14 to 15 minutes | Serves 2

2 large eggs	packed sardines
1 cup water	¼ cup fresh parsley leaves
1 tablespoon avocado oil	4 cups chopped romaine
4 slices bacon, cut into small pieces	lettuce
2 tablespoons minced shallots	2 cups baby spinach, torn into smaller pieces
1 tablespoon apple cider vinegar	¼ teaspoon ground black pepper
1 (4.4-ounce / 125-g) can oil-	1 medium avocado, sliced

Pour the water into the Instant Pot. Place the trivet inside and place the eggs on top. Set the lid in place. Select the Pressure Cook mode and set the cooking time for 10 minutes on High Pressure. Meanwhile, prepare a bowl with ice water to cool the eggs. When the timer goes off, do a quick pressure release. Carefully open the lid. Use tongs to transfer the eggs to the ice bath. When cool, peel and slice the eggs. Carefully pour the water out of the Instant Pot and wipe it dry. Set the Instant Pot to Sauté mode and heat the avocado oil. Add the bacon and cook for 3 minutes. Add the shallots and cook until the bacon is crispy, another 1 to 2 minutes. Press Cancel. Deglaze the pot with the vinegar, scraping the bottom with a wooden spoon to loosen any browned bits. Use a fork to break up the sardines and add them, along with their oil, to the pot. Stir in the parsley. Place the lettuce, spinach, and pepper in the pot and mix well to coat the greens with the oil. Divide the mixture between two large serving bowls, scraping any remaining dressing from the pot. Top each salad with half the sliced avocado and 1 sliced egg. Crack some black pepper over the top and serve immediately.

Broccoli Egg Cups

Prep time: 10 minutes | Cook time: 6 minutes | Serves 4

7 large eggs, divided	¼ teaspoon salt
1½ cups half-and-half	⅛ teaspoon cayenne pepper
3 tablespoons shredded Swiss cheese	Cooking spray
1 teaspoon minced fresh basil	1½ cups frozen broccoli florets, thawed
2 teaspoons minced fresh parsley	1 cup water

Spritz four ramekins with cooking spray and set aside. Beat together three eggs with the half-and-half, cheese, basil, parsley, salt, and cayenne pepper in a large bowl until well incorporated. Pour the egg mixture evenly into the greased ramekins. Divide the broccoli florets among the ramekins and top each with one remaining egg. Add the water and trivet to the Instant Pot, then place the ramekins on top of the trivet. Cover them loosely with foil. Lock the lid. Select the Steam mode and set the cooking time for 6 minutes at High Pressure. Once cooking is complete, do a quick pressure release. Carefully open the lid. Allow to cool for 5 minutes before removing and serving.

Pineapple and Bacon Sweet Potato Hash

Prep time: 20 minutes | Cook time: 20 minutes | Serves 6

4 bacon strips, chopped	2 cups cubed fresh pineapple
1 tablespoon canola or coconut oil	½ teaspoon salt
	¼ teaspoon paprika
2 large sweet potatoes, peeled and cut into ½-inch pieces	¼ teaspoon chili powder
	¼ teaspoon pepper
1 cup water	⅛ teaspoon ground cinnamon

Press the Sauté button on the Instant Pot and add the bacon. Cook for about 7 minutes, stirring occasionally, or until crisp. Remove the bacon with a slotted spoon and drain on paper towels. Set aside. In the Instant Pot, heat the oil until it shimmers. Working in batches, add the sweet potatoes to the pot and brown each side for 3 to 4 minutes. Transfer the sweet potatoes to a large bowl and set aside. Pour the water into the pot and cook for 1 minute, stirring to loosen browned bits from pan. Place a steamer basket in the Instant Pot. Add the pineapple, salt, paprika, chili powder, pepper, and cinnamon to the large bowl of sweet potatoes and toss well, then transfer the mixture to the steamer basket. Secure the lid. Select the Steam mode and set the cooking time for 2 minutes at High Pressure. Once cooking is complete, do a quick pressure release. Carefully open the lid. Top with the bacon and serve on a plate.

Banana and Walnut Oatmeal

Prep time: 5 minutes | Cook time: 7 minutes | Serves 2

1 cup water	sugar
1 cup unsweetened soy milk or almond milk	2 teaspoons ground cinnamon
1 cup old-fashioned oats	2 tablespoons chopped walnuts
2 medium bananas, peeled and sliced	¼ teaspoon vanilla extract
2 tablespoons light brown	Pinch salt

In the Instant Pot, combine all ingredients. Stir to combine and lock lid. Press the Manual button and adjust time to 7 minutes. When the timer beeps, let pressure release naturally until float valve drops and then unlock lid. Stir oatmeal. Spoon the oats into serving bowls. Serve warm.

Date and Almond Oatmeal

Prep time: 5 minutes | Cook time: 4 to 6 hours | Serves 8

2 cups dry rolled oats
½ cup dry Grape-Nuts cereal
½ cup slivered almonds
¼ cup chopped dates
4 cups water

Combine all ingredients in the Instant Pot. Press the Slow Cook button, and cook on low for 4 to 6 hours. (Press Slow Cook again to toggle between Low and High cooking temperatures.) Serve with fat-free milk, if desired.

Rhubarb Compote with Almonds

Prep time: 10 minutes | Cook time: 3 minutes | Serves 6

Compote:
2 cups finely chopped fresh rhubarb
¼ cup sugar
⅓ cup water
For Serving:
3 cups reduced-fat plain Greek yogurt
2 tablespoons honey
¾ cup sliced almonds, toasted

Combine the rhubarb, sugar, and water in the Instant Pot. Secure the lid. Select the Pressure Cook mode and set the cooking time for 3 minutes at High Pressure. Once cooking is complete, do a natural pressure release for 10 minutes, then release any remaining pressure. Carefully open the lid. Transfer the mixture to a bowl and let rest for a few minutes until cooled slightly. Place in the refrigerator until chilled. When ready, whisk the yogurt and honey in a small bowl until well combined. Spoon into serving dishes and top each dish evenly with the compote. Scatter with the almonds and serve immediately.

Cranberry Compote with Raisins and Apricots

Prep time: 5 minutes | Cook time: 3 minutes | Makes 2½ cups

1 (12-ounce / 340-g) package fresh or 3 cups frozen cranberries
¼ cup thawed orange juice concentrate
⅔ cup packed brown sugar
2 tablespoons raspberry vinegar
½ cup golden raisins
½ cup chopped dried apricots
½ cup chopped walnuts, toasted

Combine the cranberries, orange juice concentrate, brown sugar, and vinegar in the Instant Pot. Secure the lid. Select the Pressure Cook mode and set the cooking time for 3 minutes at High Pressure. Once cooking is complete, do a natural pressure release for 5 minutes, then release any remaining pressure. Carefully open the lid. Stir in the raisins, apricots, and walnuts and serve warm.

Quinoa with Cucumber and Chickpea Salad

Prep time: 15 minutes | Cook time: 1 minute | Serves 4

2 cups quinoa, rinsed well
2 cups vegetable or chicken broth
Salad:
1 (15-ounce / 425-g) can chickpeas, drained and rinsed
1 cucumber, diced
1 cup chopped flat-leaf parsley
¼ cup extra-virgin olive oil
1 red onion, diced
1 red bell pepper, diced
3 cloves garlic, minced
Juice of 2 lemons
2 tablespoons red wine vinegar
Salt and pepper, to taste
1 to 2 cups crumbled feta cheese (optional)

Place the quinoa and broth into the Instant Pot and stir to incorporate. Lock the lid. Select the Pressure Cook mode and set the cooking time for 1 minute at High Pressure. Once cooking is complete, do a natural pressure release for 10 minutes, then release any remaining pressure. Carefully open the lid. Fluff the quinoa with a fork and allow to cool for 5 to 10 minutes. Remove the quinoa from the pot to a large bowl and toss together with all the salad ingredients until combined. Serve immediately.

Ham and Potato Casserole

Prep time: 20 minutes | Cook time: 35 minutes | Serves 6

6 large eggs
½ cup 2% milk
½ teaspoon salt
¼ teaspoon pepper
4 cups frozen shredded hash brown potatoes, thawed
2 cups shredded Cheddar cheese
1 cup cubed fully cooked ham
½ medium onion, chopped
1 cup water

In a medium bowl, beat together the eggs with the milk, salt, and pepper until combined. In another bowl, thoroughly combine the potatoes, cheese, ham, and onion, then transfer to a greased baking dish. Pour the egg mixture over top. Cover the dish with foil. Pour the water into the Instant Pot and insert a trivet. Place the baking dish on top of the trivet. Secure the lid. Select the Pressure Cook mode and set the cooking time for 35 minutes at High Pressure. Once cooking is complete, do a natural pressure release for 10 minutes, then release any remaining pressure. Carefully open the lid. Allow the casserole cool for 5 to 10 minutes before serving.

Goat Cheese and Asparagus Strata

Prep time: 15 minutes | Cook time: 20 minutes | Serves 4

2 tablespoons unsalted butter, divided
1 small baguette, cut into 1-inch chunks
4 ounces (113 g) Goat cheese, crumbled
8 ounces (227 g) cooked asparagus, cut into 1-inch chunks (or use thawed frozen
asparagus)
3 eggs
1½ cups whole milk
¼ teaspoon kosher salt
¼ teaspoon dry mustard
⅛ teaspoon freshly ground black pepper
1 cup water

In a 2-quart tempered glass baking dish that fits into the pot of your Instant Pot, rub the bottom and insides with 1 tablespoon of butter. Arrange a layer of the bread on the bottom of the dish. Sprinkle half the Goat cheese and asparagus over the bread. Place another layer of bread in the dish and top it with the remaining Goat cheese and asparagus. Top this with any remaining bread to fill to the top of the dish. Set aside. In a medium bowl, lightly whisk the eggs. Whisk in the milk, salt, mustard, and pepper. Pour the mixture over the bread and use a wooden spoon or spatula to press the bread down to soak it with the egg mixture. Let it sit for 5 minutes to allow the bread to absorb the eggs. Place the rack inside the Instant Pot pot. Pour the water into the pot. Cut the remaining 1 tablespoon of butter into small pieces and dot them over the top of the casserole. Carefully put the casserole dish on the rack inside the Instant Pot. Lock on the lid and set the timer for 20 minutes at Low Pressure. When the timer goes off, natural release the pressure for 10 minutes. Quick release any remaining pressure and carefully take the dish out of the Instant Pot. Serve hot.

Herbed Beef Breakfast Bowl

Prep time: 5 minutes | Cook time: 10 minutes | Serves 4

2 tablespoons avocado oil	pepper
1 pound (454 g) ground grass-fed beef	½ teaspoon kosher salt
	½ teaspoon cayenne pepper
½ teaspoon dried cilantro	½ teaspoon freshly ground
½ teaspoon ground turmeric	black pepper
½ teaspoon crushed red	½ cup filtered water

Press the Sauté button on the Instant Pot and melt the avocado oil. Put the ground beef in the Instant Pot, breaking it up gently. Stir in the cilantro, turmeric, red pepper, salt, cayenne pepper, and black pepper. Pour in the water. Secure the lid. Select the Pressure Cook mode and set the cooking time for 10 minutes at High Pressure. Once cooking is complete, do a natural pressure release for 10 minutes, then release any remaining pressure. Carefully open the lid. Allow to cool for 5 minutes before serving.

Macadamia and Coconut Bowl

Prep time: 5 minutes | Cook time: 0 minutes | Serves 4

2 cups filtered water	⅓ cup Swerve, or more to taste
2 cups full-fat coconut milk	¼ cup blanched almond flour
1 cup dried unsweetened coconut	2 tablespoons unsweetened cocoa powder
1 cup sugar-free chocolate chips	½ teaspoon kosher salt
1 cup macadamia nuts	½ teaspoon ground cinnamon

Press the Sauté button on your Instant Pot. Add the filtered water and the coconut milk. Add the remaining ingredients and stir until well mixed. Secure the lid. Press the Pressure Cook button on the Instant Pot and set the cooking time for 0 minutes on High Pressure. Once the timer goes off, do a quick pressure release. Carefully open the lid. Divide the cereal among four serving bowls and serve warm.

Hawaiian Sweet Potato Hash

Prep time: 20 minutes | Cook time: 20 minutes | Serves 6

4 bacon strips, chopped	2 cups cubed fresh pineapple
1 tablespoon canola or coconut oil	½ teaspoon salt
	¼ teaspoon paprika
2 large sweet potatoes, peeled and cut into ½-inch pieces	¼ teaspoon chili powder
	¼ teaspoon pepper
1 cup water	⅛ teaspoon ground cinnamon

Press the Sauté button on the Instant Pot and add the bacon. Cook for about 7 minutes, stirring occasionally, or until crisp. Remove the bacon with a slotted spoon and drain on paper towels. Set aside. In the Instant Pot, heat the oil until it shimmers. Working in batches, add the sweet potatoes to the pot and brown each side for 3 to 4 minutes. Transfer the sweet potatoes to a large bowl and set aside. Pour the water into the pot and cook for 1 minute, stirring to loosen browned bits from pan. Place a steamer basket in the Instant Pot. Add the pineapple, salt, paprika, chili powder, pepper, and cinnamon to the large bowl of sweet potatoes and toss well, then transfer the mixture to the steamer basket. Secure the lid. Select the Steam mode and set the cooking time for 2 minutes at High Pressure. Once cooking is complete, do a quick pressure release. Carefully open the lid. Top with the bacon and serve on a plate.

Chicken and Spinach Bowls

Prep time: 5 minutes | Cook time: 10 minutes | Serves 4

2 tablespoons coconut oil	½ teaspoon dried basil
1 pound (454 g) ground chicken	½ teaspoon dried parsley
	½ teaspoon dried cilantro
1 cup shredded full-fat Cheddar cheese	1 tablespoon hot sauce
	½ teaspoon kosher salt
2 tablespoons sugar-free or low-sugar salsa	½ teaspoon freshly ground black pepper
½ cup chopped spinach	1 cup filtered water
1 teaspoon curry powder	

Press the Sauté button on the Instant Pot and heat the coconut oil. Fold in the ground chicken, cheese, salsa, spinach, curry powder, basil, parsley, cilantro, hot sauce, salt, and pepper and stir thoroughly. Pour in the water. Secure the lid. Select the Pressure Cook mode and set the cooking time for 10 minutes at High Pressure. Once cooking is complete, do a quick pressure release. Carefully open the lid. Serve warm.

Avocado and Chicken Platter

Prep time: 5 minutes | Cook time: 10 minutes | Serves 4

2 tablespoons avocado oil	1 teaspoon hot sauce
1 pound (454 g) ground chicken	1 teaspoon lime juice
	½ teaspoon kosher salt
½ cup shredded full fat Cheddar cheese (optional)	½ teaspoon freshly ground black pepper
½ cup filtered water	1 cup mashed avocado
1 jalapeño pepper, finely chopped	¾ cup low-sugar salsa

Press the Sauté button on the Instant Pot and melt the avocado oil. Add the ground chicken, cheese (if desired), water, jalapeño, hot sauce, lime juice, salt, and black pepper to the Instant Pot and stir to incorporate. Secure the lid. Select the Pressure Cook mode and set the cooking time for 10 minutes at High Pressure. Once cooking is complete, do a quick pressure release. Carefully open the lid. Serve topped with the mashed avocado and salsa.

Rhubarb Compote

Prep time: 10 minutes | Cook time: 3 minutes | Serves 6

Compote:

2 cups finely chopped fresh rhubarb	¼ cup sugar
	⅓ cup water

For Serving:

3 cups reduced-fat plain Greek yogurt	2 tablespoons honey
	¾ cup sliced almonds, toasted

Combine the rhubarb, sugar, and water in the Instant Pot. Secure the lid. Select the Manual mode and set the cooking time for 3 minutes at High Pressure. Once cooking is complete, do a natural pressure release for 10 minutes, then release any remaining pressure. Carefully open the lid. Transfer the mixture to a bowl and let rest for a few minutes until cooled slightly. Place in the refrigerator until chilled. When ready, whisk the yogurt and honey in a small bowl until well combined. Spoon into serving dishes and top each dish evenly with the compote. Scatter with the almonds and serve immediately.

Cranberry Compote

Prep time: 5 minutes | Cook time: 3 minutes | Makes 2½ cups

1 (12-ounce / 340-g) package fresh or 3 cups frozen cranberries
¼ cup thawed orange juice concentrate
⅔ cup packed brown sugar

2 tablespoons raspberry vinegar
½ cup golden raisins
½ cup chopped dried apricots
½ cup chopped walnuts, toasted

Combine the cranberries, orange juice concentrate, brown sugar, and vinegar in the Instant Pot. Secure the lid. Select the Manual mode and set the cooking time for 3 minutes at High Pressure. Once cooking is complete, do a natural pressure release for 5 minutes, then release any remaining pressure. Carefully open the lid. Stir in the raisins, apricots, and walnuts and serve warm.

Arugula Frittata

Prep time: 5 minutes | Cook time: 5 minutes | Serves 2

3 eggs, beaten
¼ cup loosely packed arugula
¼ red onion, chopped
¼ cup feta cheese crumbles
¼ teaspoon garlic powder

Kosher salt, to taste
Freshly ground black pepper, to taste
1 cup water

Stir together the eggs, arugula, onion, feta cheese crumbles, garlic powder, salt, and pepper in a medium bowl. Pour the egg mixture into a greased round cake pan and cover with foil. Add the water and trivet to the Instant Pot, then place the cake pan on top of the trivet. Lock the lid. Select the Manual mode and set the cooking time for 5 minutes at High Pressure. Once cooking is complete, do a natural pressure release for 10 minutes, then release any remaining pressure. Carefully open the lid. Let the frittata rest for 5 minutes in the pan before cutting and serving.

Herbed Bell Pepper and Bacon Omelet

Prep time: 5 minutes | Cook time: 20 minutes | Serves 2

2 tablespoons avocado oil
¼ cup red bell pepper, finely chopped
¼ cup green bell pepper, finely chopped
¼ cup onion, chopped
½ cup shredded full-fat Cheddar cheese
2 slices no-sugar-added bacon, cooked and finely cut (optional)

6 eggs
½ teaspoon dried parsley
½ teaspoon dried basil
½ teaspoon kosher salt
½ teaspoon crushed red pepper
½ teaspoon freshly ground black pepper
Cooking spray
1 cup filtered water

Press the Sauté button on your Instant Pot. Add and heat the oil. Add the bell pepper and onion and sauté for 4 minutes. Mix together the eggs, cheese, bacon (if desired), parsley, basil, salt, and pepper in a medium bowl and stir well. Spray a glass dish with cooking spray and pour in the mixture. Fold in the sautéed bell pepper and onion, scraping the bits from the pot, and mix well. Add 1 cup of filtered water to the inner pot of the Instant Pot and then place the trivet in the bottom of the pot. Carefully lower the dish into the Instant Pot with a sling. Secure the lid. Press the Manual button on the Instant Pot and set the cooking time for 20 minutes at High Pressure. When the timer beeps, use a natural pressure release for about 10 minutes and then release any remaining pressure. Carefully open the lid. Remove the dish and serve.

Leek and Asparagus Frittata

Prep time: 10 minutes | Cook time: 10 minutes | Serves 4

6 eggs
¼ teaspoon fine sea salt
Freshly ground black pepper, to taste
8 ounces (227 g) asparagus spears, woody stems removed and cut into 1-inch pieces
1 cup thinly sliced leeks

¼ cup grated Parmesan cheese
1 cup water
Chopped green onions, for garnish (optional)
Fresh flat-leaf parsley, for garnish (optional)

Whisk together the eggs, salt, and black pepper in a large mixing bowl until frothy. Add the asparagus pieces, leeks, and cheese and stir to combine. Pour the mixture into a greased round cake pan. Add the water and trivet to the Instant Pot, then place the pan on top of the trivet. Lock the lid. Select the Manual mode and set the cooking time for 10 minutes at High Pressure. Once cooking is complete, do a natural pressure release for 10 minutes, then release any remaining pressure. Carefully open the lid. Allow the frittata to cool for 5 minutes. Garnish with the green onions and parsley, if desired. Cut the frittata into wedges and serve warm.

Cheddar and Spinach Strata

Prep time: 5 minutes | Cook time: 40 minutes | Serves 4

1 cup filtered water
6 eggs
1 cup chopped spinach
1 cup shredded full-fat Cheddar cheese
¼ small onion, thinly sliced
½ tablespoon salted grass-fed butter, softened
½ teaspoon Dijon mustard

½ teaspoon kosher salt
½ teaspoon freshly ground black pepper
½ teaspoon cayenne pepper
½ teaspoon paprika
½ teaspoon dried sage
½ teaspoon dried cilantro
½ teaspoon dried parsley

Pour the water into the the Instant Pot, then place the trivet. Whisk together the eggs, spinach, cheese, onion, butter, mustard, salt, black pepper, cayenne pepper, paprika, sage, cilantro, and parsley in a large bowl until well incorporated. Pour the egg mixture into a greased baking dish. Cover the dish loosely with aluminum foil. Put the dish on top of the trivet. Secure the lid. Select the Manual mode and set the cooking time for 40 minutes at High Pressure. Once cooking is complete, do a natural pressure release for 10 minutes, then release any remaining pressure. Carefully open the lid. Let the strata rest for 5 minutes and serve warm.

Raisin and Apricot Oatmeal

Prep time: 5 minutes | Cook time: 10 minutes | Serves 2

2 cups water
1 cup old-fashioned oats, toasted
2 teaspoons vegan margarine
1 cup apple juice
1 tablespoon dried cranberries

1 tablespoon golden raisins
1 tablespoon chopped dried apricots
1 tablespoon maple syrup
¼ teaspoon ground cinnamon
Pinch salt

In the Instant Pot, combine the water, oats, margarine, apple juice, cranberries, raisins, apricots, maple syrup, cinnamon, and salt. Stir to combine and lock lid. Press the Manual button and adjust time to 10 minutes. When the timer beeps, let pressure release naturally until float valve drops and then unlock lid. Stir oatmeal. Spoon the oats into serving bowls. Serve warm.

Bacon and Spinach Quiche

Prep time: 5 minutes | Cook time: 35 minutes | Serves 3

1 cup filtered water
5 eggs, lightly beaten
½ cup spinach, chopped
½ cup full-fat coconut milk
½ cup shredded full-fat
Cheddar cheese
2 slices no-sugar-added bacon,

cooked and finely chopped
½ teaspoon dried parsley
½ teaspoon dried basil
½ teaspoon freshly ground
black pepper
¼ teaspoon kosher salt

Pour the water into the the Instant Pot, then place the trivet. Stir together the remaining ingredients in a baking dish. Cover the dish loosely with aluminum foil. Place the dish on top of the trivet. Secure the lid. Select the Manual mode and set the cooking time for 35 minutes at High Pressure. Once cooking is complete, do a natural pressure release for 10 minutes, then release any remaining pressure. Carefully open the lid. Serve warm.

Coconut, Chocolate, and Macadamia Bowl

Prep time: 5 minutes | Cook time: 0 minutes | Serves 4

2 cups filtered water
2 cups full-fat coconut milk
1 cup dried unsweetened
coconut
1 cup sugar-free chocolate
chips
1 cup macadamia nuts

⅓ cup Swerve, or more to taste
¼ cup blanched almond flour
2 tablespoons unsweetened
cocoa powder
½ teaspoon kosher salt
½ teaspoon ground cinnamon

Press the Sauté button on your Instant Pot. Add the filtered water and the coconut milk. Add the remaining ingredients and stir until well mixed. Secure the lid. Press the Manual button on the Instant Pot and set the cooking time for 0 minutes on High Pressure. Once the timer goes off, do a quick pressure release. Carefully open the lid. Divide the cereal among four serving bowls and serve warm.

Toast Casserole

Prep time: 15 minutes | Cook time: 20 minutes | Serves 4

2 tablespoons unsalted butter,
divided
8 slices stale white bread,
crusts removed, cut into 1-inch
cubes
3 eggs

1½ cups whole milk
¼ cup maple syrup
1 tablespoon vanilla extract
1 teaspoon ground cinnamon
⅛ teaspoon kosher salt
1 cup water

Rub the bottom and insides of a 2-quart tempered glass baking dish that fits into the pot of your Instant Pot with 1 tablespoon of butter. Pile the bread cubes in the dish, and set aside. In a medium bowl, lightly whisk the eggs. Whisk in the milk, maple syrup, vanilla, cinnamon, and salt. Pour the mixture over the bread and use a wooden spoon or spatula to press the bread down to soak it with the egg mixture. Let it sit for 5 minutes to allow the bread to absorb the eggs. Place the rack inside the Instant Pot pot. Pour the water into the pot. Cut the remaining 1 tablespoon of butter into small pieces and dot them over the top of the casserole. Carefully put the casserole dish on the rack inside the Instant Pot. Lock on the lid and set the timer for 20 minutes at Low Pressure. When the timer goes off, natural release the pressure for 10 minutes. Quick release any remaining pressure and carefully take the dish out of the Instant Pot. Serve hot.

Bacon and Avocado Burger

Prep time: 5 minutes | Cook time: 10 minutes | Serves 2

2 tablespoons coconut oil
2 eggs, lightly beaten
3 slices no-sugar-added bacon
½ cup shredded full-fat
Cheddar cheese
½ teaspoon kosher salt

½ teaspoon freshly ground
black pepper
1 cup shredded lettuce
1 avocado, halved and pitted
2 tablespoons sesame seeds

Press the Sauté button on the Instant Pot and melt the coconut oil. Fold in the beaten eggs, bacon, cheese, salt, and pepper and stir thoroughly and continuously. When cooked, remove the egg mixture from the pot to a bowl. Assemble the burger: Place an avocado half on a clean work surface and top with the egg mixture and shredded lettuce, and finish with the other half of the avocado. Scatter the sesame seeds on top and serve immediately.

Spinach and Chicken Breakfast Bowl

Prep time: 5 minutes | Cook time: 10 minutes | Serves 4

2 tablespoons coconut oil
1 pound (454 g) ground
chicken
1 cup shredded full-fat
Cheddar cheese
2 tablespoons sugar-free or
low-sugar salsa
½ cup chopped spinach
1 teaspoon curry powder

½ teaspoon dried basil
½ teaspoon dried parsley
½ teaspoon dried cilantro
1 tablespoon hot sauce
½ teaspoon kosher salt
½ teaspoon freshly ground
black pepper
1 cup filtered water

Press the Sauté button on the Instant Pot and heat the coconut oil. Fold in the ground chicken, cheese, salsa, spinach, curry powder, basil, parsley, cilantro, hot sauce, salt, and pepper and stir thoroughly. Pour in the water. Secure the lid. Select the Manual mode and set the cooking time for 10 minutes at High Pressure. Once cooking is complete, do a quick pressure release. Carefully open the lid. Serve warm.

Blueberry French Toast

Prep time: 15 minutes | Cook time: 20 minutes | Serves 4

1⅓ cups 2% milk
3 tablespoons sugar
2 large eggs
1 teaspoon vanilla extract
1 teaspoon ground cinnamon
¼ teaspoon salt
Cooking spray

6 cups cubed French bread,
about 6 ounces (170 g),
divided
¾ cup fresh or frozen
blueberries, divided
1 cup water
Maple syrup, for serving

Stir together the milk, sugar, eggs, vanilla, cinnamon, and salt. Spray a baking dish with cooking spray and place 3 cups of bread cubes in the dish. Place half the milk mixture and half the blueberries on top. Repeat layers. Add the water to your Instant Pot and put the trivet in the bottom of the pot. Wrap the baking dish in aluminum foil. Create a foil sling and carefully lower the baking dish into the Instant Pot. Secure the lid. Press the Manual button on the Instant Pot and set the cooking time for 20 minutes on High Pressure. Once cooking is complete, use a natural pressure release for 10 minutes and then release any remaining pressure. Carefully remove the baking dish using the foil sling. Let sit for 10 minutes. Serve with the syrup.

Spicy Chicken Platter
Prep time: 5 minutes | Cook time: 10 minutes | Serves 4

2 tablespoons avocado oil
1 pound (454 g) ground chicken
½ cup shredded full fat Cheddar cheese (optional)
½ cup filtered water
1 jalapeño pepper, finely chopped

1 teaspoon hot sauce
1 teaspoon lime juice
½ teaspoon kosher salt
½ teaspoon freshly ground black pepper
1 cup mashed avocado
¾ cup low-sugar salsa

Press the Sauté button on the Instant Pot and melt the avocado oil. Add the ground chicken, cheese (if desired), water, jalapeño, hot sauce, lime juice, salt, and black pepper to the Instant Pot and stir to incorporate. Secure the lid. Select the Manual mode and set the cooking time for 10 minutes at High Pressure. Once cooking is complete, do a quick pressure release. Carefully open the lid. Serve topped with the mashed avocado and salsa.

Pecan and Pumpkin Porridge
Prep time: 5 minutes | Cook time: 10 minutes | Serves 2 to 4

¼ cup unsweetened coconut flakes
2 cups filtered water
2 cups full-fat coconut milk
1 cup organic pumpkin purée
1 cup pecans, chopped

¼ cup organic coconut flour
½ teaspoon ground cinnamon
½ teaspoon ginger, finely grated
Swerve, to taste (optional)

Press the Sauté button on your Instant Pot and toast the coconut flakes, stirring occasionally. Pour in the filtered water and milk. Secure the lid. Press the Manual button on the Instant Pot and set the cooking time for 0 minutes on High Pressure. Once cooking is complete, use a natural pressure release for about 10 minutes and then release any remaining pressure. Carefully remove the lid. Fold in the pumpkin, pecans, flour, cinnamon, ginger, and Swerve (if desired). Let stand for 2 to 4 minutes until desired consistency, stirring occasionally. Ladle the porridge into bowls and serve warm.

Cheddar and Spinach Egg Bites
Prep time: 5 minutes | Cook time: 10 minutes | Serves 2 to 4

1 cup filtered water
6 eggs
½ cup shredded full-fat Cheddar cheese
½ cup bell peppers, finely chopped

½ cup spinach, finely chopped
½ teaspoon dried cilantro
½ teaspoon kosher salt
½ teaspoon freshly ground black pepper
Cooking spray

Place the trivet in the bottom of your Instant Pot and add the water. Mix together the eggs, cheese, bell peppers, spinach, cilantro, salt, and pepper in a large bowl. Stir well. Spritz a silicone egg mold with cooking spray and ladle the mixture into the impressions in the mold. Put the mold on the trivet with a sling and wrap loosely in aluminum foil. Secure the lid and select Press the Manual button on the Instant Pot and set the cooking time for 10 minutes at High Pressure. When the timer beeps, use a quick pressure release. Carefully open the lid. Remove the egg mold from the pot. Remove the foil and allow to cool for 5 minutes. Scoop the egg bites out of the mold with a spoon and transfer to a serving dish. Serve.

Shakshuka
Prep time: 10 minutes | Cook time: 5 minutes | Serves 4

1 tablespoon extra-virgin olive oil
2 cloves garlic, minced
½ yellow onion, chopped
Fine sea salt, to taste
2½ cups marinara sauce

1 cup chopped kale, stems removed
¼ cup water
4 eggs
Freshly ground black pepper, to taste

Press the Sauté button on your Instant Pot. Add and heat the olive oil. Add the garlic, onion, and a pinch of salt and sauté for about 5 minutes until soft. Add the marinara sauce, kale, and water and stir well with a wooden spoon, scraping the bits from the pot. Create four small wells evenly spaced in the marinara sauce with the spoon and then crack an egg into each well. Sprinkle the eggs with salt and pepper. Lock the lid. Press the Manual button on your Instant Pot and set the cooking time for 0 minutes on High Pressure. Once cooking is complete, use a quick pressure release. Carefully open the lid. Scoop the eggs, sauce, and cooked vegetables into a small serving dish with a slotted spoon. Serve immediately.

Ham and Cheese Soufflé
Prep time: 10 minutes | Cook time: 3 to 4 hours | Serves 6

8 slices bread (crusts removed), cubed or torn into squares
2 cups shredded Cheddar, Swiss, or American cheese
1 cup cooked, chopped ham
4 eggs

1 cup light cream or milk
1 cup evaporated milk
¼ teaspoon salt
1 tablespoon parsley
Paprika, to taste
Nonstick cooking spray

Lightly grease the Instant Pot with nonstick cooking spray. Alternate layers of bread and cheese and ham. Beat together eggs, milk, salt, and parsley in a bowl. Pour over bread in the Instant Pot and sprinkle with paprika. Cover and press the Slow Cook button, and cook on low for 3 to 4 hours. (Press Slow Cook again to toggle between Low and High cooking temperatures.) Serve warm.

Bacon and Spinach Scrambled Eggs
Prep time: 5 minutes | Cook time: 20 minutes | Serves 2

4 eggs
2 tablespoons coconut oil, plus more for greasing the pot
1 cup filtered water
4 slices no-sugar-added bacon, cooked and finely cut
1 cup spinach, chopped
½ cup shredded full-fat Cheddar cheese

¼ cup full-fat coconut milk
½ teaspoon chili powder
½ teaspoon dried parsley
½ teaspoon dried basil
½ teaspoon ground cumin
½ teaspoon kosher salt
½ teaspoon freshly ground black pepper

Grease the inner pot of your Instant Pot. Add all the ingredients and stir until well mixed. Add the filtered water to the pot. Secure the lid. Press the Manual button on your Instant Pot and set the cooking time for 20 minutes at High Pressure. Once cooking is complete, use a natural pressure release for about 10 minutes and then release any remaining pressure. Carefully remove the lid. Transfer to a serving dish and serve.

Breakfast Fish Congee
Prep time: 10 minutes | Cook time: 4⅓ hours | Serves 6

1½ cups long-grain white rice
1 (1-inch) piece fresh ginger, peeled and grated
3 quarts boiling water
12 ounces (340 g) firm white

fish fillets, such as flounder or cod, skin removed, thinly sliced
Coarse salt, to taste
Sliced scallions, for serving

Place the rice and ginger into the Instant Pot. Add the boiling water and stir. Cover and press the Slow Cook button, and cook on low for about 4 hours or on high for 2 hours until congee reaches consistency of loose porridge. (Press Slow Cook again to toggle between Low and High cooking temperatures.) Add fish and cook on low until fish falls apart, about 20 minutes more (or on high for 10 minutes). Season to taste with salt and serve with the sliced scallions.

Corn and Sweet Potato Scramble
Prep time: 10 minutes | Cook time: 8 hours | Serves 2

1 teaspoon butter, at room temperature, or extra-virgin olive oil
4 eggs
½ cup 2% milk
⅛ teaspoon sea salt
½ teaspoon smoked paprika
½ teaspoon ground cumin

Freshly ground black pepper, to taste
1 cup finely diced sweet potato
1 cup frozen corn kernels, thawed
½ cup diced roasted red peppers
2 tablespoons minced onion

Grease the inside of the Instant Pot with the butter. In a small bowl, whisk together the eggs, milk, salt, paprika, and cumin. Season with the freshly ground black pepper. Put the sweet potato, corn, red peppers, and onion into the Instant Pot. Pour in the egg mixture and stir gently. Cover and press the Slow Cook button, and cook on low for 8 hours or overnight. (Press Slow Cook again to toggle between Low and High cooking temperatures.) Serve warm.

Yogurt Jars
Prep time: 5 minutes | Cook time: 18 hours | Serves 4

4 cups plain soy or pea-based milk
1 (5 ounce / 142 g) container plain or vanilla vegan yogurt with live cultures

2 teaspoons vanilla bean paste, or seeds from 1 vanilla bean
Organic liquid stevia (optional), to taste

Pour the milk and yogurt into a medium bowl. Whisk until completely combined. Whisk in the vanilla bean paste or seeds. If desired, sweeten to taste with a few drops of liquid stevia. Pour the milk mixture evenly into 4 pint-sized glass jars. Place the jars directly into the inner pot, not on a trivet. (You won't need any water in the pot because it is not using pressure.) Place the glass lid on top of the Instant Pot, or use your regular lid with the steam release valve in the venting position. Select Yogurt (Medium), and set the cook time for 18 hours. Your yogurt is ready when it's thick; this may take anywhere from 13 to 20 hours. Once the yogurt is the desired consistency, remove the jars and secure with the lids. Store in the refrigerator for up to 1 week. Enjoy your homemade yogurt cold. The top half of each jar will be empty and ready to be filled with your favorite fruit or granola and a splash of maple syrup.

Potato and Ham Omelet
Prep time: 15 minutes | Cook time: 8 to 9 hours | Serves 10

1 (32-ounce / 907-g) bag frozen hash brown potatoes
1 pound (454 g) cooked ham, cubed
1 medium onion, diced
1½ cups shredded Cheddar

cheese
12 eggs
1 cup milk
1 teaspoon salt
1 teaspoon pepper

Layer one-third each of frozen potatoes, ham, onion, and cheese in the bottom of the Instant Pot. Repeat 2 times. Beat together eggs, milk, salt, and pepper in a bowl. Pour over mixture in the Instant Pot. Cover and press the Slow Cook button, and cook on low for 8 to 9 hours. (Press Slow Cook again to toggle between Low and High cooking temperatures.) Serve with orange juice and fresh fruit, if desired.

Quinoa and Dried Fruit Porridge
Prep time: 7 minutes | Cook time: 5 minutes | Serves 2

1½ cups water, divided
½ cup white quinoa
½ cup milk
¼ cup diced dried fruit

¼ teaspoon ground cinnamon
½ tablespoon maple syrup or brown sugar

Place a rack into the pot of the Instant Pot. Add 1 cup of water to the pot. In a heat-proof glass 1-quart bowl, combine the quinoa, the remaining ½ cup of water, milk, diced fruit, and cinnamon. Stir with a spoon to combine and scrape down any stray pieces of quinoa from the sides of the bowl. Place the bowl on the rack. Lock on the lid and set the timer for 5 minutes at High Pressure. When the timer goes off, natural release the pressure for 10 minutes, then quick release any remaining pressure. Stir the quinoa, then stir in the maple syrup. Serve hot.

Potato and Tofu Frittata
Prep time: 10 minutes | Cook time: 12 minutes | Serves 4

16 ounces (454 g) firm tofu, drained
½ cup unsweetened soy milk
4 teaspoons cornstarch
2 teaspoons nutritional yeast
1 teaspoon spicy mustard
½ teaspoon turmeric powder
1 teaspoon salt
2 tablespoons olive oil
1 cup peeled and diced red

potatoes
½ cup diced red onion
½ cup diced red bell pepper
½ cup diced green bell pepper
1 teaspoon minced jalapeño pepper
1 clove garlic, minced
¼ cup chopped fresh Italian flat-leaf parsley
¾ cup water

In a blender or food processor combine the tofu, soy milk, cornstarch, nutritional yeast, mustard, turmeric, and salt and process until smooth. Set aside. Add the olive oil to the Instant Pot and press the Sauté button. Add the potatoes, onion, peppers, garlic, and parsley; sauté 3 to 5 minutes. Transfer the cooked mixture to a 7 cup greased glass dish and pour the tofu mixture into the cooked potato mixture. Place the trivet in the Instant Pot. Pour in the water. Place the dish with the tofu mixture on the trivet. Lock the lid into place. Press the Manual button and adjust time to 7 minutes. When the timer beeps, let pressure release naturally until the float valve drops and then unlock lid. Remove the dish from the pot and put aside 5–10 minutes to set. Slice and serve.

Breakfast Almond Oats

Prep time: 8 minutes | Cook time: 10 minutes | Serves 2

1 tablespoon unsalted butter
1 cup steel-cut oats
1 cup whole or part-skim milk, divided
2 tablespoons brown sugar
1 teaspoon ground cinnamon
½ teaspoon vanilla extract
¼ cup slivered almonds, toasted

With the Instant Pot on the Sauté or brown setting, melt the butter. When it melts, add the oats and toast them, stirring frequently, for 2 to 3 minutes, until they're fragrant. Add 2 cups of water and ½ cup of milk, the brown sugar, and the cinnamon. Stir to combine. Lock on the lid and set the timer for 10 minutes at High Pressure. When the timer goes off, turn off the Instant Pot and natural release for 10 minutes, then quick release any remaining pressure. Open the Instant Pot and stir the liquid back into the oats. If it's still soupy, cover the Instant Pot and let the oats sit for 5 minutes. Stir in as much of the remaining ½ cup of milk as desired and the vanilla extract. Serve hot, sprinkled with the toasted almonds.

Spinach and Asparagus Frittata

Prep time: 10 minutes | Cook time: 8 minutes | Serves 6

1 cup chickpea flour (also called garbanzo bean or gram flour)
1 teaspoon baking powder
1 teaspoon garlic powder
½ teaspoon sea salt
¼ teaspoon freshly ground black pepper
2⅛ cups water, divided
¼ teaspoon apple cider vinegar
1 teaspoon Dijon mustard
1 tablespoon extra virgin olive oil
1 cup chopped leeks (about 1 leek)
1 cup (2-inch; 5 cm) asparagus pieces (about ½ of a bunch)
1 cup packed baby spinach
¼ cup chopped chives, for garnish
6 ounce (170 g) plain dairy-free yogurt or soft cheese(optional), for garnish

Coat a springform pan with cooking spray, or brush with olive oil. Set aside. In a medium mixing bowl, whisk together the chickpea flour, baking powder, garlic powder, salt, and pepper. Add 1⅛ cup water, vinegar, and mustard, and whisk vigorously until bubbly and well combined, about 1 minute. Set aside. Select Sauté (High), and heat the oil in the inner pot, or use a medium skillet over medium-high heat. Sauté the leeks and asparagus with a pinch of salt and pepper until the asparagus is just tender, about 5 minutes. Add the spinach and sauté until wilted, about 1 minute. Evenly spread the vegetables in the springform pan. If you used the inner pot to sauté, clean it out and place back in the Instant Pot. Pour the chickpea flour mixture over the vegetables. Cover the top of the pan with foil. Fit the inner pot with the trivet or steam rack, and add the remaining 1 cup water. Place the pan on the trivet. Lock the lid and ensure the steam release valve is set to the sealing position. Select Pressure Cook (High), and set the cook time for 8 minutes. Once the cook time is complete, immediately quick release the pressure. Carefully remove the lid and the pan. Remove the foil and let the pan rest on a cooling rack for 5 minutes. Use a thin knife, if needed, to release the frittata from the sides of the pan. Remove the sides of the pan. If desired, place on a cookie sheet and broil for a few minutes to brown the top. Cut into slices and serve immediately, garnished with chives and yogurt or cheese, if desired. This recipe is best served right when it's made because the frittata will become m ore dense the longer it sits.

Apple Oatmeal with Pecans

Prep time: 5 minutes | Cook time: 8 minutes | Serves 2

1 cup water
1 cup unsweeted soy milk or almond milk
2 medium Granny Smith apples, peeled, cored, and diced
1 cup old-fashioned oats
2 tablespoons light brown sugar
2 teaspoons ground cinnamon
2 tablespoons chopped pecans

In the Instant Pot, combine the water, soy milk, oats, apples, brown sugar, and cinnamon. Stir to combine and lock lid. Press the Manual button and adjust time to 8 minutes. When the timer beeps, let pressure release naturally until float valve drops and then unlock lid. Stir the oatmeal. Spoon the oats into serving bowls and top with pecans. Serve warm.

Tofu Scramble

Prep time: 10 minutes | Cook time: 14 minutes | Serves 2

16 ounces (454 g) firm tofu, drained
1 teaspoon fresh lemon juice
1 teaspoon salt
½ teaspoon freshly ground black pepper
½ teaspoon turmeric powder
1 tablespoon olive oil
¼ cup diced red onion
¼ cup diced red bell pepper
¼ cup diced tomato
1 clove garlic, minced
1 teaspoon ground cumin
½ teaspoon chipotle powder
½ teaspoon chili powder
¼ cup water
2 tablespoons chopped fresh cilantro

In a large bowl, mash the tofu with your hands or a fork, then stir in the lemon juice, salt, pepper, and turmeric. Add the olive oil to the Instant Pot and select the Sauté button. Add the onion and bell pepper; sauté 3 minutes. Add the tomato, garlic, cumin, chipotle powder, and chili powder; sauté an additional 30 seconds. Add the tofu mixture and water to the pot and stir. Lock the lid into place, press the Manual button, and adjust time to 10 minutes. When the timer beeps, let pressure release naturally until float valve drops and then unlock lid. Stir in the cilantro and spoon the scramble into serving bowls. Serve warm.

Tofu Scramble with Broccoli and Mushroom

Prep time: 10 minutes | Cook time: 15 minutes | Serves 2

16 ounces (454 g) firm tofu, drained
1 teaspoon fresh lemon juice
1 teaspoon salt
½ teaspoon freshly ground black pepper
½ teaspoon turmeric powder
1 tablespoon olive oil
½ cup broccoli florets,
blanched
½ cup sliced button mushrooms
½ cup diced tomato
1 clove garlic, minced
¼ cup water
2 tablespoons chopped fresh Italian flat-leaf parsley

In a large bowl, mash the tofu with your hands or a fork, then stir in the lemon juice, salt, pepper, and turmeric. Add the olive oil to the Instant Pot and press the Sauté button. Add the broccoli and mushrooms and sauté 4 to 5 minutes. Add the tomato and garlic and sauté an additional 30 seconds. Add the tofu mixture and water to the pot and stir. Lock the lid into place, press the Manual button, and adjust the timer to 10 minutes. When the timer beeps, let pressure release naturally until float valve drops and then unlock lid. Stir in the parsley and spoon the scramble into serving bowls. Serve warm.

Hash Browns

Prep time: 5 minutes | Cook time: 16 minutes | Serves 4

2 tablespoons olive oil
2 tablespoons vegan margarine
4 cups peeled and grated russet potatoes
¼ cup diced yellow onion
1 poblano pepper, cored, seeded, and diced
1 clove garlic, minced
Pinch salt
Pinch freshly ground black pepper
1 teaspoon ground cumin

Add the oil and margarine to the Instant Pot and press the Sauté button. Add the potatoes, onion, and poblano pepper. Sauté 5 minutes, stirring occasionally, until the potatoes just begin to brown. Add the garlic and sauté 30 seconds. Season with the salt, pepper, and cumin. Use a wide spatula to press down firmly on the potatoes in the pan. Lock the lid into place. Press the Manual button and adjust time to 10 minutes. When the timer beeps, quick-release the pressure until the float valve drops and then unlock the lid. Serve warm.

Mushroom and Spinach Muffins

Prep time: 10 minutes | Cook time: 15 minutes | Serves 2

½ cup silken tofu
1 tablespoon fresh lemon juice
1 teaspoon Dijon mustard
⅛ teaspoon cayenne pepper
⅛ teaspoon turmeric powder
1 tablespoon vegetable oil
Pinch salt
1 tablespoon olive oil
4 small portobello mushroom caps
2 cups fresh spinach leaves
2 vegan English muffins, toasted

Add the silken tofu to a food processor and purée until smooth. Add the lemon juice, mustard, cayenne, and turmeric. Blend until well combined. With the food processor still running, slowly add the vegetable oil and blend until combined. Season with salt to complete the vegan hollandaise. Pour the hollandaise into a small saucepan and heat on low. Keep warm until ready to serve. Press the Sauté button on the Instant Pot and add the olive oil. Add the mushroom caps and spinach and stir until coated with the oil and slightly softened, about 3 minutes. Lock the lid into place. Press the Manual button and adjust time to 9 minutes. When the timer beeps, let pressure release naturally until the float valve drops and then unlock lid. Place a toasted English muffin open-faced on each plate and top each half with a Portobello cap and sautéed spinach. Drizzle with a spoonful of the warm vegan hollandaise to finish.

Cinnamon Oatmeal with Applesauce

Prep time: 10 minutes | Cook time: 5 minutes | Serves 8

6 cups water
1½ cups steel-cut oats
1½ cups unsweetened applesauce
¼ cup maple syrup, plus more for topping
½ teaspoon ground nutmeg
1½ teaspoons ground cinnamon
⅛ teaspoon salt
1 large apple, chopped

Except for the apple, combine all the ingredients in the Instant Pot. Lock the lid. Select the Manual mode and set the cooking time for 5 minutes at High Pressure. Once cooking is complete, do a natural pressure release for 10 minutes, then release any remaining pressure. Carefully open the lid. Add the chopped apple and stir well. Allow the oatmeal to sit for 10 minutes. Ladle into bowls and top with a drizzle of maple syrup, if desired. Serve warm.

Black Bean and Tofu Burrito

Prep time: 10 minutes | Cook time: 12 minutes | Serves 4

2 tablespoons olive oil
16 ounces (454 g) firm tofu, drained and diced
¼ cup diced red onion
½ cup diced tomato
¼ cup chopped fresh cilantro
¼ cup water
1 teaspoon salt
4 (10-inch) flour tortillas
1 cup canned black beans, warmed
1 medium avocado, peeled and sliced
½ cup vegan sour cream (optional)
½ cup shredded vegan Cheddar cheese (optional)

Add the oil to the Instant Pot and press the Sauté button. Add the tofu, stir until well coated, and sauté until it begins to brown, about 5 minutes. Add the onion, tomato, cilantro, water, and salt. Lock the lid into place. Press the Manual button and adjust time to 7 minutes. When the timer beeps, let pressure release naturally until the float valve drops and then unlock lid. Steam or microwave the tortillas until softened, then lay the tortillas on a flat surface to build the burritos. Place equal amounts of the tofu mixture, beans, and avocado in a line down the center of each tortilla. Roll each burrito by first folding the sides of the tortilla over the filling. Then, while still holding the sides closed, fold the bottom of the tortilla over the filling. Next, roll the burrito while still holding the sides closed and pushing the filling down into the burrito if it starts to spill out. Repeat for remaining burritos. Top with vegan sour cream and/or vegan cheese if desired.

Parmesan Egg Bake

Prep time: 5 minutes | Cook time: 4 minutes | Serves 2

1 tablespoon unsalted butter, room temperature
2 tablespoons finely grated Parmesan cheese
2 eggs
Pinch kosher salt
Pinch freshly ground black pepper
1 cup water

Using a paper towel or your clean fingers, generously rub the inside of two small glass or ceramic ramekins, or egg coddlers, with butter. Divide the Parmesan cheese between each ramekin, and turn and shake the ramekins to coat the bottom and sides with the cheese. Crack an egg into each ramekin, sprinkle with the salt and pepper, and cover each tightly with aluminum foil. Place a rack in the Instant Pot. Add the water to the Instant Pot and place the ramekins on the rack. Lock on the lid and set the timer for 4 minutes at Low Pressure. When the timer goes off, quick release the pressure and open the lid. Carefully remove the ramekins, uncover, and serve immediately.

Cherry and Almond Oatmeal

Prep time: 10 minutes | Cook time: 5 minutes | Serves 6

4 cups vanilla almond milk, plus additional as needed
1 cup steel-cut oats
⅓ cup packed brown sugar
1 cup dried cherries
½ teaspoon ground cinnamon
½ teaspoon salt

Combine all ingredients in the Instant Pot. Secure the lid. Select the Manual mode and set the cooking time for 5 minutes at High Pressure. Once cooking is complete, do a natural pressure release for 10 minutes, then release any remaining pressure. Carefully open the lid. Allow the oatmeal to sit for 10 minutes. Serve with additional almond milk, if desired.

Kale and Bacon Egg Bake

Prep time: 10 minutes | Cook time: 19 minutes | Serves 2 to 3

5 eggs
3 slices bacon, cooked and finely chopped
½ cup chopped broccoli
½ cup chopped kale
½ cup heavy whipping cream
2 tablespoons avocado oil

½ teaspoon dried basil
½ teaspoon ground cayenne pepper
½ teaspoon kosher salt
½ teaspoon freshly ground black pepper
1 cup water

Pour the water and insert the trivet in the Instant Pot. In a large bowl, stir together the remaining ingredients. Transfer the mixture into a well-greased baking pan and cover loosely with aluminum foil. Lock the lid. Select the Manual mode and set the cooking time for 19 minutes on High Pressure. Once the timer goes off, perform a natural pressure release for 10 minutes, then release any remaining pressure. Carefully open the lid. Transfer the dish to a plate and serve.

Turkey Rolls

Prep time: 5 minutes | Cook time: 5 minutes | Serves 3

½ teaspoon olive oil
3 turkey lunch meat slices
3 ounces (85 g) grated

Parmesan cheese
1 tablespoon cream cheese
½ teaspoon minced garlic

Press the Sauté button on the Instant Pot and heat the olive oil. Add the turkey slices to the pot and cook for 2 minutes on each side. Meanwhile, in a bowl, stir together the remaining ingredients. Transfer the cooked turkey slices to a plate and spread the cheese mixture over the turkey slices. Roll up the turkey slices and secure them with the toothpicks. Serve immediately.

Egg and Cheese Ramekin

Prep time: 7 minutes | Cook time: 5 minutes | Serves 1

Unsalted butter for greasing
1 egg
¼ cup whole milk
¼ teaspoon kosher salt
⅛ teaspoon freshly ground black pepper

2 tablespoons shredded sharp Cheddar cheese
1 tablespoon fresh minced chives
1 cup water
½ tablespoon bread crumbs

Rub the butter over the interior of a ramekin or glass baking dish. Set aside. In a small bowl, whisk together the egg, milk, salt, and pepper. Stir in the cheese and chives. Pour the mixture into the ramekin. Place the rack in the Instant Pot pot and add the water. Place the ramekin on the rack and sprinkle the top of the egg mixture with the bread crumbs. By sprinkling on the bread crumbs just before cooking, they don't sink into the egg mixture. Lock on the lid and set the timer for 5 minutes at Low Pressure. When the timer goes off, quick release the pressure, carefully remove the ramekin from the Instant Pot, and serve immediately.

Beef Taco

Prep time: 10 minutes | Cook time: 16 minutes | Serves 6

1 teaspoon coconut oil
2 cups ground beef
1 teaspoon chili flakes
3 jalapeño peppers, chopped

2 eggs, beaten
½ avocado, chopped
¾ cup black olives, sliced
⅓ cup coconut milk

Press the Sauté button on the Instant Pot and melt the coconut oil for 2 minutes. Add the ground beef and chili flakes to the pot and sauté for 4 minutes, or until lightly browned, stirring constantly. Stir in the remaining ingredients. Set the lid in place. Select the Manual mode and set the cooking time for 10 minutes on High Pressure. When the timer goes off, do a quick pressure release. Carefully open the lid. Serve immediately.

Pineapple and Carrot Oatmeal

Prep time: 10 minutes | Cook time: 10 minutes | Serves 8

4½ cups water
2 cups shredded carrots
1 cup steel-cut oats
1 (20-ounce / 567-g) can crushed pineapple, undrained

1 cup raisins
2 teaspoons ground cinnamon
1 teaspoon pumpkin pie spice
Cooking spray
Brown sugar (optional)

Spritz the bottom of the Instant Pot with cooking spray. Place the water, carrots, oats, raisins, pineapple, cinnamon, and pumpkin pie spice into the Instant Pot and stir to combine. Secure the lid. Select the Manual mode and set the cooking time for 10 minutes at High Pressure. Once cooking is complete, do a natural pressure release for 10 minutes, then release any remaining pressure. Carefully open the lid. Let the oatmeal stand for 5 to 10 minutes. Sprinkle with the brown sugar, if desired. Serve warm.

Raisin Oatmeal

Prep time: 10 minutes | Cook time: 5 minutes | Serves 6

3 cups vanilla almond milk
¾ cup steel-cut oats
3 tablespoons brown sugar
¾ cup raisins
4½ teaspoons butter

½ teaspoon salt
¾ teaspoon ground cinnamon
1 large apple, peeled and chopped
¼ cup chopped pecans

Combine all the ingredients except the apple and pecans in the Instant Pot. Secure the lid. Select the Manual mode and set the cooking time for 5 minutes at High Pressure. Once cooking is complete, do a natural pressure release for 10 minutes, then release any remaining pressure. Carefully open the lid. Scatter with the chopped apple and stir well. Allow the oatmeal to sit for 1o minutes. Ladle into bowls and sprinkle the pecans on top. Serve immediately.

Milk and Pumpkin Oatmeal

Prep time: 5 minutes | Cook time: 4 minutes | Serves 4

2 cups rolled oats
½ cup pumpkin purée
3 tablespoons brown sugar
2½ cups water, divided

1 cup whole or part-skim milk
1 teaspoon ground cinnamon
½ teaspoon ground ginger
Dash nutmeg

In a heat-proof glass bowl that will fit inside the Instant Pot, combine the oats, pumpkin purée, brown sugar, 1½ cups of water, milk, cinnamon, ginger, and nutmeg. Place a rack in the Instant Pot pot and add the remaining 1 cup of water to the pot. Place the bowl on the rack Lock on the lid, and set the timer for 4 minutes at High Pressure. When the timer goes off, turn off the Instant Pot and natural release the pressure. If, after 10 minutes, the pressure hasn't completely been released, quick release the remaining pressure. Carefully remove the bowl from inside the Instant Pot and stir in any liquid on the surface. Serve hot.

Chapter 6 Vegetables

Mushroom and Cauliflower Risotto
Prep time: 7 minutes | Cook time: 10 minutes | Serves 3

1 cup freshly squeezed
coconut milk
1 tablespoon coconut oil
1 cauliflower head, cut into
florets

1 onion, chopped
1 pound (454 g) shiitake
mushrooms, sliced
Salt and pepper, to taste

Press the Sauté button and heat the coconut oil. Sauté the
onions for 3 minutes or until fragrant. Add the cauliflower and
shiitake mushrooms. Sprinkle salt and pepper for seasoning.
Add the coconut milk in three batches. Allow to simmer for 10
minutes. Garnish with chopped parsley if desired.

Smothered Greens
Prep time: 6 minutes | Cook time: 3 minutes | Serves 4

2 teaspoons crushed garlic
Salt and pepper, to taste
1 onion, chopped

6 cups raw greens
1 tablespoon coconut oil
1 cup water

Press the Sauté button on the Instant Pot and heat the coconut
oil. Sauté the onion and garlic for 2 minutes or until fragrant. Add
the greens and Sprinkle salt and pepper for seasoning. Add the
water. Lock the lid. Set the Instant Pot to Pressure Cook mode,
then set the timer for 3 minutes at High Pressure. Once cooking
is complete, do a quick pressure release. Carefully open the lid.
Sprinkle with red chili flakes, then serve.

Caramelized Lemony White Onions
Prep time: 6 minutes | Cook time: 35 minutes | Serves 2

1 tablespoon freshly squeezed
lemon juice
3 tablespoons coconut oil

Salt and pepper, to taste
3 white onions, sliced
1 cup water

Press the Sauté button on the Instant Pot and heat the coconut
oil. Sauté the onions for 5 minutes and add the remaining
ingredients. Add the water and stir. Lock the lid. Set the Instant
Pot to Pressure Cook mode, then set the timer for 20 minutes at
High Pressure. Once cooking is complete, do a quick pressure
release. Carefully open the lid. Press the Sauté button and
continue cooking for another 10 minutes. Serve warm.

Artichokes with Onion
Prep time: 6 minutes | Cook time: 30 minutes | Serves 8

½ cup organic chicken broth
Salt and pepper, to taste
4 large artichokes, trimmed

and cleaned
1 onion, chopped
1 garlic clove, crushed

Place all ingredients in the Instant Pot. Lock the lid. Set the
Instant Pot to Pressure Cook mode, then set the timer for 30
minutes at High Pressure. Once cooking is complete, do a quick
pressure release. Carefully open the lid. Serve the artichokes
with lemon juice.

Tomato and Zucchini Melange
Prep time: 13 minutes | Cook time: 10 minutes | Serves 4

5 garlic cloves, minced
3 medium zucchinis, chopped
1 pound (454 g) puréed
tomatoes

1 onion, chopped
1 tablespoon coconut oil
Salt and pepper, to taste
1 cup water

Place the tomatoes in a food processor and blend until smooth.
Press the Sauté button on the Instant Pot and heat the oil.
Sauté the garlic and onions for 2 minutes or until fragrant. Add
the zucchini and tomato purée. Sprinkle salt and pepper for
seasoning. Add the water to add more moisture. Lock the lid.
Set the Instant Pot to Pressure Cook mode, then set the timer
for 10 minutes at High Pressure. Once cooking is complete, do
a quick pressure release. Carefully open the lid. Serve warm.

Zucchini and Mushroom Stew
Prep time: 6 minutes | Cook time: 10 minutes | Serves 5

½ cup chopped tomatoes
1 stalk celery, minced
2 zucchinis, chopped
1 pound (454 g) mushrooms,

sliced
1 onion, chopped
Salt and pepper, to taste

Place all ingredients in the Instant Pot. Pour in enough water
until half of the vegetables are submerged. Lock the lid. Set the
Instant Pot to Pressure Cook mode, then set the timer for 10
minutes at High Pressure. Once cooking is complete, do a quick
pressure release. Carefully open the lid. Serve warm.

Bell Pepper and Zucchini Stir-Fry
Prep time: 6 minutes | Cook time: 5 minutes | Serves 6

2 large zucchinis, sliced
1 tablespoon coconut oil
4 garlic cloves, minced
2 red sweet bell peppers,

julienned
1 onion, chopped
Salt and pepper, to taste
¼ cup water

Press the Sauté button on the Instant Pot. Heat the coconut oil
and sauté the onion and garlic for 2 minutes or until fragrant.
Add the zucchini and red bell peppers. Sprinkle salt and pepper
for seasoning. Pour in the water. Lock the lid. Set the Instant
Pot to Pressure Cook mode, then set the timer for 5 minutes at
High Pressure. Once cooking is complete, do a quick pressure
release. Carefully open the lid. Serve warm.

Tofu Curry with Mango Sauce
Prep time: 15 minutes | Cook time: 35 minutes | Serves 2

1 cup vegetable broth
1 pound (454 g) vegetables,
chopped
2 tablespoons curry paste

1 pound (454 g) cubed extra
firm tofu
1 cup mango sauce
Salt and pepper, to taste

Mix all the ingredients in the Instant Pot. Lock the lid. Set the
Instant Pot to Pressure Cook mode, then set the timer for 35
minutes at High Pressure. Once cooking is complete, do a quick
pressure release. Carefully open the lid. Serve warm.

Eggplant and Zucchini Platter

Prep time: 6 minutes | Cook time: 8 minutes | Serves 6

3 zucchinis, sliced
1 eggplant, chopped
3 tablespoons olive oil
3 tomatoes, sliced

1 onion, diced
Salt and pepper, to taste
¼ cup water

Press the Sauté button on the Instant Pot and heat the olive oil. Sauté the onions for 3 minutes or until translucent, then add the eggplants. Sauté for another 2 minutes. Add the tomatoes and zucchini. Sprinkle salt and pepper for seasoning. Add the water. Lock the lid. Set the Instant Pot to Pressure Cook mode, then set the timer for 6 minutes at High Pressure. Once cooking is complete, do a quick pressure release. Carefully open the lid. Serve warm.

Garlicky Baby Bok Choy

Prep time: 9 minutes | Cook time: 4 minutes | Serves 6

1 teaspoon peanut oil
1 pound (454 g) baby Bok choy, trimmed and washed
Salt and pepper, to taste

4 garlic cloves, minced
1 teaspoon red pepper flakes
1 cup water

Press the Sauté button on the Instant Pot. Heat the oil and sauté the garlic for 1 minute until fragrant. Add the Bok choy and sprinkle salt and pepper for seasoning. Pour in the water. Lock the lid. Set the Instant Pot to Pressure Cook mode, then set the timer for 4 minutes at High Pressure. Once cooking is complete, do a quick pressure release. Carefully open the lid. Sprinkle with red pepper flakes, then serve.

Easy Sesame Bok Choy

Prep time: 6 minutes | Cook time: 4 minutes | Serves 4

1 teaspoon soy sauce
½ teaspoon sesame oil
1½ cups water

1 medium Bok choy
2 teaspoons sesame seeds

Pour the water into the Instant Pot. Place the Bok choy inside the steamer basket. Lower the basket Lock the lid. Set the Instant Pot to Pressure Cook mode, then set the timer for 4 minutes at High Pressure. Once cooking is complete, do a quick pressure release. Carefully open the lid. In a serving bowl, set in the Bok choy. Toss with the remaining ingredients to coat. Serve immediately!

Cauliflower and Chive Mash

Prep time: 12 minutes | Cook time: 10 minutes | Serves 4

1 cup water
1 cauliflower head, cut into florets
¼ teaspoon salt

¼ teaspoon ground black pepper
¼ teaspoon garlic powder
1 handful chopped chives

Set a trivet in the Instant Pot and pour in the water. Place the cauliflower. Lock the lid. Set the Instant Pot to Steam mode, then set the timer for 10 minutes at High Pressure. Once cooking is complete, do a quick pressure release. Carefully open the lid. Using a food processor, pulse the cauliflower. Add the garlic powder, salt, and pepper. Garnish with chives, then serve.

Mac and Cheese

Prep time: 30 minutes | Cook time: 4 minutes | Serves 10

4 cups water
1 teaspoon garlic powder
16 ounces (454 g) elbow macaroni pasta
Salt and pepper, to taste

2 cups frozen mixed vegetables
1 cup shredded Cheddar
1 cup milk
Fresh parsley, for garnish

To the Instant Pot, add the water, garlic powder and pasta. Sprinkle with salt and pepper. Lock the lid. Set the Instant Pot to Pressure Cook mode, then set the timer for 4 minutes at High Pressure. Once cooking is complete, do a quick pressure release. Carefully open the lid. Add the vegetables, Cheddar and milk, then cover the pot and press Sauté. Simmer until the vegetables have softened. Garnish with fresh parsley and serve.

Couscous with Bell Pepper

Prep time: 30 minutes | Cook time: 10 minutes | Serves 3

2 teaspoons olive oil
1 onion, chopped
1 red bell pepper, chopped
1 cup grated carrot

2 cups couscous
2 cups water
Salt, to taste
½ tablespoon lemon juice

Grease the Instant Pot with olive oil. Add the onion. Set to the Sauté mode and sauté the onion for 2 minutes. Add the red bell pepper and carrot. Cook for 3 minutes. Add the couscous and water. Season with salt. Lock the lid. Set the Instant Pot to Pressure Cook mode, then set the timer for 2 minutes at High Pressure. Once cooking is complete, do a natural pressure release. Carefully open the lid. Fluff the couscous with a fork. Drizzle with the lemon juice before serving.

Feta Quinoa with Cucumber and Olives

Prep time: 15 minutes | Cook time: 5 minutes | Serves 4

1½ cups water
1 cup rinsed and drained uncooked quinoa
¼ cup crumbled feta cheese

Greek seasoning and olive oil mixture
¼ cup sliced cucumber
¼ cup diced black olives

Pour the water into the Instant Pot. Add the quinoa. Lock the lid. Set the Instant Pot to Pressure Cook mode, then set the timer for 1 minute at High Pressure. Once cooking is complete, do a natural pressure release. Carefully open the lid. In a bowl, mix cucumber and black olives. Top with the quinoa and feta cheese. Drizzle with the dressing, then serve.

Sweet Potato and Kale Tofu Bowl

Prep time: 45 minutes | Cook time: 6 minutes | Serves 4

1 tablespoon tamari sauce
⅔ cup vegetable broth
1 sweet potato, cubed

2 cups chopped kale
8 ounces (227 g) cubed tofu
Salt and pepper, to taste

Add tofu in the Instant Pot. Drizzle with half of the tamari and the broth. Cook for about 3 minutes on Sauté function. Add the rest of the ingredients. Lock the lid. Set the Instant Pot to Pressure Cook mode, then set the timer for about 3 minutes at High Pressure. Once cooking is complete, do a quick pressure release. Carefully open the lid. Serve immediately!

Greek Navy Beans with Tomatoes

Prep time: 10 minutes | Cook time: 15 minutes | Serves 8

8 cups water	crushed tomatoes
3 cups navy beans	1 garlic clove, peeled
Salt and pepper, to taste	¼ cup olive oil
28 ounces (794 g) canned	1 onion, diced

In the Instant Pot, add the water and navy beans. Season with a pinch of salt. Soak for 10 hours. Lock the lid. Set the Instant Pot to Pressure Cook mode, then set the timer for 3 minutes at High Pressure. Once cooking is complete, do a natural pressure release. Carefully open the lid. Set the beans in a bowl. Set aside a cup of the cooking liquid. Drain the rest. Select the Sauté mode and heat the olive oil. Add the tomatoes, garlic and onion to sauté for about 5 minutes. Mix in the reserved cooking liquid. Add the beans back. Lock the lid. Set the Instant Pot to Pressure Cook mode, then set the timer for 5 minutes at High Pressure. Once cooking is complete, do a natural pressure release. Carefully open the lid. Add salt and pepper for seasoning.

Basil Tomato and Olive Stuffed Peppers

Prep time: 20 minutes | Cook time: 8 minutes | Serves 4

¼ cup tomato sauce	4 basil leaves, chopped
4 large bell peppers, trimmed	½ cup chopped olives
2 cup chopped tomatoes	1 cup water
Salt and pepper, to taste	

Using a bowl, mix basil leaves, olives and tomatoes. Season with salt and pepper. Stuff bell peppers with the mixture. Top with a drizzle of tomato sauce. In the Instant Pot, add the water. Add the steamer rack inside. Carefully lay the bell peppers. Lock the lid. Set the Instant Pot to Pressure Cook mode, then set the timer for 8 minutes at High Pressure. Once cooking is complete, do a quick pressure release. Carefully open the lid. Serve warm.

Lime Cauliflower Rice with Cilantro

Prep time: 5 minutes | Cook time: 8 minutes | Serves 4

1 head cauliflower, trimmed, stem removed and cut into medium florets	1 garlic clove, minced
	Juice of 1 lime
	⅛ teaspoon fine grind sea salt
1 cup water	4 sprigs fresh cilantro, chopped
2 tablespoons avocado oil	

Pour the water into the Instant Pot and put the trivet in the pot. Place the cauliflower florets in the trivet. Place a steamer basket on the trivet. Add the cauliflower to the steamer basket. Lock the lid. Select the Manual mode and set the cooking time for 2 minutes on High Pressure. When the timer goes off, perform a quick pressure release. Carefully open the lid. Remove the steamer basket and cauliflower from the pot. Place the cauliflower florets in a blender and pulse until it reaches a rice-like texture. Set aside. Pour out the water and wipe the pot dry with a paper towel. Select Sauté mode and heat the avocado oil. Add the garlic to the pot and sauté for 2 minutes, or until fragrant. Add the cauliflower rice to the pot and sauté for 2 additional minutes, or until the rice becomes soft. Stir in the lime juice and sauté for 2 additional minutes. Transfer the cauliflower rice to a serving dish. Season with the sea salt and garnish with the cilantro. Serve hot.

Spaghetti Squash Noodles

Prep time: 5 minutes | Cook time: 18 minutes | Serves 4

2 pounds (907 g) spaghetti squash	almonds
	¼ cup flat-leaf parsley
1 cup water	3 tablespoons grated
3 garlic cloves	Parmesan cheese
1 cup fresh basil leaves	½ teaspoon fine grind sea salt
½ cup olive oil	½ teaspoon ground black pepper
⅓ cup unsalted toasted	

Using a knife, pierce all sides of the squash to allow the steam to penetrate during cooking. Pour the water into the Instant Pot and put the trivet in the pot. Place the squash on the trivet. Lock the lid. Select the Manual mode and set the cooking time for 18 minutes at High Pressure. When the timer goes off, use a natural pressure release for 10 minutes, then release any remaining pressure. Carefully open the lid. Remove the trivet and squash from the pot. Set aside to cool for 15 minutes, or until the squash is cool enough to handle. Make the pesto sauce by placing the remaining ingredients in a food processor. Pulse until the ingredients are well combined and form a thick paste. Set aside. Cut the cooled spaghetti squash in half lengthwise. Using a spoon, scoop out and discard the seeds. Using a fork, scrape the flesh of the squash to create the noodles. Transfer the noodles to a large bowl. Divide the squash noodles among 4 serving bowls. Top each serving with the pesto sauce. Serve hot.

Couscous and Chickpea Stuffed Sweet Potatoes

Prep time: 42 minutes | Cook time: 17 minutes | Serves 2

1 cup cooked couscous	Salt and pepper, to taste
2 sweet potatoes	1 cup cooked chickpeas
1 tablespoon olive oil	2 spring onions, chopped
1 teaspoon paprika	

Use a fork to pierce sweet potatoes. To the Instant Pot, add enough water to cover. Add the steamer rack inside and set the potatoes on top. Lock the lid. Set the Instant Pot to Pressure Cook mode, then set the timer for 8 minutes on High Pressure. Once cooking is complete, do a natural pressure release for 5 minutes. Carefully open the lid. Set the sweet potato aside on a plate. Drain the pot. While the Instant Pot is on Sauté mode, heat the olive oil. Set in chickpeas and paprika with salt and pepper. Half the potatoes and mash the inside. Add the chickpeas and couscous. Top with the chopped spring onion and serve.

Ritzy Veggie Medley

Prep time: 50 minutes | Cook time: 8 minutes | Serves 4

1 cup water	3 tablespoons olive oil
1 tablespoon raisins	10 halved cherry tomatoes
1 zucchini, sliced	2 potatoes, cubed
1 eggplant, cubed	2 tablespoons raisins

In the Instant Pot, add the water. Add the potatoes and zucchini. Lock the lid. Set the Instant Pot to Pressure Cook mode, then set the timer for 8 minutes on High Pressure. Once cooking is complete, do a quick pressure release. Carefully open the lid. Drain water and add olive oil. Mix in the tomatoes and eggplant. Let cook for 2 minutes. Top with the raisins before serving.

Ratatouille

Prep time: 20 minutes | Cook time: 10 minutes | Serves 4

2 cups water
2 medium zucchini, sliced
3 tomatoes, sliced

2 eggplants, sliced
1 tablespoon olive oil
Salt and pepper, to taste

Pour the water into the Instant Pot. In a baking dish, arrange a layer of the zucchini. Top with a layer of the tomatoes. Place a layer of eggplant slices on top. Continue layering until you use all the ingredients. Drizzle with olive oil. Place the baking dish on the trivet and lower it. Lock the lid. Set the Instant Pot to Pressure Cook mode, then set the timer for 10 minutes at High Pressure. Once cooking is complete, do a quick pressure release. Carefully open the lid. Sprinkle with salt and pepper and serve warm!

Chili Carrots

Prep time: 25 minutes | Cook time: 5 minutes | Serves 4

1½ cups water
1 tablespoon maple syrup
1 tablespoon coconut oil

1½ pounds (680 g) carrots, chopped
1 teaspoon chili powder

Pour the water into the Instant Pot. Place the chopped carrots inside the steamer basket. Arrange the basket in the Instant Pot. Lock the lid. Set the Instant Pot to Pressure Cook mode, then set the timer for 4 minutes on High Pressure. Once cooking is complete, do a quick pressure release. Carefully open the lid. Transfer the carrots along with the remaining ingredients to a food processor. Process until puréed and smooth. Serve immediately!

Coconut Potato Mash

Prep time: 15 minutes | Cook time: 8 minutes | Serves 4

2 tablespoons coconut oil
4 medium potatoes

1 teaspoon ground nutmeg
¼ cup coconut milk

Peel the potatoes and place them in the Instant Pot. Add enough water to cover them. Lock the lid. Set the Instant Pot to Pressure Cook mode, then set the timer for 8 minutes at High Pressure. Once cooking is complete, do a quick pressure release. Carefully open the lid. Drain any water present. Mash the potatoes. Add the remaining ingredients. Serve immediately!

Cauliflower Vermicelli Pasta

Prep time: 12 minutes | Cook time: 20 minutes | Serves 6

1 cup chopped cauliflower
2 tablespoons chopped green onions
12 ounces (340 g) vermicelli

pasta
1 teaspoon olive oil
1 small green chili pepper, chopped

In the Instant Pot; add the pasta and enough water to cover. Lock the lid. Set the Instant Pot to Pressure Cook mode, then set the timer for 7 minutes at High Pressure. Once cooking is complete, do a quick pressure release. Carefully open the lid. Drain water and transfer the cooked pasta in a container. Take the Instant Pot and place over dry kitchen surface; open its top lid and switch it on. Press Sauté. Grease the pot with olive oil. Add the cauliflower; cook for 7 to 8 minutes until turn softened. Mix in the pasta and serve warm. Top with the green onions.

Spaghetti Squash Noodles with Tomatoes

Prep time: 15 minutes | Cook time: 14 to 16 minutes | Serves 4

1 medium spaghetti squash
1 cup water
2 tablespoons olive oil
1 small yellow onion, diced
6 garlic cloves, minced
2 teaspoons crushed red pepper flakes
2 teaspoons dried oregano
1 cup sliced cherry tomatoes

1 teaspoon kosher salt
½ teaspoon freshly ground black pepper
1 (14.5-ounce / 411-g) can sugar-free crushed tomatoes
¼ cup capers
1 tablespoon caper brine
½ cup sliced olives

With a sharp knife, halve the spaghetti squash crosswise. Using a spoon, scoop out the seeds and sticky gunk in the middle of each half. Pour the water into the Instant Pot and place the trivet in the pot with the handles facing up. Arrange the squash halves, cut side facing up, on the trivet. Lock the lid. Select the Manual mode and set the cooking time for 7 minutes on High Pressure. When the timer goes off, use a quick pressure release. Carefully open the lid. Remove the trivet and pour out the water that has collected in the squash cavities. Using the tines of a fork, separate the cooked strands into spaghetti-like pieces and set aside in a bowl. Pour the water out of the pot. Select the Sauté mode and heat the oil. Add the onion to the pot and sauté for 3 minutes. Add the garlic, pepper flakes and oregano to the pot and sauté for 1 minute. Stir in the cherry tomatoes, salt and black pepper and cook for 2 minutes, or until the tomatoes are tender. Pour in the crushed tomatoes, capers, caper brine and olives and bring the mixture to a boil. Continue to cook for 2 to 3 minutes to allow the flavors to meld. Stir in the spaghetti squash noodles and cook for 1 to 2 minutes to warm everything through. Transfer the dish to a serving platter and serve.

Stir-Fried Cauliflower Rice with Mushrooms

Prep time: 10 minutes | Cook time: 13 minutes | Serves 4

1 medium head cauliflower, cut into florets
1 cup water
1½ tablespoons unsalted butter
3 garlic cloves, minced
1 cup sliced fresh white mushrooms

1 teaspoon coconut aminos
1½ tablespoons olive oil
1 large egg, beaten
¼ teaspoon fine grind sea salt
⅛ teaspoon ground black pepper
½ tablespoon chopped fresh flat-leaf parsley

Place a steamer basket with legs in the inner pot and pour the water in the pot. Place the cauliflower florets in the steamer basket. Lock the lid. Select the Steam mode and set the cooking time for 3 minutes on High Pressure. When the timer goes off, perform a quick pressure release. Carefully open the lid. Transfer the cauliflower florets to a blender. Pulse until it reaches a rice-like texture. Set aside. Remove the steamer basket from the pot. Pour out the water and wipe the pot dry with a paper towel. Select Sauté setting and melt the butter. Add the garlic and mushrooms to the pot and sauté for 4 minutes, or until the mushrooms are tender. Stir in the coconut aminos, olive oil and cauliflower rice. Sauté for 3 minutes. Whisk in the beaten egg and sauté for 3 minutes, or until the egg is thoroughly cooked. Season with the sea salt and black pepper and stir to combine. Transfer the fried rice to serving bowls and sprinkle the parsley on top. Serve hot.

Broiled Cauli Bites

Prep time: 10 minutes | Cook time: 1 to 2 minutes | Serves 4

1 head cauliflower, cut into florets
1 cup water
1 cup mayonnaise
⅓ cup full-fat coconut milk yogurt
1 teaspoon dried dill
1 teaspoon onion powder

1 teaspoon garlic powder
½ teaspoon sea salt
1 teaspoon apple cider vinegar
4 tablespoons melted butter, divided
3 tablespoons hot sauce
2 celery stalks, cut into 3-inch pieces

Pour the water into the Instant Pot and put the steamer basket in the pot. Place the cauliflower florets in the steamer basket. Close and secure the lid. Select the Manual mode and set the cooking time for 0 minute at High Pressure. Meanwhile, stir together the mayonnaise, coconut milk yogurt, dill, onion powder, garlic powder, sea salt and apple cider vinegar in a bowl. Set in a refrigerator. In another bowl, whisk together the melted butter and hot sauce. Preheat the oven to 450°F (235°C). When the timer beeps, use a quick pressure release. Carefully open the lid. Transfer the florets to a large mixing bowl and coat the florets well with the butter and hot sauce mixture. Spread the coated florets on a baking pan and place the pan in the oven. Broil for 1 to 2 minutes, or until the florets are browned. Remove the mayonnaise mixture from the refrigerator. Serve the Buffalo Cauli Bites and celery sticks with the mayonnaise mixture.

Simple Cauliflower Couscous

Prep time: 5 minutes | Cook time: 0 minutes | Serves 4

1 large head cauliflower, cut into florets, rinsed and drained
½ cup water

Pour the water into the Instant Pot and put the steamer basket in the pot. Place the cauliflower florets in the steamer basket. Lock the lid. Select the Manual mode and set the cooking time for 0 minute at High Pressure. Once cooking is complete, do a quick pressure release. Carefully open the lid. Transfer the cauliflower to a large mixing bowl filled with cold water to let cool. Place the cauliflower in a blender and blend a few times. Don't over process. Serve immediately.

Savory and Rich Creamed Kale

Prep time: 10 minutes | Cook time: 5 minutes | Serves 4

2 tablespoons extra-virgin olive oil
2 cloves garlic, crushed
1 small onion, chopped
12 ounces (340 g) kale, finely chopped
½ cup chicken broth

1 teaspoon Herbes de Provence
4 ounces (113 g) cream cheese
½ cup full-fat heavy cream
1 teaspoon dried tarragon

Press the Sauté button on the Instant Pot and heat the olive oil. Add the garlic and onion to the pot and sauté for 2 minutes, or until the onion is soft. Stir in the kale, chicken broth and Herbes de Provence. Lock the lid. Select the Manual mode and set the cooking time for 3 minutes at High Pressure. When the timer goes off, perform a quick pressure release. Carefully open the lid. Stir in the cream cheese, heavy cream and tarragon. Stir well to thicken the dish. Serve immediately.

Dijon Artichokes with Lemon

Prep time: 40 minutes | Cook time: 20 minutes | Serves 4

1½ cups water
2 artichokes, rinsed and trimmed

Juice of 1 lemon
2 tablespoons Dijon mustard

Pour the water into the Instant Pot. Place the artichokes inside the steamer basket, then drizzle the lemon juice over. Arrange the basket in the Instant Pot. Lock the lid. Set the Instant Pot to Pressure Cook mode, then set the timer for 20 minutes at High Pressure. Once cooking is complete, do a quick pressure release. Carefully open the lid. Serve immediately!

Baked Tofu and Tomato

Prep time: 12 minutes | Cook time: 4 minutes | Serves 4

2 tablespoons jarred banana pepper rings
1 tofu block, crumbled
½ cup vegetable broth

1 tablespoon Italian seasoning
1 can undrained and diced tomatoes

In the Instant Pot, set in all ingredients. Give the mixture a good stir to incorporate everything well. Lock the lid. Set the Instant Pot to Pressure Cook mode, then set the timer for 4 minutes on High Pressure. Once cooking is complete, do a quick pressure release. Carefully open the lid. Serve immediately!

Penne Pasta with Onion

Prep time: 12 minutes | Cook time: 10 minutes | Serves 6

3 cups water
12 ounces (340 g) penne pasta
1 small onion, chopped

1 cup skim milk
1 teaspoon olive oil

In the Instant Pot; add the water and pasta. Lock the lid. Set the Instant Pot to Pressure Cook mode, then set the timer for 6 minutes at High Pressure. Once cooking is complete, do a natural pressure release for 5 minutes. Carefully open the lid. Drain water and transfer the cooked pasta in a container. Press Sauté. Grease the pot with olive oil. Add the onions and let cook for about 2 minutes until turn translucent and softened. Add the milk and cook for 2 to 3 minutes. Mix in the pasta and serve.

Spinach Fusilli Pasta

Prep time: 12 minutes | Cook time: 16 minutes | Serves 5

1 cup water
12 ounces (340 g) fusilli pasta
1 teaspoon olive oil
1 small onion, chopped

1 cup chopped spinach
12 ounces (340 g) diced tomatoes

In the Instant Pot; add the water and pasta. Lock the lid. Set the Instant Pot to Pressure Cook mode, then set the timer for 7 minutes at High Pressure. Once cooking is complete, do a natural pressure release for 5 minutes. Carefully open the lid. Drain water and transfer the cooked pasta in a container. Press Sauté. Grease the pot with olive oil. Add the onions and sauté for 4 minutes until turn translucent and softened. Mix in the spinach and tomatoes; cook for 4 to 5 minutes. Mix in the pasta and serve warm.

Wild Rice and Mushroom Meal
Prep time: 12 minutes | Cook time: 35 minutes | Serves 3

2 teaspoons olive oil
1 tablespoon white wine vinegar
1 small onion, chopped

1 cup wild rice
1 cup sliced button mushrooms
2 cups water

Take the Instant Pot and place over dry kitchen surface; open its top lid and switch it on. Press Sauté. Grease the pot with olive oil. Add the onions and let cook for 4 minutes until turn translucent and softened. Add the mushrooms and cook for 8 to 10 minutes. Pour in the vinegar; stir and cook for 1 minute more, then set aside the mixture in a bowl. Add the water and rice. Lock the lid. Set the Instant Pot to Pressure Cook mode, then set the timer for 20 minutes at Low Pressure. Once cooking is complete, do a natural pressure release for 10 minutes, then release any remaining pressure. Carefully open the lid. Transfer the cooked rice in a mushroom bowl. Mix well and serve.

Garlicky Buttery Whole Cauliflower
Prep time: 5 minutes | Cook time: 8 minutes | Serves 4

1 large cauliflower, rinsed and patted dry
1 cup water
4 tablespoons melted butter
2 cloves garlic, minced

Pinch of sea salt
Pinch of fresh ground black pepper
1 tablespoon chopped fresh flat leaf parsley, for garnish

Pour the water into the Instant Pot and put the trivet in the pot. Place the cauliflower on the trivet. Lock the lid. Select the Manual mode and set the cooking time for 3 minutes at High Pressure. Preheat the oven to 550ºF (288ºC). Line a baking sheet with parchment paper. In a small bowl, whisk together the butter, garlic, sea salt and black pepper. Set aside. When the timer beeps, use a quick pressure release. Carefully open the lid. Transfer the cauliflower to the lined baking sheet. Dab and dry the surface with a clean kitchen towel. Brush the cauliflower with the garlic butter. Place the baking sheet with the cauliflower in the preheated oven and roast for 5 minutes, or until the cauliflower is golden brown. Drizzle with any remaining garlic butter and sprinkle with the chopped parsley. Serve immediately.

Creamy Mashed Cauliflower
Prep time: 5 minutes | Cook time: 0 minutes | Serves 4

1 head cauliflower, cut into florets
½ cup water
2 tablespoons cream cheese
2 tablespoons full-fat heavy whipping cream

2 tablespoons collagen peptide powder
¼ teaspoon sea salt
1 tablespoon butter
¼ cup chopped fresh flat leaf parsley

Pour the water into the Instant Pot and put the steamer basket in the pot. Place the cauliflower florets in the steamer basket. Close and secure the lid. Select the Manual mode and set the cooking time for 0 minute at High Pressure. Meanwhile, whisk together the cream cheese, heavy cream, collagen peptide powder and sea salt in a small bowl. Set aside. Once cooking is complete, do a quick pressure release. Carefully open the lid. Remove the steamer basket and the florets. Pour out the water and put the florets back in the pot. Add the cream mixture and butter to the pot. Using an immersion blender, blend until smooth. Serve immediately garnished with the fresh parsley.

Cauliflower Curry
Prep time: 10 minutes | Cook time: 3 minutes | Serves 6

1 pound (454 g) cauliflower, chopped
3 ounces (85 g) scallions, chopped
1 cup coconut milk

¼ cup crushed tomatoes
1 tablespoon coconut oil
1 teaspoon garam masala
1 teaspoon ground turmeric

Add all the ingredients to the Instant Pot and stir to combine. Lock the lid. Select the Manual mode and set the cooking time for 3 minutes at High Pressure. When the timer goes off, use a natural pressure release for 5 minutes, then release any remaining pressure. Carefully open the lid. Stir the cooked dish well before serving.

Spicy Cauliflower Head
Prep time: 5 minutes | Cook time: 7 minutes | Serves 4

13 ounces (369 g) cauliflower head
1 cup water
1 tablespoon coconut cream
1 tablespoon avocado oil

1 teaspoon ground paprika
1 teaspoon ground turmeric
½ teaspoon ground cumin
½ teaspoon salt

Pour the water in the Instant Pot and insert the trivet. In the mixing bowl, stir together the coconut cream, avocado oil, paprika, turmeric, cumin and salt. Carefully brush the cauliflower head with the coconut cream mixture. Sprinkle the remaining coconut cream mixture over the cauliflower. Transfer the cauliflower head onto the trivet. Lock the lid. Select the Manual mode and set the cooking time for 7 minutes at High Pressure. When the timer goes off, use a natural pressure release for 10 minutes, then release any remaining pressure. Carefully open the lid. Serve immediately.

Lentils Dal
Prep time: 15 minutes | Cook time: 26 minutes | Serves 4

2¾ cups water, divided
½ cup chana dal
2 teaspoons avocado oil
2 dried red chiles
¼ teaspoon cumin seeds
4 garlic cloves, minced

1 cup thinly sliced red onion
1 large tomato, chopped
½ teaspoon ground turmeric
1 teaspoon salt
½ teaspoon ground cumin
¼ cup chopped fresh cilantro

Pour 1 cup of water into the Instant Pot, then place a trivet in the pot. In a heatproof bowl, combine the dal and 1 cup of water. Place the bowl on the trivet. Lock the lid. Select Pressure Cook mode and set cooking time for 6 minutes on High Pressure. When cooking is complete, let the pressure release naturally for 5 minutes, then release any remaining pressure. Unlock the lid. Meanwhile, heat a medium saucepan over medium-high heat. Add the oil. When it shimmers, add the red chiles, cumin seeds, and garlic and cook for 1 minute. Add the onion slices and cook, stirring occasionally, until the onions are crisp and lightly browned, 5 to 8 minutes. Add the tomato and mash with the back of a spoon. Sprinkle with the turmeric, salt, and cumin, mixing well. When the dal is finished, carefully remove the bowl from the Instant Pot. Transfer the dal to the saucepan and add the remaining ¾ cup of water. Stir to combine. Turn the heat to low and let it simmer for 5 to 10 minutes, or until the flavors meld. Garnish with the cilantro and serve.

Parmesan Zoodles

Prep time: 5 minutes | Cook time: 5 minutes | Serves 2

1 large zucchini, trimmed and spiralized	½ teaspoon chili flakes
1 tablespoon butter	3 ounces (85 g) Parmesan cheese, grated
1 garlic clove, diced	

Set the Instant Pot on the Sauté mode and melt the butter. Add the garlic and chili flakes to the pot. Sauté for 2 minutes, or until fragrant. Stir in the zucchini spirals and sauté for 2 minutes, or until tender. Add the grated Parmesan cheese to the pot and stir well. Continue to cook it for 1 minute, or until the cheese melts. Transfer to a plate and serve immediately

Stir Fried Asparagus and Kale

Prep time: 5 minutes | Cook time: 3 minutes | Serves 4

8 ounces (227 g) asparagus, chopped	1 tablespoon avocado oil
2 cups chopped kale	1 teaspoon apple cider vinegar
2 bell peppers, chopped	½ teaspoon minced ginger
	½ cup water

Pour the water into the Instant Pot. In the Instant Pot pan, stir together the remaining ingredients. Insert the trivet and place the pan on it. Set the lid in place. Select the Manual mode and set the cooking time for 3 minutes on High Pressure. When the timer goes off, perform a quick pressure release. Carefully open the lid. Serve immediately.

Buttery Thyme Cabbage

Prep time: 10 minutes | Cook time: 5 minutes | Serves 4

1 pound (454 g) white cabbage	½ teaspoon salt
2 tablespoons butter	1 cup water
1 teaspoon dried thyme	

Cut the white cabbage on medium size petals and sprinkle with the butter, dried thyme and salt. Place the cabbage petals in the Instant Pot pan. Pour the water and insert the trivet in the Instant Pot. Put the pan on the trivet. Set the lid in place. Select the Manual mode and set the cooking time for 5 minutes on High Pressure. When the timer goes off, do a quick pressure release. Carefully open the lid. Serve immediately.

Curried Cauliflower and Tomatoes

Prep time: 10 minutes | Cook time: 2 minutes | Serves 4 to 6

1 medium head cauliflower, cut into bite-size pieces	2 tablespoons red curry paste
1 (14-ounce / 397-g) can sugar-free diced tomatoes, undrained	1 teaspoon salt
	1 teaspoon garlic powder
	½ teaspoon onion powder
1 bell pepper, thinly sliced	½ teaspoon ground ginger
1 (14-ounce / 397-g) can full-fat coconut milk	¼ teaspoon chili powder
½ to 1 cup water	Freshly ground black pepper, to taste

Add all the ingredients, except for the black pepper, to the Instant Pot and stir to combine. Lock the lid. Select the Manual setting and set the cooking time for 2 minutes at High Pressure. Once the timer goes off, use a quick pressure release. Carefully open the lid. Sprinkle the black pepper and stir well. Serve immediately.

Lemony Broccoli

Prep time: 5 minutes | Cook time: 4 minutes | Serves 4

2 cups broccoli florets	1 teaspoon olive oil
1 tablespoon ground paprika	½ teaspoon chili powder
1 tablespoon lemon juice	1 cup water
1 teaspoon grated lemon zest	

Pour the water in the Instant Pot and insert the trivet. In the Instant Pot pan, stir together the remaining ingredients. Place the pan on the trivet. Set the lid in place. Select the Manual mode and set the cooking time for 4 minutes on High Pressure. When the timer goes off, do a quick pressure release. Carefully open the lid. Serve immediately.

Cauliflower Gnocchi

Prep time: 5 minutes | Cook time: 2 minutes | Serves 4

2 cups cauliflower, boiled	1 teaspoon salt
½ cup almond flour	1 cup water
1 tablespoon sesame oil	

In a bowl, mash the cauliflower until puréed. Mix it up with the almond flour, sesame oil and salt. Make the log from the cauliflower dough and cut it into small pieces. Pour the water in the Instant Pot and add the gnocchi. Lock the lid. Select the Manual mode and set the cooking time for 2 minutes on High Pressure. Once the timer goes off, perform a natural pressure release for 5 minutes, then release any remaining pressure. Carefully open the lid. Remove the cooked gnocchi from the water and serve.

Rosemary Baby Potatoes

Prep time: 30 minutes | Cook time: 11 minutes | Serves 4

1 tablespoon olive oil	1 sprig rosemary
3 garlic cloves	1 cup vegetable stock
2 pounds (907 g) baby potatoes	Salt and pepper, to taste

Hit the Sauté button on the Instant Pot. Add the olive oil. Add the garlic, baby potatoes and rosemary. Brown the outside of the potatoes. Pierce each potato with a fork. Add the vegetable stock. Lock the lid. Set the Instant Pot to Pressure Cook mode, then set the timer for 11 minutes at High Pressure. Once cooking is complete, do a quick pressure release. Carefully open the lid. Season with salt and pepper and serve.

Instant Pot Zucchini Sticks

Prep time: 5 minutes | Cook time: 8 minutes | Serves 2

2 zucchinis, trimmed and cut into sticks	½ teaspoon white pepper
2 teaspoons olive oil	½ teaspoon salt
	1 cup water

Place the zucchini sticks in the Instant Pot pan and sprinkle with the olive oil, white pepper and salt. Pour the water and put the trivet in the pot. Place the pan on the trivet. Lock the lid. Select the Manual setting and set the cooking time for 8 minutes at High Pressure. Once the timer goes off, use a quick pressure release. Carefully open the lid. Remove the zucchinis from the pot and serve.

Zucchini and Daikon Fritters
Prep time: 10 minutes | Cook time: 8 minutes | Serves 4

2 large zucchinis, grated
1 daikon, diced
1 egg, beaten
1 teaspoon ground flax meal
1 teaspoon salt
1 tablespoon coconut oil

In the mixing bowl, combine all the ingredients, except for the coconut oil. Form the zucchini mixture into fritters. Press the Sauté button on the Instant Pot and melt the coconut oil. Place the zucchini fritters in the hot oil and cook for 4 minutes on each side, or until golden brown. Transfer to a plate and serve.

Sesame Zoodles with Scallions
Prep time: 10 minutes | Cook time: 3 minutes | Serves 6

2 large zucchinis, trimmed and spiralized
¼ cup chicken broth
1 tablespoon chopped scallions
1 tablespoon coconut aminos
1 teaspoon sesame oil
1 teaspoon sesame seeds
¼ teaspoon chili flakes

Set the Instant Pot on the Sauté mode. Add the zucchini spirals to the pot and pour in the chicken broth. Sauté for 3 minutes and transfer to the serving bowls. Sprinkle with the scallions, coconut aminos, sesame oil, sesame seeds and chili flakes. Gently stir the zoodles. Serve immediately.

Falafel and Lettuce Salad
Prep time: 10 minutes | Cook time: 6 to 8 minutes | Serves 4

1 cup shredded cauliflower
⅓ cup coconut flour
1 teaspoon grated lemon zest
1 egg, beaten
2 tablespoons coconut oil
2 cups chopped lettuce
1 cucumber, chopped
1 tablespoon olive oil
1 teaspoon lemon juice
½ teaspoon cayenne pepper

In a bowl, combine the cauliflower, coconut flour, grated lemon zest and egg. Form the mixture into small balls. Set the Instant Pot to the Sauté mode and melt the coconut oil. Place the balls in the pot in a single layer. Cook for 3 to 4 minutes per side, or until they are golden brown. In a separate bowl, stir together the remaining ingredients. Place the cooked balls on top and serve.

Zoodles with Mediterranean Sauce
Prep time: 10 minutes | Cook time: 5 minutes | Serves 2

1 tablespoon olive oil
2 tomatoes, chopped
½ cup water
½ cup roughly chopped fresh parsley
3 tablespoons ground almonds
1 tablespoon fresh rosemary, chopped
1 tablespoon apple cider vinegar
1 teaspoon garlic, smashed
2 zucchinis, spiralized and cooked
½ avocado, pitted and sliced
Salt and ground black pepper, to taste

Add the olive oil, tomatoes, water, parsley, ground almonds, rosemary, apple cider vinegar and garlic to the Instant Pot. Lock the lid. Select the Manual mode and set the cooking time for 5 minutes on High Pressure. When the timer beeps, perform a natural pressure release for 10 minutes, then release any remaining pressure. Carefully open the lid. Divide the cooked zucchini spirals between two serving plates. Spoon the sauce over each serving. Top with the avocado slices and season with salt and black pepper. Serve immediately.

Gobi Masala
Prep time: 5 minutes | Cook time: 4 to 5 minutes | Serves 4 to 6

1 tablespoon olive oil
1 teaspoon cumin seeds
1 white onion, diced
1 garlic clove, minced
1 head cauliflower, chopped
1 tablespoon ground coriander
1 teaspoon ground cumin
½ teaspoon garam masala
½ teaspoon salt
1 cup water

Set the Instant Pot to the Sauté mode and heat the olive oil. Add the cumin seeds to the pot and sauté for 30 seconds, stirring constantly. Add the onion and sauté for 2 to 3 minutes, stirring constantly. Add the garlic and sauté for 30 seconds, stirring frequently. Stir in the remaining ingredients. Lock the lid. Select the Manual mode and set the cooking time for 1 minute on High Pressure. When the timer goes off, perform a quick pressure release. Carefully open the lid. Serve immediately.

Lemony Asparagus with Gremolata
Prep time: 15 minutes | Cook time: 2 minutes | Serves 2 to 4

Gremolata:
1 cup finely chopped fresh Italian flat-leaf parsley leaves
3 garlic cloves, peeled and
grated
Zest of 2 small lemons
Asparagus:
1½ pounds (680 g) asparagus, trimmed
1 cup water
Lemony Vinaigrette:
1½ tablespoons fresh lemon juice
1 teaspoon Swerve
1 teaspoon Dijon mustard
2 tablespoons extra-virgin olive oil
Kosher salt and freshly ground black pepper, to taste
Garnish:
3 tablespoons slivered almonds

In a small bowl, stir together all the ingredients for the gremolata. Pour the water into the Instant Pot. Arrange the asparagus in a steamer basket. Lower the steamer basket into the pot. Lock the lid. Select the Steam mode and set the cooking time for 2 minutes on Low Pressure. Meanwhile, prepare the lemony vinaigrette: In a bowl, combine the lemon juice, swerve and mustard and whisk to combine. Slowly drizzle in the olive oil and continue to whisk. Season generously with salt and pepper. When the timer goes off, perform a quick pressure release. Carefully open the lid. Remove the steamer basket from the Instant Pot. Transfer the asparagus to a serving platter. Drizzle with the vinaigrette and sprinkle with the gremolata. Serve the asparagus topped with the slivered almonds.

Chinese-Style Pe-Tsai with Onion
Prep time: 5 minutes | Cook time: 8 minutes | Serves 4

2 tablespoons sesame oil
1 yellow onion, chopped
1 pound (454 g) pe-tsai cabbage, shredded
¼ cup rice wine vinegar
1 tablespoon coconut aminos
1 teaspoon finely minced garlic
½ teaspoon salt
¼ teaspoon Szechuan pepper

Set the Instant Pot on the Sauté mode and heat the sesame oil. Add the onion to the pot and sauté for 5 minutes, or until tender. Stir in the remaining ingredients. Lock the lid. Select the Manual mode and set the cooking time for 3 minutes on High Pressure. When the timer goes off, perform a quick pressure release. Carefully open the lid. Transfer the cabbage mixture to a bowl and serve immediately.

Garlicky Broccoli with Roasted Almonds

Prep time: 10 minutes | Cook time: 4 minutes | Serves 4 to 6

6 cups broccoli florets	medium lemon
1 cup water	½ teaspoon kosher salt
1½ tablespoons olive oil	Freshly ground black pepper,
8 garlic cloves, thinly sliced	to taste
2 shallots, thinly sliced	¼ cup chopped roasted
½ teaspoon crushed red	almonds
pepper flakes	¼ cup finely slivered fresh basil
Grated zest and juice of 1	

Pour the water into the Instant Pot. Place the broccoli florets in a steamer basket and lower into the pot. Close and secure the lid. Select the Steam setting and set the cooking time for 2 minutes at Low Pressure. Once the timer goes off, use a quick pressure release. Carefully open the lid. Transfer the broccoli to a large bowl filled with cold water and ice. Once cooled, drain the broccoli and pat dry. Select the Sauté mode on the Instant Pot and heat the olive oil. Add the garlic to the pot and sauté for 30 seconds, tossing constantly. Add the shallots and pepper flakes to the pot and sauté for 1 minute. Stir in the cooked broccoli, lemon juice, salt and black pepper. Toss the ingredients together and cook for 1 minute. Transfer the broccoli to a serving platter and sprinkle with the chopped almonds, lemon zest and basil. Serve immediately.

Vinegary Broccoli with Cheese

Prep time: 5 minutes | Cook time: 5 minutes | Serves 4

1 pound (454 g) broccoli, cut	2 tablespoons balsamic
into florets	vinegar
1 cup water	1 teaspoon cumin seeds
2 garlic cloves, minced	1 teaspoon mustard seeds
1 cup crumbled Cottage	Salt and pepper, to taste
cheese	

Pour the water into the Instant Pot and put the steamer basket in the pot. Place the broccoli in the steamer basket. Close and secure the lid. Select the Manual setting and set the cooking time for 5 minutes at High Pressure. Once the timer goes off, do a quick pressure release. Carefully open the lid. Stir in the remaining ingredients. Serve immediately.

Satarash with Eggs

Prep time: 10 minutes | Cook time: 5 minutes | Serves 4

2 tablespoons olive oil	1 teaspoon paprika
1 white onion, chopped	½ teaspoon dried oregano
2 cloves garlic	½ teaspoon turmeric
2 ripe tomatoes, puréed	Kosher salt and ground black
1 green bell pepper, deseeded	pepper, to taste
and sliced	1 cup water
1 red bell pepper, deseeded	4 large eggs, lightly whisked
and sliced	

Press the Sauté button on the Instant Pot and heat the olive oil. Add the onion and garlic to the pot and sauté for 2 minutes, or until fragrant. Stir in the remaining ingredients, except for the eggs. Lock the lid. Select the Manual mode and set the cooking time for 3 minutes on High Pressure. When the timer goes off, perform a quick pressure release. Carefully open the lid. Fold in the eggs and stir to combine. Lock the lid and let it sit in the residual heat for 5 minutes. Serve warm.

Asparagus with Copoundy Cheese

Prep time: 5 minutes | Cook time: 1 minute | Serves 4

1½ pounds (680 g) fresh	Sea salt, to taste
asparagus	¼ teaspoon ground black
1 cup water	pepper
2 tablespoons olive oil	½ cup shredded Copoundy
4 garlic cloves, minced	cheese

Pour the water into the Instant Pot and put the steamer basket in the pot. Place the asparagus in the steamer basket. Drizzle the asparagus with the olive oil and sprinkle with the garlic on top. Season with salt and black pepper. Close and secure the lid. Select the Manual mode and set the cooking time for 1 minute at High Pressure. Once cooking is complete, do a quick pressure release. Carefully open the lid. Transfer the asparagus to a platter and served topped with the shredded cheese.

Chanterelle Mushrooms with Cheddar Cheese

Prep time: 10 minutes | Cook time: 5 minutes | Serves 4

1 tablespoon olive oil	2 tablespoons dry white wine
2 cloves garlic, minced	1 teaspoon dried basil
1 (1-inch) ginger root, grated	½ teaspoon dried thyme
16 ounces (454 g) Chanterelle	½ teaspoon dried dill weed
mushrooms, brushed clean	⅓ teaspoon freshly ground
and sliced	black pepper
½ cup unsweetened tomato	Kosher salt, to taste
purée	1 cup shredded Cheddar
½ cup water	cheese

Press the Sauté button on the Instant Pot and heat the olive oil. Add the garlic and grated ginger to the pot and sauté for 1 minute, or until fragrant. Stir in the remaining ingredients, except for the cheese. Lock the lid. Select the Manual mode and set the cooking time for 5 minutes on Low Pressure. When the timer goes off, perform a quick pressure release. Carefully open the lid.. Serve topped with the shredded cheese.

Spinach with Almonds and Olives

Prep time: 15 minutes | Cook time: 2 to 3 minutes | Serves 4

1 tablespoon olive oil	black pepper, to taste
3 cloves garlic, smashed	½ cup almonds, soaked
Bunch scallions, chopped	overnight and drained
2 pounds (907 g) spinach,	2 tablespoons green olives,
washed	pitted and halved
1 cup vegetable broth	2 tablespoons water
1 tablespoon champagne	1 tablespoon extra-virgin olive
vinegar	oil
½ teaspoon dried dill weed	2 teaspoons lemon juice
¼ teaspoon cayenne pepper	1 teaspoon garlic powder
Seasoned salt and ground	1 teaspoon onion powder

Press the Sauté button on the Instant Pot and heat the olive oil. Add the garlic and scallions to the pot and sauté for 1 to 2 minutes, or until fragrant. Stir in the spinach, vegetable broth, vinegar, dill, cayenne pepper, salt and black pepper. Lock the lid. Select the Manual mode and set the cooking time for 1 minute on High Pressure. When the timer goes off, perform a quick pressure release. Carefully open the lid. Stir in the remaining ingredients. Transfer to serving plates and serve immediately.

Steamed Tomato with Halloumi Cheese

Prep time: 5 minutes | Cook time: 3 minutes | Serves 4

8 tomatoes, sliced
1 cup water
½ cup crumbled Halloumi cheese
2 tablespoons extra-virgin olive

oil
2 tablespoons snipped fresh basil
2 garlic cloves, smashed

Pour the water into the Instant Pot and put the trivet in the pot. Place the tomatoes in the trivet. Lock the lid. Select the Manual mode and set the cooking time for 3 minutes on High Pressure. When the timer goes off, perform a quick pressure release. Carefully open the lid. Toss the tomatoes with the remaining ingredients and serve.

Aromatic Spicy Zucchini

Prep time: 5 minutes | Cook time: 4 minutes | Serves 4

1½ tablespoons olive oil
2 garlic cloves, minced
1½ pounds (680 g) zucchinis, sliced
½ cup vegetable broth

1 teaspoon dried basil
½ teaspoon smoked paprika
½ teaspoon dried rosemary
Salt and pepper, to taste

Set the Instant Pot to the Sauté mode and heat the olive oil. Add the garlic to the pot and sauté for 1 minute, or until fragrant. Stir in the remaining ingredients. Lock the lid. Select the Manual mode and set the cooking time for 3 minutes on Low Pressure. When the timer goes off, perform a quick pressure release. Carefully open the lid. Serve immediately.

Braised Collards with Red Wine

Prep time: 5 minutes | Cook time: 2 minutes | Serves 4

1 pound (454 g) Collards, torn into pieces
¾ cup water
¼ cup dry red wine
1½ tablespoons sesame oil

1 teaspoon ginger-garlic paste
½ teaspoon fennel seeds
½ teaspoon mustard seeds
Sea salt and ground black pepper, to taste

Add all the ingredients to the Instant Pot and stir to combine. Lock the lid. Select the Manual mode and set the cooking time for 2 minutes on High Pressure. When the timer goes off, perform a quick pressure release. Carefully open the lid. Ladle into individual bowls and serve warm.

Green Beans with Onion

Prep time: 5 minutes | Cook time: 6 to 7 minutes | Serves 6

6 slices bacon, diced
1 cup diced onion
4 cups halved green beans
¼ cup water

1 teaspoon salt
1 teaspoon freshly ground black pepper

Press the Sauté button on the Instant Pot and add the bacon and onion to the pot and sauté for 2 to 3 minutes. Stir in the remaining ingredients. Close and secure the lid. Select the Manual setting and set the cooking time for 4 minutes at High Pressure. Once the timer goes off, use a quick pressure release. Carefully open the lid. Serve immediately.

Cauliflower Spinach Medley

Prep time: 10 minutes | Cook time: 3 minutes | Serves 4

1 pound (454 g) cauliflower, cut into florets
1 yellow onion, peeled and chopped
1 red bell pepper, deseeded and chopped
1 celery stalk, chopped
2 garlic cloves, crushed

2 tablespoons olive oil
1 tablespoon grated lemon zest
1 teaspoon Hungarian paprika
Sea salt and ground black pepper, to taste
2 cups spinach, torn into pieces

Add all the ingredients, except for the spinach, to the Instant Pot. Close and secure the lid. Select the Manual setting and set the cooking time for 3 minutes at High Pressure. Once the timer goes off, use a quick pressure release. Carefully open the lid. Stir in the spinach and lock the lid. Let it sit in the residual heat for 5 minutes, or until wilted. Serve warm.

Cabbage in Cream Sauce

Prep time: 10 minutes | Cook time: 13 minutes | Serves 4

1 tablespoon unsalted butter
½ cup diced pancetta
¼ cup diced yellow onion
1 cup chicken broth
1 pound (454 g) green cabbage, finely chopped
1 bay leaf

⅓ cup heavy cream
1 tablespoon dried parsley
1 teaspoon fine grind sea salt
¼ teaspoon ground nutmeg
¼ teaspoon ground black pepper

Press the Sauté button on the Instant Pot and melt the butter. Add the pancetta and onion to the pot and sauté for about 4 minutes, or until the onion is tender and begins to brown. Pour in the chicken broth. Using a wooden spoon, stir and loosen any browned bits from the bottom of the pot. Stir in the cabbage and bay leaf. Lock the lid. Select the Manual mode and set the cooking time for 4 minutes on High Pressure. When the timer goes off, perform a quick pressure release. Carefully open the lid. Select Sauté mode and bring the ingredients to a boil. Stir in the remaining ingredients and simmer for 5 additional minutes. Remove and discard the bay leaf. Spoon into serving bowls. Serve warm.

Mediterranean Zoodles

Prep time: 10 minutes | Cook time: 5 minutes | Serves 2

1 tablespoon olive oil
2 tomatoes, chopped
½ cup water
½ cup roughly chopped fresh parsley
3 tablespoons ground almonds
1 tablespoon fresh rosemary, chopped

1 tablespoon apple cider vinegar
1 teaspoon garlic, smashed
2 zucchinis, spiralized and cooked
½ avocado, pitted and sliced
Salt and ground black pepper, to taste

Add the olive oil, tomatoes, water, parsley, ground almonds, rosemary, apple cider vinegar and garlic to the Instant Pot. Lock the lid. Select the Pressure Cook mode and set the cooking time for 5 minutes on High Pressure. When the timer beeps, perform a natural pressure release for 10 minutes, then release any remaining pressure. Carefully open the lid. Divide the cooked zucchini spirals between two serving plates. Spoon the sauce over each serving. Top with the avocado slices and season with salt and black pepper. Serve immediately.

Cheesy Cauliflower Flatbread

Prep time: 10 minutes | Cook time: 2 hours 30 minutes | Serves 8

½ medium head cauliflower, trimmed, stem removed and cut into florets
3½ tablespoons coconut flour
1½ cups grated Mouncezarella cheese, divided
¼ teaspoon fine grind sea salt
2 large eggs, beaten
2 tablespoons heavy cream
2 tablespoons unsalted butter, melted, divided
2 garlic cloves, minced
2 tablespoons fresh basil, cut into ribbons

Add the cauliflower to a blender and pulse until it reaches a rice-like texture. In a large bowl, whisk together ⅔ cup of the riced cauliflower, coconut flour, ¾ cup of the Mouncezarella cheese and sea salt. Stir in the eggs, heavy cream and 1 tablespoon of the butter. Brush the Instant Pot with the remaining 1 tablespoon of the butter. Add the cauliflower mixture and use a spoon to press the mixture flat into the bottom of the pot. Sprinkle the garlic and the remaining ¾ cup of the Mouncezarella cheese on top. Lock the lid. Select the Slow Cook mode and set the cooking time for 2 hours 30 minutes on More. While the flatbread is cooking, preheat the oven broiler to 450°F (235°C). Once the cook time is complete, transfer the flatbread to a clean work surface and cut into 8 wedges. Place the wedges on a large baking sheet and transfer to the oven to broil for 2 to 3 minutes, or until the cheese is lightly browned. Remove from the oven and transfer to a serving platter. Sprinkle the basil ribbons on top. Serve warm.

Peppery Brussels Sprouts

Prep time: 10 minutes | Cook time: 7 minutes | Serves 4

2 tablespoons olive oil
1 white onion, chopped
¾ pound (340 g) Brussels sprouts, trimmed and halved
1 red bell pepper, deseeded and chopped
1 habanero pepper, chopped
1 cup vegetable broth
1 cup water
2 tablespoons unsweetened tomato purée
1 tablespoon coconut aminos
1 teaspoon fennel seeds
½ teaspoon paprika
2 bay leaves
1 garlic clove, minced
Sea salt and freshly ground black pepper, to taste

Press the Sauté button on the Instant Pot and heat the oil. Add the onion to the pot and sauté for 3 minutes, or until tender. Stir in the remaining ingredients. Lock the lid. Select the Manual mode and set the cooking time for 4 minutes on Low Pressure. When the timer goes off, perform a quick pressure release. Carefully open the lid. Remove and discard the bay leaves. Serve warm.

Onion and Green Bean Bowl

Prep time: 5 minutes | Cook time: 6 to 7 minutes | Serves 6

1 cup diced onion
4 cups halved green beans
¼ cup water
1 teaspoon salt
1 teaspoon freshly ground black pepper

Press the Sauté button on the Instant Pot and add the onion to the pot and sauté for 2 to 3 minutes. Stir in the remaining ingredients. Close and secure the lid. Select the Pressure Cook setting and set the cooking time for 4 minutes at High Pressure. Once the timer goes off, use a quick pressure release. Carefully open the lid. Serve immediately.

Kidney Bean and Jalapeño Hummus

Prep time: 5 minutes | Cook time: 6 minutes | Serves 4

1 cup dried kidney beans, soaked in water overnight, rinsed and drained
1 seeded and diced fresh jalapeño
3 cloves garlic, minced
1 tablespoon lime juice
1 teaspoon taco seasoning
½ teaspoon cayenne pepper
1 tablespoon olive oil
½ teaspoon sea salt

Add the beans to the Instant Pot. Pour in enough water to cover about 1 inch. Secure the lid. Select Pressure Cook mode and set cooking time for 6 minutes. When timer beeps, use a natural pressure release for 5 minutes, then release any remaining pressure. Open the lid. Drain the beans. Add the beans, jalapeño, garlic, lime juice, seasonings, oil, and salt to a food processor. Pulse to a creamy consistency. Serve immediately.

Teriyaki Mushrooms with Chives

Prep time: 45 minutes | Cook time: 5 minutes | Serves 4

1½ pounds (680 g) button mushrooms
¼ cup coconut milk
¼ cup dry wine
2 tablespoons sesame oil
1 tablespoon coconut aminos
1 teaspoon ginger-garlic paste
1 teaspoon red pepper flakes
Sea salt and ground black pepper, to taste
2 tablespoons roughly chopped fresh chives

In a bowl, stir together the mushrooms, coconut milk, wine, sesame oil, coconut aminos and ginger-garlic paste. Cover in plastic and let marinate in the refrigerator for 40 minutes. Place the mushrooms along with the marinade in the Instant Pot. Season with the red pepper flakes, salt and black pepper. Lock the lid. Select the Manual mode and set the cooking time for 5 minutes on High Pressure. When the timer goes off, perform a quick pressure release. Carefully open the lid. Serve topped with the fresh chives.

Tempeh and Fennel with Beans

Prep time: 15 minutes | Cook time: 16 minutes | Serves 4

2 tablespoons olive oil
2 pounds (907 g) tempeh, chopped
1 large yellow onion, chopped
1 small fennel bulb, chopped
3 carrots, cubed
3 large garlic cloves, roughly chopped
1 cinnamon stick
1 bay leaf
1½ teaspoons ground allspice
1 teaspoon ras el hanout
½ teaspoon ginger paste
6 large tomatoes, chopped
4 cups vegetable broth
1 (15-ounce / 425-g) can white beans

Add the oil to the Instant Pot and select Sauté mode. Pour in the tempeh and fry for 3 minutes or until golden brown on all sides. Remove to a plate. Put onion, fennel, carrots, and garlic into the pot and sauté for 6 minutes. Drop in cinnamon stick, bay leaf, allspice, ras el hanout, and ginger paste. Sauté for 2 minutes. Pour in tomatoes and broth and stir. Seal the lid. Select Pressure Cook mode and set cooking time for 2 minutes on High Pressure. When timer beeps, do a natural release for 1 minutes, then release any remaining pressure and open the lid. Select Sauté mode. Stir in the tempeh and beans; cook for 3 minutes to warm through. Serve warm.

Almond Spinach with Champagne Vinegar
Prep time: 15 minutes | Cook time: 2 to 3 minutes | Serves 4

1 tablespoon olive oil
3 cloves garlic, smashed
Bunch scallions, chopped
2 pounds (907 g) spinach, washed
1 cup vegetable broth
1 tablespoon champagne vinegar
½ teaspoon dried dill weed
¼ teaspoon cayenne pepper
Seasoned salt and ground
black pepper, to taste
½ cup almonds, soaked overnight and drained
2 tablespoons green olives, pitted and halved
2 tablespoons water
1 tablespoon extra-virgin olive oil
2 teaspoons lemon juice
1 teaspoon garlic powder
1 teaspoon onion powder

Press the Sauté button on the Instant Pot and heat the olive oil. Add the garlic and scallions to the pot and sauté for 1 to 2 minutes, or until fragrant. Stir in the spinach, vegetable broth, vinegar, dill, cayenne pepper, salt and black pepper. Lock the lid. Select the Pressure Cook mode and set the cooking time for 1 minute on High Pressure. When the timer goes off, perform a quick pressure release. Carefully open the lid. Stir in the remaining ingredients. Transfer to serving plates and serve immediately.

Tahini-Lemon Hummus
Prep time: 5 minutes | Cook time: 20 minutes | Serves 4

1 cup dried chickpeas, soaked in water overnight, rinsed and drained
1 tablespoon sesame oil
½ cup diced yellow onion
4 cloves garlic, minced
½ to 1 teaspoon sea salt
¼ cup tahini
¼ cup lemon juice

In the Instant Pot, heat the oil on Sauté mode. Add the onion and garlic and sauté for 3 minutes until the onion is translucent. Add the chickpeas and pour in enough water to cover about 1-inch. Secure the lid. Select Pressure Cook mode and set cooking time for 14 minutes on High Pressure. When timer beeps, use a natural pressure release for 5 minutes, then release any remaining pressure. Remove the lid and stir in the salt. Drain the chickpeas, reserving the cooking broth. Add the chickpeas, tahini, and lemon juice to a food processor. Pulse to a creamy texture. Serve immediately.

Indian Matar
Prep time: 10 minutes | Cook time: 15 minutes | Serves 2

½ tablespoon avocado oil
¼ teaspoon cumin seeds
½ yellow onion, chopped
1 cup green peas
1 tomato, puréed
½ teaspoon garam masala
½ tablespoon coriander
2 curry leaves
½ teaspoon chili powder
Sea salt and ground black pepper, to taste
1½ cups vegetable broth
1 tablespoon chickpea flour
½ cup coconut yogurt

Press the Sauté button on the Instant Pot and heat the oil. Once hot, cook the cumin seeds for about 1 minute or until fragrant. Add the onion and continue sautéing for an additional 3 minutes. Stir in the green peas, tomatoes, garam masala, coriander, curry leaves, chili powder, salt, black pepper, and broth. Secure the lid. Choose the Pressure Cook mode and set cooking time for 12 minutes at High Pressure. Once cooking is complete, use a quick pressure release. Carefully remove the lid. Stir in the chickpea flour and let it simmer on the Sauté mode until thickened. Serve in soup bowls with yogurt on the side.

Green Lentil Salad
Prep time: 15 minutes | Cook time: 20 minutes | Serves 4 to 6

Lentils:
1 cup green lentils, rinsed
3½ cups water, divided
½ teaspoon fine sea salt
1 large carrot, diced
1 red bell pepper, diced
Vinaigrette:
1 small shallot, minced
2 teaspoons Dijon mustard
1 teaspoon dried herbes de Provence
¼ cup fresh lemon juice
2 ribs celery, diced
½ small red onion, diced
¼ cup chopped fresh flat-leaf parsley

1½ teaspoons sugar
½ teaspoon fine sea salt
½ teaspoon freshly ground black pepper
½ cup olive oil

In a heatproof bowl, stir together the lentils, 1½ cups of water, and salt. Pour the remaining 2 cups water into the Instant Pot and place a trivet in the pot. Put the bowl on the trivet. Select Pressure Cook mode and set the cooking time for 20 minutes at High Pressure. Meanwhile, in a bowl, combine the ingredients for the vinaigrette. Stir to mix well. Set aside. When timer beeps, perform a quick pressure release. Open the pot and remove the bowl of lentils. Drain the lentils in a colander, then return them to the bowl. While they are still warm, pour half of the vinaigrette over the lentils and stir gently. Let cool for 20 minutes. In a serving bowl, toss the lentils, carrot, bell pepper, celery, onion, and parsley. Taste and add more vinaigrette as needed. Serve immediately.

Kombu and Mixed Bean Bowls
Prep time: 5 minutes | Cook time: 25 minutes | Serves 6

1 teaspoon olive oil
½ cup diced sweet onion
2 cloves garlic, minced
2 cups mixed dried pinto, red
kidney, and adzuki beans
1-inch strip kombu
4 cups water
½ to 1 teaspoon dulse flakes

In the Instant Pot, heat the oil on Sauté mode. Add the onion and garlic and sauté for 3 minutes, or until the onions are translucent. Stir in the beans, kombu, and water. Secure the lid. Select Pressure Cook mode and set cooking time for 25 minutes on High Pressure. When timer beeps, use a natural pressure release for 15 minutes, then release any remaining pressure. Remove the lid. Stir in the dulse flakes. Serve immediately.

Japan Bean and Mushroom Bowl
Prep time: 10 minutes | Cook time: 16 minutes | Serves 4

1 cup dried anasazi beans, soaked in water overnight, rinsed and drained
1 tablespoon olive oil
2 cups half-moon slices onion
½ teaspoon sugar
½ cup finely diced mushrooms
¼ teaspoon liquid smoke
1 teaspoon smoked paprika
2 cups vegan beef-style broth
¼ cup water
2 teaspoons red miso

In the Instant Pot, heat the olive oil on Sauté mode. Add the onion and sugar and cook for 10 minutes or until soft and brown. Add the beans, mushrooms, liquid smoke, paprika, broth, and water. Stir to combine. Secure the lid. Select Pressure Cook mode and set cooking time for 6 minutes on High Pressure. When timer beeps, use a natural pressure release for 5 minutes, then release any remaining pressure. Remove the lid and stir in the miso. Serve immediately.

Spicy Refried Pinto Beans

Prep time: 5 minutes | Cook time: 10 minutes | Serves 6

1 cup dried pinto beans, soaked in water overnight, rinsed and drained
1 tablespoon olive oil
4 cloves garlic, minced
1 fresh jalapeños, deseeded and diced
½ cup diced yellow onion
3 cups water
1 teaspoon chili powder
½ teaspoon cumin
¼ teaspoon cayenne pepper
½ teaspoon salt

In the Instant Pot, heat the oil on Sauté mode. Add the garlic, onion, and jalapeño and sauté for 3 minutes, until the onion is soft. Add the pinto beans and enough water to cover the beans plus another 1 inch of liquid. Add the chili powder, cumin, and cayenne pepper. Stir to combine. Secure the lid. Select Pressure Cook mode and set cooking time for 6 minutes at High Pressure. When timer beeps, use a natural pressure release for 5 minutes, then release any remaining pressure. Remove the lid, drain the beans and return the beans to the Instant Pot. Add salt. Mash the beans with a hand masher. Serve immediately.

Broccoli and Tempeh Bowls

Prep time: 10 minutes | Cook time: 5 minutes | Serves 2

¼ cup tamari
1 tablespoon pure maple syrup
1 teaspoon cornstarch
¼ cup water
1 tablespoon olive oil
½ teaspoon ground ginger
1 (8- or 9-ounce / 227- or 255-g) package tempeh, cubed
½ head broccoli, cut into pieces

In the Instant Pot, stir together the tamari, maple syrup, cornstarch, water, olive oil, and ginger. Add the tempeh and broccoli. Close the lid, then select Pressure Cook mode and set cooking time for 5 minutes on High Pressure. When the cook time is complete, quick release the pressure. Open the lid and toss to combine. Serve immediately.

Collard Green and Black-Eyed Pea Bowl

Prep time: 5 minutes | Cook time: 3 to 4 minutes | Serves 4 to 6

1 yellow onion, diced
1 tablespoon olive oil
1 cup dried black-eyed peas
¼ cup chopped sun-dried tomatoes
¼ cup tomato paste
1 teaspoon smoked paprika
2 cups water
4 large collard green leaves
Salt and freshly ground black pepper, to taste

In the Instant Pot, select Sauté mode. Add the onion and olive oil and cook for 3 to 4 minutes, stirring occasionally, until the onion is softened. Add the black-eyed peas, tomatoes, tomato paste, paprika, water, and stir to combine. Close the lid, then select Pressure Cook mode and set cooking time for 30 minutes on High Pressure. Once the cook time is complete, let the pressure release naturally for about 15 minutes, then release any remaining pressure. Trim off the thick parts of the collard green stems, then slice the leaves lengthwise in half or quarters. Roll them up together, then finely slice into ribbons. Sprinkle the sliced collard greens with salt and massage it into them with hands to soften. Open the lid. Add the collard greens and ½ teaspoon of salt to the pot, stirring to combine and letting the greens wilt in the heat. Serve immediately.

Ritzy Vegetable and Navy Bean Pot

Prep time: 15 minutes | Cook time: 15 minutes | Serves 2

1 tablespoon olive oil
1 pound (454 g) white button mushrooms, quartered
1 medium white onion, diced
1 medium butternut squash, chopped
¼ teaspoon dried rosemary
1 cup chopped tomatoes
3 cups chicken broth
1 (15-ounce / 425-g) can navy beans, rinsed
2 cups baby spinach
1 lemon, juiced
Salt and ground black pepper, to taste

Set the Instant Pot to Sauté mode. Heat olive oil and sauté mushroom, onion, and squash until softened, about 6 minutes. Season with rosemary, salt, pepper, and cook for 1 minute. Stir in tomato and broth. Seal the lid, select Pressure Cook mode, and set cooking time for 3 minutes on High Pressure. When timer beeps, do a natural pressure release for 2 minutes, then release the remaining pressure and unlock the lid. Press Sauté button on the pot, add navy beans, spinach, and allow spinach to wilt, 3 minutes. Top with lemon juice and serve.

Brussels Sprouts with Peanuts

Prep time: 10 minutes | Cook time: 8 minutes | Serves 4

3 tablespoons sesame oil
1½ pounds (680 g) Brussels sprouts, halved
2 tablespoons fish sauce
1 cup chicken stock
½ cup chopped roasted peanuts

Set the Instant Pot to Sauté and heat the sesame oil until shimmering. Add and fry Brussels sprouts for 5 minutes or until golden. Mix in the fish sauce and chicken stock. Seal the lid. Select the Manual mode and set the time for 3 minutes. Once cooking is complete, do a quick pressure release, then unlock the lid. Mix in the peanuts. Serve immediately.

Rajma

Prep time: 10 minutes | Cook time: 35 minutes | Serves 6

1 tablespoon peanut oil
1 cup diced tomato
1½ cups diced onion
1 tablespoon minced ginger
1 teaspoon garam masala
1 teaspoon ground cumin
1 tablespoon minced garlic
1 teaspoon ground cayenne pepper
1 teaspoon ground turmeric
1 teaspoon salt
1 teaspoon ground coriander
1 cup dried red kidney beans
2 cups water

Put the oil into the Instant Pot, and add the tomato, onion, ginger, garam masala, cumin, garlic, cayenne, turmeric, salt, and coriander. Stir to combine. Place a trivet on top of the onion mixture. Put the beans and water into a heatproof bowl. Cover the bowl with foil. Place the covered bowl on top of the trivet. Lock the lid. Select the Pressure Cook setting and set the time for 30 minutes on High Pressure. When timer beeps, let the pressure release naturally for 10 minutes, then quick release any remaining pressure. Unlock the lid. Carefully remove the bowl of red kidney beans and the trivet. Slightly mash about half the beans with the back of a spoon. Select Sauté mode. Pour the beans and any remaining liquid into the onion masala and mix well. Bring to a boil before serving.

Korean Kongbap

Prep time: 5 minutes | Cook time: 22 minutes | Serves 6

½ cup dried whole peas
½ cup brown rice
½ cup dried black soybeans
½ cup pearl barley
7 cups water, divided
1 tablespoon sesame oil

Combine the peas, brown rice, soybeans, and pearl barley to a large bowl and add 4 cups of the water. Soak overnight. Rinse, drain, and add to the Instant Pot. Add the remaining 3 cups water. Drizzle the oil over the water. Stir to combine. Secure the lid. Select Pressure Cook mode and set cooking time for 22 minutes on High Pressure. When timer beeps, use a natural pressure release for 10 minutes, then release any remaining pressure. Open the lid. Serve immediately.

Beet and Bean Hummus

Prep time: 5 minutes | Cook time: 13 minutes | Serves 4

2 large beets, peeled and chopped
2 cups canned pinto beans, rinsed
2 cups vegetable stock
1 teaspoon garlic powder
Salt, to taste
½ lemon, juiced
¼ cup olive oil

Combine pinto beans, beets, stock, garlic powder, and salt into Instant Pot. Seal the lid, select Pressure Cook mode, and set cooking time for 13 minutes on High Pressure. When timer beeps, do a quick pressure release, and unlock the lid. Transfer mixture to a blender and process until smooth. Add lemon juice and olive oil and blend again to combine. Pour mixture into bowls and serve.

Hearty Vegetable Burgers

Prep time: 20 minutes | Cook time: 55 minutes | Serves 2

2 tablespoons olive oil, divided
½ medium red bell pepper, deseeded and chopped
½ medium yellow onion, chopped
½ medium zucchini, chopped
½ cup chopped yellow squash
4 cloves garlic, minced
1 cup dried black beans
8 cups water
1 teaspoon salt
½ cup panko bread crumbs
½ jalapeño, deseeded and minced
Pinch freshly ground black pepper
2 burger buns

Press the Sauté button on the Instant Pot and heat 1 tablespoon of olive oil until shimmering. Add the bell pepper and onion and sauté for 3 minutes or until the onion is translucent. Add the zucchini, squash, and garlic and sauté for 3 minutes. Transfer the vegetables in the pot to a small bowl and set aside. Add the beans, water, and salt to the pot. Lock the lid. Press the Bean button and set the cooking time for 30 minutes at High Pressure. When the timer beeps, let pressure release naturally for 10 minutes. Release any remaining pressure, then unlock lid. Press the Sauté button on the pot and simmer bean mixture for 10 minutes to thicken. Transfer the mixture to a large bowl and mash with forks. When cool enough to handle, quickly mix in the vegetable mixture, panko, jalapeño, and pepper and blend thoroughly. Form the mixture into 2 patties. Cook in a skillet over remaining 1 tablespoon of olive oil for 2 to 3 minutes on each side until browned. Remove from heat and assemble each patty with a bun. Serve warm.

Coconut Lentil Curry

Prep time: 5 minutes | Cook time: 15 minutes | Serves 4

1 teaspoon sesame oil
2 cubes frozen glazed onions
2 large cloves garlic, minced
1 large sweet potato, diced (about 3½ cups)
¼ cup water
¼ cup dried red lentils
1 (13.5-ounce / 383-g) can coconut milk
½ cup sushi rice
2 tablespoons gochujang
1 teaspoon curry powder
½ cup vegetable broth
1 teaspoon tamari or soy sauce
½ cup chopped unsalted roasted peanuts for garnish
¼ cup chopped fresh cilantro, for garnish

Heat the sesame oil in the Instant Pot on the Sauté function with the onions, garlic, sweet potatoes, and water for 5 minutes. Add the lentils, sushi rice, coconut milk, gochujang, curry powder, and vegetable broth. Stir well. Cover the pot, select Pressure Cook mode, and set cooking time for 7 minutes on High Pressure. When timer beeps, use a natural pressure release for 5 minutes, then release any remaining pressure. Remove the lid. Stir until potatoes have disappeared, turning into a bright cream clinging to the rice. Stir in the tamari. Spoon into bowls and garnish each serving with peanuts and cilantro.

Butternut Squash and Mushrooms

Prep time: 10 minutes | Cook time: 40 minutes | Serves 4

1 tablespoon olive oil
2 cups butternut squash, peeled and diced
1 red bell pepper, diced
½ cup onion, chopped
3 garlic cloves, minced
8 ounces (227 g) white mushrooms, sliced
1½ cups Arborio rice
3½ cup vegetable soup
¼ teaspoon oregano
2 teaspoons ground coriander
1 teaspoon salt
1 teaspoon black pepper
½ cup dry white wine
1½ tablespoons nutritional yeast

Put the oil to the Instant Pot and select the Sauté function. Add the butternut squash, bell pepper, onion, and garlic to the oil and sauté for 5 minutes. Stir in the mushrooms, rice, soup, oregano, coriander, salt, pepper, and wine. Secure the lid and select the Bean / Chili function and set the cooking time for 30 minutes at High Pressure. When the timer beeps, do a natural pressure release for 10 minutes, then release any remaining pressure. Open the lid. Mix in the nutritional yeast, then cook for another 5 minutes on Sauté setting. Serve warm.

Easy Green Beans with Toasted Peanuts

Prep time: 10 minutes | Cook time: 1 minutes | Serves 4

1 cup water
1 pound (454 g) green beans, trimmed
1 lemon, juiced
2 tablespoons olive oil
Salt and black pepper, to taste
2 tablespoons toasted peanuts

Pour the water in the Instant Pot, then fit in a steamer basket and arrange the green beans on top. Seal the lid. Select the Manual mode and set the time for 1 minute on High Pressure. Once cooking is complete, do a quick pressure release. Unlock the lid. Transfer the green beans onto a plate and mix in lemon juice, olive oil, salt, pepper, and toasted peanuts. Serve immediately.

Broccoli, Raisin, and Seed Salad

Prep time: 10 minutes | Cook time: 1 minutes | Serves 2 to 4

1 cup water
½ pound (227 g) broccoli, cut into florets
2 tablespoons raisins
2 scallion stalks, chopped
Sea salt and ground black pepper, to taste
2 tablespoons sesame seeds, toasted
2 tablespoons sunflower seeds, to toasted
1 tablespoon balsamic vinegar
⅓ cup mayonnaise
1 tablespoon fresh lemon juice
⅓ cup sour cream

Pour the water in the Instant Pot and fit in a steamer basket. Place the broccoli in the steamer basket. Secure the lid. Choose the Manual mode and set the cooking time for 1 minute at High pressure. Once cooking is complete, perform a quick pressure release. Carefully open the lid. Allow to cool for a few minutes. Transfer the broccoli florets to a serving bowl. Toss in the raisins, scallions, salt, black pepper, and seeds. Stir in the balsamic vinegar, mayo, lemon juice, and sour cream. Serve immediately.

Broccoli, Spinach, and Avocado Mash

Prep time: 15 minutes | Cook time: 3 minutes | Serves 4

1 medium broccoli, cut into florets
2 cups spinach
1 cup vegetable broth
2 avocados, halved, pitted, and peeled
2 tablespoons chopped parsley
2 tablespoons butter
Salt and black pepper, to taste
3 tablespoons Greek yogurt
2 tablespoons toasted pine nuts, for topping

Add the broccoli, spinach, and broth to the Instant Pot. Stir to mix well. Seal the lid. Select the Manual mode and set the cooking time for 3 minutes on High Pressure. Once cooking is complete, do a quick pressure release. Carefully open the lid. Stir in the avocado, parsley, butter, salt, pepper, and Greek yogurt. Pour the mixture in a food processor and pulse until smooth. Spoon into serving bowls and top with pine nuts. Serve immediately.

Cheesy Broccoli Stuffed Potatoes

Prep time: 10 minutes | Cook time: 20 minutes | Serves 4

1 cup water
1 head broccoli, cut into florets
4 small russet potatoes
¾ cup half-and-half
1 tablespoon butter
2 cups Gruyere cheese, grated
1 teaspoon cornstarch
¼ cup chopped fresh chives

Pour the water in the Instant Pot and fit in a steamer basket. Add the broccoli. Seal the lid. Select the Manual mode and set the cooking time for 1 minute at High Pressure. Once cooking is complete, do a quick pressure release, then unlock the lid and transfer the broccoli to a bowl. In the steamer basket, place the potatoes. Seal the lid again. Select the Manual mode and set the cooking time for 15 minutes on High Pressure. Once cooking is complete, do a quick pressure release. Unlock the lid and let the potatoes cool. Take out the steamer basket and discard the water. Press the Sauté button and warm half-and-half and butter until the butter melts. In a bowl, mix the cheese with cornstarch and pour the mixture into the pot. Stir until the cheese melts. Transfer the mixture in a large bowl. Toss the broccoli with the mixture to combine well. Cut a slit into each potato and stuff with the broccoli mixture. Scatter with chives to serve.

Bok Choy with Rice Wine Vinegar

Prep time: 5 minutes | Cook time: 6 minutes | Serves 4

1 teaspoon sesame oil
1 clove garlic, pressed
1 pound (454 g) Bok choy
½ cup water
1 tablespoon rice wine vinegar
2 tablespoons soy sauce

Press the Sauté button and heat the sesame oil in the Instant Pot. Add the garlic and sauté for 1 minute or until fragrant. Add the Bok choy and pour in the water. Secure the lid. Choose the Manual mode and set the cooking time for 5 minutes at High pressure. Meanwhile, in a small bowl, whisk the rice vinegar and soy sauce. Once cooking is complete, do a quick pressure release. Carefully open the lid. Drizzle the sauce over the Bok choy and serve immediately.

Beet Thoran Keralite Sadhya

Prep time: 10 minutes | Cook time: 20 minutes | Serves 4

1 cup water
½ pound (227 g) small beets
2 tablespoons olive oil
½ chili pepper, chopped
1 garlic clove, minced
½ cup shallots, chopped
5 curry leaves
⅓ teaspoon turmeric powder
Sea salt and ground black pepper, to taste

Pour the water in the Instant Pot and fit in a steamer basket. Place the beets in the steamer basket. Secure the lid. Choose the Steam mode and set the cooking time for 15 minutes at High pressure. Once cooking is complete, perform a quick pressure release. Carefully open the lid. Allow the beets to cool for a few minutes. Once the beets are cool enough to touch, transfer them to a cutting board, then peel and chop them into small pieces. Press the Sauté button and heat the olive oil until shimmering. Add and sauté the chili pepper, garlic, shallots, and curry leaves for about 4 minutes or until softened. Sprinkle with the turmeric, salt, and black pepper. Fold in the cooked beets. Serve warm.

Beet and Wheat Berry Salad

Prep time: 10 minutes | Cook time: 6 to 8 hours | Serves 4 to 6

1 cup wheat berries
2 garlic cloves, minced
2 teaspoons minced fresh thyme or ½ teaspoon dried
Salt and pepper, to taste
1 Granny Smith apple, peeled, cored, halved, and sliced ¼ inch thick
1 pound (454 g) beets, trimmed
4 ounces (113 g) baby arugula
3 tablespoons extra-virgin olive oil
3 tablespoons red wine vinegar
Pinch sugar
4 ounces (113 g) goat cheese, crumbled (1 cup)

Combine 5 cups water, wheat berries, garlic, thyme, and ½ teaspoon salt in the Instant Pot. Wrap beets individually in aluminum foil and place in the Instant Pot. Cover and press the Slow Cook button, and cook on low for 6 to 8 hours or on high for 4 to 5 hours, until wheat berries and beets are tender. (Press Slow Cook again to toggle between Low and High cooking temperatures.) Transfer beets to cutting board, open foil, and let sit until cool enough to handle. Rub off beet skins with paper towels and cut beets into ½-inch-thick wedges. Drain wheat berries, transfer to a large serving bowl, and let cool slightly. Add beets, apple, arugula, oil, vinegar, ½ teaspoon salt, pinch pepper, and sugar and toss to combine. Season with salt and pepper to taste. Sprinkle with goat cheese and serve.

Beet and Walnut Burgers

Prep time: 10 minutes | Cook time: 45 minutes | Serves 4

5 medium beets, quartered
1½ cups water
1½ cups chopped walnuts
4 teaspoons cornstarch, combined with ¼ cup warm water
½ cup chopped yellow onions
⅛ cup all-purpose flour
1 cup shredded Cheddar cheese
2 tablespoons soy sauce
2 tablespoons olive oil
Salt and ground black pepper, to taste
4 burger buns

Add the beets and water to the Instant Pot. Lock the lid, then press the Manual button, and set the timer to 15 minutes at High Pressure. When the timer beeps, let pressure release naturally for 5 minutes, then release any remaining pressure. Unlock lid. Drain the beets and add to a large bowl. Add the remaining ingredients, except for the buns, and mash the mixture with a potato masher. Form the beet mixture into 4 patties. Preheat the oven to 350ºF (180ºC). Spray a baking pan with cooking spray. Place the patties on the prepared baking pan and bake for 25 to 30 minutes. Allow the patties to cool, then assemble the patties with buns and serve.

Cheesy Asparagus

Prep time: 10 minutes | Cook time: 8 minutes | Serves 4

1 cup water
1 pound (454 g) asparagus, chopped
2 garlic cloves, minced
2 tablespoons butter, softened
Salt and black pepper, to taste
1 tablespoon olive oil
½ lemon, juiced
2 tablespoons grated Parmesan cheese

In the Instant pot, pour the water and fit in a trivet. Cut out a foil sheet, place the asparagus on top with garlic and butter. Season with salt and black pepper. Wrap the foil and place on the trivet. Seal the lid. Select the Manual mode and set to 8 minutes on High Pressure. Once cooking is complete, do a quick pressure release. Carefully open the lid. Remove the foil, then transfer the asparagus onto a platter. Drizzle with lemon juice, and top with Parmesan cheese to serve.

Cheesy Cabbage and Pepper Bake

Prep time: 15 minutes | Cook time: 25 minutes | Serves 2

1 tablespoon olive oil, divided
½ pound (227 g) green cabbage, shredded
1 garlic clove, sliced
1 onion, thinly sliced
1 Serrano pepper, chopped
1 sweet pepper, thinly sliced
Sea salt and ground black
pepper, to taste
1 teaspoon paprika
1 cup cream of mushroom soup
4 ounces (113 g) Colby cheese, shredded
1 cup water

Grease a baking dish with ½ tablespoon of olive oil. Add the cabbage, garlic, onion, and peppers. Stir to combine. Drizzle with remaining oil and season with salt, black pepper, and paprika. Pour in the mushroom soup. Top with the shredded cheese and cover with aluminum foil. Pour the water in the Instant Pot and fit in a trivet. Lower the dish onto the trivet. Secure the lid. Choose the Manual mode and set the cooking time for 25 minutes at High pressure. Once cooking is complete, perform a quick pressure release. Carefully open the lid. Serve warm.

Cauliflower and Olive Salad

Prep time: 10 minutes | Cook time: 2 minutes | Serves 4

1 cup water
½ pound (227 g) cauliflower, cut into florets
1 bell pepper, thinly sliced
½ red onion, thinly sliced
¼ cup fresh flat-leaf parsley,
coarsely chopped
¼ cup green olives, pitted and coarsely chopped
2 ounces (57 g) Mozzarella cheese, crumbled
Dressing:
1 teaspoon hot mustard
2 tablespoons fresh lime juice
3 tablespoons extra-virgin olive
oil
Sea salt and ground black pepper, to taste

Pour the water in the Instant Pot and fit in a steamer basket. Place the cauliflower in the steamer basket. Secure the lid. Choose the Steam mode and set the cooking time for 2 minutes at High pressure. Once cooking is complete, perform a quick pressure release. Carefully open the lid. Toss the cooked cauliflower with pepper, onion, parsley, and olives in a large bowl. In a small bowl, combine the ingredients for the dressing. Dress the salad and serve garnished with the crumbled Mozzarella cheese.

Cauliflower and Celeriac Mix

Prep time: 10 minutes | Cook time: 2 minutes | Serves 4

1 cup water
1 head cauliflower, cut into florets
1 carrot, sliced
½ cup celeriac, sliced
2 tablespoons butter
Salt and black pepper, to taste

Pour the water into the Instant Pot and fit in a steamer basket. Place the cauliflower, carrots, and celeriac in the basket. Seal the lid. Select the Steam mode, then set the cooking time for 2 minutes at High Pressure. Once cooking time is complete, perform a quick pressure release. Unlock the lid and transfer the veggies to a bowl. Stir in the butter and sprinkle with salt and pepper before serving.

Khoreshe Karafs

Prep time: 20 minutes | Cook time: 11 minutes | Serves 2

1 tablespoon unsalted butter
½ onion, chopped
1 garlic clove, minced
½ pound (227 g) celery stalks, diced
1 Persian lime, prick a few holes
1 tablespoon fresh cilantro,
roughly chopped
1 tablespoon fresh mint, finely chopped
½ teaspoon mustard seeds
2 cups vegetable broth
½ teaspoon cayenne pepper
Sea salt and ground black pepper, to taste

Press the Sauté button of the Instant Pot. Add and melt the butter. Add and sauté the onions and garlic for about 3 minutes or until tender and fragrant. Stir in the remaining ingredients, except for the basmati rice. Secure the lid. Choose the Manual mode and set the cooking time for 18 minutes at High pressure. Once cooking is complete, use a natural pressure release for 15 minutes, then release any remaining pressure. Carefully open the lid. Serve hot.

Golden Cauliflower Tots

Prep time: 30 minutes | Cook time: 10 minutes | Serves 4

1 cup water
1 large cauliflower
1 egg, beaten
1 cup almond meal
1 cup grated Parmesan cheese

1 cup grated Gruyere cheese
2 garlic cloves, minced
Salt, to taste
3 tablespoons olive oil

Pour the water in the Instant Pot, then fit in a trivet and place the cauliflower on top. Seal the lid. Select the Manual mode and set the time for 3 minutes at High Pressure. Once cooking is complete, do a quick pressure release. Carefully open the lid. Transfer the cauliflower to a food processor and pulse to rice the cauliflower. Pour the cauliflower rice into a bowl. Mix in the egg, almond meal, cheeses, garlic, and salt. Make the tots: Form the mixture into 2-inch oblong balls. Place on a baking sheet and chill in the refrigerator for 20 minutes. Set the Instant Pot on Sauté mode. Heat the olive oil until shimmering. Remove tots from refrigerator and fry in the oil for 6 minutes on all sides until golden brown. Flip the tots in the oil during the frying. Work in batches to avoid overcrowding. Place the tots on a paper towel-lined plate to pat dry and serve.

Gold Potato and Boiled Egg Salad

Prep time: 20 minutes | Cook time: 12 minutes | Serves 4

1 cup water
1 pound (454 g) small Yukon Gold potatoes
2 boiled eggs, peeled and chopped
1 celery rib, diced
¼ cup pickle relish
½ yellow onion, sliced

1 garlic clove, minced
⅓ cup mayonnaise
½ teaspoon fresh rosemary, chopped
½ tablespoon yellow mustard
⅓ teaspoon cayenne pepper
Sea salt and ground black pepper, to taste

Pour the water in the Instant Pot and fit in a steamer basket. Place the potatoes in the steamer basket. Secure the lid. Choose the Manual mode and set the cooking time for 12 minutes at High pressure. Once cooking is complete, do a quick pressure release. Carefully remove the lid. Allow to cool for a few minutes until cool enough to handle. Peel and slice the potatoes, then place them in a large bowl and toss with the remaining ingredients. Stir to combine. Serve immediately.

Honey Carrot Salad with Dijon Mustard

Prep time: 10 minutes | Cook time: 3 minutes | Serves 2 to 4

1 cup water
1 pound (454 g) carrots, sliced to 2-inch chunks
1 scallion, finely sliced
½ tablespoon Dijon mustard
½ tablespoon lime juice

1 teaspoon honey
¼ teaspoon red pepper flakes
½ teaspoon Himalayan salt
¼ teaspoon ground white pepper
1 tablespoon olive oil

Pour the water in the Instant Pot and fit in a steamer basket. Place the carrots in the steamer basket. Secure the lid. Choose the Steam mode and set the cooking time for 3 minutes at High pressure. Once cooking is complete, perform a quick pressure release. Carefully open the lid. Toss the carrots with the remaining ingredients in a serving bowl and serve chilled.

Italian Potato and Carrot Medley

Prep time: 15 minutes | Cook time: 11 minutes | Serves 4

2 tablespoons olive oil
1 cup potatoes, peeled and chopped
3 carrots, peeled and chopped
3 garlic cloves, minced

1 cup vegetable broth
1 teaspoon Italian seasoning
Salt and black pepper, to taste
1 tablespoon chopped parsley
1 tablespoon chopped oregano

Set the Instant Pot to the Sauté mode. Heat the olive oil until shimmering. Add and sauté the potatoes and carrots for 5 minutes or until tender. Add the garlic and cook for a minute or until fragrant. Pour in the vegetable broth, season with Italian seasoning, salt, and black pepper. Seal the lid. Select the Manual mode and set the time for 5 minutes at High Pressure. Once cooking is complete, do a quick pressure release, then unlock the lid. Spoon the potatoes and carrots into a serving bowl and mix in the parsley and oregano. Serve warm.

Cherry and Pecan Stuffed Pumpkin

Prep time: 20 minutes | Cook time: 20 minutes | Serves 4

1 (2-pound / 907-g) pumpkin, halved lengthwise, stems trimmed
2 tablespoons olive oil
1 cup water
½ cup dried cherries
1 teaspoon dried parsley

5 toasted bread slices, cubed
1 teaspoon onion powder
1½ cups vegetable broth
Salt and black pepper, to taste
½ cup chopped pecans, for topping

Brush the pumpkin with olive oil. Pour the water in the Instant Pot and fit in a trivet. Place the pumpkin, skin-side down, on the trivet. Seal the lid. Select the Manual mode and set the cooking time for 15 minutes at High Pressure. Once cooking is complete, do a quick pressure release. Carefully open the lid. Remove the pumpkin and water. Press the Sauté button, add the remaining ingredients. Stir for 5 minutes or until the liquid is reduced by half. Divide the mixture between pumpkin halves and top with pecans.

Red Beans and Rice with Okra

Prep time: 15 minutes | Cook time: 8 to 9 hours | Serves 4 to 6

2 tablespoons Cajun seasoning
2 tablespoons extra-virgin olive oil
3 garlic cloves, minced
8 ounces (227 g) dried small red beans, picked over and rinsed
1 green bell pepper, stemmed, deseeded, and cut into ½-inch

pieces
4 cups vegetable broth
1½ cups instant white rice
2 cups frozen cut okra, thawed
2 tomatoes, cored and cut into ½-inch pieces
4 scallions, thinly sliced
Salt and pepper, to taste

Microwave Cajun seasoning, oil, and garlic in bowl until fragrant, about 1 minute; transfer to the Instant Pot. Stir in broth, beans, and bell pepper. Cover and press the Slow Cook button, and cook on high for 8 to 9 hours, until beans are tender. (Press Slow Cook again to toggle between Low and High temperatures.) Stir in rice, cover, and press the Slow Cook button, and cook on high for 20 to 30 minutes, until rice is tender. (Press Slow Cook again to toggle between Low and High cooking temperatures.) Stir in okra and let sit until heated through, about 5 minutes. Stir in tomatoes and scallions, and season with salt and pepper to taste. Serve.

Summer Squash, Kale, and Quinoa Stew
Prep time: 10 minutes | Cook time: 4 hours | Serves 2

½ cup quinoa
½ cup canned chickpeas, drained and rinsed
1 cup diced summer squash
4 cups fresh kale
1 cup canned plum tomatoes, roughly chopped
2 cups low-sodium vegetable broth
1 tablespoon Italian herb blend
⅛ teaspoon sea salt

Put all the ingredients into the Instant Pot, stirring to mix them together thoroughly. Cover and press the Slow Cook button, and cook on low for 4 hours. (Press Slow Cook again to toggle between Low and High cooking temperatures.)

Rosemary Cauliflower and Lentils
Prep time: 10 minutes | Cook time: 8 hours | Serves 2

1 cup cauliflower florets
1 cup lentils
1 tablespoon fresh rosemary
1 tablespoon roasted garlic
Zest of 1 lemon
1 tablespoon extra-virgin olive oil
⅛ teaspoon sea salt
Freshly ground black pepper, to taste
3 cups low-sodium vegetable broth
Juice of 1 lemon
¼ cup roughly chopped fresh parsley

Put the cauliflower, lentils, rosemary, garlic, lemon zest, and olive oil in the Instant Pot. Season with the salt and black pepper. Pour the vegetable broth over the cauliflower and lentils. Cover and press the Slow Cook button, and cook on low for 8 hours. (Press Slow Cook again to toggle between Low and High cooking temperatures.) Just before serving, drizzle the cauliflower and lentils with the lemon juice and sprinkle the parsley over the top.

Smoky Mixed Bean Chili
Prep time: 10 minutes | Cook time: 6 to 8 hours | Serves 2

1 (16-ounce / 454-g) can mixed beans, drained and rinsed
1 cup frozen roasted corn kernels, thawed
1 cup canned fire-roasted diced tomatoes, undrained
½ cup diced onion
2 garlic cloves, minced
1 teaspoon ground cumin
1 teaspoon smoked paprika
1 teaspoon dried oregano
⅛ teaspoon sea salt

Put all the ingredients in the Instant Pot. Give them a quick stir to combine. Cover and press the Slow Cook button, and cook on low for 6 to 8 hours. (Press Slow Cook again to toggle between Low and High cooking temperatures.)

Tempeh and Corn Stuffed Bell Peppers
Prep time: 10 minutes | Cook time: 6 to 8 hours | Serves 2

1 teaspoon extra-virgin olive oil
8 ounces (227 g) tempeh, crumbled
1 cup frozen corn kernels, thawed
¼ cup minced onions
1 teaspoon minced garlic
1 teaspoon ground cumin
1 teaspoon smoked paprika
2 tablespoons Pepper Jack cheese
⅛ teaspoon sea salt
4 narrow red bell peppers

Grease the inside of the Instant Pot with the olive oil. In a medium bowl, combine the tempeh, corn, onions, garlic, cumin, paprika, cheese, and salt. Cut the tops off each of the peppers and set the tops aside. Scoop out and discard the seeds and membranes from inside each pepper. Divide the tempeh filling among the peppers. Return the tops to each of the peppers. Nestle the peppers into the Instant Pot. Cover and press the Slow Cook button, and cook on low for 6 to 8 hours, until the peppers are very tender. (Press Slow Cook again to toggle between Low and High cooking temperatures.)

Vegetarian Bean Cassoulet
Prep time: 10 minutes | Cook time: 6 to 8 hours | Serves 2

1 teaspoon extra-virgin olive oil
2 (15-ounce / 425-g) cans navy beans, drained and rinsed
16 ounces (454 g) vegan sausage, cut into 1-inch pieces
1 cup minced onion
¼ cup minced celery
1 tablespoon minced garlic
1 teaspoon minced fresh sage
1 cup low-sodium vegetable broth

Grease the inside of the Instant Pot with the olive oil. Put the beans, sausage, onion, celery, garlic, and sage in the Instant Pot. Stir to mix thoroughly. Pour in the vegetable broth. Cover and press the Slow Cook button, and cook on low for 6 to 8 hours, , until the beans are very tender but not falling apart. (Press Slow Cook again to toggle between Low and High cooking temperatures.)

Curried Sweet Potatoes and Broccoli
Prep time: 10 minutes | Cook time: 6 to 8 hours | Serves 2

2 medium sweet potatoes, cut into 1-inch pieces
1 cup broccoli florets
½ cup diced onions
1 cup light coconut milk
1 teaspoon minced fresh ginger
1 teaspoon minced garlic
Pinch red pepper flakes
1 tablespoon curry powder
1 teaspoon garam masala
¼ cup toasted cashews

Put the sweet potatoes, broccoli, and onions into the Instant Pot. In a small bowl, whisk together the coconut milk, ginger, garlic, red pepper flakes, curry powder, and garam masala. Pour this mixture over the vegetables. Cover and press the Slow Cook button, and cook on low for 6 to 8 hours, , until the vegetables are very tender but not falling apart. (Press Slow Cook again to toggle between Low and High cooking temperatures.) Just before serving, add the cashews and stir thoroughly.

Red Tofu Curry and Green Beans
Prep time: 15 minutes | Cook time: 6 hours | Serves 2

1 teaspoon extra-virgin olive oil
16 ounces (454 g) firm tofu, drained and cut into 1-inch pieces
2 cups chopped green beans
½ red onion, halved and thinly sliced
1 plum tomato, diced
1 teaspoon minced fresh ginger
1 teaspoon minced garlic
2 teaspoons Thai red curry paste
1 cup coconut milk
1 cup low-sodium vegetable broth

Grease the inside of the Instant Pot with the olive oil. Put all the ingredients into the Instant Pot and stir gently. Cover and press the Slow Cook button, and cook on low for 6 hours. (Press Slow Cook again to toggle between Low and High cooking temperatures.)

Cabbage and Tomato Rolls

Prep time: 10 minutes | Cook time: 25 minutes | Serves 4

6 cups chopped green
cabbage
2 medium onions, chopped
1 (14.5-ounce / 411-g) can
diced tomatoes
1 (8-ounce / 227-g) can tomato
sauce
1 cup fine bulgur

3 cloves garlic, minced
2 teaspoons kosher salt
1 teaspoon black pepper
1 teaspoon granulated sugar
¼ cup water
2 tablespoons apple cider
vinegar

In the Instant Pot, combine the cabbage, onion, tomatoes,
tomato sauce, bulgur, garlic, salt, pepper, sugar, and water. Stir
well to combine. Secure the lid on the pot. Close the pressure-
release valve. Select Manual and set the pot at High Pressure
for 3 minutes. At the end of the cooking time, allow the pot to sit
undisturbed for 10 minutes, then quick-release any remaining
pressure. Stir in the vinegar and serve.

Chard and Chickpea Soup

Prep time: 15 minutes | Cook time: 15 minutes | Serves 6

8 cups chopped rainbow chard
4 cups thinly sliced leeks (white
and light green parts)
2 cups vegetable broth, plus
more if needed
1 (14.5-ounce / 411-g) can
chickpeas, drained and rinsed
1 cup sliced celery
6 cloves garlic, minced

1 teaspoon dried oregano
1 teaspoon kosher salt
2 teaspoons black pepper
1 medium yellow summer
squash, halved lengthwise and
sliced
¼ cup chopped fresh parsley
4 to 6 tablespoons grated
Parmesan cheese

In the Instant Pot, combine the chard, leeks, broth, chickpeas,
celery, half the garlic, the oregano, salt, and pepper. Secure the
lid on the pot. Close the pressure-release valve. Select Manual
and set the pot at High Pressure for 3 minutes. At the end of the
cooking time, use a quick release to depressurize. Add more
broth, if needed. Select Sauté/Normal. Add the squash, parsley,
and remaining garlic and cook, stirring occasionally, 2 to 3
minutes. Ladle the soup into bowls, sprinkle with the Parmesan
cheese, and serve.

Eggplant and Tomato Stew

Prep time: 15 minutes | Cook time: 25 minutes | Serves 4

3 tablespoons vegetable oil
3 cloves garlic, minced
4 cups peeled, chopped
eggplant
1 (14.5-ounce / 411-g) can
chickpeas, drained and rinsed
2 cups chopped tomatoes or 1
(14.5-ounce / 411-g) can diced
tomatoes

1 cup chopped onion
1 cup stemmed, seeded, and
roughly chopped red, yellow, or
orange bell pepper
1 teaspoon kosher salt
1 teaspoon black pepper
¼ cup chopped fresh basil
Extra-virgin olive oil, for serving
(optional)

Select Sauté/Normal on the Instant Pot. When the pot is hot,
add the vegetable oil. Once the oil is hot, add the garlic and
allow it to sizzle for about 30 seconds. Select Cancel. Add the
eggplant, chickpeas, if using, tomatoes, onion, bell pepper,
salt, and pepper. Secure the lid on the pot. Close the pressure-
release valve. Select Manual and set the pot at High Pressure
for 4 minutes. At the end of the cooking time, allow the pot to
sit undisturbed for 5 minutes, then quick-release any remaining
pressure. Ladle the stew into bowls and garnish with the basil.

Drizzle with olive oil, if desired, and serve.

Mushroom Cheese Stroganoff

Prep time: 10 minutes | Cook time: 25 minutes | Serves 4

1 cup diced onion
3 cloves garlic, minced
1 (10-ounces / 283-g) package
frozen mixed mushrooms or
1½ cups sliced mixed fresh
mushrooms
2 tablespoons butter or olive oil
1 tablespoon Dijon mustard
1 tablespoon soy sauce

1 teaspoon kosher salt
1 teaspoon black pepper
1¼ cups water
8 ounces (227 g) fusilli or other
pasta (about 2 cups)
½ cup sour cream
½ cup shredded Parmesan
cheese
½ cup chopped fresh parsley

In the Instant Pot, combine the onion, garlic, mushrooms,
butter, mustard, soy sauce, salt, pepper, water, and pasta. Stir
well to combine. Secure the lid on the pot. Close the pressure-
release valve. Select Manual and set the pot at High Pressure
for 5 minutes. At the end of the cooking time, allow the pot to
sit undisturbed for 5 minutes, then quick-release any remaining
pressure. Open the lid, stir in the sour cream, Parmesan
cheese, and parsley, and serve.

Creamy Potato with Cabbage

Prep time: 15 minutes | Cook time: 25 minutes | Serves 10

4 cups peeled and cubed (2-
inch) russet potatoes
2½ teaspoons kosher salt
1½ cups water
3 cups coarsely chopped
cabbage
⅓ cup heavy cream

4 tablespoons (½ stick)
unsalted butter, plus additional
melted butter for serving
½ teaspoon black pepper
¼ teaspoon ground nutmeg
1 cup chopped green onions

In the Instant Pot, combine the potatoes, 1 teaspoon of the
salt, and the water. Place the cabbage in a round baking pan.
Place a trivet on top of the potatoes. Place the pan on the trivet.
Secure the lid on the pot. Close the pressure-release valve.
Select Manual and set the pot at High Pressure for 5 minutes.
At the end of the cooking time, allow the pot to sit undisturbed
for 10 minutes, then quick-release any remaining pressure.
Remove the pan with the cabbage and set aside. Drain the
potatoes. In a stand mixer fitted with the paddle attachment,
combine the potatoes, cream, butter, the remaining 1½
teaspoons salt, pepper, and nutmeg. Whip until creamy. (You
can also use a hand mixer and whip the potatoes in the pot.) Stir
in the cooked cabbage and the green onions. To serve, make a
well in the center of each serving and fill with melted butter.

Bok Choy with Sesame

Prep time: 5 minutes | Cook time: 1 minutes | Serves 4

1 cup water
4 baby bok choy heads,
quartered lengthwise
1 tablespoon rice wine vinegar

1 teaspoon sesame oil
1 tablespoon toasted sesame
seeds

Place a steamer insert in the Instant Pot. Add the water to the
Instant Pot and mound the bok choy in the steamer. Lock on the
lid and set the timer for 1 minute at High Pressure. When the
timer goes off, quick release the pressure and remove the lid.
Use a tongs to transfer the bok choy to a serving platter or bowl.
In a small bowl, whisk together the vinegar and sesame oil.
Drizzle it over the bok choy. Sprinkle the sesame seeds over the
bok choy and serve immediately.

Kale with Garlic

Prep time: 1 minutes | Cook time: 5 minutes | Serves 4

1 tablespoon extra-virgin olive oil
2 garlic cloves, minced
1 kale bunch, stemmed and chopped or 1 (1-pound / 454-g) bag chopped kale
1½ cups water
1 tablespoon red wine vinegar
½ teaspoon red pepper flakes
¼ teaspoon kosher salt

With the Instant Pot on the Sauté or brown setting, heat the olive oil. Add the garlic and sauté for 30 seconds, stirring constantly. Add the kale and water to the Instant Pot. Lock on the lid and set the timer for 5 minutes at High Pressure. When the timer goes off, quick release the pressure, remove the lid, and toss the cooked greens with the vinegar, red pepper flakes, and salt. Serve hot.

Collard Greens Bunch

Prep time: 10 minutes | Cook time: 20 minutes | Serves 4

1 tablespoon vegetable oil
1 yellow onion, diced
1 collard greens bunch, roughly chopped
2 cups vegetable broth
1 teaspoon smoked paprika
1 tablespoon cider vinegar
½ teaspoon hot sauce
⅛ teaspoon kosher salt
⅛ teaspoon freshly ground black pepper

With the Instant Pot on the Sauté or brown setting, heat the vegetable oil until it shimmers. Add the onion and sauté, stirring frequently, until it is softened and translucent, about 5 minutes. Add the collard greens, vegetable broth, and paprika. Lock on the lid and set the timer for 20 minutes at High Pressure. When the timer goes off, natural release for 10 minutes. Quick release any remaining pressure and remove the lid Stir in the vinegar, hot sauce, salt, and pepper. Serve hot.

Cabbage and Potato Curry

Prep time: 20 minutes | Cook time: 5 minutes | Serves 6

2 medium carrots, cut into 1-inch pieces
3 cups roughly shredded green cabbage
2 Yukon Gold potatoes, cut into 1-inch pieces (about ½ pound / 227 g)
1 cup water
2 teaspoons corn oil
½ onion, finely chopped
1 garlic clove, finely chopped
1 teaspoon freshly grated ginger
1 tablespoon mild curry powder
1¼ teaspoons kosher salt
1 tablespoon finely chopped fresh cilantro, for garnish

Steam the vegetables. Place the carrots, cabbage, and potatoes in the steamer rack. Add the water to the inner pot, and place the trivet inside. Place the steamer rack on the trivet. Lock the lid into place. Select Steam, and set the time to 5 minutes. Make sure the steam release knob is in the sealed position. After cooking, quick release the pressure. Unlock and remove the lid. Place the vegetables in a colander. Discard the water. Prepare the curry. Wipe the inside of the pot dry, and return it to its place. Select Sauté, and pour in the oil. Once hot, add the onion, garlic, and ginger, and sauté until the onion turns translucent, about 3 minutes. Add the curry powder and salt, and sauté for 2 minutes. Add the steamed vegetables and cook, stirring frequently, for about 2 minutes. Transfer the curry to a serving platter, garnish with the cilantro, and serve hot.

Broccoli with Tofu

Prep time: 20 minutes | Cook time: 1 minutes | Serves 4

1¼ cups water
1 tablespoon cornstarch
1 tablespoon rice vinegar
1 tablespoon soy sauce
1 tablespoon Sriracha
1 teaspoon sugar
½ teaspoon kosher salt
2 tablespoons peanut oil
10 scallions, chopped, white and green parts separated
1 garlic clove, finely chopped
3 dried Thai red chiles
1 teaspoon freshly ground black pepper
3 whole cloves
2 cups broccoli florets, cut into bite-size pieces (about 10 ounces / 283 g)
¾ cup bite-size pieces red and green bell pepper mix
½ cup (1-inch cubes) extra-firm tofu, pressed to remove water
¼ cup peanuts

Prepare the slurry. In a small mixing bowl, stir together the water and cornstarch. Mix thoroughly and set aside. Prepare the sauce. In a medium bowl, mix together the vinegar, soy sauce, Sriracha, sugar, and salt. Set aside. Sauté the vegetables. Select Sauté, and pour in the oil. Once hot, add the white parts of the scallions and the garlic, chiles, black pepper, and cloves. Sauté for 2 minutes. Add the broccoli, bell pepper, tofu, peanuts, and sauce. Mix thoroughly. Add the slurry, and stir constantly until everything is well combined. Pressure cook the kung pao. Lock the lid into place. Select Pressure Cook or Manual, and adjust the pressure to High and the time to 1 minute. After cooking, quick release the pressure. Unlock and remove the lid. Stir the kung pao once before transferring to a serving bowl. Do not keep the kung pao in Keep Warm mode, as the broccoli might become soft and mushy. Garnish with the green parts of the scallions, and serve hot.

Bok Choy Squash with Pineapple

Prep time: 5 minutes | Cook time: 15 minutes | Serves 4

1 butternut squash
4 cups chopped bok choy
1 scallion, chopped
1 to 2 teaspoons toasted sesame oil
10 ounces (283 g) bite-size pineapple chunks (about 1½ cups)
1 to 2 tablespoons tamari or soy sauce

Put the butternut squash in your electric Instant Pot's cooking pot. (If the squash won't fit, cut it in half lengthwise, scoop out the seeds with a large spoon, and stack the halves in the pot, cut-side down.) Pour in a cup or two of water. Close and lock the lid and ensure the pressure valve is sealed, then select High Pressure and set the time for 10 to 15 minutes, depending on the size of your squash. (If you've cut the squash in half, set the time for 5 to 7 minutes, depending on size.) Once the cook time is complete, let the pressure release naturally, about 10 minutes. Once all the pressure has released, carefully unlock and remove the lid. Using tongs or a large fork and spoon, carefully lift the squash out of the pot and let cool for a few minutes. Empty the water from the pot and return the pot to the Instant Pot. Select Sauté. Add the bok choy, scallion, and sesame oil. Cook for 1 minute, stirring occasionally, until the vegetables are softened. If the squash is whole, cut it in half lengthwise, scoop out the seeds, and remove the skin. Chop the squash into bite-size chunks and add them to the pot, along with the pineapple and tamari. Toss to combine until heated through.

Potato with Dill

Prep time: 5 minutes | Cook time: 10 minutes | Serves 4

2 pounds (907 g) baby potatoes, scrubbed
2 tablespoons olive oil
2 tablespoons freshly squeezed lemon juice

1 teaspoon dried dill
2 tablespoons nutritional yeast (optional)
Salt, to taste

Pour a cup or two of water into your electric Instant Pot's cooking pot and add the potatoes. Close and lock the lid and ensure the pressure valve is sealed, then select High Pressure and set the time for 10 minutes. Once the cook time is complete, let the pressure release naturally, about 10 minutes. Once all the pressure has released, carefully unlock and remove the lid. Drain the potatoes. In a small bowl, whisk together the olive oil, lemon juice, dill, and nutritional yeast (if using). Add to the pot and toss the potatoes to coat.

Carrot with Butter

Prep time: 8 minutes | Cook time: 2 minutes | Serves 4

1 cup water
1 pound (454 g) baby carrots
1½ tablespoons unsalted butter
1½ tablespoons pure maple syrup

¼ teaspoon kosher salt
Pinch freshly ground black pepper
1 teaspoon fresh minced thyme

Place the water and carrots in the Instant Pot. Lock on the lid and set the timer for 2 minutes at High Pressure. When the timer goes off, quick release the pressure, open the Instant Pot, and switch to the brown setting. Add the butter, maple syrup, salt, and pepper. Sauté the carrots for 2 to 3 minutes, or until most of the remaining liquid evaporates. Sprinkle with the fresh thyme. Serve hot or warm.

Potato Salad with Yogurt

Prep time: 10 minutes | Cook time: 6 minutes | Serves 4 to 6

4 to 6 medium russet potatoes, scrubbed and cut in large uniform cubes (4 to 5 cups)
½ cup unsweetened nondairy yogurt
2 teaspoons Dijon mustard
1½ teaspoons apple cider vinegar

½ teaspoon onion powder (optional)
¼ teaspoon salt
3 or 4 celery stalks, chopped
2 scallions, chopped
Freshly ground black pepper, to taste

Put the potatoes in a steaming basket. Put a trivet in your electric Instant Pot's cooking pot, pour in a cup or two of water, and set the steaming basket on the trivet. (Alternatively, you can cook the potatoes right in the water, though they will end up quite a bit softer.) Close and lock the lid and ensure the pressure valve is sealed, then select High Pressure and set the time for 6 minutes. Once the cook time is complete, let the pressure release naturally, about 10 minutes. Meanwhile, in a large bowl, stir together the yogurt, mustard, vinegar, onion powder (if using), and salt. Add the celery and scallions and stir to combine. Once all the pressure has released, carefully unlock and remove the lid. Using oven mitts, carefully lift the steaming basket out of the pot (or drain the potatoes if you cooked them directly in the water). Let the potatoes cool for a few minutes, then stir them into the bowl with the vegetables and dressing. Taste and season with pepper.

Squash and Tomato Curry

Prep time: 20 minutes | Cook time: 8 minutes | Serves 8

3 Roma tomatoes, chopped
½ cup roughly chopped yellow onion
1 Thai green chile, chopped
1 dried red chile
2 garlic cloves, finely chopped
1 teaspoon finely chopped fresh ginger
½ cup water
2 teaspoons corn oil
2 cups (1-inch cubes) butternut

squash
1 (14-ounce / 397-g) can full-fat coconut milk
1¼ teaspoons kosher salt
1 medium eggplant, cut into bite-size pieces
1 cup chopped red, orange, or yellow bell pepper or a mix
2 tablespoons chopped fresh cilantro

Prepare the tomato paste. In a blender, roughly grind the tomatoes, onion, green chile, red chile, garlic, and ginger with the water. Sauté the tomato paste. Select Sauté, and pour the oil into the inner pot. Once hot, slowly pour in the tomato paste mixture. Sauté for about 5 minutes, until the onions are translucent. Add the butternut squash, coconut milk, and salt. Pressure cook the butternut squash. Lock the lid into place. Select Pressure Cook or Manual, and adjust the pressure to High and the time to 5 minutes. Make sure the steam release knob in in the sealed position. After cooking, quick release the pressure. Pressure cook the eggplant. Unlock and remove the lid. Scrape the bottom of the pot with a wooden spoon, ensuring nothing is sticking to the bottom. Add the eggplant and bell pepper. Lock the lid into place. Select Manual, and adjust the pressure to High and the time to 3 minutes. After cooking, quick release the pressure. Unlock and remove the lid. Stir the curry, and garnish with the cilantro. Serve hot.

Pea and Squash Primavera

Prep time: 5 minutes | Cook time: 15 minutes | Serves 3 to 4

1 spaghetti squash
2 or 3 garlic cloves, minced
1 to 2 tablespoons olive oil or vegan margarine, plus more as needed
1 cup peas

2 to 3 tablespoons nutritional yeast, plus more as needed
Salt and freshly ground black pepper, to taste
1 cup cherry tomatoes, halved

Put the spaghetti squash in your electric Instant Pot's cooking pot. (If the squash won't fit, cut it in half, scoop out the seeds with a large spoon, and stack the halves in the pot cut-side down.) Pour in a cup or two of water. Close and lock the lid and ensure the pressure valve is sealed, then select High Pressure and set the time for 10 to 15 minutes, depending on the size of your squash. (If you've cut the squash in half, set the time for 5 to 7 minutes, depending on size.) Once the cook time is complete, let the pressure release naturally, about 10 minutes. Once all the pressure has released, carefully unlock and remove the lid. Using tongs or a large fork and spoon, carefully lift out the squash and set it aside to cool. Empty the water from the pot and return the pot to the Instant Pot. Select Sauté. Add the garlic and olive oil and cook for about 2 minutes, stirring occasionally, until the garlic is lightly browned. Add the peas and cook for 1 to 2 minutes to soften. If the squash is whole, cut it in half and scoop out the seeds. Using a fork, scrape the squash flesh into strands and return them to the pot. Sprinkle the strands with the nutritional yeast and season with salt. Toss to coat in the oil. Add the cherry tomatoes, plus more nutritional yeast, olive oil, salt, and pepper, if needed.

Carrot and Potato Curry

Prep time: 20 minutes | Cook time: 2 minutes | Serves 6

The Thai Curry Paste:

3 dried red Thai chiles
½ teaspoon cumin seeds
1 teaspoon coriander seeds
½ teaspoon whole black peppercorns
2 garlic cloves
1 tablespoon finely chopped

fresh cilantro
¼ cup chopped onion
1 tablespoon finely chopped fresh ginger
1 tablespoon sliced lemongrass
3 tablespoons water

The Vegetable Curry:

2 teaspoons corn oil
½ cup (1-inch pieces) chopped carrots
½ cup (1-inch cubed) peeled potatoes
5 fresh snap peas
5 fresh baby corn ears, cut into bite-size pieces
1 teaspoon kosher salt

1 teaspoon sugar
¼ teaspoon ground turmeric
1 (12-ounce / 340-g) can full-fat coconut milk
½ cup (½-inch cubes) extra-firm tofu, pressed to remove water
6 fresh basil leaves, roughly chopped

Prepare the Thai curry paste. In a blender, blend the chiles, cumin seeds, coriander seeds, peppercorns, garlic, cilantro, onion, ginger, lemongrass, and water into a smooth paste. Sauté the vegetables. Select Sauté, and pour in the oil. Once hot, add the carrots, potatoes, snap peas, baby corn, salt, sugar, and turmeric, and sauté for 1 minute. Add the curry paste, and sauté for 2 more minutes. Add the coconut milk, tofu, and half of the basil, and mix thoroughly. Pressure cook the vegetable curry. Lock the lid into place. Select Pressure Cook or Manual, and adjust the pressure to High and the time to 2 minutes. After cooking, naturally release the pressure for 5 minutes, then quick release any remaining pressure. Unlock and remove the lid. Serve, garnished with the remaining basil.

Cauliflower Cream Korma

Prep time: 20 minutes | Cook time: 5 minutes | Serves 6

½ cup chopped onion
10 raw cashews
1 green Thai chile, finely chopped
1 cup water, divided
1 large carrot, chopped into 1-inch cubes (about ¾ cup)
1 medium potato, peeled and cut into 1-inch cubes (about ½ cup)
1¼ cups cauliflower florets

(about ½ pound / 227 g)
¼ cup frozen peas
1 teaspoon curry powder
½ teaspoon ground allspice
1 teaspoon kosher salt
⅓ cup heavy (whipping) cream
2 tablespoons finely chopped fresh cilantro
1 tablespoon roughly chopped fresh mint leaves
Naan bread, for serving

Pressure cook the onion-cashew paste. Add the onion, cashews, green chile, and ½ cup of water to the inner pot. Lock the lid into place. Select Pressure Cook or Manual, and adjust the pressure to High and the time to 2 minutes. Make sure the steam release knob is in the sealed position. After cooking, quick release the pressure. Unlock and remove the lid. Use an immersion blender to purée the mixture. Pressure cook the korma. Select Sauté. Once hot, add the carrot, potato, cauliflower, peas, curry powder, allspice, salt, cream, and remaining ½ cup of water to the onion-cashew paste. Mix thoroughly, and sauté for 2 minutes. Lock the lid into place. Select Pressure Cook or Manual, and adjust the pressure to High and the time to 3 minutes. Make sure the steam release knob is in the sealed position. After cooking, quick release the pressure. Unlock and remove the lid. Add the chopped cilantro and mint leaves, and stir the korma one last time. Serve hot with naan bread.

Butternut Squash Soup

Prep time: 20 minutes | Cook time: 20 minutes | Serves 4

4 cups cubed peeled butternut squash
1 (13.5-ounce / 383-g) can full-fat coconut milk
1 cup diced onion
3 cloves garlic, minced
1 tablespoon minced fresh

ginger
1 teaspoon kosher salt
1 teaspoon black pepper
1 teaspoon ground turmeric
½ teaspoon ground nutmeg, plus more for garnish (optional)

In the Instant Pot, combine the squash, coconut milk, onion, garlic, ginger, salt, pepper, turmeric, and the ½ teaspoon nutmeg. Mix well. Secure the lid on the pot. Close the pressure-release valve. Select Manual and set the pot at High Pressure for 8 minutes. At the end of the cooking time, allow the pot to sit undisturbed for 10 minutes, then quick-release any remaining pressure. Using an immersion blender, purée the soup until smooth. Add a little water, if necessary, to reach desired consistency. Ladle the soup into bowls. Garnish with nutmeg, if desired, and serve.

Red Wine Mushrooms

Prep time: 5 minutes | Cook time: 2 minutes | Serves 4

¼ cup dry red wine
¼ cup water
2 tablespoons balsamic vinegar
1 tablespoon olive oil
1 teaspoon cornstarch or arrowroot powder
½ teaspoon dried basil or

mixed herbs
¼ teaspoon salt, plus more as needed
Freshly ground black pepper, to taste
1 pound (454 g) white mushrooms, quartered

In your electric Instant Pot's cooking pot, stir together the red wine, water, vinegar, olive oil, cornstarch, basil, and salt. Season with pepper. Add the mushrooms to the sauce. Close and lock the lid and ensure the pressure valve is sealed, then select High Pressure and set the time for 2 minutes. Once the cook time is complete, quick release the pressure, being careful not to get your fingers or face near the steam release. Once all the pressure has released, carefully unlock and remove the lid. Taste and season with more salt and pepper, if needed.

Pea and Tomato Curry

Prep time: 5 minutes | Cook time: 2 minutes | Serves 4

1 (1-inch) piece fresh ginger, peeled and minced (optional)
1 tablespoon coconut oil or olive oil
1 head cauliflower, chopped
1 (28-ounce / 794-g) can crushed tomatoes

2 cups frozen peas
1 cup water
2 tablespoons tomato paste
1 tablespoon curry powder
Salt and freshly ground black pepper, to taste

On your electric Instant Pot, Select Sauté. Add the ginger (if using) and coconut oil and cook for 2 to 3 minutes, stirring occasionally, until the ginger is softened. Add the cauliflower, tomatoes, peas, water, tomato paste, and curry powder and stir to combine. Cancel Sauté. Close and lock the lid and ensure the pressure valve is sealed, then select Low Pressure and set the time for 1 to 2 minutes, depending on how soft you like your cauliflower. Once the cook time is complete, quick release the pressure, being careful not to get your fingers or face near the steam release. Once all the pressure has released, carefully unlock and remove the lid. Taste and season with salt and pepper.

Herbed Mahi-Mahi and Bell Peppers

Prep time: 10 minutes | Cook time: 3 minutes | Serves 3

2 sprigs fresh rosemary	melted
2 sprigs dill, tarragon	Sea salt and ground black
1 sprig fresh thyme	pepper, to taste
1 cup water	1 serrano pepper, seeded and
1 lemon, sliced	sliced
3 mahi-mahi fillets	1 green bell pepper, sliced
2 tablespoons coconut oil,	1 red bell pepper, sliced

Add the herbs, water, and lemon slices to the Instant Pot and insert a steamer basket. Arrange the mahi-mahi fillets in the steamer basket. Drizzle the melted coconut oil over the top and season with the salt and black pepper. Lock the lid. Select the Pressure Cook mode and set the cooking time for 3 minutes at Low Pressure. When the timer beeps, perform a natural pressure release for 10 minutes, then release any remaining pressure. Carefully remove the lid. Place the peppers on top. Select the Sauté mode and let it simmer for another 1 minute. Serve immediately.

Monkfish Stew

Prep time: 5 minutes | Cook time: 6 minutes | Serves 6

Juice of 1 lemon	peppercorns
1 tablespoon fresh basil	¼ teaspoon turmeric powder
1 tablespoon fresh parsley	¼ teaspoon ground cumin
1 tablespoon olive oil	Sea salt and ground black
1 teaspoon garlic, minced	pepper, to taste
1½ pounds (680 g) monkfish	2 cups fish stock
1 tablespoon butter	½ cup water
1 bell pepper, chopped	¼ cup dry white wine
1 onion, sliced	2 bay leaves
½ teaspoon cayenne pepper	1 ripe tomato, crushed
½ teaspoon mixed	

Stir together the lemon juice, basil, parsley, olive oil, and garlic in a ceramic dish. Add the monkfish and marinate for 30 minutes. Set your Instant Pot to Sauté. Add and melt the butter. Once hot, cook the bell pepper and onion until fragrant. Stir in the remaining ingredients. Lock the lid. Select the Pressure Cook mode and set the cooking time for 6 minutes at High Pressure. When the timer beeps, perform a quick pressure release. Carefully remove the lid. Discard the bay leaves and divide your stew into serving bowls. Serve hot.

Salmon Tandoori

Prep time: 2 hours | Cook time: 6 minutes | Serves 4

1½ pounds (680 g) salmon	Salt and pepper, to taste
fillets	1 tablespoon tandoori spice
3 tablespoons coconut oil	mix

In a bowl, add all the ingredients. Toss well until the fish is fully coated. Allow the fish to marinate for 2 hours in the fridge. Place the marinated salmon in the Instant Pot. Lock the lid. Select the Pressure Cook mode and cook for 6 minutes at Low Pressure. Flip the fish halfway through the cooking time. Once cooking is complete, do a quick pressure release. Carefully open the lid. Remove from the pot and serve on a plate.

Haddock and Shrimp Soup

Prep time: 10 minutes | Cook time: 8 minutes | Serves 4

2 teaspoons olive oil	fillets
1 yellow onion, chopped	1 cup shrimp
1 bell pepper, sliced	1 tablespoon sweet Hungarian
1 celery, diced	paprika
2 garlic cloves, minced	1 teaspoon hot Hungarian
3 cups fish stock	paprika
2 ripe tomatoes, crushed	½ teaspoon caraway seeds
¾ pound (340 g) haddock	

Set the Instant Pot to Sauté. Add and heat the oil. Once hot, add the onions and sauté until soft and fragrant. Add the pepper, celery, and garlic and continue to sauté until soft. Stir in the remaining ingredients. Lock the lid. Select the Pressure Cook mode and set the cooking time for 5 minutes at High Pressure. When the timer beeps, perform a quick pressure release. Carefully remove the lid. Divide into serving bowls and serve hot.

Herbed Haddock Foil Packets

Prep time: 5 minutes | Cook time: 10 minutes | Serves 4

1½ cups water	4 haddock fillets
1 lemon, sliced	Sea salt, to taste
2 bell peppers, sliced	⅓ teaspoon ground black
1 brown onion, sliced into rings	pepper, or more to taste
4 sprigs parsley	2 tablespoons extra-virgin olive
2 sprigs thyme	oil
2 sprigs rosemary	

Pour the water and lemon into your Instant Pot and insert a steamer basket. Assemble the packets with large sheets of heavy-duty foil. Place the peppers, onion rings, parsley, thyme, and rosemary in the center of each foil. Place the fish fillets on top of the veggies. Sprinkle with the salt and black pepper and drizzle the olive oil over the fillets. Place the packets in the steamer basket. Lock the lid. Select the Pressure Cook mode and set the cooking time for 10 minutes at Low Pressure. When the timer beeps, perform a quick pressure release. Carefully remove the lid. Serve warm.

Herbed Cod Steaks

Prep time: 5 minutes | Cook time: 4 minutes | Serves 4

1½ cups water	peppercorns, crushed
2 tablespoons garlic-infused oil	2 sprigs thyme
4 cod steaks, 1½-inch thick	1 sprig rosemary
Sea salt, to taste	1 yellow onion, sliced
½ teaspoon mixed	

Pour the water into your Instant Pot and insert a trivet. Rub the garlic-infused oil into the cod steaks and season with the salt and crushed peppercorns. Lower the cod steaks onto the trivet, skin-side down. Top with the thyme, rosemary, and onion. Lock the lid. Select the Pressure Cook mode and set the cooking time for 4 minutes at High Pressure. When the timer beeps, perform a quick pressure release. Carefully remove the lid. Serve immediately.

Fish Fillets with Asparagus

Prep time: 5 minutes | Cook time: 3 minutes | Serves 4

2 lemons
2 cups cold water
2 tablespoons extra-virgin olive oil
4 (4-ounce / 113-g) white fish fillets, such as cod or haddock
1 teaspoon fine sea salt
1 teaspoon ground black pepper
1 bundle asparagus, ends trimmed
2 tablespoons lemon juice
Fresh dill, for garnish

Grate the zest off the lemons until you have about 1 tablespoon and set the zest aside. Slice the lemons into ⅛-inch slices. Pour the water into the Instant Pot. Add 1 tablespoon of the olive oil to each of two stackable steamer pans. Sprinkle the fish on all sides with the lemon zest, salt, and pepper. Arrange two fillets in each steamer pan and top each with the lemon slices and then the asparagus. Sprinkle the asparagus with the salt and drizzle the lemon juice over the top. Stack the steamer pans in the Instant Pot. Cover the top steamer pan with its lid. Lock the lid. Select the Pressure Cook mode and set the cooking time for 3 minutes at High Pressure. Once cooking is complete, do a natural pressure release for 7 minutes, then release any remaining pressure. Carefully open the lid. Lift the steamer pans out of the Instant Pot. Transfer the fish and asparagus to a serving plate. Garnish with the lemon slices and dill. Serve immediately.

Lemony Salmon Foil-Packet

Prep time: 2 minutes | Cook time: 7 minutes | Serves 2

2 (3-ounce / 85-g) salmon fillets
¼ teaspoon garlic powder
1 teaspoon salt
¼ teaspoon pepper
¼ teaspoon dried dill
½ lemon
1 cup water

Place each filet of salmon on a square of foil, skin-side down. Season with garlic powder, salt, and pepper and squeeze the lemon juice over the fish. Cut the lemon into four slices and place two on each filet. Close the foil packets by folding over edges. Add the water to the Instant Pot and insert a trivet. Place the foil packets on the trivet. Secure the lid. Select the Steam mode and set the cooking time for 7 minutes at Low Pressure. Once cooking is complete, do a quick pressure release. Carefully open the lid. Check the internal temperature with a meat thermometer to ensure the thickest part of the filets reached at least 145ºF (63ºC). Salmon should easily flake when fully cooked. Serve immediately.

Basil Pesto Salmon

Prep time: 6 minutes | Cook time: 6 minutes | Serves 6

3 garlic cloves, minced
1½ pounds (680 g) salmon fillets
2 cups basil leaves
2 tablespoons freshly squeezed lemon juice
½ cup olive oil
Salt and pepper, to taste

Make the pesto sauce: Put the basil leaves, olive oil, lemon juice, and garlic in a food processor, and pulse until smooth. Season with salt and pepper. Place the salmon fillets in the Instant Pot and add the pesto sauce. Lock the lid. Select the Pressure Cook mode and set the cooking time for 6 minutes at Low Pressure. Once cooking is complete, do a quick pressure release. Carefully open the lid. Divide the salmon among six plates and serve.

Pesto Fish Packets

Prep time: 8 minutes | Cook time: 6 minutes | Serves 4

1½ cups cold water.
4 (4-ounce / 113-g) white fish fillets, such as cod or haddock
1 teaspoon fine sea salt
½ teaspoon ground black pepper
1 (4-ounce / 113-g) jar pesto
½ cup shredded Parmesan cheese (about 2 ounces / 57 g)
Halved cherry tomatoes, for garnish

Pour the water into your Instant Pot and insert a steamer basket. Sprinkle the fish on all sides with the salt and pepper. Take four sheets of parchment paper and place a fillet in the center of each sheet. Dollop 2 tablespoons of the pesto on top of each fillet and sprinkle with 2 tablespoons of the Parmesan cheese. Wrap the fish in the parchment by folding in the edges and folding down the top like an envelope to close tightly. Stack the packets in the steamer basket, seam-side down. Lock the lid. Select the Pressure Cook mode and set the cooking time for 6 minutes at Low Pressure. Once cooking is complete, do a natural pressure release for 10 minutes, then release any remaining pressure. Carefully open the lid. Remove the fish packets from the pot. Transfer to a serving plate and garnish with the cherry tomatoes. Serve immediately.

Italian Cod Fillets

Prep time: 2 minutes | Cook time: 15 minutes | Serves 4

2 tablespoons butter
¼ cup diced onion
1 clove garlic, minced
1 cup cherry tomatoes, halved
¼ cup chicken broth
¼ teaspoon dried thyme
¼ teaspoon salt
⅛ teaspoon pepper
4 (4-ounce / 113-g) cod fillets
1 cup water
¼ cup fresh chopped Italian parsley

Set your Instant Pot to Sauté. Add and melt the butter. Once hot, add the onions and cook until softened. Add the garlic and cook for another 30 seconds. Add the tomatoes, chicken broth, thyme, salt, and pepper. Continue to cook for 5 to 7 minutes, or until the tomatoes start to soften. Pour the sauce into a glass bowl. Add the fish fillets. Cover with foil. Pour the water into the Instant Pot and insert a trivet. Place the bowl on top. Lock the lid. Select the Pressure Cook mode and set the cooking time for 3 minutes at Low Pressure. Once cooking is complete, do a quick pressure release. Carefully open the lid. Sprinkle with the fresh parsley and serve.

Red Curry Perch

Prep time: 5 minutes | Cook time: 6 minutes | Serves 4

1 cup water
2 sprigs rosemary
1 large-sized lemon, sliced
1 pound (454 g) perch fillets
1 teaspoon cayenne pepper
Sea salt and ground black pepper, to taste
1 tablespoon red curry paste
1 tablespoons butter

Add the water, rosemary, and lemon slices to the Instant Pot and insert a trivet. Season the perch fillets with the cayenne pepper, salt, and black pepper. Spread the red curry paste and butter over the fillets. Arrange the fish fillets on the trivet. Lock the lid. Select the Pressure Cook mode and set the cooking time for 6 minutes at Low Pressure. When the timer beeps, perform a quick pressure release. Carefully remove the lid. Serve with your favorite keto sides.

Cod Garam Masala

Prep time: 10 minutes | Cook time: 10 minutes | Serves 4

2 tablespoons sesame oil
½ teaspoon cumin seeds
½ cup chopped leeks
1 teaspoon ginger-garlic paste
1 pound (454 g) cod fillets, boneless and sliced
2 ripe tomatoes, chopped
1½ tablespoons fresh lemon juice
½ teaspoon garam masala
½ teaspoon turmeric powder
1 tablespoon chopped fresh dill leaves
1 tablespoon chopped fresh curry leaves
1 tablespoon chopped fresh parsley leaves
Coarse sea salt, to taste
½ teaspoon smoked cayenne pepper
¼ teaspoon ground black pepper, or more to taste

Set the Instant Pot to Sauté. Add and heat the sesame oil until hot. Sauté the cumin seeds for 30 seconds. Add the leeks and cook for another 2 minutes until translucent. Add the ginger-garlic paste and cook for an additional 40 seconds. Stir in the remaining ingredients. Lock the lid. Select the Pressure Cook mode and set the cooking time for 6 minutes at Low Pressure. When the timer beeps, perform a quick pressure release. Carefully remove the lid. Serve immediately.

Snapper and Peppers with Spicy Tomato Sauce

Prep time: 5 minutes | Cook time: 5 minutes | Serves 6

2 teaspoons coconut oil, melted
1 teaspoon celery seeds
½ teaspoon fresh grated ginger
½ teaspoon cumin seeds
1 yellow onion, chopped
2 cloves garlic, minced
1½ pounds (680 g) snapper fillets
¾ cup vegetable broth
1 (14-ounce / 113-g) can fire-roasted diced tomatoes
1 bell pepper, sliced
1 jalapeño pepper, minced
Sea salt and ground black pepper, to taste
¼ teaspoon chili flakes
½ teaspoon turmeric powder

Set the Instant Pot to Saute. Add and heat the sesame oil until hot. Sauté the celery seeds, fresh ginger, and cumin seeds. Add the onion and continue to sauté until softened and fragrant. Mix in the minced garlic and continue to cook for 30 seconds. Add the remaining ingredients and stir well. Lock the lid. Select the Pressure Cook mode and set the cooking time for 3 minutes at Low Pressure. When the timer beeps, perform a quick pressure release. Carefully remove the lid. Serve warm

Garlicky Yogurt Salmon Steaks

Prep time: 2 minutes | Cook time: 4 minutes | Serves 4

1 cup water
2 tablespoons olive oil
4 salmon steaks

Coarse sea salt and ground black pepper, to taste

Garlicky Yogurt:
1 (8-ounce / 227-g) container full-fat Greek yogurt
2 cloves garlic, minced
2 tablespoons mayonnaise
⅓ teaspoon Dijon mustard

Pour the water into the Instant Pot and insert a trivet. Rub the olive oil into the fish and sprinkle with the salt and black pepper on all sides. Put the fish on the trivet. Lock the lid. Select the Pressure Cook mode and set the cooking time for 4 minutes at High Pressure. When the timer beeps, perform a quick pressure release. Carefully remove the lid. Meanwhile, stir together all the ingredients for the garlicky yogurt in a bowl. Serve the salmon steaks alongside the garlicky yogurt.

Garlic-Lemony Salmon

Prep time: 7 minutes | Cook time: 21 minutes | Serves 4

1 tablespoon unsalted butter
3 cloves garlic, minced
¼ cup lemon juice
1¼ cups fresh or canned diced tomatoes
1 tablespoon chopped fresh flat-leaf parsley, plus more for
garnish
¼ teaspoon ground black pepper
4 (6-ounce / 170-g) skinless salmon fillets
1 teaspoon fine sea salt
Lemon wedges, for garnish

Add the butter to your Instant Pot and select the Sauté mode. Once melted, add the garlic (if using) and sauté for 1 minute. Add the roasted garlic, lemon juice, tomatoes, parsley, and pepper. Let simmer for 5 minutes, or until the liquid has reduced a bit. Meanwhile, rinse the salmon and pat dry with a paper towel. Sprinkle on all sides with the salt. Using a spatula, push the reduced sauce to one side of the pot and place the salmon on the other side. Spoon the sauce over the salmon. Sauté uncovered for another 15 minutes, or until the salmon flakes easily with a fork. The timing will depend on the thickness of the fillets. Transfer the salmon to a serving plate. Serve with the sauce and garnish with the parsley and lemon wedges.

Salmon with Bok Choy

Prep time: 5 minutes | Cook time: 8 minutes | Serves 4

1½ cups water
2 tablespoons unsalted butter
4 (1-inch thick) salmon fillets
½ teaspoon cayenne pepper
Sea salt and freshly ground pepper, to taste
2 cups Bok choy, sliced
1 cup chicken broth
3 cloves garlic, minced
1 teaspoon grated lemon zest
½ teaspoon dried dill weed

Pour the water into your Instant Pot and insert a trivet. Brush the salmon with the melted butter and season with the cayenne pepper, salt, and black pepper on all sides. Lock the lid. Select the Pressure Cook mode and set the cooking time for 3 minutes at Low Pressure. When the timer beeps, perform a quick pressure release. Carefully remove the lid. Add the remaining ingredients. Lock the lid. Select the Pressure Cook mode and set the cooking time for 5 minutes at High Pressure. When the timer beeps, perform a quick pressure release. Carefully remove the lid. Serve the poached salmon with the veggies on the side.

Tuna Fillets with Lemon Butter

Prep time: 5 minutes | Cook time: 3 minutes | Serves 4

1 cup water
⅓ cup lemon juice
2 sprigs fresh thyme
2 sprigs fresh parsley
2 sprigs fresh rosemary
1 pound (454 g) tuna fillets
4 cloves garlic, pressed
Sea salt, to taste
¼ teaspoon black pepper, or more to taste
2 tablespoons butter, melted
1 lemon, sliced

Pour the water into your Instant Pot. Add the lemon juice, thyme, parsley, and rosemary and insert a steamer basket. Put the tuna fillets in the basket. Top with the garlic and season with the salt and black pepper. Drizzle the melted butter over the fish fillets and place the lemon slices on top. Lock the lid. Select the Manual mode and set the cooking time for 3 minutes at Low Pressure. When the timer beeps, perform a quick pressure release. Carefully remove the lid. Serve immediately.

Steamed Salmon Fillets

Prep time: 6 minutes | Cook time: 10 minutes | Serves 3

1 cup water
2 tablespoons freshly squeezed lemon juice
2 tablespoons soy sauce
10 ounces (283 g) salmon

fillets
Salt and pepper, to taste
1 teaspoon toasted sesame seeds

Set a trivet in the Instant Pot and pour the water into the pot. Using a heat-proof dish, combine all ingredients. Place the heat-proof dish on the trivet. Lock the lid. Select the Pressure Cook mode and cook for 10 minutes at Low Pressure. Once cooking is complete, do a quick pressure release. Carefully open the lid. Garnish with toasted sesame seeds and serve.

Curried Salmon

Prep time: 6 minutes | Cook time: 8 minutes | Serves 4

2 cups coconut milk
2 tablespoons coconut oil
1 onion, chopped

1 pound (454 g) raw salmon, diced
1½ tablespoons minced garlic

Press the Sauté button on the Instant Pot and heat the oil. Sauté the garlic and onions until fragrant, about 2 minutes. Add the diced salmon and stir for 1 minute. Pour in the coconut milk. Lock the lid. Select the Pressure Cook mode and cook for 4 minutes at Low Pressure. Once cooking is complete, do a quick pressure release. Carefully open the lid. Let the salmon cool for 5 minutes before serving.

Garlic Tuna Casserole

Prep time: 7 minutes | Cook time: 9 minutes | Serves 4

1 cup grated Parmesan or shredded Cheddar cheese, plus more for topping
1 (8-ounce / 227-g) package cream cheese (1 cup), softened
½ cup chicken broth
1 tablespoon unsalted butter
For Garnish:
Chopped fresh flat-leaf parsley
Sliced green onions

½ small head cauliflower, cut into 1-inch pieces
1 cup diced onions
2 cloves garlic, minced, or more to taste
2 (4-ounce / 113-g) cans chunk tuna packed in water, drained
1½ cups cold water

Cherry tomatoes, halved
Ground black pepper

In a blender, add the Parmesan cheese, cream cheese, and broth and blitz until smooth. Set aside. Set your Instant Pot to Sauté. Add and melt the butter. Add the cauliflower and onions and sauté for 4 minutes, or until the onions are softened. Fold in the garlic and sauté for an additional 1 minute. Place the cheese sauce and tuna in a large bowl. Mix in the veggies and stir well. Transfer the mixture to a casserole dish. Place a trivet in the bottom of your Instant Pot and add the cold water. Use a foil sling, lower the casserole dish onto the trivet. Tuck in the sides of the sling. Lock the lid. Select the Manual mode and set the cooking time for 5 minutes for al dente cauliflower or 8 minutes for softer cauliflower at High Pressure. Once cooking is complete, do a quick pressure release. Carefully open the lid. Serve topped with the cheese and garnished with the parsley, green onions, cherry tomatoes, and freshly ground pepper.

Herbed Salmon with Carrot and Zucchini

Prep time: 15 minutes | Cook time: 5 minutes | Serves 4

1 cup water
1 teaspoon ground dill
1 teaspoon ground tarragon
1 teaspoon ground basil
4 salmon fillets

2 tablespoons olive oil
Salt, to taste
4 lemon slices
1 carrot, sliced
1 zucchini, sliced

In the Instant Pot, add the water, dill, tarragon, and basil. Place the steamer basket inside. Set in the salmon. Drizzle with a tablespoon of olive oil, pepper and salt. Top with lemon slices. Lock the lid. Select the Steam mode and cook for 3 minutes at Low Pressure. Once cooking is complete, do a quick pressure release. Carefully open the lid. Transfer the fish to a plate and discard the lemon slices. Drizzle the Instant Pot with remaining olive oil. Add the carrot and zucchini to the Instant Pot. Set to Sauté mode, then sauté for 2minutes or until the vegetables are tender. Serve the salmon with the veggies. Garnish with fresh lemon wedges.

Tuna Salad with Tomatoes and Peppers

Prep time: 10 minutes | Cook time: 4 minutes | Serves 4

1½ cups water
1 pound (454 g) tuna steaks
1 green bell pepper, sliced
1 red bell pepper, sliced
2 Roma tomatoes, sliced
1 head lettuce
1 red onion, chopped
2 tablespoons Kalamata olives,

pitted and halved
2 tablespoons extra-virgin olive oil
2 tablespoons balsamic vinegar
½ teaspoon chili flakes
Sea salt, to taste

Add the water to the Instant Pot and insert a steamer basket. Arrange the tuna steaks in the basket. Put the bell peppers and tomato slices on top. Lock the lid. Select the Manual mode and set the cooking time for 4 minutes at High Pressure. When the timer beeps, perform a quick pressure release. Carefully remove the lid. Flake the fish with a fork. Divide the lettuce leaves among 4 serving plates to make a bed for your salad. Add the onion and olives. Drizzle with the olive oil and balsamic vinegar. Season with the chili flakes and salt. Place the prepared fish, tomatoes, and bell peppers on top. Serve immediately.

Ahi Tuna and Cherry Tomato Salad

Prep time: 5 minutes | Cook time: 4 minutes | Serves 4

1 cup water
2 sprigs thyme
2 sprigs rosemary
2 sprigs parsley
1 lemon, sliced
1 pound (454 g) ahi tuna
⅓ teaspoon ground black pepper

1 head lettuce
1 cup cherry tomatoes, halved
1 red bell pepper, julienned
2 tablespoons extra-virgin olive oil
1 teaspoon Dijon mustard
Sea salt, to taste

Pour the water into your Instant Pot. Add the thyme, rosemary, parsley, and lemon and insert a trivet. Lay the fish on the trivet and season with the ground black pepper. Lock the lid. Select the Manual mode and set the cooking time for 4 minutes at High Pressure. When the timer beeps, perform a quick pressure release. Carefully remove the lid. In a salad bowl, place the remaining ingredients and toss well. Add the flaked tuna and toss again. Serve chilled.

Cheesy Trout Casserole

Prep time: 5 minutes | Cook time: 10 minutes | Serves 3

1½ cups water	or more to taste
1½ tablespoons olive oil	⅓ teaspoon black pepper
3 plum tomatoes, sliced	Salt, to taste
½ teaspoon dried oregano	1 bay leaf
1 teaspoon dried basil	1 cup shredded Pepper Jack
3 trout fillets	cheese
½ teaspoon cayenne pepper,	

Pour the water into your Instant Pot and insert a trivet. Grease a baking dish with the olive oil. Add the tomatoes slices to the baking dish and sprinkle with the oregano and basil. Add the fish fillets and season with the cayenne pepper, black pepper, and salt. Add the bay leaf. Lower the baking dish onto the trivet. Lock the lid. Select the Manual mode and set the cooking time for 10 minutes at High Pressure. When the timer beeps, perform a quick pressure release. Carefully remove the lid. Scatter the Pepper Jack cheese on top, lock the lid, and allow the cheese to melt. Serve warm.

Rainbow Trout with Mixed Greens

Prep time: 5 minutes | Cook time: 12 minutes | Serves 4

1 cup water	1 pound (454 g) mixed greens,
1½ (680 g) pounds rainbow	trimmed and torn into pieces
trout fillets	1 bunch of scallions
4 tablespoons melted butter,	½ cup chicken broth
divided	1 tablespoon apple cider
Sea salt and ground black	vinegar
pepper, to taste	1 teaspoon cayenne pepper

Pour the water into your Instant Pot and insert a steamer basket. Add the fish to the basket. Drizzle with 1 tablespoon of the melted butter and season with the salt and black pepper. Lock the lid. Select the Manual mode and set the cooking time for 12 minutes at Low pressure. When the timer beeps, perform a quick pressure release. Carefully remove the lid. Wipe down the Instant Pot with a damp cloth. Add and warm the remaining 3 tablespoons of butter. Once hot, add the greens, scallions, broth, vinegar, and cayenne pepper and cook until the greens are wilted, stirring occasionally. Serve the prepared trout fillets with the greens on the side.

Haddock and Veggie Foil Packets

Prep time: 5 minutes | Cook time: 10 minutes | Serves 4

1½ cups water	4 haddock fillets
1 lemon, sliced	Sea salt, to taste
2 bell peppers, sliced	⅓ teaspoon ground black
1 brown onion, sliced into rings	pepper, or more to taste
4 sprigs parsley	2 tablespoons extra-virgin olive
2 sprigs thyme	oil
2 sprigs rosemary	

Pour the water and lemon into your Instant Pot and insert a steamer basket. Assemble the packets with large sheets of heavy-duty foil. Place the peppers, onion rings, parsley, thyme, and rosemary in the center of each foil. Place the fish fillets on top of the veggies. Sprinkle with the salt and black pepper and drizzle with the olive oil over the fillets. Place the packets in the steamer basket. Lock the lid. Select the Manual mode and set the cooking time for 10 minutes at Low Pressure. When the timer beeps, perform a quick pressure release. Carefully remove the lid. Serve warm.

Lemony Tilapia Fillets with Arugula

Prep time: 5 minutes | Cook time: 4 minutes | Serves 4

1 lemon, juiced	2 teaspoons butter, melted
1 cup water	Sea salt and ground black
1 pound (454 g) tilapia fillets	pepper, to taste
½ teaspoon cayenne pepper,	½ teaspoon dried basil
or more to taste	2 cups arugula

Pour the fresh lemon juice and water into your Instant Pot and insert a steamer basket. Brush the fish fillets with the melted butter. Sprinkle with the cayenne pepper, salt, and black pepper. Place the tilapia fillets in the basket. Sprinkle the dried basil on top. Lock the lid. Select the Manual mode and set the cooking time for 4 minutes at Low Pressure. When the timer beeps, perform a quick pressure release. Carefully remove the lid. Serve with the fresh arugula.

Cheesy Fish Bake with Veggies

Prep time: 10 minutes | Cook time: 5 minutes | Serves 4

1½ cups water	florets
Cooking spray	1 pound (454 g) tilapia fillets,
2 ripe tomatoes, sliced	sliced
2 cloves garlic, minced	Sea salt, to taste
1 teaspoon dried oregano	1 tablespoon olive oil
1 teaspoon dried basil	1 cup crumbled feta cheese
½ teaspoon dried rosemary	⅓ cup Kalamata olives, pitted
1 red onion, sliced	and halved
1 head cauliflower, cut into	

Pour the water into your Instant Pot and insert a trivet. Spritz a casserole dish with cooking spray. Add the tomato slices to the dish. Scatter the top with the garlic, oregano, basil, and rosemary. Mix in the onion and cauliflower. Arrange the fish fillets on top. Sprinkle with the salt and drizzle with the olive oil. Place the feta cheese and Kalamata olives on top. Lower the dish onto the trivet. Lock the lid. Select the Manual mode and set the cooking time for 5 minutes at High Pressure. When the timer beeps, perform a quick pressure release. Carefully remove the lid. Allow to cool for 5 minutes before serving.

Halibut Stew with Bacon and Cheese

Prep time: 10 minutes | Cook time: 10 minutes | Serves 4

4 slices bacon, chopped	softened
1 celery, chopped	¼ teaspoon ground allspice
½ cup chopped shallots	Sea salt and crushed black
1 teaspoon garlic, smashed	peppercorns, to taste
1 pound (454 g) halibut	1 cup Cottage cheese, at room
2 cups fish stock	temperature
1 tablespoon coconut oil,	1 cup heavy cream

Set the Instant Pot to Sauté. Cook the bacon until crispy. Add the celery, shallots, and garlic and sauté for another 2 minutes, or until the vegetables are just tender. Mix in the halibut, stock, coconut oil, allspice, salt, and black peppercorns. Stir well. Lock the lid. Select the Manual mode and set the cooking time for 7 minutes at Low Pressure. When the timer beeps, perform a natural pressure release for 10 minutes, then release any remaining pressure. Carefully remove the lid. Stir in the cheese and heavy cream. Select the Sauté mode again and let it simmer for a few minutes until heated through. Serve immediately.

Lemony Mahi-Mahi fillets with Peppers

Prep time: 10 minutes | Cook time: 3 minutes | Serves 3

2 sprigs fresh rosemary
2 sprigs dill, tarragon
1 sprig fresh thyme
1 cup water
1 lemon, sliced
3 mahi-mahi fillets
2 tablespoons coconut oil,

melted
Sea salt and ground black pepper, to taste
1 serrano pepper, seeded and sliced
1 green bell pepper, sliced
1 red bell pepper, sliced

Add the herbs, water, and lemon slices to the Instant Pot and insert a steamer basket. Arrange the mahi-mahi fillets in the steamer basket. Drizzle the melted coconut oil over the top and season with the salt and black pepper. Lock the lid. Select the Manual mode and set the cooking time for 3 minutes at Low Pressure. When the timer beeps, perform a natural pressure release for 10 minutes, then release any remaining pressure. Carefully remove the lid. Place the peppers on top. Select the Sauté mode and let it simmer for another 1 minute. Serve immediately.

Aromatic Monkfish Stew

Prep time: 5 minutes | Cook time: 6 minutes | Serves 6

Juice of 1 lemon
1 tablespoon fresh basil
1 tablespoon fresh parsley
1 tablespoon olive oil
1 teaspoon garlic, minced
1½ pounds (680 g) monkfish
1 tablespoon butter
1 bell pepper, chopped
1 onion, sliced
½ teaspoon cayenne pepper
½ teaspoon mixed

peppercorns
¼ teaspoon turmeric powder
¼ teaspoon ground cumin
Sea salt and ground black pepper, to taste
2 cups fish stock
½ cup water
¼ cup dry white wine
2 bay leaves
1 ripe tomato, crushed

Stir together the lemon juice, basil, parsley, olive oil, and garlic in a ceramic dish. Add the monkfish and marinate for 30 minutes. Set your Instant Pot to Sauté. Add and melt the butter. Once hot, cook the bell pepper and onion until fragrant. Stir in the remaining ingredients. Lock the lid. Select the Manual mode and set the cooking time for 6 minutes at High Pressure. When the timer beeps, perform a quick pressure release. Carefully remove the lid. Discard the bay leaves and divide your stew into serving bowls. Serve hot.

Chunky Fish Soup with Tomatoes

Prep time: 10 minutes | Cook time: 8 minutes | Serves 4

2 teaspoons olive oil
1 yellow onion, chopped
1 bell pepper, sliced
1 celery, diced
2 garlic cloves, minced
3 cups fish stock
2 ripe tomatoes, crushed
¾ pound (340 g) haddock

fillets
1 cup shrimp
1 tablespoon sweet Hungarian paprika
1 teaspoon hot Hungarian paprika
½ teaspoon caraway seeds

Set the Instant Pot to Sauté. Add and heat the oil. Once hot, add the onions and sauté until soft and fragrant. Add the pepper, celery, and garlic and continue to sauté until soft. Stir in the remaining ingredients. Lock the lid. Select the Manual mode and set the cooking time for 5 minutes at High Pressure. When the timer beeps, perform a quick pressure release. Carefully remove the lid. Divide into serving bowls and serve hot.

Herb-Crusted Cod Steaks

Prep time: 5 minutes | Cook time: 4 minutes | Serves 4

1½ cups water
2 tablespoons garlic-infused oil
4 cod steaks, 1½-inch thick
Sea salt, to taste
½ teaspoon mixed

peppercorns, crushed
2 sprigs thyme
1 sprig rosemary
1 yellow onion, sliced

Pour the water into your Instant Pot and insert a trivet. Rub the garlic-infused oil into the cod steaks and season with the salt and crushed peppercorns. Lower the cod steaks onto the trivet, skin-side down. Top with the thyme, rosemary, and onion. Lock the lid. Select the Manual mode and set the cooking time for 4 minutes at High Pressure. When the timer beeps, perform a quick pressure release. Carefully remove the lid. Serve immediately.

Lemony Fish and Asparagus

Prep time: 5 minutes | Cook time: 3 minutes | Serves 4

2 lemons
2 cups cold water
2 tablespoons extra-virgin olive oil
4 (4-ounce / 113-g) white fish fillets, such as cod or haddock
1 teaspoon fine sea salt

1 teaspoon ground black pepper
1 bundle asparagus, ends trimmed
2 tablespoons lemon juice
Fresh dill, for garnish

Grate the zest off the lemons until you have about 1 tablespoon and set the zest aside. Slice the lemons into ⅛-inch slices. Pour the water into the Instant Pot. Add 1 tablespoon of the olive oil to each of two stackable steamer pans. Sprinkle the fish on all sides with the lemon zest, salt, and pepper. Arrange two fillets in each steamer pan and top each with the lemon slices and then the asparagus. Sprinkle the asparagus with the salt and drizzle the lemon juice over the top. Stack the steamer pans in the Instant Pot. Cover the top steamer pan with its lid. Lock the lid. Select the Manual mode and set the cooking time for 3 minutes at High Pressure. Once cooking is complete, do a natural pressure release for 7 minutes, then release any remaining pressure. Carefully open the lid. Lift the steamer pans out of the Instant Pot. Transfer the fish and asparagus to a serving plate. Garnish with the lemon slices and dill. Serve immediately.

Perch Fillets with Red Curry

Prep time: 5 minutes | Cook time: 6 minutes | Serves 4

1 cup water
2 sprigs rosemary
1 large-sized lemon, sliced
1 pound (454 g) perch fillets
1 teaspoon cayenne pepper

Sea salt and ground black pepper, to taste
1 tablespoon red curry paste
1 tablespoons butter

Add the water, rosemary, and lemon slices to the Instant Pot and insert a trivet. Season the perch fillets with the cayenne pepper, salt, and black pepper. Spread the red curry paste and butter over the fillets. Arrange the fish fillets on the trivet. Lock the lid. Select the Manual mode and set the cooking time for 6 minutes at Low Pressure. When the timer beeps, perform a quick pressure release. Carefully remove the lid. Serve with your favorite keto sides.

Fish Packets with Pesto and Cheese

Prep time: 8 minutes | Cook time: 6 minutes | Serves 4

1½ cups cold water.
4 (4-ounce / 113-g) white fish fillets, such as cod or haddock
1 teaspoon fine sea salt
½ teaspoon ground black pepper

1 (4-ounce / 113-g) jar pesto
½ cup shredded Parmesan cheese (about 2 ounces / 57 g)
Halved cherry tomatoes, for garnish

Pour the water into your Instant Pot and insert a steamer basket. Sprinkle the fish on all sides with the salt and pepper. Take four sheets of parchment paper and place a fillet in the center of each sheet. Dollop 2 tablespoons of the pesto on top of each fillet and sprinkle with 2 tablespoons of the Parmesan cheese. Wrap the fish in the parchment by folding in the edges and folding down the top like an envelope to close tightly. Stack the packets in the steamer basket, seam-side down. Lock the lid. Select the Manual mode and set the cooking time for 6 minutes at Low Pressure. Once cooking is complete, do a natural pressure release for 10 minutes, then release any remaining pressure. Carefully open the lid. Remove the fish packets from the pot. Transfer to a serving plate and garnish with the cherry tomatoes. Serve immediately.

Cod Fillets with Cherry Tomatoes

Prep time: 2 minutes | Cook time: 15 minutes | Serves 4

2 tablespoons butter
¼ cup diced onion
1 clove garlic, minced
1 cup cherry tomatoes, halved
¼ cup chicken broth
¼ teaspoon dried thyme

¼ teaspoon salt
⅛ teaspoon pepper
4 (4-ounce / 113-g) cod fillets
1 cup water
¼ cup fresh chopped Italian parsley

Set your Instant Pot to Sauté. Add and melt the butter. Once hot, add the onions and cook until softened. Add the garlic and cook for another 30 seconds. Add the tomatoes, chicken broth, thyme, salt, and pepper. Continue to cook for 5 to 7 minutes, or until the tomatoes start to soften. Pour the sauce into a glass bowl. Add the fish fillets. Cover with foil. Pour the water into the Instant Pot and insert a trivet. Place the bowl on top. Lock the lid. Select the Manual mode and set the cooking time for 3 minutes at Low Pressure. Once cooking is complete, do a quick pressure release. Carefully open the lid. Sprinkle with the fresh parsley and serve.

Pesto Salmon with Almonds

Prep time: 5 minutes | Cook time: 12 minutes | Serves 4

1 tablespoon butter
¼ cup sliced almonds
4 (3-ounce / 85-g) salmon fillets

½ cup pesto
¼ teaspoon pepper
½ teaspoon salt
1 cup water

Press the Sauté button on the Instant Pot and add the butter and almonds. Sauté for 3 to 5 minutes until they start to soften. Remove and set aside. Brush salmon fillets with pesto and season with salt and pepper. Pour the water into Instant Pot and insert the trivet. Place the salmon fillets on the trivet. Secure the lid. Select the Steam mode and set the cooking time for 7 minutes at High Pressure. Once cooking is complete, do a quick pressure release. Carefully open the lid. Serve the salmon with the almonds sprinkled on top.

Garam Masala Fish

Prep time: 10 minutes | Cook time: 10 minutes | Serves 4

2 tablespoons sesame oil
½ teaspoon cumin seeds
½ cup chopped leeks
1 teaspoon ginger-garlic paste
1 pound (454 g) cod fillets, boneless and sliced
2 ripe tomatoes, chopped
1½ tablespoons fresh lemon juice
½ teaspoon garam masala
½ teaspoon turmeric powder

1 tablespoon chopped fresh dill leaves
1 tablespoon chopped fresh curry leaves
1 tablespoon chopped fresh parsley leaves
Coarse sea salt, to taste
½ teaspoon smoked cayenne pepper
¼ teaspoon ground black pepper, or more to taste

Set the Instant Pot to Sauté. Add and heat the sesame oil until hot. Sauté the cumin seeds for 30 seconds. Add the leeks and cook for another 2 minutes until translucent. Add the ginger-garlic paste and cook for an additional 40 seconds. Stir in the remaining ingredients. Lock the lid. Select the Manual mode and set the cooking time for 6 minutes at Low Pressure. When the timer beeps, perform a quick pressure release. Carefully remove the lid. Serve immediately.

Snapper in Spicy Tomato Sauce

Prep time: 5 minutes | Cook time: 5 minutes | Serves 6

2 teaspoons coconut oil, melted
1 teaspoon celery seeds
½ teaspoon fresh grated ginger
½ teaspoon cumin seeds
1 yellow onion, chopped
2 cloves garlic, minced
1½ pounds (680 g) snapper fillets

¾ cup vegetable broth
1 (14-ounce / 113-g) can fire-roasted diced tomatoes
1 bell pepper, sliced
1 jalapeño pepper, minced
Sea salt and ground black pepper, to taste
¼ teaspoon chili flakes
½ teaspoon turmeric powder

Set the Instant Pot to Sauté. Add and heat the sesame oil until hot. Sauté the celery seeds, fresh ginger, and cumin seeds. Add the onion and continue to sauté until softened and fragrant. Mix in the minced garlic and continue to cook for 30 seconds. Add the remaining ingredients and stir well. Lock the lid. Select the Manual mode and set the cooking time for 3 minutes at Low Pressure. When the timer beeps, perform a quick pressure release. Carefully remove the lid. Serve warm

Foil-Packet Salmon

Prep time: 2 minutes | Cook time: 7 minutes | Serves 2

2 (3-ounce / 85-g) salmon fillets
¼ teaspoon garlic powder
1 teaspoon salt

¼ teaspoon pepper
¼ teaspoon dried dill
½ lemon
1 cup water

Place each filet of salmon on a square of foil, skin-side down. Season with garlic powder, salt, and pepper and squeeze the lemon juice over the fish. Cut the lemon into four slices and place two on each filet. Close the foil packets by folding over edges. Add the water to the Instant Pot and insert a trivet. Place the foil packets on the trivet. Secure the lid. Select the Steam mode and set the cooking time for 7 minutes at Low Pressure. Once cooking is complete, do a quick pressure release. Carefully open the lid. Check the internal temperature with a meat thermometer to ensure the thickest part of the filets reached at least 145°F (63°C). Salmon should easily flake when fully cooked. Serve immediately.

Lemony Salmon with Tomatoes

Prep time: 7 minutes | Cook time: 21 minutes | Serves 4

1 tablespoon unsalted butter
3 cloves garlic, minced
1¼ cups fresh or canned diced tomatoes
1 tablespoon chopped fresh flat-leaf parsley, plus more for garnish

¼ cup lemon juice
¼ teaspoon ground black pepper
4 (6-ounce / 170-g) skinless salmon fillets
1 teaspoon fine sea salt
Lemon wedges, for garnish

Add the butter to your Instant Pot and select the Sauté mode. Once melted, add the garlic (if using) and sauté for 1 minute. Add the roasted garlic, lemon juice, tomatoes, parsley, and pepper. Let simmer for 5 minutes, or until the liquid has reduced a bit. Meanwhile, rinse the salmon and pat dry with a paper towel. Sprinkle on all sides with the salt. Using a spatula, push the reduced sauce to one side of the pot and place the salmon on the other side. Spoon the sauce over the salmon. Sauté uncovered for another 15 minutes, or until the salmon flakes easily with a fork. The timing will depend on the thickness of the fillets. Transfer the salmon to a serving plate. Serve with the sauce and garnish with the parsley and lemon wedges.

Salmon Fillets and Bok Choy

Prep time: 5 minutes | Cook time: 8 minutes | Serves 4

1½ cups water
2 tablespoons unsalted butter
4 (1-inch thick) salmon fillets
½ teaspoon cayenne pepper
Sea salt and freshly ground pepper, to taste

2 cups Bok choy, sliced
1 cup chicken broth
3 cloves garlic, minced
1 teaspoon grated lemon zest
½ teaspoon dried dill weed

Pour the water into your Instant Pot and insert a trivet. Brush the salmon with the melted butter and season with the cayenne pepper, salt, and black pepper on all sides. Lock the lid. Select the Manual mode and set the cooking time for 3 minutes at Low Pressure. When the timer beeps, perform a quick pressure release. Carefully remove the lid. Add the remaining ingredients. Lock the lid. Select the Manual mode and set the cooking time for 5 minutes at High Pressure. When the timer beeps, perform a quick pressure release. Carefully remove the lid. Serve the poached salmon with the veggies on the side.

Salmon Steaks with Garlicky Yogurt

Prep time: 2 minutes | Cook time: 4 minutes | Serves 4

1 cup water
2 tablespoons olive oil
4 salmon steaks

Coarse sea salt and ground black pepper, to taste

Garlicky Yogurt:

1 (8-ounce / 227-g) container full-fat Greek yogurt
2 cloves garlic, minced

2 tablespoons mayonnaise
⅓ teaspoon Dijon mustard

Pour the water into the Instant Pot and insert a trivet. Rub the olive oil into the fish and sprinkle with the salt and black pepper on all sides. Put the fish on the trivet. Lock the lid. Select the Manual mode and set the cooking time for 4 minutes at High Pressure. When the timer beeps, perform a quick pressure release. Carefully remove the lid. Meanwhile, stir together all the ingredients for the garlicky yogurt in a bowl. Serve the salmon steaks alongside the garlicky yogurt.

Avocado Salmon Burgers

Prep time: 5 minutes | Cook time: 5 minutes | Serves 4

2 tablespoons coconut oil
1 pound (454 g) salmon fillets
⅓ cup finely ground pork rinds
2 tablespoons finely diced onion
2 tablespoons mayonnaise

½ teaspoon salt
¼ teaspoon chili powder
¼ teaspoon garlic powder
1 egg
1 avocado, pitted
Juice of ½ lime

Set your Instant Pot to Sauté. Add and heat the coconut oil. Remove skin from the salmon filets. Finely mince the salmon and add to a large bowl. Stir in the remaining ingredients except the avocado and lime and form 4 patties. Place the burgers into the pot and sear for about 3 to 4 minutes per side, or until the center feels firm and reads at least 145ºF (63ºC) on a meat thermometer. Scoop flesh out of the avocado. In a small bowl, mash the avocado with a fork and squeeze the lime juice over the top. Divide the mash into four sections and place on top of salmon burgers. Serve warm.

Lemony Salmon with Avocados

Prep time: 10 minutes | Cook time: 7 minutes | Serves 2

2 (3-ounce / 85-g) salmon fillets
½ teaspoon salt
¼ teaspoon pepper
1 cup water

⅓ cup mayonnaise
Juice of ½ lemon
2 avocados
½ teaspoon chopped fresh dill

Season the salmon fillets on all sides with the salt and pepper. Add the water to the Instant Pot and insert a trivet. Arrange the salmon fillets on the trivet, skin-side down. Secure the lid. Select the Steam mode and set the cooking time for 7 minutes at Low Pressure. Once cooking is complete, do a quick pressure release. Carefully open the lid. Set aside to cool. Mix together the mayonnaise and lemon juice in a large bowl. Cut the avocados in half. Remove the pits and dice the avocados. Add the avocados to the large bowl and gently fold into the mixture. Flake the salmon into bite-sized pieces with a fork and gently fold into the mixture. Serve garnished with the fresh dill.

Salmon Packets

Prep time: 8 minutes | Cook time: 6 minutes | Serves 4

1½ cups cold water
4 (5-ounce / 142-g) salmon fillets
½ teaspoon fine sea salt
¼ teaspoon ground black

pepper
1 lime, thinly sliced
4 teaspoons extra-virgin olive oil, divided
Fresh thyme leaves

Pour the cold water into the Instant Pot and insert a steamer basket. Sprinkle the fish on all sides with the salt and pepper. Take four sheets of parchment paper and place 3 lime slices on each sheet. Top the lime slices with a piece of fish. Drizzle with 1 teaspoon of olive oil and place a few thyme leaves on top. Cover each fillet with the parchment by folding in the edges and folding down the top like an envelope to close tightly. Stack the packets in the steamer basket, seam-side down. Secure the lid. Select the Manual mode and set the cooking time for 6 minutes at Low Pressure. When the timer beeps, perform a natural pressure release for 10 minutes, then release any remaining pressure. Carefully remove the lid. Remove the fish packets from the pot. Serve the fish garnished with the fresh thyme.

Crispy Salmon Fillets

Prep time: 5 minutes | Cook time: 5 minutes | Serves 2

1 tablespoon avocado oil
2 (3-ounce / 85-g) salmon fillets
1 teaspoon paprika
½ teaspoon salt
¼ teaspoon dried thyme
¼ teaspoon onion powder
¼ teaspoon pepper
⅛ teaspoon cayenne pepper

Drizzle the avocado oil over salmon fillets. Combine the remaining ingredients in a small bowl and rub all over fillets. Press the Sauté button on the Instant Pot. Add the salmon fillets and sear for 2 to 5 minutes until the salmon easily flakes with a fork. Serve warm.

Lemon-Dill Salmon

Prep time: 3 minutes | Cook time: 5 minutes | Serves 2

2 (3-ounce / 85-g) salmon fillets, 1-inch thick
1 teaspoon chopped fresh dill
½ teaspoon salt
¼ teaspoon pepper
1 cup water
2 tablespoons lemon juice
½ lemon, sliced

Season salmon with dill, salt, and pepper. Pour the water into the Instant Pot and insert the trivet. Place the salmon on the trivet, skin-side down. Squeeze lemon juice over fillets and scatter the lemon slices on top. Lock the lid. Select the Steam mode and set the cooking time for 5 minutes at High Pressure. Once cooking is complete, do a quick pressure release. Carefully open the lid. Serve warm.

Swai with Port Wine Sauce

Prep time: 5 minutes | Cook time: 10 minutes | Serves 4

1 tablespoon butter
1 teaspoon fresh grated ginger
2 garlic cloves, minced
2 tablespoon chopped green onions
1 pound (454 g) swai fish fillets
½ cup port wine
1 teaspoon parsley flakes
½ tablespoon lemon juice
½ teaspoon chili flakes
½ teaspoon cayenne pepper
½ teaspoon fennel seeds
¼ teaspoon ground bay leaf
Coarse sea salt and ground black pepper, to taste

Set your Instant Pot to Sauté and melt the butter. Cook the ginger, garlic, and green onions for 2 minutes until softened. Add the remaining ingredients and gently stir to incorporate. Lock the lid. Select the Manual mode and set the cooking time for 6 minutes at Low Pressure. When the timer beeps, perform a quick pressure release. Carefully remove the lid. Serve warm.

Salmon Fillets with Broccoli

Prep time: 5 minutes | Cook time: 5 minutes | Serves 2

1 cup water
8 ounces (227 g) broccoli, cut into florets
8 ounces (227 g) salmon fillets
Salt and ground black pepper, to taste

Pour the water into the Instant Pot and insert a trivet. Season the salmon and broccoli florets with salt and pepper. Put them on the trivet. Secure the lid. Select the Steam mode and set the cooking time for 5 minutes at High Pressure. Once cooking is complete, do a natural pressure release for 10 minutes, then release any remaining pressure. Carefully open the lid. Serve hot.

Tarragon Bluefish in Vermouth Sauce

Prep time: 5 minutes | Cook time: 5 minutes | Serves 4

2 teaspoons butter
½ yellow onion, chopped
1 garlic clove, minced
1 pound (454 g) bluefish fillets
¼ cup vermouth
1 tablespoon rice vinegar
2 teaspoons coconut aminos
1 teaspoon chopped fresh tarragon leaves
Sea salt and ground black pepper, to taste

Set your Instant Pot to Sauté and melt the butter. Add the onion and sauté for 2 minutes until softened. Add garlic and sauté for 1 minute more or until fragrant. Stir in the remaining ingredients. Lock the lid. Select the Manual mode and set the cooking time for 3 minutes at Low Pressure. When the timer beeps, perform a quick pressure release. Carefully remove the lid. Serve warm.

Smoked Sausage and Grouper

Prep time: 5 minutes | Cook time: 10 minutes | Serves 4

2 tablespoons butter
½ pound (227 g) smoked turkey sausage, casing removed
1 pound (454 g) cremini mushrooms, sliced
2 garlic cloves, minced
4 grouper fillets
½ cup dry white wine
Sea salt, to taste
½ teaspoon freshly cracked black peppercorns
1 tablespoon fresh lime juice
2 tablespoons chopped fresh cilantro

Set your Instant Pot to Sauté and melt the butter. Add the sausage and cook until nicely browned on all sides. Remove the sausage and set aside. Add the mushrooms and cook for about 3 minutes or until fragrant. Add the garlic and continue to sauté for another 30 seconds. Add the fish, wine, salt, and black peppercorns. Return the sausage to the Instant Pot. Lock the lid. Select the Manual mode and set the cooking time for 3 minutes at Low Pressure. When the timer beeps, perform a quick pressure release. Carefully remove the lid. Drizzle with the lime juice and serve garnished with fresh cilantro.

Bacon and Seafood Chowder

Prep time: 10 minutes | Cook time: 15 minutes | Serves 6

¼ pound (113 g) meaty bacon, chopped
1 serrano pepper, minced
1 celery with leaves, diced
½ cup diced leeks
3 cups fish stock
½ cup Rose wine
1½ pounds (680 g) halibut fillets, cut into 2-inch pieces
10 ounces (283 g) clams,
minced and juice reserved
2 garlic cloves, pressed
Sea salt and ground black pepper, to taste
2 sprigs fresh rosemary
2 sprigs fresh thyme
2 cups heavy cream
2 tablespoons chopped fresh chives

Press the Sauté button to heat the Instant Pot. Cook the bacon for about 5 minutes until crisp, stirring occasionally. Remove the bacon and set aside. Add the pepper, celery, and leeks and sauté for an additional 3 minutes or until softened. Add the remaining ingredients except the heavy cream and chives to the Instant Pot and stir well. Lock the lid. Select the Manual mode and set the cooking time for 7 minutes at Low Pressure. When the timer beeps, perform a quick pressure release. Carefully remove the lid. Stir in heavy cream. Press the Sauté button again and let it simmer until heated through. Serve topped with the cooked bacon and fresh chives.

Cheesy Mussel Stew

Prep time: 15 minutes | Cook time: 3 minutes | Serves 6

1½ pounds (680 g) mussels, scrubbed and debearded
1 cup chicken broth
½ cup dry red wine
2 tablespoons olive oil
2 heaping tablespoons chopped green onions
2 tablespoons chopped fresh coriander
½ teaspoon paprika
½ teaspoon dried marjoram
A pinch ground nutmeg
Sea salt and ground black pepper, to taste
½ (28-ounce / 794-g) can San Marzano tomatoes, crushed
2 cloves garlic, crushed
1 cup shredded Asiago cheese
1 tablespoon chopped fresh dill
1 lemon, sliced

Combine all the ingredients except the cheese, dill and lemon in the Instant Pot. Lock the lid. Select the Manual mode and set the cooking time for 3 minutes at Low Pressure. When the timer beeps, perform a quick pressure release. Carefully remove the lid. Sprinkle with the cheese and dill. Serve topped with the lemon slices.

Cheesy Shrimp Salad

Prep time: 10 minutes | Cook time: 2 minutes | Serves 4

28 ounces (794 g) shrimp, peeled and deveined
½ cup water
½ cup apple cider vinegar
⅓ cup mayonnaise
¼ cup cream cheese
2 tablespoons roughly chopped cilantro
1 red onion, chopped
1 celery with leaves, chopped
1 large-sized cucumber, sliced
1 tablespoon lime juice

Combine the shrimp, water, and apple cider vinegar in the Instant Pot. Lock the lid. Select the Manual mode and set the cooking time for 2 minutes at Low Pressure. When the timer beeps, perform a quick pressure release. Carefully remove the lid. Allow the shrimp to cool completely. Toss the shrimp with the remaining ingredients. Serve chilled.

White Fish Fillets with Asparagus

Prep time: 5 minutes | Cook time: 3 minutes | Serves 4

2 lemons
2 cups cold water
2 tablespoons extra-virgin olive oil
4 (4-ounce / 113-g) white fish fillets, such as cod or haddock
1 teaspoon fine sea salt
1 teaspoon ground black pepper
1 bundle asparagus, ends trimmed
2 tablespoons lemon juice
Fresh dill, for garnish

Grate the zest off the lemons until you have about 1 tablespoon and set the zest aside. Slice the lemons into ⅛-inch slices. Pour the water into the Instant Pot. Add 1 tablespoon of the olive oil to each of two stackable steamer pans. Sprinkle the fish on all sides with the lemon zest, salt, and pepper. Arrange two fillets in each steamer pan and top each with the lemon slices and then the asparagus. Sprinkle the asparagus with the salt and drizzle the lemon juice over the top. Stack the steamer pans in the Instant Pot. Cover the top steamer pan with its lid. Lock the lid. Select the Pressure Cook mode and set the cooking time for 3 minutes at High Pressure. Once cooking is complete, do a natural pressure release for 7 minutes, then release any remaining pressure. Carefully open the lid. Lift the steamer pans out of the Instant Pot. Transfer the fish and asparagus to a serving plate. Garnish with the lemon slices and dill. Serve immediately.

Garlic Halibut Steaks

Prep time: 2 minutes | Cook time: 5 minutes | Serves 3

1½ cups water
3 halibut steaks
Coarse sea salt, to taste
¼ teaspoon ground black pepper, to taste
4 garlic cloves, crushed

Pour the water into the Instant Pot and insert a steamer basket. Put the halibut steaks in the steamer basket and season with salt and black pepper. Scatter with the garlic. Lock the lid. Select the Manual mode and set the cooking time for 5 minutes at High Pressure. When the timer beeps, perform a quick pressure release. Carefully remove the lid. Serve warm.

Creamy Mackerel Chowder

Prep time: 5 minutes | Cook time: 8 minutes | Serves 4

1 tablespoon olive oil
1 yellow onion, chopped
1 teaspoon grated ginger
1 pound (454 g) mackerel fillets, sliced
2 garlic cloves, minced
2 cups chicken stock
1½ cups coconut milk
½ cup heavy cream
1 tablespoon butter

Set your Instant Pot to Sauté and heat the olive oil. Sauté the onion until softened, about 2 minutes. Sauté the garlic and ginger for 30 to 40 seconds more. Add the remaining ingredients to the Instant Pot and stir until combined. Lock the lid. Select the Manual mode and set the cooking time for 6 minutes at High Pressure. When the timer beeps, perform a quick pressure release. Carefully remove the lid. Serve warm.

Parsley Scallops

Prep time: 5 minutes | Cook time: 5 minutes | Serves 3

1 tablespoon sesame oil
¾ pound (340 g) scallops
2 garlic cloves, crushed
1 cup chicken broth
¼ cup dry white wine
½ teaspoon paprika
Sea salt, to taste
⅓ teaspoon ground black pepper
2 tablespoons chopped fresh parsley
1 tablespoon fresh lemon juice

Set your Instant Pot to Sauté and heat the sesame oil. Add the scallops and sauté for 1 to 2 minutes. Add the garlic and continue to sauté for 30 seconds more. Add the broth, wine, paprika, salt, and pepper. Lock the lid. Select the Manual mode and set the cooking time for 2 minutes at Low Pressure. When the timer beeps, perform a quick pressure release. Carefully remove the lid. Transfer the scallops to a bowl and toss with fresh parsley and lemon juice. Serve immediately.

Easy Steamed Salmon

Prep time: 5 minutes | Cook time: 10 minutes | Serves 2

1 cup water
2 salmon fillets
Salt and ground black pepper, to taste

Pour the water into the Instant Pot and add a trivet. Season the salmon fillets with salt and black pepper to taste. Put the salmon fillets on the trivet. Secure the lid. Select the Steam mode and set the cooking time for 10 minutes at High Pressure. Once cooking is complete, do a natural pressure release for 10 minutes, then release any remaining pressure. Carefully open the lid. Serve hot.

Lemon-Chili Sockeye Salmon Fillets

Prep time: 5 minutes | Cook time: 5 minutes | Serves 4

4 wild sockeye salmon fillets
¼ cup lemon juice
2 tablespoons assorted chili pepper seasoning

Salt and ground black pepper, to taste
1 cup water

Drizzle the salmon fillets with lemon juice. Season with the chili pepper seasoning, salt, and pepper. Pour the water into the Instant Pot and add a steamer basket. Put the salmon fillets in the steamer basket. Secure the lid. Select the Pressure Cook mode and set the cooking time for 5 minutes at High Pressure. Once cooking is complete, do a quick pressure release. Carefully open the lid. Remove from the Instant Pot and serve.

Easy Sea Scallops

Prep time: 5 minutes | Cook time: 5 minutes | Serves 4

2 teaspoons butter
1½ pounds (680 g) sea scallops
2 garlic cloves, finely chopped
1 (1-inch) piece fresh ginger root, grated
⅔ cup fish stock

⅓ cup dry white wine
1 teaspoon Creole seasoning blend
Coarse sea salt and ground black pepper, to taste
2 tablespoons chopped fresh parsley

Set your Instant Pot to Sauté and melt the butter. Cook the sea scallops until browned on all sides, about 2 minutes. Stir in the garlic and ginger and continue sautéing for 1 minute more. Add the remaining ingredients, except for the fresh parsley, into the Instant Pot. Lock the lid. Select the Manual mode and set the cooking time for 1 minute at Low Pressure. When the timer beeps, perform a quick pressure release. Carefully remove the lid. Serve garnished with the fresh parsley.

Cheesy Salmon Casserole

Prep time: 10 minutes | Cook time: 2½ to 3½ hours | Serves 6

1 (14¾-ounce / 418-g) can salmon with liquid
1 (4-ounce / 113-g) can mushrooms, drained
1½ cups bread crumbs

⅓ cup eggbeaters
1 cup shredded fat-free cheese
1 tablespoon lemon juice
1 tablespoon minced onion

Flake fish in a bowl, removing bones. Stir in remaining ingredients. Pour into lightly greased Instant Pot. Cover. Press the Slow Cook button, and cook on low for 2½ to 3½ hours. (Press Slow Cook again to toggle between Low and High cooking temperatures.)

Tuna and Egg Casserole

Prep time: 10 minutes | Cook time: 5 to 8 hours | Serves 4

2 (7-ounce / 198-g) cans tuna
1 (10¾-ounce / 305-g) can cream of celery soup
3 hard-boiled eggs, chopped
½ to 1½ cups diced celery

½ cup diced onions
½ cup mayonnaise
¼ teaspoon ground pepper
1½ cups crushed potato chips

Combine all ingredients except ¼ cup potato chips in Instant Pot. Top with remaining chips. Cover. Press the Slow Cook button, and cook on low for 5 to 8 hours. (Press Slow Cook again to toggle between Low and High cooking temperatures.)

Dijon Salmon

Prep time: 5 minutes | Cook time: 5 minutes | Serves 2

1 cup water
2 fish fillets or steaks, such as salmon, cod, or halibut (1-inch thick)

Salt and ground black pepper, to taste
2 teaspoons Dijon mustard

Add the water to the Instant Pot and insert a trivet. Season the fish with salt and pepper to taste. Put the fillets, skin-side down, on the trivet and top with the Dijon mustard. Secure the lid. Select the Manual mode and set the cooking time for 5 minutes at High Pressure. Once cooking is complete, do a quick pressure release. Carefully open the lid. Divide the fish between two plates and serve.

Steamed Cod and Veggies

Prep time: 5 minutes | Cook time: 2 to 4 minutes | Serves 2

½ cup water
Kosher salt and freshly ground black pepper, to taste
2 tablespoons freshly squeezed lemon juice, divided
2 tablespoons melted butter
1 zucchini or yellow summer squash, cut into thick slices

1 garlic clove, minced
1 cup cherry tomatoes
1 cup whole Brussels sprouts
2 (6-ounce / 170-g) cod fillets
2 thyme sprigs or ½ teaspoon dried thyme
Hot cooked rice, for serving

Pour the water into your Instant Pot and insert a steamer basket. Sprinkle the fish with the salt and pepper. Mix together 1 tablespoon of the lemon juice, the butter, and garlic in a small bowl. Set aside. Add the zucchini, tomatoes, and Brussels sprouts to the basket. Sprinkle with the salt and pepper and drizzle the remaining 1 tablespoon of lemon juice over the top. Place the fish fillets on top of the veggies. Brush with the mixture and then turn the fish and repeat on the other side. Drizzle any remaining mixture all over the veggies. Place the thyme sprigs on top. Lock the lid. Select the Steam mode and set the cooking time for 2 to 4 minutes on High Pressure, depending on the thickness of the fish. Once cooking is complete, use a quick pressure release. Carefully open the lid. Serve the cod and veggies over the cooked rice.

Shrimp Spaghetti

Prep time: 5 minutes | Cook time: 10 minutes | Serves 4

6 tablespoons butter, divided
12 ounces (340 g) small shrimp, peeled and deveined
½ teaspoon salt
4 cups chicken broth

1 pound (454 g) spaghetti
1 cup grated Parmesan cheese
1 cup heavy whipping cream
1 teaspoon lemon pepper

Set your Instant Pot to Sauté and add 2 tablespoons of butter. Add the shrimp and salt to the Instant Pot and sauté for 4 minutes, or until the flesh is pink and opaque. Remove the shrimp and set aside. Add the broth and scrape up any bits on the bottom of the pot. Break the spaghetti in half and add to the pot. Place the remaining 4 tablespoons of butter on top. Secure the lid. Press the Pressure Cook button on the Instant Pot and cook for 5 minutes on High Pressure. Once the timer goes off, use a quick pressure release. Carefully open the lid. Fold in the cooked shrimp, Parmesan, cream, and lemon pepper. Stir until thoroughly combined. Transfer to a serving plate and serve hot.

Pesto White Fish Packets

Prep time: 8 minutes | Cook time: 6 minutes | Serves 4

1½ cups cold water.
4 (4-ounce / 113-g) white fish fillets, such as cod or haddock
1 teaspoon fine sea salt
½ teaspoon ground black pepper

1 (4-ounce / 113-g) jar pesto
½ cup shredded Parmesan cheese (about 2 ounces / 57 g)
Halved cherry tomatoes, for garnish

Pour the water into your Instant Pot and insert a steamer basket. Sprinkle the fish on all sides with the salt and pepper. Take four sheets of parchment paper and place a fillet in the center of each sheet. Dollop 2 tablespoons of the pesto on top of each fillet and sprinkle with 2 tablespoons of the Parmesan cheese. Wrap the fish in the parchment by folding in the edges and folding down the top like an envelope to close tightly. Stack the packets in the steamer basket, seam-side down. Lock the lid. Select the Pressure Cook mode and set the cooking time for 6 minutes at Low Pressure. Once cooking is complete, do a natural pressure release for 10 minutes, then release any remaining pressure. Carefully open the lid. Remove the fish packets from the pot. Transfer to a serving plate and garnish with the cherry tomatoes. Serve immediately.

Cod and Cherry Tomato Bowls

Prep time: 2 minutes | Cook time: 15 minutes | Serves 4

2 tablespoons butter
¼ cup diced onion
1 clove garlic, minced
1 cup cherry tomatoes, halved
¼ cup chicken broth
¼ teaspoon dried thyme

¼ teaspoon salt
⅛ teaspoon pepper
4 (4-ounce / 113-g) cod fillets
1 cup water
¼ cup fresh chopped Italian parsley

Set your Instant Pot to Sauté. Add and melt the butter. Once hot, add the onions and cook until softened. Add the garlic and cook for another 30 seconds. Add the tomatoes, chicken broth, thyme, salt, and pepper. Continue to cook for 5 to 7 minutes, or until the tomatoes start to soften. Pour the sauce into a glass bowl. Add the fish fillets. Cover with foil. Pour the water into the Instant Pot and insert a trivet. Place the bowl on top. Lock the lid. Select the Pressure Cook mode and set the cooking time for 3 minutes at Low Pressure. Once cooking is complete, do a quick pressure release. Carefully open the lid. Sprinkle with the fresh parsley and serve.

Tuna, Egg Noodle, and Pea Casserole

Prep time: 5 minutes | Cook time: 4 minutes | Serves 4

3 cups water
28 ounces (794 g) cream of mushroom soup
14 ounces (397 g) canned tuna, drained
20 ounces (567 g) egg noodles

1 cup frozen peas
Salt and ground black pepper, to taste
4 ounces (113 g) grated Cheddar cheese
¼ cup bread crumbs (optional)

Combine the water and mushroom soup in the Instant Pot. Stir in the tuna, egg noodles, and peas. Season with salt and pepper. Secure the lid. Select the Pressure Cook mode and set the cooking time for 4 minutes at High Pressure. When the timer beeps, perform a quick pressure release. Carefully remove the lid. Scatter the grated cheese and bread crumbs (if desired) on top. Lock the lid and allow to sit for 5 minutes. Serve warm.

Cod and Leek Garam Masala

Prep time: 10 minutes | Cook time: 10 minutes | Serves 4

2 tablespoons sesame oil
½ teaspoon cumin seeds
½ cup chopped leeks
1 teaspoon ginger-garlic paste
1 pound (454 g) cod fillets, boneless and sliced
2 ripe tomatoes, chopped
1½ tablespoons fresh lemon juice
½ teaspoon garam masala
½ teaspoon turmeric powder

1 tablespoon chopped fresh dill leaves
1 tablespoon chopped fresh curry leaves
1 tablespoon chopped fresh parsley leaves
Coarse sea salt, to taste
½ teaspoon smoked cayenne pepper
¼ teaspoon ground black pepper, or more to taste

Set the Instant Pot to Sauté. Add and heat the sesame oil until hot. Sauté the cumin seeds for 30 seconds. Add the leeks and cook for another 2 minutes until translucent. Add the ginger-garlic paste and cook for an additional 40 seconds. Stir in the remaining ingredients. Lock the lid. Select the Pressure Cook mode and set the cooking time for 6 minutes at Low Pressure. When the timer beeps, perform a quick pressure release. Carefully remove the lid. Serve immediately.

Salmon with Honey Sauce

Prep time: 10 minutes | Cook time: o minutes | Serves 4

Salmon:
1 cup water
1 pound (454 g) salmon fillets

½ teaspoon salt
¼ teaspoon black pepper

Sauce:
½ cup honey
4 cloves garlic, minced
4 tablespoons soy sauce

2 tablespoons rice vinegar
1 teaspoon sesame seeds

Pour the water into the Instant Pot and insert a trivet. Season the salmon fillets with salt and pepper to taste, then place on the trivet. Secure the lid. Select the Pressure Cook mode and set the cooking time for 0 minutes at High Pressure. Once cooking is complete, do a natural pressure release for 10 minutes, then release any remaining pressure. Carefully open the lid. Meanwhile, whisk together all the ingredients for the sauce in a small bowl until well mixed. Transfer the fillets to a plate and pour the sauce over them. Serve hot.

Garlicky Salmon

Prep time: 5 minutes | Cook time: 15 minutes | Serves 4 to 6

½ cup mayonnaise
4 cloves garlic, minced
1 tablespoon lemon juice
1 teaspoon dried basil leaves
2 pounds (907 g) salmon fillets

Salt and ground pepper, to taste
2 tablespoons olive oil
Chopped green onion, for garnish

Stir together the mayo, garlic, lemon juice, and basil in a bowl. Set aside. Season the salmon fillets with salt and pepper to taste. Press the Sauté button on the Instant Pot and heat the olive oil. Add the seasoned fillets and brown each side for 5 minutes. Add the mayo mixture to the Instant Pot and coat the fillets. Continue cooking for another 5 minutes, flipping occasionally. Remove from the Instant Pot to a plate and serve garnished with the green onions.

Broiled Shrimp with Kielbasa Sausage

Prep time: 5 minutes | Cook time: 4 minutes | Serves 2

½ pound (227 g) red potatoes, halved
1 cup water
2 ears of corn, shucked and broken in half
½ pound (227 g) fully cooked kielbasa sausage, cut into 2-inch slices
1 medium sweet onion, chopped
2 tablespoons crab boil seasoning (optional)
2 tablespoons Old Bay seasoning, plus more for seasoning
½ teaspoon kosher salt
1 pound (454 g) peel-on large raw shrimp, deveined

Mix together the potatoes, water, corn, onion, kielbasa, the crab boil seasoning (if desired), 2 tablespoons of Old Bay, and salt in your Instant pot. Lock the lid. Select the Pressure Cook mode and cook for 4 minutes on High Pressure. Once cooking is complete, do a quick pressure release. Carefully open the lid. Mix in the shrimp and stir well. Replace the lid loosely and let stand for 3 to 4 minutes. Sprinkle with the salt and Old Bay. Transfer the shrimp to a large colander and drain. Serve.

Lemon-Wine Shrimp

Prep time: 10 minutes | Cook time: 3 minutes | Serves 4 to 6

2 tablespoons butter
1 tablespoon lemon juice
1 tablespoon garlic, minced
½ cup chicken stock
½ cup white wine
2 pounds (907 g) shrimp
Salt and ground black pepper, to taste
1 tablespoon parsley, for garnish

Place the butter, lemon juice, and garlic in your Instant Pot. Stir in the stock and wine. Add the shrimp and sprinkle with the salt and pepper. Stir well. Secure the lid. Press the Pressure Cook button on your Instant Pot and set the cooking time for 3 minutes at High Pressure. Once the timer beeps, do a quick pressure release. Carefully remove the lid. Serve topped with the parsley.

Saffron Shrimp Paella

Prep time: 10 minutes | Cook time: 8 minutes | Serves 4

1¾ cups store-bought chicken or vegetable broth
2 big pinches of saffron
3 tablespoons olive oil
1 medium yellow onion, chopped
1 cup drained, chopped roasted bell peppers
1½ cups long-grain rice
1 cup drained canned fire-roasted tomatoes with garlic
Salt and freshly ground black pepper, to taste
1 pound (454 g) frozen large/jumbo shell-on, deveined shrimp

Mix together the broth and saffron in a mixing bowl and set aside. Set your Instant Pot to Sauté. Add and heat the oil. Add the onion and sauté for 4 minutes until tender. Mix in the rice and stir to coat. Stir in the broth-saffron mixture, roasted peppers, tomatoes, ¾ teaspoon of salt, and pepper. Arrange the frozen shrimp on the rice mixture. Secure the lid. Select the Pressure Cook mode and cook for 4 minutes on High Pressure. When the timer beeps, do a natural pressure release for 10 minutes and then release any remaining pressure. Carefully open the lid. Transfer the paella to a serving dish. Serve immediately.

Coconut-Curry Shrimp

Prep time: 10 minutes | Cook time: 4 minutes | Serves 2 to 4

2 cups water
1 pound (454 g) shrimp, peeled and deveined
8 ounces (227 g) unsweetened coconut milk
1 teaspoon curry powder
1 tablespoon garlic, minced
Salt and ground black pepper, to taste

Pour the water into the Instant Pot and insert a trivet. Mix together the shrimp, coconut milk, curry powder, and garlic in a large bowl. Sprinkle with the salt and pepper. Add the mixture to the pan and place the dish onto the trivet, uncovered. Secure the lid. Press the Pressure Cook button on the Instant Pot and cook for 4 minutes at Low Pressure. Once cooking is complete, use a quick pressure release. Carefully open the lid. Stir well and serve.

Parmesan Scampi with Tomatoes

Prep time: 10 minutes | Cook time: 3 minutes | Serves 2 to 4

2 tablespoons olive oil
1 clove garlic, minced
1 pound (454 g) shrimp, peeled and deveined
10 ounces (284 g) canned tomatoes, chopped
⅓ cup tomato paste
⅓ cup water
1 tablespoon parsley, finely chopped
¼ teaspoon dried oregano
½ teaspoon kosher salt
½ teaspoon ground black pepper, to taste
1 cup grated Parmesan Cheese

Set the Instant Pot to Sauté. Add and heat the oil. Add the garlic and sauté for 1 minute until fragrant. Stir in the shrimp, tomatoes, tomato paste, water, parsley, oregano, salt and pepper. Secure the lid. Select the Pressure Cook mode and cook for 3 minutes on High Pressure. When the timer beeps, do a quick pressure release. Carefully remove the lid. Serve scattered with the Parmesan Cheese.

Braised Tomato Squid

Prep time: 5 minutes | Cook time: 27 minutes | Serves 4

2 tablespoons olive oil
1 medium yellow onion, chopped
1 teaspoon dried oregano
4 medium garlic cloves, chopped
1 pound (454 g) frozen cleaned and sliced squid
¼ cup dry red wine
1 (14-ounce / 397-g) can diced tomatoes with Italian herbs, with juice
Salt and freshly ground black pepper, to taste
Lemon wedges, for garnish

Set your Instant Pot to Sauté. Add and heat the oil. Add the onion and sauté for 6 minutes until slightly browned. Fold in the oregano and garlic and cook for 45 seconds until fragrant. Pour in the wine and let simmer for 1 minute, scraping any browned bits out of the bottom of the pot. Mix in the squid, tomatoes, and several grinds of pepper. Secure the lid. Select the Pressure Cook setting and cook for 20 minutes at High Pressure. Once cooking is complete, do a quick pressure release. Carefully remove the lid. Sprinkle with the salt and pepper. Transfer to a serving plate and serve with the lemon wedges, if desired.

Crab and Bell Pepper Bisque

Prep time: 5 minutes | Cook time: 3 minutes | Serves 4

4 tablespoons grass-fed butter, softened
1 pound (454 g) frozen crab meat, thawed
3 cups grass-fed bone broth
1 (14-ounce / 397-g) can sugar-free crushed tomatoes
8 ounces (227 g) full-fat cream cheese, softened
¼ cup heavy whipping cream

¼ cup chopped bell peppers
2 stalks celery, chopped
¼ small onion, thinly sliced
1 teaspoon Old Bay seasoning
½ teaspoon ground cayenne pepper
½ teaspoon kosher salt
½ teaspoon freshly ground black pepper

Press the Sauté button on the Instant Pot and melt the butter. Add the remaining ingredients to the Instant Pot and stir to combine. Secure the lid. Select the Pressure Cook mode and set the cooking time for 3 minutes at Low Pressure. Once cooking is complete, do a quick pressure release. Carefully open the lid. If you prefer a smoother soup, you can purée it with an immersion blender. Ladle into bowls and serve hot.

Cajun Shrimp and Asparagus

Prep time: 10 minutes | Cook time: 2 minutes | Serves 2

1 pound (454 g) shrimp, frozen or fresh, peeled and deveined
1 cup water
6 ounces (170 g) asparagus

1 teaspoon olive oil
½ tablespoon Cajun seasoning (or your choice of seasoning)

Pour the water into the Instant pot and place the trivet inside the pot. Place the asparagus onto the trivet. Arrange the shrimp on the asparagus and drizzle the olive oil over the top. Season with Cajun seasoning. Press the Steam button on the Instant pot and cook for 2 minutes at Low Pressure. Once the timer beeps, do a quick pressure release. Carefully remove the lid. Transfer to a serving plate and serve immediately.

Shrimp Paella with Saffron

Prep time: 10 minutes | Cook time: 8 minutes | Serves 4

1¾ cups store-bought chicken or vegetable broth
2 big pinches of saffron
3 tablespoons olive oil
1 medium yellow onion, chopped
1 cup drained, chopped roasted bell peppers

1½ cups long-grain rice
1 cup drained canned fire-roasted tomatoes with garlic
Salt and freshly ground black pepper, to taste
1 pound (454 g) frozen large/jumbo shell-on, deveined shrimp

Mix together the broth and saffron in a mixing bowl and set aside. Set your Instant Pot to Sauté. Add and heat the oil. Add the onion and sauté for 4 minutes until tender. Mix in the rice and stir to coat. Stir in the broth-saffron mixture, roasted peppers, tomatoes, ¾ teaspoon of salt, and pepper. Arrange the frozen shrimp on the rice mixture. Secure the lid. Select the Manual mode and cook for 4 minutes on High Pressure. When the timer beeps, do a natural pressure release for 10 minutes and then release any remaining pressure. Carefully open the lid. Transfer the paella to a serving dish. Serve immediately.

Coconut and Lemongrass Crabs

Prep time: 10 minutes | Cook time: 9 minutes | Serves 2 to 4

1 tablespoon olive oil
1 onion, chopped
3 cloves garlic, minced
1 pound (454 g) crabs, halved
1 can coconut milk

1 lemongrass stalk
1 thumb-size ginger, sliced
Salt and ground black pepper, to taste

Set the Instant Pot to Sauté. Add and heat the oil. Add the onion and sauté for 2 minutes until tender. Mix in the garlic and sauté for another 1 minute until fragrant. Add the crabs, coconut milk, lemongrass stalk, ginger, salt, and pepper. Secure the lid. Select the Pressure Cook mode and set the cooking time for 6 minutes at High Pressure. Once the timer beeps, do a quick pressure release. Carefully remove the lid. Transfer to a serving plate and serve immediately.

Steamed Crab Legs

Prep time: 5 minutes | Cook time: 3 minutes | Serves 5

1 cup water
2 pounds (907 g) crab legs, thawed

Pour the water into the Instant Pot and add a trivet. Put the crab legs on the trivet. Secure the lid. Select the Pressure Cook mode and set the cooking time for 3 minutes at High Pressure. Once cooking is complete, do a quick pressure release. Carefully open the lid. Transfer the crab legs to a plate and serve.

Almond-Crusted Tilapia

Prep time: 5 minutes | Cook time: 5 minutes | Serves 4

1 cup water
2 tablespoons Dijon mustard
1 teaspoon olive oil

¼ teaspoon lemon pepper
4 tilapia fillets
⅔ cup sliced almonds

Pour the water into the Instant Pot and add a trivet. Whisk together the Dijon mustard, olive oil, and lemon pepper in a small bowl. Brush both sides of the tilapia fillets with the mixture. Spread the almonds on a plate. Roll the fillets in the almonds until well coated. Place the fillets on top of the trivet. Secure the lid. Select the Manual mode and set the cooking time for 5 minutes at High Pressure. Once cooking is complete, do a quick pressure release. Carefully open the lid. Divide the fillets among the plates and serve.

Teriyaki Salmon

Prep time: 5 minutes | Cook time: 0 minutes | Serves 4

1 pound (454 g) salmon fillets
½ cup packed light brown sugar
½ cup rice vinegar

½ cup soy sauce
1 tablespoon cornstarch
1 teaspoon minced ginger
¼ teaspoon garlic powder

Place the salmon fillets into the Instant Pot. Whisk together the remaining ingredients in a small bowl until well combined. Pour the mixture over the salmon fillets, turning to coat. Secure the lid. Select the Manual mode and set the cooking time for 0 minutes at High Pressure. Once cooking is complete, do a natural pressure release for 10 minutes, then release any remaining pressure. Carefully open the lid. Serve hot.

Salmon Cakes

Prep time: 15 minutes | Cook time: 9 minutes | Serves 4

½ pound (227 g) cooked salmon, shredded	1 tablespoon Worcestershire sauce
2 medium green onions, sliced	1 teaspoon salt
2 large eggs, lightly beaten	½ tablespoon garlic powder
1 cup bread crumbs	½ teaspoon cayenne pepper
½ cup chopped flat leaf parsley	¼ teaspoon celery seed
¼ cup soy sauce	4 tablespoons olive oil, divided

Stir together all the ingredients except the olive oil in a large mixing bowl until combined. Set your Instant Pot to Sauté and heat 2 tablespoons of olive oil. Scoop out golf ball-sized clumps of the salmon mixture and roll them into balls, then flatten to form cakes. Working in batches, arrange the salmon cakes in an even layer in the Instant Pot. Cook each side for 2 minutes until golden brown. Transfer to a paper towel-lined plate. Repeat with the remaining 2 tablespoons of olive oil and salmon cakes. Serve immediately.

Honey Salmon

Prep time: 10 minutes | Cook time: o minutes | Serves 4

Salmon:

1 cup water	½ teaspoon salt
1 pound (454 g) salmon fillets	¼ teaspoon black pepper

Sauce:

½ cup honey	2 tablespoons rice vinegar
4 cloves garlic, minced	1 teaspoon sesame seeds
4 tablespoons soy sauce	

Pour the water into the Instant Pot and insert a trivet. Season the salmon fillets with salt and pepper to taste, then place on the trivet. Secure the lid. Select the Manual mode and set the cooking time for 0 minutes at High Pressure. Once cooking is complete, do a natural pressure release for 10 minutes, then release any remaining pressure. Carefully open the lid. Meanwhile, whisk together all the ingredients for the sauce in a small bowl until well mixed. Transfer the fillets to a plate and pour the sauce over them. Serve hot.

White Fish and Vegetables

Prep time: 15 minutes | Cook time: 15 minutes | Serves 2

1 cup water	¼ long red chili, sliced
2 fillets white fish	2 tablespoons soy sauce
½ pound (227 g) frozen vegetables of your choice	1 tablespoon honey
2 teaspoons grated ginger	Salt and ground black pepper, to taste
1 clove garlic, minced	

Pour the water into the Instant Pot and place the trivet in the bottom of the pot. Place the vegetables in a pan. Put the pan on the trivet. Stir together the ginger, garlic, red chili, soy sauce, honey, salt, and pepper in a bowl. Add the fillets and stir until well coated. Lay the fish fillets on the vegetables. Secure the lid. Select the Steam function and cook for 15 minutes at Low Pressure. When the timer goes off, do a natural pressure release for 10 minutes and then release any remaining pressure. Carefully open the lid. Transfer to a serving plate and serve.

Fast Salmon with Broccoli

Prep time: 5 minutes | Cook time: 5 minutes | Serves 2

1 cup water	8 ounces (227 g) salmon fillets
8 ounces (227 g) broccoli, cut into florets	Salt and ground black pepper, to taste

Pour the water into the Instant Pot and insert a trivet. Season the salmon and broccoli florets with salt and pepper. Put them on the trivet. Secure the lid. Select the Steam mode and set the cooking time for 5 minutes at High Pressure. Once cooking is complete, do a natural pressure release for 10 minutes, then release any remaining pressure. Carefully open the lid. Serve hot.

Chili-Lemon Sockeye Salmon

Prep time: 5 minutes | Cook time: 5 minutes | Serves 4

4 wild sockeye salmon fillets	Salt and ground black pepper, to taste
¼ cup lemon juice	1 cup water
2 tablespoons assorted chili pepper seasoning	

Drizzle the salmon fillets with lemon juice. Season with the chili pepper seasoning, salt, and pepper. Pour the water into the Instant Pot and add a steamer basket. Put the salmon fillets in the steamer basket. Secure the lid. Select the Manual mode and set the cooking time for 5 minutes at High Pressure. Once cooking is complete, do a quick pressure release. Carefully open the lid. Remove from the Instant Pot and serve.

Mayonnaise Salmon

Prep time: 5 minutes | Cook time: 15 minutes | Serves 4 to 6

½ cup mayonnaise	Salt and ground pepper, to taste
4 cloves garlic, minced	2 tablespoons olive oil
1 tablespoon lemon juice	Chopped green onion, for garnish
1 teaspoon dried basil leaves	
2 pounds (907 g) salmon fillets	

Stir together the mayo, garlic, lemon juice, and basil in a bowl. Set aside. Season the salmon fillets with salt and pepper to taste. Press the Sauté button on the Instant Pot and heat the olive oil. Add the seasoned fillets and brown each side for 5 minutes. Add the mayo mixture to the Instant Pot and coat the fillets. Continue cooking for another 5 minutes, flipping occasionally. Remove from the Instant Pot to a plate and serve garnished with the green onions.

Cod Fillets with Lemon and Dill

Prep time: 5 minutes | Cook time: 5 minutes | Serves 2

1 cup water	Salt and ground black pepper, to taste
2 cod fillets	4 slices lemon
¼ teaspoon garlic powder	2 tablespoons butter
2 sprigs fresh dill	

Add the water to the Instant Pot and put the trivet in the bottom of the pot. Arrange the cod fillets on the trivet. Sprinkle with the garlic powder, salt, and pepper. Layer 1 sprig of dill, 2 lemon slices, and 1 tablespoon of butter on each fillet. Secure the lid. Select the Manual mode and set the cooking time for 5 minutes on High Pressure. Once the timer beeps, use quick pressure release. Carefully remove the lid. Serve.

Tuna Noodle Casserole

Prep time: 5 minutes | Cook time: 4 minutes | Serves 4

3 cups water
28 ounces (794 g) cream of mushroom soup
14 ounces (397 g) canned tuna, drained
20 ounces (567 g) egg noodles

1 cup frozen peas
Salt and ground black pepper, to taste
4 ounces (113 g) grated Cheddar cheese
¼ cup bread crumbs (optional)

Combine the water and mushroom soup in the Instant Pot. Stir in the tuna, egg noodles, and peas. Season with salt and pepper. Secure the lid. Select the Manual mode and set the cooking time for 4 minutes at High Pressure. When the timer beeps, perform a quick pressure release. Carefully remove the lid. Scatter the grated cheese and bread crumbs (if desired) on top. Lock the lid and allow to sit for 5 minutes. Serve warm.

Creamy Tuna and Eggs

Prep time: 5 minutes | Cook time: 15 minutes | Serves 4

2 cans tuna, drained
2 eggs, beaten
1 can cream of celery soup
2 carrots, peeled and chopped
1 cup frozen peas
½ cup water

¾ cup milk
¼ cup diced onions
2 tablespoons butter
Salt and ground black pepper, to taste

Combine all the ingredients in the Instant Pot and stir to mix well. Secure the lid. Select the Manual mode and set the cooking time for 15 minutes at High Pressure. Once cooking is complete, do a quick pressure release. Carefully open the lid. Divide the mix into bowls and serve.

Wild Alaskan Cod with Cherry Tomatoes

Prep time: 5 minutes | Cook time: 8 minutes | Serves 2

1 large fillet wild Alaskan Cod
1 cup cherry tomatoes, chopped

Salt and ground black pepper, to taste
2 tablespoons butter

Add the tomatoes to your Instant Pot. Top with the cod fillet. Sprinkle with the salt and pepper. Secure the lid. Press the Manual button on your Instant Pot and set the cooking time for 8 minutes on High Pressure. Once the timer goes off, perform a quick pressure release. Carefully remove the lid. Add the butter to the cod fillet. Secure the lid and let stand for 1 minute. Transfer to a serving plate and serve.

Lemony Shrimp

Prep time: 10 minutes | Cook time: 3 minutes | Serves 4 to 6

2 tablespoons butter
1 tablespoon lemon juice
1 tablespoon garlic, minced
½ cup chicken stock
½ cup white wine

2 pounds (907 g) shrimp
Salt and ground black pepper, to taste
1 tablespoon parsley, for garnish

Place the butter, lemon juice, and garlic in your Instant Pot. Stir in the stock and wine. Add the shrimp and sprinkle with the salt and pepper. Stir well. Secure the lid. Press the Manual button on your Instant Pot and set the cooking time for 3 minutes at High Pressure. Once the timer beeps, do a quick pressure release. Carefully remove the lid. Serve topped with the parsley.

Garlic and Lemon Cod

Prep time: 10 minutes | Cook time: 5 minutes | Serves 4

1 pound (454 g) cod fillets
4 cloves garlic, smashed
1 medium lemon, cut into wedges

½ teaspoon salt
¼ teaspoon black pepper
1 tablespoon olive oil
1 cup water

Place the cod, garlic, and lemon in the center of aluminum foil. Sprinkle with the salt and pepper. Drizzle the oil over the top. Fold the foil up on all sides and crimp the edges tightly. Place the trivet in the bottom of your Instant Pot. Pour in the water. Carefully lower the foil packet into the pot. Secure the lid. Select the Manual mode and cook for 5 minutes on Low Pressure. Once the timer goes off, do a quick release pressure. Carefully open the lid. Lift the foil packet out of your Instant Pot. Carefully open the foil packet. Squeeze fresh lemon juice over the cod and serve.

Citrus Mahi Mahi

Prep time: 5 minutes | Cook time: 4 minutes | Serves 4

½ cup filtered water
3 tablespoons grass-fed butter, softened
1 tablespoon grated ginger
½ lime, juiced
½ lemon, juiced
½ teaspoon dried basil

½ teaspoon garlic, minced
½ teaspoon kosher salt
½ teaspoon freshly ground black pepper
4 mahi mahi fillets
Cooking spray

Add the water to the Instant Pot and place the trivet inside the pot. Mix together the butter, ginger, lime juice, lemon juice, basil, garlic, salt, and black pepper in a large bowl. Stir well. Add the mahi mahi filets to this mixture and stir to coat. Spray an Instant Pot-friendly dish with cooking spray and place the fillets in the dish. Place the dish onto the pot and wrap loosely in aluminum foil. Secure the lid. Select the Manual mode and cook for 4 minutes on Low Pressure. Once cook is complete, do a quick pressure release. Carefully open the lid. Transfer the fillets to a serving plate and serve immediately.

Braised Squid in Tomato Sauce

Prep time: 5 minutes | Cook time: 27 minutes | Serves 4

2 tablespoons olive oil
1 medium yellow onion, chopped
1 teaspoon dried oregano
4 medium garlic cloves, chopped
1 pound (454 g) frozen cleaned and sliced squid

¼ cup dry red wine
1 (14-ounce / 397-g) can diced tomatoes with Italian herbs, with juice
Salt and freshly ground black pepper, to taste
Lemon wedges, for garnish

Set your Instant Pot to Sauté. Add and heat the oil. Add the onion and sauté for 6 minutes until slightly browned. Fold in the oregano and garlic and cook for 45 seconds until fragrant. Pour in the wine and let simmer for 1 minute, scraping any browned bits out of the bottom of the pot. Mix in the squid, tomatoes, and several grinds of pepper. Secure the lid. Select the Manual setting and cook for 20 minutes at High Pressure. Once cooking is complete, do a quick pressure release. Carefully remove the lid. Sprinkle with the salt and pepper. Transfer to a serving plate and serve with the lemon wedges, if desired.

Cod with Orange Sauce

Prep time: 10 minutes | Cook time: 7 minutes | Serves 4

4 cod fillets, boneless
1 cup white wine
Juice from 1 orange
A small grated ginger piece

Salt and ground black pepper, to taste
4 spring onions, chopped

Combine the wine, orange juice, and ginger in your Instant Pot and stir well. Insert a steamer basket. Arrange the cod fillets on the basket. Sprinkle with the salt and pepper. Secure the lid. Press the Manual button on your Instant Pot and set the cooking time for 7 minutes on High Pressure. Once the timer beeps, do a quick pressure release. Carefully remove the lid. Drizzle the sauce all over the fish and sprinkle with the green onions. Transfer to a serving plate and serve immediately.

Steamed Shrimp with Asparagus

Prep time: 10 minutes | Cook time: 2 minutes | Serves 2

1 pound (454 g) shrimp, frozen or fresh, peeled and deveined
1 cup water
6 ounces (170 g) asparagus

1 teaspoon olive oil
½ tablespoon Cajun seasoning (or your choice of seasoning)

Pour the water into the Instant pot and place the trivet inside the pot. Place the asparagus onto the trivet. Arrange the shrimp on the asparagus and drizzle the olive oil over the top. Season with Cajun seasoning. Press the Steam button on the Instant pot and cook for 2 minutes at Low Pressure. Once the timer beeps, do a quick pressure release. Carefully remove the lid. Transfer to a serving plate and serve immediately.

Fish Tacos with Cabbage

Prep time: 15 minutes | Cook time: 5 minutes | Serves 4

1 cup water
3 tablespoons olive oil
1 (1-ounce / 28-g) packet taco seasoning
1 pound (454 g) cod fillets
3 tablespoons full-fat sour cream

3 tablespoons mayonnaise
1 tablespoon lime juice
1 teaspoon sriracha
⅛ teaspoon cumin
⅛ teaspoon garlic powder
8 small corn tortillas
1 cup shredded red cabbage

Add the water to your Instant Pot and place the trivet inside the pot. Combine the oil and taco seasoning in a small bowl. Brush the cod with the mixture. Lay the seasoned cod on the trivet. Lock the lid. Select the Manual mode and cook for 5 minutes at Low Pressure. Once cooking is complete, perform a quick pressure release. Carefully open the lid. Meanwhile, stir together the sour cream, mayonnaise, lime juice, sriracha, cumin, and garlic powder in another small bowl. Serve the cod wrapped in the tortillas with the sauce and cabbage.

Steamed Fish with Tomatoes and Olives

Prep time: 15 minutes | Cook time: 10 minutes | Serves 4

4 white fish fillets
1 cup water
1 cup olives, pitted and chopped
1 pound (454 g) cherry tomatoes, cut into halves

1 tablespoon olive oil
½ teaspoon dried thyme
1 clove garlic, minced
Salt and ground black pepper, to taste

Pour the water into the Instant Pot and insert a steamer basket. Add the fish fillets to the basket. Top with the olives and tomato halves. Stir in the olive oil, thyme, garlic, salt, and pepper. Secure the lid. Press the Manual button on your Instant Pot and set the cooking time for 10 minutes on Low Pressure. Once the timer beeps, do a natural pressure release for 10 minutes. Carefully remove the lid. Serve the fish with the mix.

Red Snapper Poached in Salsa

Prep time: 5 minutes | Cook time: 3 to 4 minutes | Serves 2

2 (6-ounce / 170-g) snapper fillets
1 teaspoon kosher salt
½ teaspoon freshly ground black pepper

1½ cups fresh salsa
¼ cup pale lager beer or water
½ lime
Cooked rice, for serving

Place the trivet inside the inner pot of your Instant Pot. Sprinkle the fish with the salt and pepper. Pour the salsa and beer into the pot and top with the fish. Squeeze the fresh lime juice over the fish and salsa. Lock the lid. Select the Manual mode and set the cooking time for 3 to 4 minutes on High Pressure, depending on the thickness of the fish. Once the cooking is complete, use a quick pressure release. Carefully open the lid. Transfer the fish to a serving plate and serve over rice.

Shrimp Spaghetti with Parmesan

Prep time: 5 minutes | Cook time: 10 minutes | Serves 4

6 tablespoons butter, divided
12 ounces (340 g) small shrimp, peeled and deveined
½ teaspoon salt
4 cups chicken broth

1 pound (454 g) spaghetti
1 cup grated Parmesan cheese
1 cup heavy whipping cream
1 teaspoon lemon pepper

Set your Instant Pot to Sauté and add 2 tablespoons of butter. Add the shrimp and salt to the Instant Pot and sauté for 4 minutes, or until the flesh is pink and opaque. Remove the shrimp and set aside. Add the broth and scrape up any bits on the bottom of the pot. Break the spaghetti in half and add to the pot. Place the remaining 4 tablespoons of butter on top. Secure the lid. Press the Manual button on the Instant Pot and cook for 5 minutes on High Pressure. Once the timer goes off, use a quick pressure release. Carefully open the lid. Fold in the cooked shrimp, Parmesan, cream, and lemon pepper. Stir until thoroughly combined. Transfer to a serving plate and serve hot.

Lemon-Dijon Orange Roughy

Prep time: 5 minutes | Cook time: 3 hours | Serves 4

1½ pounds (680 g) orange roughy fillets
2 tablespoons Dijon mustard
3 tablespoons butter, melted

1 teaspoon Worcestershire sauce
1 tablespoon lemon juice

Cut fillets to fit in the Instant Pot. In a bowl, mix remaining ingredients together. Pour sauce over fish. (If you have to stack the fish, spoon a portion of the sauce over the first layer of fish before adding the second layer.) Cover and press the Slow Cook button, and cook on low for 3 hours, or until fish flakes easily but is not dry or overcooked. (Press Slow Cook again to toggle between Low and High cooking temperatures.)

Shrimp and Sausage Boil

Prep time: 5 minutes | Cook time: 4 minutes | Serves 2

½ pound (227 g) red potatoes, halved
1 cup water
2 ears of corn, shucked and broken in half
½ pound (227 g) fully cooked kielbasa sausage, cut into 2-inch slices
1 medium sweet onion, chopped
2 tablespoons crab boil seasoning (optional)
2 tablespoons Old Bay seasoning, plus more for seasoning
½ teaspoon kosher salt
1 pound (454 g) peel-on large raw shrimp, deveined

Mix together the potatoes, water, corn, onion, kielbasa, the crab boil seasoning (if desired), 2 tablespoons of Old Bay, and salt in your Instant pot. Lock the lid. Select the Manual mode and cook for 4 minutes on High Pressure. Once cooking is complete, do a quick pressure release. Carefully open the lid. Mix in the shrimp and stir well. Replace the lid loosely and let stand for 3 to 4 minutes. Sprinkle with the salt and Old Bay. Transfer the shrimp to a large colander and drain. Serve.

Curry-Flavored Shrimp

Prep time: 10 minutes | Cook time: 4 minutes | Serves 2 to 4

2 cups water
1 pound (454 g) shrimp, peeled and deveined
8 ounces (227 g) unsweetened coconut milk
1 teaspoon curry powder
1 tablespoon garlic, minced
Salt and ground black pepper, to taste

Pour the water into the Instant Pot and insert a trivet. Mix together the shrimp, coconut milk, curry powder, and garlic in a large bowl. Sprinkle with the salt and pepper. Add the mixture to the pan and place the dish onto the trivet, uncovered. Secure the lid. Press the Manual button on the Instant Pot and cook for 4 minutes at Low Pressure. Once cooking is complete, use a quick pressure release. Carefully open the lid. Stir well and serve.

Smoky Salmon Fettuccine

Prep time: 10 minutes | Cook time: 1 to 2 hours | Serves 4

2 cups heavy cream
3 to 4 ounces (85 to 113 g) top quality lox or smoked salmon, chopped or flaked into ½-inch pieces
1 pound (454 g) fresh
fettuccine, regular egg or spinach flavored
2 tablespoons olive oil (optional)
Freshly ground black pepper, to taste

Combine the cream and the lox in the Instant Pot. Cover and press the Slow Cook button, and cook on low for 1 to 2 hours, until very hot. (Press Slow Cook again to toggle between Low and High cooking temperatures.) Meanwhile, cook the fettuccine in boiling water until tender to the bite, about 3 minutes. Take care not to overcook. Toss with the olive oil if the pasta is to stand for over 5 minutes. Add the fettuccine to the hot sauce and toss to coat evenly. If your Instant Pot is large enough, just add the pasta; if not, pour the sauce over the pasta in a shallow, heated bowl. Garnish with a few grinds of black pepper and serve immediately.

Shrimp Scampi with Tomatoes

Prep time: 10 minutes | Cook time: 3 minutes | Serves 2 to 4

2 tablespoons olive oil
1 clove garlic, minced
1 pound (454 g) shrimp, peeled and deveined
10 ounces (284 g) canned tomatoes, chopped
⅓ cup tomato paste
⅓ cup water
1 tablespoon parsley, finely chopped
¼ teaspoon dried oregano
½ teaspoon kosher salt
½ teaspoon ground black pepper, to taste
1 cup grated Parmesan Cheese

Set the Instant Pot to Sauté. Add and heat the oil. Add the garlic and sauté for 1 minute until fragrant. Stir in the shrimp, tomatoes, tomato paste, water, parsley, oregano, salt and pepper. Secure the lid. Select the Manual function and cook for 3 minutes on High Pressure. When the timer beeps, do a quick pressure release. Carefully remove the lid. Serve scattered with the Parmesan Cheese.

Crabs with Coconut Milk

Prep time: 10 minutes | Cook time: 9 minutes | Serves 2 to 4

1 tablespoon olive oil
1 onion, chopped
3 cloves garlic, minced
1 pound (454 g) crabs, halved
1 can coconut milk
1 lemongrass stalk
1 thumb-size ginger, sliced
Salt and ground black pepper, to taste

Set the Instant Pot to Sauté. Add and heat the oil. Add the onion and sauté for 2 minutes until tender. Mix in the garlic and sauté for another 1 minute until fragrant. Add the crabs, coconut milk, lemongrass stalk, ginger, salt, and pepper. Secure the lid. Select the Manual function and set the cooking time for 6 minutes at High Pressure. Once the timer beeps, do a quick pressure release. Carefully remove the lid. Transfer to a serving plate and serve immediately.

Miso-Honey Poached Salmon

Prep time: 5 minutes | Cook time: 1½ hours | Serves 8

3 pounds (1.4 kg) salmon fillets
3 tablespoons white Miso
3 tablespoons honey
¼ cup rice wine (mirin) or dry
sherry
2 teaspoons freshly grated ginger

Place the salmon in the insert of the Instant Pot. Combine the miso, honey, rice wine, and ginger in a mixing bowl and stir. Pour the sauce over the salmon in the Instant Pot. Cover and press the Slow Cook button, and cook on high for 1½ hours, until the salmon is cooked through and registers 165ºF (74ºC) on an instant-read thermometer inserted in the center of a thick fillet. (Press Slow Cook again to toggle between Low and High cooking temperatures.) Carefully remove the salmon from the Instant Pot insert with a large spatula. Remove the skin from the underside of the salmon (if necessary) and arrange the salmon on a serving platter. Strain the sauce through a fine-mesh sieve into a saucepan. Boil the sauce, reduce it to a syrupy consistency, and serve with the salmon.

Buttery Halibut with Garlic
Prep time: 10 minutes | Cook time: 4¾ hours | Serves 6

1 cup (2 sticks) unsalted butter
½ cup olive oil
6 cloves garlic, sliced
1 teaspoon sweet paprika
½ cup lemon juice
Grated zest of 1 lemon

¼ cup finely chopped fresh chives
2 to 3 pounds (907 g to 1.4 kg) halibut fillets
½ cup finely chopped fresh Italian parsley

Combine the butter, oil, garlic, paprika, lemon juice, zest, and chives in the insert of the Instant Pot and stir to combine. Cover and press the Slow Cook button, and cook on low for 4 hours. (Press Slow Cook again to toggle between Low and High cooking temperatures.) Add the halibut to the pot, spooning the sauce over the halibut. Cover and cook for an additional 40 minutes, until the halibut is cooked through and opaque. Sprinkle the parsley evenly over the fish and serve immediately.

Cheesy Halibut with Salsa
Prep time: 10 minutes | Cook time: 2½ to 2¾ hours | Serves 6

3 cups prepared medium-hot salsa
2 tablespoons fresh lime juice
2 to 3 pounds (907 g to 1.4 kg) halibut fillets

1 teaspoon ground cumin
1½ cup finely shredded Monterey Jack cheese (or Pepper Jack for a spicy topping)

Combine the salsa, lime juice, and cumin in the insert of the Instant Pot and stir. Cover the Instant Pot and press the Slow Cook button, and cook on low for 2 hours. (Press Slow Cook again to toggle between Low and High cooking temperatures.) Put the halibut in the Instant Pot and spoon some of the sauce over the top of the fish. Sprinkle the cheese evenly over the fish. Cover and cook for an additional 30 to 45 minutes. Remove the halibut from the Instant Pot and serve on a bed of the sauce.

Scallops Braised in Dry Sherry
Prep time: 10 minutes | Cook time: 4½ hours | Serves 6

1 cup (2 sticks) unsalted butter
2 tablespoons olive oil
2 cloves garlic, minced
2 teaspoons sweet paprika
¼ cup dry sherry

2 pounds (907 g) dry-pack sea scallops
½ cup finely chopped fresh Italian parsley

Put the butter, oil, garlic, paprika, and sherry in the insert of a Instant Pot. Cover and press the Slow Cook button, and cook on low for 4 hours. (Press Slow Cook again to toggle between Low and High cooking temperatures.) Add the scallops, tossing them in the butter sauce. Cover and press the Slow Cook button, and cook on high for 30 to 40 minutes, until the scallops are opaque. (Press Slow Cook again to toggle between Low and High cooking temperatures.) Transfer the scallops and sauce from the Instant Pot to a serving platter. Sprinkle with the parsley and serve.

Garlicky Crab in White Wine
Prep time: 10 minutes | Cook time: 5½ hours | Serves 6 to 8

1 cup (2 sticks) unsalted butter
½ cup olive oil
10 cloves garlic, sliced
2 tablespoons Old Bay seasoning
2 cups dry white wine or

vermouth
1 lemon, thinly sliced
3 to 4 pounds (1.4 to 1.8 kg) cooked crab legs and claws, cracked

Put the butter, oil, garlic, seasoning, wine, and lemon in the insert of the Instant Pot. Cover and press the Slow Cook button, and cook on low for 4 hours. (Press Slow Cook again to toggle between Low and High cooking temperatures.) Add the crab, spoon the sauce over the crab, and cook for an additional 1½ hours, turning the crab in the sauce during cooking. Serve the crab from the Instant Pot set on warm.

Sweet and Hot Salmon
Prep time: 5 minutes | Cook time: 1½ hours | Serves 6

3 pounds (1.4 kg) salmon fillets
½ cup Colman's English mustard

¼ cup honey
2 tablespoons finely chopped fresh dill

Place the salmon in the insert of the Instant Pot. Put the mustard, honey, and dill in a small bowl and stir to combine. Pour the mixture over the salmon, spreading evenly. Cover and press the Slow Cook button, and cook on high for 1½ hours, until the salmon is cooked through. (Press Slow Cook again to toggle between Low and High cooking temperatures.) Serve the salmon from the Instant Pot topped with some of the sauce.

Pork Steaks with Pico de Gallo

Prep time: 15 minutes | Cook time: 12 minutes | Serves 6

1 tablespoon butter
2 pounds (907 g) pork steaks
1 bell pepper, deseeded and sliced
½ cup shallots, chopped
2 garlic cloves, minced
¼ cup dry red wine
1 cup chicken bone broth
¼ cup water
Salt, to taste
¼ teaspoon freshly ground

black pepper, or more to taste
Pico de Gallo:
1 tomato, chopped
1 chili pepper, seeded and minced
½ cup red onion, chopped
2 garlic cloves, minced
1 tablespoon fresh cilantro, finely chopped
Sea salt, to taste

Press the Sauté button to heat up the Instant Pot. Melt the butter and sear the pork steaks about 4 minutes or until browned on both sides. Add bell pepper, shallot, garlic, wine, chicken bone broth, water, salt, and black pepper to the Instant Pot. Secure the lid. Choose the Pressure Cook mode and set cooking time for 8 minutes at High pressure. Meanwhile, combine the ingredients for the Pico de Gallo in a small bowl. Refrigerate until ready to serve. Once cooking is complete, use a quick pressure release. Carefully remove the lid. Serve warm pork steaks with the chilled Pico de Gallo on the side.

Beef and Riced Cauliflower Casserole

Prep time: 15 minutes | Cook time: 26 minutes | Serves 5

2 cups fresh cauliflower florets
1 pound (454 g) ground beef
5 slices uncooked bacon, chopped
8 ounces (227 g) unsweetened tomato purée
1 cup shredded Cheddar cheese, divided

1 teaspoon garlic powder
½ teaspoon paprika
½ teaspoon sea salt
¼ teaspoon ground black pepper
¼ teaspoon celery seed
1 cup water
1 medium Roma tomato, sliced

Spray a round soufflé dish with coconut oil cooking spray. Set aside. Add the cauliflower florets to a food processor and pulse until a riced. Set aside. Select Sauté mode. Once the pot is hot, crumble the ground beef into the pot and add the bacon. Sauté for 6 minutes or until the ground beef is browned and the bacon is cooked through. Transfer the beef, bacon, and rendered fat to a large bowl. Add the cauliflower rice, tomato purée, ½ cup Cheddar cheese, garlic powder, paprika, sea salt, black pepper, and celery seed to the bowl with the beef and bacon. Mix well to combine. Add the mixture to the prepared dish and use a spoon to press and smooth the mixture into an even layer. Place the trivet in the Instant Pot and add the water to the bottom of the pot. Place the dish on top of the trivet. Lock the lid. Select Pressure Cook mode and set cooking time for 20 minutes on High Pressure. When cooking is complete, quick release the pressure. Open the lid. Arrange the tomato slices in a single layer on top of the casserole and sprinkle the remaining cheese over top. Secure the lid and let the residual heat melt the cheese for 5 minutes. Open the lid, remove the dish from the pot. Transfer the casserole to a serving plate and slice into 5 equal-sized wedges. Serve warm.

Paprika Beef Short Ribs with Radishes

Prep time: 20 minutes | Cook time: 56 minutes | Serves 4

¼ teaspoon ground coriander
¼ teaspoon ground cumin
1 teaspoon kosher salt, plus more to taste
½ teaspoon smoked paprika
Pinch of ground allspice (optional)
4 (8-ounce / 227-g) bone-in

beef short ribs
2 tablespoons avocado oil
1 cup water
2 radishes, ends trimmed, leaves rinsed and roughly chopped
Freshly ground black pepper, to taste

In a small bowl, mix together the coriander, cumin, salt, paprika, and allspice. Rub the spice mixture all over the short ribs. Set the Instant Pot to Sauté mode and add the oil to heat. Add the short ribs, bone side up. Brown for 4 minutes on each side. Pour the water into the Instant Pot. Secure the lid. Press the Pressure Cook button and set cooking time for 45 minutes on High Pressure. When timer beeps, allow the pressure to release naturally for 10 minutes, then release any remaining pressure. Open the lid. Remove the short ribs to a serving plate. Add the radishes to the sauce in the pot. Place a metal steaming basket directly on top of the radishes and place the radish leaves in the basket. Secure the lid. Press the Pressure Cook button and set cooking time for 3 minutes on High Pressure. When timer beeps, quick release the pressure. Open the lid. Transfer the leaves to a serving bowl. Sprinkle with with salt and pepper. Remove the radishes and place on top of the leaves. Serve hot with the short ribs.

Carnitas with Avocado

Prep time: 10 minutes | Cook time: 45 minutes | Serves 4

1 onion, sliced
4 garlic cloves, sliced
1 pound (454 g) pork shoulder, cut into cubes, visible fat removed
Juice of 1 lemon
¼ teaspoon ancho chili powder
¼ teaspoon chipotle chili powder
½ teaspoon dried oregano

½ teaspoon roasted cumin powder
¼ teaspoon smoked paprika
1 to 2 teaspoons salt
1 teaspoon freshly ground black pepper
½ cup water
1 to 2 tablespoons coconut oil
½ cup sour cream
½ avocado, diced

Place the onion and garlic in the Instant Pot to help them release water when the meat is cooking. In a large bowl, mix together the pork and lemon juice. Add the ancho chili powder, chipotle chili powder, oregano, cumin, paprika, salt, and pepper, and stir to combine. Place the pork on top of the onions and garlic. Pour the water into the bowl and swirl to get the last of the spices, then pour the liquid onto the pork. Lock the lid. Select Pressure Cook mode. Set cooking time for 35 minutes on High Pressure. When cooking is complete, let the pressure release naturally for 10 minutes, then release any remaining pressure. Unlock the lid. Remove the pork, leaving the liquid in the pot. Switch the pot to Sauté and bring the sauce to a boil until it is thickened. Place a cast iron skillet over medium-high heat. Once it is hot, add the oil. Shred the pork, then place in the skillet. Let the meat brown for 4 minutes. When the meat is browned on the bottom, stir and continue cooking until it's crisp in parts. Add the sauce from the pot. Serve with the sour cream and diced avocado.

Barbecue Pork Ribs

Prep time: 6 minutes | Cook time: 35 minutes | Serves 5

1½ cups beef broth
2 pounds (907 g) country-style boneless pork ribs
For the Sauce:

1½ tablespoons unsalted butter	1 tablespoon apple cider vinegar
½ tablespoon Worcestershire sauce	1½ teaspoons liquid smoke
½ teaspoon blackstrap molasses	2 tablespoons Erythritol
1 cup unsweetened tomato purée	1 teaspoon garlic powder
	½ teaspoon sea salt
	½ teaspoon onion powder

For the Dry Rub:

1½ teaspoons smoked paprika	1 teaspoon sea salt
1½ teaspoons onion powder	1 teaspoon ground black pepper
1 teaspoon garlic powder	⅛ teaspoon cayenne pepper
1 teaspoon ground cumin	

Add the butter to a small saucepan and heat over medium heat. Once the butter is melted, add the Worcestershire sauce, molasses, tomato purée, vinegar, liquid smoke, Erythritol, garlic powder, sea salt, and onion powder. Stir until well combined and then remove from the heat. Set aside. Comb the paprika, onion powder, garlic powder, cumin, sea salt, black pepper, and cayenne pepper in a small bowl. Mix well to combine. Set aside. Add the beef broth to the Instant Pot and place the trivet in the pot. Generously sprinkle the dry rub over the pork and gently rub the spices into the meat. Stack the seasoned ribs on the trivet. Pour half the barbecue sauce over the ribs, reserving the remaining sauce for serving. Lock the lid. Select Pressure Cook mode and set cooking time for 35 minutes on High Pressure. When cooking is complete, allow the pressure to release naturally for 20 minutes, then release any remaining pressure. Open the lid and use tongs to carefully transfer the ribs to a serving plate. Using a pastry brush, brush the reserved sauce over the ribs. Serve warm.

Barbecue-Glazed Beef Back Ribs

Prep time: 10 minutes | Cook time: 35 minutes | Serves 4

½ cup water	¼ teaspoon garlic powder
1 (3-pound / 1.4-kg) rack beef back ribs, prepared with rub of choice	2 teaspoons apple cider vinegar
¼ cup unsweetened tomato purée	¼ teaspoon liquid smoke
¼ teaspoon Worcestershire sauce	¼ teaspoon smoked paprika
	3 tablespoons Swerve
	Dash of cayenne pepper

Pour the water in the pot and place the trivet inside. Arrange the ribs on top of the trivet. Close the lid. Select Pressure Cook mode and set cooking time for 25 minutes on High Pressure. Meanwhile, prepare the glaze by whisking together the tomato purée, Worcestershire sauce, garlic powder, vinegar, liquid smoke, paprika, Swerve, and cayenne in a medium bowl. Heat the broiler. When timer beeps, quick release the pressure. Open the lid. Remove the ribs and place on a baking sheet. Brush a layer of glaze on the ribs. Put under the broiler for 5 minutes. Remove from the broiler and brush with glaze again. Put back under the broiler for 5 more minutes, or until the tops are sticky. Serve immediately.

Lamb Shanks with Red Wine

Prep time: 10 minutes | Cook time: 55 minutes | Serves 4

2 tablespoons olive oil	¾ cup red wine
2 pounds (907 g) lamb shanks	2 cups crushed tomatoes
Salt and black pepper, to taste	1 teaspoon dried oregano
6 garlic cloves, minced	¼ cup chopped parsley, for garnish
1 cup chicken broth	

Press the Sauté button on the Instant Pot. Heat the olive oil and add the lamb to the pot. Season with salt and pepper. Sear the lamb on both sides for 6 minutes, or until browned. Transfer the lamb to a plate and set aside. Add the garlic to the pot and sauté for 30 seconds, or until fragrant. Stir in the chicken broth and red wine and cook for 2 minutes, stirring constantly. Add the tomatoes and oregano. Stir and cook for 2 minutes. Return the lamb to the pot and baste with the chicken broth mixture. Lock the lid. Select the Pressure Cook setting and set the cooking time for 45 minutes on High Pressure. When the timer beeps, do a natural pressure release for 15 minutes, then release any remaining pressure. Open the lid. Top with the chopped parsley and adjust the taste with salt and pepper. Divide among 4 plates and serve warm.

Pork Meatloaf with Boiled Eggs

Prep time: 20 minutes | Cook time: 25 minutes | Serves 6

1 tablespoon avocado oil	pepper
1½ cup ground pork	2 tablespoons coconut flour
1 teaspoon chives	3 eggs, hard-boiled, peeled
1 teaspoon salt	1 cup water
½ teaspoon ground black	

Brush a loaf pan with avocado oil. In the mixing bowl, mix the ground pork, chives, salt, ground black pepper, and coconut flour. Transfer the mixture in the loaf pan and flatten with a spatula. Fill the meatloaf with hard-boiled eggs. Pour water and insert the trivet in the Instant Pot. Lower the loaf pan over the trivet in the Instant Pot. Close the lid. Select Pressure Cook mode and set cooking time for 25 minutes on High Pressure. When timer beeps, use a natural pressure release for 10 minutes, then release any remaining pressure. Open the lid. Serve immediately.

Pork and Eggplant Lasagna

Prep time: 20 minutes | Cook time: 30 minutes | Serves 6

2 eggplants, sliced	1 tablespoon unsweetened tomato purée
1 teaspoon salt	1 teaspoon butter, softened
10 ounces (283 g) ground pork	1 cup chicken stock
1 cup Mozzarella, shredded	

Sprinkle the eggplants with salt and let sit for 10 minutes, then pat dry with paper towels. In a mixing bowl, mix the ground pork, butter, and tomato purée. Make a layer of the sliced eggplants in the bottom of the Instant Pot and top with ground pork mixture. Top the ground pork with Mozzarella and repeat with remaining ingredients. Pour in the chicken stock. Close the lid. Select Pressure Cook mode and set cooking time for 30 minutes on High Pressure. When timer beeps, use a natural pressure release for 10 minutes, then release the remaining pressure and open the lid. Cool for 10 minutes and serve.

Hawaiian Roasted Pulled Pork

Prep time: 10 minutes | Cook time: 1 hour 2 minutes | Serves 6

1½ tablespoons olive oil
3 pounds (1.4 kg) pork shoulder roast, cut into 4 equal-sized pieces
3 cloves garlic, minced

1 tablespoon liquid smoke
2 cups water, divided
1 tablespoon sea salt
2 cups shredded cabbage

Select Sauté mode and add the olive oil to the Instant Pot. Once the oil is hot, add the pork cuts and sear for 5 minutes per side or until browned. Once browned, transfer the pork to a platter and set aside. Add the garlic, liquid smoke, and 1½ cups water to the Instant Pot. Stir to combine. Return the pork to the pot and sprinkle the salt over top. Lock the lid. Select Pressure Cook mode and set cooking time for 1 hour on High Pressure. When cooking is complete, allow the pressure to release naturally for 20 minutes, then release any remaining pressure. Open the lid and transfer the pork to a large platter. Using two forks, shred the pork. Set aside. Add the shredded cabbage and remaining water to the liquid in the pot. Stir. Lock the lid. Select Pressure Cook mode and set cooking time for 2 minutes on High Pressure. When cooking is complete, quick release the pressure. Transfer the cabbage to the serving platter with the pork. Serve warm.

Pot Roast

Prep time: 15 minutes | Cook time: 1 hour 8 minutes | Serves 6

¼ cup dry red wine
1 tablespoon dried thyme
1½ cups beef broth
½ tablespoon dried rosemary
1 teaspoon paprika
1 teaspoon garlic powder
1½ teaspoons sea salt
½ teaspoon ground black pepper
1½ tablespoons avocado oil

3 pounds (1.4 kg) boneless chuck roast
2 tablespoons unsalted butter
½ medium yellow onion, chopped
2 garlic cloves, minced
1 cup sliced mushrooms
4 stalks celery, chopped
2 sprigs fresh thyme
1 bay leaf

In a medium bowl, combine the wine, dried thyme, beef broth, and dried rosemary. Stir to combine. Set aside. In a small bowl, combine the paprika, garlic powder, sea salt, and black pepper. Mix well. Generously rub the dry spice mixture into the roast. Set aside. Select Sauté mode. Once the pot becomes hot, add the avocado oil and butter and heat until the butter is melted, about 2 minutes. Add the roast to the pot. Sauté for 3 minutes per side or until a crust is formed. Transfer the browned roast to a plate and set aside. Add the onions and garlic to the pot. Sauté for 3 minutes or until the onions soften and the garlic becomes fragrant. Add half the broth and wine mixture to the pot. Place the trivet in the Instant Pot and place the roast on top of the trivet. Add the mushrooms and celery to the pot, and pour the remaining broth and wine mixture over the roast. Place the thyme sprigs and bay leaf on top of the roast. Lock the lid. Select Pressure Cook mode and set cooking time for 1 hour on High Pressure. When cooking is complete, allow the pressure to release naturally for 10 minutes and then release the remaining pressure. Open the lid, discard the bay leaf and thyme sprigs. Transfer the roast to a serving platter. Transfer the vegetables to the platter and spoon the remaining broth over the roast and vegetables. Slice the roast and ladle ¼ cup of the broth over each serving. Serve hot.

Rosemary Lamb Loin Chops

Prep time: 10 minutes | Cook time: 29 minutes | Serves 2

1½ tablespoons butter
1 pound (454 g) lamb loin chops
½ small onion, sliced
1 garlic clove, crushed
1 cup carrots, peeled and sliced
¾ cup diced sugar-free

tomatoes
½ cup bone broth
¾ teaspoon crushed dried rosemary
Salt and black pepper, to taste
1 tablespoon arrowroot starch
½ tablespoon cold water

Select the Sauté mode and heat the butter in the Instant Pot. Add the lamb chops to the pot and cook for 3 minutes on each side, or until lightly browned. Transfer the lamb chops to plates. Add the onion and garlic to the pot and cook for 3 minutes. Stir in the carrots, tomatoes, bone broth, rosemary, salt and pepper. Lock the lid. Select the Pressure Cook mode and set the cooking time for 15 minutes at High Pressure. When the timer goes off, do a quick pressure release. Carefully open the lid. In a small bowl, whisk together the arrowroot starch and water. Pour the slurry in the pot. Select the Sauté mode and cook for 5 minutes. Spread the sauce over the cooked chops and serve hot.

Bacon-Stuffed Beef Meatloaf

Prep time: 15 minutes | Cook time: 32 minutes | Serves 4

1 pound (454 g) ground beef
1 large egg, beaten
½ cup unsweetened tomato purée
2 tablespoons golden flaxseed meal
1 teaspoon garlic powder
1 teaspoon sea salt
For The Glaze:
⅓ cup unsweetened tomato purée
1 teaspoon apple cider vinegar
¼ teaspoon onion powder

½ teaspoon paprika
¼ teaspoon ground black pepper
4 slices uncooked bacon
⅓ cup shredded Cheddar cheese
1 cup water

¼ teaspoon garlic powder
2 teaspoons Erythritol
⅛ teaspoon sea salt
⅛ teaspoon allspice

In a large bowl, combine the ground beef, egg, tomato purée, flaxseed meal, garlic powder, sea salt, paprika, and black pepper. Mix to combine well. Place a sheet of aluminum foil on a flat surface. Place half of the meat mixture in the center of the foil sheet and use the hands to mold the mixture into a flat oval shape that is about 6 inches long. Place the bacon slices on top of the meat and sprinkle the Cheddar over. Place the remaining meat mixture on top and shape the mixture into an oval-shaped loaf. Fold the sides of the foil up and around the sides of the meatloaf to form a loaf pan. Set aside. Make the tomato glaze by combining the tomato purée, vinegar, onion powder, garlic powder, Erythritol, sea salt, and allspice in a small bowl. Mix well. Spoon the glaze over the meatloaf. Add the water to the Instant Pot. Place the loaf on the trivet and lower the trivet into the pot. Lock the lid. Select Pressure Cook mode and set cooking time for 30 minutes on High Pressure. While the meatloaf is cooking, preheat the oven broiler to 550°F (288°C). When cooking time is complete, quick release the pressure, then open the lid and carefully remove the meatloaf from the pot. Transfer the loaf pan to a large baking sheet. Place the meatloaf under the broiler to brown for 2 minutes or until the glaze is bubbling. Transfer the browned meatloaf to a serving plate, discard the foil, and cut the loaf into 8 equal-sized slices. Serve hot.

Garlicky Beef Brisket with Green Cabbage

Prep time: 15 minutes | Cook time: 1 hour 7 minutes | Serves 8

3 pounds (1.4 kg) corned beef brisket
4 cups water
3 garlic cloves, minced
2 teaspoons yellow mustard seed

2 teaspoons black peppercorns
3 celery stalks, chopped
½ large white onion, chopped
1 green cabbage, cut into quarters

Add the brisket to the Instant Pot. Pour the water into the pot. Add the garlic, mustard seed, and black peppercorns. Lock the lid. Select Pressure Cook mode and set cooking time for 50 minutes on High Pressure. When cooking is complete, allow the pressure to release naturally for 20 minutes, then release any remaining pressure. Open the lid and transfer only the brisket to a platter. Add the celery, onion, and cabbage to the pot. Lock the lid. Select Pressure Cook mode and set cooking time for 12 minutes on High Pressure. When cooking is complete, quick release the pressure. Open the lid, add the brisket back to the pot and let warm in the pot for 5 minutes. Transfer the warmed brisket back to the platter and thinly slice. Transfer the vegetables to the platter. Serve hot.

Beef Roast Masala

Prep time: 10 minutes | Cook time: 20 minutes | Serves 4

2 tomatoes, quartered
1 small onion, quartered
4 garlic cloves, chopped
½ cup fresh cilantro leaves
1 teaspoon garam masala
½ teaspoon ground coriander

1 teaspoon ground cumin
½ teaspoon cayenne
1 teaspoon salt
1 pound (454 g) beef chuck roast, cut into 1-inch cubes

In a blender, combine the tomatoes, onion, garlic, and cilantro. Process until the vegetables are puréed. Add the garam masala, coriander, cumin, cayenne, and salt. Process for several more seconds. To the Instant Pot, add the beef and pour the vegetable purée on top. Lock the lid. Select Pressure Cook mode and set cooking time for 20 minutes on High Pressure. When timer beeps, let the pressure release naturally for 10 minutes, then release any remaining pressure. Unlock the lid. Stir and serve immediately.

Carne Guisada

Prep time: 10 minutes | Cook time: 20 minutes | Serves 4

2 tomatoes, chopped
1 red bell pepper, chopped
½ onion, chopped
3 garlic cloves, chopped
1 teaspoon ancho chili powder
1 tablespoon ground cumin
½ teaspoon dried oregano
1 teaspoons salt

1 teaspoon freshly ground black pepper
1 teaspoon smoked paprika
1 pound (454 g) beef chuck, cut into large pieces
¾ cup water, plus 2 tablespoons
¼ teaspoon xanthan gum

In a blender, purée the tomatoes, bell pepper, onion, garlic, chili powder, cumin, oregano, salt, pepper, and paprika. Put the beef pieces in the Instant Pot. Pour in the blended mixture. Use ¾ cup of water to wash out the blender and pour the liquid into the pot. Lock the lid. Select Pressure Cook mode and set cooking time for 20 minutes on High Pressure. When cooking is complete, quick release the pressure. Unlock the lid. Switch the pot to Sauté mode. Bring the stew to a boil. Put the xanthan gum and 2 tablespoons of water into the boiling stew and stir until it thickens. Serve immediately.

Beef and Cheddar Burger Pie

Prep time: 15 minutes | Cook time: 30 minutes | Serves 6

1 tablespoon olive oil
1 pound (454 g) ground beef
3 eggs (1 beaten)
½ cup unsweetened tomato purée
2 tablespoons golden flaxseed meal
1 garlic clove, minced
½ teaspoon Italian seasoning blend

½ teaspoon sea salt
½ teaspoon smoked paprika
½ teaspoon onion powder
2 tablespoons heavy cream
½ teaspoon ground mustard
¼ teaspoon ground black pepper
2 cups water
½ cup grated Cheddar cheese

Coat a round cake pan with the olive oil. Select Sauté mode. Once the pot is hot, add the ground beef and sauté for 5 minutes or until the beef is browned. Transfer the beef to a large bowl. Add the 1 beaten egg, tomato purée, flaxseed meal, garlic, Italian seasoning, sea salt, smoked paprika, and onion powder to the bowl. Mix until well combined. Transfer the meat mixture to the prepared cake pan and use a knife to spread the mixture into an even layer. Set aside. In a separate medium bowl, combine the 2 remaining eggs, heavy cream, ground mustard, and black pepper. Whisk until combined. Pour the egg mixture over the meat mixture. Tightly cover the pan with a sheet of aluminum foil. Place the trivet in the Instant Pot and add the water to the bottom of the pot. Place the pan on the trivet. Lock the lid. Select Pressure Cook mode and set cooking time for 20 minutes on High Pressure. When cooking is complete, allow the pressure to release naturally for 10 minutes and then release the remaining pressure. Allow the pie to rest in the pot for 5 minutes. Preheat the oven broiler to 450°F (235°C). Open the lid, remove the pan from the pot. Remove the foil and sprinkle the Cheddar over top of the pie. Place the pie in the oven and broil for 2 minutes or until the cheese is melted and the top becomes golden brown. Slice into six equal-sized wedges. Serve hot.

Braised Tri-Tip Steak with Turnip

Prep time: 20 minutes | Cook time: 54 minutes | Serves 4

2 pounds (907 g) tri-tip steak, pat dry
2 teaspoons coarse sea salt
3 tablespoons avocado oil
½ medium onion, diced
2 cloves garlic, smashed
1 tablespoon unsweetened tomato purée

1½ cups dry red wine
½ tablespoon dried thyme
2 bay leaves
1 Roma (plum) tomato, diced
1 stalk celery, including leaves, chopped
1 small turnip, chopped
½ cup water

Season the tri-tip with the coarse salt. Set the Instant Pot to Sauté mode and heat the avocado oil until shimmering. Cook the steak in the pot for 2 minutes per side or until well browned. Remove the steak from the pot and place it in a shallow bowl. Set aside. Add the onion to the pot and sauté for 3 minutes. Add the garlic and sauté for 1 minute. Add the unsweetened tomato purée and cook for 1 minute, stirring constantly. Pour in the red wine. Stir in the thyme and bay leaves. Return the tri-tip steak to the pot. Scatter the tomato, celery, and turnip around the steak. Pour in the water. Secure the lid. Press the Pressure Cook button and set cooking time for 35 minutes on High Pressure. When timer beeps, allow the pressure to release naturally for 20 minutes, then release any remaining pressure. Open the lid. Discard the bay leaves. Remove the steak and place in a dish. Press the Sauté button and bring the braising liquid to a boil. Cook for 10 minutes or until the liquid is reduced by about half. Slice the steak thinly and serve with braising liquid over.

Beef Shawarma Salad Bowls

Prep time: 10 minutes | Cook time: 19 minutes | Serves 4

2 teaspoons olive oil	½ cup Greek yogurt
1½ pounds (680 g) beef flank steak, thinly sliced	2 tablespoons sesame oil
	1 tablespoon fresh lime juice
Sea salt and freshly ground black pepper, to taste	2 English cucumbers, chopped
	1 cup cherry tomatoes, halved
1 teaspoon cayenne pepper	1 red onion, thinly sliced
½ teaspoon ground bay leaf	½ head romaine lettuce, chopped
½ teaspoon ground allspice	
½ teaspoon cumin, divided	

Press the Sauté button to heat up the Instant Pot. Then, heat the olive oil and cook the beef for about 4 minutes. Add all seasonings, 1½ cups of water, and secure the lid. Choose Pressure Cook mode. Set the cook time for 15 minutes on High Pressure. Once cooking is complete, use a natural pressure release. Carefully remove the lid. Allow the beef to cool completely. To make the dressing, whisk Greek yogurt, sesame oil, and lime juice in a mixing bowl. Then, divide cucumbers, tomatoes, red onion, and romaine lettuce among four serving bowls. Dress the salad and top with the reserved beef flank steak. Serve warm.

Beef Stuffed Kale Rolls

Prep time: 15 minutes | Cook time: 30 minutes | Serves 4

8 ounces (227 g) ground beef	1 tablespoon cream cheese
1 teaspoon chives	¼ cup heavy cream
¼ teaspoon cayenne pepper	½ cup chicken broth
4 kale leaves	

In the mixing bowl, combine the ground beef, chives, and cayenne pepper. Then fill and roll the kale leaves with ground beef mixture. Place the kale rolls in the Instant Pot. Add cream cheese, heavy cream, and chicken broth. Close the lid. Select Manual mode mode and set cooking time for 30 minutes on High Pressure When timer beeps, make a quick pressure release. Open the lid. Serve warm.

Beef Shoulder Roast with Champagne Vinegar

Prep time: 15 minutes | Cook time: 46 minutes | Serves 6

2 tablespoons peanut oil	2 tablespoons champagne vinegar
2 pounds (907 g) shoulder roast	
	½ teaspoon hot sauce
¼ cup coconut aminos	1 teaspoon celery seeds
1 teaspoon porcini powder	1 cup purple onions, cut into wedges
1 teaspoon garlic powder	
1 cup beef broth	1 tablespoon flaxseed meal, plus 2 tablespoons water
2 cloves garlic, minced	

Press the Sauté button to heat up the Instant Pot. Then, heat the peanut oil and cook the beef shoulder roast for 3 minutes on each side. In a mixing dish, combine coconut aminos, porcini powder, garlic powder, broth, garlic, vinegar, hot sauce, and celery seeds. Pour the broth mixture into the Instant Pot. Add the onions to the top. Secure the lid. Choose Pressure Cook mode and set cooking time for 40 minutes on High Pressure. Once cooking is complete, use a natural pressure release for 15 mintues, then release any remaining pressure. Carefully remove the lid. Make the slurry by mixing flaxseed meal with 2 tablespoons of water. Add the slurry to the Instant Pot. Press the Sauté button and allow it to cook until the cooking liquid is reduced and thickened slightly. Serve warm.

Beef Shawarma and Veggie Salad Bowls

Prep time: 10 minutes | Cook time: 19 minutes | Serves 4

2 teaspoons olive oil	½ cup Greek yogurt
1½ pounds (680 g) beef flank steak, thinly sliced	2 tablespoons sesame oil
	1 tablespoon fresh lime juice
Sea salt and freshly ground black pepper, to taste	2 English cucumbers, chopped
	1 cup cherry tomatoes, halved
1 teaspoon cayenne pepper	1 red onion, thinly sliced
½ teaspoon ground bay leaf	½ head romaine lettuce, chopped
½ teaspoon ground allspice	
½ teaspoon cumin, divided	

Press the Sauté button to heat up the Instant Pot. Then, heat the olive oil and cook the beef for about 4 minutes. Add all seasonings, 1½ cups of water, and secure the lid. Choose Manual mode. Set the cook time for 15 minutes on High Pressure. Once cooking is complete, use a natural pressure release. Carefully remove the lid. Allow the beef to cool completely. To make the dressing, whisk Greek yogurt, sesame oil, and lime juice in a mixing bowl. Then, divide cucumbers, tomatoes, red onion, and romaine lettuce among four serving bowls. Dress the salad and top with the reserved beef flank steak. Serve warm.

Rogan Josh

Prep time: 5 minutes | Cook time: 15 minutes | Serves 4

1 pound (454 g) lamb shoulder, boneless, chopped	½ teaspoon coriander powder
	½ teaspoon ground turmeric
1 teaspoon unsweetened tomato purée	1 teaspoon ground cardamom
	¼ teaspoon chili powder
½ cup unsweetened almond milk	1 teaspoon coconut oil

Put all ingredients in the Instant Pot. Stir to mix well. Close the lid. Select Manual mode and set cooking time for 15 minutes on High Pressure. When timer beeps, use a quick pressure release. Open the lid and stir well. Serve immediately.

Galbijjim

Prep time: 10 minutes | Cook time: 12 minutes | Serves 8

2 pounds (907 g) meaty short ribs	1 teaspoon Swerve
	¼ teaspoon powdered stevia
2 tablespoons gochujang	1 teaspoon salt
4 garlic cloves, crushed	2 teaspoons freshly ground black pepper
1 tablespoon mirin	
3 tablespoons coconut aminos	1 tablespoon sesame oil
2 teaspoons minced fresh ginger	¼ cup water
	¼ teaspoon xanthan gum

Put the ribs into a large zip-top bag. Whisk in the remaining ingredients, except for the water and xanthan gum. Shake to coat the ribs well and seal the bag. Marinate the ribs in the refrigerator for at least 1 hour. Put the ribs and marinade in the Instant Pot along with the water. Lock the lid. Select Manual mode and set cooking time for 12 minutes on High Pressure. When cooking is complete, let the pressure release naturally for 5 minutes, then release any remaining pressure. Unlock the lid. Turn the Instant Pot on Sauté mode. Transfer the ribs to a platter. Bring the sauce to a boil, then fold in the xanthan gum and stir until the sauce thickens. Pour the sauce over the ribs and serve.

Ropa Vieja

Prep time: 10 minutes | Cook time: 35 minutes | Serves 4

1 pound (454 g) beef chuck steak
2 cups canned diced fire-roasted tomatoes, with their juices
1 cup sliced bell peppers
1½ cups sliced onions
6 garlic cloves, peeled
½ teaspoon ancho chili powder
1 teaspoon ground cumin
½ teaspoon dried oregano
1 teaspoon smoked paprika
1 teaspoon salt
½ cup sliced olives, for garnish

Put all the ingredients, except for the olives, in the Instant Pot. Stir to mix well. Lock the lid. Select Meat/Stew mode. Set cooking time for 30 minutes on High Pressure. When cooking is complete, let the pressure release naturally for 10 minutes, then release any remaining pressure. Unlock the lid. Remove the steak from the pot. Switch the Instant Pot to Sauté mode. Bring the sauce to a boil. Meanwhile, cut the steak into long slices, then put back into the sauce. Garnish with the sliced olives and serve warm..

New York Strip with Heavy Cream

Prep time: 15 minutes | Cook time: 30 minutes | Serves 4

1 tablespoon sesame oil
1 pound (454 g) New York strip, sliced into thin strips
½ leek, sliced
1 carrot, sliced
⅓ cup dry red wine
½ tablespoon tamari
½ cup cream of mushroom soup
1 clove garlic, sliced
Kosher salt and ground black pepper, to taste
¼ cup heavy cream

Press the Sauté button of the Instant Pot. Heat the sesame oil until sizzling. Add and brown the beef strips in batches for 4 minutes. Stir in the remaining ingredients, except for the heavy cream. Secure the lid. Choose the Manual mode and set the cooking time for 20 minutes at High pressure. Once cooking is complete, use a quick pressure release. Carefully open the lid. Transfer the beef on a serving plate. Mash the vegetables in the pot with a potato masher. Press the Sauté button. Bring to a boil, then Stir in the heavy cream. Spoon the mixture over the New York strip and serve immediately.

Philly Steak Sub

Prep time: 20 minutes | Cook time: 13 minutes | Serves 4

1½ pounds (680 g) flat iron steak
1 tablespoon olive oil
4 teaspoons garlic seasoning
1 cup beef broth
1 large red bell pepper, cut into
1-inch-wide strips
2 tablespoons soy sauce
4 crusty sub sandwich rolls, split lengthwise
4 slices provolone cheese

Select the Sauté mode. Brush the steak with the olive oil and rub with garlic seasoning. Add the steaks in batches to the pot and cook for 8 minutes until well browned. Flip the steaks halfway through. Transfer the steaks to a cutting board and slice into ¼- to ½-inch-thick slices. Return the meat to the pot. Add the broth, bell peppers, and soy sauce. Lock the lid, select the Manual function, and set the cooking time for 5 minutes on High Pressure. When timer beeps, let the pressure release naturally for 10 minutes, then release any remaining pressure. Carefully open the lid. Remove the beef and vegetables from the pot. Mound the beef and peppers on the rolls. Top with slices of cheese and serve.

Bacon Stuffed Meatloaf with Tomato Glaze

Prep time: 15 minutes | Cook time: 32 minutes | Serves 4

1 pound (454 g) ground beef
1 large egg, beaten
½ cup unsweetened tomato purée
2 tablespoons golden flaxseed meal
1 teaspoon garlic powder
1 teaspoon sea salt
For The Glaze:
⅓ cup unsweetened tomato purée
1 teaspoon apple cider vinegar
¼ teaspoon onion powder
½ teaspoon paprika
¼ teaspoon ground black pepper
4 slices uncooked bacon
⅓ cup shredded Cheddar cheese
1 cup water

¼ teaspoon garlic powder
2 teaspoons Erythritol
⅛ teaspoon sea salt
⅛ teaspoon allspice

In a large bowl, combine the ground beef, egg, tomato purée, flaxseed meal, garlic powder, sea salt, paprika, and black pepper. Mix to combine well. Place a sheet of aluminum foil on a flat surface. Place half of the meat mixture in the center of the foil sheet and use the hands to mold the mixture into a flat oval shape that is about 6 inches long. Place the bacon slices on top of the meat and sprinkle the Cheddar over. Place the remaining meat mixture on top and shape the mixture into an oval-shaped loaf. Fold the sides of the foil up and around the sides of the meatloaf to form a loaf pan. Set aside. Make the tomato glaze by combining the tomato purée, vinegar, onion powder, garlic powder, Erythritol, sea salt, and allspice in a small bowl. Mix well. Spoon the glaze over the meatloaf. Add the water to the Instant Pot. Place the loaf on the trivet and lower the trivet into the pot. Lock the lid. Select Pressure Cook mode and set cooking time for 30 minutes on High Pressure. While the meatloaf is cooking, preheat the oven broiler to 550°F (288°C). When cooking time is complete, quick release the pressure, then open the lid and carefully remove the meatloaf from the pot. Transfer the loaf pan to a large baking sheet. Place the meatloaf under the broiler to brown for 2 minutes or until the glaze is bubbling. Transfer the browned meatloaf to a serving plate, discard the foil, and cut the loaf into 8 equal-sized slices. Serve hot.

Indian Lamb Korma

Prep time: 15 minutes | Cook time: 25 minutes | Serves 6

1 (6-inch) Anaheim chile, minced
1 clove garlic, grated
½ medium onion, chopped
2 tablespoons coconut oil
½ teaspoon grated fresh ginger
1 teaspoon garam masala
¼ teaspoon ground cardamom
Pinch of ground cinnamon
2 teaspoons ground cumin
1 teaspoon coriander seeds
1 teaspoon sea salt
½ teaspoon cayenne pepper
½ tablespoon unsweetened tomato purée
1 cup chicken broth
3 pounds (1.4 kg) lamb shoulder, cut into 1-inch cubes
¼ cup full-fat coconut milk
½ cup full-fat Greek yogurt

Preheat the Instant Pot on Sauté mode. Add the chile, garlic, onion, coconut oil, and ginger and sauté for 2 minutes. Add the garam masala, cardamom, cinnamon, cumin, coriander seeds, salt, cayenne, and unsweetened tomato purée and sauté for a minute or until fragrant. Pour in the broth. Add the lamb and stir well. Secure the lid. Press the Manual button and set cooking time for 15 minutes on High Pressure. When timer beeps, quick release the pressure. Open the lid. Stir in the coconut milk and yogurt. Switch to Sauté mode and bring the mixture to a simmer for 5 minutes, stirring occasionally until thickened. Serve hot.

Cheesy Bacon Stuffed Meatloaf

Prep time: 15 minutes | Cook time: 32 minutes | Serves 4

1 pound (454 g) ground beef
1 large egg, beaten
½ cup unsweetened tomato purée
2 tablespoons golden flaxseed meal
1 teaspoon garlic powder
1 teaspoon sea salt

½ teaspoon paprika
¼ teaspoon ground black pepper
4 slices uncooked bacon
⅓ cup shredded Cheddar cheese
1 cup water

For The Glaze:

⅓ cup unsweetened tomato purée
1 teaspoon apple cider vinegar
¼ teaspoon onion powder

¼ teaspoon garlic powder
2 teaspoons erythritol
⅛ teaspoon sea salt
⅛ teaspoon allspice

In a large bowl, combine the ground beef, egg, tomato purée, flaxseed meal, garlic powder, sea salt, paprika, and black pepper. Mix to combine well. Place a sheet of aluminum foil on a flat surface. Place half of the meat mixture in the center of the foil sheet and use the hands to mold the mixture into a flat oval shape that is about 6 inches long. Place the bacon slices on top of the meat and sprinkle the Cheddar over. Place the remaining meat mixture on top and shape the mixture into an oval-shaped loaf. Fold the sides of the foil up and around the sides of the meatloaf to form a loaf pan. Set aside. Make the tomato glaze by combining the tomato purée, vinegar, onion powder, garlic powder, erythritol, sea salt, and allspice in a small bowl. Mix well. Spoon the glaze over the meatloaf. Add the water to the Instant Pot. Place the loaf on the trivet and lower the trivet into the pot. Lock the lid. Select Manual mode and set cooking time for 30 minutes on High Pressure. While the meatloaf is cooking, preheat the oven broiler to 550°F (288°C). When cooking time is complete, quick release the pressure, then open the lid and carefully remove the meatloaf from the pot. Transfer the loaf pan to a large baking sheet. Place the meatloaf under the broiler to brown for 2 minutes or until the glaze is bubbling. Transfer the browned meatloaf to a serving plate, discard the foil, and cut the loaf into 8 equal-sized slices. Serve hot.

Beef Shoulder Roast

Prep time: 15 minutes | Cook time: 46 minutes | Serves 6

2 tablespoons peanut oil
2 pounds (907 g) shoulder roast
¼ cup coconut aminos
1 teaspoon porcini powder
1 teaspoon garlic powder
1 cup beef broth
2 cloves garlic, minced

2 tablespoons champagne vinegar
½ teaspoon hot sauce
1 teaspoon celery seeds
1 cup purple onions, cut into wedges
1 tablespoon flaxseed meal, plus 2 tablespoons water

Press the Sauté button to heat up the Instant Pot. Then, heat the peanut oil and cook the beef shoulder roast for 3 minutes on each side. In a mixing dish, combine coconut aminos, porcini powder, garlic powder, broth, garlic, vinegar, hot sauce, and celery seeds. Pour the broth mixture into the Instant Pot. Add the onions to the top. Secure the lid. Choose Meat/Stew mode and set cooking time for 40 minutes on High Pressure. Once cooking is complete, use a natural pressure release for 15 mintues, then release any remaining pressure. Carefully remove the lid. Make the slurry by mixing flaxseed meal with 2 tablespoons of water. Add the slurry to the Instant Pot. Press the Sauté button and allow it to cook until the cooking liquid is reduced and thickened slightly. Serve warm.

Pot Roast

Prep time: 15 minutes | Cook time: 1 hour 8 minutes | Serves 6

¼ cup dry red wine
1 tablespoon dried thyme
1½ cups beef broth
½ tablespoon dried rosemary
1 teaspoon paprika
1 teaspoon garlic powder
1½ teaspoons sea salt
½ teaspoon ground black pepper
1½ tablespoons avocado oil

3 pounds (1.4 kg) boneless chuck roast
2 tablespoons unsalted butter
½ medium yellow onion, chopped
2 garlic cloves, minced
1 cup sliced mushrooms
4 stalks celery, chopped
2 sprigs fresh thyme
1 bay leaf

In a medium bowl, combine the wine, dried thyme, beef broth, and dried rosemary. Stir to combine. Set aside. In a small bowl, combine the paprika, garlic powder, sea salt, and black pepper. Mix well. Generously rub the dry spice mixture into the roast. Set aside. Select Sauté mode. Once the pot becomes hot, add the avocado oil and butter and heat until the butter is melted, about 2 minutes. Add the roast to the pot. Sauté for 3 minutes per side or until a crust is formed. Transfer the browned roast to a plate and set aside. Add the onions and garlic to the pot. Sauté for 3 minutes or until the onions soften and the garlic becomes fragrant. Add half the broth and wine mixture to the pot. Place the trivet in the Instant Pot and place the roast on top of the trivet. Add the mushrooms and celery to the pot, and pour the remaining broth and wine mixture over the roast. Place the thyme sprigs and bay leaf on top of the roast. Lock the lid. Select Manual mode and set cooking time for 1 hour on High Pressure. When cooking is complete, allow the pressure to release naturally for 10 minutes and then release the remaining pressure. Open the lid, discard the bay leaf and thyme sprigs. Transfer the roast to a serving platter. Transfer the vegetables to the platter and spoon the remaining broth over the roast and vegetables. Slice the roast and ladle ¼ cup of the broth over each serving. Serve hot.

Lamb Burgers

Prep time: 10 minutes | Cook time: 14 minutes | Serves 2

10 ounces (283 g) ground lamb
½ teaspoon chili powder
1 teaspoon dried cilantro
1 teaspoon garlic powder

½ teaspoon salt
¼ cup water
1 tablespoon coconut oil

In a mixing bowl, mix the ground lamb, chili powder, dried cilantro, garlic powder, salt, and water. Shape the mixture into 2 burgers. Melt the coconut oil on Sauté mode. Put the burgers in the hot oil and cook for 7 minutes on each side or until well browned. Serve immediately.

Greek Lamb Leg

Prep time: 10 minutes | Cook time: 50 minutes | Serves 4

1 pound (454 g) lamb leg
½ teaspoon dried thyme
1 teaspoon paprika powder
¼ teaspoon cumin seeds

1 tablespoon softened butter
2 garlic cloves
¼ cup water

Rub the lamb leg with dried thyme, paprika powder, and cumin seeds on a clean work surface. Brush the leg with softened butter and transfer to the Instant Pot. Add garlic cloves and water. Close the lid. Select Manual mode and set cooking time for 50 minutes on High Pressure. When timer beeps, use a quick pressure release. Open the lid. Serve warm.

Beef, Bacon and Cauliflower Rice Casserole

Prep time: 15 minutes | Cook time: 26 minutes | Serves 5

2 cups fresh cauliflower florets	1 teaspoon garlic powder
1 pound (454 g) ground beef	½ teaspoon paprika
5 slices uncooked bacon, chopped	½ teaspoon sea salt
8 ounces (227 g) unsweetened tomato purée	¼ teaspoon ground black pepper
1 cup shredded Cheddar cheese, divided	¼ teaspoon celery seed
	1 cup water
	1 medium Roma tomato, sliced

Spray a round soufflé dish with coconut oil cooking spray. Set aside. Add the cauliflower florets to a food processor and pulse until a riced. Set aside. Select Sauté mode. Once the pot is hot, crumble the ground beef into the pot and add the bacon. Sauté for 6 minutes or until the ground beef is browned and the bacon is cooked through. Transfer the beef, bacon, and rendered fat to a large bowl. Add the cauliflower rice, tomato purée, ½ cup Cheddar cheese, garlic powder, paprika, sea salt, black pepper, and celery seed to the bowl with the beef and bacon. Mix well to combine. Add the mixture to the prepared dish and use a spoon to press and smooth the mixture into an even layer. Place the trivet in the Instant Pot and add the water to the bottom of the pot. Place the dish on top of the trivet. Lock the lid. Select Manual mode and set cooking time for 20 minutes on High Pressure. When cooking is complete, quick release the pressure. Open the lid. Arrange the tomato slices in a single layer on top of the casserole and sprinkle the remaining cheese over top. Secure the lid and let the residual heat melt the cheese for 5 minutes. Open the lid, remove the dish from the pot. Transfer the casserole to a serving plate and slice into 5 equal-sized wedges. Serve warm.

Classic Osso Buco with Gremolata

Prep time: 35 minutes | Cook time: 1 hour 2 minutes | Serves 6

4 bone-in beef shanks	1 tablespoon unsweetened tomato purée
Sea salt, to taste	½ cup dry white wine
2 tablespoons avocado oil	1 cup chicken broth
1 small turnip, diced	1 sprig fresh rosemary
1 medium onion, diced	2 sprigs fresh thyme
1 medium stalk celery, diced	3 Roma tomatoes, diced
4 cloves garlic, smashed	
For the Gremolata:	
½ cup loosely packed parsley leaves	1 clove garlic, crushed
	Grated zest of 2 lemons

On a clean work surface, season the shanks all over with salt. Set the Instant Pot to Sauté and add the oil. When the oil shimmers, add 2 shanks and sear for 4 minutes per side. Remove the shanks to a bowl and repeat with the remaining shanks. Set aside. Add the turnip, onion, and celery to the pot and cook for 5 minutes or until softened. Add the garlic and unsweetened tomato purée and cook 1 minute more, stirring frequently. Deglaze the pot with the wine, scraping the bottom with a wooden spoon to loosen any browned bits. Bring to a boil. Add the broth, rosemary, thyme, and shanks, then add the tomatoes on top of the shanks. Secure the lid. Press the Manual button and set cooking time for 40 minutes on High Pressure. Meanwhile, for the gremolata: In a small food processor, combine the parsley, garlic, and lemon zest and pulse until the parsley is finely chopped. Refrigerate until ready to use. When timer beeps, allow the pressure to release naturally for 20 minutes, then release any remaining pressure. Open the lid. To serve, transfer the shanks to large, shallow serving bowl. Ladle the braising sauce over the top and sprinkle with the gremolata.

Creamy Lamb Curry

Prep time: 10 minutes | Cook time: 30 minutes | Serves 4

1 teaspoon curry paste	chopped
2 tablespoons coconut cream	1 tablespoon fresh cilantro, chopped
¼ teaspoon chili powder	
1 pound (454 g) lamb shoulder,	½ cup heavy cream

In a bowl, mix the curry paste and coconut cream. Add the chili powder and chopped lamb shoulder. Toss to coat the lamb in the curry mixture well. Transfer the lamb and all remaining curry paste mixture in the Instant Pot. Add cilantro and heavy cream. Close the lid and select Manual mode. Set cooking time for 30 minutes on High Pressure. When timer beeps, do a quick pressure release. Open the lid. Serve warm.

Ground Beef with Okra

Prep time: 10 minutes | Cook time: 20 minutes | Serves 4

1 tablespoon avocado oil	1 teaspoon ground black pepper
7 ounces (198 g) ground beef	¼ cup water
1 cup okra, sliced	
1 teaspoon salt	

Heat the avocado oil in the Instant Pot on Sauté mode and add the ground beef. Sprinkle with salt and ground black pepper and sauté for 10 minutes or until the beef is browned. Add the sliced okra and stir to well. Pour in the water. Select Manual mode and set cooking time for 10 minutes on High Pressure. When timer beeps, use a quick pressure release. Open the lid. Serve immediately.

Braised Tri-Tip Steak

Prep time: 20 minutes | Cook time: 54 minutes | Serves 4

2 pounds (907 g) tri-tip steak, patted dry	1½ cups dry red wine
2 teaspoons coarse sea salt	½ tablespoon dried thyme
3 tablespoons avocado oil	2 bay leaves
½ medium onion, diced	1 Roma (plum) tomato, diced
2 cloves garlic, smashed	1 stalk celery, including leaves, chopped
1 tablespoon unsweetened tomato purée	1 small turnip, chopped
	½ cup water

Season the tri-tip with the coarse salt. Set the Instant Pot to Sauté mode and heat the avocado oil until shimmering. Cook the steak in the pot for 2 minutes per side or until well browned. Remove the steak from the pot and place it in a shallow bowl. Set aside. Add the onion to the pot and sauté for 3 minutes. Add the garlic and sauté for 1 minute. Add the unsweetened tomato purée and cook for 1 minute, stirring constantly. Pour in the red wine. Stir in the thyme and bay leaves. Return the tri-tip steak to the pot. Scatter the tomato, celery, and turnip around the steak. Pour in the water. Secure the lid. Press the Manual button and set cooking time for 35 minutes on High Pressure. When timer beeps, allow the pressure to release naturally for 20 minutes, then release any remaining pressure. Open the lid. Discard the bay leaves. Remove the steak and place in a dish. Press the Sauté button and bring the braising liquid to a boil. Cook for 10 minutes or until the liquid is reduced by about half. Slice the steak thinly and serve with braising liquid over.

Harissa Lamb

Prep time: 30 minutes | Cook time: 40 minutes | Serves 4

1 tablespoon keto-friendly Harissa sauce
1 teaspoon dried thyme
½ teaspoon salt
1 pound (454 g) lamb shoulder
2 tablespoons sesame oil
2 cups water

In a bowl, mix the Harissa, dried thyme, and salt. Rub the lamb shoulder with the Harissa mixture and brush with sesame oil. Heat the the Instant Pot on Sauté mode for 2 minutes and put the lamb shoulder inside. Cook the lamb for 3 minutes on each side, then pour in the water. Close the lid. Select Manual mode and set cooking time for 40 minutes on High Pressure. When timer beeps, use a natural pressure release for 25 minutes, then release any remaining pressure. Open the lid. Serve warm.

Herbed Lamb Shank

Prep time: 15 minutes | Cook time: 35 minutes | Serves 2

2 lamb shanks
1 rosemary spring
1 teaspoon coconut flour
¼ teaspoon onion powder
¼ teaspoon chili powder
¾ teaspoon ground ginger
½ cup beef broth
½ teaspoon avocado oil

Put all ingredients in the Instant Pot. Stir to mix well. Close the lid. Select Manual mode and set cooking time for 35 minutes on High Pressure. When timer beeps, use a natural pressure release for 15 minutes, then release any remaining pressure. Open the lid. Discard the rosemary sprig and serve warm.

Coconut Pork Muffins

Prep time: 5 minutes | Cook time: 9 minutes | Serves 2

1 egg, beaten
2 tablespoons coconut flour
1 teaspoon parsley
¼ teaspoon salt
1 tablespoon coconut cream
4 ounces (113 g) ground pork, fried
1 cup water

Whisk together the egg, coconut flour, parsley, salt, and coconut cream. Add the fried ground pork. Mix the the mixture until homogenous. Pour the mixture into a muffin pan. Pour the water in the Instant Pot and place in the trivet. Lower the muffin pan on the trivet and close the Instant Pot lid. Set the Manual mode and set cooking time for 4 minutes on High Pressure. When timer beeps, perform a natural pressure release for 5 minutes, then release any remaining pressure. Open the lid. Serve warm.

Hibachi Steak with Cremini Mushroom

Prep time: 10 minutes | Cook time: 10 minutes | Serves 4

1 pound (454 g) beef sirloin, roughly chopped
1 teaspoon ground ginger
¼ teaspoon garlic powder
¼ cup cremini mushrooms, sliced
2 tablespoons apple cider vinegar
1 tablespoon avocado oil
¼ cup water

Mix the beef sirloin, mushrooms, garlic powder, apple cider vinegar, ground ginger, and avocado oil in the Instant Pot. Pour in the water. Close the lid and select Manual mode. Set cooking time for 10 minutes on High Pressure. When timer beeps, allow a natural pressure release for 10 minutes, then release any remaining pressure. Open the lid. Serve warm.

Hearty Turkish Kebab Gyros

Prep time: 15 minutes | Cook time: 15 minutes | Serves 6

1 red onion, roughly chopped
6 garlic cloves
1 pound (454 g) ground beef
1 pound (454 g) ground pork or ground lamb
2 teaspoons dried rosemary
2 teaspoons dried oregano
2 teaspoons ground marjoram
2 teaspoons kosher salt
2 teaspoons freshly ground black pepper
2 cups water
1 cup tzatziki sauce

Put the onion and garlic into the food processor and process until finely chopped but not liquefied. Put the ground beef and ground pork in the bowl of a sturdy stand mixer with a paddle attachment. Sprinkle the meat with the rosemary, oregano, marjoram, salt, and pepper. Add the onions and garlic. Mix until sticky. Pour the water into the Instant Pot, then place a trivet in the pot. Lay out a sheet of aluminum foil, and make two 4-inch-thick meatloaf on top. Put this sheet of foil and the meat loaves on top of the trivet. Lock the lid. Select Manual mode. Set the time for 15 minutes on High Pressure. When cooking is complete, let the pressure release naturally for 5 minutes, then release any remaining pressure. Unlock the lid. Take out the meat loaves and cover them with foil. Place something heavy on top to compress them. Let the meat rest for 30 minutes and then cut into thin slices. Serve with the tzatziki sauce.

Hearty Chimichurri Skirt Steak

Prep time: 15 minutes | Cook time: 30 minutes | Serves 4

1 pound (454 g) skirt steak, trimmed and cut into 4 equal-sized pieces
½ teaspoon sea salt
Chimichurri:
⅓ cup chopped flat-leaf parsley
3 large garlic cloves, minced
2½ tablespoons red wine vinegar
½ teaspoon dried oregano
¼ teaspoon crushed red
½ teaspoon black pepper
1 tablespoon avocado oil
1 cup water

pepper
½ teaspoon sea salt
½ teaspoon black pepper
1 teaspoon lemon juice
½ cup extra virgin olive oil

Add the parsley to a food processor and pulse until finely chopped. Add the garlic, red wine vinegar, oregano, crushed red pepper, ½ teaspoon sea salt, ½ teaspoon black pepper, and lemon juice. Pulse until combined. Add the olive oil and pulse until the ingredients are well blended. Set aside. Season both sides of the steaks with the remaining salt and pepper. Select Sauté mode. Once the Instant Pot is hot, add the avocado oil and let heat for 1 minute. Add the steaks to the pot, two at a time, and sauté for 2 minutes per side or until browned on both sides. Transfer the browned steaks to a plate and repeat with the remaining steaks. Place one sheet on a flat surface. Place two steaks in the center of the sheet and pour half the chimichurri sauce over top of the steaks. Place the remaining steaks on top and pour the remaining sauce over top. Place another sheet of foil over the steaks and tightly roll and crimp the ends to create a foil packet. Place the trivet in the pot and add the water to the bottom of the pot. Place the foil packet on top of the trivet. Lock the lid. Select Manual mode and set cooking time for 25 minutes on High Pressure. When cooking is complete, allow the pressure to release naturally for 6 minutes and then release the remaining pressure. Open the lid, remove the steaks from the pot. Set the steaks aside to rest for 2 minutes. Open the packet and transfer the steaks to a cutting board. Thinly slice and transfer to a serving platter. Serve warm.

Icelandic Lamb with Turnip
Prep time: 5 minutes | Cook time: 45 minutes | Serves 4

12 ounces (340 g) lamb fillet, chopped
4 ounces (113 g) turnip, chopped
1 teaspoon unsweetened tomato purée
3 ounces (85 g) celery ribs,
chopped
¼ cup scallions, chopped
½ teaspoon salt
½ teaspoon ground black pepper
4 cups water

Put all ingredients in the Instant Pot and stir well. Close the lid. Select Manual mode and set cooking time for 45 minutes on High Pressure. When timer beeps, use a quick pressure release. Open the lid. Serve hot.

Italian Beef and Pork Rind Meatloaf
Prep time: 6 minutes | Cook time: 25 minutes | Serves 6

1 pound (454 g) ground beef
1 cup crushed pork rinds
1 egg
¼ cup grated Parmesan cheese
¼ cup Italian dressing
2 teaspoons Italian seasoning
½ cup water
½ cup unsweetened tomato purée
1 tablespoon chopped fresh parsley
1 clove garlic, minced

In large bowl, combine the beef, pork rinds, egg, cheese, dressing, and Italian seasoning. Stir to mix well. Pour the mixture in a baking pan and level with a spatula. Place the trivet in the pot and add the water. Place the pan on top of the trivet. Close the lid. Select Manual mode and set cooking time for 20 minutes on High Pressure. When timer beeps, use a quick pressure release. Open the lid. Meanwhile, whisk together the tomato purée, parsley, and garlic in a small bowl. Heat the broiler. Remove the pan from the pot. Spread the tomato purée mixture on top. Broil for 5 minutes or until sticky. Slice and serve.

Hawaiian Pulled Pork Roast with Cabbage
Prep time: 10 minutes | Cook time: 1 hour 2 minutes minutes | Serves 6

1½ tablespoons olive oil
3 pounds (1.4 kg) pork shoulder roast, cut into 4 equal-sized pieces
3 cloves garlic, minced
1 tablespoon liquid smoke
2 cups water, divided
1 tablespoon sea salt
2 cups shredded cabbage

Select Sauté mode and add the olive oil to the Instant Pot. Once the oil is hot, add the pork cuts and sear for 5 minutes per side or until browned. Once browned, transfer the pork to a platter and set aside. Add the garlic, liquid smoke, and 1½ cups water to the Instant Pot. Stir to combine. Return the pork to the pot and sprinkle the salt over top. Lock the lid. Select Manual mode and set cooking time for 1 hour on High Pressure. When cooking is complete, allow the pressure to release naturally for 20 minutes, then release any remaining pressure. Open the lid and transfer the pork to a large platter. Using two forks, shred the pork. Set aside. Add the shredded cabbage and remaining water to the liquid in the pot. Stir. Lock the lid. Select Manual mode and set cooking time for 2 minutes on High Pressure. When cooking is complete, quick release the pressure. Transfer the cabbage to the serving platter with the pork. Serve warm.

Chile Verde Pulled Pork with Tomatillos
Prep time: 15 minutes | Cook time: 1 hour 3 minutes | Serves 6

2 pounds (907 g) pork shoulder, cut into 6 equal-sized pieces
1 teaspoon sea salt
½ teaspoon ground black pepper
2 jalapeño peppers, deseeded and stemmed
1 pound (454 g) tomatillos, husks removed and quartered
3 garlic cloves
1 tablespoon lime juice
3 tablespoons fresh cilantro, chopped
1 medium white onion, chopped
1 teaspoon ground cumin
½ teaspoon dried oregano
1⅔ cups chicken broth
1½ tablespoons olive oil

Season the pork pieces with the salt and pepper. Gently rub the seasonings into the pork cuts. Set aside. Combine the jalapeños, tomatillos, garlic cloves, lime juice, cilantro, onions, cumin, oregano, and chicken broth in the blender. Pulse until well combined. Set aside. Select Sauté mode and add the olive oil to the pot. Once the oil is hot, add the pork cuts and sear for 4 minutes per side or until browned. Pour the jalapeño sauce over the pork and lightly stir to coat well. Lock the lid. Select Manual mode and set cooking time for 55 minutes on High Pressure. When cooking is complete, allow the pressure to release naturally for 10 minutes and then release the remaining pressure. Open the lid. Transfer the pork pieces to a cutting board and use two forks to shred the pork. Transfer the shredded pork back to the pot and stir to combine the pork with the sauce. Transfer to a serving platter. Serve warm.

Creamy Pork Liver
Prep time: 5 minutes | Cook time: 7 minutes | Serves 3

14 ounces (397 g) pork liver, chopped
1 teaspoon salt
1 teaspoon butter
½ cup heavy cream
3 tablespoons scallions, chopped

Rub the liver with the salt on a clean work surface. Put the butter in the Instant Pot and melt on the Sauté mode. Add the heavy cream, scallions, and liver. Stir and close the lid. Select Manual mode and set cooking time for 12 minutes on High Pressure. When timer beeps, perform a natural pressure release for 5 minutes, then release any remaining pressure. Open the lid. Serve immediately.

Braised Pork Belly
Prep time: 15 minutes | Cook time: 37 minutes | Serves 4

1 pound (454 g) pork belly
1 tablespoon olive oil
Salt and ground black pepper to taste
1 clove garlic, minced
1 cup dry white wine
Rosemary sprig

Select the Sauté mode on the Instant Pot and heat the oil. Add the pork belly and sauté for 2 minutes per side, until starting to brown. Season the meat with salt and pepper, add the garlic. Pour in the wine and add the rosemary sprig. Bring to a boil. Select the Manual mode and set the cooking time for 35 minutes at High pressure. Once cooking is complete, use a natural pressure release for 10 minutes, then release any remaining pressure. Open the lid. Slice the meat and serve.

Korean Beef and Pickled Vegetable Bowls

Prep time: 15 minutes | Cook time: 10 minutes | Serves 6

1 tablespoon vegetable oil	divided
5 garlic cloves, thinly sliced	1 tablespoon coconut aminos
1 tablespoon julienned fresh ginger	1 teaspoon Swerve
2 dried red chiles	2 tablespoons freshly squeezed lime juice
1 cup sliced onions	1 teaspoon salt
1 pound (454 g) 80% lean ground beef	1 teaspoon freshly ground pepper
1 tablespoon gochujang, adjusted to taste	¼ cup water
1 cup fresh basil leaves,	1 teaspoon sesame oil

For the Pickled Vegetables:

1 cucumber, peeled, coarsely grated	¼ cup white vinegar
1 turnip, coarsely grated	½ teaspoon salt
	½ teaspoon Swerve

Select Sauté mode of the Instant Pot. When the pot is hot, add the oil and heat until it is shimmering. Add the garlic, ginger, and chiles and sauté for 1 minute. Add the onions and sauté for 1 minute. Add the ground beef and cooking for 4 minutes.. Add the gochujang, ½ cup of basil, coconut aminos, sweetener, lime juice, salt, pepper, water, and sesame oil, and stir to combine. Lock the lid. Select Manual mode. Set the time for 4 minutes on High Pressure. When cooking is complete, let the pressure release naturally for 5 minutes, then release any remaining pressure. Unlock the lid and stir in the remaining ½ cup of basil. Meanwhile, put the cucumber and turnip in a medium bowl and mix with the vinegar, salt, and sweetener. To serve, portion the basil beef into individual bowls and serve with the pickled salad.

Lamb and Tomato Bhuna

Prep time: 15 minutes | Cook time: 20 minutes | Serves 2

¼ teaspoon minced ginger	chopped
¼ teaspoon garlic paste	2 ounces (57 g) scallions, chopped
1 teaspoon coconut oil	¼ cup water
¼ cup crushed tomatoes	
10 ounces (283 g) lamb fillet,	

Put the minced ginger, garlic paste, coconut oil, and crushed tomatoes in the Instant Pot. Sauté for 10 minutes on Sauté mode. Add the chopped lamb fillet, scallions, and water. Select Manual mode and set cooking time for 10 minutes on High Pressure. When timer beeps, use a natural pressure release for 15 minutes, then release any remaining pressure. Open the lid. Serve warm.

Lamb Kleftiko with Turnip

Prep time: 25 minutes | Cook time: 50 minutes | Serves 6

¼ cup apple cider vinegar	½ teaspoon fresh thyme
½ cup chicken broth	1 pound (454 g) lamb shoulder, chopped
1 tablespoon lemon juice	½ cup turnip, chopped
½ teaspoon lemon zest	

In the mixing bowl, mix the apple cider vinegar, chicken broth, lemon juice, lemon zest, and thyme. Put the lamb shoulder in the Instant Pot. Add the lemon juice mixture and turnip. Close the lid. Select Manual mode and set cooking time for 50 minutes on High Pressure. When the time is over, use a natural pressure release for 20 minutes, then release any remaining pressure. Open the lid. Serve warm.

Lamb Kofta Curry

Prep time: 15 minutes | Cook time: 20 minutes | Serves 4

1 pound (454 g) ground lamb	½ teaspoon chili flakes
4 ounces (113 g) scallions, chopped	1 tablespoon dried cilantro
1 tablespoon curry powder, divided	1 tablespoon coconut oil
	1 cup chicken broth
	⅓ cup coconut cream

In a mixing bowl, mix the ground lamb, scallions, and ½ tablespoon of curry powder. Add chili flakes and dried cilantro. Stir the mixture until homogenous and shape the mixture into medium size koftas (meatballs). Heat the coconut oil in the Instant Pot on Sauté mode until melted. Put the koftas in the hot oil and cook for 2 minutes on each side. Meanwhile, mix the chicken broth, coconut cream and remaining curry powder in a small bowl. Pour the mixture over the koftas. Select Manual mode and set timer for 12 minutes on High Pressure. When timer beeps, use a natural pressure release for 10 minutes, then release any remaining pressure. Open the lid. Serve warm.

Classic Pork and Cauliflower Keema

Prep time: 15 minutes | Cook time: 8 minutes | Serves 6

1 tablespoon sesame oil	minced
½ cup yellow onion, chopped	4 cloves, whole
1 garlic cloves, minced	1 teaspoon garam masala
1 (1-inch) piece fresh ginger, minced	½ teaspoon ground cumin
1½ pounds (680 g) ground pork	¼ teaspoon turmeric powder
1 cup cauliflower, chopped into small florets	1 teaspoon brown mustard seeds
1 ripe tomatoes, puréed	½ teaspoon hot paprika
1 jalapeño pepper, seeded and	Sea salt and ground black pepper, to taste
	1 cup water

Press the Sauté button to heat up the Instant Pot. Heat the sesame oil. Once hot, sauté yellow onion for 3 minutes or until softened. Stir in garlic and ginger; cook for an additional minute. Add the remaining ingredients. Secure the lid. Choose the Manual mode and set cooking time for 5 minutes on High pressure. Once cooking is complete, use a quick pressure release. Carefully remove the lid. Serve immediately.

Teriyaki Pork Tenderloin

Prep time: 5 minutes | Cook time: 3 hours | Serves 6

2 tablespoons vegetable oil	3 tablespoons light brown sugar
2 cloves garlic, minced	2 (1-pound / 454-g) pork tenderloins
1 teaspoon grated fresh ginger	
1 cup soy sauce	
¼ cup rice vinegar	

Whisk the oil, garlic, ginger, soy sauce, vinegar, and sugar together in a bowl until blended. Remove the silver skin from the outside of the pork with a boning knife and discard. Place the tenderloins in a 1-gallon zipper-top plastic bag or 13-by-9-inch baking dish. Pour the marinade over the tenderloins and seal the bag or cover the dish with plastic wrap. Marinate for at least 4 hours or overnight, turning the meat once or twice during that time. Place the marinade and pork in the insert of the Instant Pot. Cover and press the Slow Cook button, and cook on high for 3 hours. (Press Slow Cook again to toggle between Low and High cooking temperatures.) Remove the meat from the sauce, cover loosely with aluminum foil, and allow the meat to rest for about 10 minutes. Skim off any fat from the top of the sauce. Cut the meat diagonally in ½-inch-thick slices. Nap each serving of pork with some of the sauce.

Lamb Rostelle

Prep time: 20 minutes | Cook time: 30 minutes | Serves 4

1 pound (454 g) lamb loin, slice into strips
½ teaspoon apple cider vinegar
1 teaspoon ground black pepper
1 teaspoon olive oil
½ teaspoon salt
1 cup water, for cooking

Combine the apple cider vinegar, ground black pepper, olive oil, and salt in a bowl. Stir to mix well. Put the lamb strips in the bowl and toss to coat well. Run the lamb strips through four skewers and put in a baking pan. Pour water in the Instant Pot and then insert the trivet. Put the baking pan on the trivet. Close the lid. Select Manual mode and set cooking time for 30 minutes on High Pressure. When timer beeps, use a natural pressure release for 10 minutes, then release any remaining pressure. Open the lid. Serve immediately.

Lamb Sirloin Masala

Prep time: 10 minutes | Cook time: 25 minutes | Serves 3

12 ounces (340 g) lamb sirloin, sliced
1 tablespoon garam masala
1 tablespoon lemon juice
1 tablespoon olive oil
¼ cup coconut cream

Sprinkle the sliced lamb sirloin with garam masala, lemon juice, olive oil, and coconut cream in a large bowl. Toss to mix well. Transfer the mixture in the Instant Pot. Cook on Sauté mode for 25 minutes. Flip the lamb for every 5 minutes. When cooking is complete, allow to cool for 10 minutes, then serve warm.

Pork Carnitas

Prep time: 10 minutes | Cook time: 45 minutes | Serves 4

1 onion, sliced
4 garlic cloves, sliced
1 pound (454 g) pork shoulder, cut into cubes, visible fat removed
Juice of 1 lemon
¼ teaspoon ancho chili powder
¼ teaspoon chipotle chili powder
½ teaspoon dried oregano
½ teaspoon roasted cumin powder
¼ teaspoon smoked paprika
1 to 2 teaspoons salt
1 teaspoon freshly ground black pepper
½ cup water
1 to 2 tablespoons coconut oil
½ cup sour cream
½ avocado, diced

Place the onion and garlic in the Instant Pot to help them release water when the meat is cooking. In a large bowl, mix together the pork and lemon juice. Add the ancho chili powder, chipotle chili powder, oregano, cumin, paprika, salt, and pepper, and stir to combine. Place the pork on top of the onions and garlic. Pour the water into the bowl and swirl to get the last of the spices, then pour the liquid onto the pork. Lock the lid. Select Meat/Stew mode. Set cooking time for 35 minutes on High Pressure. When cooking is complete, let the pressure release naturally for 10 minutes, then release any remaining pressure. Unlock the lid. Remove the pork, leaving the liquid in the pot. Switch the pot to Sauté and bring the sauce to a boil until it is thickened. Place a cast iron skillet over medium-high heat. Once it is hot, add the oil. Shred the pork, then place in the skillet. Let the meat brown for 4 minutes. When the meat is browned on the bottom, stir and continue cooking until it's crisp in parts. Add the sauce from the pot. Serve with the sour cream and diced avocado.

Easy Ginger Pork Meatballs

Prep time: 10 minutes | Cook time: 7 minutes | Serves 3

11 ounces (312 g) ground pork
1 teaspoon ginger paste
1 teaspoon lemon juice
¼ teaspoon chili flakes
1 tablespoon butter
¼ cup water

Combine the ground pork and ginger paste in a large bowl. Mix in the lemon juice and chili flakes. Put the butter in the Instant Pot and melt on Sauté mode. Meanwhile, shape the mixture into small meatballs. Place the meatballs in the Instant Pot and cook for 2 minutes on each side. Add water and lock the lid. Set the Manual mode and set cooking time for 3 minutes on High Pressure. When timer beeps, perform a quick pressure release. Open the lid. Serve warm.

Easy Pork Steaks with Pico de Gallo

Prep time: 15 minutes | Cook time: 12 minutes | Serves 6

1 tablespoon butter
2 pounds (907 g) pork steaks
1 bell pepper, deseeded and sliced
½ cup shallots, chopped
2 garlic cloves, minced
Pico de Gallo:
1 tomato, chopped
1 chili pepper, seeded and minced
½ cup red onion, chopped
¼ cup dry red wine
1 cup chicken bone broth
¼ cup water
Salt, to taste
¼ teaspoon freshly ground black pepper, or more to taste

2 garlic cloves, minced
1 tablespoon fresh cilantro, finely chopped
Sea salt, to taste

Press the Sauté button to heat up the Instant Pot. Melt the butter and sear the pork steaks about 4 minutes or until browned on both sides. Add bell pepper, shallot, garlic, wine, chicken bone broth, water, salt, and black pepper to the Instant Pot. Secure the lid. Choose the Manual mode and set cooking time for 8 minutes at High pressure. Meanwhile, combine the ingredients for the Pico de Gallo in a small bowl. Refrigerate until ready to serve. Once cooking is complete, use a quick pressure release. Carefully remove the lid. Serve warm pork steaks with the chilled Pico de Gallo on the side.

Pork Tenderloin with Mango Sauce

Prep time: 20 minutes | Cook time: 3 hours | Serves 6

4 tablespoons (½ stick) unsalted butter, melted
2 large mangoes, peeled, pitted, and coarsely chopped
2 navel oranges, peeled and sectioned
2 tablespoons soy sauce
½ cup dark rum
½ cup beef broth
2 (1-pound / 454-g) pork tenderloins
2 tablespoons Jamaican jerk seasoning
6 green onions, finely chopped, using the white and tender green parts for garnish

Stir the butter, mangoes, oranges, soy sauce, rum, and broth together in the insert of the Instant Pot. Remove the silver skin from the outside of the pork with a boning knife and discard. Rub the jerk seasoning on the pork and arrange it in the Instant Pot. Cover and press the Slow Cook button, and cook on high for 3 hours, until the pork is tender and cooked through. (The pork should register 175ºF (79ºC) on an instant-read thermometer.) (Press Slow Cook again to toggle between Low and High cooking temperatures.) Remove the pork from the sauce, cover with aluminum foil, and allow to rest for 20 minutes. Skim off any fat from the top of the sauce. Slice the meat and garnish with the green onions. Serve the sauce on the side.

Eggplant Pork Lasagna

Prep time: 20 minutes | Cook time: 30 minutes | Serves 6

2 eggplants, sliced
1 teaspoon salt
10 ounces (283 g) ground pork
1 cup Mozzarella, shredded
1 tablespoon unsweetened tomato purée
1 teaspoon butter, softened
1 cup chicken stock

Sprinkle the eggplants with salt and let sit for 10 minutes, then pat dry with paper towels. In a mixing bowl, mix the ground pork, butter, and tomato purée. Make a layer of the sliced eggplants in the bottom of the Instant Pot and top with ground pork mixture. Top the ground pork with Mozzarella and repeat with remaining ingredients. Pour in the chicken stock. Close the lid. Select Manual mode and set cooking time for 30 minutes on High Pressure. When timer beeps, use a natural pressure release for 10 minutes, then release the remaining pressure and open the lid. Cool for 10 minutes and serve.

Pork and Spinach Florentine

Prep time: 20 minutes | Cook time: 45 minutes | Serves 6

12 ounces (340 g) pork roast, roll cut
1 cup spinach
1 tablespoon olive oil
½ teaspoon ground black pepper
3 ounces (85 g) Monterey Jack cheese, shredded
1 cup water

Pound the pork roast with a kitchen hammer on a clean work surface. Put the spinach in the blender and add olive oil, and ground black pepper. Pulse until smooth. Transfer the mixture over the pork roast, spread and top with shredded cheese. Roll the meat and wrap in the foil. Pour water and insert the trivet in the Instant Pot. Put the wrapped pork on the trivet. Close the lid. Select Manual mode mode and set cooking time for 45 minutes on High Pressure. When timer beeps, use a natural pressure release for 15 minutes, then release any remaining pressure. Open the lid. Serve warm.

Italian Sausage Stuffed Bell Peppers

Prep time: 15 minutes | Cook time: 17 minutes | Serves 4

4 medium bell peppers, tops and seeds removed
1 pound (454 g) ground pork sausage
1 large egg
3 tablespoons unsweetened tomato purée
½ tablespoon Italian seasoning blend
2 garlic cloves, minced
½ teaspoon sea salt
¼ teaspoon ground black pepper
½ teaspoon onion powder
⅓ cup tomato, puréed
1 cup water
4 slices Mozzarella cheese

Using a fork, pierce small holes into the bottoms of the peppers. Set aside. In a large mixing bowl, combine the sausage, egg, tomato purée, garlic, Italian seasoning, sea salt, black pepper, and onion powder. Mix to combine. Stuff each bell pepper with the meat mixture. Place the trivet in the Instant Pot and add the water. Place the stuffed peppers on the trivet. Pour the puréed tomato over. Lock the lid. Select Manual mode and set cooking time for 15 minutes on High Pressure. When cooking is complete, allow the pressure to release naturally for 5 minutes and then release the remaining pressure. Open the lid and top each pepper with 1 slice of the Mozzarella. Secure the lid, select Keep Warm / Cancel, and set cooking time for 2 minutes to melt the cheese. Open the lid and use tongs to carefully transfer the peppers to a large serving platter. Serve warm.

Marinara Sausage with Bell Peppers

Prep time: 10 minutes | Cook time: 16 minutes | Serves 4

2 tablespoons extra-virgin olive oil
1 pound (454 g) mild or hot Italian sausage links
2½ cups keto-friendly Marinara sauce
1 Roma (plum) tomato, diced
2 green bell peppers, cut into thick strips
¾ cup shredded Parmesan cheese
Pinch of red pepper flakes

Set the Instant Pot to Sauté mode and add the oil to heat. Add the sausages. Sauté for 6 minutes on both sides or until browned. Carefully pour in the Marinara and stir to mix. Layer the diced tomato and bell peppers on top of the sausages without mixing. Secure the lid. Press the Manual button and set cooking time for 10 minutes on High Pressure. When timer beeps, allow the pressure to release naturally for 5 minutes, then release any remaining pressure. Open the lid. Use tongs to remove the sausages and peppers and arrange them on a serving platter. Ladle the sauce over the sausages. Sprinkle the Parmesan and pepper flakes over the top and serve hot.

Golden Bacon Sticks

Prep time: 5 minutes | Cook time: 6 minutes | Serves 4

6 ounces (170 g) bacon, sliced
2 tablespoons almond flour
1 tablespoon water
¾ teaspoon chili pepper

Sprinkle the sliced bacon with the almond flour and drizzle with water. Add the chili pepper. Put the bacon in the Instant Pot. Cook on Sauté mode for 3 minutes per side. Serve immediately.

Riced Cauliflower and Beef Casserole

Prep time: 15 minutes | Cook time: 26 minutes | Serves 5

2 cups fresh cauliflower florets
1 pound (454 g) ground beef
5 slices uncooked bacon, chopped
8 ounces (227 g) unsweetened tomato purée
1 cup shredded Cheddar cheese, divided
1 teaspoon garlic powder
½ teaspoon paprika
½ teaspoon sea salt
¼ teaspoon ground black pepper
¼ teaspoon celery seed
1 cup water
1 medium Roma tomato, sliced

Spray a round soufflé dish with coconut oil cooking spray. Set aside. Add the cauliflower florets to a food processor and pulse until a riced. Set aside. Select Sauté mode. Once the pot is hot, crumble the ground beef into the pot and add the bacon. Sauté for 6 minutes or until the ground beef is browned and the bacon is cooked through. Transfer the beef, bacon, and rendered fat to a large bowl. Add the cauliflower rice, tomato purée, ½ cup Cheddar cheese, garlic powder, paprika, sea salt, black pepper, and celery seed to the bowl with the beef and bacon. Mix well to combine. Add the mixture to the prepared dish and use a spoon to press and smooth the mixture into an even layer. Place the trivet in the Instant Pot and add the water to the bottom of the pot. Place the dish on top of the trivet. Lock the lid. Select Pressure Cook mode and set cooking time for 20 minutes on High Pressure. When cooking is complete, quick release the pressure. Open the lid. Arrange the tomato slices in a single layer on top of the casserole and sprinkle the remaining cheese over top. Secure the lid and let the residual heat melt the cheese for 5 minutes. Open the lid, remove the dish from the pot. Transfer the casserole to a serving plate and slice into 5 equal-sized wedges. Serve warm.

Hearty Barbecue Pork Ribs

Prep time: 6 minutes | Cook time: 35 minutes | Serves 5

1½ cups beef broth
2 pounds (907 g) country-style boneless pork ribs
For the Sauce:

1½ tablespoons unsalted butter	1 tablespoon apple cider vinegar
½ tablespoon Worcestershire sauce	1½ teaspoons liquid smoke
½ teaspoon blackstrap molasses	2 tablespoons erythritol
1 cup unsweetened tomato purée	1 teaspoon garlic powder
	½ teaspoon sea salt
	½ teaspoon onion powder

For the Dry Rub:

1½ teaspoons smoked paprika	1 teaspoon sea salt
1½ teaspoons onion powder	1 teaspoon ground black pepper
1 teaspoon garlic powder	
1 teaspoon ground cumin	⅛ teaspoon cayenne pepper

Add the butter to a small saucepan and heat over medium heat. Once the butter is melted, add the Worcestershire sauce, molasses, tomato purée, vinegar, liquid smoke, erythritol, garlic powder, sea salt, and onion powder. Stir until well combined and then remove from the heat. Set aside. Comb the paprika, onion powder, garlic powder, cumin, sea salt, black pepper, and cayenne pepper in a small bowl. Mix well to combine. Set aside. Add the beef broth to the Instant Pot and place the trivet in the pot. Generously sprinkle the dry rub over the pork and gently rub the spices into the meat. Stack the seasoned ribs on the trivet. Pour half the barbecue sauce over the ribs, reserving the remaining sauce for serving. Lock the lid. Select Manual mode and set cooking time for 35 minutes on High Pressure. When cooking is complete, allow the pressure to release naturally for 20 minutes, then release any remaining pressure. Open the lid and use tongs to carefully transfer the ribs to a serving plate. Using a pastry brush, brush the reserved sauce over the ribs. Serve warm.

Mediterranean Rum Pork

Prep time: 15 minutes | Cook time: 14 minutes | Serves 6

3 tablespoons olive oil, divided	1 sprig lemon thyme, chopped
Juice of 1 lemon	2 pounds (907 g) pork cutlets, bone-in
1 bunch fresh cilantro leaves, chopped	Coarse sea salt and ground black pepper, to taste
1 tablespoons stone ground mustard	¼ cup white rum
2 sprigs fresh rosemary, chopped	1 cup chicken stock
2 garlic cloves, finely minced	½ cup black olives, pitted and sliced

Add 2 tablespoons of olive oil, lemon juice, cilantro, mustard, rosemary, garlic, and lemon thyme to a ceramic dish. Add the bone-in pork cutlets and let marinate at least 3 hours in the refrigerator. Press the Sauté button to heat up the Instant Pot. Heat the remaining tablespoon of olive oil and brown the pork for 3 minutes or until browned on each side. Season with salt and pepper. Pour in the rum and stock. Secure the lid. Choose Manual mode and set cooking time for 8 minutes on High Pressure. Once cooking is complete, use a quick pressure release. Carefully remove the lid. Serve warm garnished with black olives.

Herbed Pork Roast with Asparagus

Prep time: 25 minutes | Cook time: 17 minutes | Serves 6

1 teaspoon dried thyme	½ medium white onion, chopped
½ teaspoon garlic powder	2 garlic cloves, minced
½ teaspoon onion powder	⅔ cup chicken broth
½ teaspoon dried oregano	2 tablespoons Worcestershire sauce
1½ teaspoons smoked paprika	
½ teaspoon ground black pepper	1 cup water
1 teaspoon sea salt	20 fresh asparagus spears, cut in half and woody ends removed
2 tablespoons olive oil, divided	
2 pounds (907 g) boneless pork loin roast	

In a small bowl, combine the thyme, garlic powder, onion powder, oregano, smoked paprika, black pepper, and sea salt. Mix until well combined and then add 1½ tablespoons olive oil. Stir until blended. Brush all sides of the pork roast with the oil and spice mixture. Place the roast in a covered dish and transfer to the refrigerator to marinate for 30 minutes. Select Sauté mode and brush the Instant Pot with remaining olive oil. Once the oil is hot, add the pork roast and sear for 5 minutes per side or until browned. Remove the roast from the pot and set aside. Add the onions and garlic to the pot and Sauté for 2 minutes, or until the onions soften and garlic becomes fragrant. Add the chicken broth and Worcestershire sauce. Lock the lid. Select Manual mode and set cooking time for 15 minutes on High pressure. When cooking is complete, allow the pressure release naturally for 10 minutes and then release the remaining pressure. Open the lid. Transfer the roast to a cutting board, cover with aluminum foil, and set aside to rest. Transfer the broth to a measuring cup. Set aside. Place the trivet in the Instant Pot and add the water to the bottom of the pot. Place the asparagus in an ovenproof bowl that will fit in the Instant Pot and place the bowl on top of the trivet. Lock the lid. Select Steam mode and set cooking time for 2 minutes. Once the cook time is complete, quick release the pressure. Open the lid and transfer the asparagus to a large serving platter. Thinly slice the roast and transfer to the serving platter with the asparagus. Drizzle the reserved broth over top. Serve warm.

Korean Galbijjim

Prep time: 10 minutes | Cook time: 12 minutes | Serves 8

2 pounds (907 g) meaty short ribs	1 teaspoon Swerve
2 tablespoons gochujang	¼ teaspoon powdered stevia
4 garlic cloves, crushed	1 teaspoon salt
1 tablespoon mirin	2 teaspoons freshly ground black pepper
3 tablespoons coconut aminos	
2 teaspoons minced fresh ginger	1 tablespoon sesame oil
	¼ cup water
	¼ teaspoon xanthan gum

Put the ribs into a large zip-top bag. Whisk in the remaining ingredients, except for the water and xanthan gum. Shake to coat the ribs well and seal the bag. Marinate the ribs in the refrigerator for at least 1 hour. Put the ribs and marinade in the Instant Pot along with the water. Lock the lid. Select Pressure Cook mode and set cooking time for 12 minutes on High Pressure. When cooking is complete, let the pressure release naturally for 5 minutes, then release any remaining pressure. Unlock the lid. Turn the Instant Pot on Sauté mode. Transfer the ribs to a platter. Bring the sauce to a boil, then fold in the xanthan gum and stir until the sauce thickens. Pour the sauce over the ribs and serve.

Beef Chuck Roast Masala

Prep time: 10 minutes | Cook time: 20 minutes | Serves 4

2 tomatoes, quartered
1 small onion, quartered
4 garlic cloves, chopped
½ cup fresh cilantro leaves
1 teaspoon garam masala
½ teaspoon ground coriander
1 teaspoon ground cumin
½ teaspoon cayenne
1 teaspoon salt
1 pound (454 g) beef chuck roast, cut into 1-inch cubes

In a blender, combine the tomatoes, onion, garlic, and cilantro. Process until the vegetables are puréed. Add the garam masala, coriander, cumin, cayenne, and salt. Process for several more seconds. To the Instant Pot, add the beef and pour the vegetable purée on top. Lock the lid. Select Pressure Cook mode and set cooking time for 20 minutes on High Pressure. When timer beeps, let the pressure release naturally for 10 minutes, then release any remaining pressure. Unlock the lid. Stir and serve immediately.

Rosemary Pork Tenderloin with Cherry

Prep time: 5 minutes | Cook time: 25 minutes | Serves 6

2 tablespoons avocado oil
2 (3-pound / 1.4 kg) pork tenderloins, halved
½ cup balsamic vinegar
¼ cup finely chopped fresh rosemary
¼ cup cherry preserves
¼ cup olive oil
½ teaspoon sea salt
¼ teaspoon ground black pepper
4 garlic cloves, minced

Set your Instant Pot to Sauté. Add and heat the oil. Add the pork and brown for about 2 minutes on each side. Stir together the remaining ingredients in a small bowl and pour over the pork. Secure the lid. Select the Pressure Cook mode and cook for 20 minutes on High Pressure. Once cooking is complete, use a natural pressure release for 5 minutes and then release any remaining pressure. Carefully open the lid. Remove the tenderloin from the Instant Pot to a cutting board. Let stand for 5 minutes. Cut into medallions before serving.

Herbed Pork Cutlets with Mustard Sauce

Prep time: 20 minutes | Cook time: 13 minutes | Serves 6

6 pork cutlets
½ teaspoon dried rosemary
½ teaspoon dried marjoram
¼ teaspoon paprika
¼ teaspoon cayenne pepper
Kosher salt and ground black pepper, to taste
2 tablespoons olive oil
½ cup water
½ cup vegetable broth
1 tablespoon butter
1 cup heavy cream
1 tablespoon yellow mustard
½ cup shredded Cheddar cheese

Sprinkle both sides of the pork cutlets with rosemary, marjoram, paprika, cayenne pepper, salt, and black pepper. Press the Sauté button on the Instant Pot and heat the olive oil until sizzling. Add the pork cutlets and sear both sides for about 3 minutes until lightly browned. Pour in the water and vegetable broth. Secure the lid. Select the Pressure Cook mode and set the cooking time for 8 minutes at High Pressure. When the timer beeps, perform a quick pressure release. Carefully open the lid. Transfer the pork cutlets to a plate and set aside. Press the Sauté button again and melt the butter. Stir in the heavy cream, mustard, and cheese and cook for another 2 minutes until heated through. Add the pork cutlets to the sauce, turning to coat. Remove from the Instant Pot and serve.

Beef and Cheddar Burger Pie

Prep time: 15 minutes | Cook time: 30 minutes | Serves 6

1 tablespoon olive oil
1 pound (454 g) ground beef
3 eggs (1 beaten)
½ cup unsweetened tomato purée
2 tablespoons golden flaxseed meal
1 garlic clove, minced
½ teaspoon Italian seasoning blend
½ teaspoon sea salt
½ teaspoon smoked paprika
½ teaspoon onion powder
2 tablespoons heavy cream
½ teaspoon ground mustard
¼ teaspoon ground black pepper
2 cups water
½ cup grated Cheddar cheese

Coat a round cake pan with the olive oil. Select Sauté mode. Once the pot is hot, add the ground beef and sauté for 5 minutes or until the beef is browned. Transfer the beef to a large bowl. Add the 1 beaten egg, tomato purée, flaxseed meal, garlic, Italian seasoning, sea salt, smoked paprika, and onion powder to the bowl. Mix until well combined. Transfer the meat mixture to the prepared cake pan and use a knife to spread the mixture into an even layer. Set aside. In a separate medium bowl, combine the 2 remaining eggs, heavy cream, ground mustard, and black pepper. Whisk until combined. Pour the egg mixture over the meat mixture. Tightly cover the pan with a sheet of aluminum foil. Place the trivet in the Instant Pot and add the water to the bottom of the pot. Place the pan on the trivet. Lock the lid. Select Pressure Cook mode and set cooking time for 20 minutes on High Pressure. When cooking is complete, allow the pressure to release naturally for 10 minutes and then release the remaining pressure. Allow the pie to rest in the pot for 5 minutes. Preheat the oven broiler to 450°F (235°C). Open the lid, remove the pan from the pot. Remove the foil and sprinkle the Cheddar over top of the pie. Place the pie in the oven and broil for 2 minutes or until the cheese is melted and the top becomes golden brown. Slice into six equal-sized wedges. Serve hot.

Roasted Beef Shoulder with Purple Onions

Prep time: 15 minutes | Cook time: 46 minutes | Serves 6

2 tablespoons peanut oil
2 pounds (907 g) beef shoulder roast
¼ cup coconut aminos
1 teaspoon porcini powder
1 teaspoon garlic powder
1 cup beef broth
2 cloves garlic, minced
2 tablespoons champagne vinegar
½ teaspoon hot sauce
1 teaspoon celery seeds
1 cup purple onions, cut into wedges
1 tablespoon flaxseed meal, plus 2 tablespoons water

Press the Sauté button to heat up the Instant Pot. Then, heat the peanut oil and cook the beef shoulder roast for 3 minutes on each side. In a mixing dish, combine coconut aminos, porcini powder, garlic powder, broth, garlic, vinegar, hot sauce, and celery seeds. Pour the broth mixture into the Instant Pot. Add the onions to the top. Secure the lid. Choose Pressure Cook mode and set cooking time for 40 minutes on High Pressure. Once cooking is complete, use a natural pressure release for 15 mintues, then release any remaining pressure. Carefully remove the lid. Make the slurry by mixing flaxseed meal with 2 tablespoons of water. Add the slurry to the Instant Pot. Press the Sauté button and allow it to cook until the cooking liquid is reduced and thickened slightly. Serve warm.

Milk Pork Belly

Prep time: 5 minutes | Cook time: 48 minutes | Serves 8

2 pounds (907 g) pork belly, skin scored
Seasoned salt and ground black pepper, to taste
1 teaspoon cayenne pepper
⅓ cup full-fat coconut milk
1 teaspoon hot sauce
1 teaspoon oyster sauce
1 cup water

Season the pork with salt, black pepper, and cayenne pepper. Add the remaining ingredients. Secure the lid. Choose the Soup mode and set cooking time for 40 minutes on High pressure. Once cooking is complete, use a natural pressure release for 15 minutes, then release any remaining pressure. Carefully remove the lid. Strain cooking liquid into a saucepan. Bring to the boil over high heat. Cook, stirring occasionally, for 8 minutes or until sauce reduces. Cut the pork into thick slices and serve with the milk sauce.

Pork Adovada

Prep time: 15 minutes | Cook time: 20 minutes | Serves 8

¼ cup raisins
¼ cup hot water
2 pounds (907 g) pork shoulder, cut into large pieces
½ teaspoon ancho chili powder
1 chipotle chile in adobo sauce, chopped
1 teaspoon dried oregano
2 teaspoons vegetable oil
1 cup chopped red onion
3 garlic cloves, chopped
1 teaspoon salt
¼ cup Mexican red chili powder
1 tablespoon cider vinegar
¼ cup coconut aminos
½ cup water
½ teaspoon xanthan gum

Put the raisins in a blender jar and cover them with the hot water. Let them sit until ready to use. Place the pork in the Instant Pot. In a microwave-safe bowl, combine the ancho chili powder, chipotle chiles with sauce, oregano, oil, onions, garlic, salt, and red chili powder. Microwave on high for 5 to 7 minutes, stirring once or twice. Pour this mixture, the cider vinegar, and coconut aminos into the blender jar with the raisins. Purée until smooth. Pour this mixture over the pork. Use the water to wash out the blender jar, and pour the liquid into the pot. Lock the lid. Select Manual mode. Set cooking time for 20 minutes on High Pressure. When cooking is complete, naturally release the pressure for 5 minutes, then release any remaining pressure. Unlock the lid. Set the pot on Sauté mode. Fold the xanthan gum in and let the sauce boil and thicken. Serve the pork baste with the thickened sauce.

Jamaican Pork Roast

Prep time: 10 minutes | Cook time: 55 minutes | Serves 6

¼ cup Jamaican jerk spice blend
¾ tablespoon olive oil
2 pounds (907 g) pork shoulder
¼ cup beef broth

Rub the jerk spice blend and olive oil all over the pork shoulder and set aside to marinate for 10 minutes. When ready, press the Sauté button on the Instant Pot and add the pork. Sear for 4 minutes. Flip the pork and cook for 4 minutes. Pour the beef broth into the Instant Pot. Secure the lid. Select the Manual mode and set the cooking time for 45 minutes at High Pressure. Once cooking is complete, do a natural pressure release for 10 minutes, then release any remaining pressure. Carefully open the lid. Serve hot.

Pork Roast with Sweet Potatoes

Prep time: 10 minutes | Cook time: 40 minutes | Serves 4

1 tablespoon olive oil
2 red onions, chopped
2 pounds (907 g) pork shoulder, sliced
2 sweet potatoes, peeled and cubed
1 cup beef stock
1 teaspoon chili powder
½ teaspoon chopped rosemary
A pinch of salt and black pepper
1 cup coconut cream
1 tablespoon chopped parsley

Press the Sauté button on the Instant Pot and heat the olive oil. Add the onions and pork and brown for 5 minutes. Stir in the sweet potatoes, beef stock, chili powder, rosemary, salt, and black pepper. Secure the lid. Select the Manual mode and set the cooking time for 25 minutes at High Pressure. Once cooking is complete, do a natural pressure release for 10 minutes, then release any remaining pressure. Carefully open the lid. Press the Sauté button again and add the coconut cream, toss, and cook for an additional 10 minutes. Serve with the parsley sprinkled on top.

Pork, Green Beans, and Corn

Prep time: 10 minutes | Cook time: 35 minutes | Serves 4

2 pounds (907 g) pork shoulder, boneless and cubed
1 cup green beans, trimmed and halved
1 cup corn
1 cup beef stock
2 garlic cloves, minced
1 teaspoon ground cumin
A pinch of salt and black pepper

Combine all the ingredients in the Instant Pot. Secure the lid. Select the Manual mode and set the cooking time for 35 minutes at High Pressure. Once cooking is complete, do a natural pressure release for 10 minutes, then release any remaining pressure. Carefully open the lid. Divide the mix among four plates and serve.

Pulled Pork with Cabbage

Prep time: 10 minutes | Cook time: 1 hour 2 minutes minutes | Serves 6

1½ tablespoons olive oil
3 pounds (1.4 kg) pork shoulder roast, cut into 4 equal-sized pieces
3 cloves garlic, minced
1 tablespoon liquid smoke
2 cups water, divided
1 tablespoon sea salt
2 cups shredded cabbage

Select Sauté mode and add the olive oil to the Instant Pot. Once the oil is hot, add the pork cuts and sear for 5 minutes per side or until browned. Once browned, transfer the pork to a platter and set aside. Add the garlic, liquid smoke, and 1½ cups water to the Instant Pot. Stir to combine. Return the pork to the pot and sprinkle the salt over top. Lock the lid. Select Pressure Cook mode and set cooking time for 1 hour on High Pressure. When cooking is complete, allow the pressure to release naturally for 20 minutes, then release any remaining pressure. Open the lid and transfer the pork to a large platter. Using two forks, shred the pork. Set aside. Add the shredded cabbage and remaining water to the liquid in the pot. Stir. Lock the lid. Select Pressure Cook mode and set cooking time for 2 minutes on High Pressure. When cooking is complete, quick release the pressure. Transfer the cabbage to the serving platter with the pork. Serve warm.

Braised Tri-Tip Steak with Turnip
Prep time: 20 minutes | Cook time: 54 minutes | Serves 4

2 pounds (907 g) tri-tip steak, pat dry
2 teaspoons coarse sea salt
3 tablespoons avocado oil
½ medium onion, diced
2 cloves garlic, smashed
1 tablespoon unsweetened tomato purée
1½ cups dry red wine
½ tablespoon dried thyme
2 bay leaves
1 Roma (plum) tomato, diced
1 stalk celery, including leaves, chopped
1 small turnip, chopped
½ cup water

Season the tri-tip with the coarse salt. Set the Instant Pot to Sauté mode and heat the avocado oil until shimmering. Cook the steak in the pot for 2 minutes per side or until well browned. Remove the steak from the pot and place it in a shallow bowl. Set aside. Add the onion to the pot and sauté for 3 minutes. Add the garlic and sauté for 1 minute. Add the unsweetened tomato purée and cook for 1 minute, stirring constantly. Pour in the red wine. Stir in the thyme and bay leaves. Return the tri-tip steak to the pot. Scatter the tomato, celery, and turnip around the steak. Pour in the water. Secure the lid. Press the Pressure Cook button and set cooking time for 35 minutes on High Pressure. When timer beeps, allow the pressure to release naturally for 20 minutes, then release any remaining pressure. Open the lid. Discard the bay leaves. Remove the steak and place in a dish. Press the Sauté button and bring the braising liquid to a boil. Cook for 10 minutes or until the liquid is reduced by about half. Slice the steak thinly and serve with braising liquid over.

Pot Roast
Prep time: 15 minutes | Cook time: 1 hour 8 minutes | Serves 6

¼ cup dry red wine
1 tablespoon dried thyme
1½ cups beef broth
½ tablespoon dried rosemary
1 teaspoon paprika
1 teaspoon garlic powder
1½ teaspoons sea salt
½ teaspoon ground black pepper
1½ tablespoons avocado oil
3 pounds (1.4 kg) boneless chuck roast
2 tablespoons unsalted butter
½ medium yellow onion, chopped
2 garlic cloves, minced
1 cup sliced mushrooms
4 stalks celery, chopped
2 sprigs fresh thyme
1 bay leaf

In a medium bowl, combine the wine, dried thyme, beef broth, and dried rosemary. Stir to combine. Set aside. In a small bowl, combine the paprika, garlic powder, sea salt, and black pepper. Mix well. Generously rub the dry spice mixture into the roast. Set aside. Select Sauté mode. Once the pot becomes hot, add the avocado oil and butter and heat until the butter is melted, about 2 minutes. Add the roast to the pot. Sauté for 3 minutes per side or until a crust is formed. Transfer the browned roast to a plate and set aside. Add the onions and garlic to the pot. Sauté for 3 minutes or until the onions soften and the garlic becomes fragrant. Add half the broth and wine mixture to the pot. Place the trivet in the Instant Pot and place the roast on top of the trivet. Add the mushrooms and celery to the pot, and pour the remaining broth and wine mixture over the roast. Place the thyme sprigs and bay leaf on top of the roast. Lock the lid. Select Pressure Cook mode and set cooking time for 1 hour on High Pressure. When cooking is complete, allow the pressure to release naturally for 10 minutes and then release the remaining pressure. Open the lid, discard the bay leaf and thyme sprigs. Transfer the roast to a serving platter. Transfer the vegetables to the platter and spoon the remaining broth over the roast and vegetables. Slice the roast and ladle ¼ cup of the broth over each serving. Serve hot.

Italian Osso Buco
Prep time: 35 minutes | Cook time: 1 hour 2 minutes | Serves 6

4 bone-in beef shanks
Sea salt, to taste
2 tablespoons avocado oil
1 small turnip, diced
1 medium onion, diced
1 medium stalk celery, diced
4 cloves garlic, smashed
For the Gremolata:
½ cup loosely packed parsley leaves
1 tablespoon unsweetened tomato purée
½ cup dry white wine
1 cup chicken broth
1 sprig fresh rosemary
2 sprigs fresh thyme
3 Roma tomatoes, diced

1 clove garlic, crushed
Grated zest of 2 lemons

On a clean work surface, season the shanks all over with salt. Set the Instant Pot to Sauté and add the oil. When the oil shimmers, add 2 shanks and sear for 4 minutes per side. Remove the shanks to a bowl and repeat with the remaining shanks. Set aside. Add the turnip, onion, and celery to the pot and cook for 5 minutes or until softened. Add the garlic and unsweetened tomato purée and cook 1 minute more, stirring frequently. Deglaze the pot with the wine, scraping the bottom with a wooden spoon to loosen any browned bits. Bring to a boil. Add the broth, rosemary, thyme, and shanks, then add the tomatoes on top of the shanks. Secure the lid. Press the Pressure Cook button and set cooking time for 40 minutes on High Pressure. Meanwhile, for the gremolata: In a small food processor, combine the parsley, garlic, and lemon zest and pulse until the parsley is finely chopped. Refrigerate until ready to use. When timer beeps, allow the pressure to release naturally for 20 minutes, then release any remaining pressure. Open the lid. To serve, transfer the shanks to large, shallow serving bowl. Ladle the braising sauce over the top and sprinkle with the gremolata.

Maple-Coffee Pork Ribs
Prep time: 40 minutes | Cook time: 30 minutes | Serves 6

2 racks (about 3 pounds / 1.4 kg) baby back pork ribs, cut into 2-rib sections
1 teaspoon instant coffee crystals
1 teaspoon sea salt
½ teaspoon ground cumin
½ teaspoon chili powder
½ teaspoon ground mustard
½ teaspoon cayenne pepper
½ teaspoon onion powder
½ teaspoon garlic powder
¼ teaspoon ground coriander
¼ cup soy sauce
¼ cup pure maple syrup
2 tablespoons tomato paste
1 tablespoon apple cider vinegar
1 tablespoon olive oil
1 medium onion, peeled and large diced

Mix together the coffee, salt, cumin, chili powder, mustard, cayenne pepper, onion powder, garlic powder, and coriander in a mixing bowl. Rub the mixture into the rib sections with your hands. Refrigerate for at least 30 minutes, covered. Set aside. Stir together the soy sauce, maple syrup, tomato paste, and apple cider vinegar in a small mixing bowl. Set your Instant Pot to Sauté and heat the olive oil. Add the onions and sauté for 3 to 5 minutes until translucent. Stir in the soy sauce mixture. Add a few ribs at a time with tongs and gently stir to coat. Arrange the ribs standing upright, meat-side outward. Secure the lid. Select the Pressure Cook mode and cook for 25 minutes on High Pressure. Once cooking is complete, use a natural pressure release for 10 minutes and then release any remaining pressure. Carefully open the lid. Transfer the ribs to a serving plate and serve warm.

Skirt Steak with Chimichurri

Prep time: 15 minutes | Cook time: 30 minutes | Serves 4

1 pound (454 g) skirt steak, trimmed and cut into 4 equal-sized pieces
½ teaspoon sea salt
Chimichurri:
⅓ cup chopped flat-leaf parsley
3 large garlic cloves, minced
2½ tablespoons red wine vinegar
½ teaspoon dried oregano
¼ teaspoon crushed red

½ teaspoon black pepper
1 tablespoon avocado oil
1 cup water

pepper
½ teaspoon sea salt
½ teaspoon black pepper
1 teaspoon lemon juice
½ cup extra virgin olive oil

Add the parsley to a food processor and pulse until finely chopped. Add the garlic, red wine vinegar, oregano, crushed red pepper, ½ teaspoon sea salt, ½ teaspoon black pepper, and lemon juice. Pulse until combined. Add the olive oil and pulse until the ingredients are well blended. Set aside. Season both sides of the steaks with the remaining salt and pepper. Select Sauté mode. Once the Instant Pot is hot, add the avocado oil and let heat for 1 minute. Add the steaks to the pot, two at a time, and sauté for 2 minutes per side or until browned on both sides. Transfer the browned steaks to a plate and repeat with the remaining steaks. Place one sheet on a flat surface. Place two steaks in the center of the sheet and pour half the chimichurri sauce over top of the steaks. Place the remaining steaks on top and pour the remaining sauce over top. Place another sheet of foil over the steaks and tightly roll and crimp the ends to create a foil packet. Place the trivet in the pot and add the water to the bottom of the pot. Place the foil packet on top of the trivet. Lock the lid. Select Pressure Cook mode and set cooking time for 25 minutes on High Pressure. When cooking is complete, allow the pressure to release naturally for 6 minutes and then release the remaining pressure. Open the lid, remove the steaks from the pot. Set the steaks aside to rest for 2 minutes. Open the packet and transfer the steaks to a cutting board. Thinly slice and transfer to a serving platter. Serve warm.

Barbecue-Honey Baby Back Ribs

Prep time: 10 minutes | Cook time: 25 minutes | Serves 4

2 racks baby back ribs (3 pounds / 1.4 kg; about 4 ribs each), cut into 5- to 6-inch portions
2 tablespoons chili powder
2 tablespoons toasted sesame

oil
3 tablespoons grainy mustard
1 tablespoon red wine vinegar
1 cup ketchup
⅓ cup honey
½ cup chicken broth

Rub the ribs all over with the chili powder. Mix together the remaining ingredients in your Instant Pot and stir until the honey has dissolved. Dip the ribs in the sauce to coat. Using tongs, arrange the ribs standing upright against the sides of the pot. Secure the lid. Select the Pressure Cook mode and cook for 25 minutes on High Pressure. Preheat the broiler and adjust an oven rack so that it is 4 inches below the broiler element. Line a baking sheet with aluminum foil. When the timer beeps, use a natural pressure release for 15 minutes and then release any remaining pressure. Carefully open the lid. Transfer the ribs with tongs to the prepared baking sheet, meaty side up. Stir the cooking liquid and pour over the ribs with a spoon. Broil the ribs for 5 minutes until browned in places. Transfer the ribs to a serving plate and serve warm.

Paprika Pork and Brussels Sprouts

Prep time: 10 minutes | Cook time: 30 minutes | Serves 4

2 pounds (907 g) pork shoulder, cubed
2 cups Brussels sprouts, trimmed and halved

1½ cups beef stock
1 tablespoon sweet paprika
1 tablespoon chopped parsley
2 tablespoons olive oil

Press the Sauté button on the Instant Pot and heat the olive oil. Add the pork and brown for 5 minutes. Stir in the remaining ingredients. Secure the lid. Select the Manual mode and set the cooking time for 25 minutes at High Pressure. Once cooking is complete, do a natural pressure release for 10 minutes, then release any remaining pressure. Carefully open the lid. Divide the mix between plates and serve warm.

Carolina-Style Pork Barbecue

Prep time: 10 minutes | Cook time: 40 minutes | Serves 4 to 6

1 (4-pound / 1.8-kg) boneless pork shoulder or pork butt roast
3 tablespoons packed brown sugar
1½ teaspoons smoked paprika

1 tablespoon seasoning salt
1 cup ketchup
½ cup water
½ cup cider vinegar

On a clean work surface, trim any excess fat off the outside of the pork shoulder, then cut the pork into four large pieces. Mix together the brown sugar, paprika, and seasoning salt in a small bowl. Rub this mixture all over the pork pieces. Place the ketchup, water, and vinegar into the Instant Pot and stir well. Add the pork pieces to the pot, turning to coat. Secure the lid. Select the Manual mode and set the cooking time for 40 minutes at High Pressure. Once cooking is complete, do a natural pressure release for 5 minutes, then release any remaining pressure. Carefully open the lid. Remove the pork pieces from the pot to a cutting board. Using two forks to shred them and discard any large chunks of fat. Spoon the sauce over the pork and serve immediately.

Balsamic Pork with Asparagus

Prep time: 10 minutes | Cook time: 30 minutes | Serves 4

1 tablespoon olive oil
4 garlic cloves, minced
1 yellow onion, chopped
2 pounds (907 g) pork roast
1 cup beef stock
1 tablespoon chopped basil
1 teaspoon smoked paprika

A pinch of salt and black pepper
1 bunch asparagus, trimmed
2 tablespoons balsamic vinegar
1 teaspoon chopped chives

Press the Sauté button on the Instant Pot and heat the olive oil. Add the garlic and onion and sauté for 2 minutes until fragrant. Add the pork and brown for an additional 5 minutes. Fold in the beef stock, basil, paprika, salt, and pepper and stir to combine. Secure the lid. Select the Manual mode and set the cooking time for 20 minutes at High Pressure. Once cooking is complete, do a natural pressure release for 10 minutes, then release any remaining pressure. Carefully open the lid. Press the Sauté button again and stir in the asparagus, vinegar, and chives. Cook for an additional 7 minutes until the asparagus is tender. Divide the mix among four plates and serve.

Herbed Tenderloin in Tomato Salsa
Prep time: 20 minutes | Cook time: 15 minutes | Serves 8

2 teaspoons grapeseed oil
3 pounds (1.4 kg) pork tenderloin, cut into slices
1 teaspoon granulated garlic
½ teaspoon dried marjoram
½ teaspoon dried thyme
1 teaspoon paprika
Salsa:
1 cup puréed tomatoes
1 teaspoon granulated garlic
2 bell peppers, deveined and chopped
1 cup chopped onion

1 teaspoon ground cumin
Sea salt and ground black pepper, to taste
1 cup water
1 avocado, pitted, peeled, and sliced

2 tablespoons minced fresh cilantro
3 teaspoons lime juice
1 minced jalapeño, chopped
Avocado slices, for serving

Press the Sauté button on your Instant Pot. Add and hear the oil. Sear the pork until nicely browned on all sides. Stir in the garlic, seasonings, and water. Lock the lid. Select the Pressure Cook mode and set the cooking time for 12 minutes at High Pressure. Once the timer beeps, use a natural pressure release for 10 minutes. Carefully open the lid. Remove the tenderloin. Shred with two forks and reserve. Meanwhile, stir together all the ingredients for the salsa in a mixing bowl. Spoon the salsa over the prepared pork. Divide the pork among bowls and serve garnished with the avocado slices.

Lush Pork Curry
Prep time: 15 minutes | Cook time: 15 minutes | Serves 6

1 teaspoon cumin seeds
1 teaspoon fennel seeds
½ teaspoon mustard seeds
2 chili peppers, deseeded and minced
1 teaspoon mixed peppercorns
½ teaspoon ground bay leaf
1 tablespoon sesame oil
1½ pounds (680 g) pork steak, sliced
1 cup chicken broth
3 tablespoons coconut cream
2 tablespoons balsamic

vinegar
2 tablespoons chopped scallions
2 cloves garlic, finely minced
1 teaspoon curry powder
1 teaspoon grated fresh ginger
¼ teaspoon crushed red pepper flakes
¼ teaspoon ground black pepper
1 cup vegetable broth
Sea salt, to taste

Heat a skillet over medium-high heat and roast the cumin seeds, fennel seeds, mustard seeds, peppers, peppercorns, and ground bay leaf and until aromatic. Set the Instant Pot to Sauté. Add and heat the sesame oil until sizzling. Sear the pork steak until nicely browned. Stir in the roasted seasonings and the remaining ingredients. Lock the lid. Select the Pressure Cook mode and set the cooking time for 8 minutes at High Pressure. When the timer beeps, do a quick pressure release. Carefully open the lid. Divide the mix among bowls and serve immediately.

Green Bean and Pork Shoulder Bowl
Prep time: 10 minutes | Cook time: 35 minutes | Serves 4

2 pounds (907 g) pork shoulder, boneless and cubed
1 cup green beans, trimmed and halved
1 cup corn

1 cup beef stock
2 garlic cloves, minced
1 teaspoon ground cumin
A pinch of salt and black pepper

Combine all the ingredients in the Instant Pot. Secure the lid. Select the Pressure Cook mode and set the cooking time for 35 minutes at High Pressure. Once cooking is complete, do a natural pressure release for 10 minutes, then release any remaining pressure. Carefully open the lid. Divide the mix among four plates and serve.

Lamb Shoulder with Anchovies
Prep time: 10 minutes | Cook time: 1 hour 5 minutes | Serves 4

2 tablespoons olive oil
2 pounds (907 g) boneless lamb shoulder, cut into 4 pieces
2 cups chicken stock
6 tinned anchovies, chopped

1 teaspoon garlic purée
3 green chilies, minced
1 sprig rosemary
1 teaspoon dried oregano
Salt, to taste
2 tablespoons chopped parsley

Press the Sauté button on the Instant Pot. Heat the olive oil and sear the lamb shoulder on both sides for 5 minutes, or until browned. Transfer the lamb to a plate and set aside. Pour the chicken stock into the Instant Pot and add the anchovies and garlic. Return the lamb to the pot and sprinkle the green chilies, rosemary, oregano and salt on top. Set the lid in place, select the Pressure Cook mode and set the cooking time for 60 minutes on High Pressure. When the timer goes off, use a natural pressure release for 15 minutes, then release any remaining pressure. Open the lid, shred the lamb with two forks and top with the chopped parsley. Serve warm.

Spicy Lamb and Onion
Prep time: 10 minutes | Cook time: 20 minutes | Serves 2

½ pound (227 g) ground lamb meat
½ cup onion, chopped
½ tablespoon minced ginger
½ tablespoon garlic

½ teaspoon salt
¼ teaspoon ground coriander
¼ teaspoon cayenne pepper
¼ teaspoon cumin
¼ teaspoon turmeric

Press the Sauté button on the Instant Pot. Add the onion, ginger and garlic to the pot and sauté for 5 minutes. Add the remaining ingredients to the pot and lock the lid. Select the Pressure Cook mode and set the cooking time for 15 minutes on High Pressure. Once the timer goes off, perform a natural pressure release for 15 minutes. Open the lid and serve immediately.

Pork Shoulder and Celery
Prep time: 10 minutes | Cook time: 30 minutes | Serves 4

2 tablespoons avocado oil
4 garlic cloves, minced
2 pounds (907 g) pork shoulder, boneless and cubed
1½ cups beef stock

2 celery stalks, chopped
2 tablespoons chili powder
1 tablespoon chopped sage
A pinch of salt and black pepper

Press the Sauté button on the Instant Pot and heat the avocado oil. Add the garlic and sauté for 2 minutes until fragrant. Stir in the pork and brown for another 3 minutes. Add the remaining ingredients to the Instant Pot and mix well. Secure the lid. Select the Manual mode and set the cooking time for 25 minutes at High Pressure. Once cooking is complete, do a natural pressure release for 10 minutes, then release any remaining pressure. Carefully open the lid. Serve warm.

Chili Pork Roast and Tomatoes

Prep time: 10 minutes | Cook time: 35 minutes | Serves 4

1 tablespoon olive oil
4 garlic cloves, minced
1 yellow onion, chopped
1½ pounds (680 g) pork roast
12 ounces (340 g) tomatoes, crushed
1 cup beef stock
2 tablespoons chili powder
1 tablespoon apple cider vinegar
1 teaspoon dried oregano
A pinch of salt and black pepper

Press the Sauté button on the Instant Pot and heat the olive oil. Add the garlic and onion and sauté for 5 minutes, stirring occasionally. Add the remaining ingredients to the Instant Pot and stir. Secure the lid. Select the Manual mode and set the cooking time for 30 minutes at High Pressure. Once cooking is complete, do a natural pressure release for 10 minutes, then release any remaining pressure. Carefully open the lid. Serve hot.

Cheesy Pork and Broccoli

Prep time: 10 minutes | Cook time: 30 minutes | Serves 4

1 tablespoon olive oil
1½ pounds (680 g) pork stew meat, cubed
2 cups broccoli florets
1½ cups beef stock
¼ cup tomato purée
1 tablespoon grated ginger
A pinch of salt and black pepper
¾ cup grated Parmesan cheese
1 tablespoon chopped basil

Press the Sauté button on the Instant Pot and heat the olive oil. Add the pork and brown for 5 minutes. Stir in the broccoli, beef stock, tomato purée, ginger, salt, and pepper. Secure the lid. Select the Manual mode and set the cooking time for 25 minutes at High Pressure. Once cooking is complete, do a natural pressure release for 5 minutes, then release any remaining pressure. Carefully open the lid. Scatter the grated cheese and basil all over. Lock the lid and allow to sit for 5 minutes. Divide the mix among four plates and serve.

Beef Roast with Cauliflower

Prep time: 10 minutes | Cook time: 15 minutes | Serves 2

2 teaspoons sesame oil
12 ounces (340 g) sliced beef roast
Freshly ground black pepper, to taste
½ small onion, chopped
3 garlic cloves, minced
½ cup beef stock
¼ cup soy sauce
2 tablespoons brown sugar
Pinch red pepper flakes
1 tablespoon cornstarch
8 ounces (227 g) fresh cauliflower, cut into florets

Set the Instant Pot pot on Sauté mode. Add the sesame oil, beef, and black pepper. Sear for 2 minutes on all sides. Transfer the beef to a plate and set aside. Add the onion and garlic to the pot and sauté for 2 minutes or until softened. Stir in the stock, soy sauce, brown sugar, and red pepper flakes. Stir until the sugar is dissolved, then return the beef to the pot. Secure the lid and set to the Manual mode. Set the cooking time for 10 minutes on High Pressure. When timer beeps, quick release the pressure and open the lid. Set to the Sauté mode. Transfer 2 tablespoons of liquid from the pot to a small bowl. Whisk it with the cornstarch, then add back to the pot along with the cauliflower. Cover the lid and let simmer for 3 to 4 minutes, or until the sauce is thickened and the cauliflower is softened. Serve the beef and cauliflower.

Dill Pork, Spinach and Tomatoes

Prep time: 10 minutes | Cook time: 25 minutes | Serves 4

2 tablespoons olive oil
½ cup chopped yellow onion
1½ pounds (680 g) pork stew meat, cubed
2 cups baby spinach
2 tomatoes, cubed
1½ cups beef stock
1 tablespoon chopped dill
1 teaspoon hot paprika
1 teaspoon dried cumin
A pinch of salt and black pepper

Press the Sauté button on the Instant Pot and heat the olive oil. Add the onion and pork and brown for 3 minutes. Add the remaining ingredients to the Instant Pot and stir well. Secure the lid. Select the Manual mode and set the cooking time for 20 minutes at High Pressure. Once cooking is complete, do a natural pressure release for 10 minutes, then release any remaining pressure. Carefully open the lid. Serve hot.

Beef Meatballs with Roasted Tomatoes

Prep time: 15 minutes | Cook time: 16 minutes | Serves 4

2 tablespoons avocado oil
1 pound (454 g) ground beef
½ teaspoon dried basil
½ teaspoon crushed red pepper
½ teaspoon ground cayenne
pepper
½ teaspoon kosher salt
½ teaspoon freshly ground black pepper
2 (14-ounce / 397-g) cans fire roasted tomatoes

Set the Instant Pot to Sauté mode and heat the avocado oil. In a large bowl, mix the remaining ingredients, except for the tomatoes. Form the mixture into 1½-inch meatballs and place them into the Instant Pot. Spread the tomatoes evenly over the meatballs. Close the lid. Select the Manual mode, set the cooking time for 16 minutes on High Pressure. When timer beeps, perform a natural pressure release for 5 minutes, then release any remaining pressure. Open the lid and serve.

Lamb Tagine with Carrots

Prep time: 15 minutes | Cook time: 32 to 34 minutes | Serves 4

2 tablespoons ghee
1½ pounds (680 g) lamb stew meat, cubed
4 large carrots, peeled and chopped
1 large red onion, chopped
6 cloves garlic, minced
2 teaspoons coriander powder
2 teaspoons ginger powder
2 teaspoons cumin powder
½ teaspoon turmeric
¼ teaspoon clove powder
¼ teaspoon cinnamon powder
¼ teaspoon red chili flakes
2 bay leaves
1 lemon, zested and juiced
Salt and black pepper, to taste
2 cups vegetable stock
2 cups green olives, pitted
3 tablespoons chopped parsley

Select the Sauté setting. Melt the ghee and add the lamb to the pot. Cook for 6 to 7 minutes, or until the lamb is lightly browned. Stir in the carrots, onion and garlic and cook for 5 minutes, or until the vegetables are tender. Add the coriander, ginger, cumin, turmeric, clove, cinnamon, red chili flakes, bay leaves, lemon zest, lemon juice, salt and pepper to the pot. Cook for 1 to 2 minutes, or until fragrant. Pour the vegetable stock into the pot. Lock the lid. Select Manual mode and set the cooking time for 20 minutes on High Pressure. Once cooking is complete, use a natural pressure release for 10 minutes, then release any remaining pressure. Open the lid. Discard the bay leaves and stir in the green olives and parsley. Divide the dish among 4 serving bowls and serve warm.

Beef Rice Noodles

Prep time: 15 minutes | Cook time: 16 minutes | Serves 4

6 cups boiled water
8 ounces (227 g) rice noodles
1 tablespoon sesame oil
1 pound (454 g) ground beef
2 cups sliced shitake mushrooms
Sauce:
¼ cup tamarind sauce
1 tablespoon hoisin sauce

½ cup julienned carrots
1 yellow onion, sliced
1 cup shredded green cabbage
¼ cup sliced scallions, for garnish
Sesame seeds, for garnish

1 teaspoon grated ginger
1 teaspoon maple syrup

In a medium bowl, whisk together the ingredients for the sauce. Set aside. Pour boiling water into a bowl and add rice noodles. Cover the bowl and allow the noodles to soften for 5 minutes. Drain and set aside. Set the Instant Pot to Sauté mode and heat the sesame oil. Cook the beef in the pot for 5 minutes or until browned. Stir in the mushrooms, carrots, onion, and cabbage. Cook for 5 minutes or until softened. Add the noodles. Top with the sauce and mix well. Cook for 1 more minute. Garnish with scallions and sesame seeds and serve immediately.

Beef Steaks with Mushrooms

Prep time: 15 minutes | Cook time: 25 minutes | Serves 2

2 beef steaks, boneless
Salt and black pepper, to taste
2 tablespoons olive oil
4 ounces (113 g) mushrooms, sliced

½ onion, chopped
1 garlic clove, minced
1 cup vegetable soup
1½ tablespoons cornstarch
1 tablespoon half-and-half

Rub the beef steaks with salt and pepper on a clean work surface. Set the Instant Pot to Sauté mode and warm the olive oil until shimmering. Sear the beef for 2 minutes per side until browned. Transfer to a plate. Add the mushrooms and sauté for 5 minutes or until soft. Add the onion and garlic and sauté for 2 minutes until fragrant. Return the steaks to the pot and pour in the soup. Seal the lid, select the Manual mode, and set the time to 15 minutes on High Pressure. When cooking is complete, do a quick pressure release and unlock the lid and transfer the chops to a plate. Press the Sauté button. In a bowl, combine the cornstarch and half-and-half and mix well. Pour the mixture into the pot and cook until the sauce is thickened. Serve warm.

Beery Back Ribs

Prep time: 20 minutes | Cook time: 50 minutes | Serves 2 to 4

½ pound (227 g) back ribs
4 ounces (113 g) beers
½ cup BBQ sauce
½ red chili, sliced
½ onion, chopped
1 garlic clove, minced
1-inch piece fresh ginger,

minced
2 tablespoons tamari
1 tablespoon agave nectar
Sea salt and ground black pepper, to taste
1 teaspoon toasted sesame seeds

Place the back ribs, beers, BBQ sauce, red chili, onion, garlic, and ginger in the Instant Pot. Secure the lid. Choose the Manual mode and set the cooking time for 40 minutes at High pressure. Once cooking is complete, perform a natural pressure release for 10 minutes, then release any remaining pressure. Carefully open the lid. Add the tamari sauce, agave, salt and pepper and place the beef ribs under the broiler. Broil ribs for 10 minutes or until well browned. Serve with sesame seeds.

Beef Tips with Portobello Mushrooms

Prep time: 20 minutes | Cook time: 16 minutes | Serves 4

2 teaspoons olive oil
1 beef top sirloin steak (1-pound / 454-g), cubed
½ teaspoon salt
¼ teaspoon ground black pepper
½ pound (227 g) sliced baby portobello mushrooms

⅓ cup dry red wine
1 small onion, halved and sliced
2 cups beef broth
1 tablespoon Worcestershire sauce
3 to 4 tablespoons cornstarch
¼ cup cold water

Select the Sauté setting of the Instant Pot. Add the olive oil. Sprinkle the beef with salt and pepper. Brown meat in batches in the pot for 10 minutes. Flip constantly. Transfer meat to a bowl. Add the wine to the pot. Return beef to the pot and add mushrooms, onion, broth, and Worcestershire sauce. Lock the lid. Select the Manual setting and set the cooking time for 15 minutes at High Pressure. When timer beeps, quick release the pressure. Carefully open the lid. Select the Sauté setting and bring to a boil. Meanwhile, in a small bowl, mix cornstarch and water until smooth. Gradually stir the cornstarch into beef mixture. Sauté for 1 more minute or until sauce is thickened. Serve immediately.

Beef with Red and Green Cabbage

Prep time: 20 minutes | Cook time: 22 minutes | Serves 4

1 tablespoon olive oil
1 pound (454 g) ground beef
1 tablespoon grated ginger
3 garlic cloves, minced
Salt and black pepper, to taste
1 medium red cabbage, shredded
1 medium green cabbage, shredded

1 red bell pepper, chopped
1 cup water
2 tablespoons tamarind sauce
½ tablespoon honey
1 tablespoon hot sauce
1 tablespoon sesame oil
2 tablespoons walnuts
1 teaspoon toasted sesame seeds

Set the Instant Pot to Sauté mode and heat the olive oil. Add the beef, then season with ginger, garlic, salt, black pepper. Cook for 5 minutes. Add the red and green cabbage, bell pepper, and sauté for 5 minutes. Pour in the water and seal the lid. Select the Manual mode and set the time to 10 minutes on High Pressure. When timer beeps, allow a natural release for 10 minutes, then release any remaining pressure. Unlock the lid. Meanwhile, in a bowl, combine the tamarind sauce, honey, hot sauce, and sesame oil. Stir in the pot, add walnuts, and cook for 1 to 2 minutes on Sauté mode. Dish out and garnish with sesame seeds. Serve warm.

Japanese Beef Shanks

Prep time: 15 minutes | Cook time: 30 minutes | Serves 4

1 pound (454 g) beef shank
½ teaspoon Five-spice powder
1 teaspoon instant dashi granules
½ teaspoon garlic, minced
1 tablespoon tamari or soy

sauce
¼ cup rice wine
1 clove star anise
½ dried red chili, sliced
1 tablespoon sesame oil
¾ cup water

Combine all ingredients to the Instant Pot. Secure the lid. Choose the Manual mode and set the cooking time for 30 minutes at High pressure. Once cooking is complete, use a natural pressure release for 10 minutes, then release any remaining pressure. Carefully open the lid. Slice the beef shank and serve hot.

Milky Lamb with Potatoes

Prep time: 10 minutes | Cook time: 1 hour | Serves 4

2 pounds (907 g) boneless lamb shoulder, cubed	2 rosemary sprigs
1 pound (454 g) potatoes, cubed	4 cups milk
3 carrots, cubed	2 cups water
5 garlic cloves	1 tablespoon Vegeta seasoning
	Salt and black pepper, to taste

Add all the ingredients to the Instant Pot and stir to combine. Lock the lid. Select the Manual mode and set the cooking time for 60 minutes on High Pressure. Once cooking is complete, use a natural pressure release for 10 minutes, then release any remaining pressure. Carefully open the lid. Remove and discard the rosemary springs. Divide the dish among four serving bowls and serve warm.

Herbed Beef Ribs with Leek

Prep time: 40 minutes | Cook time: 1 hour 40 minutes | Serves 4

1 pound (454 g) beef short ribs, bone-in	1 sprig thyme
½ medium leek, sliced	1 sprig rosemary
½ teaspoon celery seeds	1 tablespoon olive oil
1 teaspoon onion soup mix	Sea salt and ground black pepper, to taste
1 clove garlic, sliced	1 cup water

Place all ingredients in the Instant Pot. Secure the lid. Choose the Manual mode and set the cooking time for 90 minutes at High pressure. Once cooking is complete, do a natural pressure release for 30 minutes, then release any remaining pressure. Carefully open the lid. Transfer the short ribs in the broiler and broil for 10 minutes or until crispy. Transfer the ribs to a platter and serve.

Cheesy and Creamy Delmonico Steak

Prep time: 10 minutes | Cook time: 20 minutes | Serves 4

1 tablespoon butter	¼ cup sour cream
1 pound (454 g) Delmonico steak, cubed	1 teaspoon cayenne pepper
½ cup double cream	Sea salt and ground black pepper, to taste
½ cup beef broth	¼ cup gorgonzola cheese, shredded
1 clove garlic, minced	

Press the Sauté button of the Instant Pot. Melt the butter and brown the beef cubes in batches for about 4 minutes per batch. Add the double cream, broth, garlic, and sour cream to the Instant Pot, then season with cayenne pepper, salt, and black pepper. Secure the lid. Choose the Manual mode and set the cooking time for 10 minutes at High pressure. Once cooking is complete, use a quick pressure release. Carefully open the lid. Top with gorgonzola cheese and serve.

Citrus Beef Carnitas

Prep time: 15 minutes | Cook time: 25 minutes | Serves 8

2½ pounds (1.1 kg) bone-in country ribs	1 onion, cut into wedges
Salt, to taste	2 garlic cloves, smashed and peeled
¼ cup orange juice	1 teaspoon chili powder
1½ cups beef stock	1 cup shredded Jack cheese

Season the ribs with salt on a clean work surface. In the Instant Pot, combine the orange juice and stock. Fold in the onion and garlic. Put the ribs in the pot. Sprinkle with chili powder. Seal the lid, select the Manual mode and set the cooking time for 25 minutes at High Pressure. Once cooking is complete, do a natural pressure release for 10 minutes, then release any remaining pressure. Carefully open the lid. Transfer beef to a plate to cool. Remove and discard the bones. Shred the ribs with two forks. Top the beef with the sauce remains in the pot. Sprinkled with cheese and serve.

Classic Sloppy Joes

Prep time: 10 minutes | Cook time: 19 minutes | Serves 4

1 pound (454 g) ground beef, divided	1 garlic clove, minced
½ cup chopped onion	1 tablespoon Dijon mustard
½ cup chopped green bell pepper	¾ cup ketchup
¼ cup water	2 teaspoons brown sugar
2 teaspoons Worcestershire sauce	¼ teaspoon sea salt
	½ teaspoon hot sauce
	4 soft hamburger buns

Select the Sauté mode of the Instant Pot. Put about ½ cup of the ground beef in the pot and cook for about 4 minutes or until browned. Stir in the onion, bell pepper, and water. Add the remaining beef and cook for about 3 minutes or until well browned. Mix in the Worcestershire sauce, garlic, mustard, ketchup, brown sugar, and salt. Lock the lid. Select the Manual mode. Set the time for 12 minutes at High Pressure. When timer beeps, quick release the pressure, then unlock the lid. Stir in the hot sauce. Select the Sauté mode and simmer until lightly thickened. Spoon the meat and sauce into the buns. Serve immediately.

Dijon Lemony Leg of Lamb

Prep time: 10 minutes | Cook time: 3 to 4 hours | Serves 8

½ cup Dijon mustard	black pepper
¼ cup fresh lemon juice	1 (3- to 4-pound / 1.4- to 1.8-kg) boneless leg of lamb, butterflied, fat trimmed
Grated zest of 2 lemons	1 cup dry white wine
6 garlic cloves, minced	½ cup finely chopped fresh Italian parsley
¼ cup extra-virgin olive oil	
1 teaspoon dried oregano	
1 teaspoon salt	
½ teaspoon freshly ground	

Combine the mustard, lemon juice, zest, garlic, oil, oregano, salt, and pepper in a mixing bowl. Pour the marinade into a zipper-top plastic bag, add the lamb to the bag, and turn it to coat. Seal the bag and refrigerate for at least 8 hours or up to 24 hours. Drain the marinade, and roll the meat into a compact cylinder, tying the meat at 1-inch intervals with kitchen string or silicone loops, and put the lamb in insert of the Instant Pot. Add the wine. Cover and press the Slow Cook button, and cook on high for 3 hours to 4 hours, until the meat is tender. (Press Slow Cook again to toggle between Low and High cooking temperatures.) Remove the meat from the Instant Pot, cover with aluminum foil, and allow to rest for 20 minutes. Strain the sauce through a fine-mesh sieve into a saucepan and remove any fat from the surface. Boil until the sauce is reduced by half. Taste and adjust the seasonings, adding the parsley to the sauce. Cut the meat into ½-inch-thick slices and serve with the sauce on the side.

Greek Beef and Spinach Ravioli

Prep time: 15 minutes | Cook time: 20 minutes | Serves 4

1 cup cheese ravioli
3 cups water
Salt, to taste
1 tablespoon olive oil
1 pound (454 g) ground beef
1 cup canned diced tomatoes

1 tablespoon dried mixed herbs
3 cups chicken broth
1 cup baby spinach
¼ cup Kalamata olives, sliced
¼ cup crumbled feta cheese

Put ravioli, water, and salt in Instant Pot. Seal the lid, select the Manual mode and set the time for 3 minutes at High Pressure. Once cooking is complete, do a quick pressure release. Carefully open the lid. Drain the ravioli through a colander and set aside. Set the pot to Sauté mode, then heat the olive oil. Add and brown the beef for 5 minutes. Mix in the tomatoes, mixed herbs, and chicken broth. Seal the lid, select the Manual mode and set cooking time for 10 minutes on High Pressure. When timer beeps, do a quick pressure release. Carefully open the lid. Set the pot to Sauté mode, then mix in ravioli, spinach, olives and cook for 2 minutes or until spinach wilts. Stir in the feta cheese and serve.

Ground Beef and Mushroom Stroganoff

Prep time: 25 minutes | Cook time: 20 minutes | Serves 8

2 pounds (907 g) ground beef, divided
1½ teaspoons salt, divided
1 teaspoon ground black pepper, divided
½ pound (227 g) sliced fresh mushrooms
1 tablespoon butter
2 medium onions, chopped

2 garlic cloves, minced
1 (10½-ounce / 298-g) can condensed beef consomme, undiluted
⅓ cup all-purpose flour
2 tablespoons tomato paste
1½ cups sour cream
Hot cooked noodles, for serving

Select the Sauté setting of the Instant Pot. Add half of ground beef, salt and pepper. Sauté for 8 minutes or until no longer pink. Remove the beef. Repeat with remaining ground beef, salt and pepper. Add mushrooms, butter, and onions to Instant Pot. Sauté for 6 minutes or until mushrooms are tender. Add garlic and sauté for 1 minute more until fragrant. Return the beef to the pot. Lock the lid. Select the Manual setting and set the cooking time for 5 minutes at High Pressure. When timer beeps, quick release pressure. Carefully open the lid. Select the Sauté setting. In a small bowl, whisk together consomme, flour and tomato paste. Pour over the beef and stir to combine. Sauté for 3 more minutes or until thickened. Stir in sour cream; cook for a minute more until heated through. Serve with noodles.

Spicy Minced Lamb Meat

Prep time: 10 minutes | Cook time: 20 minutes | Serves 2

½ pound (227 g) ground lamb meat
½ cup onion, chopped
½ tablespoon minced ginger
½ tablespoon garlic

½ teaspoon salt
¼ teaspoon ground coriander
¼ teaspoon cayenne pepper
¼ teaspoon cumin
¼ teaspoon turmeric

Press the Sauté button on the Instant Pot. Add the onion, ginger and garlic to the pot and sauté for 5 minutes. Add the remaining ingredients to the pot and lock the lid. Select the Manual mode and set the cooking time for 15 minutes on High Pressure. Once the timer goes off, perform a natural pressure release for 15 minutes. Open the lid and serve immediately.

Hot Sirloin with Snap Peas

Prep time: 15 minutes | Cook time: 8 minutes | Serves 4

½ teaspoon hot sauce
1 teaspoon balsamic vinegar
1 cup chicken stock
¼ cup soy sauce
2 tablespoons sesame oil, divided
2 tablespoons maple syrup

½ cup plus 2 teaspoons cornstarch, divided
1 pound (454 g) beef sirloin, sliced
2 cups snap peas
3 garlic cloves, minced
3 scallions, sliced

In a bowl, combine the hot sauce, vinegar, stock, soy sauce, 1 tablespoon of sesame oil, maple syrup, and 2 tablespoons of cornstarch. Set aside. Pour the remaining cornstarch on a plate. Season beef with salt, and pepper; toss lightly in cornstarch. Set the Instant Pot to Sauté mode, heat the remaining sesame oil and fry the beef in batches for 5 minutes or until browned and crispy. Remove the beef from the pot and set aside. Wipe the Instant Pot clean and pour in hot sauce mixture. Return meat to the pot, then add snow peas and garlic. Seal the lid, select the Manual mode and set the time for 3 minutes on High Pressure. When cooking is complete, perform natural pressure release for 10 minutes, then release the remaining pressure. Unlock the lid. Dish out and garnish with scallions.

Pork Chili Verde

Prep time: 10 minutes | Cook time: 5 to 6 hours | Serves 12

1 boneless pork shoulder roast (4 to 5 pounds / 1.8 to 2.3 kg), cut into 1-inch pieces
3 (10-ounce / 283-g) cans green enchilada sauce
1 cup salsa verde

1 (4-ounce / 113-g) can chopped green chilies
½ teaspoon salt
Hot cooked rice, for serving
Sour cream (optional)

In the Instant Pot, combine pork, enchilada sauce, salsa verde, green chilies and salt. Cover and press the Slow Cook button, and cook on low for 5 to 6 hours or until pork is tender. (Press Slow Cook again to toggle between Low and High cooking temperatures.) Serve with rice. If desired, top with sour cream.

Indian Spicy Beef with Basmati

Prep time: 15 minutes | Cook time: 15 minutes | Serves 4

1 tablespoon olive oil
1 pound (454 g) beef stew meat, cubed
Salt and black pepper, to taste
½ teaspoon garam masala powder
½ teaspoon grated ginger
2 white onions, sliced
2 garlic cloves, minced
1 tablespoon cilantro leaves

½ teaspoon red chili powder
1 teaspoon cumin powder
¼ teaspoon turmeric powder
1 cup basmati rice
1 cup grated carrots
2 cups beef broth
¼ cup cashew nuts
¼ cup coconut yogurt, for serving

Set the Instant Pot to Sauté mode, then heat the olive oil. Season the beef with salt and pepper, and brown both sides for 5 minutes. Transfer to a plate and set aside. Add and sauté the garam masala, ginger, onions, garlic, cilantro, red chili, cumin, turmeric, salt, and pepper for 2 minutes. Stir in beef, rice, carrots, and broth. Seal the lid, select the Manual mode, and set the time to 6 minutes on High Pressure. When cooking is complete, do a natural pressure release for 5 minutes, then release any remaining pressure. Unlock the lid. Fluff the rice and stir in cashews. Serve with coconut yogurt.

Korean Flavor Beef Ribs

Prep time: 10 minutes | Cook time: 15 minutes | Serves 6

3 pounds (1.4 kg) beef short ribs
1 cup beef broth
Sauce:
½ teaspoon gochujang
½ cup rice wine
½ cup soy sauce
½ teaspoon garlic powder

2 green onions, sliced
1 tablespoon toasted sesame seeds

½ teaspoon ground ginger
½ cup pure maple syrup
1 teaspoon white pepper
1 tablespoon sesame oil

In a large bowl, combine the ingredients for the sauce. Dunk the rib in the bowl and press to coat well. Cover the bowl in plastic and refrigerate for at least an hour. Add the beef broth to the Instant Pot. Insert a trivet. Arrange the ribs standing upright over the trivet. Lock the lid. Press the Manual button and set the cooking time for 25 minutes at High Pressure. When timer beeps, let pressure release naturally for 10 minutes, then release any remaining pressure. Unlock the lid. Transfer ribs to a serving platter and garnish with green onions and sesame seeds. Serve immediately.

Spicy Lamb Shoulder

Prep time: 10 minutes | Cook time: 50 minutes | Serves 4

2 pounds (907 g) lamb shoulder
1 cup chopped fresh thyme
¼ cup rice wine
¼ cup chicken stock
1 tablespoon turmeric
1 tablespoon ground black

pepper
1 teaspoon oregano
1 teaspoon paprika
1 teaspoon sugar
1 tablespoon olive oil
½ cup water
4 tablespoons butter

In a large bowl, whisk together the thyme, rice wine, chicken stock, turmeric, black pepper, oregano, paprika and sugar. Rub all sides of the lamb shoulder with the spice mix. Press the Sauté button on the Instant Pot and heat the oil. Add the lamb to the pot and sear for 6 minutes on both sides, or until browned. Add the remaining spice mixture, water and butter to the pot. Stir until the butter is melted. Lock the lid. Select the Manual mode and set the cooking time for 45 minutes on High Pressure. Once cooking is complete, do a natural pressure release for 10 minutes, then release any remaining pressure. Carefully open the lid. Serve hot.

Mexican Beef Shred

Prep time: 20 minutes | Cook time: 30 minutes | Serves 4

1 pound (454 g) tender chuck roast, cut into half
3 tablespoons chipotle sauce
1 (8-ounce / 227-g) can tomato sauce
1 cup beef broth
½ cup chopped cilantro

1 lime, zested and juiced
2 teaspoons cumin powder
1 teaspoon cayenne pepper
Salt and ground black pepper, to taste
½ teaspoon garlic powder
1 tablespoon olive oil

In the Instant Pot, add the beef, chipotle sauce, tomato sauce, beef broth, cilantro, lime zest, lime juice, cumin powder, cayenne pepper, salt, pepper, and garlic powder. Seal the lid, then select the Manual mode and set the cooking time for 30 minutes at High Pressure. Once cooking is complete, allow a natural pressure release for 10 minutes, then release any remaining pressure. Unlock the lid and using two forks to shred the beef into strands. Stir in the olive oil. Serve warm.

Spicy Lamb with Anchovies

Prep time: 10 minutes | Cook time: 1 hour 5 minutes | Serves 4

2 tablespoons olive oil
2 pounds (907 g) boneless lamb shoulder, cut into 4 pieces
2 cups chicken stock
6 tinned anchovies, chopped

1 teaspoon garlic purée
3 green chilies, minced
1 sprig rosemary
1 teaspoon dried oregano
Salt, to taste
2 tablespoons chopped parsley

Press the Sauté button on the Instant Pot. Heat the olive oil and sear the lamb shoulder on both sides for 5 minutes, or until browned. Transfer the lamb to a plate and set aside. Pour the chicken stock into the Instant Pot and add the anchovies and garlic. Return the lamb to the pot and sprinkle the green chilies, rosemary, oregano and salt on top. Set the lid in place, select the Manual mode and set the cooking time for 60 minutes on High Pressure. When the timer goes off, use a natural pressure release for 15 minutes, then release any remaining pressure. Open the lid, shred the lamb with two forks and top with the chopped parsley. Serve warm.

Saucy Italian Beef Chuck

Prep time: 10 minutes | Cook time: 19 minutes | Serves 6

1 tablespoon olive oil
1 pound (454 g) 95% lean ground chuck
1 medium yellow onion, chopped
3 tablespoons tomato paste
3 medium garlic cloves,

chopped
2 teaspoons Italian seasoning
1 (28-ounce / 794-g) can tomatoes, chopped, with juice
½ cup beef broth
Salt and freshly ground black pepper, to taste

Put the olive oil in the pot, select the Sauté mode. Add the ground beef and onion and sauté for 8 minutes or until the beef is browned. Push the meat and onion mixture to one side of the pot. Add the tomato paste, garlic, and Italian seasoning to the other side of the pot and sauté for 1 minute or until fragrant. Add the tomatoes and the broth to the pot. Lock on the lid, select the Manual function, and set the cooking time for 10 minutes on High Pressure. When the cooking time is up, quick release the pressure. Season with salt and pepper and serve.

Ribeye Steak with Cauliflower Rice

Prep time: 15 minutes | Cook time: 20 minutes | Serves 4

1 cup water
1 ribeye steak
½ teaspoon dried parsley
½ teaspoon ground cumin
½ teaspoon ground turmeric
½ teaspoon paprika

½ teaspoon freshly ground black pepper
½ teaspoon kosher salt
1 head cauliflower, riced
2 tablespoons butter, softened

Pour the water into the Instant Pot, then insert a trivet. In a small bowl, mix the parsley, cumin, turmeric, paprika, black pepper, and salt. Coat the steak evenly with the mixture. Place the steak into a greased baking pan. Arrange the cauliflower rice beside the steak. Place the pan onto the trivet, and cover with aluminum foil. Close the lid, then select the Manual mode. Set the cooking time for 20 minutes on High Pressure. When timer beeps, naturally release the pressure for about 10 minutes, then release any remaining pressure. Carefully open the lid. Remove the pan. Add the butter to the steak. Serve immediately.

Lemongrass Beef and Rice Pot

Prep time: 45 minutes | Cook time: 15 minutes | Serves 4

1 pound (454 g) beef stew
meat, cut into cubes
2 tablespoons olive oil
1 green bell pepper, chopped
1 red bell pepper, chopped
1 lemongrass stalk, sliced
Marinade:
1 tablespoon rice wine
½ teaspoon Five-spice
½ teaspoon miso paste
1 teaspoon garlic purée
1 teaspoon chili powder
1 teaspoon cumin powder

1 onion, chopped
2 garlic cloves, minced
1 cup jasmine rice
2 cups chicken broth
2 tablespoons chopped
parsley, for garnish

1 tablespoon soy sauce
1 teaspoon plus ½ tablespoon
ginger paste, divided
½ teaspoon sesame oil
Salt and black pepper, to taste

In a bowl, add beef and top with the ingredients for the
marinade. Mix and wrap the bowl in plastic. Marinate in the
refrigerate for 30 minutes. Set the Instant Pot to Sauté mode,
then heat the olive oil. Drain beef from marinade and brown
in the pot for 5 minutes. Flip frequently. Stir in bell peppers,
lemongrass, onion, and garlic. Sauté for 3 minutes. Stir in rice,
cook for 1 minute. Pour in the broth. Seal the lid, select the
Manual mode and set the time for 5 minutes on High Pressure.
When timer beeps, perform a quick pressure release. Carefully
open the lid. Dish out and garnish with parsley. Serve warm.

Lamb with Peppers and Tomatoes

Prep time: 10 minutes | Cook time: 30 minutes | Serves 10

2 tablespoons olive oil
2 pounds (907 g) boneless
lamb, trimmed
Salt and black pepper, to taste
4 cups chopped tomatoes
3 cups sugar-free tomato
sauce
2 cups water
2 teaspoons crushed dried

rosemary
6 garlic cloves, minced
2 large yellow bell peppers,
deseeded and sliced
2 large red bell peppers,
deseeded and sliced
2 large green bell peppers,
deseeded and sliced

Press the Sauté button on the Instant Pot and heat the olive oil.
Add the lamb meat to the pot and season with salt and pepper.
Cook for 5 minutes. Transfer the lamb meat to a plate. Stir
together all the remaining ingredients in the pot and add the
lamb meat. Lock the lid. Select the Manual function and set the
cooking time for 25 minutes at High Pressure. Once cooking
is complete, use a quick pressure release. Open the lid. Serve
hot.

Lamb Curry with Tomatoes

Prep time: 15 minutes | Cook time: 59 minutes | Serves 4

¼ cup olive oil, divided
2 pounds (907 g) lamb
shoulder, cubed
4 green onions, sliced
2 tomatoes, peeled and
chopped
2 tablespoons garlic paste
1 tablespoon ginger paste
1½ cups vegetable stock
2 teaspoons ground coriander
2 teaspoons allspice

1 teaspoon ground cumin
½ teaspoon ground red chili
pepper
½ teaspoon curry powder
1 large carrot, sliced
1 potato, cubed
2 bay leaves
Salt, to taste
2 tablespoons mint leaves,
chopped

Press the Sauté button on the Instant Pot and heat 2
tablespoons of the olive oil. Add the green onions and sauté
for 3 minutes, or until softened, stirring constantly. Transfer the
green onions to a blender. Mix in the tomatoes, garlic paste
and ginger paste. Blend until smooth. Heat the remaining 2
tablespoons of the olive oil in the pot and add the lamb to the
pot. Cook for 6 minutes. Stir in the vegetable stock, coriander,
allspice, cumin, red chili pepper, curry powder, carrot, potato,
bay leaves and salt. Lock the lid. Select the Manual function and
set the cooking time for 50 minutes on High Pressure. When the
timer beeps, use a natural pressure release for 10 minutes, then
release any remaining pressure. Open the lid. Discard the bay
leaves. Top with the mint leaves and serve immediately.

Leg of Lamb and Cabbage

**Prep time: 10 minutes | Cook time: 5⅓ to 6⅓ hours | Serves
4 to 6**

½ teaspoon allspice berries
½ teaspoon black peppercorns
½ teaspoon whole cloves
1 small leg of lamb (about 2
pounds / 907 g), bone-in or
boned and tied
2 cups hot chicken broth

(optional)
½ cup dry white wine (optional)
¾ teaspoon to 1 teaspoon salt,
to your taste
1 head cabbage, cored and cut
into 8 wedges

Put the allspice berries, peppercorns, and cloves in a
cheesecloth bag or tea ball and set aside. Put the lamb in the
Instant Pot. Add the broth and wine, if using. Add hot water to
cover the lamb by an inch. Add the salt, using the lesser amount
if you used salted chicken broth. Add the spice ball. Cover and
press the Slow Cook button, and cook on high for 1 hour. (Press
Slow Cook again to toggle between Low and High cooking
temperatures.) Turn the Instant Pot to cook on low for 4 to 5
hours, until the lamb is fork-tender. (Press Slow Cook again to
toggle between Low and High cooking temperatures.) About
20 minutes before it is done, preheat the oven to 200ºF (93ºC).
Transfer the lamb to a platter, tent with aluminum foil, and place
in the oven to keep warm. Put the cabbage wedges in the hot
broth remaining in the Instant Pot, cover, and turn the heat to
high. Cook until tender, 20 to 30 minutes. Just before cabbage
is done, carve the meat. Serve the lamb in shallow bowls with 1
or 2 wedges of cabbage and some of the broth.

Mongolian Arrowroot Glazed Beef

Prep time: 15 minutes | Cook time: 20 minutes | Serves 4

1 tablespoon sesame oil
1 (2-pound / 907-g) skirt steak,
sliced into thin strips
½ cup pure maple syrup
¼ cup soy sauce
4 cloves garlic, minced

1-inch knob fresh ginger root,
peeled and grated
½ cup plus 2 tablespoons
water, divided
2 tablespoons arrowroot
powder

Press the Sauté button on the Instant Pot. Heat the sesame
oil. Add and sear the steak strips for 3 minutes on all sides. In
a medium bowl, whisk together maple syrup, soy sauce, garlic,
ginger, and ½ cup water. Pour the mixture over beef. Lock the
lid. Press the Manual button and set the cooking time for 10
minutes at High Pressure. When timer beeps, quick release the
pressure, then unlock the lid. Meanwhile, in a small dish, whisk
together the arrowroot and 2 tablespoons water until smooth
and chunky. Stir the arrowroot into the beef mixture. Press
the Sauté button and simmer for 5 minutes or until the sauce
thickens. Ladle the beef and sauce on plates and serve.

Slow Cooked Lamb Shanks

Prep time: 10 minutes | Cook time: 55 minutes | Serves 4

2 tablespoons olive oil
2 pounds (907 g) lamb shanks
Salt and black pepper, to taste
6 garlic cloves, minced
1 cup chicken broth

¾ cup red wine
2 cups crushed tomatoes
1 teaspoon dried oregano
¼ cup chopped parsley, for garnish

Press the Sauté button on the Instant Pot. Heat the olive oil and add the lamb to the pot. Season with salt and pepper. Sear the lamb on both sides for 6 minutes, or until browned. Transfer the lamb to a plate and set aside. Add the garlic to the pot and sauté for 30 seconds, or until fragrant. Stir in the chicken broth and red wine and cook for 2 minutes, stirring constantly. Add the tomatoes and oregano. Stir and cook for 2 minutes. Return the lamb to the pot and baste with the chicken broth mixture. Lock the lid. Select the Manual setting and set the cooking time for 45 minutes on High Pressure. When the timer beeps, do a natural pressure release for 15 minutes, then release any remaining pressure. Open the lid. Top with the chopped parsley and adjust the taste with salt and pepper. Divide among 4 plates and serve warm.

Lamb Curry with Zucchini

Prep time: 40 minutes | Cook time: 25 minutes | Serves 3

1 pound (454 g) cubed lamb stew meat
2 garlic cloves, minced
½ cup coconut milk
1 tablespoon grated fresh ginger
½ teaspoon lime juice
¼ teaspoon salt

¼ teaspoon black pepper
1 tablespoon olive oil
1½ medium carrots, sliced
½ medium onion, diced
¾ cup diced tomatoes
½ teaspoon turmeric powder
½ medium zucchini, diced

In a bowl, stir together the garlic, coconut milk, ginger, lime juice, salt and pepper. Add the lamb to the bowl and marinate for 30 minutes. Combine the remaining ingredients, except for the zucchini, in the Instant Pot. Add the meat and the marinade to the pot. Set the lid in place. Select the Manual mode and set the cooking time for 20 minutes on High Pressure. Once the timer goes off, use a natural pressure release for 15 minutes, then release any remaining pressure. Open the lid. Add the zucchini to the pot. Select the Sauté mode and cook for 5 minutes. Serve hot.

Sauce Glazed Lamb Chops

Prep time: 10 minutes | Cook time: 29 minutes | Serves 2

1½ tablespoons butter
1 pound (454 g) lamb loin chops
½ small onion, sliced
1 garlic clove, crushed
1 cup carrots, peeled and sliced
¾ cup diced sugar-free

tomatoes
½ cup bone broth
¾ teaspoon crushed dried rosemary
Salt and black pepper, to taste
1 tablespoon arrowroot starch
½ tablespoon cold water

Select the Sauté mode and heat the butter in the Instant Pot. Add the lamb chops to the pot and cook for 3 minutes on each side, or until lightly browned. Transfer the lamb chops to plates. Add the onion and garlic to the pot and cook for 3 minutes. Stir in the carrots, tomatoes, bone broth, rosemary, salt and pepper. Lock the lid. Select the Manual mode and set the cooking time for 15 minutes at High Pressure. When the timer goes off, do a

quick pressure release. Carefully open the lid. In a small bowl, whisk together the arrowroot starch and water. Pour the slurry in the pot. Select the Sauté mode and cook for 5 minutes. Spread the sauce over the cooked chops and serve hot.

Lamb Koobideh

Prep time: 15 minutes | Cook time: 30 minutes | Serves 4

1 pound (454 g) ground lamb
1 egg, beaten
1 tablespoon lemon juice
1 teaspoon ground turmeric
½ teaspoon garlic powder

1 teaspoon chives, chopped
½ teaspoon ground black pepper
1 cup water

In a mixing bowl, combine all the ingredients except for water. Shape the mixture into meatballs and press into ellipse shape. Pour the water and insert the trivet in the Instant Pot. Put the prepared ellipse meatballs in a baking pan and transfer on the trivet. Close the lid and select Manual mode. Set cooking time for 30 minutes on High Pressure. When timer beeps, make a quick pressure release. Open the lid. Serve immediately.

Saucy Short Ribs

Prep time: 20 minutes | Cook time: 40 minutes | Serves 4

2 tablespoons olive oil
1½ pounds (680 g) large beef short ribs
Salt and ground black pepper, to taste
3 garlic cloves, minced
1 medium onion, finely

chopped
½ cup apple cider vinegar
1 tablespoon honey
1 cup beef broth
2 tablespoons tomato paste
1 tablespoon cornstarch

Select the Sauté mode of the Instant Pot, then heat the olive oil. Season ribs with salt and pepper, and fry in the pot for 8 minutes or until browned. Remove from the pot and set aside. Sauté the garlic, onion, and cook for 4 minutes until fragrant. Stir in apple cider vinegar, honey, broth, tomato paste. Bring to a simmer. Add ribs. Seal the lid, then select the Manual mode and set the time for 25 minutes at High Pressure. Once cooking is complete, allow a natural pressure release for 10 minutes, then release any remaining pressure. Unlock the lid. Transfer the ribs to serving plates. Stir cornstarch into the sauce in the pot and stir for 1 minute or until thickened, on Sauté mode. Spoon sauce over ribs and serve.

Egg Meatloaf

Prep time: 20 minutes | Cook time: 25 minutes | Serves 6

1 tablespoon avocado oil
1½ cup ground pork
1 teaspoon chives
1 teaspoon salt
½ teaspoon ground black

pepper
2 tablespoons coconut flour
3 eggs, hard-boiled, peeled
1 cup water

Brush a loaf pan with avocado oil. In the mixing bowl, mix the ground pork, chives, salt, ground black pepper, and coconut flour. Transfer the mixture in the loaf pan and flatten with a spatula. Fill the meatloaf with hard-boiled eggs. Pour water and insert the trivet in the Instant Pot. Lower the loaf pan over the trivet in the Instant Pot. Close the lid. Select Manual mode and set cooking time for 25 minutes on High Pressure. When timer beeps, use a natural pressure release for 10 minutes, then release any remaining pressure. Open the lid. Serve immediately.

Green Chile Chicken Verde
Prep time: 5 minutes | Cook time: 15 minutes | Serves 4

3 pounds (1.4 kg) bone-in, skin-on chicken drumsticks and/or thighs
1 (27-ounce / 765-g) can roasted poblano peppers, drained
1 (15-ounce / 425-g) jar salsa verde (green chile salsa)

1 (7-ounce / 198-g) jar chopped green chiles, drained
1 onion, chopped
1 tablespoon chopped jalapeño (optional)
1 tablespoon ground cumin
4 teaspoons minced garlic
1 teaspoon fine sea salt

Mix together all the ingredients in your Instant Pot and stir to combine. Secure the lid. Press the Pressure Cook button and set the cooking time for 15 minutes on High Pressure. Once the timer goes off, use a quick pressure release. Carefully open the lid. Remove the chicken from the Instant Pot to a plate with tongs. Let cool for 5 minutes. Remove the bones and skin and discard. Shred the chicken with two forks. Transfer the chicken back to the sauce and stir to combine. Serve immediately.

Garlic-Honey Chicken
Prep time: 5 minutes | Cook time: 15 minutes | Serves 6

1½ pounds (680 g) chicken breasts, cut into cubes
3 cloves of garlic, minced
6 tablespoons honey
2 tablespoons online powder
1½ tablespoons soy sauce

½ tablespoon sriracha sauce
1 cup water
1 tablespoon cornstarch plus 2 tablespoons water
1 tablespoon sesame oil
Green onions, chopped

Add all the ingredients except the cornstarch slurry, sesame oil, and green onions to the Instant Pot and stir to combine. Secure the lid. Select the Pressure Cook mode and cook for 15 minutes on High Pressure. Once the timer goes off, use a quick pressure release. Carefully open the lid. Select the Sauté mode. Fold in the cornstarch slurry. Stir well. Let simmer until the sauce is thickened. Mix in the sesame oil and green onions and stir to combine. Serve immediately.

Cheesy Chicken with Ranch Dressing
Prep time: 5 minutes | Cook time: 15 minutes | Serves 2

½ cup grass-fed bone broth
½ pound (227 g) boneless, skinless chicken breasts
2 ounces (57 g) cream cheese, softened
¼ cup tablespoons keto-

friendly ranch dressing
3 slices bacon, cooked, chopped into small pieces
½ cup shredded full-fat Cheddar cheese

Add the bone broth, chicken, cream cheese, and ranch dressing to your Instant Pot and stir to combine. Secure the lid. Press the Pressure Cook button and set the cooking time for 15 minutes on High Pressure. When the timer goes off, do a quick pressure release. Carefully open the lid. Add the bacon and cheese and stir until the cheese has melted. Serve.

Orange Chicken Tacos
Prep time: 5 minutes | Cook time: 20 minutes | Serves 12

¼ cup olive oil
12 chicken breasts, skin and bones removed
8 cloves of garlic, minced
⅔ cup orange juice, freshly squeezed
⅔ cup lime juice, freshly

squeezed
2 tablespoons ground cumin
1 tablespoon dried oregano
1 tablespoon orange peel
Salt and pepper, to taste
¼ cup cilantro, chopped

Set your Instant Pot to Sauté. Add and heat the oil. Add the chicken breasts and garlic. Cook until the chicken pieces are lightly browned. Add the orange juice, lime juice, cumin, oregano, orange peel, salt, and pepper. Stir well. Secure the lid. Select the Pressure Cook mode and cook for 15 minutes on High Pressure. Once cooking is complete, do a quick pressure release. Carefully remove the lid. Serve garnished with the cilantro.

Chicken and Moringa Soup
Prep time: 3 minutes | Cook time: 18 minutes | Serves 8

1½ pounds (680 g) chicken breasts
5 cups water
1 cup chopped tomatoes
2 cloves garlic, minced

1 onion, chopped
1 thumb-size ginger
Salt and pepper, to taste
2 cups moringa leaves or kale leaves

Combine all the ingredients except the moringa leaves in the Instant Pot. Secure the lid. Select the Pressure Cook mode and set the cooking time for 15 minutes at High Pressure. Once cooking is complete, do a natural pressure release for 10 minutes, then release any remaining pressure. Carefully open the lid. Set your Instant Pot to Sauté and stir in the moringa leaves. Allow to simmer for 3 minutes until softened. Divide into bowls and serve warm.

Chicken Tacos with Fried Cheese Shells
Prep time: 5 minutes | Cook time: 25 minutes | Serves 6

Chicken:
4 (6-ounce / 170-g) boneless, skinless chicken breasts
1 cup chicken broth
1 teaspoon salt
Cheese Shells:
1½ cups shredded whole-milk Mozzarella cheese

¼ teaspoon pepper
1 tablespoon chili powder
2 teaspoons garlic powder
2 teaspoons cumin

Combine all ingredients for the chicken in the Instant Pot. Secure the lid. Select the Manual mode and set the cooking time for 20 minutes at High Pressure. Once cooking is complete, do a quick pressure release. Carefully open the lid. Shred the chicken and serve in bowls or cheese shells. Make the cheese shells: Heat a nonstick skillet over medium heat. Sprinkle ¼ cup of Mozzarella cheese in the skillet and fry until golden. Flip and turn off the heat. Allow the cheese to get brown. Fill with chicken and fold. The cheese will harden as it cools. Repeat with the remaining cheese and filling. Serve warm.

Chipotle Chicken and Bell Pepper Fajita

Prep time: 15 minutes | Cook time: 10 minutes | Serves 2

1 tablespoon oil
½ green bell pepper, sliced
¼ red onion, sliced
2 skinless, boneless chicken breasts
½ cup water
2 canned chipotle chiles in adobo sauce, deseeded and

minced
Kosher salt, to taste
3 tablespoons mayonnaise
¼ cup sour cream
½ tablespoon freshly squeezed lime juice
Freshly ground black pepper, to taste

Set your Instant Pot to Sauté and heat the oil until it shimmers. Add the bell pepper and onion and sauté for 3 to 4 minutes until tender. Remove from the Instant Pot to a small bowl and set aside to cool. Add the chicken breasts, water, and a few teaspoons of adobo sauce to the pot and season with salt to taste. Lock the lid. Select the Pressure Cook mode and set the cooking time for 6 minutes at High Pressure. Once cooking is complete, do a natural pressure release for 5 minutes, then release any remaining pressure. Carefully open the lid. Remove the chicken from the pot to a cutting board and allow to cool for 10 minutes. Slice the chicken breasts into cubes and place in a medium bowl. Add the cooked bell pepper and onion, mayo, sour cream, chipotle chiles, lime juice, salt, and pepper to the bowl of chicken and toss to coat. Serve immediately.

Chicken with Orange-Barbecue Sauce

Prep time: 5 minutes | Cook time: 18 minutes | Serves 4

4 chicken breasts
¾ cup orange marmalade
¾ cup barbecue sauce
¼ cup water
2 tablespoons soy sauce

1 tablespoon cornstarch, mixed with 2 tablespoons water
2 tablespoons green onions, chopped

Combine all the ingredients except the cornstarch mixture and green onions in the Instant Pot. Secure the lid. Select the Pressure Cook mode and set the cooking time for 15 minutes at High Pressure. Once cooking is complete, do a quick pressure release. Carefully open the lid. Set your Instant Pot to Sauté and stir in the cornstarch mixture. Simmer for a few minutes until the sauce is thickened. Add the green onions and stir well. Serve immediately.

Chili Chicken with Zoodles

Prep time: 10 minutes | Cook time: 20 minutes | Serves 4

2 chicken breasts, skinless, boneless and halved
1½ cups chicken stock
3 celery stalks, chopped
1 tablespoon tomato sauce

1 teaspoon chili powder
A pinch of salt and black pepper
2 zucchinis, spiralized
1 tablespoon chopped cilantro

Mix together all the ingredients except the zucchini noodles and cilantro in the Instant Pot. Secure the lid. Select the Pressure Cook mode and set the cooking time for 15 minutes at High Pressure. Once cooking is complete, do a natural pressure release for 10 minutes, then release any remaining pressure. Carefully open the lid. Set your Instant Pot to Sauté and add the zucchini noodles. Cook for about 5 minutes, stirring often, or until softened. Sprinkle the cilantro on top for garnish before serving.

Chicken, Broccoli, and Pea Lo Mein

Prep time: 10 minutes | Cook time: 10 minutes | Serves 4

1 tablespoon toasted sesame oil
1 garlic clove, minced
1½ pounds (680 g) boneless, skinless chicken breast, cut into bite-size pieces
Sauce:
1½ cups low-sodium chicken broth
1 tablespoon fish sauce
1 tablespoon soy sauce

8 ounces (227 g) dried linguine, broken in half
1 cup broccoli florets
1 carrot, peeled and thinly sliced
1 cup snow peas

1 tablespoon Shaoxing rice wine
1 tablespoon brown sugar
1 teaspoon grated fresh ginger

Press the Sauté button on the Instant Pot and heat the sesame oil until shimmering. Add the garlic and chicken and sauté for about 5 minutes, stirring occasionally, or until the garlic is lightly browned. Fan the noodles across the bottom of the Instant Pot. Top with the broccoli florets, carrot, finished by snow peas. Whisk together all the ingredients for the sauce in a medium bowl until the sugar is dissolved. Pour the sauce over the top of the vegetables. Secure the lid. Select the Pressure Cook mode and set the cooking time for 5 minutes at High Pressure. Once cooking is complete, do a quick pressure release. Carefully open the lid. Stir the noodles, breaking up any clumps, or until the liquid has absorbed. Serve warm.

Chicken with Cucumber and Avocado Salad

Prep time: 10 minutes | Cook time: 20 minutes | Serves 4

1 tablespoon olive oil
1 yellow onion, chopped
2 chicken breasts, skinless, boneless and halved
Salad:
2 cucumbers, sliced
1 tomato, cubed
1 avocado, peeled, pitted, and

1 cup chicken stock
1 tablespoon sweet paprika
½ teaspoon cinnamon powder

cubed
1 tablespoon chopped cilantro

Press the Sauté button on the Instant Pot and heat the olive oil until it shimmers. Add the onion and chicken breasts and sauté for 5 minutes, stirring occasionally, or until the onion is translucent. Stir in the chicken stock, paprika, and cinnamon powder. Secure the lid. Select the Pressure Cook mode and set the cooking time for 15 minutes at High Pressure. Meanwhile, toss all the ingredients for the salad in a bowl. Set aside. Once cooking is complete, do a natural pressure release for 10 minutes, then release any remaining pressure. Carefully open the lid. Divide the chicken breasts between four plates and serve with the salad on the side.

Garlic-Chili Chicken

Prep time: 10 minutes | Cook time: 20 minutes | Serves 4

2 chicken breasts, skinless, boneless and halved
1 cup tomato sauce
¼ cup sweet chili sauce

¼ cup chicken stock
4 garlic cloves, minced
1 tablespoon chopped basil

Combine all the ingredients in the Instant Pot. Secure the lid. Select the Pressure Cook mode and set the cooking time for 20 minutes at High Pressure. Once cooking is complete, do a natural pressure release for 10 minutes, then release any remaining pressure. Carefully open the lid. Divide the chicken breasts among four plates and serve.

Creole Chicken with Bell Peppers

Prep time: 10 minutes | Cook time: 25 minutes | Serves 4

2 tablespoons olive oil
1 yellow onion, chopped
2 chicken breasts, skinless, boneless and cubed
1 cup cubed mixed bell peppers
1 cup cubed tomato
1 cup chicken stock
1 teaspoon Creole seasoning
A pinch of cayenne pepper

Set your Instant Pot to Sauté and heat the olive oil until hot. Add the onion and chicken cubes and brown for 5 minutes. Stir in the remaining ingredients. Secure the lid. Select the Pressure Cook mode and set the cooking time for 20 minutes at High Pressure. Once cooking is complete, do a natural pressure release for 10 minutes, then release any remaining pressure. Carefully open the lid. Serve warm.

Chicken with Coconut Cream

Prep time: 5 minutes | Cook time: 25 minutes | Serves 4

2 chicken breasts, skinless, boneless and halved
1 cup tomato sauce
1 cup plain Greek yogurt
¾ cup coconut cream
¼ cup chopped cilantro
2 teaspoons garam masala
2 teaspoons ground cumin
A pinch of salt and black pepper

Thoroughly combine all the ingredients in the Instant Pot. Lock the lid. Select the Pressure Cook mode and set the cooking time for 25 minutes at High Pressure. Once cooking is complete, do a natural pressure release for 5 minutes, then release any remaining pressure. Carefully open the lid. Transfer the chicken breasts to a plate and serve.

Greek Chicken Salad

Prep time: 10 minutes | Cook time: 14 minutes | Serves 4

4 bone-in, skin-on chicken thighs
1 teaspoon fine sea salt
¾ teaspoon ground black pepper
2 tablespoons unsalted butter
2 cloves garlic, minced
Greek Salad:
2 cups Greek olives, pitted
1 medium tomato, diced
1 medium cucumber, diced
¼ cup diced red onions
2 tablespoons extra-virgin olive
¼ cup red wine vinegar
2 tablespoons lemon or lime juice
2 teaspoons Dijon mustard
½ teaspoon dried oregano leaves
½ teaspoon dried basil leaves

oil
4 sprigs fresh oregano
1 cup crumbled feta cheese, for garnish

Sprinkle the chicken thighs on all sides with the salt and pepper. Set your Instant Pot to Sauté and melt the butter. Add the chicken thighs to the Instant Pot, skin-side down. Add the garlic and sauté for 4 minutes until golden brown. Turn the chicken thighs over and stir in the vinegar, lemon juice, mustard, oregano, and basil. Secure the lid. Select the Manual mode and set the cooking time for 10 minutes at High Pressure. Once cooking is complete, do a quick pressure release. Carefully open the lid. Meanwhile, toss all the salad ingredients except the cheese in a large serving dish. When the chicken is finished, take ¼ cup of the liquid from the Instant Pot and stir into the salad. Place the chicken on top of the salad and serve garnished with the cheese.

Chicken with Mushroom Sauce

Prep time: 5 minutes | Cook time: 22 minutes | Serves 12

2 tablespoons vegetable oil
4 cloves garlic, minced
1 onion, chopped
6 chicken breasts, halved
1¼ pounds (567 g) cremini mushrooms, sliced
1½ cups dry white wine
1 cup chicken broth
1 tablespoon lemon juice, freshly squeezed
1 tablespoon thyme
2 bay leaves
Salt and pepper, to taste
2 tablespoons cornstarch, mixed with 2 tablespoons water

Set your Instant Pot to Sauté and heat the vegetable oil. Add the garlic, onion, and chicken and brown for about 5 minutes. Fold in the mushrooms, white wine, chicken broth, lemon juice, thyme, bay leaves, salt, and pepper and stir to incorporate. Secure the lid. Select the Pressure Cook mode and set the cooking time for 15 minutes at High Pressure. Once cooking is complete, do a quick pressure release. Carefully open the lid. Set your Instant Pot to Sauté again and stir in the cornstarch mixture. Let simmer for a few minutes until the sauce is thickened. Allow to cool for 5 minutes before serving.

Shredded Chicken

Prep time: 3 minutes | Cook time: 30 minutes | Serves 8

4 pounds (1.8 kg) chicken breasts
½ cup water
Salt and pepper, to taste

Combine all the ingredients in the Instant Pot. Secure the lid. Select the Pressure Cook mode and set the cooking time for 30 minutes at High Pressure. Once cooking is complete, do a natural pressure release for 10 minutes, then release any remaining pressure. Carefully open the lid. Transfer the chicken breasts to a plate and shred them with two forks. Serve warm.

Cheesy Pesto Chicken

Prep time: 5 minutes | Cook time: 25 minutes | Serves 2

2 (6-ounce / 170-g) boneless, skinless chicken breasts, butterflied
½ teaspoon salt
¼ teaspoon pepper
¼ teaspoon dried parsley
¼ teaspoon garlic powder
2 tablespoons coconut oil
1 cup water
¼ cup whole-milk ricotta cheese
¼ cup pesto
¼ cup shredded whole-milk Mozzarella cheese
Chopped parsley, for garnish (optional)

Sprinkle the chicken breasts with salt, pepper, parsley, and garlic powder. Set your Instant Pot to Sauté and melt the coconut oil. Add the chicken and brown for 3 to 5 minutes. Remove the chicken from the pot to a 7-cup glass bowl. Pour the water into the Instant Pot and use a wooden spoon or rubber spatula to make sure no seasoning is stuck to bottom of pot. Scatter the ricotta cheese on top of the chicken. Pour the pesto over chicken, and sprinkle the Mozzarella cheese over chicken. Cover with aluminum foil. Add the trivet to the Instant Pot and place the bowl on the trivet. Secure the lid. Select the Manual mode and set the cooking time for 20 minutes at High Pressure. Once cooking is complete, do a natural pressure release for 10 minutes, then release any remaining pressure. Carefully open the lid. Serve the chicken garnished with the chopped parsley, if desired.

Honey-Sesame Chicken

Prep time: 5 minutes | Cook time: 25 minutes | Serves 6

1 tablespoon olive oil
2 cloves garlic, minced
½ cup diced onions
4 large boneless, skinless chicken breasts
Salt and pepper, to taste
½ cup soy sauce
½ cup honey
¼ cup ketchup
2 teaspoons sesame oil
¼ teaspoon red pepper flakes
2 green onions, chopped
1 tablespoon sesame seeds, toasted

Press the Sauté button on the Instant Pot and heat the olive oil. Add the garlic and onions and sauté for about 3 minutes until fragrant. Add the chicken breasts and sprinkle with the salt and pepper. Brown each side for 3 minutes. Stir in the soy sauce, honey, ketchup, sesame oil, and red pepper flakes. Secure the lid. Select the Pressure Cook mode and set the cooking time for 20 minutes at High Pressure. Once cooking is complete, do a natural pressure release for 10 minutes, then release any remaining pressure. Carefully open the lid. Sprinkle the onions and sesame seeds on top for garnish before serving.

Mongolian Garlicky Chicken

Prep time: 5 minutes | Cook time: 20 minutes | Serves 6

2 tablespoons olive oil
10 cloves garlic, minced
1 onion, minced
4 large boneless, skinless chicken breasts, cut into cubes
1 cup water
1 cup soy sauce
1 cup brown sugar
1 cup chopped carrots
1 tablespoon garlic powder
1 tablespoon grated ginger
1 teaspoons red pepper flakes
1 tablespoon cornstarch, mixed with 2 tablespoons water

Set your Instant Pot to Sauté and heat the olive oil. Add the garlic and onion and sauté for about 3 minutes until fragrant. Add the chicken cubes and brown each side for 3 minutes. Add the remaining ingredients except the cornstarch mixture to the Instant Pot and stir well. Secure the lid. Select the Pressure Cook mode and set the cooking time for 15 minutes at High Pressure. Once cooking is complete, do a natural pressure release for 10 minutes, then release any remaining pressure. Carefully open the lid. Set your Instant Pot to Sauté again and whisk in the cornstarch mixture until the sauce thickens. Serve warm.

Pea and Chicken Casserole

Prep time: 10 minutes | Cook time: 30 minutes | Serves 4

2 pounds (907 g) chicken breast, skinless, boneless and cubed
1 cup veggie stock
1 cup peas
1 tablespoon Italian seasoning
1 tablespoon sweet paprika
A pinch of salt and black pepper
1 cup coconut cream
1 cup shredded Cheddar cheese

Stir together the chicken cubes, veggie stock, peas, Italian seasoning, paprika, salt, and pepper in the Instant Pot. Pour the coconut cream over top. Secure the lid. Select the Pressure Cook mode and set the cooking time for 20 minutes at High Pressure. Once cooking is complete, do a quick pressure release. Remove the lid. Scatter the shredded cheese all over. Put the lid back on and cook on High Pressure for an additional 10 minutes. Once cooking is complete, do a quick pressure release. Carefully open the lid. Serve warm.

Belizean Chicken Leg Stew

Prep time: 5 minutes | Cook time: 20 minutes | Serves 8

1 tablespoon coconut oil
3 cloves garlic, minced
1 onion, sliced
4 whole chicken legs
2 cups chicken stock
3 tablespoons Worcestershire sauce
2 tablespoons white vinegar
2 tablespoons achiote seasoning
1 tablespoon granulated sugar
1 teaspoon dried oregano
1 teaspoon ground cumin
Salt and pepper, to taste

Set your Instant Pot to Sauté and melt the coconut oil. Add the garlic, onion, and chicken legs and keep stirring until the chicken legs are golden brown. Add the remaining ingredients to the Instant Pot and stir to combine. Secure the lid. Select the Pressure Cook mode and set the cooking time for 15 minutes at High Pressure. Once cooking is complete, do a quick pressure release. Carefully open the lid. Divide the chicken legs among plates and serve.

Murgh Makhani

Prep time: 3 minutes | Cook time: 20 minutes | Serves 4

1 pound (454 g) chicken meat
1 can crushed tomatoes
6 cloves garlic
2 teaspoons grated ginger
1 teaspoon garam masala
1 teaspoon turmeric
1 teaspoon paprika
1 teaspoon cumin
½ teaspoon cayenne pepper

Combine all the ingredients in the Instant Pot. Lock the lid. Select the Pressure Cook mode and set the cooking time for 20 minutes at High Pressure. Once cooking is complete, do a natural pressure release for 10 minutes, then release any remaining pressure. Carefully open the lid. Serve warm.

BLT Chicken Salad

Prep time: 15 minutes | Cook time: 17 minutes | Serves 4

4 slices bacon
2 (6-ounce / 170-g) chicken breasts
1 teaspoon salt
½ teaspoon garlic powder
¼ teaspoon dried parsley
Sauce:
⅓ cup mayonnaise
1 ounce (28 g) chopped pecans
¼ teaspoon pepper
¼ teaspoon dried thyme
1 cup water
2 cups chopped romaine lettuce
½ cup diced Roma tomatoes
½ avocado, diced
1 tablespoon lemon juice

Press the Sauté button to heat your Instant Pot. Add the bacon and cook for about 7 minutes, flipping occasionally, until crisp. Remove and place on a paper towel to drain. When cool enough to handle, crumble the bacon and set aside. Sprinkle the chicken with salt, garlic powder, parsley, pepper, and thyme. Pour the water into the Instant Pot. Use a wooden spoon to ensure nothing is stuck to the bottom of the pot. Add the trivet to the pot and place the chicken on top of the trivet. Secure the lid. Select the Manual mode and set the cooking time for 10 minutes at High Pressure. Meanwhile, whisk together all the ingredients for the sauce in a large salad bowl. Once cooking is complete, do a quick pressure release. Carefully open the lid. Remove the chicken and let sit for 10 minutes. Cut the chicken into cubes and transfer to the salad bowl, along with the cooked bacon. Gently stir until the chicken is thoroughly coated. Mix in the lettuce right before serving.

Easy Kung Pao Chicken

Prep time: 5 minutes | Cook time: 17 minutes | Serves 5

2 tablespoons coconut oil
1 pound (454 g) boneless, skinless chicken breasts, cubed
1 cup cashews, chopped
6 tablespoons hot sauce

½ teaspoon chili powder
½ teaspoon finely grated ginger
½ teaspoon kosher salt
½ teaspoon freshly ground black pepper

Set the Instant Pot to Sauté and melt the coconut oil. Add the remaining ingredients to the Instant Pot and mix well. Secure the lid. Select the Manual mode and set the cooking time for 17 minutes at High Pressure. Once cooking is complete, do a quick pressure release. Carefully open the lid. Serve warm.

Crack Chicken Breasts

Prep time: 5 minutes | Cook time: 15 minutes | Serves 2

½ pound (227 g) boneless, skinless chicken breasts
2 ounces (57 g) cream cheese, softened
½ cup grass-fed bone broth
¼ cup tablespoons keto-

friendly ranch dressing
½ cup shredded full-fat Cheddar cheese
3 slices bacon, cooked and chopped into small pieces

Combine all the ingredients except the Cheddar cheese and bacon in the Instant Pot. Secure the lid. Select the Manual mode and set the cooking time for 15 minutes at High Pressure. Once cooking is complete, do a quick pressure release. Carefully open the lid. Add the Cheddar cheese and bacon and stir well, then serve.

Chicken and Broccoli Rice

Prep time: 5 minutes | Cook time: 10 minutes | Serves 4

Cooking spray
2 boneless, skinless chicken breasts, cut into 1-inch pieces
4 cups broccoli florets
4 cups low-sodium chicken broth

1 cup long-grain white rice
½ teaspoon fine sea salt
¼ teaspoon ground black pepper
1½ cups shredded Cheddar cheese

Spitz the inner pot of your Instant Pot with cooking spray. Add the chicken, broccoli, broth, rice, salt, and pepper. Secure the lid. Press the Manual button and set the cooking time for 10 minutes on High Pressure. Once cooking is complete, do a quick pressure release. Carefully open the lid. Add the cheese and stir until melted. Serve immediately.

Keto Bruschetta Chicken

Prep time: 5 minutes | Cook time: 20 minutes | Serves 2

½ cup filtered water
2 boneless, skinless chicken breasts
1 (14-ounce / 397-g) can sugar-free or low-sugar

crushed tomatoes
¼ teaspoon dried basil
½ cup shredded full-fat Cheddar cheese
¼ cup heavy whipping cream

Add the filtered water, chicken breasts, tomatoes, and basil to your Instant Pot. Lock the lid. Press the Manual button and set the cooking time for 20 minutes on High Pressure. Once cooking is complete, use a quick pressure release. Carefully open the lid. Fold in the cheese and cream and stir until the cheese is melted. Serve immediately.

Bruschetta Chicken

Prep time: 5 minutes | Cook time: 20 minutes | Serves 2

2 boneless, skinless chicken breasts
½ cup filtered water
1 (14-ounce / 397-g) can sugar-free or low-sugar

crushed tomatoes
¼ teaspoon dried basil
½ cup shredded full-fat Cheddar cheese
¼ cup heavy whipping cream

Combine all the ingredients except the cheese and whipping cream in the Instant Pot. Secure the lid. Select the Manual mode and set the cooking time for 20 minutes at High Pressure. Once cooking is complete, do a quick pressure release. Carefully open the lid. Stir in the cheese and whipping cream until the cheese melts, and serve.

Baked Cheesy Mushroom Chicken

Prep time: 5 minutes | Cook time: 15 minutes | Serves 4

1 tablespoon butter
2 cloves garlic, smashed
½ cup chopped yellow onion
1 pound (454 g) chicken breasts, cubed
10 ounces (283 g) button mushrooms, thinly sliced
1 cup chicken broth
½ teaspoon shallot powder

½ teaspoon turmeric powder
½ teaspoon dried basil
½ teaspoon dried sage
½ teaspoon cayenne pepper
⅓ teaspoon ground black pepper
Kosher salt, to taste
½ cup heavy cream
1 cup shredded Colby cheese

Set your Instant Pot to Sauté and melt the butter. Add the garlic, onion, chicken, and mushrooms and sauté for about 4 minutes, or until the vegetables are softened. Add the remaining ingredients except the heavy cream and cheese to the Instant Pot and stir to incorporate. Lock the lid. Select the Meat/Stew mode and set the cooking time for 6 minutes at High Pressure. When the timer beeps, perform a natural pressure release for 10 minutes, then release any remaining pressure. Carefully remove the lid. Stir in the heavy cream until heated through. Pour the mixture into a baking dish and scatter the cheese on top. Bake in the preheated oven at 400°F (205°C) until the cheese bubbles. Allow to cool for 5 minutes and serve.

Chicken and Bacon Ranch Casserole

Prep time: 5 minutes | Cook time: 30 minutes | Serves 4

4 slices bacon
4 (6-ounce / 170-g) boneless, skinless chicken breasts, cut into 1-inch cubes
½ teaspoon salt
¼ teaspoon pepper

1 tablespoon coconut oil
½ cup chicken broth
½ cup ranch dressing
½ cup shredded Cheddar cheese
2 ounces (57 g) cream cheese

Press the Sauté button to heat your Instant Pot. Add the bacon slices and cook for about 7 minutes until crisp, flipping occasionally. Remove from the pot and place on a paper towel to drain. Set aside. Season the chicken cubes with salt and pepper. Set your Instant Pot to Sauté and melt the coconut oil. Add the chicken cubes and brown for 3 to 4 minutes until golden brown. Stir in the broth and ranch dressing. Secure the lid. Select the Manual mode and set the cooking time for 20 minutes at High Pressure. Once cooking is complete, do a quick pressure release. Carefully open the lid. Stir in the Cheddar and cream cheese. Crumble the cooked bacon and scatter on top. Serve immediately.

Chicken Piccata

Prep time: 5 minutes | Cook time: 25 minutes | Serves 4

4 (6-ounce / 170-g) boneless, skinless chicken breasts
½ teaspoon salt
½ teaspoon garlic powder
¼ teaspoon pepper
2 tablespoons coconut oil

1 cup water
2 cloves garlic, minced
4 tablespoons butter
Juice of 1 lemon
¼ teaspoon xanthan gum

Sprinkle the chicken with salt, garlic powder, and pepper. Set your Instant Pot to Sauté and melt the coconut oil. Add the chicken and sear each side for about 5 to 7 minutes until golden brown. Remove the chicken and set aside on a plate. Pour the water into the Instant Pot. Using a wooden spoon, scrape the bottom if necessary to remove any stuck-on seasoning or meat. Insert the trivet and place the chicken on the trivet. Secure the lid. Select the Manual mode and set the cooking time for 10 minutes at High Pressure. Once cooking is complete, do a natural pressure release for 10 minutes, then release any remaining pressure. Carefully open the lid. Remove the chicken and set aside. Strain the broth from the Instant Pot into a large bowl and return to the pot. Set your Instant Pot to Sauté again and add the remaining ingredients. Cook for at least 5 minutes, stirring frequently, or until the sauce is cooked to your desired thickness. Pour the sauce over the chicken and serve warm.

Italian Chicken Thighs

Prep time: 10 minutes | Cook time: 15 minutes | Serves 4

4 bone-in chicken thighs
2 cloves garlic, minced
1 teaspoon salt
½ teaspoon dried oregano

¼ teaspoon pepper
¼ teaspoon dried parsley
¼ teaspoon dried basil
1 cup water

Place all the ingredients except the water into a large bowl and toss to evenly coat. Pour the water into the Instant Pot and insert the trivet. Arrange the chicken thighs on the trivet. Secure the lid. Select the Manual mode and set the cooking time for 15 minutes at High Pressure. Once cooking is complete, do a quick pressure release. Carefully open the lid. Serve warm.

Instant Pot Ranch Chicken

Prep time: 5 minutes | Cook time: 20 minutes | Serves 6

1 teaspoon salt
½ teaspoon garlic powder
¼ teaspoon pepper
¼ teaspoon dried oregano
3 (6-ounce / 170-g) skinless chicken breasts

1 stick butter
8 ounces (227 g) cream cheese
1 dry ranch packet
1 cup chicken broth

In a small bowl, combine the salt, garlic powder, pepper, and oregano. Rub this mixture over both sides of chicken breasts. Place the chicken breasts into the Instant Pot, along with the butter, cream cheese, ranch seasoning, and chicken broth. Secure the lid. Select the Manual mode and set the cooking time for 20 minutes at High Pressure. Once cooking is complete, do a natural pressure release for 10 minutes, then release any remaining pressure. Carefully open the lid. Remove the chicken and shred with two forks, then return to the Instant Pot. Use a rubber spatula to stir and serve on a plate.

Keto Chicken Enchilada Bowl

Prep time: 10 minutes | Cook time: 35 minutes | Serves 4

2 (6-ounce / 170-g) boneless, skinless chicken breasts
2 teaspoons chili powder
½ teaspoon garlic powder
½ teaspoon salt
¼ teaspoon pepper
2 tablespoons coconut oil
¾ cup red enchilada sauce
¼ cup chicken broth

1 (4-ounce / 113-g) can green chilies
¼ cup diced onion
2 cups cooked cauliflower rice
1 avocado, diced
½ cup sour cream
1 cup shredded Cheddar cheese

Sprinkle the chili powder, garlic powder, salt, and pepper on chicken breasts. Set your Instant Pot to Sauté and melt the coconut oil. Add the chicken breasts and sear each side for about 5 minutes until golden brown. Pour the enchilada sauce and broth over the chicken. Using a wooden spoon or rubber spatula, scrape the bottom of pot to make sure nothing is sticking. Stir in the chilies and onion. Secure the lid. Select the Manual mode and set the cooking time for 25 minutes at High Pressure. Once cooking is complete, do a quick pressure release. Carefully open the lid. Remove the chicken and shred with two forks. Serve the chicken over the cauliflower rice and place the avocado, sour cream, and Cheddar cheese on top.

Chicken and Mixed Greens Salad

Prep time: 5 minutes | Cook time: 20 minutes | Serves 4

Chicken:
2 tablespoons avocado oil
1 pound (454 g) chicken breast, cubed
½ cup filtered water
½ teaspoon ground turmeric
Salad:
1 avocado, mashed
1 cup chopped arugula
1 cup chopped Swiss chard
1 cup chopped kale

½ teaspoon dried parsley
½ teaspoon dried basil
½ teaspoon kosher salt
½ teaspoon freshly ground black pepper

½ cup chopped spinach
2 tablespoons pine nuts, toasted

Combine all the chicken ingredients in the Instant Pot. Secure the lid. Select the Manual mode and set the cooking time for 20 minutes at High Pressure. Meanwhile, toss all the salad ingredients in a large salad bowl. Once cooking is complete, do a quick pressure release. Carefully open the lid. Remove the chicken to the salad bowl and serve.

Barbecue Wings

Prep time: 5 minutes | Cook time: 12 minutes | Serves 4

1 pound (454 g) chicken wings
1 teaspoon salt
½ teaspoon pepper
¼ teaspoon garlic powder

1 cup sugar-free barbecue sauce, divided
1 cup water

Toss the chicken wings with the salt, pepper, garlic powder, and half of barbecue sauce in a large bowl until well coated. Pour the water into the Instant Pot and insert the trivet. Place the wings on the trivet. Secure the lid. Select the Manual mode and set the cooking time for 12 minutes at High Pressure. Once cooking is complete, do a quick pressure release. Carefully open the lid. Transfer the wings to a serving bowl and toss with the remaining sauce. Serve immediately.

Chicken Alfredo with Bacon

Prep time: 10 minutes | Cook time: 27 minutes | Serves 4

2 (6-ounce / 170-g) boneless, skinless chicken breasts, butterflied
½ teaspoon garlic powder
¼ teaspoon dried parsley
¼ teaspoon dried thyme
¼ teaspoon salt
⅛ teaspoon pepper
2 tablespoons coconut oil
1 cup water
1 stick butter
2 cloves garlic, finely minced
¼ cup heavy cream
½ cup grated Parmesan cheese
¼ cup cooked crumbled bacon

Sprinkle the chicken breasts with the garlic powder, parsley, thyme, salt, and pepper. Set your Instant Pot to Sauté and melt the coconut oil. Add the chicken and sear for 3 to 5 minutes until golden brown on both sides. Remove the chicken with tongs and set aside. Pour the water into the Instant Pot and insert the trivet. Place the chicken on the trivet. Secure the lid. Select the Manual mode and set the cooking time for 20 minutes at High Pressure. Once cooking is complete, do a quick pressure release. Carefully open the lid. Remove the chicken from the pot to a platter and set aside. Pour the water out of the Instant Pot, reserving ½ cup; set aside. Set your Instant Pot to Sauté again and melt the butter. Add the garlic, heavy cream, cheese, and reserved water to the Instant Pot. Cook for 3 to 4 minutes until the sauce starts to thicken, stirring frequently. Stir in the crumbled bacon and pour the mixture over the chicken. Serve immediately.

Herbed Whole Chicken

Prep time: 5 minutes | Cook time: 25 minutes | Serves 6

4 tablespoons grass-fed butter, softened
1 teaspoon dried cilantro
1 teaspoon dried basil
½ teaspoon kosher salt
½ teaspoon freshly ground black pepper
½ cup grass-fed bone broth
1 whole chicken

Stir together the softened butter, cilantro, basil, salt, and pepper in a large bowl until combined. Pour the bone broth into the Instant Pot. Place the chicken in the Instant Pot with the breast facing down and lightly baste with the butter mixture. Secure the lid. Select the Pressure Cook mode and set the cooking time for 25 minutes at High Pressure. Once cooking is complete, do a natural pressure release for 15 minutes, then release any remaining pressure. Carefully open the lid. Remove the chicken from the Instant Pot and serve.

Paprika Whole Chicken

Prep time: 5 minutes | Cook time: 40 minutes | Serves 6

1¾ tablespoons olive oil
1½ teaspoons salt
½ teaspoon pepper
1 teaspoon minced garlic
1 teaspoon paprika
1 whole chicken
1 cup chicken broth

Stir together the olive oil, salt, pepper, garlic, and paprika in a small bowl. Rub the mixture all over the chicken until evenly coated. Pour the chicken broth into the Instant Pot and add the coated chicken. Secure the lid. Select the Pressure Cook mode and set the cooking time for 40 minutes at High Pressure. Once cooking is complete, do a natural pressure release for 15 minutes, then release any remaining pressure. Carefully open the lid. Serve warm.

Stuffed Chicken with Spinach and Feta

Prep time: 10 minutes | Cook time: 25 minutes | Serves 4

½ cup frozen spinach
⅓ cup crumbled feta cheese
1¼ teaspoons salt, divided
4 (6-ounce / 170-g) boneless, skinless chicken breasts, butterflied
¼ teaspoon pepper
¼ teaspoon dried oregano
¼ teaspoon dried parsley
¼ teaspoon garlic powder
2 tablespoons coconut oil
1 cup water

Combine the spinach, feta cheese, and ¼ teaspoon of salt in a medium bowl. Divide the mixture evenly and spoon onto the chicken breasts. Close the chicken breasts and secure with toothpicks or butcher's string. Sprinkle the chicken with the remaining 1 teaspoon of salt, pepper, oregano, parsley, and garlic powder. Set your Instant Pot to Sauté and heat the coconut oil. Sear each chicken breast until golden brown, about 4 to 5 minutes per side. Remove the chicken breasts and set aside. Pour the water into the Instant Pot and scrape the bottom to remove any chicken or seasoning that is stuck on. Add the trivet to the Instant Pot and place the chicken on the trivet. Secure the lid. Select the Manual mode and set the cooking time for 15 minutes at High Pressure. Once cooking is complete, do a natural pressure release for 15 minutes, then release any remaining pressure. Carefully open the lid. Serve warm.

Simple Shredded Chicken

Prep time: 5 minutes | Cook time: 14 minutes | Serves 4

½ teaspoon salt
½ teaspoon pepper
½ teaspoon dried oregano
½ teaspoon dried basil
½ teaspoon garlic powder
2 (6-ounce / 170-g) boneless, skinless chicken breasts
1 tablespoon coconut oil
1 cup water

In a small bowl, combine the salt, pepper, oregano, basil, and garlic powder. Rub this mix over both sides of the chicken. Set your Instant Pot to Sauté and heat the coconut oil until sizzling. Add the chicken and sear for 3 to 4 minutes until golden on both sides. Remove the chicken and set aside. Pour the water into the Instant Pot and use a wooden spoon or rubber spatula to make sure no seasoning is stuck to bottom of pot. Add the trivet to the Instant Pot and place the chicken on top. Secure the lid. Select the Manual mode and set the cooking time for 10 minutes at High Pressure. Once cooking is complete, do a natural pressure release for 5 minutes, then release any remaining pressure. Carefully open the lid. Remove the chicken and shred, then serve.

Salsa Curry Chicken

Prep time: 15 minutes | Cook time: 3 to 4½ hours | Serves 10

10 skinless, bone-in chicken breast halves, divided
1 (16-ounce / 454-g) jar salsa, your choice of heat
1 medium onion, chopped
2 tablespoons curry powder
1 cup sour cream

Place half the chicken in the Instant Pot. Combine salsa, onion, and curry powder in a medium-sized bowl. Pour half the sauce over the meat in the Instant Pot. Repeat Steps 1 and 2. Cover and press the Slow Cook button, and cook on high for 3 hours. Or cook on high for 1½ hours and then turn Instant Pot to low and cook 3 more hours. (Press Slow Cook again to toggle between Low and High cooking temperatures.). Remove chicken to serving platter and cover to keep warm. Add sour cream to Instant Pot and stir into salsa until well blended. Serve over the chicken.

Chicken Fajita Bowls

Prep time: 5 minutes | Cook time: 10 minutes | Serves 2

1 pound (454 g) boneless, skinless chicken breasts, cut into 1-inch pieces
2 cups chicken broth
1 cup salsa
1 teaspoon paprika
1 teaspoon fine sea salt, or more to taste
1 teaspoon chili powder
½ teaspoon ground cumin
½ teaspoon ground black pepper
1 lime, halved

Combine all the ingredients except the lime in the Instant Pot. Lock the lid. Select the Manual mode and set the cooking time for 10 minutes at High Pressure. When the timer beeps, perform a quick pressure release. Carefully remove the lid. Shred the chicken with two forks and return to the Instant Pot. Squeeze the lime juice into the chicken mixture. Taste and add more salt, if needed. Give the mixture a good stir. Ladle the chicken mixture into bowls and serve.

Prosciutto-Wrapped Chicken

Prep time: 5 minutes | Cook time: 15 minutes | Serves 5

1½ cups water
5 chicken breast halves, butterflied
2 garlic cloves, halved
1 teaspoon marjoram
Sea salt, to taste
½ teaspoon red pepper flakes
¼ teaspoon ground black pepper, or more to taste
10 strips prosciutto

Pour the water into the Instant Pot and insert the trivet. Rub the chicken breast halves with garlic. Sprinkle with marjoram, salt, red pepper flakes, and black pepper. Wrap each chicken breast into 2 prosciutto strips and secure with toothpicks. Put the chicken on the trivet. Lock the lid. Select the Poultry mode and set the cooking time for 15 minutes at High Pressure. When the timer beeps, perform a natural pressure release for 10 minutes, then release any remaining pressure. Carefully remove the lid. Remove the toothpicks and serve warm.

Parmesan Drumsticks

Prep time: 5 minutes | Cook time: 25 minutes | Serves 4

2 pounds (907 g) chicken drumsticks (about 8 pieces)
1 teaspoon salt
1 teaspoon dried parsley
½ teaspoon garlic powder
½ teaspoon dried oregano
¼ teaspoon pepper
1 cup water
1 stick butter
2 ounces (57 g) cream cheese, softened
½ cup grated Parmesan cheese
½ cup chicken broth
¼ cup heavy cream
⅛ teaspoon pepper

Sprinkle the salt, parsley, garlic powder, oregano, and pepper evenly over the chicken drumsticks. Pour the water into the Instant Pot and insert the trivet. Arrange the drumsticks on the trivet. Secure the lid. Select the Manual mode and set the cooking time for 15 minutes at High Pressure. Once cooking is complete, do a quick pressure release. Carefully open the lid. Transfer the drumsticks to a foil-lined baking sheet and broil each side for 3 to 5 minutes, or until the skin begins to crisp. Meanwhile, pour the water out of the Instant Pot. Set your Instant Pot to Sauté and melt the butter. Add the remaining ingredients to the Instant Pot and whisk to combine. Pour the sauce over the drumsticks and serve warm.

Creamy Chicken Cordon Bleu

Prep time: 12 minutes | Cook time: 15 minutes | Serves 6

4 boneless, skinless chicken breast halves, butterflied
4 (1-ounce / 28-g) slices Swiss cheese
Sauce:
1½ ounces (43 g) cream cheese (3 tablespoons)
¼ cup chicken broth
1 tablespoon unsalted butter
8 (1-ounce / 28-g) slices ham
1 cup water
Chopped fresh flat-leaf parsley, for garnish

¼ teaspoon ground black pepper
¼ teaspoon fine sea salt

Lay the chicken breast halves on a clean work surface. Top each with a slice of Swiss cheese and 2 slices of ham. Roll the chicken around the ham and cheese, then secure with toothpicks. Set aside. Whisk together all the ingredients for the sauce in a small saucepan over medium heat, stirring until the cream cheese melts and the sauce is smooth. Place the chicken rolls, seam-side down, in a casserole dish. Pour half of the sauce over the chicken rolls. Set the remaining sauce aside. Pour the water into the Instant Pot and insert the trivet. Place the dish on the trivet. Lock the lid. Select the Manual mode and set the cooking time for 15 minutes at High Pressure. When the timer beeps, perform a natural pressure release for 10 minutes, then release any remaining pressure. Carefully remove the lid. Remove the chicken rolls from the Instant Pot to a plate. Pour the remaining sauce over them and serve garnished with the parsley.

Orange Chicken Breasts

Prep time: 5 minutes | Cook time: 18 minutes | Serves 4

4 chicken breasts
¾ cup orange marmalade
¾ cup barbecue sauce
¼ cup water
2 tablespoons soy sauce
1 tablespoon cornstarch, mixed with 2 tablespoons water
2 tablespoons green onions, chopped

Combine all the ingredients except the cornstarch mixture and green onions in the Instant Pot. Secure the lid. Select the Poultry mode and set the cooking time for 15 minutes at High Pressure. Once cooking is complete, do a quick pressure release. Carefully open the lid. Set your Instant Pot to Sauté and stir in the cornstarch mixture. Simmer for a few minutes until the sauce is thickened. Add the green onions and stir well. Serve immediately.

Greek Chicken with Coconut Cream

Prep time: 5 minutes | Cook time: 25 minutes | Serves 4

2 chicken breasts, skinless, boneless and halved
1 cup tomato sauce
1 cup plain Greek yogurt
¾ cup coconut cream
¼ cup chopped cilantro
2 teaspoons garam masala
2 teaspoons ground cumin
A pinch of salt and black pepper

Thoroughly combine all the ingredients in the Instant Pot. Lock the lid. Select the Pressure Cook mode and set the cooking time for 25 minutes at High Pressure. Once cooking is complete, do a natural pressure release for 5 minutes, then release any remaining pressure. Carefully open the lid. Transfer the chicken breasts to a plate and serve.

Chicken Cacciatore

Prep time: 5 minutes | Cook time: 22 minutes | Serves 4 to 5

6 tablespoons coconut oil
5 chicken legs
1 bell pepper, diced
½ onion, chopped
1 (14-ounce / 397-g) can sugar-free or low-sugar diced tomatoes
½ teaspoon dried basil
½ teaspoon dried parsley
½ teaspoon kosher salt
½ teaspoon freshly ground black pepper
½ cup filtered water

Press the Sauté button on the Instant Pot and melt the coconut oil. Add the chicken legs and sauté until the outside is browned. Remove the chicken and set aside. Add the bell pepper, onion, tomatoes, basil, parsley, salt, and pepper to the Instant Pot and cook for about 2 minutes. Pour in the water and return the chicken to the pot. Lock the lid. Select the Manual mode and set the cooking time for 18 minutes at High Pressure. Once cooking is complete, do a quick pressure release. Carefully open the lid. Serve warm.

Cheesy Chicken Drumsticks

Prep time: 3 minutes | Cook time: 23 minutes | Serves 5

1 tablespoon olive oil
5 chicken drumsticks
½ cup chicken stock
¼ cup unsweetened coconut milk
¼ cup dry white wine
2 garlic cloves, minced
1 teaspoon shallot powder
½ teaspoon marjoram
½ teaspoon thyme
6 ounces (170 g) ricotta cheese
4 ounces (113 g) Cheddar cheese
½ teaspoon cayenne pepper
¼ teaspoon ground black pepper
Sea salt, to taste

Set your Instant Pot to Sauté and heat the olive oil until sizzling. Add the chicken drumsticks and brown each side for 3 minutes. Stir in the chicken stock, milk, wine, garlic, shallot powder, marjoram, thyme. Lock the lid. Select the Manual mode and set the cooking time for 15 minutes at High Pressure. When the timer beeps, perform a natural pressure release for 10 minutes, then release any remaining pressure. Carefully remove the lid. Shred the chicken with two forks and return to the Instant Pot. Set your Instant Pot to Sauté again and add the remaining ingredients and stir well. Cook for another 2 minutes, or until the cheese is melted. Taste and add more salt, if desired. Serve immediately.

Chili Chicken Zoodles

Prep time: 10 minutes | Cook time: 20 minutes | Serves 4

2 chicken breasts, skinless, boneless and halved
1½ cups chicken stock
3 celery stalks, chopped
1 tablespoon tomato sauce
1 teaspoon chili powder
A pinch of salt and black pepper
2 zucchinis, spiralized
1 tablespoon chopped cilantro

Mix together all the ingredients except the zucchini noodles and cilantro in the Instant Pot. Secure the lid. Select the Manual mode and set the cooking time for 15 minutes at High Pressure. Once cooking is complete, do a natural pressure release for 10 minutes, then release any remaining pressure. Carefully open the lid. Set your Instant Pot to Sauté and add the zucchini noodles. Cook for about 5 minutes, stirring often, or until softened. Sprinkle the cilantro on top for garnish before serving.

Jamaican Curry Chicken Drumsticks

Prep time: 5 minutes | Cook time: 20 minutes | Serves 4

1½ pounds (680 g) chicken drumsticks
1 tablespoon Jamaican curry powder
1 teaspoon salt
1 cup chicken broth
½ medium onion, diced
½ teaspoon dried thyme

Sprinkle the salt and curry powder over the chicken drumsticks. Place the chicken drumsticks into the Instant Pot, along with the remaining ingredients. Secure the lid. Select the Manual mode and set the cooking time for 20 minutes at High Pressure. Once cooking is complete, do a quick pressure release. Carefully open the lid. Serve warm.

Chicken Legs with Mayo Sauce

Prep time: 5 minutes | Cook time: 20 minutes | Serves 4

4 chicken legs, bone-in, skinless
2 garlic cloves, peeled and halved
½ teaspoon coarse sea salt
½ teaspoon crushed red
Dipping Sauce:
¾ cup mayonnaise
2 tablespoons stone ground mustard
1 teaspoon fresh lemon juice
pepper flakes
¼ teaspoon ground black pepper, or more to taste
1 tablespoon olive oil
¼ cup chicken broth

½ teaspoon Sriracha
For Garnish:
¼ cup roughly chopped fresh cilantro

Rub the chicken legs with the garlic. Sprinkle with salt, red pepper flakes, and black pepper. Set your Instant Pot to Sauté and heat the olive oil. Add the chicken legs and brown for 4 to 5 minutes. Add a splash of chicken broth to deglaze the bottom of the pot. Pour the remaining chicken broth into the Instant Pot and mix well. Lock the lid. Select the Manual mode and set the cooking time for 14 minutes at High Pressure. Meanwhile, whisk together all the sauce ingredients in a small bowl. When the timer beeps, perform a natural pressure release for 10 minutes, then release any remaining pressure. Carefully remove the lid. Sprinkle the cilantro on top for garnish and serve with the prepared dipping sauce.

Butter-Parmesan Wings

Prep time: 5 minutes | Cook time: 12 minutes | Serves 4

2 pounds (907 g) chicken wings, patted dry
1 teaspoon seasoned salt
½ teaspoon garlic powder
½ teaspoon pepper
1 cup water
3 tablespoons butter
1 teaspoon lemon pepper
¼ cup grated Parmesan cheese

Season the chicken wings with the salt, garlic powder, and pepper. Pour the water into the Instant Pot and insert the trivet. Arrange the wings on the trivet. Secure the lid. Select the Manual mode and set the cooking time for 10 minutes at High Pressure. Once cooking is complete, do a quick pressure release. Carefully open the lid. Remove the chicken wings and set aside on a plate. For crispy wings, you can place them on a foil-lined baking sheet and broil for 3 to 5 minutes, or until the skin is crispy. Pour the water out of the Instant Pot. Set your Instant Pot to Sauté and melt the butter. Stir in the lemon pepper and return the wings to the pot, tossing to coat. Scatter with the cheese and serve warm.

Chicken With Cheese Mushroom Sauce

Prep time: 8 minutes | Cook time: 14 minutes | Serves 4

2 tablespoons unsalted butter or coconut oil
2 cloves garlic, minced
¼ cup diced onions
2 cups sliced button or cremini mushrooms
4 boneless, skinless chicken breast halves
½ cup chicken broth
¼ cup heavy cream
1 teaspoon fine sea salt

1 teaspoon dried tarragon leaves
½ teaspoon dried thyme leaves
½ teaspoon ground black pepper
2 bay leaves
½ cup grated Parmesan cheese
Fresh thyme leaves, for garnish

Set your Instant Pot to Sauté and melt the butter. Add the garlic, onions, and mushrooms and sauté for 4 minutes, stirring often, or until the onions are softened. Add the remaining ingredients except the Parmesan cheese and thyme leaves to the Instant Pot and stir to combine. Lock the lid. Select the Manual mode and set the cooking time for 10 minutes at High Pressure. When the timer beeps, perform a natural pressure release for 10 minutes, then release any remaining pressure. Carefully remove the lid. Discard the bay leaves and transfer the chicken to a serving platter. Add the Parmesan cheese to the Instant Pot with the sauce and stir until the cheese melts. Pour the mushroom sauce from the pot over the chicken. Serve garnished with the fresh thyme leaves.

Salsa Chicken Legs

Prep time: 5 minutes | Cook time: 16 minutes | Serves 5

5 chicken legs, skinless and boneless
½ teaspoon sea salt
Salsa Sauce:
1 cup puréed tomatoes
1 cup onion, chopped
1 jalapeño, chopped
2 bell peppers, deveined and chopped

2 tablespoons minced fresh cilantro
3 teaspoons lime juice
1 teaspoon granulated garlic

Press the Sauté button to heat your Instant Pot. Add the chicken legs and sear each side for 2 to 3 minutes until evenly browned. Season with sea salt. Thoroughly combine all the ingredients for the salsa sauce in a mixing bowl. Spoon the salsa mixture evenly over the browned chicken legs. Lock the lid. Select the Manual mode and set the cooking time for 10 minutes at High Pressure. When the timer beeps, perform a natural pressure release for 10 minutes, then release any remaining pressure. Carefully remove the lid. Serve warm.

Italian BBQ Chicken with Potatoes

Prep time: 5 minutes | Cook time: 10 minutes | Serves 8

2 pounds (907 g) chicken
3 large potatoes, peeled and chopped
1 large onion, sliced
1 cup BBQ sauce

½ cup water
1 tablespoon minced garlic
1 tablespoon Italian seasoning

Combine all the ingredients in the Instant Pot. Secure the lid. Select the Pressure Cook mode and set the cooking time for 10 minutes at High Pressure. Once cooking is complete, do a quick pressure release. Carefully open the lid. Serve warm.

Crack Chicken with Bacon

Prep time: 5 minutes | Cook time: 15 minutes | Serves 2

½ cup grass-fed bone broth
½ pound (227 g) boneless, skinless chicken breasts
2 ounces (57 g) cream cheese, softened
¼ cup tablespoons keto-

friendly ranch dressing
3 slices bacon, cooked, chopped into small pieces
½ cup shredded full-fat Cheddar cheese

Add the bone broth, chicken, cream cheese, and ranch dressing to your Instant Pot and stir to combine. Secure the lid. Press the Manual button and set the cooking time for 15 minutes on High Pressure. When the timer goes off, do a quick pressure release. Carefully open the lid. Add the bacon and cheese and stir until the cheese has melted. Serve.

Curried Mustard Chicken Legs

Prep time: 10 minutes | Cook time: 20 minutes | Serves 5

5 chicken legs, boneless, skin-on
2 garlic cloves, halved
Sea salt, to taste
½ teaspoon smoked paprika
¼ teaspoon ground black pepper

2 teaspoons olive oil
1 tablespoon yellow mustard
1 teaspoon curry paste
4 strips pancetta, chopped
1 shallot, peeled and chopped
1 cup vegetable broth

Rub the chicken legs with the garlic halves. Sprinkle with salt, paprika, and black pepper. Set your Instant Pot to Sauté and heat the olive oil. Add the chicken legs and brown for 4 to 5 minutes. Add a splash of chicken broth to deglaze the bottom of the pot. Spread the chicken legs with mustard and curry paste. Add the pancetta strips, shallot, and remaining vegetable broth to the Instant Pot. Lock the lid. Select the Manual mode and set the cooking time for 14 minutes at High Pressure. When the timer beeps, perform a natural pressure release for 10 minutes, then release any remaining pressure. Carefully remove the lid. Serve warm.

Chicken Fillets with Cheese Sauce

Prep time: 5 minutes | Cook time: 10 minutes | Serves 4

1 tablespoon olive oil
1 pound (454 g) chicken fillets
½ teaspoon dried basil
Cheese Sauce:
3 teaspoons butter, at room temperature
⅓ cup grated Gruyère cheese
⅓ cup Neufchâtel cheese, at room temperature

Salt and freshly ground black pepper, to taste
1 cup chicken broth

⅓ cup heavy cream
3 tablespoons unsweetened coconut milk
1 teaspoon shallot powder
½ teaspoon granulated garlic

Set your Instant Pot to Sauté and heat the olive oil until sizzling. Add the chicken and sear each side for 3 minutes. Sprinkle with the basil, salt, and black pepper. Pour the broth into the Instant Pot and stir well. Lock the lid. Select the Manual mode and set the cooking time for 6 minutes at High Pressure. When the timer beeps, perform a natural pressure release for 10 minutes, then release any remaining pressure. Carefully remove the lid. Transfer the chicken to a platter and set aside. Clean the Instant Pot. Press the Sauté button and melt the butter. Add the cheeses, heavy cream, milk, shallot powder, and garlic, stirring until everything is heated through. Pour the cheese sauce over the chicken and serve.

Buffalo Wings
Prep time: 5 minutes | Cook time: 12 minutes | Serves 4

2 pounds (907 g) chicken
wings, patted dry
1 teaspoon seasoned salt
¼ teaspoon pepper
½ teaspoon garlic powder

¼ cup buffalo sauce
¾ cup chicken broth
⅓ cup blue cheese crumbles
¼ cup cooked bacon crumbles
2 stalks green onion, sliced

Season the chicken wings with salt, pepper, and garlic powder.
Pour the buffalo sauce and broth into the Instant Pot. Stir in the
chicken wings. Lock the lid. Select the Manual mode and set
the cooking time for 12 minutes at High Pressure. Once cooking
is complete, do a quick pressure release. Carefully open the lid.
Gently stir to coat wings with the sauce. If you prefer crispier
wings, you can broil them for 3 to 5 minutes until the skin is
crispy. Remove the chicken wings from the pot to a plate. Brush
them with the leftover sauce and serve topped with the blue
cheese, bacon, and green onions.

Chicken Wingettes with Cilantro Sauce
Prep time: 5 minutes | Cook time: 6 minutes | Serves 6

12 chicken wingettes
10 fresh cayenne peppers,
trimmed and chopped
3 garlic cloves, minced
1½ cups white vinegar
Dipping Sauce:
½ cup sour cream
½ cup mayonnaise
½ cup cilantro, chopped

1 teaspoon sea salt
1 teaspoon onion powder
½ teaspoon black pepper
2 tablespoons olive oil

2 cloves garlic, minced
1 teaspoon smoked paprika

In a large bowl, toss the chicken wingettes, cayenne peppers,
garlic, white vinegar, salt, onion powder, and black pepper.
Cover and marinate for 1 hour in the refrigerator. When ready,
transfer the chicken wingettes to the Instant Pot, along with
the marinade and olive oil. Lock the lid. Select the Manual
mode and set the cooking time for 6 minutes at High Pressure.
Meanwhile, thoroughly combine all the sauce ingredients in a
mixing bowl. When the timer beeps, perform a quick pressure
release. Carefully remove the lid. Serve the chicken warm
alongside the dipping sauce.

Chicken Liver Pâté
Prep time: 5 minutes | Cook time: 15 minutes | Serves 8

2 tablespoons olive oil
1 pound (454 g) chicken livers
2 garlic cloves, crushed
½ cup chopped leeks
1 tablespoon poultry
seasonings
1 teaspoon dried rosemary
½ teaspoon paprika
½ teaspoon dried marjoram

½ teaspoon red pepper flakes
½ teaspoon ground black
pepper
¼ teaspoon dried dill weed
Salt, to taste
1 cup water
1 tablespoon stone ground
mustard

Set your Instant Pot to Sauté and heat the olive oil. Add the
chicken livers and sauté for about 3 minutes until no longer
pink. Add the remaining ingredients except the mustard to the
Instant Pot and stir to combine. Lock the lid. Select the Manual
mode and set the cooking time for 10 minutes at High Pressure.
When the timer beeps, perform a quick pressure release.
Carefully remove the lid. Transfer the cooked mixture to a food
processor, along with the mustard. Pulse until the mixture is
smooth. Serve immediately.

Creamy Chicken and Cauliflower Soup
Prep time: 5 minutes | Cook time: 13 minutes | Serves 4

1½ tablespoons olive oil
4 chicken thighs
1 teaspoon minced garlic
1 leek, chopped
1 tablespoon chopped sage
½ pound (227 g) cauliflower,

broken into small florets
4 cups chicken broth
½ cup heavy cream
3 ounces (85 g) mild blue
cheese, crumbled

Set your Instant Pot to Sauté and heat the olive oil. Add the
chicken thighs and brown each side for 2 to 3 minutes. Remove
and set aside. Add the garlic and leek to the Instant Pot and
sauté for about 2 minutes until softened. Add the cooked
chicken thighs, sage, cauliflower, and broth to the pot. Stir well.
Lock the lid. Select the Manual mode and set the cooking time
for 6 minutes at High Pressure. When the timer beeps, perform
a natural pressure release for 10 minutes, then release any
remaining pressure. Carefully remove the lid. Shred the chicken
with two forks and discard the bones, then return to the Instant
Pot. Add the heavy cream and blue cheese and stir until the
cheese is melted. Ladle the chicken mixture into four bowls and
serve immediately.

Sesame Chicken
Prep time: 5 minutes | Cook time: 24 minutes | Serves 4

1 pound (454 g) boneless,
skinless chicken thighs, cut
into bite-sized pieces and
patted dry
Fine sea salt, to taste
2 tablespoons avocado oil or
coconut oil
1 clove garlic, smashed to a
paste
For Garnish:
Sesame seeds

½ cup chicken broth
½ cup coconut aminos
⅓ cup Swerve
2 tablespoons toasted sesame
oil
1 tablespoon lime juice
¼ teaspoon peeled and grated
fresh ginger

Sliced green onions

Season all sides of chicken thighs with salt. Set your Instant
Pot to Sauté and heat the avocado oil. Add the chicken thighs
and sear for about 4 minutes, or until lightly browned on all
sides. Remove the chicken and set aside. Add the remaining
ingredients to the Instant Pot and cook for 10 minutes, stirring
occasionally, or until the sauce is reduced and thickened. Return
the chicken thighs to the pot and cook for 10 minutes, stirring
occasionally, or until the chicken is cooked through. Sprinkle the
sesame seeds and green onions on top for garnish and serve.

Honey Butter Baked Chicken
Prep time: 15 minutes | Cook time: 3 hours | Serves 4

4 skinless, bone-in chicken
breast halves
2 tablespoons butter, melted
2 tablespoons honey

2 teaspoons prepared mustard
2 teaspoons curry powder
Salt and pepper, to taste
(optional)

Spray Instant Pot with nonstick cooking spray and add chicken
Mix butter, honey, mustard, and curry powder together in a
small bowl. Pour sauce over chicken. Cover and press the Slow
Cook button, and cook on low for 5 to 6 hours or on high for 3
hours. (Press Slow Cook again to toggle between Low and High
cooking temperatures.)

Chicken Adobo

Prep time: 6 minutes | Cook time: 21 minutes | Serves 6

2 pounds (907 g) bone-in, skin-on chicken thighs
½ cup chicken broth
⅓ cup coconut aminos
¼ cup coconut vinegar or apple cider vinegar
6 cloves garlic, minced
3 tablespoons Swerve
2 shallots, minced
½ teaspoon ground black pepper
¼ teaspoon cayenne pepper
2 bay leaves

Combine all the ingredients in the Instant Pot. Secure the lid. Select the Manual mode and set the cooking time for 10 minutes at High Pressure. Once cooking is complete, do a quick pressure release. Carefully open the lid. Transfer the chicken thighs to a rimmed baking sheet. Strain the remaining sauce from the Instant Pot into a saucepan and cook over medium-high heat for about 8 minutes, stirring frequently, until the sauce is reduced by half. Brush both sides of the chicken thighs with the sauce. Place the baking sheet in the oven and broil for 2 to 3 minutes, or until the chicken is slightly charred and crispy. Cool for 5 minutes and serve the chicken thighs with the sauce.

Garlic Turkey Breast Tenderloins

Prep time: 2 minutes | Cook time: 38 minutes | Serves 6

6 turkey breast tenderloins
4 cloves garlic, halved
2 tablespoons olive oil, divided
½ teaspoon paprika
½ teaspoon dried oregano
½ teaspoon dried basil
½ teaspoon dried marjoram
Sea salt, to taste
¼ teaspoon ground black pepper, or more to taste
1 cup water

Rub the turkey with the garlic halves. Massage 1 tablespoon of olive oil into the turkey and sprinkle with paprika, oregano, basil, marjoram, salt, and black pepper. Set your Instant Pot to Sauté and heat the remaining 1 tablespoon of olive oil. Add the turkey and brown each side for 3 to 4 minutes. Pour in the water. Secure the lid. Select the Manual mode and set the cooking time for 30 minutes at High Pressure. When the timer beeps, perform a natural pressure release for 15 minutes, then release any remaining pressure. Carefully remove the lid. Serve warm.

Creamed Turkey Breasts with Mushrooms

Prep time: 10 minutes | Cook time: 15 minutes | Serves 6

3 teaspoons butter
1½ pounds (680 g) turkey breasts, cubed
2 cloves garlic, minced
½ leek, chopped
1 cup thinly sliced white mushrooms
½ cup broth
½ teaspoon basil
½ teaspoon dried parsley flakes
¼ teaspoon ground allspice
Salt and black pepper, to taste
½ cup heavy cream

Set your Instant Pot to Sauté and melt the butter. Add the turkey and sear for about 4 minutes, stirring constantly. Remove the turkey and set aside on a plate. Add the garlic, leek, and mushrooms to the Instant Pot and cook for 3 minutes, or until the garlic is fragrant. Stir in the cooked turkey, broth, basil, parsley flakes, allspice, salt, and pepper. Lock the lid. Select the Manual mode and set the cooking time for 8 minutes at High Pressure. When the timer beeps, perform a quick pressure release. Carefully remove the lid. Stir in the heavy cream until heated through. Ladle the turkey mixture into six bowls and serve warm.

Paprika Turkey Breasts with Pesto Sauce

Prep time: 5 minutes | Cook time: 26 minutes | Serves 6

2 pounds (907 g) turkey breasts
Sea salt and ground black pepper, to taste
1 teaspoon paprika
1 tablespoon olive oil
1 cup water

Pesto Sauce:

⅓ cup olive oil
½ cup fresh basil leaves
⅓ cup grated Parmesan cheese
2 tablespoons pine nuts,
toasted
1 garlic clove, halved
Salt and ground black pepper, to taste

Season the turkey breasts on both sides with salt, black pepper, and paprika. Set your Instant Pot to Sauté and heat the olive oil. Add the turkey breasts and sear each side for 2 to 3 minutes. Pour in the water. Secure the lid. Select the Poultry mode and set the cooking time for 20 minutes at High Pressure. Meanwhile, place all the ingredients for the pesto sauce into a food processor. Pulse until everything is well combined. When the timer beeps, perform a quick pressure release. Carefully remove the lid. Spoon the pesto sauce onto the turkey breasts and serve.

Cheese and Mayo Turkey

Prep time: 5 minutes | Cook time: 26 minutes | Serves 8

2 pounds (907 g) turkey breasts
2 garlic cloves, halved
Sea salt and ground black pepper, to taste
1 teaspoon paprika
1 tablespoon butter
10 slices Colby cheese, shredded
1 cup grated Romano cheese, divided
⅔ cup mayonnaise
⅓ cup sour cream

Rub the turkey breasts with the garlic halves. Season with salt, black pepper, and paprika. Set your Instant Pot to Sauté and melt the butter. Add the turkey breasts and sear each side for 2 to 3 minutes. Meanwhile, thoroughly combine the Colby cheese, ½ cup of Romano cheese, mayonnaise, and sour cream in a mixing bowl. Spread this mixture over turkey breasts. Scatter the remaining ½ cup of Romano cheese on top. Secure the lid. Select the Manual mode and set the cooking time for 20 minutes at High Pressure. When the timer beeps, perform a quick pressure release. Carefully remove the lid. Cool for 5 minutes before serving.

Moringa Chicken Soup

Prep time: 3 minutes | Cook time: 18 minutes | Serves 8

1½ pounds (680 g) chicken breasts
5 cups water
1 cup chopped tomatoes
2 cloves garlic, minced
1 onion, chopped
1 thumb-size ginger
Salt and pepper, to taste
2 cups moringa leaves or kale leaves

Combine all the ingredients except the moringa leaves in the Instant Pot. Secure the lid. Select the Poultry mode and set the cooking time for 15 minutes at High Pressure. Once cooking is complete, do a natural pressure release for 10 minutes, then release any remaining pressure. Carefully open the lid. Set your Instant Pot to Sauté and stir in the moringa leaves. Allow to simmer for 3 minutes until softened. Divide into bowls and serve warm.

Stir-Fried Turkey and Cauliflower

Prep time: 10 minutes | Cook time: 35 minutes | Serves 4

2 tablespoons olive oil	A pinch of salt and black
2 garlic cloves, minced	pepper
1 yellow onion, chopped	1 cup chicken stock
1 cup cauliflower florets	2 pounds (907 g) turkey breast,
A pinch of dried rosemary	skinless, boneless and sliced

Press the Sauté button on the Instant Pot and heat the olive oil. Add the garlic, onion, cauliflower, rosemary, salt, and pepper to the Instant Pot, toss and sauté for 10 minutes, stirring occasionally. Stir in the chicken stock and turkey. Secure the lid. Select the Pressure Cook mode and set the cooking time for 25 minutes at High Pressure. Once cooking is complete, do a natural pressure release for 10 minutes, then release any remaining pressure. Carefully open the lid. Divide the mixture among four plates and serve.

Spicy Turkey Meatballs

Prep time: 5 minutes | Cook time: 25 minutes | Serves 5

1 pound (454 g) ground turkey	½ teaspoon chili powder
¼ cup hot sauce, or more to	½ teaspoon kosher salt
taste	½ teaspoon freshly ground
2 tablespoons coconut oil	black pepper
1 teaspoon finely grated ginger	1 cup filtered water
½ teaspoon dried basil	

Shape the ground turkey into 1½ inch meatballs with your hands and place in a greased dish in a single layer. Whisk together the hot sauce, oil, ginger, basil, chili powder, salt, and pepper in a small bowl until combined. Sprinkle evenly over the meatballs. Pour the water into the Instant Pot and insert the trivet. Using a sling, put the dish with the meatballs on the trivet. Lock the lid. Select the Manual mode and set the cooking time for 25 minutes at High Pressure. When the timer beeps, perform a natural pressure release for 10 minutes, then release any remaining pressure. Carefully remove the lid. Cool for 5 minutes and serve warm.

Coconut Chicken

Prep time: 10 minutes | Cook time: 15 minutes | Serves 4

1 tablespoon coconut oil	1 tomato, peeled and chopped
1 pound (454 g) chicken,	1 cup vegetable broth
cubed	⅓ cup unsweetened coconut
2 cloves garlic, minced	milk
1 shallot, peeled and chopped	2 tablespoons coconut aminos
1 teaspoon Thai chili, minced	1 teaspoon Thai curry paste
1 teaspoon fresh ginger root,	Salt and freshly ground black
julienned	pepper, to taste
⅓ teaspoon cumin powder	

Set your Instant Pot to Sauté and heat the coconut oil. Brown the chicken cubes for 2 to 3 minutes, stirring frequently. Reserve the chicken in a bowl. Add the garlic and shallot and sauté for 2 minutes until tender. Add a splash of vegetable broth to the pot, if needed. Stir in the Thai chili, ginger, and cumin powder and cook for another 1 minute or until fragrant. Add the cooked chicken, tomato, vegetable broth, milk, coconut aminos, and curry paste to the Instant Pot and stir well. Lock the lid. Select the Pressure Cook mode and set the cooking time for 10 minutes at High Pressure. When the timer beeps, perform a quick pressure release. Carefully remove the lid. Season with salt and pepper to taste and serve.

Honey Chicken

Prep time: 5 minutes | Cook time: 25 minutes | Serves 6

1 tablespoon olive oil	½ cup honey
2 cloves garlic, minced	¼ cup ketchup
½ cup diced onions	2 teaspoons sesame oil
4 large boneless, skinless	¼ teaspoon red pepper flakes
chicken breasts	2 green onions, chopped
Salt and pepper, to taste	1 tablespoon sesame seeds,
½ cup soy sauce	toasted

Press the Sauté button on the Instant Pot and heat the olive oil. Add the garlic and onions and sauté for about 3 minutes until fragrant. Add the chicken breasts and sprinkle with the salt and pepper. Brown each side for 3 minutes. Stir in the soy sauce, honey, ketchup, sesame oil, and red pepper flakes. Secure the lid. Select the Pressure Cook mode and set the cooking time for 20 minutes at High Pressure. Once cooking is complete, do a natural pressure release for 10 minutes, then release any remaining pressure. Carefully open the lid. Sprinkle the onions and sesame seeds on top for garnish before serving.

Mongolian Chicken with Carrots

Prep time: 5 minutes | Cook time: 20 minutes | Serves 6

2 tablespoons olive oil	1 cup brown sugar
10 cloves garlic, minced	1 cup chopped carrots
1 onion, minced	1 tablespoon garlic powder
4 large boneless, skinless	1 tablespoon grated ginger
chicken breasts, cut into cubes	1 teaspoons red pepper flakes
1 cup water	1 tablespoon cornstarch, mixed
1 cup soy sauce	with 2 tablespoons water

Set your Instant Pot to Sauté and heat the olive oil. Add the garlic and onion and sauté for about 3 minutes until fragrant. Add the chicken cubes and brown each side for 3 minutes. Add the remaining ingredients except the cornstarch mixture to the Instant Pot and stir well. Secure the lid. Select the Pressure Cook mode and set the cooking time for 15 minutes at High Pressure. Once cooking is complete, do a natural pressure release for 10 minutes, then release any remaining pressure. Carefully open the lid. Set your Instant Pot to Sauté again and whisk in the cornstarch mixture until the sauce thickens. Serve warm.

Spicy Chicken with Roasted Tomatoes

Prep time: 5 minutes | Cook time: 17 minutes | Serves 4

2 tablespoons avocado oil	½ teaspoon crushed red
½ cup water	pepper
1 pound (454 g) ground	½ teaspoon coriander
chicken	½ teaspoon chili powder
1 (14-ounce / 397-g) can low-	½ teaspoon curry powder
sugar fire roasted tomatoes	½ teaspoon kosher salt
½ jalapeño, finely chopped	½ teaspoon freshly ground
¼ poblano chili pepper, finely	black pepper
chopped	

Press the Sauté button on the Instant Pot and heat the avocado oil. Pour the water into the Instant Pot and stir in the remaining ingredients. Secure the lid. Select the Pressure Cook mode and set the cooking time for 17 minutes at High Pressure. Once cooking is complete, do a quick pressure release. Carefully open the lid. Let the chicken cool for 5 minutes and serve.

Chicken and Thyme Salad

Prep time: 5 minutes | Cook time: 12 minutes | Serves 8

2 pounds (907 g) chicken breasts	pepper
1 cup vegetable broth	1 cup mayonnaise
2 sprigs fresh thyme	2 stalks celery, chopped
1 teaspoon granulated garlic	2 tablespoons chopped fresh chives
1 teaspoon onion powder	1 teaspoon fresh lemon juice
1 bay leaf	1 teaspoon Dijon mustard
½ teaspoon ground black	½ teaspoon coarse sea salt

Combine the chicken, broth, thyme, garlic, onion powder, bay leaf, and black pepper in the Instant Pot. Lock the lid. Select the Pressure Cook mode and set the cooking time for 12 minutes at High Pressure. When the timer beeps, perform a natural pressure release for 10 minutes, then release any remaining pressure. Carefully remove the lid. Remove the chicken from the Instant Pot and let rest for a few minutes until cooled slightly. Slice the chicken breasts into strips and place in a salad bowl. Add the remaining ingredients and gently stir until well combined. Serve immediately.

BLT Chicken Salad with Pecan-Avocado Sauce

Prep time: 15 minutes | Cook time: 17 minutes | Serves 4

4 slices bacon	¼ teaspoon pepper
2 (6-ounce / 170-g) chicken breasts	¼ teaspoon dried thyme
1 teaspoon salt	1 cup water
½ teaspoon garlic powder	2 cups chopped romaine lettuce
¼ teaspoon dried parsley	
Sauce:	
⅓ cup mayonnaise	½ cup diced Roma tomatoes
1 ounce (28 g) chopped pecans	½ avocado, diced
	1 tablespoon lemon juice

Press the Sauté button to heat your Instant Pot. Add the bacon and cook for about 7 minutes, flipping occasionally, until crisp. Remove and place on a paper towel to drain. When cool enough to handle, crumble the bacon and set aside. Sprinkle the chicken with salt, garlic powder, parsley, pepper, and thyme. Pour the water into the Instant Pot. Use a wooden spoon to ensure nothing is stuck to the bottom of the pot. Add the trivet to the pot and place the chicken on top of the trivet. Secure the lid. Select the Pressure Cook mode and set the cooking time for 10 minutes at High Pressure. Meanwhile, whisk together all the ingredients for the sauce in a large salad bowl. Once cooking is complete, do a quick pressure release. Carefully open the lid. Remove the chicken and let sit for 10 minutes. Cut the chicken into cubes and transfer to the salad bowl, along with the cooked bacon. Gently stir until the chicken is thoroughly coated. Mix in the lettuce right before serving.

Chicken and Mushroom Bake

Prep time: 5 minutes | Cook time: 15 minutes | Serves 4

1 tablespoon butter	½ teaspoon turmeric powder
2 cloves garlic, smashed	½ teaspoon dried basil
½ cup chopped yellow onion	½ teaspoon dried sage
1 pound (454 g) chicken breasts, cubed	½ teaspoon cayenne pepper
10 ounces (283 g) button mushrooms, thinly sliced	⅓ teaspoon ground black pepper
1 cup chicken broth	Kosher salt, to taste
½ teaspoon shallot powder	½ cup heavy cream
	1 cup shredded Colby cheese

Set your Instant Pot to Sauté and melt the butter. Add the garlic, onion, chicken, and mushrooms and sauté for about 4 minutes, or until the vegetables are softened. Add the remaining ingredients except the heavy cream and cheese to the Instant Pot and stir to incorporate. Lock the lid. Select the Pressure Cook mode and set the cooking time for 6 minutes at High Pressure. When the timer beeps, perform a natural pressure release for 10 minutes, then release any remaining pressure. Carefully remove the lid. Stir in the heavy cream until heated through. Pour the mixture into a baking dish and scatter the cheese on top. Bake in the preheated oven at 400°F (205°C) until the cheese bubbles. Allow to cool for 5 minutes and serve.

Piccata

Prep time: 5 minutes | Cook time: 25 minutes | Serves 4

4 (6-ounce / 170-g) boneless, skinless chicken breasts	1 cup water
½ teaspoon salt	2 cloves garlic, minced
½ teaspoon garlic powder	4 tablespoons butter
¼ teaspoon pepper	Juice of 1 lemon
2 tablespoons coconut oil	¼ teaspoon xanthan gum

Sprinkle the chicken with salt, garlic powder, and pepper. Set your Instant Pot to Sauté and melt the coconut oil. Add the chicken and sear each side for about 5 to 7 minutes until golden brown. Remove the chicken and set aside on a plate. Pour the water into the Instant Pot. Using a wooden spoon, scrape the bottom if necessary to remove any stuck-on seasoning or meat. Insert the trivet and place the chicken on the trivet. Secure the lid. Select the Pressure Cook mode and set the cooking time for 10 minutes at High Pressure. Once cooking is complete, do a natural pressure release for 10 minutes, then release any remaining pressure. Carefully open the lid. Remove the chicken and set aside. Strain the broth from the Instant Pot into a large bowl and return to the pot. Set your Instant Pot to Sauté again and add the remaining ingredients. Cook for at least 5 minutes, stirring frequently, or until the sauce is cooked to your desired thickness. Pour the sauce over the chicken and serve warm.

Chicken and Cauliflower Rice Enchilada

Prep time: 10 minutes | Cook time: 35 minutes | Serves 4

2 (6-ounce / 170-g) boneless, skinless chicken breasts	1 (4-ounce / 113-g) can green chilies
2 teaspoons chili powder	¼ cup diced onion
½ teaspoon garlic powder	2 cups cooked cauliflower rice
½ teaspoon salt	1 avocado, diced
¼ teaspoon pepper	½ cup sour cream
2 tablespoons coconut oil	1 cup shredded Cheddar cheese
¾ cup red enchilada sauce	
¼ cup chicken broth	

Sprinkle the chili powder, garlic powder, salt, and pepper on chicken breasts. Set your Instant Pot to Sauté and melt the coconut oil. Add the chicken breasts and sear each side for about 5 minutes until golden brown. Pour the enchilada sauce and broth over the chicken. Using a wooden spoon or rubber spatula, scrape the bottom of pot to make sure nothing is sticking. Stir in the chilies and onion. Secure the lid. Select the Pressure Cook mode and set the cooking time for 25 minutes at High Pressure. Once cooking is complete, do a quick pressure release. Carefully open the lid. Remove the chicken and shred with two forks. Serve the chicken over the cauliflower rice and place the avocado, sour cream, and Cheddar cheese on top.

Pesto Chicken with Cheeses

Prep time: 5 minutes | Cook time: 25 minutes | Serves 2

2 (6-ounce / 170-g) boneless, skinless chicken breasts, butterflied
½ teaspoon salt
¼ teaspoon pepper
¼ teaspoon dried parsley
¼ teaspoon garlic powder
2 tablespoons coconut oil

1 cup water
¼ cup whole-milk ricotta cheese
¼ cup pesto
¼ cup shredded whole-milk Mozzarella cheese
Chopped parsley, for garnish (optional)

Sprinkle the chicken breasts with salt, pepper, parsley, and garlic powder. Set your Instant Pot to Sauté and melt the coconut oil. Add the chicken and brown for 3 to 5 minutes. Remove the chicken from the pot to a 7-cup glass bowl. Pour the water into the Instant Pot and use a wooden spoon or rubber spatula to make sure no seasoning is stuck to bottom of pot. Scatter the ricotta cheese on top of the chicken. Pour the pesto over chicken, and sprinkle the Mozzarella cheese over chicken. Cover with aluminum foil. Add the trivet to the Instant Pot and place the bowl on the trivet. Secure the lid. Select the Pressure Cook mode and set the cooking time for 20 minutes at High Pressure. Once cooking is complete, do a natural pressure release for 10 minutes, then release any remaining pressure. Carefully open the lid. Serve the chicken garnished with the chopped parsley, if desired.

Chicken Alfredo

Prep time: 10 minutes | Cook time: 27 minutes | Serves 4

2 (6-ounce / 170-g) boneless, skinless chicken breasts, butterflied
½ teaspoon garlic powder
¼ teaspoon dried parsley
¼ teaspoon dried thyme
¼ teaspoon salt
⅛ teaspoon pepper

2 tablespoons coconut oil
1 cup water
1 stick butter
2 cloves garlic, finely minced
¼ cup heavy cream
½ cup grated Parmesan cheese
¼ cup cooked crumbled bacon

Sprinkle the chicken breasts with the garlic powder, parsley, thyme, salt, and pepper. Set your Instant Pot to Sauté and melt the coconut oil. Add the chicken and sear for 3 to 5 minutes until golden brown on both sides. Remove the chicken with tongs and set aside. Pour the water into the Instant Pot and insert the trivet. Place the chicken on the trivet. Secure the lid. Select the Pressure Cook mode and set the cooking time for 20 minutes at High Pressure. Once cooking is complete, do a quick pressure release. Carefully open the lid. Remove the chicken from the pot to a platter and set aside. Pour the water out of the Instant Pot, reserving ½ cup; set aside. Set your Instant Pot to Sauté again and melt the butter. Add the garlic, heavy cream, cheese, and reserved water to the Instant Pot. Cook for 3 to 4 minutes until the sauce starts to thicken, stirring frequently. Stir in the crumbled bacon and pour the mixture over the chicken. Serve immediately.

Spinach Stuffed Chicken

Prep time: 10 minutes | Cook time: 25 minutes | Serves 4

½ cup frozen spinach
⅓ cup crumbled feta cheese
1¼ teaspoons salt, divided
4 (6-ounce / 170-g) boneless, skinless chicken breasts, butterflied

¼ teaspoon pepper
¼ teaspoon dried oregano
¼ teaspoon dried parsley
¼ teaspoon garlic powder
2 tablespoons coconut oil
1 cup water

Combine the spinach, feta cheese, and ¼ teaspoon of salt in a medium bowl. Divide the mixture evenly and spoon onto the chicken breasts. Close the chicken breasts and secure with toothpicks or butcher's string. Sprinkle the chicken with the remaining 1 teaspoon of salt, pepper, oregano, parsley, and garlic powder. Set your Instant Pot to Sauté and heat the coconut oil. Sear each chicken breast until golden brown, about 4 to 5 minutes per side. Remove the chicken breasts and set aside. Pour the water into the Instant Pot and scrape the bottom to remove any chicken or seasoning that is stuck on. Add the trivet to the Instant Pot and place the chicken on the trivet. Secure the lid. Select the Pressure Cook mode and set the cooking time for 15 minutes at High Pressure. Once cooking is complete, do a natural pressure release for 15 minutes, then release any remaining pressure. Carefully open the lid. Serve warm.

White Wine Chicken with Mushroom

Prep time: 5 minutes | Cook time: 22 minutes | Serves 12

2 tablespoons vegetable oil
4 cloves garlic, minced
1 onion, chopped
6 chicken breasts, halved
1¼ pounds (567 g) cremini mushrooms, sliced
1½ cups dry white wine
1 cup chicken broth

1 tablespoon lemon juice, freshly squeezed
1 tablespoon thyme
2 bay leaves
Salt and pepper, to taste
2 tablespoons cornstarch, mixed with 2 tablespoons water

Set your Instant Pot to Sauté and heat the vegetable oil. Add the garlic, onion, and chicken and brown for about 5 minutes. Fold in the mushrooms, white wine, chicken broth, lemon juice, thyme, bay leaves, salt, and pepper and stir to incorporate. Secure the lid. Select the Pressure Cook mode and set the cooking time for 15 minutes at High Pressure. Once cooking is complete, do a quick pressure release. Carefully open the lid. Set your Instant Pot to Sauté again and stir in the cornstarch mixture. Let simmer for a few minutes until the sauce is thickened. Allow to cool for 5 minutes before serving.

Chicken Salad with Cranberries

Prep time: 10 minutes | Cook time: 6 to 10 minutes | Serves 2

1 pound (454 g) skinless, boneless chicken breasts
½ cup water
2 teaspoons kosher salt, plus more for seasoning
½ cup mayonnaise
1 celery stalk, diced
2 tablespoons diced red onion
½ cup chopped dried

cranberries
¼ cup chopped walnuts
1 tablespoon freshly squeezed lime juice
¼ shredded unpeeled organic green apple
Freshly ground black pepper, to taste

Add the chicken, water, and 2 teaspoons of salt to your Instant Pot. Lock the lid. Press the Poultry button on the Instant Pot and cook for 6 minutes on High Pressure. Once cooking is complete, use a natural pressure release for 5 minutes and then release any remaining pressure. Carefully open the lid. Remove the chicken from the Instant Pot to a cutting board and let sit for 5 to 10 minutes. Shred the meat, transfer to a bowl, and add ¼ cup of the cooking liquid. Mix in the mayonnaise and stir until well coated. Add the celery, onion, cranberries, walnuts, lime juice, and apple. Sprinkle with the salt and pepper. Serve immediately.

Cacciatore

Prep time: 15 minutes | Cook time: 15 minutes | Serves 6

1 broiler/fryer chicken (3 to 4 pounds / 1.4 to 1.8 kg), cut up and skin removed
1 (4-ounce / 113-g) can mushroom stems and pieces, drained
1 (14½-ounce / 411-g) can diced tomatoes, undrained
1 (8-ounce / 227-g) can tomato sauce
¼ cup white wine or water
2 medium onions, thinly sliced
2 garlic cloves, minced
1 bay leaf
1 to 2 teaspoon dried oregano
½ teaspoon dried basil
1 teaspoon salt
¼ teaspoon pepper

Combine all the ingredients in the Instant Pot. Secure the lid. Select the Pressure Cook mode and set the cooking time for 15 minutes at High Pressure. Once cooking is complete, do a natural pressure release for 10 minutes, then release any remaining pressure. Carefully open the lid. Discard the bay leaf and serve on a plate.

Lemony Chicken With Potatoes

Prep time: 5 minutes | Cook time: 21 minutes | Serves 4

2 pounds (907 g) chicken thighs
1 teaspoon fine sea salt
½ teaspoon ground black pepper
2 tablespoons olive oil
¼ cup freshly squeezed lemon juice
¾ cup low-sodium chicken broth
2 tablespoons Italian seasoning
2 to 3 tablespoons Dijon mustard
2 to 3 pounds (907 to 1361 g) red potatoes, quartered

Sprinkle the chicken with the salt and pepper. Add the oil to your Instant Pot. Select the Sauté mode. Add the chicken and sauté for 3 minutes until browned on both sides. Meanwhile, make the sauce by stirring together the lemon juice, chicken broth, Italian seasoning, and mustard in a medium mixing bowl. Drizzle the sauce over the chicken. Fold in the potatoes. Secure the lid. Press the Manual button on the Instant Pot and cook for 15 minutes on High Pressure. Once cooking is complete, do a quick pressure release. Carefully remove the lid. Transfer the chicken to a serving dish and serve immediately.

Paprika Chicken with Cucumber Salad

Prep time: 10 minutes | Cook time: 20 minutes | Serves 4

1 tablespoon olive oil
1 yellow onion, chopped
2 chicken breasts, skinless, boneless and halved
Salad:
2 cucumbers, sliced
1 tomato, cubed
1 avocado, peeled, pitted, and
1 cup chicken stock
1 tablespoon sweet paprika
½ teaspoon cinnamon powder

cubed
1 tablespoon chopped cilantro

Press the Sauté button on the Instant Pot and heat the olive oil until it shimmers. Add the onion and chicken breasts and sauté for 5 minutes, stirring occasionally, or until the onion is translucent. Stir in the chicken stock, paprika, and cinnamon powder. Secure the lid. Select the Manual mode and set the cooking time for 15 minutes at High Pressure. Meanwhile, toss all the ingredients for the salad in a bowl. Set aside. Once cooking is complete, do a natural pressure release for 10 minutes, then release any remaining pressure. Carefully open the lid. Divide the chicken breasts between four plates and serve with the salad on the side.

Indian Butter Chicken

Prep time: 10 minutes | Cook time: 15 minutes | Serves 4

1 medium yellow onion, halved and sliced through the root end
1 (10-ounce / 284-g) can Ro-Tel tomatoes with green chilies, with juice
1½ pounds (680 g) boneless, skinless chicken thighs, fat trimmed, cut into 2- to 3-inch pieces
2 tablespoons mild Indian curry paste
3 tablespoons butter or ghee, at room temperature, divided
2 tablespoons all-purpose flour
Salt and freshly ground black pepper, to taste

Add 1 tablespoon of the butter in the Instant Pot and select the Sauté mode. Add the onion and sauté for 6 minutes until browned. Stir in the tomatoes and scrape any browned bits from the pot. Add the curry paste and stir well. Fold in the chicken and stir to coat. Secure the lid. Press the Manual button on the Instant Pot and cook for 8 minutes on High Pressure. Once cooking is complete, use a quick pressure release. Combine the remaining 2 tablespoons of butter and the flour in a small bowl and stir until smooth. Select the Sauté mode. Add the flour mixture to the chicken in two additions, stirring between additions. Sauté for 1 minute, or until the sauce is thickened. Sprinkle with the salt and pepper and serve.

Cashew Chicken

Prep time: 3 minutes | Cook time: 15 minutes | Serves 6

2 pounds (907 g) chicken thighs, bones, and skin removed
¼ cup soy sauce
¼ teaspoon black pepper
2 tablespoons ketchup
2 tablespoons rice vinegar
1 clove of garlic, minced
1 tablespoon brown sugar
1 teaspoon grated ginger
1 tablespoon cornstarch + 2 tablespoons water
⅓ cup cashew nuts, toasted
2 tablespoons sesame seeds, toasted
¼ cup green onions, chopped

Add all the ingredients except for the cashew nuts, sesame seeds, cornstarch slurry, and green onions to the Instant Pot and stir to combine. Secure the lid. Select the Manual mode and cook for 15 minutes on High Pressure. Once cooking is complete, use a quick pressure release. Carefully open the lid. Select the Sauté mode and stir in the cornstarch slurry. Let simmer until the sauce is thickened. Stir in the cashew nuts, sesame seeds, and green onions. Transfer to a serving dish and serve immediately.

Cheesy Black Bean Chicken

Prep time: 10 minutes | Cook time: 8 minutes | Serves 8

1½ pounds (680 g) boneless, skinless chicken breasts
2 (16-ounce /454-g) jars black bean and corn salsa
1 medium green pepper, chopped
1 medium sweet red pepper, chopped
1 (12-ounce / 340-g) package tortilla chips
2 cups shredded Mexican cheese blend

Add the chicken, peppers, and salsa to your Instant Pot. Secure the lid. Press the Manual button on the Instant Pot and set the cooking time for 8 minutes on High Pressure. Once cooking is complete, use a natural pressure release for 7 minutes and then release any remaining pressure. Carefully open the lid. Remove the chicken from the pot to a plate and shred with two forks. Transfer the chicken back to the Instant Pot and stir to combine. Serve the chicken over chips with a slotted spoon. Scatter the cheese on top.

Spicy Chicken and Smoked Sausage
Prep time: 35 minutes | Cook time: 15 minutes | Serves 11

1 (6-ounce / 170-g) can tomato paste
1 (14½-ounce / 411-g) can diced tomatoes, undrained
1 (14½-ounce / 411-g) can beef broth or chicken broth
2 medium green peppers, chopped
1 medium onion, chopped
5 garlic cloves, minced
3 celery ribs, chopped
3 teaspoons dried parsley flakes
2 teaspoons dried basil
1½ teaspoons dried oregano
½ teaspoon hot pepper sauce
1¼ teaspoons salt
½ teaspoon cayenne pepper
1 pound (454 g) smoked sausage, halved and cut into ¼-inch slices
1 pound (454 g) boneless, skinless chicken breasts, cut into 1-inch cubes
½ pound (227 g) uncooked shrimp, peeled and deveined
Hot cooked rice, for serving

Mix together the tomato paste, tomatoes, and broth in your Instant Pot. Stir in the green peppers, onion, garlic, celery, and seasonings. Fold in the sausage and chicken. Secure the lid. Press the Manual button and set the cooking time for 8 minutes on High Pressure. Once the timer goes off, do a quick pressure release. Carefully open the lid. Set the Instant Pot to sauté. Add the shrimp and stir well. Cook for another 5 minutes, or until the shrimp turn pink, stirring occasionally. Serve over the cooked rice.

Garlic Chicken
Prep time: 10 minutes | Cook time: 20 minutes | Serves 4

2 chicken breasts, skinless, boneless and halved
1 cup tomato sauce
¼ cup sweet chili sauce
¼ cup chicken stock
4 garlic cloves, minced
1 tablespoon chopped basil

Combine all the ingredients in the Instant Pot. Secure the lid. Select the Poultry mode and set the cooking time for 20 minutes at High Pressure. Once cooking is complete, do a natural pressure release for 10 minutes, then release any remaining pressure. Carefully open the lid. Divide the chicken breasts among four plates and serve.

Chipotle Chicken Fajita
Prep time: 15 minutes | Cook time: 10 minutes | Serves 2

1 tablespoon oil
½ green bell pepper, sliced
¼ red onion, sliced
2 skinless, boneless chicken breasts
½ cup water
2 canned chipotle chiles in adobo sauce, deseeded and
minced
Kosher salt, to taste
3 tablespoons mayonnaise
¼ cup sour cream
½ tablespoon freshly squeezed lime juice
Freshly ground black pepper, to taste

Set your Instant Pot to Sauté and heat the oil until it shimmers. Add the bell pepper and onion and sauté for 3 to 4 minutes until tender. Remove from the Instant Pot to a small bowl and set aside to cool. Add the chicken breasts, water, and a few teaspoons of adobo sauce to the pot and season with salt to taste. Lock the lid. Select the Poultry mode and set the cooking time for 6 minutes at High Pressure. Once cooking is complete, do a natural pressure release for 5 minutes, then release any remaining pressure. Carefully open the lid. Remove the chicken from the pot to a cutting board and allow to cool for 10 minutes. Slice the chicken breasts into cubes and place in a medium bowl. Add the cooked bell pepper and onion, mayo, sour cream, chipotle chiles, lime juice, salt, and pepper to the bowl of chicken and toss to coat. Serve immediately.

Browned Chicken with Veggies
Prep time: 10 minutes | Cook time: 25 minutes | Serves 4

2 tablespoons olive oil
1 yellow onion, chopped
2 chicken breasts, skinless, boneless and cubed
1 cup cubed mixed bell
peppers
1 cup cubed tomato
1 cup chicken stock
1 teaspoon Creole seasoning
A pinch of cayenne pepper

Set your Instant Pot to Sauté and heat the olive oil until hot. Add the onion and chicken cubes and brown for 5 minutes. Stir in the remaining ingredients. Secure the lid. Select the poultry mode and set the cooking time for 20 minutes at High Pressure. Once cooking is complete, do a natural pressure release for 10 minutes, then release any remaining pressure. Carefully open the lid. Serve warm.

Chicken Pasta Puttanesca
Prep time: 10 minutes | Cook time: 9 minutes | Serves 4

2 (6- to 7-ounce / 170- to 198-g) boneless, skinless chicken breasts
Salt and freshly ground black pepper, to taste
2 tablespoons olive oil
12 ounces (340 g) dry penne pasta
1 (14.5-ounce / 411-g) can diced tomatoes with Italian
herbs, with juices
2½ cups store-bought chicken or vegetable broth, or homemade
4 oil-packed rolled anchovies with capers, plus 1 tablespoon oil from the jar
½ cup oil-cured black or Kalamata olives
Pinch of red pepper flakes

Using paper towels, pat the chicken dry. Sprinkle with the salt and pepper. Press the Sauté button on your Instant Pot. Add and heat the oil. Add the chicken and cook for 3 minutes, or until the chicken is nicely browned on one side. Stir in the penne, tomatoes, broth, anchovies and oil, olives, red pepper flakes, and pepper. Place the chicken on top. Secure the lid. Select the Manual mode and set the cooking time for 6 minutes on Low Pressure. When the timer beeps, do a quick pressure release. Carefully open the lid. Remove the chicken from the Instant Pot to a cutting board and cut into bite-size pieces. Transfer the chicken back to the pot and stir until well mixed. Lock the lid and let sit for 5 minutes, or until the liquid is thickened. Serve immediately.

Asian Honey Garlic Chicken
Prep time: 5 minutes | Cook time: 15 minutes | Serves 6

1½ pounds (680 g) chicken breasts, cut into cubes
3 cloves of garlic, minced
6 tablespoons honey
2 tablespoons online powder
1½ tablespoons soy sauce
½ tablespoon sriracha sauce
1 cup water
1 tablespoon cornstarch + 2 tablespoons water
1 tablespoon sesame oil
Green onions, chopped

Add all the ingredients except the cornstarch slurry, sesame oil, and green onions to the Instant Pot and stir to combine. Secure the lid. Select the Poultry mode and cook for 15 minutes on High Pressure. Once the timer goes off, use a quick pressure release. Carefully open the lid. Select the Sauté mode. Fold in the cornstarch slurry. Stir well. Let simmer until the sauce is thickened. Mix in the sesame oil and green onions and stir to combine. Serve immediately.

Citrusy Chicken Tacos

Prep time: 5 minutes | Cook time: 20 minutes | Serves 12

¼ cup olive oil
12 chicken breasts, skin and bones removed
8 cloves of garlic, minced
⅔ cup orange juice, freshly squeezed
⅔ cup lime juice, freshly

squeezed
2 tablespoons ground cumin
1 tablespoon dried oregano
1 tablespoon orange peel
Salt and pepper, to taste
¼ cup cilantro, chopped

Set your Instant Pot to Sauté. Add and heat the oil. Add the chicken breasts and garlic. Cook until the chicken pieces are lightly browned. Add the orange juice, lime juice, cumin, oregano, orange peel, salt, and pepper. Stir well. Secure the lid. Select the Poultry mode and cook for 15 minutes on High Pressure. Once cooking is complete, do a quick pressure release. Carefully remove the lid. Serve garnished with the cilantro.

Picnic Chicken

Prep time: 5 minutes | Cook time: 6 to 7 hours | Serves 4

2 pounds (907 g) or 4 large chicken thighs
¼ cup dill pickle relish

¼ cup Dijon mustard
¼ cup mayonnaise
½ cup chicken broth

Rinse chicken well. Pat dry. Place in the Instant Pot with the skin side up. In a mixing bowl, stir together the relish, mustard, and mayonnaise. When well blended, stir in chicken broth. Mix well. Pour sauce over chicken. Cover Instant Pot and press the Slow Cook button, and cook on low for 6 to 7 hours, or until chicken is tender but not dry or mushy. (Press Slow Cook again to toggle between Low and High cooking temperatures.)

Butter Chicken (Murgh Makhani)

Prep time: 3 minutes | Cook time: 20 minutes | Serves 4

1 pound (454 g) chicken meat
1 can crushed tomatoes
6 cloves garlic
2 teaspoons grated ginger
1 teaspoon garam masala

1 teaspoon turmeric
1 teaspoon paprika
1 teaspoon cumin
½ teaspoon cayenne pepper

Combine all the ingredients in the Instant Pot. Lock the lid. Select the Poultry mode and set the cooking time for 20 minutes at High Pressure. Once cooking is complete, do a natural pressure release for 10 minutes, then release any remaining pressure. Carefully open the lid. Serve warm.

Lemon Pepper Chicken

Prep time: 5 minutes | Cook time: 6 to 8 hours | Serves 4

1 onion, chopped
1 pound (454 g) boneless, skinless chicken thighs

1 teaspoon lemon pepper
½ teaspoon dried oregano
½ cup plain yogurt

Combine first 3 ingredients in the Instant Pot. Cover and press the Slow Cook button, and cook on low for 6 to 8 hours, or until chicken is tender. (Press Slow Cook again to toggle between Low and High cooking temperatures.) Just before serving, remove chicken and shred with two forks. Add shredded chicken back into the Instant Pot and stir in oregano and yogurt. Serve as a filling for pita bread.

Chicken Lo Mein

Prep time: 10 minutes | Cook time: 10 minutes | Serves 4

1 tablespoon toasted sesame oil
1 garlic clove, minced
1½ pounds (680 g) boneless, skinless chicken breast, cut into bite-size pieces
Sauce:
1½ cups low-sodium chicken broth
1 tablespoon fish sauce
1 tablespoon soy sauce

8 ounces (227 g) dried linguine, broken in half
1 cup broccoli florets
1 carrot, peeled and thinly sliced
1 cup snow peas

1 tablespoon Shaoxing rice wine
1 tablespoon brown sugar
1 teaspoon grated fresh ginger

Press the Sauté button on the Instant Pot and heat the sesame oil until shimmering. Add the garlic and chicken and sauté for about 5 minutes, stirring occasionally, or until the garlic is lightly browned. Fan the noodles across the bottom of the Instant Pot. Top with the broccoli florets, carrot, finished by snow peas. Whisk together all the ingredients for the sauce in a medium bowl until the sugar is dissolved. Pour the sauce over the top of the vegetables. Secure the lid. Select the Manual mode and set the cooking time for 5 minutes at High Pressure. Once cooking is complete, do a quick pressure release. Carefully open the lid. Stir the noodles, breaking up any clumps, or until the liquid has absorbed. Serve warm.

Creamy Chicken with Cilantro

Prep time: 5 minutes | Cook time: 25 minutes | Serves 4

2 chicken breasts, skinless, boneless and halved
1 cup tomato sauce
1 cup plain Greek yogurt
¾ cup coconut cream

¼ cup chopped cilantro
2 teaspoons garam masala
2 teaspoons ground cumin
A pinch of salt and black pepper

Thoroughly combine all the ingredients in the Instant Pot. Lock the lid. Select the Poultry mode and set the cooking time for 25 minutes at High Pressure. Once cooking is complete, do a natural pressure release for 5 minutes, then release any remaining pressure. Carefully open the lid. Transfer the chicken breasts to a plate and serve.

Chicken with White Wine Mushroom Sauce

Prep time: 5 minutes | Cook time: 22 minutes | Serves 12

2 tablespoons vegetable oil
4 cloves garlic, minced
1 onion, chopped
6 chicken breasts, halved
1¼ pounds (567 g) cremini mushrooms, sliced
1½ cups dry white wine
1 cup chicken broth

1 tablespoon lemon juice, freshly squeezed
1 tablespoon thyme
2 bay leaves
Salt and pepper, to taste
2 tablespoons cornstarch, mixed with 2 tablespoons water

Set your Instant Pot to Sauté and heat the vegetable oil. Add the garlic, onion, and chicken and brown for about 5 minutes. Fold in the mushrooms, white wine, chicken broth, lemon juice, thyme, bay leaves, salt, and pepper and stir to incorporate. Secure the lid. Select the Poultry mode and set the cooking time for 15 minutes at High Pressure. Once cooking is complete, do a quick pressure release. Carefully open the lid. Set your Instant Pot to Sauté again and stir in the cornstarch mixture. Let simmer for a few minutes until the sauce is thickened. Allow to cool for 5 minutes before serving.

Simple Shredded Chicken

Prep time: 3 minutes | Cook time: 30 minutes | Serves 8

4 pounds (1.8 kg) chicken breasts
½ cup water
Salt and pepper, to taste

Combine all the ingredients in the Instant Pot. Secure the lid. Select the Poultry mode and set the cooking time for 30 minutes at High Pressure. Once cooking is complete, do a natural pressure release for 10 minutes, then release any remaining pressure. Carefully open the lid. Transfer the chicken breasts to a plate and shred them with two forks. Serve warm.

Honey-Glazed Chicken with Sesame

Prep time: 5 minutes | Cook time: 25 minutes | Serves 6

1 tablespoon olive oil
2 cloves garlic, minced
½ cup diced onions
4 large boneless, skinless chicken breasts
Salt and pepper, to taste
½ cup soy sauce
½ cup honey
¼ cup ketchup
2 teaspoons sesame oil
¼ teaspoon red pepper flakes
2 green onions, chopped
1 tablespoon sesame seeds, toasted

Press the Sauté button on the Instant Pot and heat the olive oil. Add the garlic and onions and sauté for about 3 minutes until fragrant. Add the chicken breasts and sprinkle with the salt and pepper. Brown each side for 3 minutes. Stir in the soy sauce, honey, ketchup, sesame oil, and red pepper flakes. Secure the lid. Select the Poultry mode and set the cooking time for 20 minutes at High Pressure. Once cooking is complete, do a natural pressure release for 10 minutes, then release any remaining pressure. Carefully open the lid. Sprinkle the onions and sesame seeds on top for garnish before serving.

Mongolian Chicken

Prep time: 5 minutes | Cook time: 20 minutes | Serves 6

2 tablespoons olive oil
10 cloves garlic, minced
1 onion, minced
4 large boneless, skinless chicken breasts, cut into cubes
1 cup water
1 cup soy sauce
1 cup brown sugar
1 cup chopped carrots
1 tablespoon garlic powder
1 tablespoon grated ginger
1 teaspoon red pepper flakes
1 tablespoon cornstarch, mixed with 2 tablespoons water

Set your Instant Pot to Sauté and heat the olive oil. Add the garlic and onion and sauté for about 3 minutes until fragrant. Add the chicken cubes and brown each side for 3 minutes. Add the remaining ingredients except the cornstarch mixture to the Instant Pot and stir well. Secure the lid. Select the Poultry mode and set the cooking time for 15 minutes at High Pressure. Once cooking is complete, do a natural pressure release for 10 minutes, then release any remaining pressure. Carefully open the lid. Set your Instant Pot to Sauté again and whisk in the cornstarch mixture until the sauce thickens. Serve warm.

Basil Chicken

Prep time: 5 minutes | Cook time: 5 to 6 hours | Serves 6

6 boneless, skinless chicken breast halves
2 (10¾-ounce / 305-g) cans broccoli cheese soup
2 cups milk
1 small onion, chopped
½ to 1 teaspoon salt
½ to 1 teaspoon dried basil
⅛ teaspoon pepper

Place chicken pieces in the Instant Pot. Combine remaining ingredients. Pour over chicken. Cover. Press the Slow Cook button, and cook on high for 1 hour. Turn the Instant Pot to cook on low for 5 to 6 hours. (Press Slow Cook again to toggle between Low and High cooking temperatures.) Serve over noodles.

Garlic and Citrus Chicken

Prep time: 15 minutes | Cook time: 5 to 6 hours | Serves 6

6 skinless, bone-in chicken breast halves
1½ teaspoons dry thyme
6 cloves garlic, minced
1 cup orange juice concentrate
2 tablespoons balsamic vinegar

Rub thyme and garlic over chicken. (Reserve any leftover thyme and garlic.) Place chicken in the Instant Pot. Mix orange juice concentrate and vinegar together in a small bowl. Stir in reserved thyme and garlic. Spoon over chicken. Cover and press the Slow Cook button, and cook on low for 5 to 6 hours or on high for 2½ to 3 hours, until chicken is tender but not dry. (Press Slow Cook again to toggle between Low and High cooking temperatures.)

Chicken and Peas Casserole with Cheese

Prep time: 10 minutes | Cook time: 30 minutes | Serves 4

2 pounds (907 g) chicken breast, skinless, boneless and cubed
1 cup veggie stock
1 cup peas
1 tablespoon Italian seasoning
1 tablespoon sweet paprika
A pinch of salt and black pepper
1 cup coconut cream
1 cup shredded Cheddar cheese

Stir together the chicken cubes, veggie stock, peas, Italian seasoning, paprika, salt, and pepper in the Instant Pot. Pour the coconut cream over top. Secure the lid. Select the Poultry mode and set the cooking time for 20 minutes at High Pressure. Once cooking is complete, do a quick pressure release. Remove the lid. Scatter the shredded cheese all over. Put the lid back on and cook on High Pressure for an additional 10 minutes. Once cooking is complete, do a quick pressure release. Carefully open the lid. Serve warm.

Authentic Belizean Stewed Chicken

Prep time: 5 minutes | Cook time: 20 minutes | Serves 8

1 tablespoon coconut oil
3 cloves garlic, minced
1 onion, sliced
4 whole chicken legs
2 cups chicken stock
3 tablespoons Worcestershire sauce
2 tablespoons white vinegar
2 tablespoons achiote seasoning
1 tablespoon granulated sugar
1 teaspoon dried oregano
1 teaspoon ground cumin
Salt and pepper, to taste

Set your Instant Pot to Sauté and melt the coconut oil. Add the garlic, onion, and chicken legs and keep stirring until the chicken legs are golden brown. Add the remaining ingredients to the Instant Pot and stir to combine. Secure the lid. Select the Poultry mode and set the cooking time for 15 minutes at High Pressure. Once cooking is complete, do a quick pressure release. Carefully open the lid. Divide the chicken legs among plates and serve.

Sweet and Sour Chicken
Prep time: 5 minutes | Cook time: 20 minutes | Serves 8

1 tablespoon olive oil
4 cloves garlic, minced
1 onion, chopped
2 pounds (907 g) chicken meat
1 green bell pepper, julienned

½ cup molasses
½ cup ketchup
¼ cup soy sauce
1 tablespoon cornstarch, mixed
with 2 tablespoons water

Set your Instant Pot to Sauté and heat the olive oil. Add the garlic, onion, and chicken and stir-fry for about 5 minutes until lightly golden. Stir in the bell pepper, molasses, ketchup, and soy sauce. Secure the lid. Select the Poultry mode and set the cooking time for 15 minutes at High Pressure. Once cooking is complete, do a quick pressure release. Carefully open the lid. Set your Instant Pot to Sauté again and whisk in the cornstarch mixture until thickened. Allow to cool for 5 minutes before serving.

Stuffed Chicken with Bacon and Feta
Prep time: 10 minutes | Cook time: 1½ to 3 hours | Serves 4

¼ cup crumbled cooked bacon
¼ cup crumbled feta cheese
4 boneless, skinless chicken
breast halves

2 (14½-ounce / 411-g) cans
diced tomatoes
1 tablespoon dried basil

In a small bowl, mix bacon and cheese together lightly. Cut a pocket in the thicker side of each chicken breast. Fill each with ¼ of the bacon and cheese. Pinch shut and secure with toothpicks. Place chicken in the Instant Pot. Top with tomatoes and sprinkle with basil. Cover and press the Slow Cook button, and cook on high for 1½ to 3 hours, or until chicken is tender, but not dry or mushy. (Press Slow Cook again to toggle between Low and High cooking temperatures.)

Asian Ginger Chicken
Prep time: 15 minutes | Cook time: 3 to 5 hours | Serves 6

6 chicken breast halves,
uncooked, cut up
1 cup diced carrots
½ cup minced onion
½ cup low-sodium soy sauce
¼ cup rice vinegar
¼ cup sesame seeds

1 tablespoon ground ginger, or
¼ cup grated ginger
¾ teaspoon salt
1 teaspoon sesame oil
2 cups broccoli florets
1 cup cauliflower florets

Combine all ingredients except broccoli and cauliflower in the Instant Pot. Cover. Press the Slow Cook button, and cook on low for 3 to 5 hours. (Press Slow Cook again to toggle between Low and High cooking temperatures.) Stir in broccoli and cauliflower and cook an additional hour. Serve over brown rice.

Shredded Chicken
Prep time: 3 minutes | Cook time: 30 minutes | Serves 8

4 pounds (1.8 kg) chicken
breasts

½ cup water
Salt and pepper, to taste

Combine all the ingredients in the Instant Pot. Secure the lid. Select the Pressure Cook mode and set the cooking time for 30 minutes at High Pressure. Once cooking is complete, do a natural pressure release for 10 minutes, then release any remaining pressure. Carefully open the lid. Transfer the chicken breasts to a plate and shred them with two forks. Serve warm.

Chicken and Potato Bake
Prep time: 15 minutes | Cook time: 4½ to 5½ hours | Serves 6 to 8

¼ cup chopped green peppers
½ cup chopped onions
1½ cups diced Velveeta
cheese
7 to 8 medium potatoes, sliced
Salt, to taste

1 (10¾-ounce / 305-g) can
cream of celery soup
1 cup milk
3 to 4 whole boneless, skinless
chicken breasts

Place layers of green peppers, onions, cheese, and potatoes and a sprinkling of salt in the Instant Pot. Sprinkle salt over chicken breasts and lay on top of potatoes. Combine soup and milk and pour into the Instant Pot, pushing meat down into liquid. Cover. Press the Slow Cook button, and cook on high for 1½ hours. Turn the Instant Pot to cook on low for 3 to 4 hours (Press Slow Cook again to toggle between Low and High cooking temperatures.) Test that potatoes are soft. If not, continue cooking on low another hour and test again, continuing to cook until potatoes are finished.

Creamy Lemon Garlic Chicken
Prep time: 15 minutes | Cook time: 3 to 4 hours | Serves 6

1 cup vegetable broth
1½ teaspoons grated lemon
peel
3 tablespoons lemon juice
2 tablespoons capers, drained
3 garlic cloves, minced
½ teaspoon pepper

6 boneless skinless chicken
breast halves (6 ounces / 170
g each)
2 tablespoons butter
2 tablespoons all-purpose flour
½ cup heavy whipping cream
Hot cooked rice

In a small bowl, combine the first six ingredients. Place chicken in the Instant Pot; pour broth mixture over chicken. Cover and press the Slow Cook button, and cook on low for 3 to 5 hours or until chicken is tender. (Press Slow Cook again to toggle between Low and High cooking temperatures.) Remove chicken from Instant Pot; keep warm. In a large saucepan, melt butter over medium heat. Stir in flour until smooth; gradually whisk in cooking juices. Bring to a boil, stirring constantly; cook and stir 1-2 minutes or until thickened. Remove from heat and stir in cream. Serve chicken and rice with sauce.

Chicken Verde with Green Chile
Prep time: 5 minutes | Cook time: 15 minutes | Serves 4

3 pounds (1.4 kg) bone-in,
skin-on chicken drumsticks
and/or thighs
1 (27-ounce / 765-g) can
roasted poblano peppers,
drained
1 (15-ounce / 425-g) jar salsa
verde (green chile salsa)

1 onion, chopped
1 (7-ounce / 198-g) jar
chopped green chiles, drained
1 tablespoon chopped jalapeño
(optional)
1 tablespoon ground cumin
4 teaspoons minced garlic
1 teaspoon fine sea salt

Mix together all the ingredients in your Instant Pot and stir to combine. Secure the lid. Press the Manual button and set the cooking time for 15 minutes on High Pressure. Once the timer goes off, use a quick pressure release. Carefully open the lid. Remove the chicken from the Instant Pot to a plate with tongs. Let cool for 5 minutes. Remove the bones and skin and discard. Shred the chicken with two forks. Transfer the chicken back to the sauce and stir to combine. Serve immediately.

Chapter 10 Soups, Stews, and Chilies

Potato and Beef Stew

Prep time: 15 minutes | Cook time: 46 minutes | Serves 6

2 tablespoons olive oil
2 pounds (907 g) beef stew cubes
1 medium sweet onion, peeled and diced
4 cloves garlic, peeled and minced
3 cups beef broth
½ cup dry red wine
1 (14.5-ounce / 411-g) can crushed tomatoes, undrained
2 medium carrots, peeled and diced

2 medium Russet potatoes, scrubbed and small-diced
1 stalk celery, chopped
2 tablespoons chopped fresh rosemary
1 teaspoon salt
½ teaspoon ground black pepper
2 tablespoons gluten-free all-purpose flour
4 tablespoons water
¼ cup chopped fresh Italian flat-leaf parsley

Press the Sauté button on the Instant Pot and heat the oil. Add the beef and onion to the pot and sauté for 5 minutes, or until the beef is seared and the onion is translucent. Add the garlic and sauté for 1 minute. Pour in the beef broth and wine and deglaze the pot by scraping up any bits from the sides and bottom of the pot. Stir in the tomatoes with juice, carrots, potatoes, celery, rosemary, salt and pepper. Set the lid in place. Select the Pressure Cook mode and set the cooking time for 35 minutes on High Pressure. When the timer goes off, perform a natural pressure release for 10 minutes, then release any remaining pressure. Open the lid. Create a slurry by whisking together the flour and water in a small bowl. Add the slurry to the pot. Select the Sauté mode and let simmer for 5 minutes, stirring constantly. Ladle the stew into 6 bowls and serve topped with the parsley.

Beef, Bean, and Spaghtti Chili

Prep time: 20 minutes | Cook time: 19 minutes | Serves 8

2 pounds (907 g) 90% lean ground beef
3 large yellow onions, peeled and diced, divided
3 cloves garlic, peeled and minced
2 (16-ounce / 454-g) cans kidney beans, rinsed and drained
1 (15-ounce / 425-g) can tomato sauce
1 cup beef broth
2 tablespoons semisweet chocolate chips
2 tablespoons honey

2 tablespoons red wine vinegar
2 tablespoons chili powder
1 tablespoon pumpkin pie spice
1 teaspoon ground cumin
½ teaspoon ground cardamom
½ teaspoon salt
½ teaspoon freshly cracked black pepper
¼ teaspoon ground cloves
1 pound (454 g) cooked spaghetti
4 cups shredded Cheddar cheese

Press the Sauté button on the Instant Pot. Add the ground beef and ¾ of the diced onions to the pot and sauté for 8 minutes, or until the beef is browned and the onions are transparent. Drain the beef mixture and discard any excess fat. Add the garlic to the pot and sauté for 30 seconds. Stir in the remaining ingredients, except for the reserved onions, spaghetti and cheese. Cook for 1 minute, or until fragrant. Set the lid in place. Select the Pressure Cook mode and set the cooking time for 10 minutes on High Pressure. When the timer goes off, perform a quick pressure release. Carefully open the lid. Serve over the cooked spaghetti and top with the reserved onions and cheese.

Pork and Beef Chili

Prep time: 10 minutes | Cook time: 40 minutes | Serves 4

1 tablespoon olive oil
½ pound (227 g) ground beef
½ pound (227 g) ground pork
1 medium onion, peeled and diced
1 (28-ounce / 794-g) can puréed tomatoes, undrained
1 large carrot, peeled and diced

1 small green bell pepper, deseeded and diced
1 small jalapeño, deseeded and diced
3 cloves garlic, minced
2 tablespoons chili powder
1 teaspoon sea salt
2 teaspoons ground black pepper

Press the Sauté button on the Instant Pot and heat the olive oil. Add the ground beef, ground pork and onion to the pot and sauté for 5 minutes, or until the pork is no longer pink. Stir in the remaining ingredients. Close and secure the lid. Select the Pressure Cook mode and set the cooking time for 35 minutes on High Pressure. Once cooking is complete, use a natural pressure release for 15 minutes, then release any remaining pressure. Open the lid. Serve warm.

Okra and Beef Stew

Prep time: 15 minutes | Cook time: 25 minutes | Serves 3

8 ounces (227 g) beef sirloin, chopped
¼ teaspoon cumin seeds
1 teaspoon dried basil
1 tablespoon avocado oil

¼ cup coconut cream
1 cup water
6 ounces (170 g) okra, chopped

Sprinkle the beef sirloin with cumin seeds and dried basil and put in the Instant Pot. Add avocado oil and roast the meat on Sauté mode for 5 minutes. Flip occasionally. Add coconut cream, water, and okra. Close the lid and select Pressure Cook mode. Set cooking time for 25 minutes on High Pressure. When timer beeps, use a natural pressure release for 10 minutes, the release any remaining pressure. Open the lid. Serve warm.

Potato, Zucchini, and Orzo Soup

Prep time: 15 minutes | Cook time: 10 minutes | Serves 4

1 medium potato, peeled and small-diced
1 medium zucchini, diced
1 small carrot, peeled and diced
1 small yellow onion, peeled and diced
2 stalks celery, diced
1 (15-ounce / 425-g) can diced tomatoes, undrained
2 cloves garlic, peeled and minced

½ cup gluten-free orzo
5 cups vegetable broth
2 teaspoons dried oregano leaves
2 teaspoons dried thyme leaves
1 teaspoon salt
1 teaspoon ground black pepper
3 cups fresh baby spinach
4 tablespoons grated Parmesan cheese

Add all the ingredients, except for the spinach and Parmesan cheese, to the Instant Pot. Lock the lid. Select the Pressure Cook setting and set the cooking time for 10 minutes at High Pressure. Once the timer goes off, use a quick pressure release. Carefully open the lid. Stir in the spinach until wilted. Ladle the soup into four bowls and garnish with the Parmesan cheese. Serve warm.

Spinach and Beef Stew

Prep time: 20 minutes | Cook time: 30 minutes | Serves 4

1 pound (454 g) beef sirloin, chopped
2 cups spinach, chopped
3 cups chicken broth
1 cup coconut milk
1 teaspoon allspices
1 teaspoon coconut aminos

Put all ingredients in the Instant Pot. Stir to mix well. Close the lid. Set the Pressure Cook mode and set cooking time for 30 minutes on High Pressure. When timer beeps, use a natural pressure release for 10 minutes, then release any remaining pressure. Open the lid. Blend with an immersion blender until smooth. Serve warm.

Beef and Pinto Bean Chili

Prep time: 20 minutes | Cook time: 40 minutes | Serves 8

1 pound (454 g) 80% lean ground beef
1 medium onion, peeled and chopped
2 cloves garlic, peeled and minced
¼ cup chili powder
2 tablespoons brown sugar
1 teaspoon ground cumin
½ teaspoon ground coriander
½ teaspoon salt
½ teaspoon ground black pepper
1 (14.5-ounce / 411-g) can diced tomatoes
2 cups dried pinto beans, soaked overnight in water and drained
2 cups beef broth
1 tablespoon lime juice

Press the Sauté button on the Instant Pot and brown the beef for 10 minutes, or until no pink remains. Add the onion, garlic, chili powder, brown sugar, cumin, coriander, salt and pepper to the pot and sauté for 10 minutes, or until the onion is just softened. Stir in the tomatoes, soaked beans and beef broth. Lock the lid. Select the Pressure Cook mode and set the cooking time for 20 minutes on High Pressure. When the timer goes off, do a natural pressure release for 20 minutes, then release any remaining pressure. Carefully open the lid. Add the lime juice and stir well. Serve hot.

Chipotle Chili with Beer

Prep time: 15 minutes | Cook time: 55 minutes | Serves 8

2 pounds (907 g) chili meat, made from chuck roast
1 medium onion, peeled and chopped
3 cloves garlic, peeled and minced
3 tablespoons minced chipotle in adobo
2 tablespoons chili powder
2 tablespoons light brown sugar
1 teaspoon ground cumin
½ teaspoon ground coriander
½ teaspoon salt
½ teaspoon ground black pepper
2 cups beef broth
1 (12-ounce / 340-g) bottle lager-style beer
½ cup water
¼ cup corn masa
1 tablespoon lime juice

Press the Sauté button on the Instant Pot and brown the chili meat for 10 minutes. Add the onion, garlic, chipotle, chili powder, brown sugar, cumin, coriander, salt and pepper to the pot and cook for 10 minutes, or until the onion is just softened. Pour in the beef broth and beer and stir well. Lock the lid. Select the Pressure Cook mode and set the cooking time for 30 minutes on High Pressure. When the timer goes off, perform a quick pressure release. Carefully open the lid. Select the Sauté mode. Whisk in the water and masa and cook for 5 minutes, stirring constantly, or until it starts to thicken. Stir in the lime juice. Serve hot.

Bacon and Coconut Milk Curry Soup

Prep time: 10 minutes | Cook time: 20 minutes | Serves 4

3 ounces (85 g) bacon, chopped
1 tablespoon chopped scallions
1 teaspoon curry powder
1 cup coconut milk
3 cups beef broth
1 cup Cheddar cheese, shredded

Heat the the Instant Pot on Sauté mode for 3 minutes and add bacon. Cook for 5 minutes. Flip constantly. Add the scallions and curry powder. Sauté for 5 minutes more. Pour in the coconut milk and beef broth. Add the Cheddar cheese and stir to mix well. Select Pressure Cook mode and set cooking time for 10 minutes on High Pressure. When timer beeps, use a quick pressure release. Open the lid. Blend the soup with an immersion blender until smooth. Serve warm.

Cauliflower and Leek Soup

Prep time: 15 minutes | Cook time: 15 minutes | Serves 6

6 slices bacon
1 leek, remove the dark green end and roots, sliced in half lengthwise, rinsed, cut into ½-inch-thick slices crosswise
½ medium yellow onion, sliced
4 cloves garlic, minced
3 cups chicken broth
1 large head cauliflower,
roughly chopped into florets
1 cup water
1 teaspoon kosher salt
1 teaspoon ground black pepper
⅔ cup shredded sharp Cheddar cheese, divided
½ cup heavy whipping cream

Set the Instant Pot to Sauté mode. When heated, place the bacon on the bottom of the pot and cook for 5 minutes or until crispy. Transfer the bacon slices to a plate. Let stand until cool enough to handle, crumble it with forks. Add the leek and onion to the bacon fat remaining in the pot. Sauté for 5 minutes or until fragrant and the onion begins to caramelize. Add the garlic and sauté for 30 seconds more or until fragrant. Stir in the chicken broth, cauliflower florets, water, salt, pepper, and three-quarters of the crumbled bacon. Secure the lid. Press the Pressure Cook button and set cooking time for 3 minutes on High Pressure. When timer beeps, perform a quick pressure release. Open the lid. Stir in ½ cup of the Cheddar and the cream. Use an immersion blender to purée the soup until smooth. Ladle into bowls and garnish with the remaining Cheddar and crumbled bacon. Serve immediately.

Creamy Bacon and Cauliflower Chowder

Prep time: 10 minutes | Cook time: 25 minutes | Serves 6

2 cups chicken broth
8 ounces (227 g) diced bacon, uncooked
5 ounces (142 g) diced onion (about 1 small onion)
1 teaspoon salt
½ teaspoon black pepper
1 (2-pound / 907-g) large head
cauliflower, stem and core removed, cut into florets
8 ounces (227 g) cream cheese, softened and cut into small cubes
½ cup heavy cream, at room temperature

Pour the chicken broth into the pot. Add the bacon, onion, salt, and pepper. Stir to combine. Place the large florets in the pot. Close the lid. Select Manual mode and set cooking time for 25 minutes on High Pressure. When timer beeps, perform a quick pressure release. Open the lid. Use a potato masher to break the cauliflower apart into little pieces. Stir in the cream cheese and heavy cream. Serve warm.

Quinoa and Black Bean Chili

Prep time: 10 minutes | Cook time: 16 minutes | Serves 6

1 tablespoon vegetable oil
1 medium onion, peeled and chopped
1 medium red bell pepper, deseeded and chopped
2 cloves garlic, peeled and minced
3 tablespoons chili powder
1 teaspoon ground cumin

½ teaspoon salt
½ teaspoon ground black pepper
2 cups vegetable broth
1 cup water
¾ cup quinoa
2 (15-ounce / 425-g) cans black beans, drained and rinsed

Press the Sauté button on the Instant Pot and heat the oil. Add the onion and bell pepper to the pot and sauté for 5 minutes, or until tender. Add the garlic, chili powder, cumin, salt and black pepper to the pot and sauté for 1 minute, or until fragrant. Stir in the remaining ingredients. Lock the lid. Select the Pressure Cook mode and set the cooking time for 10 minutes on High Pressure. When the timer goes off, do a quick pressure release. Carefully open the lid. Serve hot.

Chinese Pork Belly and Rice Stew

Prep time: 10 minutes | Cook time: 42 minutes | Serves 8

½ cup plus 2 tablespoons soy sauce, divided
¼ cup Chinese cooking wine
½ cup packed light brown sugar
2 pounds (907 g) pork belly, skinned and cubed

12 scallions, cut into pieces
3 cloves garlic, minced
3 tablespoons vegetable oil
1 teaspoon Chinese five-spice powder
2 cups vegetable broth
4 cups cooked white rice

In a large bowl, whisk together ½ cup of the soy sauce, wine and brown sugar. Place the pork into the bowl and turn to coat evenly. Cover in plastic and refrigerate for at least 4 hours. Drain the pork and pat dry. Reserve the marinade. Press the Sauté button on the Instant Pot and heat the oil. Add half the pork to the pot in an even layer, making sure there is space between pork cubes to prevent steam from forming. Sear the pork for 3 minutes on each side, or until lightly browned. Transfer the browned pork to a plate. Repeat with the remaining pork. Stir in the remaining ingredients, except for the rice. Return the browned pork to the pot with the reserved marinade. Lock the lid. Select the Pressure Cook mode and set the cooking time for 30 minutes on High Pressure. When the timer beeps, perform a natural pressure release for 20 minutes, then release any remaining pressure. Carefully open the lid. Serve hot over cooked rice.

Cabbage Beef Stew

Prep time: 10 minutes | Cook time: 19 minutes | Serves 4 to 6

3 tablespoons extra-virgin olive oil
2 large carrots, peeled and sliced into ¼-inch disks and then quartered
1 large Spanish onion, diced
2 pounds (907 g) ground beef
3 cloves garlic, minced
1 (46-ounce / 1.3-kg) can tomato juice
2 cups vegetable broth

Juice of 2 lemons
1 head cabbage, cored and roughly chopped
½ cup jasmine rice
¼ cup dark brown sugar
1 tablespoon Worcestershire sauce
2 teaspoons seasoned salt
1 teaspoon black pepper
3 bay leaves

Set the Instant Pot to the Sauté mode and heat the oil for 3 minutes. Add the carrots and onion to the pot and sauté for 3 minutes, or until just tender. Add the ground beef and garlic to the pot and sauté for 3 minutes, or until the beef is lightly browned. Stir in the remaining ingredients. Lock the lid. Select the Pressure Cook mode and set the cooking time for 10 minutes on High Pressure. When the timer goes off, perform a quick pressure release. Carefully open the lid. Let rest for 5 minutes to thicken and cool before serving.

Beef and Lettuce Soup

Prep time: 10 minutes | Cook time: 16 minutes | Serves 4

1 tablespoon olive oil
1 pound (454 g) ground beef
1 medium yellow onion, peeled and diced
1 small green bell pepper, deseeded and diced
1 medium carrot peeled and shredded
1 (15-ounce / 425-g) can diced tomatoes, undrained

2 teaspoons yellow mustard
1 teaspoon garlic powder
1 teaspoon smoked paprika
½ teaspoon salt
4 cups beef broth
2 cups shredded iceberg lettuce
1 cup shredded Cheddar cheese, divided
½ cup diced dill pickles

Set the Instant Pot to the Sauté mode and heat the olive oil for 30 seconds. Add the beef, onion and green bell pepper to the pot and sauté for 5 minutes, or until the beef is lightly browned. Add the carrot and sauté for 1 minute. Stir in the tomatoes with juice, mustard, garlic powder, paprika, salt and beef broth. Close and secure the lid. Select the Pressure Cook mode and set the cooking time for 7 minutes on High Pressure. When the timer goes off, use a quick pressure release. Carefully open the lid. Whisk in the lettuce and ½ cup of the cheese. Select the Sauté mode and cook for 3 minutes. Divide the soup among 4 bowls and serve topped with the remaining ½ cup of the cheese and dill pickles.

Chicken and Egg Noodle Soup

Prep time: 15 minutes | Cook time: 24 minutes | Serves 8

1 (3½-pound / 1.5-kg) chicken, cut into pieces
4 cups low-sodium chicken broth
3 stalks celery, chopped
2 medium carrots, peeled and chopped
1 medium yellow onion, peeled and chopped

1 clove garlic, and smashed
1 bay leaf
1 teaspoon poultry seasoning
½ teaspoon dried thyme
1 teaspoon salt
¼ teaspoon ground black pepper
4 ounces (113 g) dried egg noodles

Add all the ingredients, except for the egg noodles, to the Instant Pot and stir to combine. Set the lid in place. Select the Pressure Cook mode and set the cooking time for 20 minutes at High Pressure. Once cooking is complete, use a natural pressure release for 20 to 25 minutes, then release any remaining pressure. Carefully open the lid. Remove and discard the bay leaf. Transfer the chicken to a clean work surface. Shred chicken and discard the skin and bones. Return the shredded chicken to the pot and stir to combine. Stir in the noodles. Lock the lid. Select the Pressure Cook mode and set the cooking time for 4 minutes at High Pressure. Once cooking is complete, use a quick pressure release. Carefully open the lid. Serve hot.

Lamb and Chickpea Soup

Prep time: 10 minutes | Cook time: 13 minutes | Serves 4

1 tablespoon olive oil
1 pound (454 g) ground lamb
1 medium red onion, peeled and diced
1 medium carrot, peeled and shredded
3 cloves garlic, peeled and minced
1 (15-ounce / 425-g) can diced tomatoes, undrained

1 (15.5-ounce / 439-g) can chickpeas, rinsed and drained
4 cups chicken broth
½ teaspoon ground ginger
½ teaspoon turmeric
½ teaspoon salt
¼ teaspoon ground cinnamon
½ cup chopped fresh cilantro
4 tablespoons plain full-fat Greek yogurt

Set the Instant Pot to the Sauté mode and heat the olive oil. Add the lamb and onion to the pot and sauté for 5 minutes, or until the lamb is lightly browned. Add the carrot and garlic to the pot and sauté for 1 minute. Stir in the remaining ingredients, except for the cilantro and Greek yogurt. Set the lid in place. Select the Pressure Cook mode and set the cooking time for 7 minutes on High Pressure. When the timer goes off, perform a quick pressure release. Carefully open the lid. Ladle the soup into 4 bowls and garnish with the cilantro and yogurt. Serve warm.

Jamaican Red Bean and Bacon Soup

Prep time: 10 minutes | Cook time: 50 minutes | Serves 4

2 teaspoons olive oil
3 slices bacon, diced
2 large carrots, peeled and diced
5 green onions, sliced
1 stalk celery, chopped
1 Scotch bonnet, deseeded, veins removed and minced
1 (15-ounce / 425-g) can diced tomatoes, undrained
½ pound (227 g) dried small

red beans
1 (13.5-ounce / 383-g) can coconut milk
2 cups chicken broth
1 tablespoon Jamaican jerk seasoning
1 teaspoon salt
4 cups cooked basmati rice
1 cup chopped fresh parsley
1 lime, quartered

Press the Sauté button on the Instant Pot and heat the oil. Add the bacon, carrots, onions, celery and Scotch bonnet to the pot and sauté for 5 minutes, or until the onions are translucent. Stir in the tomatoes with juice, red beans, coconut milk, chicken broth, Jamaican jerk seasoning and salt. Lock the lid. Select the Pressure Cook mode and set the cooking time for 45 minutes on High Pressure. When the timer goes off, do a natural pressure release for 10 minutes, then release any remaining pressure. Carefully open the lid. Ladle the soup into four bowls over cooked rice and garnish with parsley. Squeeze a quarter of lime over each bowl. Serve warm.

Eggplant and Beef Tagine

Prep time: 15 minutes | Cook time: 25 minutes | Serves 6

1 pound (454 g) beef fillet, chopped
1 eggplant, chopped
6 ounces (170 g) scallions, chopped

4 cups beef broth
1 teaspoon ground allspices
1 teaspoon erythritol
1 teaspoon coconut oil

Put all ingredients in the Instant Pot. Stir to mix well. Close the lid. Select Pressure Cook mode and set cooking time for 25 minutes on High Pressure. When timer beeps, use a natural pressure release for 15 minutes, then release any remaining pressure. Open the lid. Serve warm.

Cauliflower and Beef Soup

Prep time: 10 minutes | Cook time: 14 minutes | Serves 4

1 cup ground beef
½ cup cauliflower, shredded
1 teaspoon unsweetened tomato purée
¼ cup coconut milk

1 teaspoon minced garlic
1 teaspoon dried oregano
½ teaspoon salt
4 cups water

Put all ingredients in the Instant Pot and stir well. Close the lid. Select Pressure Cook mode and set cooking time for 14 minutes on High Pressure. When timer beeps, make a quick pressure release and open the lid. Blend with an immersion blender until smooth. Serve warm.

Buffalo and Mozzarella Chicken Soup

Prep time: 7 minutes | Cook time: 10 minutes | Serves 2

1 ounce (28 g) celery stalk, chopped
4 tablespoons coconut milk
¾ teaspoon salt
¼ teaspoon white pepper
1 cup water

2 ounces (57 g) Mozzarella, shredded
6 ounces (170 g) cooked chicken, shredded
2 tablespoons keto-friendly Buffalo sauce

Place the chopped celery stalk, coconut milk, salt, white pepper, water, and Mozzarella in the Instant Pot. Stir to mix well. Set the Pressure Cook mode and set timer for 7 minutes on High Pressure. When timer beeps, use a quick pressure release and open the lid. Transfer the soup on the bowls. Stir in the chicken and Buffalo sauce. Serve warm.

Rich Beef and Vegetable Chili

Prep time: 15 minutes | Cook time: 35 minutes | Serves 4 to 6

½ tablespoon olive oil
1¼ pounds (567 g) ground beef
½ medium yellow onion, chopped
2 garlic cloves, minced
1 cup diced zucchini
⅔ cup finely chopped cauliflower
1½ cups canned diced tomatoes
1½ tablespoons chili powder
¼ teaspoon coriander powder

2 teaspoons ground cumin
4 tablespoons unsweetened tomato purée
1 teaspoon sea salt
1 teaspoon smoked paprika
⅛ teaspoon cayenne pepper
1 teaspoon garlic powder
⅔ cup water
½ medium avocado, chopped
⅔ cup grated Cheddar cheese
2½ tablespoons full-fat sour cream

Select the Instant Pot on Sauté mode. Once the pot is hot, add the olive oil and ground beef and sauté for 6 minutes or until the beef is browned. Add the onions and garlic to the pot. Sauté for 3 minutes or until the garlic becomes fragrant and the onions is softened. Add the zucchini, cauliflower, diced tomatoes (with canning liquid), chili powder, coriander powder, unsweetened tomato purée, cumin, sea salt, paprika, cayenne pepper, garlic powder, and water to the pot. Stir to combine. Lock the lid. Select Manual mode and set cooking time for 25 minutes on High Pressure. When cooking is complete, allow the pressure to release naturally for 10 minutes and then release the remaining pressure. Open the lid and stir. Ladle the chili into serving bowls and top each serving with 2 tablespoons avocado, 2 tablespoons Cheddar cheese, and ½ tablespoon sour cream. Serve hot.

Leek and Crab Soup

Prep time: 10 minutes | Cook time: 21 minutes | Serves 4

4 tablespoons unsalted butter
2 large carrots, peeled and diced
1 cup chopped leeks
2 stalks celery, chopped
4 cloves garlic, peeled and minced
2 teaspoons Italian seasoning

1 teaspoon salt
5 cups vegetable broth
1 pound (454 g) lump crabmeat, divided
2 tablespoons cooking sherry
¼ cup heavy cream
2 tablespoons fresh thyme leaves

Press the Sauté button on the Instant Pot and melt the butter. Add the carrots, leeks and celery to the pot and sauté for 5 minutes, or until the leeks are translucent. Add the garlic and sauté for 1 minute. Stir in the Italian seasoning, salt, vegetable broth and ½ pound (227 g) of the crabmeat. Lock the lid, select the Pressure Cook mode and set the cooking time for 15 minutes on High Pressure. Once cooking is complete, use a natural pressure release for 10 minutes, then release any remaining pressure. Carefully open the lid. Use an immersion blender to blend the soup in the pot until smooth. Stir in the remaining ½ pound (227 g) of the crabmeat, sherry and heavy cream. Ladle soup into four bowls and serve garnished with the thyme.

Bacon, Potato, and Broccoli Soup

Prep time: 15 minutes | Cook time: 30 minutes | Serves 4

2 teaspoons unsalted butter
6 slices bacon, diced
1 large carrot, peeled and diced
1 medium sweet onion, peeled and diced
1 small Russet potato, scrubbed and diced
1 pound (454 g) fresh broccoli,

chopped
¼ cup grated Cheddar cheese
1 tablespoon Dijon mustard
1 teaspoon salt
1 teaspoon ground black pepper
4 cups chicken broth
¼ cup whole milk
4 tablespoons sour cream

Set the Instant Pot to the Sauté mode and melt the butter. Add the bacon to the pot and sear for 5 minutes, or until crispy. Transfer the bacon to a plate lined with paper towels and let rest for 5 minutes. Crumble the bacon when cooled. Add the carrot, onion and potato to the pot. Sauté for 5 minutes, or until the onion is translucent. Stir in the remaining ingredients, except for the milk and sour cream. Set the lid in place. Select the Pressure Cook mode and set the cooking time for 20 minutes at High Pressure. Once cooking is complete, use a quick pressure release. Carefully open the lid. Pour the milk into the pot. Use an immersion blender to blend the soup in the pot until it achieves the desired smoothness. Ladle the soup into 4 bowls and garnish with the crumbled bacon and sour cream. Serve warm.

Cod and Red Potato Stew

Prep time: 10 minutes | Cook time: 14 minutes | Serves 4

1 tablespoon olive oil
1 large carrot, peeled and diced
1 stalk celery, diced
1 small yellow onion, peeled and diced
4 cloves garlic, peeled and minced
2 cups baby red potatoes, scrubbed and small-diced

1 (28-ounce / 794-g) can diced tomatoes, undrained
1 pound (454 g) skinless cod, cut into cubes
1 (8-ounce / 227-g) bottle clam juice
2 cups water
1 tablespoon Italian seasoning
1 teaspoon salt
1 bay leaf

Press the Sauté button on the Instant Pot and heat the oil. Add the carrot, celery and onion to the pot and sauté for 5 minutes, or until the onion is translucent. Add the garlic and sauté for 1 minute. Stir in the remaining ingredients. Set the lid in place. Select the Pressure Cook setting and set the cooking time for 8 minutes on High Pressure. Once cooking is complete, perform a natural pressure release for 10 minutes, then release any remaining pressure. Open the lid. Ladle the stew into 4 bowls and serve warm.

Tuscan Kale and Sausage Soup

Prep time: 15 minutes | Cook time: 13 minutes | Serves 3

1 bacon slice, chopped
6 ounces (170 g) Italian sausages, chopped
2 ounces (57 g) scallions, diced

½ teaspoon garlic powder
¼ cup cauliflower, chopped
1 cup kale, chopped
3 cups chicken broth
¼ cup heavy cream

Heat the the Instant Pot on Sauté mode for 3 minutes. Add chopped bacon and cook for 2 minutes on Sauté mode until curls and buckles. Mix in the Italian sausages, scallions, garlic powder, and cauliflower. Cook for 5 minutes on Sauté mode. Add kale, chicken broth, and heavy cream. Select Pressure Cook mode and set cooking time for 6 minutes on High Pressure. When timer beeps, make a quick pressure release. Open the lid. Serve immediately.

Easy Egg Drop Soup

Prep time: 5 minutes | Cook time: 10 minutes | Serves 4

4 cups chicken broth
1 teaspoon salt
2 eggs, beaten

2 tablespoons fresh dill, chopped

Pour chicken broth in the Instant Pot. Add the salt and bring to a boil on Sauté mode. Add beaten eggs and stir the mix well. Add dill and Sauté for 5 minutes. Serve immediately.

Pea and Mushroom Soup with Miso

Prep time: 6 minutes | Cook time: 8 minutes | Serves 4

1 teaspoon avocado oil or other neutral oil
½-inch knob ginger, peeled and finely grated
4 ounces (113 g) fresh shiitake mushrooms, stems removed, thinly sliced
2 cloves garlic, finely grated

4 cups water
2 cups (8 ounces / 227 g) sugar snap peas, cut into ½-inch pieces
¼ cup white miso paste
2 green onions, white and tender green parts, thinly sliced

Select the Sauté setting on the Instant Pot, add the oil, garlic, and ginger, and heat for 2 minutes, until bubbling. Add the mushrooms and sauté for 1 minute, until they begin to wilt and the ginger and garlic begin to brown on the bottom of the pot. Stir in the water and peas, using a wooden spoon to nudge loose any browned bits from the bottom of the pot. Cover with the glass lid and let come up to a simmer (this will take about 8 minutes). Remove the lid and press the Cancel button to turn off the pot. Put the miso paste in a small bowl. Ladle ¼ cup of the liquid from the pot into the bowl, then mash the miso against the side of the bowl and stir until it is fully dissolved. Add the miso mixture and the green onions to the pot and stir to combine. Ladle the soup into bowls and serve piping hot.

Mexican Chicken and Avocado Soup

Prep time: 15 minutes | Cook time: 25 minutes | Serves 5

2 tablespoons olive oil	Juice of 2 limes
1 pound (454 g) boneless, skinless chicken thighs, cut into bite-sized pieces	2 teaspoons sea salt
	1 teaspoon chili powder
4 garlic cloves, minced	½ teaspoon garlic powder
½ medium yellow onion, diced	¼ teaspoon ground black pepper
2 jalapeño, stems and seeds removed, chopped	1 medium avocado, chopped
½ cup diced fresh tomato	⅓ cup shredded pepper Jack cheese
5 cups chicken broth	

Select the Instant Pot on Sauté mode and add the olive oil. Once the oil is hot, add the chicken and sauté for 3 minutes per side or until browned. Add the garlic, onions, and jalapeños to the pot. Continue sautéing or until the vegetables are softened. Add the diced tomatoes, chicken broth, lime juice, sea salt, chili powder, garlic powder, and black pepper. Stir to combine. Lock the lid. Select Manual mode and set cooking time for 20 minutes on High Pressure. When cooking is complete, allow the pressure to release naturally for 15 minutes and then release the remaining pressure. Open the lid and ladle the soup into serving bowls. Top each serving with equal amounts of the avocado and pepper Jack cheese. Serve hot.

Creamy Beef Soup

Prep time: 15 minutes | Cook time: 20 minutes | Serves 6

1 tablespoon coconut oil	2 tablespoons cream cheese
1 cup ground beef	1 bell pepper, chopped
1 teaspoon taco seasonings	1 garlic clove, diced
½ cup crushed tomatoes	4 cups beef broth

Heat the the coconut oil in the Instant Pot on Sauté mode. Add the ground beef and sprinkle with taco seasonings. Stir well and cook the meat on Sauté mode for 5 minutes. Add crushed tomatoes, cream cheese, bell pepper, garlic clove, and beef broth. Close the lid and select Manual mode. Set cooking time for 15 minutes on High Pressure. When cooking is complete, perform a natural pressure release for 10 minutes and open the lid. Ladle the soup and serve.

Cannellini Bean Chili with Salsa Verde

Prep time: 10 minutes | Cook time: 10 minutes | Serves 4 to 6

1 tablespoon olive oil	1 cup salsa verde
1 yellow onion, diced	1 teaspoon ground cumin
1 green bell pepper, deseeded and diced	1 teaspoon ground coriander
1 jalapeño pepper, deseeded and diced	¼ teaspoon cayenne pepper
1 clove garlic, grated	4 cups vegetable stock
2 (15.5-ounce / 439-g) cans cannellini beans, drained and rinsed	Salt and freshly ground black pepper, to taste
	4 ounces (113 g) plant-based cheese, softened

Press Sauté button on the Instant Pot and allow the pot to heat for 2 minutes. Add the oil, onion, bell pepper and jalapeño to the pot. Sauté for 3 minutes. Stir in the garlic. Add the beans, salsa verde, cumin, coriander, cayenne, stock, and salt and black pepper, to taste. Stir to combine. Secure the lid. Press Pressure Cook button and set cooking time for 5 minutes on High Pressure. When timer beeps, quick release the pressure. Remove the lid and mix in the plant-based cheese. Serve immediately.

Beef Meatball and Squash Minestrone

Prep time: 5 minutes | Cook time: 35 minutes | Serves 6

1 pound (454 g) ground beef	2 garlic cloves, minced
1 large egg	½ medium yellow onion, minced
1½ tablespoons golden flaxseed meal	¼ cup pancetta, diced
⅓ cup shredded Mozzarella cheese	1 cup sliced yellow squash
	1 cup sliced zucchini
¼ cup unsweetened tomato purée	½ cup sliced turnips
	4 cups beef broth
1½ tablespoons Italian seasoning, divided	14 ounces (397 g) can diced tomatoes
1½ teaspoons garlic powder, divided	½ teaspoon ground black pepper
1½ teaspoons sea salt, divided	3 tablespoons shredded Parmesan cheese
1 tablespoon olive oil	

Preheat the oven to 400°F (205°C) and line a large baking sheet with aluminum foil. In a large bowl, combine the ground beef, egg, flaxseed meal, Mozzarella, unsweetened tomato purée, ½ tablespoon of Italian seasoning, ½ teaspoon of garlic powder, and ½ teaspoon of sea salt. Mix the ingredients until well combined. Make the meatballs by shaping 1 heaping tablespoon of the ground beef mixture into a meatball. Repeat with the remaining mixture and then transfer the meatballs to the prepared baking sheet. Place the meatballs in the oven and bake for 15 minutes. When the baking time is complete, remove from the oven and set aside. Select Sauté mode of the Instant Pot. Once the pot is hot, add the olive oil, garlic, onion, and pancetta. Sauté for 2 minutes or until the garlic becomes fragrant and the onions begin to soften. Add the yellow squash, zucchini, and turnips to the pot. Sauté for 3 more minutes. Add the beef broth, diced tomatoes, black pepper, and remaining garlic powder, sea salt, and Italian seasoning to the pot. Stir to combine and then add the meatballs. Lock the lid. Select Pressure Cook mode and set cooking time for 15 minutes on High Pressure. When cooking is complete, allow the pressure to release naturally for 10 minutes and then release the remaining pressure. Open the lid and gently stir the soup. Ladle into serving bowls and top with Parmesan. Serve hot.

Texas Roasted Tomato Chili

Prep time: 10 minutes | Cook time: 15 minutes | Serves 4

1 cup chopped onions	3 teaspoons Mexican red chili powder
1 tablespoon minced garlic	2 teaspoons ground cumin
1 pound (454 g) 80% lean ground beef	1 tablespoon avocado oil
1 cup canned diced fire-roasted tomatoes, with juices	2 teaspoons salt
	1 teaspoon dried oregano
1 tablespoon chopped chipotle chiles in adobo sauce	½ cup water

Preheat the Instant Pot on Sauté mode. Add the oil and heat until shimmering. Add the onions and garlic. Sauté for 30 seconds and add the ground beef. Break up the ground beef with two forks and brown for 4 minutes. Meanwhile, put the tomatoes and chipotle chiles with adobo sauce in a food processor and purée until smooth. In a small bowl, combine the chili powder, cumin, salt, and oregano. When the ground beef is browned, add the chili powder mixture and cook for 30 seconds. Add the tomato and chipotle mixture to the Instant Pot. Lock the lid. Select Manual mode. Set cooking time for 10 minutes on High Pressure. When cooking is complete, let the pressure release naturally for 10 minutes, then release any remaining pressure. Unlock the lid. Mix well and serve.

Pork and Woodear Soup

Prep time: 10 minutes | Cook time: 13 minutes | Serves 8

1 pound (454 g) boneless pork center loin chop, thinly sliced
1 cup dried woodear mushrooms
5 cups low-sodium chicken broth
3 tablespoons coconut aminos
1 tablespoon white vinegar

2 tablespoons rice vinegar
½ teaspoon xanthan gum
1 teaspoon salt
2 teaspoons freshly ground black pepper
3 tablespoons water
4 eggs, lightly beaten

In the Instant Pot, put the pork, mushrooms, broth, coconut aminos, white vinegar, rice vinegar, xanthan gum, salt, pepper, and water. Lock the lid. Select Soup mode. Set cooking time for 10 minutes at High Pressure. When cooking is complete, let the pressure release naturally for 10 minutes, then release any remaining pressure. Unlock the lid. Turn the Instant Pot on Sauté mode and keep the soup hot. Remove the mushrooms to a cutting board with tongs. Cut into thin slices, then stir them back into the soup. Slowly pour in the eggs. Mix the eggs three times around with chopsticks. Cover the pot and cook for about 1 minute, then serve.

Winter Black Bean Chili

Prep time: 10 minutes | Cook time: 15 minutes | Serves 4 to 6

3 tablespoons olive oil
2 cloves garlic, minced
2 leeks, white and tender green parts, halved lengthwise and thinly sliced
2 jalapeño chiles, deseeded and diced
1 teaspoon fine sea salt
1 canned chipotle chile in adobo sauce, minced
3 tablespoons chili powder

1 cup vegetable broth
2 carrots, peeled and diced
1 (15-ounce / 425-g) can black beans, rinsed and drained
1 (1-pound / 454-g) delicata squash, deseeded and diced
1 (14.5-ounce / 411-g) can diced fire-roasted tomatoes
Chopped fresh cilantro, for serving

Select the Sauté setting on the Instant Pot, add the oil and garlic, and heat for 2 minutes, until the garlic is bubbling. Add the leeks, jalapeños, and salt and sauté for 5 minutes, until the leeks are wilted. Add the chipotle chile and chili powder and sauté for 1 minute more. Stir in the broth. Add the carrots, beans and the squash. Pour the tomatoes and their liquid over the top. Do not stir. Secure the lid. Select Pressure Cook mode and set the cooking time for 5 minutes at High Pressure. When timer beeps, perform a quick pressure release. Open the pot, give a stir. Ladle the chili into bowls and sprinkle with cilantro. Serve hot.

Pork and Pumpkin Soup

Prep time: 15 minutes | Cook time: 37 minutes | Serves 4

1½ pounds (680 g) boneless pork shoulder, cut into 1½-inch cubes
½ teaspoon garlic powder
1 teaspoon ground cumin
½ teaspoon sea salt
¼ teaspoon ground black pepper
2 tablespoons butter
1 cup unsweetened pumpkin

purée
1 cup water
2 cups chicken broth
½ cup chopped onion
1 (4.5-ounce / 128-g) can chopped green chilies
1 fresh jalapeño, seeded and ribs removed, minced
4 cups chopped Swiss chard

In a large bowl, toss the pork with the garlic powder, cumin, salt, and pepper. Allow it to sit for 20 minutes. Set the Instant Pot to Sauté mode and heat the butter. When it is hot, add the pork shoulder and let brown for 4 minutes, then flip and brown another 4 minutes. Meanwhile, in a bowl, whisk together the pumpkin purée and water. Add the bone broth to the pot. Stir in the pumpkin mixture, onion, chilies, and jalapeño. Secure the lid. Press the Manual button and set cooking time for 30 minutes on High Pressure. When timer beeps, allow the pressure to release naturally for 10 minutes, then release any remaining pressure. Open the lid. Stir in the chard and cook on Keep Warm / Cancel for 3 minutes or until wilted. Ladle the soup into bowls. Serve hot.

Mushroom and Blue Cheese Soup

Prep time: 15 minutes | Cook time: 20 minutes | Serves 4

2 cups chopped white mushrooms
3 tablespoons cream cheese
4 ounces (113 g) scallions, diced
4 cups chicken broth

1 teaspoon olive oil
½ teaspoon ground cumin
1 teaspoon salt
2 ounces (57 g) blue cheese, crumbled

Combine the mushrooms, cream cheese, scallions, chicken broth, olive oil, and ground cumin in the Instant Pot. Seal the lid. Select Pressure Cook mode and set cooking time for 20 minutes on High Pressure. When timer beeps, use a quick pressure release and open the lid. Add the salt and blend the soup with an immersion blender. Ladle the soup in the bowls and top with blue cheese. Serve warm.

Bacon and Broccoli Super Cheese Soup

Prep time: 6 minutes | Cook time: 10 minutes | Serves 6

3 tablespoons butter
2 stalks celery, diced
½ yellow onion, diced
3 garlic cloves, minced
3½ cups chicken stock
4 cups chopped fresh broccoli florets
3 ounces (85 g) block-style cream cheese, softened and cubed
½ teaspoon ground nutmeg
½ teaspoon sea salt

1 teaspoon ground black pepper
3 cups shredded Cheddar cheese
½ cup shredded Monterey Jack cheese
2 cups heavy cream
4 slices cooked bacon, crumbled
1 tablespoon finely chopped chives

Select Sauté mode. Once the Instant Pot is hot, add the butter and heat until the butter is melted. Add the celery, onions, and garlic. Continue sautéing for 5 minutes or until the vegetables are softened. Add the chicken stock and broccoli florets to the pot. Bring the liquid to a boil. Lock the lid,. Select Pressure Cook mode and set cooking time for 5 minutes on High Pressure. When cooking is complete, allow the pressure to release naturally for 10 minutes and then release the remaining pressure. Open the lid and add the cream cheese, nutmeg, sea salt, and black pepper. Stir to combine. Select Sauté mode. Bring the soup to a boil and then slowly stir in the Cheddar and Jack cheeses. Once the cheese has melted, stir in the heavy cream. Ladle the soup into serving bowls and top with bacon and chives. Serve hot.

Mushroom Pizza Soup

Prep time: 10 minutes | Cook time: 22 minutes | Serves 3

1 teaspoon coconut oil	½ teaspoon Italian seasoning
¼ cup cremini mushrooms, sliced	1 teaspoon unsweetened tomato purée
5 ounces (142 g) Italian sausages, chopped	1 cup water
½ jalapeño pepper, sliced	4 ounces (113 g) Mozzarella, shredded

Melt the coconut oil in the Instant Pot on Sauté mode. Add the mushrooms and cook for 10 minutes. Add the chopped sausages, sliced jalapeño, Italian seasoning, and unsweetened tomato purée. Pour in the water and stir to mix well. Close the lid and select Manual mode. Set cooking time for 12 minutes on High Pressure. When timer beeps, use a quick pressure release and open the lid. Ladle the soup in the bowls. Top it with Mozzarella. Serve warm.

T-Bone Beef Steak Broth

Prep time: 20 minutes | Cook time: 50 minutes | Serves 4

1 pound (454 g) T-bone beef steak, chopped	1 teaspoon peppercorns
1 bay leaf	1 teaspoon salt
	3 cups water

Put all ingredients in the Instant Pot. Stir to mix well. Close the lid. Set Pressure Cook mode and set cooking time for 50 minutes on High Pressure. When timer beeps, use a natural pressure release for 15 minutes, then release the remaining pressure and open the lid. Strain the cooked mixture and shred the meat. Serve the beef broth with the shredded beef.

Broccoli and Coconut Cream Soup

Prep time: 10 minutes | Cook time: 25 minutes | Serves 4

1 cup broccoli, chopped	4 cups beef broth
½ cup coconut cream	1 teaspoon chili flakes
1 teaspoon unsweetened tomato purée	6 ounces (170 g) feta, crumbled

Put broccoli, coconut cream, tomato purée, and beef broth in the Instant Pot. Sprinkle with chili flakes and stir to mix well. Close the lid and select Pressure Cook mode. Set cooking time for 8 minutes on High Pressure. When timer beeps, make a quick pressure release and open the lid. Add the feta cheese and stir the soup on Sauté mode for 5 minutes or until the cheese melt. Serve immediately.

Creamy Pancetta Chowder

Prep time: 5 minutes | Cook time: 8 minutes | Serves 3

1 cup coconut milk	¼ teaspoon salt
1 ounce (28 g) celery stalk, chopped	4 ounces (113 g) pancetta, chopped, fried
1 teaspoon ground paprika	

Pour the coconut milk in the Instant Pot, then add celery stalk in the Instant Pot. Sprinkle with paprika and salt. Lock the lid. Press the Manual button and set the timer for 3 minutes on High Pressure. When timer beeps, use a naturally pressure release for 5 minutes, then release any remaining pressure. Open the lid. Top the chowder with fried pancetta. Serve warm.

Easy Chicken Soup

Prep time: 10 minutes | Cook time: 20 minutes | Serves 2

2 cups water	1 teaspoon salt
8 ounces (227 g) chicken breast, skinless, boneless	1 tablespoon fresh dill, chopped
1 tablespoon scallions, diced	

Pour water in the Instant Pot. Chop the chicken breast and add it in the water. Add scallions and salt. Close the lid. Select Manual mode. Set cooking time for 20 minutes at High Pressure. When timer beeps, make a quick pressure release and carefully open the lid. Ladle the soup in the bowls. Top the soup with fresh dill. Serve immediately.

Chorizo Soup

Prep time: 10 minutes | Cook time: 17 minutes | Serves 3

1 teaspoon avocado oil	1 tablespoon dried cilantro
8 ounces (227 g) chorizo, chopped	4 ounces (113 g) scallions, diced
1 teaspoon unsweetened tomato purée	½ teaspoon chili powder
	2 cups beef broth

Heat the avocado oil on Sauté mode for 1 minute. Add the chorizo and cook for 6 minutes, stirring frequently. Add the tomato purée, cilantro, scallions, and chili powder. Stir well. Pour in the beef broth. Close the lid. Select Manual mode and set cooking time for 10 minutes on High Pressure. When timer beeps, make a quick pressure release. Open the lid. Serve warm.

Flu-Fighter Spinach and Mushroom Soup

Prep time: 10 minutes | Cook time: 15 minutes | Serves 4

1 cup spinach, chopped	1 cup unsweetened almond milk
1 cup mushrooms, chopped	2 cups chicken broth
2 ounces (57 g) Cheddar cheese, shredded	1 teaspoon cayenne pepper
3 ounces (85 g) scallions, diced	½ teaspoon salt

Put all ingredients in the Instant Pot and close the lid. Stir to mix well. Set the Manual mode and set cooking time for 15 minutes on High Pressure. When timer beeps, make a quick pressure release. Open the lid. Blend the soup with an immersion blender until smooth. Serve warm.

Green Garden Soup

Prep time: 20 minutes | Cook time: 29 minutes | Serves 5

1 tablespoon olive oil	2 tablespoons chives, chopped
1 garlic clove, diced	1 teaspoon sea salt
½ cup cauliflower florets	6 cups beef broth
1 cup kale, chopped	

Heat the olive oil in the Instant Pot on Sauté mode for 2 minutes and add the garlic. Sauté for 2 minutes or until fragrant. Add cauliflower, kale, chives, sea salt, and beef broth. Close the lid. Select Manual mode and set cooking time for 5 minutes on High Pressure. When timer beeps, use a quick pressure release and open the lid. Ladle the soup into the bowls. Serve warm.

Hearty Chuck Roast and Vegetable Stew

Prep time: 20 minutes | Cook time: 40 minutes | Serves 4

1 pound (454 g) beef chuck roast, cut into 1-inch cubes
2 teaspoons arrowroot powder
1½ tablespoons olive oil
1 cup chopped mushrooms
1 cup chopped zucchini
½ cup sliced turnips
3 ribs celery, sliced
¾ cup unsweetened tomato purée
4 cups beef broth

2 garlic cloves, minced
1 tablespoon dried thyme
1 tablespoon paprika
1 teaspoon dried rosemary
1 teaspoon dried parsley
1 teaspoon garlic powder
1 teaspoon celery seed
1 teaspoon onion powder
2½ teaspoons sea salt
1 teaspoon ground black pepper

In a large bowl, combine the chuck roast and arrowroot powder. Toss to coat well. Select Sauté mode and add the olive oil to the pot. Once the oil is hot, add the meat and sauté for 5 minutes or until the meat is browned on all sides. Once the meat is browned, add the mushrooms, zucchini, turnips, celery, tomato purée, beef broth, garlic, thyme, paprika, rosemary, parsley, garlic powder, celery seed, sea salt, black pepper, and onion powder to the pot. Stir well to combine. Lock the lid. Select Meat/Stew and set cooking time for 35 minutes on High Pressure. When cooking is complete, allow the pressure to release naturally for 15 minutes and then release the remaining pressure. Open the lid, stir, and then ladle the stew into serving bowls. Serve hot.

Italian Lamb and Turnip Stew

Prep time: 10 minutes | Cook time: 52 minutes | Serves 4

1 teaspoon olive oil
1 pound (454 g) lamb shank, chopped
1 turnip, chopped
1 teaspoon dried rosemary

½ teaspoon salt
1 teaspoon unsweetened tomato purée
2 cups water

Heat the olive oil on Sauté mode for 2 minutes or until shimmering. Add the chopped lamb shank, turnip, and dried rosemary. Sprinkle with salt. Sauté the ingredients for 5 minutes. Pour in the unsweetened tomato purée and water. Close the lid and set to Manual mode. Set cooking time for 15 minutes on High Pressure. When timer beeps, use a natural pressure release for 5 minutes, then release any remaining pressure. Open the lid. Serve warm.

Kale Curry Soup

Prep time: 10 minutes | Cook time: 15 minutes | Serves 3

2 cups kale
1 teaspoon almond butter
1 tablespoon fresh cilantro
½ cup ground chicken

1 teaspoon curry paste
½ cup heavy cream
1 cup chicken stock
½ teaspoon salt

Put the kale in the Instant Pot. Add the almond butter, cilantro, and ground chicken. Sauté the mixture for 5 minutes. Meanwhile, mix the curry paste and heavy cream in the Instant Pot until creamy. Add chicken stock and salt, and close the lid. Select Manual mode and set cooking time for 10 minutes on High Pressure. When timer beeps, make a quick pressure release. Open the lid. Serve warm.

Lamb and Broccoli Soup

Prep time: 10 minutes | Cook time: 25 minutes | Serves 4

7 ounces (198 g) lamb fillet, chopped
1 tablespoon avocado oil
½ cup broccoli, roughly chopped

¼ daikon, chopped
2 bell peppers, chopped
¼ teaspoon ground cumin
5 cups beef broth

Sauté the lamb fillet with avocado oil in the Instant Pot for 5 minutes. Add the broccoli, daikon, bell peppers, ground cumin, and beef broth. Close the lid. Select Manual mode and set cooking time for 20 minutes on High Pressure. When timer beeps, use a natural pressure release for 10 minutes, then release any remaining pressure. Open the lid. Serve warm.

Leek and Jack Cheese Soup

Prep time: 10 minutes | Cook time: 15 minutes | Serves 4

4 tablespoons butter
7 ounces (198 g) leek, chopped
½ teaspoon salt

1 teaspoon Italian seasonings
2 cups chicken broth
2 ounces (57 g) Monterey Jack cheese, shredded

Heat the butter in the Instant Pot for 4 minutes or until melted. Add the chopped leek, salt, and Italian seasonings. Sauté the leek on Sauté mode for 5 minutes. Pour in the chicken broth and close the lid. Select Manual mode and set cooking time for 10 minutes on High Pressure. When timer beeps, use a quick pressure release. Open the lid. Add the shredded cheese and stir until the cheese is melted. Serve immediately.

Mushroom, Artichoke, and Spinach Soup

Prep time: 15 minutes | Cook time: 20 minutes | Serves 4

3 tablespoons salted butter
8 ounces (227 g) cremini mushrooms, sliced
1 (6-ounce / 170-g) small jar artichoke hearts packed in water or olive oil, drained, chopped
4 ounces (113 g) full-fat cream cheese
1 teaspoon dried sage
1 teaspoon dried thyme
1 tablespoon Dijon mustard

½ teaspoon garlic powder
½ teaspoon kosher salt
¼ teaspoon ground black pepper
2 cups chicken broth
1 cup water
2 cups roughly chopped baby spinach
½ cup heavy whipping cream
½ cup grated Parmesan cheese

Set the Instant Pot to Sauté mode and add the butter. When butter melts, add the mushrooms and sauté for about 8 minutes or until soft. Add the cream cheese to the pot and stir until it is melted. Stir in the sage, thyme, mustard, garlic powder, salt, and black pepper, then mix in the bone broth, water, and artichoke hearts. Secure the lid. Press the Manual button and set cooking time for 5 minutes on High Pressure. When timer beeps, allow the pressure to release naturally for 5 minutes, then release any remaining pressure. Open the lid. Stir in the baby spinach and secure the lid. Allow the spinach to cook for 2 minutes in the soup on Keep Warm / Cancel. Open the lid and stir. Use an immersion blender to blend the soup until smooth and creamy. Stir in the cream. To serve, ladle the soup into bowls and sprinkle with Parmesan cheese. Serve hot.

Pancetta and Jalapeño Soup

Prep time: 10 minutes | Cook time: 10 minutes | Serves 4

3 ounces (85 g) pancetta, chopped
1 teaspoon coconut oil
2 jalapeño peppers, sliced
½ teaspoon garlic powder
½ teaspoon smoked paprika
½ cup heavy cream
2 cups water
½ cup Monterey Jack cheese, shredded

Toss the pancetta in the Instant Pot, then add the coconut oil and cook for 4 minutes on Sauté mode. Stir constantly. Add the sliced jalapeños, garlic powder, and smoked paprika. Sauté for 1 more minute. Pour in the heavy cream and water. Add the Monterey Jack cheese and stir to mix well. Close the lid and select Manual mode and set cooking time on High Pressure. When timer beeps, make a quick pressure release. Open the lid. Serve warm.

Pork and Daikon Stew

Prep time: 15 minutes | Cook time: 3 minutes | Serves 6

1 pound (454 g) pork tenderloin, chopped
1 ounce (28 g) green onions, chopped
½ cup daikon, chopped
1 lemon slice
1 tablespoon heavy cream
1 tablespoon butter
1 teaspoon ground black pepper
3 cups water

Put all ingredients in the Instant Pot and stir to mix with a spatula. Seal the lid. Set Manual mode and set cooking time for 20 minutes on High Pressure. When cooking is complete, use a natural pressure release for 15 minutes, then release any remaining pressure. Open the lid. Serve warm.

Pork Cheeseburger Soup

Prep time: 10 minutes | Cook time: 11 minutes | Serves 5

1 cup ground pork
1 teaspoon mustard powder
1 teaspoon cayenne pepper
1 teaspoon coconut oil
2 tablespoons cream cheese
3 tablespoons heavy cream
4 cups beef broth
½ cup Monterey Jack cheese, shredded

In a mixing bowl, combine the ground pork, mustard powder, and cayenne pepper. Melt the coconut oil in the Instant Pot on Sauté mode. Add the ground pork mixture and sauté for 6 minutes. Stir in the cream cheese, heavy cream, and beef broth. Close the lid. Select Manual mode and set cooking time for 5 minutes on High Pressure. When timer beeps, use a quick pressure release and open the lid. Ladle the soup in the bowls. Top the soup with Monterey Jack cheese. Serve warm.

Ritzy Chicken Sausage and Veg Soup

Prep time: 10 minutes | Cook time: 15 minutes | Serves 6

2 tablespoons olive oil
12 ounces (340 g) fully cooked chicken sausage, sliced
½ medium onion, chopped
2 cloves garlic, minced
5 cups chicken broth
3 cups roughly chopped curly kale leaves
8 ounces (227 g) mushrooms, sliced
½ cup peeled and diced rutabaga
2 tablespoons apple cider vinegar
½ teaspoon red pepper flakes
1 teaspoon sea salt
¼ teaspoon ground black pepper
1 cup full-fat coconut milk

Set the Instant Pot to Sauté mode. When hot, add the oil and swirl to coat the bottom. Add the sliced sausage and sauté for 4 minutes or until browned. Add the onion and garlic and sauté for 3 minutes or until the onions are translucent and the garlic turns golden. Stir in the mushrooms, rutabaga, kale, broth, vinegar, pepper flakes, salt, and black pepper. Secure the lid. Press the Manual button and set cooking time for 8 minutes on High Pressure. When timer beeps, use a quick pressure release. Open the lid and stir in the milk. Allow the soup to rest for 3 minutes on Keep Warm / Cancel before ladling into serving bowls and serving hot.

Salmon and Tomatillos Stew

Prep time: 15 minutes | Cook time: 12 minutes | Serves 2

10 ounces (283 g) salmon fillet, chopped
2 tomatillos, chopped
½ teaspoon ground turmeric
1 cup coconut cream
1 teaspoon ground paprika
½ teaspoon salt

Put all ingredients in the Instant Pot. Stir to mix well. Close the lid. Select Manual mode and set cooking time for 12 minutes on Low Pressure. When timer beeps, use a quick pressure release. Open the lid. Serve warm.

Pork Meatball Soup

Prep time: 15 minutes | Cook time: 19 minutes | Serves 4

Meatballs:

½ pound (227 g) ground pork
2 tablespoons gluten-free bread crumbs
2 tablespoons grated Parmesan cheese
1 tablespoon Italian seasoning
½ teaspoon cayenne pepper
½ teaspoon salt
1 large egg, whisked
2 cloves garlic, peeled and minced
2 tablespoons olive oil, divided

Soup:

1 tablespoon olive oil
1 medium carrot, peeled and shredded
1 Russet potato, scrubbed and small-diced
1 small red onion, peeled and diced
1 (15-ounce / 425-g) can diced fire-roasted tomatoes,
undrained
4 cups beef broth
½ teaspoon salt
½ teaspoon ground black pepper
½ teaspoon red pepper flakes
½ cup chopped fresh basil leaves

In a medium bowl, stir together all the ingredients for the meatballs, except for the olive oil. Shape the mixture into 24 meatballs. Set the Instant Pot to the Sauté mode and heat 1 tablespoon of the olive oil for 30 seconds. Add half the meatballs to the pot and sear for 3 minutes, turning them to brown all sides. Remove the first batch and set aside. Add the remaining 1 tablespoon of the olive oil to the pot and repeat with the remaining meatballs. Remove the meatballs from the pot. Select the Sauté mode and heat the olive oil for 30 seconds. Add the carrot, potato and onion to the pot and sauté for 5 minutes, or until the onion becomes translucent. Add the meatballs to the pot along with the remaining ingredients for the soup. Close and secure the lid. Select the Manual mode and set the cooking time for 7 minutes at High Pressure. Once cooking is complete, use a quick pressure release. Carefully open the lid. Serve warm.

Thai Shrimp and Mushroom Soup

Prep time: 15 minutes | Cook time: 10 minutes | Serves 6

2 tablespoons unsalted butter, divided
½ pound (227 g) medium uncooked shrimp, shelled and deveined
½ medium yellow onion, diced
2 cloves garlic, minced
1 cup sliced fresh white mushrooms
1 tablespoon freshly grated ginger root
4 cups chicken broth
2 tablespoons fish sauce
2½ teaspoons red curry paste

2 tablespoons lime juice
1 stalk lemongrass, outer stalk removed, crushed, and finely chopped
2 tablespoons coconut aminos
1 teaspoon sea salt
½ teaspoon ground black pepper
13.5 ounces (383 g) can unsweetened, full-fat coconut milk
3 tablespoons chopped fresh cilantro

Select the Instant Pot on Sauté mode. Add 1 tablespoon butter. Once the butter is melted, add the shrimp and sauté for 3 minutes or until opaque. Transfer the shrimp to a medium bowl. Set aside. Add the remaining butter to the pot. Once the butter is melted, add the onions and garlic and sauté for 2 minutes or until the garlic is fragrant and the onions are softened. Add the mushrooms, ginger root, chicken broth, fish sauce, red curry paste, lime juice, lemongrass, coconut aminos, sea salt, and black pepper to the pot. Stir to combine. Lock the lid. Select Manual mode and set cooking time for 5 minutes on High Pressure. When cooking is complete, allow the pressure to release naturally for 5 minutes, then release the remaining pressure. Open the lid. Stir in the cooked shrimp and coconut milk. Select Sauté mode. Bring the soup to a boil and then press Keep Warm / Cancel. Let the soup rest in the pot for 2 minutes. Ladle the soup into bowls and sprinkle the cilantro over top. Serve hot.

Salsa Chicken and Cheese Soup

Prep time: 15 minutes | Cook time: 35 minutes | Serves 6

1⅓ cups chunky salsa
½ teaspoon ground chipotle powder
3 cups chicken broth
½ teaspoon ground coriander
½ teaspoon ground cumin
1 teaspoon garlic powder
1 teaspoon sea salt
½ teaspoon ground black

pepper
½ dried parsley
1 pound (454 g) boneless, skinless chicken thighs
8 ounces (227 g) block-style cream cheese, softened and cubed
½ cup Monterey Jack cheese
¼ cup queso fresco, crumbled

Combine the salsa, chipotle powder, chicken broth, coriander, cumin, garlic powder, sea salt, black pepper, and parsley in the Instant Pot. Stir until well combined. Add the chicken thighs to the pot. Lock the lid. Select Manual mode and set cooking time for 20 minutes on High Pressure. When cooking is complete, allow the pressure to release naturally for 10 minutes and then release the remaining pressure. Open the lid, use a slotted spoon to transfer the chicken thighs to a cutting board, and use two forks to shred the chicken. Return the shredded chicken to the pot. Stir to combine. Select Sauté mode. Bring the soup to a boil and then add the cream cheese. Whisk continuously until the cream cheese is melted. Turn off the pot. Add the Jack cheese and stir until the cheese is melted into the soup. Ladle the soup into bowls. Sprinkle ½ tablespoon queso fresco over each serving. Serve hot.

Simple Chicken Paprikash

Prep time: 10 minutes | Cook time: 18 minutes | Serves 4

1 teaspoon coconut oil
4 chicken thighs, skinless
1 bell pepper, chopped
¼ cup scallions, diced

1 tablespoon ground paprika
½ teaspoon salt
½ teaspoon ground cumin
4 cups chicken broth

Melt the coconut oil in the Instant Pot on Sauté mode. Add chicken thighs and cook for 4 minutes per side until lightly browned. Stir in the bell pepper, scallions, paprika, salt, and ground cumin. Pour in the chicken broth and close the lid. Select Manual mode and set cooking time for 10 minutes on High Pressure. When timer beeps, perform a quick pressure release. Open the lid. Ladle the paprikash in bowls and serve.

Super Easy Bok Choy Soup

Prep time: 5 minutes | Cook time: 2 minutes | Serves 1

1 Bok Choy stalk, chopped
¼ teaspoon nutritional yeast
1 cup chicken broth

¼ teaspoon chili flakes
½ teaspoon onion powder

Put all ingredients in the Instant Pot. Stir to mix well. Close the lid and select Manual mode. Set cooking time for 2 minutes on High Pressure. When timer beeps, make a quick pressure release. Open the lid. Serve warm.

Tomato Beef Chili

Prep time: 10 minutes | Cook time: 25 minutes | Serves 2

½ cup ground beef
1 teaspoon dried oregano
½ teaspoon chili powder
1 teaspoon avocado oil

2 ounces (57 g) scallions, diced
¼ cup water
¼ cup crushed tomatoes

Mix the ground beef, dried oregano, chili powder, avocado oil, and scallions in the Instant Pot and cook on Sauté mode for 10 minutes. Add water and crushed tomatoes. Stir the mixture with a spatula until homogenous. Close the lid and select Manual mode. Set cooking time for 15 minutes on High Pressure. When timer beeps, make a quick pressure release. Open the lid. Serve warm.

Cauliflower and Bacon Chowder

Prep time: 10 minutes | Cook time: 25 minutes | Serves 6

2 cups chicken broth
8 ounces (227 g) diced bacon, uncooked
5 ounces (142 g) diced onion (about 1 small onion)
1 teaspoon salt
½ teaspoon black pepper
1 (2-pound / 907-g) large head

cauliflower, stem and core removed, cut into florets
8 ounces (227 g) cream cheese, softened and cut into small cubes
½ cup heavy cream, at room temperature

Pour the chicken broth into the pot. Add the bacon, onion, salt, and pepper. Stir to combine. Place the large florets in the pot. Close the lid. Select Pressure Cook mode and set cooking time for 25 minutes on High Pressure. When timer beeps, perform a quick pressure release. Open the lid. Use a potato masher to break the cauliflower apart into little pieces. Stir in the cream cheese and heavy cream. Serve warm.

Turkey and Orzo Soup

Prep time: 10 minutes | Cook time: 10 minutes | Serves 2

2 teaspoons oil	dried thyme
1 small onion, diced	1 bay leaf
1 celery stalk, diced	Kosher salt, to taste
2 carrots, diced	Freshly ground black pepper,
2 garlic cloves, minced	to taste
½ pound (227 g) chopped	2 cups chopped kale
turkey breast tenderloin	1 tablespoon chopped fresh
3 cups low-sodium turkey	parsley
stock, divided	1 tablespoon freshly squeezed
⅓ cup orzo	lemon juice
1 thyme sprig or ¼ teaspoon	

Press the Sauté button on the Instant Pot and heat the oil. Add the onion, celery, and carrots and sauté for 3 minutes until softened. Stir in the garlic and cook for 1 minute. Add the turkey, 2 cups of turkey stock, orzo, thyme sprig, and bay leaf. Sprinkle with the salt and black pepper and stir well. Secure the lid. Select the Pressure Cook mode and set the cooking time for 6 minutes at High Pressure. Once cooking is complete, do a natural pressure release for 4 minutes, then release any remaining pressure. Carefully open the lid. Discard the thyme sprig and bay leaf. Set your Instant Pot to Sauté. Add the remaining 1 cup of turkey stock, kale, parsley, and lemon juice and stir to combine. Taste and season with salt and black pepper to taste. Let the mixture simmer for 2 minutes until heated through. Serve warm.

Bok Choy and Eggplant Stew

Prep time: 15 minutes | Cook time: 7 minutes | Serves 6

1 eggplant, chopped roughly	½ cup white rice
1 cup bok choy, chopped	5 cups vegetable broth
1 cup spinach, chopped	1 teaspoon salt
½ cup fresh cilantro, chopped	1 teaspoon thyme
1 red onion, cut into petals	1 teaspoon dried parsley
2 sweet peppers, chopped	

Put the eggplant, bok choy, spinach, cilantro, onion, and sweet peppers in the Instant Pot. Add rice, vegetable broth, salt, thyme, and dried parsley. Mix up the vegetables. Close the lid. Set Pressure Cook mode set cooking time for 7 minutes on High Pressure. When timer beeps, use a natural pressure release for 5 minutes, then release any remaining pressure. Mix up the stew before serving.

Summer Peruano Bean Chili

Prep time: 10 minutes | Cook time: 15 minutes | Serves 6

2 tablespoons olive oil	¼ teaspoon cayenne pepper
1 poblano chile or green bell	2 zucchini, diced
pepper, deseeded and diced	1 (15-ounce / 425-g) can
1 jalapeño chile, deseeded and	peruano beans, rinsed and
diced	drained
1 celery stalk, diced	1 (12-ounce / 340-g) bag
2 cloves garlic, minced	frozen corn
1 yellow onion, diced	1 cup vegetable broth
½ teaspoon fine sea salt, plus	1 (14.5-ounce / 411-g) can
more as needed	diced fire-roasted tomatoes
2 tablespoons chili powder	¼ cup chopped fresh cilantro
1 teaspoon dried oregano	2 green onions, white and
½ teaspoon ground cumin	tender green parts, thinly sliced

Select the Sauté setting on the Instant Pot, add the oil, and heat for 1 minute. Add the poblano and jalapeño chiles, celery, garlic, onion, and salt, and sauté for about 5 minutes, until the vegetables soften. Add the chili powder, oregano, cumin, and cayenne and sauté for about 1 minute more. Add the zucchini, beans, corn, and broth and stir to combine. Pour the tomatoes and their liquid over the top. Do not stir. Secure the lid. Select Pressure Cook mode and set the cooking time for 5 minutes at High Pressure. When timer beeps, perform a quick pressure release. Open the pot, give a stir. Ladle the chili into bowls and sprinkle with cilantro and green onions. Serve hot.

Rutabaga and Seitan Stew

Prep time: 10 minutes | Cook time: 15 minutes | Serves 4 to 6

1 pound (454 g) seitan, patted	rosemary
dry	1 cup vegetable broth
¼ teaspoon fine sea salt	2 teaspoons Dijon mustard
½ teaspoon freshly ground	1 (1-pound / 454-g) large
black pepper	rutabaga, peeled and cut into
1 tablespoon avocado oil	1-inch pieces
1 yellow onion, diced	4 medium carrots (about 8
4 cloves garlic, minced	ounces / 227 g in total), peeled
½ cup red wine	and sliced into 1-inch rounds
1 teaspoon fresh thyme leaves	3 waxy potatoes (about 1
1 teaspoon chopped fresh	pound / 454 g in total), cut into
sage leaves	1-inch pieces
1 teaspoon chopped fresh	1 tablespoon tomato paste

Sprinkle the seitan with the salt and pepper. Select the Sauté setting on the Instant Pot, add the oil, and heat for 2 minutes. Add the seitan and sear for 4 minutes until golden brown. Flip and sear for 3 minutes more. Transfer the seitan to a dish and set aside. Add the onion and garlic to the pot and sauté for 4 minutes until the onion softens. Stir in the wine. Let the wine simmer until it has mostly evaporated, about 4 minutes. Add the thyme, sage, and rosemary, and sauté for 1 minute more. Add the broth and mustard and stir to dissolve. Bring the mixture up to a simmer, then stir in the seitan, rutabaga, carrots, and potatoes. Add the tomato paste on top. Do not stir. Secure the lid. Select the Pressure Cook setting and set the cooking time for 4 minutes at High Pressure. When timer beeps, perform a quick pressure release. Open the pot and gently stir the stew to incorporate the tomato paste and make sure everything is coated with the cooking liquid. Ladle the stew into bowls and serve hot.

Zucchini and Soybean Stew

Prep time: 20 minutes | Cook time: 20 minutes | Serves 4

1 cup soybeans, soaked	1 jalapeño pepper, sliced
¼ cup tomatoes, chopped	1 tablespoon soy sauce
3 cups water	3 ounces (85 g) vegan
1 zucchini, chopped	Parmesan, grated
1 teaspoon mustard	

Place the soybeans and tomatoes in the Instant Pot. Pour in the water. Add the zucchini, mustard, jalapeño pepper, soy sauce, and close the lid. Set Pressure Cook mode and set cooking time for 20 minutes on High Pressure. When timer beeps, use a natural pressure release for 10 minutes, then release any remaining pressure. Open the lid. Transfer the cooked stew in the serving bowls and top with grated cheese.

Potato and Split Pea Barley Stew

Prep time: 10 minutes | Cook time: 15 minutes | Serves 6

½ cup chopped celery
2 cups chopped carrots
3 cups diced russet potatoes
(about 3 large potatoes)
1½ cups half-moon slices
onions
3 large cloves garlic, minced
1 teaspoon avocado oil
¾ cup dried split peas, rinsed
and drained
¼ cup dried pearled barley
1 cup sliced baby bella

mushrooms
½ teaspoon dried fennel seed
¼ teaspoon dried anise seed
1 teaspoon ground ginger
¾ teaspoon dried dill weed
1 bay leaf
2 tablespoons tomato paste
4 cups water
1 teaspoon sea salt, to taste
½ teaspoon ground black
pepper

Combine the celery, carrots, potatoes, onions, and garlic in the Instant Pot. Drizzle the avocado oil over the vegetables and sauté for 5 minutes on Sauté mode. Add the split peas, barley, mushrooms, fennel, anise, ginger, dill, bay leaf, tomato paste, and water. Stir to mix well. Cover the pot, select Pressure Cook mode, and set the timer for 7 minutes on High Pressure. When timer beeps, use a natural pressure release for 15 minutes, then release any remaining pressure. Remove the lid, stir in salt and pepper, and serve.

Eggplant and Zucchini Rainbow Stew

Prep time: 10 minutes | Cook time: 30 minutes | Serves 4

1 eggplant, sliced
1 zucchini, sliced
2 tomatoes, sliced
½ cup corn kernels
1 teaspoon paprika

1 teaspoon salt
1 teaspoon cayenne pepper
1 tablespoon coconut oil
1 cup water
¼ cup red beans, canned

In the mixing bowl, combine the sliced eggplant, zucchini, tomatoes, corn kernels, paprika, salt, and cayenne pepper. Shake the mixture well. Transfer the vegetables in the Instant Pot. Add the coconut oil, water, and red beans. Close the lid and select Pressure Cook mode. Set cooking time for 30 minutes on High Pressure. When timer beeps, perform a quick pressure release. Open the lid, stir gently and let rest for 5 minutes before serving.

Triple Beans Chili

Prep time: 15 minutes | Cook time: 10 minutes | Serves 6

¼ cup onion, chopped
¼ cup carrots, sliced
2 cloves garlic, minced
1 (10-ounce / 283-g) can black-
eyed peas, rinsed, drained
1 (10-ounce / 283-g) can
cannellini beans, rinsed,
drained
1 (10-ounce / 283-g) can red
kidney beans, rinsed, drained

1 (12-ounce / 340-g) can
crushed tomatoes
2 cups vegetable stock
1 tablespoon olive oil
1 teaspoon chili powder
1 teaspoon dried oregano
1 teaspoon smoked paprika
Salt and ground black pepper,
to taste

Heat the olive oil in the Instant pot on Sauté mode. Add the onion and carrots. Sauté for 4 minutes or until the onion is translucent. Add the garlic and sauté for 1 minute or until fragrant. Add the remaining ingredients and stir gently. Lock the lid. Select Pressure Cook mode and set cooking time for 5 minutes on High Pressure. When timer beeps, use a quick pressure release and open the lid. Serve warm.

Black Bean and Broccoli Chili

Prep time: 3 minutes | Cook time: 2 minutes | Serves 4

2 cups canned black beans,
rinsed and drained
2 cups canned fire-roasted
tomatoes, crushed
½ cup frozen broccoli
½ cup frozen cauliflower
¼ cup frozen corn, thawed

¼ cup frozen carrots, thawed
2 cups salsa
4 tablespoons coconut butter
1 teaspoon chili pepper
½ cup water
Salt and ground black pepper,
to taste

Combine all the ingredients in the Instant Pot. Stir to mix well. Lock the lid and select Pressure Cook mode. Set cooking time for 2 minutes on High Pressure. When timer beeps, use a natural pressure release for 1 minute, then release any remaining pressure. Open the lid and serve warm.

Spring Bean and Radish Chili

Prep time: 3 minutes | Cook time: 9 minutes | Serves 4

1 (8-ounce / 227-g) can
cannellini beans, rinsed
2 radishes, trimmed, sliced
1 cup sliced carrots
1 cup fennel bulb, sliced
¼ cup onion, chopped
2 tablespoon shallots, chopped
¼ cup chopped celery
2 cloves garlic, chopped
1 cup tomato paste
1 teaspoon chipotle powder

½ cup vegetable broth
½ teaspoon cumin
1 teaspoon dried oregano
Pinch of rosemary
Pinch of cayenne
Salt and ground black pepper,
to taste
1 medium zucchini, cubed
½ cup corn kernels
2 cherry tomatoes, quartered

Combine all ingredients, into the Instant pot, except the zucchinis, corn, and cherry tomatoes. Lock the lid and select Pressure Cook mode. Set cooking time for 8 minutes on High Pressure. When timer beeps, use a natural pressure release for 5 minutes, then release any remaining pressure. Open the lid. Stir in the zucchinis, corn, and tomatoes. Lock the lid and set cooking time for 1 minute on High Pressure on Pressure Cook mode. When timer beeps, perform a quick pressure release and open the lid. Serve warm.

Potato Bisque with Bacon

Prep time: 10 minutes | Cook time: 20 minutes | Serves 4

2 tablespoons unsalted butter
1 slice bacon, diced
3 leeks, trimmed, rinsed and
diced
6 cups diced Yukon Gold
potatoes

4 cups chicken broth
2 teaspoons dried thyme
leaves
1 teaspoon sriracha
½ teaspoon sea salt
¼ cup whole milk

Set the Instant Pot on the Sauté mode and melt the butter. Add the bacon and leeks to the pot and sauté for 5 minutes, or until the fat is rendered and leeks become tender. Stir in the remaining ingredients, except for the milk. Lock the lid. Select the Manual mode and set the cooking time for 15 minutes at High Pressure. When the timer goes off, use a natural pressure release for 5 minutes, then release any remaining pressure. Carefully open the lid. Pour the milk into the pot. Use an immersion blender to blend the soup in the pot until it achieves the desired consistency. Ladle the bisque into 4 bowls and serve warm.

Millet and Flageolet Bean Stew

Prep time: 10 minutes | Cook time: 20 minutes | Serves 6

1 teaspoon olive oil	½ cup millet
¼ cup sliced shallot	1 bay leaf
1 apple, diced	1 teaspoon whole fennel seed,
½ cup diced parsnip	crumbled
1 golden beet, diced	1 teaspoon dried thyme
1½ cups dried flageolet beans,	1 teaspoon dried sweet basil
soaked in water overnight,	2½ cups vegetable broth
rinsed and drained	2½ cups water
1 (14-ounce / 398-g) can diced	1 to 2 tablespoons lemon juice
tomatoes	¼ teaspoon black pepper

In the Instant Pot, heat the oil on Sauté mode. Add the shallot and sauté for 1 minute to soften a bit. Add the apple, parsnip, and beet and sauté for 4 minutes. Add the beans, millet, diced tomatoes, bay leaf, fennel, thyme, and basil. Stir to combine. Cover the vegetables and beans with broth and water by 3 inches. Secure the lid. Select Pressure Cook mode and set cooking time for 10 minutes on High Pressure. When timer beeps, use a natural pressure release for 15 minutes, then release any remaining pressure. Remove the lid and stir in the lemon juice. Remove the bay leaf before serving. Add ground pepper and serve.

African Sweet Potato and Chickpea Stew

Prep time: 5 minutes | Cook time: 7 minutes | Serves 6

1½ tablespoons refined	1 pound (454 g) sweet
coconut oil	potatoes, peeled and cut into
1 large yellow onion, diced	¾-inch cubes
6 garlic cloves, minced	1½ teaspoons kosher salt
2-inch piece fresh ginger,	½ cup peanut butter
grated or minced	1 (15-ounce / 425-g) can
1 Scotch bonnet pepper,	chickpeas, drained and rinsed
deseeded and minced	1 (28-ounce / 794-g) can
1 teaspoon ground coriander	crushed tomatoes
1 teaspoon ground turmeric	3 tablespoons tomato paste
¼ teaspoon ground cinnamon	4 cups kale, stems and midribs
½ teaspoon dried thyme	removed and sliced into strips
1½ teaspoons ground cumin	½ cup fresh cilantro, roughly
½ teaspoon freshly cracked	chopped
black pepper	1 tablespoon fresh lime juice
¼ teaspoon ground cloves	⅓ cup roasted peanuts,
2 cups vegetable broth	roughly chopped

Select the Sauté setting on the Instant Pot and let the pot heat for a few minutes before adding the oil. Once the oil is hot, add the onion. Cook until the onion is softened, about 3 to 4 minutes. Add the garlic, ginger, and chile pepper and cook for 1 minute, tossing frequently. Add the coriander, turmeric, cinnamon, thyme, cumin, black pepper, and cloves. Stir the spices into the vegetables and cook until the mixture is fragrant, about 30 seconds. Pour in the vegetable broth to deglaze the pan, using a wooden spoon to scrape up any browned bits on the bottom of the pot. Add the sweet potatoes, salt, peanut butter, and chickpeas. Stir to combine. Pour the crushed tomatoes and tomato paste on top, but do not stir, allowing the tomatoes and paste to sit on top. Secure the lid. Select the Pressure Cook mode and set the cook time to 5 minutes on High Pressure. When timer beeps, allow a natural pressure release for 5 minutes, then release any remaining pressure. Open the pot and stir in the kale. Select the Sauté setting and cook until wilted and cooked through, about 2 minutes. Stir in the cilantro and lime juice. Transfer the stew to bowls and garnish with the roasted peanuts. Serve immediately.

Apricot and Chickpea Stew

Prep time: 10 minutes | Cook time: 5 minutes | Serves 4 to 6

3 cups cooked chickpeas (from	1 tablespoon unrefined sugar
1 cup dried)	2 teaspoons curry powder
¼ cup chopped dried apricots	1 teaspoon ground cinnamon
2 or 3 carrots, scrubbed or	2 cups water
peeled and chopped	½ teaspoon salt
1 (28-ounce / 794-g) can diced	Freshly ground black pepper,
tomatoes, with juices	to taste
¼ cup chopped green olives	

In the Instant Pot, combine the chickpeas, apricots, carrots, tomatoes with juice, olives, sugar, curry powder, cinnamon, water, and salt. Season with pepper. Close the lid, then select Pressure Cook mode and set cooking time for 5 minutes on High Pressure. Once the cook time is complete, let the pressure release naturally, about 20 minutes, then release any remaining pressure. Serve immediately.

Black Bean and Sweet Potato Stew

Prep time: 5 minutes | Cook time: 30 minutes | Serves 6

2 tablespoons avocado oil	3 stalks celery, chopped
4 cups vegetable broth	½ teaspoon ground cinnamon
½ cup chopped onion	1 teaspoon garam masala
4 cloves garlic, minced	1 cup dried black beans, rinsed
2 carrots, chopped	and drained
1 large sweet potato, diced into	2 bay leaves
equal, bite-size pieces	½ teaspoon sea salt
2 small tomatoes, diced	¼ teaspoon black pepper

In the Instant Pot, heat the oil on Sauté mode. Add the onion and garlic and sauté for 2 minutes until the onion is soft. Add the carrots and sweet potato and sauté for another 3 minutes. Add the tomatoes, celery, cinnamon, and garam masala and stir to coat all the vegetables with the spices. Add the black beans, bay leaves, and vegetable broth. Stir to combine. Secure the lid. Select Pressure Cook mode and set cooking time for 24 minutes. When timer beeps, use a natural pressure release for 15 minutes, then release any remaining pressure. Remove the lid, remove the bay leaves, stir in the salt and pepper, and serve.

Creamy Carrot and Broccoli Soup

Prep time: 15 minutes | Cook time: 2½ to 3 hours | Serves 6 to 8

1 medium onion, finely	2 tablespoons unsalted butter
chopped	1 teaspoon baking soda
3 medium carrots, cut into	3 cups chicken or vegetable
½-inch dice	broth
2 bunches broccoli (about	Salt and freshly ground black
1½ pounds / 680 g), stems	pepper, to taste
trimmed and cut into florets	1 cup heavy cream

Turn the Instant Pot on high, add the butter to the insert, and cover until the butter is melted. Add the onion, carrots, and broccoli and toss the vegetables in the butter. Dissolve the baking soda in the broth and add to the vegetables. Press the Slow Cook button, and cook on high for 2½ to 3 hours or on low for 5 to 6 hours. (Press Slow Cook again to toggle between Low and High cooking temperatures.) Season with salt and pepper and stir in the cream. Turn off the Instant Pot and let the soup rest for 15 minutes to come to serving temperature.

Pinto Bean and Refried Tempeh Stew

Prep time: 10 minutes | Cook time: 15 minutes | Serves 6

1 teaspoon olive oil
1 small onion, cut into half-moon slices
2 large cloves garlic, minced
1½ cups vegetable broth, divided
1 (8-ounce, 227-g) package tempeh, quartered
1 (15-ounce / 425-g) can pinto beans, rinsed and drained, divided

1 small jalapeño, deseeded and finely diced
4 ounces (113 g) canned chopped green chiles
1 (14-ounce / 398-g) can fire-roasted diced tomatoes
1½ cups water
½ teaspoon chipotle or Ancho chile pepper
½ teaspoon salt

Heat the olive oil in the Instant Pot on the Sauté function. Add the onion and garlic, and sauté for about 3 minutes. Add the quartered tempeh and ½ cup of the broth to the pot. Sauté and crumble the tempeh with a spoon for 5 minutes. Meanwhile, in a small bowl, add ½ cup of the pinto beans and the diced jalapeño. Mash with a potato masher. Continue to stir and sauté and crumble the tempeh until it resembles small white beans. Transfer the mashed beans to the pot and, using the potato masher, mash into the tempeh. Add the remaining whole beans, green chilies, tomatoes, water, and vegetable broth to the pot, combining well. Cover the pot, select the Pressure Cook mode, set the timer for 5 minutes at Low Pressure. When timer beeps, use a natural pressure release for 15 minutes, then release any remaining pressure. Open the lid and serve immediately.

Acorn Squash and Double-Bean Chili

Prep time: 15 minutes | Cook time: 16 minutes | Serves 6

1 tablespoon olive oil
½ cup chopped onion
1 cup sliced carrots
1 large celery stalks, chopped
2 cloves garlic, minced
1½ cups cubed acorn squash
10 ounces (283 g) can red kidney beans, drained
10 ounces (283 g) can cannellini beans, drained

2 (10-ounce / 283-g) can crushed tomatoes
¾ cup corn kernels
1 teaspoon Tabasco sauce
1 teaspoon mesquite powder
1 teaspoon chili flakes
1 teaspoon dried oregano
1 teaspoon ground cumin
1 teaspoon smoked paprika

Heat the oil in the Instant pot on Sauté mode. Add the onion and carrots. Sauté for 3 minutes or until soft. Add the celery and sauté for 2 minutes. Add the garlic and sauté for 1 minute. Add the remaining ingredients and lock the lid. Select Pressure Cook mode and set cooking time for 10 minutes on High Pressure. When timer beeps, use a natural pressure release for 5 minutes, then release any remaining pressure. Open the lid. Serve warm.

Creamy Crab Soup

Prep time: 10 minutes | Cook time: 21 minutes | Serves 4

4 tablespoons unsalted butter
2 large carrots, peeled and diced
1 cup chopped leeks
2 stalks celery, chopped
4 cloves garlic, peeled and minced
2 teaspoons Italian seasoning

1 teaspoon salt
5 cups vegetable broth
1 pound (454 g) lump crabmeat, divided
2 tablespoons cooking sherry
¼ cup heavy cream
2 tablespoons fresh thyme leaves

Press the Sauté button on the Instant Pot and melt the butter. Add the carrots, leeks and celery to the pot and sauté for 5 minutes, or until the leeks are translucent. Add the garlic and sauté for 1 minute. Stir in the Italian seasoning, salt, vegetable broth and ½ pound (227 g) of the crabmeat. Lock the lid, select the Manual mode and set the cooking time for 15 minutes on High Pressure. Once cooking is complete, use a natural pressure release for 10 minutes, then release any remaining pressure. Carefully open the lid. Use an immersion blender to blend the soup in the pot until smooth. Stir in the remaining ½ pound (227 g) of the crabmeat, sherry and heavy cream. Ladle soup into four bowls and serve garnished with the thyme

Millet and Brown Lentil Chili

Prep time: 10 minutes | Cook time: 20 minutes | Serves 6

2 tablespoons olive oil
1 cup finely diced yellow onion
2 cloves garlic, minced
1 seeded and finely diced fresh jalapeño
½ teaspoon ground cinnamon
1 teaspoon chili powder
1 teaspoon ground cumin
1 cup dried brown lentils, rinsed and drained
1 cup millet, rinsed and drained

½ cup diced summer squash
4 cups diced fresh tomatoes
2 cups bite-size pieces kale
1 bay leaf
2 cups vegetable broth
4 cups water
Juice of 1 lemon
1 tablespoon chopped fresh sweet basil
½ teaspoon sea salt

Heat the olive oil in the Instant Pot. Add the onion and cook for 3 to 4 minutes, stirring occasionally, until softened. Add the garlic, stir, then add the jalapeño, cinnamon, chili powder, and cumin and sauté for a few minutes more, until the jalapeño softens. Add the lentils, millet, squash, tomatoes, kale, bay leaf, broth, and water and stir to combine. Cover the lid. Select Pressure Cook mode and set cooking time for 8 minutes on High Pressure. When timer beeps, use a natural pressure release for 15 minutes, then release any remaining pressure. Carefully remove the lid. Select Sauté mode and bring to a simmer, then add the lemon juice, basil, and salt. Stir and let simmer for a few minutes more. Serve immediately.

Quinoa and Beans Chili

Prep time: 10 minutes | Cook time: 7 minutes | Serves 6

1 large yellow onion, diced
3 cloves garlic, minced
1 green bell pepper, deseeded and diced
1 cup peeled and diced sweet potato cubes (about 1 inch)
1 (15-ounce / 425-g) can black beans, drained and rinsed
1 (15-ounce / 425-g) can kidney beans, drained and rinsed
½ cup uncooked quinoa, rinsed and drained

1 (4-ounce / 113-g) can diced green chiles
1 (26-ounce / 737-g) box chopped or diced tomatoes
1½ tablespoons chili powder
1 tablespoon ground cumin
½ teaspoon smoked paprika
½ teaspoon sea salt
2 cups vegetable broth
1 tablespoon olive oil
Fresh cilantro leaves, for garnish
1 avocado, sliced, for garnish

Select Sauté mode, and heat the oil in the Instant Pot until hot. Add the onion and sauté for 1 minute. Add the garlic, bell pepper, and sweet potatoes, and sauté 1 minute more. Add the black beans, kidney beans, quinoa, chiles, tomatoes, chili powder, cumin, paprika, salt, and broth, and stir. Lock the lid. Select Pressure Cook mode and set the cook time for 5 minutes on High Pressure. Once the cook time is complete, quick release the pressure and carefully remove the lid. Serve warm, garnished with cilantro and avocado.

Beef Meatball and Squash Minestrone

Prep time: 5 minutes | Cook time: 35 minutes | Serves 6

1 pound (454 g) ground beef
1 large egg
1½ tablespoons golden flaxseed meal
⅓ cup shredded Mozzarella cheese
¼ cup unsweetened tomato purée
1½ tablespoons Italian seasoning, divided
1½ teaspoons garlic powder, divided
1½ teaspoons sea salt, divided
1 tablespoon olive oil

2 garlic cloves, minced
½ medium yellow onion, minced
¼ cup pancetta, diced
1 cup sliced yellow squash
1 cup sliced zucchini
½ cup sliced turnips
4 cups beef broth
14 ounces (397 g) can diced tomatoes
½ teaspoon ground black pepper
3 tablespoons shredded Parmesan cheese

Preheat the oven to 400°F (205°C) and line a large baking sheet with aluminum foil. In a large bowl, combine the ground beef, egg, flaxseed meal, Mozzarella, unsweetened tomato purée, ½ tablespoon of Italian seasoning, ½ teaspoon of garlic powder, and ½ teaspoon of sea salt. Mix the ingredients until well combined. Make the meatballs by shaping 1 heaping tablespoon of the ground beef mixture into a meatball. Repeat with the remaining mixture and then transfer the meatballs to the prepared baking sheet. Place the meatballs in the oven and bake for 15 minutes. When the baking time is complete, remove from the oven and set aside. Select Sauté mode of the Instant Pot. Once the pot is hot, add the olive oil, garlic, onion, and pancetta. Sauté for 2 minutes or until the garlic becomes fragrant and the onions begin to soften. Add the yellow squash, zucchini, and turnips to the pot. Sauté for 3 more minutes. Add the beef broth, diced tomatoes, black pepper, and remaining garlic powder, sea salt, and Italian seasoning to the pot. Stir to combine and then add the meatballs. Lock the lid. Select Pressure Cook mode and set cooking time for 15 minutes on High Pressure. When cooking is complete, allow the pressure to release naturally for 10 minutes and then release the remaining pressure. Open the lid and gently stir the soup. Ladle into serving bowls and top with Parmesan. Serve hot.

Fish Stew with Carrot

Prep time: 10 minutes | Cook time: 14 minutes | Serves 4

1 large carrot, peeled and diced
1 stalk celery, diced
1 small yellow onion, peeled and diced
4 cloves garlic, peeled and minced
2 cups baby red potatoes, scrubbed and small-diced
1 (28-ounce / 794-g) can diced

tomatoes, undrained
1 pound (454 g) skinless cod, cut into cubes
1 (8-ounce / 227-g) bottle clam juice
1 tablespoon olive oil
2 cups water
1 tablespoon Italian seasoning
1 teaspoon salt
1 bay leaf

Press the Sauté button on the Instant Pot and heat the oil. Add the carrot, celery and onion to the pot and sauté for 5 minutes, or until the onion is translucent. Add the garlic and sauté for 1 minute. Stir in the remaining ingredients. Set the lid in place. Select the Manual setting and set the cooking time for 8 minutes on High Pressure. Once cooking is complete, perform a natural pressure release for 10 minutes, then release any remaining pressure. Open the lid. Ladle the stew into 4 bowls and serve warm.

White Mushroom and Blue Cheese Soup

Prep time: 15 minutes | Cook time: 20 minutes | Serves 4

2 cups chopped white mushrooms
3 tablespoons cream cheese
4 ounces (113 g) scallions, diced
4 cups chicken broth

1 teaspoon olive oil
½ teaspoon ground cumin
1 teaspoon salt
2 ounces (57 g) blue cheese, crumbled

Combine the mushrooms, cream cheese, scallions, chicken broth, olive oil, and ground cumin in the Instant Pot. Seal the lid. Select Pressure Cook mode and set cooking time for 20 minutes on High Pressure. When timer beeps, use a quick pressure release and open the lid. Add the salt and blend the soup with an immersion blender. Ladle the soup in the bowls and top with blue cheese. Serve warm.

Italian Jack Cheese and Leek Soup

Prep time: 10 minutes | Cook time: 15 minutes | Serves 4

4 tablespoons butter
7 ounces (198 g) leek, chopped
½ teaspoon salt

1 teaspoon Italian seasonings
2 cups chicken broth
2 ounces (57 g) Monterey Jack cheese, shredded

Heat the butter in the Instant Pot for 4 minutes or until melted. Add the chopped leek, salt, and Italian seasonings. Sauté the leek on Sauté mode for 5 minutes. Pour in the chicken broth and close the lid. Select Pressure Cook mode and set cooking time for 10 minutes on High Pressure. When timer beeps, use a quick pressure release. Open the lid. Add the shredded cheese and stir until the cheese is melted. Serve immediately.

Super Cheesy Bacon and Broccoli Soup

Prep time: 6 minutes | Cook time: 10 minutes | Serves 6

3 tablespoons butter
2 stalks celery, diced
½ yellow onion, diced
3 garlic cloves, minced
3½ cups chicken stock
4 cups chopped fresh broccoli florets
3 ounces (85 g) block-style cream cheese, softened and cubed
½ teaspoon ground nutmeg
½ teaspoon sea salt

1 teaspoon ground black pepper
3 cups shredded Cheddar cheese
½ cup shredded Monterey Jack cheese
2 cups heavy cream
4 slices cooked bacon, crumbled
1 tablespoon finely chopped chives

Select Sauté mode. Once the Instant Pot is hot, add the butter and heat until the butter is melted. Add the celery, onions, and garlic. Continue sautéing for 5 minutes or until the vegetables are softened. Add the chicken stock and broccoli florets to the pot. Bring the liquid to a boil. Lock the lid,. Select Pressure Cook mode and set cooking time for 5 minutes on High Pressure. When cooking is complete, allow the pressure to release naturally for 10 minutes and then release the remaining pressure. Open the lid and add the cream cheese, nutmeg, sea salt, and black pepper. Stir to combine. Select Sauté mode. Bring the soup to a boil and then slowly stir in the Cheddar and Jack cheeses. Once the cheese has melted, stir in the heavy cream. Ladle the soup into serving bowls and top with bacon and chives. Serve hot.

Chicken and Riced Cauliflower Soup

Prep time: 15 minutes | Cook time: 13 minutes | Serves 5

2 cups cauliflower florets
1 pound (454 g) boneless, skinless chicken thighs
4½ cups chicken broth
½ yellow onion, chopped
2 garlic cloves, minced
1 tablespoon unflavored gelatin powder
2 teaspoons sea salt
½ teaspoon ground black

pepper
½ cup sliced zucchini
⅓ cup sliced turnips
1 teaspoon dried parsley
3 celery stalks, chopped
1 teaspoon ground turmeric
½ teaspoon dried marjoram
1 teaspoon dried thyme
½ teaspoon dried oregano

Add the cauliflower florets to a food processor and pulse until a ricelike consistency is achieved. Set aside. Add the chicken thighs, chicken broth, onions, garlic, gelatin powder, sea salt, and black pepper to the pot. Gently stir to combine. Lock the lid. Select Pressure Cook mode and set cooking time for 10 minutes on High Pressure. When cooking is complete, quick release the pressure and open the lid. Transfer the chicken thighs to a cutting board. Chop the chicken into bite-sized pieces and then return the chopped chicken to the pot. Add the cauliflower rice, zucchini, turnips, parsley, celery, turmeric, marjoram, thyme, and oregano to the pot. Stir to combine. Lock the lid. Select Pressure Cook mode and set cooking time for 3 minutes on High Pressure. When cooking is complete, quick release the pressure. Open the lid. Ladle the soup into serving bowls. Serve hot.

Chili Verde Chicken and Cheddar Soup

Prep time: 10 minutes | Cook time: 25 minutes | Serves 4

1 pound (454 g) chicken breast, skinless, boneless
5 cups chicken broth
½ cup Cheddar cheese,

shredded
2 ounces (57 g) chili Verde sauce
1 tablespoon dried cilantro

Put chicken breast and chicken broth in the Instant Pot. Add the cilantro, Close the lid. Select Pressure Cook mode and set cooking time for 15 minutes on High Pressure. When timer beeps, make a quick pressure release and open the lid. Shred the chicken breast with a fork. Add the Cheddar and chili Verde sauce in the soup and cook on Sauté mode for 10 minutes. Mix in the dried cilantro. Serve immediately.

Beef and Bell Pepper Soup

Prep time: 15 minutes | Cook time: 20 minutes | Serves 6

1 tablespoon coconut oil
1 cup ground beef
1 teaspoon taco seasonings
½ cup crushed tomatoes

2 tablespoons cream cheese
1 bell pepper, chopped
1 garlic clove, diced
4 cups beef broth

Heat the the coconut oil in the Instant Pot on Sauté mode. Add the ground beef and sprinkle with taco seasonings. Stir well and cook the meat on Sauté mode for 5 minutes. Add crushed tomatoes, cream cheese, bell pepper, garlic clove, and beef broth. Close the lid and select Pressure Cook mode. Set cooking time for 15 minutes on High Pressure. When cooking is complete, perform a natural pressure release for 10 minutes and open the lid. Ladle the soup and serve.

Cauliflower and Kale Soup

Prep time: 20 minutes | Cook time: 29 minutes | Serves 5

1 tablespoon olive oil
1 garlic clove, diced
½ cup cauliflower florets
1 cup kale, chopped

2 tablespoons chives, chopped
1 teaspoon sea salt
6 cups beef broth

Heat the olive oil in the Instant Pot on Sauté mode for 2 minutes and add the garlic. Sauté for 2 minutes or until fragrant. Add cauliflower, kale, chives, sea salt, and beef broth. Close the lid. Select Pressure Cook mode and set cooking time for 5 minutes on High Pressure. When timer beeps, use a quick pressure release and open the lid. Ladle the soup into the bowls. Serve warm.

Beef, Mushroom, and Zucchini Stew

Prep time: 20 minutes | Cook time: 40 minutes | Serves 4

1 pound (454 g) beef chuck roast, cut into 1-inch cubes
2 teaspoons arrowroot powder
1½ tablespoons olive oil
1 cup chopped mushrooms
1 cup chopped zucchini
½ cup sliced turnips
3 ribs celery, sliced
¾ cup unsweetened tomato purée
4 cups beef broth

2 garlic cloves, minced
1 tablespoon dried thyme
1 tablespoon paprika
1 teaspoon dried rosemary
1 teaspoon dried parsley
1 teaspoon garlic powder
1 teaspoon celery seed
1 teaspoon onion powder
2½ teaspoons sea salt
1 teaspoon ground black pepper

In a large bowl, combine the chuck roast and arrowroot powder. Toss to coat well. Select Sauté mode and add the olive oil to the pot. Once the oil is hot, add the meat and sauté for 5 minutes or until the meat is browned on all sides. Once the meat is browned, add the mushrooms, zucchini, turnips, celery, tomato purée, beef broth, garlic, thyme, paprika, rosemary, parsley, garlic powder, celery seed, sea salt, black pepper, and onion powder to the pot. Stir well to combine. Lock the lid. Select Pressure Cook and set cooking time for 35 minutes on High Pressure. When cooking is complete, allow the pressure to release naturally for 15 minutes and then release the remaining pressure. Open the lid, stir, and then ladle the stew into serving bowls. Serve hot.

Ham Hock and Bean Soup

Prep time: 5 minutes | Cook time: 45 minutes | Serves 4

1 ham hock
½ pound (227 g) dried great northern beans, rinsed
1 (8-ounce / 227-g) can tomato sauce
1 large carrot, peeled and diced
1 small yellow onion, peeled and diced

4 cloves garlic, peeled and minced
2 stalks celery, chopped
1 bay leaf
4 cups chicken broth
4 tablespoons fresh thyme leaves
½ teaspoon salt

Add all the ingredients to the Instant Pot and stir to combine. Set the lid in place. Select the Manual mode and set the cooking time for 45 minutes at High Pressure. Once the timer goes off, use a natural pressure release for 10 minutes, then release any remaining pressure. Carefully open the lid. Remove and discard the bay leaf. Use two forks to shred the meat off the ham bone. Discard the bone. Divide the soup among 4 bowls and serve warm.

Coconut Red Bean Soup

Prep time: 10 minutes | Cook time: 50 minutes | Serves 4

3 slices bacon, diced
2 large carrots, peeled and diced
5 green onions, sliced
1 stalk celery, chopped
1 Scotch bonnet, deseeded, veins removed and minced
1 (15-ounce / 425-g) can diced tomatoes, undrained
½ pound (227 g) dried small red beans

1 (13.5-ounce / 383-g) can coconut milk
2 cups chicken broth
2 teaspoons olive oil
1 tablespoon Jamaican jerk seasoning
1 teaspoon salt
4 cups cooked basmati rice
1 cup chopped fresh parsley
1 lime, quartered

Press the Sauté button on the Instant Pot and heat the oil. Add the bacon, carrots, onions, celery and Scotch bonnet to the pot and sauté for 5 minutes, or until the onions are translucent. Stir in the tomatoes with juice, red beans, coconut milk, chicken broth, Jamaican jerk seasoning and salt. Lock the lid. Select the Manual mode and set the cooking time for 45 minutes on High Pressure. When the timer goes off, do a natural pressure release for 10 minutes, then release any remaining pressure. Carefully open the lid. Ladle the soup into four bowls over cooked rice and garnish with parsley. Squeeze a quarter of lime over each bowl. Serve warm.

Pork and Black Bean Chili

Prep time: 10 minutes | Cook time: 6 to 8 hours | Serves 8

1 pound (454 g) pork tenderloin, cut into 1-inch chunks
1 (16-ounce / 454-g) jar thick chunky salsa
3 (15-ounce / 425-g) cans black beans, rinsed and drained
½ cup chicken broth

1 medium red bell pepper, chopped
1 medium onion, chopped
1 teaspoon ground cumin
2 to 3 teaspoons chili powder
1 to 1½ teaspoons dried oregano
¼ cup sour cream

Combine all ingredients except sour cream in the Instant Pot. Cover. Press the Slow Cook button, and cook on low for 6 to 8 hours, or until pork is tender. (Press Slow Cook again to toggle between Low and High cooking temperatures.) Garnish individual servings with sour cream.

Kimchi Stew with Tofu

Prep time: 10 minutes | Cook time: 20 minutes | Serves 4

2 cups kimchi
1 cup chopped onion
1 cup dried shiitake mushrooms
3 cloves garlic, minced
1 tablespoon minced fresh ginger
1 tablespoon toasted sesame oil
1 tablespoon dark soy sauce

½ teaspoon granulated sugar
1 tablespoon gochugaru (Korean ground red pepper) or ½ teaspoon cayenne pepper
½ teaspoon kosher salt
2 cups water
½ cup chopped green onions
1 (8-ounce / 227-g) package firm tofu, diced

In the Instant Pot, combine the kimchi, onion, mushrooms, garlic, ginger, sesame oil, soy sauce, gochugaru, sugar, salt, and water. Secure the lid on the pot. Close the pressure-release valve. Select Manual and set the pot at High Pressure for 3 minutes. At the end of the cooking time, allow the pot to sit undisturbed for 10 minutes, then quick-release any remaining pressure. Stir in the green onions and tofu and serve.

Creamy Broccoli Soup with Bacon

Prep time: 15 minutes | Cook time: 30 minutes | Serves 4

6 slices bacon, diced
1 large carrot, peeled and diced
1 medium sweet onion, peeled and diced
1 small Russet potato, scrubbed and diced
1 pound (454 g) fresh broccoli, chopped

¼ cup grated Cheddar cheese
1 tablespoon Dijon mustard
2 teaspoons unsalted butter
1 teaspoon salt
1 teaspoon ground black pepper
4 cups chicken broth
¼ cup whole milk
4 tablespoons sour cream

Set the Instant Pot to the Sauté mode and melt the butter. Add the bacon to the pot and sear for 5 minutes, or until crispy. Transfer the bacon to a plate lined with paper towels and let rest for 5 minutes. Crumble the bacon when cooled. Add the carrot, onion and potato to the pot. Sauté for 5 minutes, or until the onion is translucent. Stir in the remaining ingredients, except for the milk and sour cream. Set the lid in place. Select the Soup mode and set the cooking time for 20 minutes at High Pressure. Once cooking is complete, use a quick pressure release. Carefully open the lid. Pour the milk into the pot. Use an immersion blender to blend the soup in the pot until it achieves the desired smoothness. Ladle the soup into 4 bowls and garnish with the crumbled bacon and sour cream. Serve warm.

Peppery Red Kidney Bean Chili

Prep time: 20 minutes | Cook time: 14 minutes | Serves 4 to 6

3 tablespoons salted butter
1 medium yellow onion, finely diced
1 Scotch bonnet pepper, deseeded and sliced in half
1 jalapeño pepper, deseeded and diced
1 poblano pepper, deseeded and diced
3 cloves garlic, minced
1½ pounds (680 g) ground beef
½ cup beer
1 (14.5-ounce / 411-g) can diced tomatoes
1 (10-ounce / 284-g) can Rotel tomatoes

1 (8-ounce / 227-g) can tomato sauce
¼ cup taco sauce
1 tablespoon hoisin sauce
1 teaspoon Worcestershire sauce
2 tablespoons cumin
1½ teaspoons seasoned salt
1 teaspoon dried cilantro
1 teaspoon Italian seasoning
1 teaspoon celery salt
½ teaspoon chili powder
1 teaspoon Tony Chachere's Creole Seasoning
2 (15.5-ounce / 439-g) cans red kidney beans, drained and rinsed

Press the Sauté button on the Instant Pot and melt the butter. Add the onion, Scotch bonnet pepper, jalapeño pepper and poblano pepper to the pot and sauté for 5 minutes, or until tender. Add the garlic and sauté for 1 minute. Add the ground beef to the pot and sauté for 3 minutes, crumbling and breaking the pieces up with a wooden spoon, or until slightly browned. Stir in the beer, diced tomatoes, Rotel tomatoes, tomato sauce, taco sauce, hoisin sauce and Worcestershire sauce. Scrape up any browned bits from the bottom of the pot. Stir in the cumin, seasoned salt, dried cilantro, Italian seasoning, celery salt, chili powder and Creole seasoning. Gently fold in the kidney beans. Set the lid in place. Select the Manual mode and set the cooking time for 5 minutes on High Pressure. When the timer goes off, do a quick pressure release. Carefully open the lid. Serve warm.

Lentil Soup with Gremolata

Prep time: 10 minutes | Cook time: 16 minutes | Serves 4 to 6

Soup:

2 tablespoons extra-virgin olive oil, plus more for serving
1 large yellow onion, diced
2 carrots, peeled and diced
2 celery stalks, diced
2 cloves garlic, minced
1 teaspoon fine sea salt, plus more as needed

½ cup French green (Puy) lentils
½ cup beluga lentils
4 cups low-sodium vegetable broth
2 tablespoons fresh lemon juice

Gremolata:

1 cup loosely packed fresh flat-leaf parsley leaves
1 clove garlic, peeled

Finely grated zest of 1 lemon
Crusty bread for serving

To make the soup: Select the Sauté setting on the Instant Pot, add the oil, and heat for 1 minute. Add the onion, carrots, celery, garlic, and salt and sauté for about 5 minutes, until the onion softens. Add the lentils and broth and stir to combine. Secure the lid and set the Pressure Release to Sealing. Press the Cancel button to reset the cooking program. Then select the Soup/Broth setting and set the cooking time for 15 minutes at High Pressure. (The pot will take about 10 minutes to come up to pressure before the cooking program begins.) While the soup is cooking, make the gremolata: Pile the parsley onto a cutting board, along with the garlic. Chop them together until the parsley is finely chopped and there are no large bits of garlic. Add the lemon zest and chop a little more, until the mixture is combined. When the cooking program ends, let the pressure release naturally for 10 minutes, then move the Pressure Release to Venting to release any remaining steam. Open the pot, then stir in the gremolata and lemon juice. Taste and adjust the seasoning with salt, if needed. Ladle the soup into bowls and drizzle with oil. Serve piping hot, with crusty bread alongside.

Sumptuous Cioppino

Prep time: 15 minutes | Cook time: 23 minutes | Serves 8

2 tablespoons unsalted butter
1 medium red bell pepper, deseeded and diced
1 medium yellow onion, peeled and diced
2 stalks celery, chopped
3 cloves garlic, minced
1 teaspoon dried oregano
½ teaspoon Italian seasoning
½ teaspoon salt
½ teaspoon black pepper
2 tablespoons tomato paste
1 cup white wine
1 (15-ounce / 425-g) can

crushed tomatoes
4 cups seafood stock
1 bay leaf
1 pound (454 g) fresh mussels, scrubbed clean and beards removed
1 pound (454 g) fresh clams, scrubbed clean
½ pound (227 g) large shrimp, peeled and deveined
½ pound (227 g) fresh scallops
½ pound (227 g) calamari rings
1 tablespoon lemon juice

Press the Sauté button on the Instant Pot and melt the butter. Add the bell pepper, onion and celery to the pot and sauté for 8 minutes, or until tender. Add the garlic, oregano, Italian seasoning, salt and black pepper to the pot and cook for 30 seconds. Add the tomato paste and cook for 1 minute. Pour in the white wine and scrape the bottom of the pot well. Stir in the tomatoes, seafood stock and bay leaf. Set the lid in place. Select the Manual mode and set the cooking time for 5 minutes on High Pressure. When the timer goes off, perform a quick pressure release. Carefully open the lid. Stir in the remaining ingredients, except for the lemon juice. Select the Sauté mode and allow the soup to simmer for 10 minutes, or until the seafood is cooked through. Remove and discard the bay leaf and stir in the lemon juice. Serve hot.

Pea Soup with Croutons

Prep time: 10 minutes | Cook time: 25 minutes | Serves 8

Soup:

2 tablespoons extra-virgin olive oil, plus more for serving
1 yellow onion, diced
2 carrots, peeled and diced
2 celery stalks, diced
1 tablespoon Old Bay seasoning
1 teaspoon smoked paprika

½ teaspoon freshly ground black pepper
4 cups low-sodium vegetable broth
2⅓ cups (1 pound (454 g)) green split peas
4 cups water
1 bay leaf

Croutons:

4 slices crusty bread, cut into ½-inch cubes
2 tablespoons extra-virgin olive

oil
1 teaspoon Old Bay seasoning
Smoked paprika for serving

To make the soup: Select the Sauté setting on the Instant Pot, add the oil, and heat for 1 minute. Add the onion, carrots, and celery and sauté for 5 minutes, until the onion softens. Add the Old Bay, smoked paprika, pepper, split peas, broth, water, and bay leaf. Stir to combine. Secure the lid and set the Pressure Release to Sealing. Press the Cancel button to reset the cooking program. Then select the Manual or Pressure Cook setting and set the cooking time for 20 minutes at High Pressure. (The pot will take about 25 minutes to come up to pressure before the cooking program begins.) When the cooking program ends, let the pressure release naturally (this will take about 45 minutes). Open the pot, then remove and discard the bay leaf. When you're ready to serve the soup, make the croutons: In a bowl, toss the cubed bread with the oil and Old Bay until the bread is evenly coated. Spread out the bread in an even layer on a foil-lined baking sheet, and toast in a toaster oven or under a broiler for about 3 to 5 minutes, until lightly browned. Ladle the soup into bowls and serve piping hot, with the croutons and smoked paprika sprinkled on top and a drizzle of oil.

Lamb and Carrot Stew

Prep time: 20 minutes | Cook time: 7 to 9 hours | Serves 6

½ cup all-purpose flour
½ teaspoon salt
¼ teaspoon pepper
1½ pounds (680 g) lamb stew meat, cubed
2 shallots, sliced
2 tablespoons olive oil
½ cup red wine
2 (14½-ounce / 411-g) cans beef broth
2 medium potatoes, cubed

1 large sweet potato, peeled and cubed
2 large carrots, cut into 1-inch pieces
2 medium parsnips, peeled and cubed
1 garlic clove, minced
1 tablespoon mint jelly
4 bacon strips, cooked and crumbled

In a large resealable plastic bag, combine the flour, salt and pepper. Add the meat, a few pieces at a time, and shake to coat. In a large skillet, brown meat and shallots in oil in batches. Transfer to the Instant Pot. Add wine to the skillet, stirring to loosen browned bits from pan. Bring to a boil. Reduce heat; simmer, uncovered, for 1-2 minutes. Add to the Instant Pot. Stir in the broth, potatoes, sweet potato, carrots, parsnips and garlic. Cover and press the Slow Cook button, and cook on low for 7 to 9 hours or until meat is tender. (Press Slow Cook again to toggle between Low and High cooking temperatures.) Stir in jelly; sprinkle with bacon.

Green Lentil Chicken Sausage Stew

Prep time: 10 minutes | Cook time: 36 minutes | Serves 6

2 tablespoons vegetable oil
1 pound (454 g) chicken sausage, sliced
3 stalks celery, cut into pieces
2 medium carrots, peeled and cut into pieces
1 medium yellow onion, peeled and roughly chopped
2 cloves garlic, peeled and

minced
½ teaspoon salt
1 large Russet potato, peeled and cut into pieces
4 cups chicken stock
2 cups green lentils
¼ cup chopped fresh flat-leaf parsley

Press the Sauté button on the Instant Pot and heat the oil. Add the sausage and cook for 8 minutes, or until the edges are browned. Transfer the sausage to a plate and set aside. Add the celery, carrots and onion to the pot and sauté for 3 minutes, or until just softened. Add the garlic and salt to the pot and cook for 30 seconds, or until fragrant. Place the sausage back to the pot along with the remaining ingredients. Lock the lid, select the Manual mode and set the cooking time for 25 minute on High Pressure. When the timer goes off, do a natural pressure release for 15 minutes, then release any remaining pressure. Open the lid. Serve warm.

Lamb Stew with Apricots

Prep time: 15 minutes | Cook time: 39 to 41 minutes | Serves 6

2 tablespoons olive oil
2 pounds (907 g) cubed boneless lamb
1 medium onion, peeled and diced
4 garlic cloves, minced
2 cups beef broth
¼ cup freshly squeezed orange juice
1 cup crushed tomatoes
¼ cup diced dried apricots

¼ cup diced pitted dates
2 teaspoons ground cumin
2 teaspoons minced fresh ginger
¼ teaspoon cayenne pepper
¼ teaspoon ground cinnamon
1 teaspoon sea salt
½ teaspoon ground black pepper
½ cup chopped fresh cilantro

Press the Sauté button on the Instant Pot and heat the olive oil. Add the lamb cubes and onion to the pot and sauté for 3 to 5 minutes, or until the onion is translucent. Add the garlic and sauté for 1 minute. Pour in the beef broth and orange juice and deglaze by scraping any of the bits from the side of the pot. Stir in the remaining ingredients, except for the cilantro. Lock the lid, select the Meat/Stew mode and set the cooking time for 35 minutes on High Pressure. When the timer goes off, do a natural pressure release for 10 minutes, then release any remaining pressure. Open the lid. Ladle into individual bowls and serve garnished with the cilantro.

Potato and Fish Stew

Prep time: 15 minutes | Cook time: 28 minutes | Serves 8

2 tablespoons unsalted butter
2 stalks celery, chopped
1 medium carrot, peeled and diced
1 medium yellow onion, peeled and diced
2 cloves garlic, peeled and minced
1 teaspoon Italian seasoning
¼ teaspoon dried thyme
¼ teaspoon salt
¼ teaspoon ground black

pepper
1 cup lager-style beer
1 (28-ounce / 794-g) can diced tomatoes
2 large Russet potatoes, peeled and diced
3 cups seafood stock
1 bay leaf
2 pounds (907 g) cod, cut into pieces
2 tablespoons lemon juice

Set the Instant Pot to the Sauté mode and melt the butter. Add the celery, carrot and onion to the pot and sauté for 8 minutes, or until softened. Add the garlic, Italian seasoning, thyme, salt and pepper to the pot and cook for 30 seconds. Pour in the beer and scrape the bottom of the pot well. Stir in the tomatoes, potatoes, seafood stock and bay leaf. Set the lid in place. Select the Manual mode and set the cooking time for 10 minutes on High Pressure. When the timer goes off, perform a quick pressure release. Carefully open the lid. Stir in the fish. Select the Sauté mode and allow the soup to simmer for 10 minutes, or until the fish is cooked through. Remove and discard the bay leaf and stir in lemon juice. Serve hot.

Peppery Chicken Chili

Prep time: 15 minutes | Cook time: 36 minutes | Serves 8

2 tablespoons unsalted butter
1 medium yellow onion, peeled and chopped
½ pound (227 g) Anaheim peppers, deseeded and roughly chopped
½ pound (227 g) poblano peppers, deseeded and roughly chopped
½ pound (227 g) tomatillos, husked and quartered
2 small jalapeño peppers, deseeded and roughly chopped

2 cloves garlic, peeled and minced
1 teaspoon ground cumin
6 bone-in, skin-on chicken thighs (2½ pounds / 1.1 kg total)
2 cups chicken stock
2 cups water
⅓ cup roughly chopped fresh cilantro
3 (15-ounce / 425-g) cans Great Northern beans, drained and rinsed

Press the Sauté button on the Instant Pot and melt the butter. Add the onion and sauté for 3 minutes, or until tender. Add Anaheim peppers, poblano peppers, tomatillos and jalapeño peppers to the pot and sauté for 3 minutes. Add the garlic and cumin to the pot and sauté for 30 seconds, or until fragrant. Stir in the chicken thighs, stock and water. Lock the lid. Select the Bean/Chili mode and set the cooking time for 30 minutes on High Pressure. When the timer goes off, perform a quick pressure release. Carefully open the lid. Transfer the chicken thighs to a clean work surface. Use two forks to remove the skin off the chicken and shred the meat. Use an immersion blender to purée the mixture in the pot until smooth. Stir in the shredded chicken, cilantro and beans. Serve warm.

Red Pear and Pumpkin Soup

Prep time: 10 minutes | Cook time: 3 hours | Serves 8

4 tablespoons (½ stick) unsalted butter
½ cup finely chopped sweet onion
½ cup finely chopped celery
½ cup finely chopped carrot
2 medium red pears, peeled, cored, and finely chopped

½ teaspoon ground ginger
2 (15-ounce / 425-g) cans pumpkin purée
3 cups chicken broth
Salt and freshly ground black pepper, to taste
1 cup heavy cream

Melt the butter in a medium skillet over medium-high heat. Add the onion, celery, carrot, pears, and ginger and sauté until the vegetables begin to soften, about 3 minutes. Transfer the contents of the skillet to the insert of the Instant Pot. Stir in the pumpkin and broth. Cover and press the Slow Cook button, and cook on high for 3 hours or on low for 5 to 6 hours. (Press Slow Cook again to toggle between Low and High cooking temperatures.) Season with salt and pepper. Stir in the cream, cover, and leave on warm for 30 minutes before serving.

Split Pea and Ham Soup

Prep time: 15 minutes | Cook time: 21 minutes | Serves 4

3 tablespoons unsalted butter
3 large carrots, peeled and diced
2 stalks celery, diced
1 small yellow onion, peeled and diced
1 pound (454 g) dried split green peas, rinsed
1 ham hock
4 cups chicken broth
2 cups water
1 tablespoon cooking sherry
1 tablespoon dried thyme leaves
1 teaspoon salt
1 teaspoon ground black pepper
1 bay leaf
4 tablespoons sour cream

Set the Instant Pot to the Sauté mode and melt the butter. Add the carrot, celery, and onion to the pot and sauté for 5 minutes, or until the onion is translucent. Add the rinsed peas and ham hock to the pot and cook for 1 minute. Stir in the remaining ingredients, except for the sour cream. Lock the lid. Select the Manual mode and set the cooking time for 15 minutes at High Pressure. When the timer goes off, use a natural pressure release for 10 minutes, then release any remaining pressure. Carefully open the lid. Remove and discard the bay leaf. Use two forks to shred meat off the ham bone. Discard the bone. Ladle the soup into 4 bowls and garnish with the sour cream. Serve warm.

Spicy Ground Chicken Chili

Prep time: 15 minutes | Cook time: 40 minutes | Serves 8

1 pound (454 g) ground chicken
1 medium yellow onion, peeled and diced
3 cloves garlic, minced
1 (30-ounce / 850-g) can diced tomatoes, undrained
1 (4-ounce / 113-g) can diced green chilies, undrained
1 (15-ounce / 425-g) can dark red kidney beans, drained and rinsed
1 (15-ounce / 425-g) can black beans, drained and rinsed
3 canned chipotle chilies in adobo sauce
1 tablespoon olive oil
2 teaspoons hot sauce
1 teaspoon smoked paprika
1 teaspoon chili powder
1 teaspoon Worcestershire sauce
1 teaspoon sea salt

Press the Sauté button on the Instant Pot and heat the oil. Add the ground chicken and onion to the pot and sauté for 5 minutes, or until the chicken is no longer pink. Stir in the remaining ingredients. Set the lid in place. Select the Meat/Stew setting and set the cooking time for 35 minutes on High Pressure. When the timer goes off, perform a natural pressure release for 15 minutes, then release any remaining pressure. Open the lid. Ladle the chili into individual bowls and serve warm.

Spicy Turkey Chili

Prep time: 15 minutes | Cook time: 43 minutes | Serves 8

2 pounds (907 g) ground turkey
1 medium carrot, peeled and finely chopped
1 medium onion, peeled and chopped
3 cloves garlic, peeled and minced
1 small jalapeño pepper, deseeded and minced
¼ cup chili powder
1 teaspoon ground cumin
½ teaspoon smoked paprika
1 tablespoon light brown sugar
½ teaspoon salt
½ teaspoon ground black pepper
2 cups chicken broth
1 cup water
1 (15-ounce / 425-g) can kidney beans, drained and rinsed
1 tablespoon lime juice

Set the Instant Pot to the Sauté mode. Add the turkey to the pot and sear for 10 minutes, or until browned. Add the carrot, onion, garlic, jalapeño pepper, chili powder, cumin and paprika to the pot and sauté for 3 minutes, or until fragrant. Season with the brown sugar, salt and pepper and cook for 30 seconds. Pour in the chicken broth and water and stir well. Close and secure the lid. Select the Bean/Chili mode and set the cooking time for 30 minutes at High Pressure. When the timer goes off, use a quick pressure release. Carefully open the lid. Stir in the kidney beans and lime juice and let sit in the residual heat for 10 minutes until the beans are heat through. Serve warm.

Spicy Corn and Bean Chili

Prep time: 15 minutes | Cook time: 44 minutes | Serves 4

1 medium red bell pepper, deseeded and diced
2 stalks celery, chopped
1 small yellow onion, peeled and diced
½ pound (227 g) ground pork
4 cloves garlic, peeled and minced
1 cup sliced white mushrooms
1 (28-ounce / 794-g) can diced tomatoes, undrained
1 (15.5-ounce / 439-g) can corn, drained
1 (15-ounce / 425-g) can black beans, drained and rinsed
2 tablespoons chili powder
1 tablespoon olive oil
1 teaspoon smoked paprika
1 teaspoon adobo sauce
1 teaspoon salt
¼ cup beef broth
2 chipotles in adobo sauce, finely diced
1 cup shredded Cheddar cheese

Set the Instant Pot to the Sauté mode and heat the oil. Add the bell pepper, celery and onion to the pot and sauté for 3 minutes, or until the onion is tender. Add the pork to the pot and sauté for 5 minutes, or until the pork is no longer pink. Add the garlic and sauté for 1 minute. Stir in the remaining ingredients, except for the cheese. Set the lid in place. Select the Meat/Stew setting and set the cooking time for 35 minutes on High Pressure. Once cooking is complete, do a natural pressure release for 15 minutes, then release any remaining pressure. Open the lid. Ladle the chili into 4 bowls and serve warm garnished with the cheese.

Tomato and Red Pepper Bisque

Prep time: 10 minutes | Cook time: 15 minutes | Serves 4

2 teaspoons balsamic vinegar
1 small sweet onion, peeled and diced
1 stalk celery, thinly chopped
8 medium tomatoes, deseeded and quartered
1 (12-ounce / 340-g) jar roasted red peppers, drained and diced
4 cups chicken broth
1 tablespoon cooking sherry
½ cup julienned fresh basil leaves, divided
1 tablespoon olive oil
1 teaspoon salt
1 teaspoon ground black pepper
1 cup whole milk

Set the Instant Pot to the Sauté mode and heat the olive oil and balsamic vinegar for 30 seconds. Add the onion and celery to the pot and sauté for 5 minutes, or until the onion is translucent. Add the tomatoes and sauté for 3 minutes, or until the tomatoes break down. Stir in the roasted red peppers, chicken broth, sherry, ¼ cup of the basil, salt and pepper. Close and secure the lid. Select the Manual mode and set the cooking time for 7 minutes on High Pressure. Once cooking is complete, use a quick pressure release. Carefully open the lid. Pour in the milk. Use an immersion blender to purée the mixture in the pot. Divide the dish among 4 bowls and serve topped with the remaining ¼ cup of the basil.

Serrano Chile and Avocado Soup

Prep time: 10 minutes | Cook time: 7 minutes | Serves 4

2 avocados
1 small fresh tomatillo, quartered
2 cups chicken broth
2 tablespoons avocado oil
1 tablespoon butter
2 tablespoons finely minced onion
1 clove garlic, minced

½ Serrano chile, deseeded and ribs removed, minced, plus thin slices for garnish
¼ teaspoon sea salt
Pinch of ground white pepper
½ cup full-fat coconut milk
Fresh cilantro sprigs, for garnish

Scoop the avocado flesh into a food processor. Add the tomatillo and chicken broth and purée until smooth. Set aside. Set the Instant Pot to Sauté mode and add the avocado oil and butter. When the butter melts, add the onion and garlic and sauté for a minute or until softened. Add the Serrano chile and sauté for 1 minute more. Pour the puréed avocado mixture into the pot, add the salt and pepper, and stir to combine. Secure the lid. Press the Pressure Cook button and set cooking time for 5 minutes on High Pressure. When timer beeps, use a quick pressure release. Open the lid and stir in the coconut milk. Serve hot topped with thin slices of Serrano chile, and cilantro sprigs.

Pork Chili with Black-Eyed Peas

Prep time: 15 minutes | Cook time: 49 minutes | Serves 6

2 tablespoons vegetable oil
2 pounds (907 g) boneless pork shoulder, cut into pieces
1 medium onion, peeled and finely chopped
3 cloves garlic, peeled and minced
1 (14.5-ounce / 411-g) can diced tomatoes, drained
3 tablespoons chili powder

1 teaspoon ground cumin
½ teaspoon ground coriander
½ teaspoon salt
½ teaspoon ground black pepper
4 cups chicken broth
2 cups dried black-eyed peas, soaked overnight in water and drained
1 tablespoon lime juice

Set the Instant Pot to the Sauté mode and heat the oil. Add half the pork to the pot in an even layer, working in batches to prevent meat from steaming. Sear the pork for 3 minutes on each side, or until lightly browned. Transfer the browned pork to a plate. Repeat with the remaining pork. Add the onion to the pot and sauté for 5 minutes, or until softened. Add the garlic, tomatoes, chili powder, cumin, coriander, salt and pepper to the pot and cook for 2 minutes, or until fragrant. Stir in the browned pork, chicken broth and black-eyed peas. Lock the lid. Select the Manual mode and set the cooking time for 30 minutes on High Pressure. Once the timer goes off, perform a natural pressure release for 20 minutes, then release any remaining pressure. Carefully open the lid. Stir in the lime juice. Serve hot.

Guinness Beef Stew

Prep time: 15 minutes | Cook time: 52 minutes | Serves 8

2 pounds (907 g) boneless beef chuck steak, cubed
2 tablespoons all-purpose flour
½ teaspoon salt
¼ teaspoon black pepper
2 tablespoons vegetable oil
1 medium onion, peeled and chopped
1 clove garlic, chopped
½ teaspoon dried thyme

1 cup Guinness stout
1 cup beef broth
2 large carrots, peeled and chopped
2 medium Russet potatoes, chopped
1 bay leaf
¼ cup chopped fresh flat-leaf parsley

In a medium bowl, whisk together the flour, salt and pepper. Add the beef to the bowl and toss until well coated. Set aside. Press the Sauté button on the Instant Pot and heat the oil. Arrange half the beef in the pot in an even layer, making sure there is space between beef cubes to prevent steam from forming. Sear the beef for 6 minutes on both sides, or until lightly browned. Transfer the beef to a plate. Repeat with the remaining beef. Add the onion, garlic and thyme to the pot and cook for 5 minutes, or until the onion is tender. Pour in half the Guinness and scrape off all the browned bits from the bottom of the pot. Stir in the remaining half of the Guinness, beef broth, carrots, potatoes, bay leaf and the cooked beef. Lock the lid. Select the Manual mode and set the cooking time for 35 minutes at High Pressure. When the timer goes off, use a natural pressure release for 20 minutes, then release any remaining pressure. Carefully open the lid. Remove and discard the bay leaf and serve hot with the fresh parsley on top.

Broccoli and Tomato Stew

Prep time: 10 minutes | Cook time: 8 minutes | Serves 4

2 teaspoons corn oil
1 yellow onion, finely chopped
3 Roma tomatoes, finely chopped
½ cup chopped red bell pepper
1½ cups broccoli florets
1 zucchini, cut into 1-inch chunks
¼ cup frozen corn kernels, thawed to room temperature
¼ cup (½-inch pieces) diced

carrot
½ cup quinoa, rinsed
2 teaspoons kosher salt
1 teaspoon ground coriander
½ teaspoon paprika
½ teaspoon ground cumin
1 (32-ounce / 907-g) container vegetable broth
4 tablespoons finely chopped fresh cilantro, divided

Sauté the vegetables. Select Sauté, and pour in the oil. Once hot, add the onion, and cook until the onion is translucent, about 5 minutes. Add the tomatoes, bell pepper, broccoli, zucchini, corn, and carrot, and mix well. Add the quinoa, salt, coriander, paprika, cumin, and broth. Add 2 tablespoons of cilantro, and mix thoroughly. Pressure cook the quinoa. Lock the lid into place. Select Pressure Cook or Manual, and adjust the pressure to High and the time to 8 minutes. Make sure the steam release knob is in the sealed position. After cooking, naturally release the pressure. Unlock and remove the lid. Stir in the remaining 2 tablespoons of cilantro, and serve hot.

Leek and Potato Soup

Prep time: 10 minutes | Cook time: 3 hours | Serves 8 to 10

4 tablespoons (½ stick) unsalted butter
4 leeks, finely chopped, using the white and a bit of the tender green parts
4 large russet potatoes, peeled and cut into 1-inch chunks

3 cups chicken broth
Salt and freshly ground black pepper, to taste
1 cup heavy cream
½ cup snipped fresh chives, for garnish

Turn the Instant Pot on high, add the butter to the insert, and cover until the butter is melted. Add the leeks and toss with the butter. Add the potatoes and broth. Cover the Instant Pot and press the Slow Cook button, and cook on high for 3 hours or on low for 5 to 6 hours, until the potatoes are tender. (Press Slow Cook again to toggle between Low and High cooking temperatures.) Purée the soup with an immersion blender, or mash with a potato masher. Season with salt and pepper. Stir in the cream and turn off the Instant Pot. Cool the soup, then refrigerate until chilled. Serve the soup in chilled bowls and garnish with the chives.

Creole Pancetta and Cheese Balls

Prep time: 5 minutes | Cook time: 5 minutes | Serves 6

1 cup water
6 eggs
4 slices pancetta, chopped
⅓ cup grated Cheddar cheese
¼ cup cream cheese

¼ cup mayonnaise
1 teaspoon Creole seasonings
Sea salt and ground black pepper, to taste

Pour the water into the Instant Pot and insert a steamer basket. Place the eggs in the basket. Lock the lid. Select the Manual mode and set the cooking time for 5 minutes at Low Pressure. When the timer beeps, perform a quick pressure release. Carefully remove the lid. Allow the eggs to cool for 10 to 15 minutes. Peel the eggs and chop them, then transfer to a bowl. Add the remaining ingredients and stir to combine well. Shape the mixture into balls with your hands. Serve chilled.

Chinese Spare Ribs

Prep time: 3 minutes | Cook time: 24 minutes | Serves 6

1½ pounds (680 g) spare ribs
Salt and ground black pepper, to taste
2 tablespoons sesame oil
½ cup chopped green onions
½ cup chicken stock
2 tomatoes, crushed
2 tablespoons sherry

1 tablespoon coconut aminos
1 teaspoon ginger-garlic paste
½ teaspoon crushed red pepper flakes
½ teaspoon dried parsley
2 tablespoons sesame seeds, for serving

Season the spare ribs with salt and black pepper to taste. Set your Instant Pot to Sauté and heat the sesame oil. Add the seasoned spare ribs and sear each side for about 3 minutes. Add the remaining ingredients except the sesame seeds to the Instant Pot and stir well. Secure the lid. Select the Meat/Stew mode and set the cooking time for 18 minutes at High Pressure. When the timer beeps, perform a natural pressure release for 10 minutes, then release any remaining pressure. Carefully remove the lid. Serve topped with the sesame seeds.

Herbed Shrimp

Prep time: 5 minutes | Cook time: 5 minutes | Serves 4

2 tablespoons olive oil
¾ pound (340 g) shrimp, peeled and deveined
1 teaspoon paprika
1 teaspoon garlic powder
1 teaspoon onion powder
1 teaspoon dried parsley flakes
½ teaspoon dried oregano

½ teaspoon dried thyme
½ teaspoon dried basil
½ teaspoon dried rosemary
¼ teaspoon red pepper flakes
Coarse sea salt and ground black pepper, to taste
1 cup chicken broth

Set your Instant Pot to Sauté and heat the olive oil. Add the shrimp and sauté for 2 to 3 minutes. Add the remaining ingredients to the Instant Pot and stir to combine. Secure the lid. Select the Manual mode and set the cooking time for 2 minutes at Low Pressure. When the timer beeps, perform a quick pressure release. Carefully remove the lid. Transfer the shrimp to a plate and serve.

Cayenne Beef Bites

Prep time: 5 minutes | Cook time: 23 minutes | Serves 6

2 tablespoons olive oil
1 pound (454 g) beef steak, cut into cubes
1 cup beef bone broth
¼ cup dry white wine

1 teaspoon cayenne pepper
½ teaspoon dried marjoram
Sea salt and ground black pepper, to taste

Set your Instant Pot to Sauté and heat the olive oil. Add the beef and sauté for 2 to 3 minutes, stirring occasionally. Add the remaining ingredients to the Instant Pot and combine well. Lock the lid. Select the Manual mode and set the cooking time for 20 minutes at High Pressure. When the timer beeps, perform a natural pressure release for 10 minutes, then release any remaining pressure. Carefully remove the lid. Remove the beef from the Instant Pot to a platter and serve warm.

Bok Choy Salad Boats with Shrimp

Prep time: 8 minutes | Cook time: 2 minutes | Serves 8

26 shrimp, cleaned and deveined
2 tablespoons fresh lemon juice
1 cup water
Sea salt and ground black pepper, to taste
4 ounces (113 g) feta cheese, crumbled
2 tomatoes, diced

⅓ cup olives, pitted and sliced
4 tablespoons olive oil
2 tablespoons apple cider vinegar
8 Bok choy leaves
2 tablespoons fresh basil leaves, snipped
2 tablespoons chopped fresh mint leaves

Toss the shrimp and lemon juice in the Instant Pot until well coated. Pour in the water. Lock the lid. Select the Manual mode and set the cooking time for 2 minutes at Low Pressure. When the timer beeps, perform a quick pressure release. Carefully remove the lid. Season the shrimp with salt and pepper to taste, then let them cool completely. Toss the shrimp with the feta cheese, tomatoes, olives, olive oil, and vinegar until well incorporated. Divide the salad evenly onto each Bok choy leaf and place them on a serving plate. Scatter the basil and mint leaves on top and serve immediately.

Sesame Mushrooms

Prep time: 2 minutes | Cook time: 10 minutes | Serves 6

3 tablespoons sesame oil
¾ pound (340 g) small button mushrooms
1 teaspoon minced garlic

½ teaspoon smoked paprika
½ teaspoon cayenne pepper
Salt and ground black pepper, to taste

Set your Instant Pot to Sauté and heat the sesame oil. Add the mushrooms and sauté for 4 minutes until just tender, stirring occasionally. Add the remaining ingredients to the Instant Pot and stir to mix well. Lock the lid. Select the Manual mode and set the cooking time for 5 minutes at High Pressure. When the timer beeps, perform a quick pressure release. Carefully remove the lid. Serve warm.

Cheese Stuffed Bell Peppers

Prep time: 10 minutes | Cook time: 5 minutes | Serves 5

1 cup water
10 baby bell peppers, seeded and sliced lengthwise
4 ounces (113 g) Monterey Jack cheese, shredded
4 ounces (113 g) cream cheese

2 tablespoons chopped scallions
1 tablespoon olive oil
1 teaspoon minced garlic
½ teaspoon cayenne pepper
¼ teaspoon ground black pepper, or more to taste

Pour the water into the Instant Pot and insert a steamer basket. Stir together the remaining ingredients except the bell peppers in a mixing bowl until combined. Stuff the peppers evenly with the mixture. Arrange the stuffed peppers in the basket. Lock the lid. Select the Manual mode and set the cooking time for 5 minutes at High Pressure. When the timer beeps, perform a quick pressure release. Carefully remove the lid. Cool for 5 minutes and serve.

Fast Spring Kale Appetizer

Prep time: 5 minutes | Cook time: 2 minutes | Serves 6

3 teaspoons butter
1 cup chopped spring onions
1 pound (454 g) kale, torn into pieces
1 cup water

½ teaspoon cayenne pepper
Himalayan salt and ground black pepper, to taste
½ cup shredded Colby cheese, for serving

Set your Instant Pot to Sauté and melt the butter. Add the spring onions and sauté for 1 minute until wilted. Add the remaining ingredients except the cheese to the Instant Pot and mix well. Lock the lid. Select the Manual mode and set the cooking time for 1 minute at High Pressure. When the timer beeps, perform a quick pressure release. Carefully remove the lid. Transfer the kale mixture to a bowl and serve topped with the cheese.

Cauliflower and Broccoli Salad

Prep time: 5 minutes | Cook time: 10 minutes | Serves 4

2 tablespoons coconut oil
2 cups boneless, skinless chicken breasts, cubed
1 cup water
2 eggs, hard-boiled and sliced
1 avocado, mashed
¼ cup green thinly sliced onions
½ teaspoon dried sage

½ teaspoon ground nutmeg
½ teaspoon ground turmeric
½ teaspoon freshly ground black pepper
1 cup chopped cauliflower
1 cup chopped broccoli
2 tablespoons extra-virgin olive oil

Set your Instant Pot to Sauté and melt the coconut oil. Add the chicken and water and mix well. Secure the lid. Select the Manual mode and set the cooking time for 10 minutes at High Pressure. Meanwhile, stir together the egg slices, avocado, green onions, sage, nutmeg, turmeric, and black pepper in a large salad bowl well incorporated. Set aside. Once cooking is complete, do a quick pressure release. Carefully open the lid. Add the cauliflower and broccoli to the Instant Pot, cover, and let sit for 2 minutes. Drain out any excess liquid from the chicken and vegetable mixture. Allow them to cool to room temperature. When cooled, transfer them to the salad bowl and drizzle with the olive oil. Toss well and serve immediately.

Lemon-Cheese Cauliflower Bites

Prep time: 5 minutes | Cook time: 8 minutes | Serves 6

1 pound (454 g) cauliflower, broken into florets
Sea salt and ground black pepper, to taste
2 tablespoons extra-virgin olive

oil
2 tablespoons lemon juice
1 cup grated Cheddar cheese
1 cup water

Pour the water into the Instant Pot and insert a steamer basket. Place the cauliflower florets in the basket. Lock the lid. Select the Manual mode and set the cooking time for 3 minutes at Low Pressure. When the timer beeps, perform a quick pressure release. Carefully remove the lid. Season the cauliflower with salt and pepper. Drizzle with olive oil and lemon juice. Sprinkle the grated cheese all over the cauliflower. Press the Sauté button to heat the Instant Pot. Allow to cook for about 5 minutes, or until the cheese melts. Serve warm.

Herbed Zucchini Slices

Prep time: 5 minutes | Cook time: 5 minutes | Serves 4

2 tablespoons olive oil
2 garlic cloves, chopped
1 pound (454 g) zucchini, sliced
½ cup water

½ cup sugar-free tomato purée
1 teaspoon dried thyme
½ teaspoon dried rosemary
½ teaspoon dried oregano

Set your Instant Pot to Sauté and heat the olive oil. Add the garlic and sauté for 2 minutes until fragrant. Add the remaining ingredients to the Instant Pot and stir well. Lock the lid. Select the Manual mode and set the cooking time for 3 minutes at Low Pressure. When the timer beeps, perform a quick pressure release. Carefully remove the lid. Serve warm.

Stuffed Jalapeños with Bacon

Prep time: 10 minutes | Cook time: 6 minutes | Serves 2

1 ounce (28 g) bacon, chopped, fried
2 ounces (57 g) Cheddar cheese, shredded
1 tablespoon coconut cream

1 teaspoon chopped green onions
2 jalapeños, trimmed and seeded

Mix together the chopped bacon, cheese, coconut cream, and green onions in a mixing bowl and stir until well incorporated. Stuff the jalapeños evenly with the bacon mixture. Press the Sauté button to heat your Instant Pot. Place the stuffed jalapeños in the Instant Pot and cook each side for 3 minutes until softened. Transfer to a paper towel-lined plate and serve.

Creamy Keto Beans

Prep time: 5 minutes | Cook time: 2 minutes | Serves 4

11 ounces (312 g) green beans
1 cup coconut cream

2 teaspoons butter

Combine all the ingredients in the Instant Pot. Secure the lid. Select the Manual mode and set the cooking time for 2 minutes at High Pressure. Once cooking is complete, do a quick pressure release. Carefully open the lid. Serve warm.

Mayo Chicken Celery

Prep time: 15 minutes | Cook time: 15 minutes | Serves 4

14 ounces (397 g) chicken breast, skinless, boneless
1 cup water
4 celery stalks
1 teaspoon salt
½ teaspoon onion powder
1 teaspoon mayonnaise

Combine all the ingredients except the mayo in the Instant Pot. Secure the lid. Select the Manual mode and set the cooking time for 15 minutes at High Pressure. Once cooking is complete, do a natural pressure release for 6 minutes, then release any remaining pressure. Carefully open the lid. Remove the chicken and shred with two forks, then return to the Instant Pot. Add the mayo and stir well. Serve immediately.

Parmesan Chicken Balls with Chives

Prep time: 10 minutes | Cook time: 15 minutes | Serves 4

1 teaspoon coconut oil, softened
1 cup ground chicken
¼ cup chicken broth
1 tablespoon chopped chives
1 teaspoon cayenne pepper
3 ounces (85 g) Parmesan cheese, grated

Set your Instant Pot to Sauté and heat the coconut oil. Add the remaining ingredients except the cheese to the Instant Pot and stir to mix well. Secure the lid. Select the Manual mode and set the cooking time for 15 minutes at High Pressure. Once cooking is complete, do a quick pressure release. Carefully open the lid. Add the grated cheese and stir until combined. Form the balls from the cooked chicken mixture and allow to cool for 10 minutes, then serve.

Chicken and Cabbage Salad

Prep time: 15 minutes | Cook time: 10 minutes | Serves 4

12 ounces (340 g) chicken fillet, chopped
1 teaspoon Cajun seasoning
1 tablespoon coconut oil
1 cup chopped Chinese cabbage
1 tablespoon avocado oil
1 teaspoon sesame seeds

Sprinkle the chopped chicken with the Cajun seasoning. Set your Instant Pot to Sauté and heat the coconut oil. Add the chicken and cook for 10 minutes, stirring occasionally. When the chicken is cooked, transfer to a salad bowl. Add the cabbage, avocado oil, and sesame seeds and gently toss to combine. Serve immediately.

Cauliflower Fritters with Cheese

Prep time: 10 minutes | Cook time: 8 minutes | Serves 4

1 cup cauliflower, boiled
2 eggs, beaten
2 tablespoons almond flour
2 ounces (57 g) Cheddar
cheese, shredded
½ teaspoon garlic powder
1 tablespoon avocado oil

In a medium bowl, mash the cauliflower. Add the beaten eggs, flour, cheese, and garlic powder and stir until well incorporated. Make the fritters from the cauliflower mixture. Set your Instant Pot to Sauté and heat the avocado oil. Add the fritters to the hot oil and cook each side for 3 minutes until golden brown. Serve hot.

Creamy Spinach

Prep time: 5 minutes | Cook time: 4 minutes | Serves 4

2 cups chopped spinach
2 ounces (57 g) Monterey Jack cheese, shredded
1 cup almond milk
1 tablespoon butter
1 teaspoon minced garlic
½ teaspoon salt

Combine all the ingredients in the Instant Pot. Secure the lid. Select the Manual mode and set the cooking time for 4 minutes at High Pressure. Once cooking is complete, do a quick pressure release. Carefully open the lid. Give the mixture a good stir and serve warm.

Lemon-Butter Mushrooms

Prep time: 10 minutes | Cook time: 4 minutes | Serves 2

1 cup cremini mushrooms, sliced
½ cup water
1 tablespoon lemon juice
1 teaspoon almond butter
1 teaspoon grated lemon zest
½ teaspoon salt
½ teaspoon dried thyme

Combine all the ingredients in the Instant Pot. Secure the lid. Select the Manual mode and set the cooking time for 4 minutes at High Pressure. Once cooking is complete, do a natural pressure release for 5 minutes, then release any remaining pressure. Carefully open the lid. Serve warm.

Chili Broccoli Sprouts

Prep time: 5 minutes | Cook time: 10 minutes | Serves 4

1 cup water
1 pound (454 g) broccoli sprouts
1 teaspoon sesame oil
1 teaspoon coconut aminos
1 teaspoon minced garlic
½ teaspoon chopped chili pepper
½ teaspoon salt

Pour the water into the Instant Pot. Lock the lid and bring the water to a boil on Sauté mode for about 10 minutes. Open the lid and add the broccoli sprouts to the Instant Pot. Let sit in the hot water for 1 minute, then transfer to a bowl. Whisk together the remaining ingredients in a separate bowl until combined. Pour the mixture over the broccoli sprouts and gently toss to combine. Serve immediately.

Lemon Brussels Sprouts

Prep time: 5 minutes | Cook time: 5 minutes | Serves 4

2 tablespoons extra-virgin olive oil
1 pound (454 g) Brussels sprouts, outer leaves removed, and washed
1 lemon, juiced
½ teaspoon fresh paprika
½ teaspoon kosher salt
½ teaspoon black ground pepper
1 cup bone broth

Set your Instant Pot to Sauté and heat the olive oil. Add the remaining ingredients except the bone broth to the Instant Pot and cook for 1 minute. Pour in the broth. Secure the lid. Select the Manual mode and set the cooking time for 3 minutes at Low Pressure. Once cooking is complete, do a quick pressure release. Carefully open the lid. Remove the Brussels sprouts from the Instant Pot to a plate and serve.

Italian-Style Kale
Prep time: 5 minutes | Cook time: 3 minutes | Serves 3

10 ounces (283 g) Italian dark-leaf kale, chopped roughly
1 tablespoon Italian
seasonings
1 cup water

Place the kale in a steamer basket and sprinkle with the Italian seasonings. Stir well. Pour the water into the Instant Pot and insert the steamer basket. Secure the lid. Select the Steam mode and set the cooking time for 3 minutes at High Pressure. Once cooking is complete, do a quick pressure release. Carefully open the lid. Serve warm.

Sesame Bok Choy
Prep time: 5 minutes | Cook time: 3 minutes | Serves 2

1 cup water
2 cups bok choy, sliced
1 tablespoon apple cider vinegar
1 teaspoon sesame oil
1 teaspoon sesame seeds
¾ teaspoon salt

Pour the water into the Instant Pot and insert a steamer basket. Place the bok choy in the basket. Secure the lid. Select the Steam mode and set the cooking time for 3 minutes at High Pressure. Once cooking is complete, do a quick pressure release. Carefully open the lid. Transfer the bok choy to a plate. Sprinkle with the vinegar, oil, sesame seeds, and salt and gently toss to combine. Serve immediately.

Butter Purple Petals
Prep time: 10 minutes | Cook time: 5 minutes | Serves 2

7 ounces (198 g) purple cabbage, cut into petals
¼ teaspoon salt
½ cup chicken broth
1 teaspoon butter

Season the cabbage with salt, then place in the Instant Pot. Stir in the broth and butter. Secure the lid. Select the Steam mode and set the cooking time for 5 minutes at High Pressure. Once cooking is complete, do a quick pressure release. Carefully open the lid. Serve warm.

Paprika Egg Salad
Prep time: 5 minutes | Cook time: 7 minutes | Serves 2

6 eggs
1 cup water
¼ cup mayonnaise
½ teaspoon ground turmeric
½ teaspoon fresh paprika
½ teaspoon kosher salt
½ teaspoon freshly ground black pepper
¼ cup thinly sliced green onions

Beat the eggs in a bowl until frothy. Pour the water into the Instant Pot and insert the trivet. Place the bowl with the eggs on the trivet. Secure the lid. Select the Manual mode and set the cooking time for 7 minutes at High Pressure. Meanwhile, stir together the mayo, turmeric, paprika, salt, and pepper in a small bowl until well combined. When the timer beeps, perform a natural pressure release for 10 minutes, then release any remaining pressure. Carefully open the lid. Remove the eggs and allow to cool for a few minutes. Stir in the mayo mixture and serve topped with the green onions.

Cheesy Zucchini Rings
Prep time: 15 minutes | Cook time: 3 minutes | Serves 2

1 zucchini
2 teaspoon butter, softened
1 cup shredded Cheddar
cheese
2 cup water

Slice the zucchini into rings and remove the center of every ring. Coat a baking pan with the softened butter and place the zucchini rings in a single layer. Fill each ring with the shredded cheese. Pour the water into the Instant Pot and insert the trivet. Place the baking pan with zucchini rings on the trivet. Secure the lid. Select the Manual mode and set the cooking time for 3 minutes at High Pressure. Once cooking is complete, do a quick pressure release. Carefully open the lid. Let the zucchini rings cool for 5 minutes and serve.

Scrambled Eggs Salad with Tomato
Prep time: 10 minutes | Cook time: 5 minutes | Serves 2

1 teaspoon butter
2 eggs
2 tablespoons coconut milk
1 bell pepper, chopped
1 tomato, chopped

Set your Instant Pot to Sauté and melt the butter. Crack the eggs in the butter. Pour in the coconut milk and stir the egg mixture until smooth. Sauté for 2 minutes and then scramble again. Cook the eggs for an additional 2 minutes. Transfer the eggs to a salad bowl. Add the chopped bell pepper and tomato and stir well. Serve immediately.

Salmon Salad with Feta Cheese
Prep time: 10 minutes | Cook time: 4 minutes | Serves 2

6 ounces (170 g) salmon
½ teaspoon salt
1 cup water
1 cup chopped lettuce
1 teaspoon olive oil
2 ounces (57 g) feta cheese, crumbled

Season the salmon with salt and wrap in foil. Pour the water into the Instant Pot and insert the trivet. Place the salmon on the trivet. Secure the lid. Select the Manual mode and set the cooking time for 4 minutes at High Pressure. Meanwhile, toss the lettuce with the olive oil in a salad bowl. When the timer beeps, perform a quick pressure release. Carefully remove the lid. Remove the salmon and chop it roughly, then transfer to the salad bowl. Sprinkle with the feta cheese and gently toss to combine. Serve immediately.

Broccoli Purée
Prep time: 10 minutes | Cook time: 6 minutes | Serves 2

7 ounces (198 g) broccoli, chopped
½ cup heavy cream

Combine the broccoli and heavy cream in the Instant Pot. Secure the lid. Select the Manual mode and set the cooking time for 6 minutes at High Pressure. Once cooking is complete, do a quick pressure release. Carefully open the lid. Transfer the broccoli and ¼ of the cooking liquid to a blender and blend until a smooth purée is achieved. Serve immediately.

Turmeric Shredded Cauliflower

Prep time: 5 minutes | Cook time: 5 minutes | Serves 2

1 teaspoon butter
8 ounces (227 g) cauliflower, shredded

Salt, to taste
½ cup chicken broth
1 teaspoon ground turmeric

Set your Instant Pot to Sauté and melt the butter. Stir in the shredded cauliflower and salt and sauté for 1 minute. Pour in the chicken broth and sprinkle with the turmeric. Secure the lid. Select the Manual mode and set the cooking time for 1 minute at High Pressure. Once cooking is complete, do a quick pressure release. Carefully open the lid. Allow to cool for 5 minutes before serving.

Parsley Fennel Slices

Prep time: 10 minutes | Cook time: 5 minutes | Serves 2

1 cup water
1 fennel bulb, sliced
¾ cup chopped fresh parsley

1 tablespoon olive oil
1 tablespoon coconut aminos
1 teaspoon apple cider vinegar

Pour the water into the Instant Pot and insert a steamer basket. Place the sliced fennel in the basket. Secure the lid. Select the Steam mode and set the cooking time for 5 minutes at High Pressure. Once cooking is complete, do a quick pressure release. Carefully open the lid. Remove the fennel from the Instant Pot to a bowl. Add the remaining ingredients to the bowl and gently toss until combined. Serve immediately.

Celery Stalk Chicken Salad

Prep time: 10 minutes | Cook time: 15 minutes | Serves 2

4 ounces (113 g) chicken fillet
1 cup water
1 teaspoon ground black pepper

7 ounces (198 g) celery stalks, chopped
½ teaspoon salt

Place the chicken, water, and pepper in the Instant Pot. Secure the lid. Select the Manual mode and set the cooking time for 15 minutes at High Pressure. Once cooking is complete, do a natural pressure release for 5 minutes, then release any remaining pressure. Carefully open the lid. Remove the chicken and shred with forks, then transfer to a bowl. Add the celery stalks and salt and toss well, then serve.

Mashed Cauliflower with Cheese

Prep time: 5 minutes | Cook time: 4 minutes | Serves 4

1 cup water
1 head cauliflower, broken into florets
¼ cup heavy whipping cream
2 tablespoons grass-fed butter

Pinch of kosher salt
Pinch of freshly ground black pepper
¼ cup shredded full-fat Cheddar cheese

Add the water and cauliflower to the Instant Pot. Secure the lid. Select the Manual mode and set the cooking time for 4 minutes at High Pressure. Once cooking is complete, do a quick pressure release. Carefully open the lid. Mash the cauliflower with a potato masher. If necessary, strain out the excess liquid. Stir in the whipping cream and butter. Sprinkle with the salt and pepper. Transfer the cauliflower mixture to a bowl and serve sprinkled with the cheese.

Sautéed Kale with Flax Seeds

Prep time: 5 minutes | Cook time: 5 minutes | Serves 2

1 teaspoon butter
1 cup chopped kale, Italian dark-leaf
Salt, to taste

¾ teaspoon ground nutmeg
¼ cup water
1 teaspoon olive oil
1 tablespoon flax seeds

Set your Instant Pot to Sauté and melt the butter. Add the kale and sprinkle with the salt and nutmeg. Pour in the water and stir well. Cook for 4 minutes, stirring occasionally. Transfer the kale onto a plate and scatter the olive oil and flax seeds on top. Serve immediately.

Asparagus and Eggplant Mix

Prep time: 5 minutes | Cook time: 30 minutes | Serves 2

3 ounces (85 g) asparagus, chopped
8 ounces (227 g) eggplant, chopped

1 bell pepper, chopped
1 cup chicken broth
1 teaspoon salt
1 teaspoon ground cumin

Set your Instant Pot to Sauté. Combine all the ingredients in the Instant Pot. Secure the lid and cook for 30 minutes. When done, stir the mixture and serve.

Soft Celery Cubes

Prep time: 6 minutes | Cook time: 15 minutes | Serves 2

1 cup chopped celery root
½ cup coconut milk
1 garlic clove, chopped
1 teaspoon butter

½ teaspoon salt
½ teaspoon ground coriander
¾ teaspoon ground cinnamon

Set your Instant Pot to Sauté. Combine all the ingredients in the Instant Pot. Secure the lid and cook for 15 minutes until you get a soft vegetable texture. Cool for 5 minutes before serving.

Keto Buffalo Chicken Lettuce Wraps

Prep time: 5 minutes | Cook time: 24 minutes | Serves 4

1 tablespoon coconut oil
1 clove garlic, minced
2 stalks celery, thinly sliced
¼ cup diced onions
1 pound (454 g) boneless,
For Serving:
Boston or romaine lettuce leaves
Ranch dressing (optional)

skinless chicken breasts
2 cups chicken broth
1 teaspoon fine sea salt
½ cup hot sauce

Set your Instant Pot to Sauté and melt the coconut oil. Add the garlic, celery, and onions and sauté for 4 minutes, stirring occasionally, or until the onions are softened. Stir in the chicken breasts, broth, and salt. Secure the lid. Select the Manual mode and set the cooking time for 20 minutes at High Pressure. Once cooking is complete, do a quick pressure release. Carefully open the lid. Remove the chicken and shred with two forks. Transfer the shredded chicken to a serving bowl and add ½ cup of the cooking liquid from the Instant Pot. Pour in the hot sauce and stir to combine. To serve, place ½ cup of the Buffalo chicken into a lettuce leaf. Serve topped with the ranch dressing, if desired.

Cream Cremini Mushrooms Stew

Prep time: 8 minutes | Cook time: 25 minutes | Serves 2

2 teaspoons butter
½ cup heavy cream
1 cup sliced cremini

mushrooms
½ teaspoon white pepper
¼ teaspoon turmeric

Set your Instant Pot to Sauté and melt the butter. Add the remaining ingredients to the Instant Pot and stir to combine. Secure the lid and cook for 20 minutes, or until the mushrooms are tender. Serve warm.

Pepperoni Pizza Bites

Prep time: 5 minutes | Cook time: 5 minutes | Serves 4 to 5

2 cups shredded full-fat mozzarella cheese
1 cup grated full-fat Parmesan cheese
1 (14-ounce / 397-g) can sugar-free or low-sugar diced

tomatoes, drained
16 uncured pepperoni slices, cut in half
1 teaspoon dried oregano
1 teaspoon dried basil
1 cup water

Pour the water into the Instant Pot and insert the trivet. Combine the remaining ingredients in a large bowl and stir to incorporate. Spoon the mixture into a greased egg bites mold. Work in batches, if needed. I prefer to stack 2 egg bites molds on top of each other, separated by Mason jar lids. Put the molds on the trivet and loosely cover with aluminum foil. Secure the lid. Select the Manual mode and set the cooking time for 5 minutes at High Pressure. Once cooking is complete, do a natural pressure release for 10 minutes, then release any remaining pressure. Carefully open the lid. Remove the molds and cool for 5 minutes, then serve.

Chinese Flavor Chicken Wings

Prep time: 10 minutes | Cook time: 16 minutes | Serves 6

1 teaspoon Sriracha sauce
2 teaspoons Chinese five-spice powder
¼ cup tamari
¼ cup apple cider vinegar
3 cloves garlic, minced
1 tablespoon light brown sugar
2 tablespoons sesame oil

5 scallions, sliced and separated into whites and greens
3 pounds (1.4 kg) chicken wings, separated at the joint
1 cup water
¼ cup toasted sesame seeds

In a large bowl, combine the Sriracha, Chinese five-spice powder, tamari, apple cider vinegar, garlic, brown sugar, sesame oil, and whites of scallions. Stir to mix well. Transfer 2 tablespoons of the sauce mixture to a small bowl and reserve until ready to use. Add wings to the remaining sauce and toss to coat well. Wrap the bowl in plastic and refrigerate for at least 1 hour or up to overnight. Add the water to the Instant Pot and insert a steamer basket. Place the chicken wings in the single layer in the steamer basket. Lock the lid. Press the Pressure Cook button and set the cook time for 10 minutes on High Pressure. When the timer beeps, let pressure release naturally for 5 minutes, then release any additional pressure and unlock the lid. Using a slotted spoon, transfer the wings to a baking sheet. Brush with 2 tablespoons of reserved sauce. Broil the wings in the oven for 3 minutes on each side to crisp the chicken. Transfer the wings to a serving dish and garnish with sesame seeds and greens of scallions. Serve immediately.

Artichoke With Butter Garlic Sauce

Prep time: 5 minutes | Cook time: 5 minutes | Serves 2

½ cup water
1 artichoke, stem, top, and thorns removed
5 tablespoons salted grass-fed butter

1 teaspoon minced garlic
¼ teaspoon dried oregano
¼ teaspoon dried cilantro
¼ teaspoon fresh lime juice

Pour the water into the Instant Pot and insert the trivet. Place the artichoke on the trivet. Secure the lid. Select the Manual mode and set the cooking time for 5 minutes at High Pressure. Once cooking is complete, do a quick pressure release. Carefully open the lid. Remove the artichoke and set aside. Whisk together the remaining ingredients in a small bowl and microwave for about 30 to 40 seconds until melted. Serve the artichoke with the sauce on the side.

Italian Tomato and Mussel Appetizer

Prep time: 20 minutes | Cook time: 10 minutes | Serves 4

¼ cup olive oil
28 ounces (794 g) canned tomatoes, chopped
2 jalapeño peppers, chopped
½ cup chopped white onion
¼ cup balsamic vinegar
¼ cup veggie stock

2 garlic cloves, minced
2 tablespoons crushed red pepper flakes
2 pounds (907 g) mussels, scrubbed
½ cup chopped basil
Salt, to taste

Press the Sauté button on the Instant Pot and heat the olive oil. Add the tomatoes, jalapeño, onion, vinegar, veggie stock, garlic, and red pepper flakes and stir well. Cook for 5 minutes. Stir in the mussels. Secure the lid. Select the Pressure Cook mode and set the cooking time for 4 minutes at Low Pressure. Once cooking is complete, do a quick pressure release. Carefully open the lid. Sprinkle with the basil and salt and stir well. Divide the mussels among four bowls and serve.

Pepper Hummus

Prep time: 10 minutes | Cook time: 30 minutes | Makes 1½ cups

½ cup dried chickpeas
2 cups water
1 cup jarred roasted red peppers with liquid, chopped and divided
1 tablespoon tahini paste
1 tablespoon lemon juice
1 teaspoon lemon zest

¼ teaspoon ground cumin
2 cloves garlic, minced
¼ teaspoon smoked paprika
⅛ teaspoon cayenne pepper
¼ teaspoon salt
1 teaspoon sesame oil
1 tablespoon olive oil

Add chickpeas and water to the Instant Pot. Drain liquid from the roasted peppers into the pot. Set aside the drained peppers. Lock the lid. Press the Pressure Cook button and set the time to 30 minutes on High Pressure. When the timer beeps, let pressure release naturally for 5 minutes, then release any remaining pressure. Unlock the lid. Drain pot, reserving the liquid in a small bowl. Make the hummus: Transfer the chickpeas into a food processor. Add ¼ cup of chopped red peppers, tahini paste, lemon juice and zest, cumin, garlic, smoked paprika, cayenne pepper, salt, sesame oil, and olive oil. If consistency is too thick, slowly add reserved liquid, 1 tablespoon at a time until it has a loose paste consistency. Transfer the hummus to a serving dish. Garnish with remaining chopped roasted red peppers and serve.

Bacon and Crab Cheese Dip

Prep time: 30 minutes | Cook time: 14 minutes | Serves 8

8 bacon strips, sliced
½ cup coconut cream
1 cup grated Parmesan cheese, divided
2 poblano pepper, chopped
½ cup mayonnaise
2 tablespoons lemon juice
8 ounces (227 g) cream cheese
4 garlic cloves, minced
4 green onions, minced
Salt and black pepper, to taste
12 ounces (340 g) crab meat

Set the Instant Pot on sauté mode. Add the bacon and cook for 8 minutes or until crispy. Transfer onto a plate and pat dry with paper towels. Set aside. In a bowl, mix the coconut cream with half of the Parmesan, poblano peppers, mayo, lemon juice, cream cheese, garlic, green onions, salt, pepper, crab meat and bacon and stir well. Add the mixture to the Instant Pot. Spread the remaining Parmesan on top. Seal the Instant Pot lid and select the Pressure Cook mode. Set the cooking time 14 minutes on High Pressure. Once cooking is complete, perform a quick pressure release. Carefully open the lid. Divide into 8 bowls and serve immediately.

Lettuce-Wrapped Chicken

Prep time: 15 minutes | Cook time: 13 to 15 minutes | Serves 4

6 ounces (170 g) chicken breasts
1 cup water
1 teaspoon sesame oil
½ small onion, finely diced
1 garlic clove, minced
½ teaspoon ginger, minced
Kosher salt and ground black pepper, to taste
1 tablespoon hoisin sauce
½ tablespoon soy sauce
1 tablespoon rice vinegar
½ head butter lettuce, leaves separated

Add the chicken breasts and water to the Instant Pot. Secure the lid. Choose the Pressure Cook mode and set the cooking time for 8 minutes at High pressure. Once cooking is complete, perform a quick pressure release. Carefully open the lid. Shred the chicken with forks. Press the Sauté button and heat the sesame oil. Add and cook the garlic and onion for 3 to 4 minutes or until softened. Add the chicken and cook for 2 to 3 minutes more. Stir in the hoisin sauce, rice vinegar, soy sauce, ginger, salt, and black pepper. Cook for another minute. Spoon the chicken mixture over the lettuce leaves on a large plate, wrap and serve immediately.

Olive and Eggplant Spread

Prep time: 20 minutes | Cook time: 8 minutes | Serves 6

¼ cup olive oil
2 pounds (907 g) eggplant, peeled and cut into medium chunks
4 garlic cloves, minced
½ cup water
Salt and black pepper, to taste
1 tablespoon sesame seed paste
¼ cup lemon juice
1 bunch thyme, chopped
3 olives, pitted and sliced

Set the Instant Pot on Sauté mode. Add the olive oil and heat until shimmering. Add eggplant pieces and Sauté for 5 minutes. Add the garlic, water, salt and pepper, then stir well. Close the lid, set to the Pressure Cook mode and set the cooking time for 3 minutes on High Pressure. Once cooking is complete, perform a quick pressure release. Carefully open the lid. Transfer to a blender, then add sesame seed paste, lemon juice and thyme, pulse to combine well. Transfer to bowls, sprinkle olive slices on top and serve.

Plum Cornmeal Squares

Prep time: 15 minutes | Cook time: 55 minutes | Serves 4

1¼ cup water, divided
1 cup yellow cornmeal
1 cup yogurt
1 egg, beaten
½ cups sour cream
1 teaspoon baking soda
2 tablespoons safflower oil
¼ teaspoon salt
4 tablespoons plum jam

Pour 1 cup of water in the Instant Pot. Set a trivet in the pot. Spritz a baking pan with cooking spray. Combine the cornmeal, yogurt, egg, sour cream, baking soda, ¼ cup of water, safflower oil, and salt in a large bowl. Stir to mix well. Pour the mixture into the prepared baking pan. Spread the plum jam over. Cover with aluminum foil. Lower the pan onto the trivet. Secure the lid. Choose the Pressure Cook mode and set the cooking time for 55 minutes at High pressure. Once cooking is complete, perform a quick pressure release, carefully open the lid. Transfer the corn meal chunk onto a cooling rack and allow to cool for 10 minutes. Slice into squares and serve.

Polenta Herb Squares

Prep time: 1 hour 15 minutes | Cook time: 15 minutes | Serves 4

½ cup cornmeal
½ cup milk
1½ cups water
½ teaspoon kosher salt
½ tablespoon butter
⅓ cup cream cheese
1 tablespoon chives, finely chopped
1 tablespoon cilantro, finely chopped
½ teaspoon basil
½ tablespoon thyme
½ teaspoon rosemary
⅓ cup bread crumbs
1 tablespoon olive oil

Make the polenta: Add the cornmeal, milk, water, and salt to the Instant Pot. Stir to mix well. Press the Sauté button and bring the mixture to a simmer. Secure the lid. Choose the Pressure Cook mode and set the cooking time for 8 minutes at High pressure. Once cooking is complete, perform a quick pressure release. Carefully open the lid. Grease a baking pan with butter. Add the cream cheese and herbs to the polenta. Scoop the polenta into the prepared baking pan and refrigerate for an hour or until firm. Cut into small squares. Spread the breadcrumbs on a large plate, coat the polenta squares with breadcrumbs. Heat the olive oil in a skillet over medium heat. Cook the polenta squares in the skillet for about 3 minutes per side or until golden brown. Serve immediately.

Chorizo Sausage Queso Fundido

Prep time: 15 minutes | Cook time: 6 minutes | Serves 4 to 6

1 pound (454 g) chorizo sausage, chopped
½ cup tomato salsa
1 red onion, chopped
1 cup cream cheese
1 teaspoon Mexican oregano
½ teaspoon cayenne pepper
½ cup water
¼ teaspoon ground black pepper
1 teaspoon coriander
1 cup Cotija cheese

Combine the sausage, tomato salsa, red onion, cream cheese, oregano, cayenne pepper, water, black pepper, and coriander in the Instant Pot. Secure the lid. Choose the Pressure Cook mode and set the cooking time for 6 minutes at High Pressure. Once cooking is complete, perform a natural pressure release for 5 minutes, then release any remaining pressure. Carefully open the lid. Add the Cotija cheese and press the Sauté button. Sauté until heated through. Serve warm.

Roasted Chickpeas and Nuts with Sultanas

Prep time: 10 minutes | Cook time: 11 minutes | Serves 2 to 4

2 tablespoons pecans halves
¼ cup canned chickpeas
2 tablespoons almonds
1 tablespoon pumpkin seeds
1 tablespoon sunflower seeds
¼ teaspoon grated nutmeg
¼ teaspoon ground ginger
2 tablespoons maple syrup
1 tablespoon butter
¼ teaspoon kosher salt
¼ cup Sultanas

Place all ingredients, except for the Sultanas, in the Instant Pot. Stir to combine well. Press the Sauté button and sauté for 1 minute until the butter melts and the nuts are well coated. Secure the lid. Choose the Pressure Cook mode and set the cooking time for 10 minutes at High pressure. Once cooking is complete, perform a quick pressure release. Carefully open the lid. Transfer them on a baking pan and bake in the preheated oven at 375ºF (190ºC) for about 8 minutes. Remove the pan from the oven. Add the Sultanas and stir to combine. Serve immediately.

Dill Deviled Eggs with Potato Chips

Prep time: 15 minutes | Cook time: 4 minutes | Makes 12 deviled eggs

1 cup water
6 large eggs
1 teaspoon finely diced dill pickles
½ teaspoon dill pickle juice
1 teaspoon yellow mustard
3 tablespoons mayonnaise
⅛ teaspoon smoked paprika
⅛ teaspoon salt
⅛ teaspoon ground black pepper
½ cup crushed dill pickle flavored potato chips

Add water to the Instant Pot and insert a steamer basket. Place the eggs in the basket. Lock the lid. Press the Pressure Cook button and set the cook time for 4 minutes on High Pressure. When timer beeps, quick release pressure, and then unlock the lid. Transfer the eggs in a large bowl of ice water. Peel the eggs under the water. Slice each egg in half lengthwise and place yolks in a small bowl. Place egg white halves on a serving tray. Add the diced pickles, pickle juice, mustard, mayonnaise, smoked paprika, salt, and pepper to the small bowl with yolks. Stir until smooth. Spoon the yolk mixture into egg white halves. Sprinkle with crushed chips. Serve immediately.

Hungarian Cornmeal Squares

Prep time: 15 minutes | Cook time: 55 minutes | Serves 4

1¼ cup water, divided
1 cup yellow cornmeal
1 cup yogurt
1 egg, beaten
½ cups sour cream
1 teaspoon baking soda
2 tablespoons safflower oil
¼ teaspoon salt
4 tablespoons plum jam

Pour 1 cup of water in the Instant Pot. Set a trivet in the pot. Spritz a baking pan with cooking spray. Combine the cornmeal, yogurt, egg, sour cream, baking soda, ¼ cup of water, safflower oil, and salt in a large bowl. Stir to mix well. Pour the mixture into the prepared baking pan. Spread the plum jam over. Cover with aluminum foil. Lower the pan onto the trivet. Secure the lid. Choose the Manual mode and set the cooking time for 55 minutes at High pressure. Once cooking is complete, perform a quick pressure release, carefully open the lid. Transfer the corn meal chunk onto a cooling rack and allow to cool for 10 minutes. Slice into squares and serve.

Grape Jelly Smokies

Prep time: 10 minutes | Cook time: 2 minutes | Serves 4

3 ounces (85 g) little smokies
2 ounces (57 g) grape jelly
¼ teaspoon jalapeño, minced
¼ cup light beer
¼ cup chili sauce
1 tablespoon white vinegar
½ cup roasted vegetable broth
2 tablespoons brown sugar

Place all ingredients in the Instant Pot. Stir to mix. Secure the lid. Choose the Pressure Cook mode and set the cooking time for 2 minutes at High pressure. Once cooking is complete, perform a quick pressure release. Carefully open the lid. Serve hot.

Mushroom and Onion Stuffed Tomatoes

Prep time: 20 minutes | Cook time: 10 minutes | Serves 4

4 tomatoes
1 tablespoon ghee
2 tablespoons celery, chopped
1 yellow onion, chopped
½ cup mushrooms, chopped
1 tablespoon parsley, chopped
1 cup cottage cheese
Salt and black pepper, to taste
¼ teaspoon caraway seeds
½ cup water

On a clean work surface, remove the tops of each tomato about 1 inch, then scoop the tomato pulp out and reserve in a small bowl. Set aside. Set the Instant Pot on Sauté mode. Add the ghee and heat until melted. Add the celery and onion. Sauté for 3 minutes or until softened. Add the mushrooms, tomato pulp, parsley, cheese, salt, pepper, and caraway seeds, then stir well. Sauté for 3 minutes more. Stuff the hollowed tomatoes with the mixture. Pour the water in the Instant Pot, then arrange the steamer basket in the pot. Place the stuffed tomatoes inside. Seal the Instant Pot lid and set to the Pressure Cook mode. Set the cooking time for 4 minutes on High Pressure. Once cooking is complete, perform a quick pressure release. Carefully open the lid. Arrange the stuffed tomatoes on a platter and serve immediately.

Pork Sausage Stuffed Mushrooms

Prep time: 10 minutes | Cook time: 7 minutes | Makes 10 mushrooms

1 tablespoon olive oil
4 ounces (113 g) ground pork sausage
1 tablespoon diced yellow onion
1 tablespoon horseradish
1 tablespoon bread crumbs
1 teaspoon yellow mustard
2 tablespoons cream cheese,
at room temperature
¼ teaspoon garlic salt
1 cup water
8 ounces (227 g) whole baby bella mushrooms, stem removed
2 tablespoons chopped fresh Italian flat-leaf parsley

Press the Sauté button on the Instant Pot and heat the olive oil until shimmering. Add the sausage and onion to the pot. Sauté for 5 minutes until the sausage is lightly browned. Transfer the sausage and onion to a small bowl and use paper towels to pat dry. Add the horseradish, bread crumbs, yellow mustard, cream cheese, and garlic salt. Pour the water into the Instant Pot. Stuff the sausage mixture into each mushroom cap and place in a steamer basket. Insert the steamer basket in the pot and lock the lid. Press the Pressure Cook button and set the cook time for 2 minutes on Low Pressure. When timer beeps, quick release the pressure. Unlock lid. Transfer the stuffed mushrooms to a serving dish. Garnish with chopped parsley. Serve warm.

Short Ribs with Port Wine
Prep time: 20 minutes | Cook time: 1 hour 45 minutes | Serves 4

½ tablespoon lard
1 pound (454 g) short ribs
¼ cup port wine
1 tablespoon rice vinegar
1 tablespoon molasses
1 thyme sprig

1 rosemary sprig
1 garlic clove
½ cup beef bone broth
½ teaspoon cayenne pepper
Sea salt and ground black
pepper, to season

Press the Sauté button and melt the lard in the Instant Pot. Add the short ribs and cook for 4 to 5 minutes, flipping periodically to ensure even cooking. Add the remaining ingredients and stir to mix well. Secure the lid. Choose the Pressure Cook mode and set the cooking time for 90 minutes at High pressure. Once cooking is complete, perform a natural pressure release for 30 minutes, then release any remaining pressure. Carefully open the lid. Transfer the short ribs into the broiler and broil for 10 minutes or until crispy. Transfer the ribs to a platter and serve immediately.

Broiled Baby Carrots with Raisins
Prep time: 10 minutes | Cook time: 2 minutes | Serves 4

½ pound (227 g) baby carrots, trimmed and scrubbed
1 tablespoon raisins
¼ cup orange juice
1 tablespoon red wine vinegar
½ tablespoon soy sauce
½ teaspoon mustard powder
¼ teaspoon cumin seeds

½ teaspoon shallot powder
½ teaspoon garlic powder
1 teaspoon butter, at room temperature
½ cup water
1 tablespoon sesame seeds, toasted

Place all ingredients, except for the sesame seeds, in the Instant Pot. Stir to mix well. Secure the lid. Choose the Pressure Cook mode and set the cooking time for 2 minutes at High pressure. Once cooking is complete, perform a quick pressure release. Carefully open the lid. Transfer them into a large bowl, sprinkle the sesame seeds over and serve.

Shrimp and Bok Choy Salad Boats
Prep time: 8 minutes | Cook time: 2 minutes | Serves 8

26 shrimp, cleaned and deveined
2 tablespoons fresh lemon juice
1 cup water
Sea salt and ground black pepper, to taste
4 ounces (113 g) feta cheese, crumbled
2 tomatoes, diced

⅓ cup olives, pitted and sliced
4 tablespoons olive oil
2 tablespoons apple cider vinegar
8 Bok choy leaves
2 tablespoons fresh basil leaves, snipped
2 tablespoons chopped fresh mint leaves

Toss the shrimp and lemon juice in the Instant Pot until well coated. Pour in the water. Lock the lid. Select the Pressure Cook mode and set the cooking time for 2 minutes at Low Pressure. When the timer beeps, perform a quick pressure release. Carefully remove the lid. Season the shrimp with salt and pepper to taste, then let them cool completely. Toss the shrimp with the feta cheese, tomatoes, olives, olive oil, and vinegar until well incorporated. Divide the salad evenly onto each Bok choy leaf and place them on a serving plate. Scatter the basil and mint leaves on top and serve immediately.

Cinnamon Popcorn Kernels
Prep time: 5 minutes | Cook time: 1 minute | Serves 2

1 tablespoon coconut oil
¼ cup popcorn kernels
½ tablespoon ground

cinnamon
3 tablespoons icing sugar

Press the Sauté button and melt the coconut oil in the Instant Pot. Stir in the popcorn kernels and stir to cover. Cook for about a minute or until the popping slows down. Transfer the popped corn to a large bowl and toss with cinnamon and icing sugar to coat well. Serve immediately.

Prosciutto Wrapped Asparagus Spears
Prep time: 10 minutes | Cook time: 4 minutes | Serves 4

8 asparagus spears
8 ounces (227 g) prosciutto slices

2 cups water
Salt, to taste

Wrap the asparagus spears into prosciutto slices and arrange them on a cutting board. Pour the water to the Instant Pot and sprinkle with a pinch of salt. Set a steamer basket in the Instant Pot and place the asparagus inside. Seal the Instant Pot lid and set to the Pressure Cook mode. Set the cooking time for 4 minutes on High Pressure. Once cooking is complete, perform a quick pressure release. Carefully open the lid. Arrange the asparagus on a platter and serve.

Turkey Meatballs with Garlic and Pesto
Prep time: 10 minutes | Cook time: 4 to 5 hours | Serves 12 to 14

4 cups lightly packed fresh basil leaves
4 garlic cloves, minced
⅓ cup extra-virgin olive oil
2 ounces (57 g) Parmesan cheese, grated (1 cup)
1⅓ cups panko bread crumbs

2 large egg yolks
Salt and pepper, to taste
2 pounds (907 g) ground turkey
1 (28-ounce / 794-g) can crushed tomatoes
Vegetable oil spray

Preheat the oven to 475ºF (245ºC). Set a wire rack in aluminum foil-lined rimmed baking sheet and coat with vegetable oil spray. Set aside. Process basil and garlic in a food processor until finely ground, about 30 seconds, scraping down sides of bowl as needed. With processor running, slowly add oil and process until smooth, about 30 seconds. Measure out and reserve 2 tablespoons of pesto for serving. Transfer remaining pesto to a large bowl. Stir Parmesan, panko, egg yolks, ½ teaspoon salt, and ¼ teaspoon pepper into remaining pesto. Add ground turkey and knead with hands until well combined. Pinch off and roll turkey mixture into tablespoon-size meatballs (about 60 meatballs) and arrange on the prepared rack. Bake in the preheated oven until no longer pink, about 10 minutes. Transfer meatballs to Instant Pot. Gently stir tomatoes and ½ teaspoon salt into the Instant Pot, cover, and press the Slow Cook button, and cook on low for 4 to 5 hours or until meatballs are tender. (Press Slow Cook again to toggle between Low and High cooking temperatures.) Using a large spoon, skim excess fat from surface of sauce. Stir reserved pesto into meatballs and season with salt and pepper to taste. Serve. (Meatballs can be held on warm or low setting for up to 2 hours. Adjust sauce consistency with hot water as needed, adding 2 tablespoons at a time.)

Blue Cheese Shrimp Cocktail Sticks

Prep time: 10 minutes | Cook time: 1 minute | Serves 6

1 pound (454 g) shrimp, shelled and deveined
¼ cup rice wine vinegar
¾ cup water
4 ounces (113 g) blue cheese, cubed
1 celery stalk, diced
½ cup olives, pitted
2 bell peppers, sliced
1 cup cherry tomatoes
1 tablespoon olive oil
½ teaspoon cayenne pepper
Sea salt and ground black pepper, to taste
½ teaspoon paprika

Special Equipment:
6 cocktail sticks

Place the shrimp, rice wine vinegar, and water in the Instant Pot. Secure the lid. Choose the Pressure Cook mode and set the cooking time for 1 minute at Low Pressure. Once cooking is complete, perform a quick pressure release. Carefully open the lid. Thread the shrimp, blue cheese, celery, olives, peppers, and cherry tomatoes onto the cocktail sticks. Drizzle olive oil over and sprinkle with cayenne pepper, salt, black pepper, and paprika. Arrange the skewers on a serving platter and serve.

Herbed Polenta Squares

Prep time: 1 hour 15 minutes | Cook time: 15 minutes | Serves 4

½ cup cornmeal
½ cup milk
1½ cups water
½ teaspoon kosher salt
½ tablespoon butter
⅓ cup cream cheese
1 tablespoon chives, finely chopped
1 tablespoon cilantro, finely chopped
½ teaspoon basil
½ tablespoon thyme
½ teaspoon rosemary
⅓ cup bread crumbs
1 tablespoon olive oil

Make the polenta: Add the cornmeal, milk, water, and salt to the Instant Pot. Stir to mix well. Press the Sauté button and bring the mixture to a simmer. Secure the lid. Choose the Manual mode and set the cooking time for 8 minutes at High pressure. Once cooking is complete, perform a quick pressure release. Carefully open the lid. Grease a baking pan with butter. Add the cream cheese and herbs to the polenta. Scoop the polenta into the prepared baking pan and refrigerate for an hour or until firm. Cut into small squares. Spread the breadcrumbs on a large plate, coat the polenta squares with breadcrumbs. Heat the olive oil in a skillet over medium heat. Cook the polenta squares in the skillet for about 3 minutes per side or until golden brown. Serve immediately.

Honey Carrots with Raisins

Prep time: 5 minutes | Cook time: 5 minutes | Serves 3

1 pound (454 g) carrots, peeled and cut into chunks
2 tablespoons golden raisins
½ cup water
½ tablespoon honey
⅔ teaspoon crushed red pepper flakes
½ tablespoon melted butter
Salt, to taste

Add the carrots, raisins, and water to the Instant Pot Secure the lid and select the Manual function. Set the cooking time for 5 minutes on Low Pressure. When the timer beeps, do a quick release, then open the lid. Strain the carrots and transfer them to a large bowl. Put the remaining ingredients into the bowl and toss well. Serve warm.

Herbed Button Mushrooms

Prep time: 10 minutes | Cook time: 4 minutes | Serves 4

6 ounces (170 g) button mushrooms, rinsed and drained
1 clove garlic, minced
½ cup vegetable broth
½ teaspoon dried basil
½ teaspoon onion powder
½ teaspoon dried oregano
⅓ teaspoon dried rosemary
½ teaspoon smoked paprika
Coarse sea salt and ground black pepper, to taste
1 tablespoon tomato paste
1 tablespoon butter

Put all the ingredients, except for the tomato paste and butter, in the Instant Pot. Stir to mix well. Secure the lid. Choose the Manual mode and set the cooking time for 4 minutes at High pressure. Once cooking is complete, perform a quick pressure release. Carefully open the lid. Stir in the tomato paste and butter. Serve immediately.

Jalapeño Peanuts

Prep time: 3 hours 20 minutes | Cook time: 45 minutes | Serves 4

4 ounces (113 g) raw peanuts in the shell
1 jalapeño, sliced
1 tablespoon Creole seasoning
½ tablespoon cayenne pepper
½ tablespoon garlic powder
1 tablespoon salt

Add all ingredients to the Instant Pot. Pour in enough water to cover. Stir to mix well. Use a steamer to gently press down the peanuts. Secure the lid. Choose the Manual mode and set the cooking time for 45 minutes at High pressure. Once cooking is complete, perform a natural pressure release for 15 minutes, then release any remaining pressure. Carefully open the lid. Transfer the peanut and the liquid in a bowl, then refrigerate for 3 hours before serving.

Bean Dip with Butter

Prep time: 5 minutes | Cook time: 0 minutes | Makes 2½ cups

1 cup dried cannellini beans, soaked and drained
¾ cup vegetable stock
3 cloves garlic, peeled
1 (1-inch) piece peeled fresh ginger
1 to 2 tablespoons peanut butter, to taste
1½ teaspoons rice vinegar
1 tablespoon mellow white or any other miso
1 tablespoon or more cilantro leaves
1 tablespoon Sucanat or coconut palm sugar; or 1 small pitted date
1 scallion, sliced

Combine the beans, stock, and 1 clove garlic in the Instant Pot. Lock on the lid. Bring to High Pressure; cook for 8 minutes. Let the pressure come down naturally. Carefully open the Instant Pot, tilting the lid away from you. Drain the beans into a colander set over a bowl and set aside the drained beans and their cooking liquid. Add the remaining garlic and the ginger to the food processor and process until finely chopped. Add the beans to the food processor along with the peanut butter, vinegar, miso, and 3 tablespoons of the bean-cooking liquid. Add more bean liquid to reach the desired consistency. Process until slightly chunky. Add the cilantro, sweetener, and scallion and process briefly, until combined. Taste and adjust the seasonings to your liking by adding more vinegar, miso, or sugar. Refrigerate for up to 3 days or freeze for up to 1 month.

Sausage Stuffed Bella Mushrooms

Prep time: 10 minutes | Cook time: 7 minutes | Makes 10 mushrooms

1 tablespoon olive oil
4 ounces (113 g) ground pork sausage
1 tablespoon diced yellow onion
1 tablespoon horseradish
1 tablespoon bread crumbs
1 teaspoon yellow mustard
2 tablespoons cream cheese,

at room temperature
¼ teaspoon garlic salt
1 cup water
8 ounces (227 g) whole baby bella mushrooms, stem removed
2 tablespoons chopped fresh Italian flat-leaf parsley

Press the Sauté button on the Instant Pot and heat the olive oil until shimmering. Add the sausage and onion to the pot. Sauté for 5 minutes until the sausage is lightly browned. Transfer the sausage and onion to a small bowl and use paper towels to pat dry. Add the horseradish, bread crumbs, yellow mustard, cream cheese, and garlic salt. Pour the water into the Instant Pot. Stuff the sausage mixture into each mushroom cap and place in a steamer basket. Insert the steamer basket in the pot and lock the lid. Press the Manual button and set the cook time for 2 minutes on Low Pressure. When timer beeps, quick release the pressure. Unlock lid. Transfer the stuffed mushrooms to a serving dish. Garnish with chopped parsley. Serve warm.

Lentil and Beef Slider Patties

Prep time: 25 minutes | Cook time: 25 minutes | Makes 15 patties

1 cup dried yellow lentils
2 cups beef broth
½ pound (227 g) 80/20 ground beef
½ cup chopped old-fashioned oats

2 large eggs, beaten
2 teaspoons Sriracha sauce
2 tablespoons diced yellow onion
½ teaspoon salt

Add the lentils and broth to the Instant Pot. Lock the lid. Press the Manual button and set the cook time for 15 minutes on High Pressure. When the timer beeps, let pressure release naturally for 10 minutes, then release any remaining pressure. Unlock the lid. Transfer the lentils to a medium bowl with a slotted spoon. Smash most of the lentils with the back of a spoon until chunky. Add beef, oats, eggs, Sriracha, onion, and salt. Whisk to combine them well. Form the mixture into 15 patties. Cook in a skillet on stovetop over medium-high heat in batches for 10 minutes. Flip the patties halfway through. Transfer patties to serving dish and serve warm.

Lemony Potato Cubes

Prep time: 5 minutes | Cook time: 10 minutes | Serves 2

2½ medium potatoes, scrubbed and cubed
1 tablespoon chopped fresh rosemary
½ tablespoon olive oil

Freshly ground black pepper, to taste
1 tablespoon fresh lemon juice
½ cup vegetable broth

Put the potatoes, rosemary, oil, and pepper to the Instant Pot. Stir to mix well. Set to the Sauté mode and sauté for 4 minutes. Fold in the remaining ingredients. Secure the lid and select the Manual function. Set the cooking time for 6 minutes at High Pressure. Once cooking is complete, do a quick release, then open the lid. Serve warm.

Little Smokies with Grape Jelly

Prep time: 10 minutes | Cook time: 2 minutes | Serves 4

3 ounces (85 g) little smokies
2 ounces (57 g) grape jelly
¼ teaspoon jalapeño, minced
¼ cup light beer

¼ cup chili sauce
1 tablespoon white vinegar
½ cup roasted vegetable broth
2 tablespoons brown sugar

Place all ingredients in the Instant Pot. Stir to mix. Secure the lid. Choose the Manual mode and set the cooking time for 2 minutes at High pressure. Once cooking is complete, perform a quick pressure release. Carefully open the lid. Serve hot.

Cajun Shrimp and Asparagus

Prep time: 7 minutes | Cook time: 3 minutes | Serves 4

1 cup water
1 pound (454 g) shrimp, peeled and deveined

1 bunch asparagus, trimmed
½ tablespoon Cajun seasoning
1 teaspoon extra virgin olive oil

Pour the water into the the Instant Pot and insert a steamer basket. Put the shrimp and asparagus in the basket. Sprinkle with the Cajun seasoning and drizzle with the olive oil. Toss a bit. Secure the lid. Select the Manual mode and set the cooking time for 3 minutes at High Pressure. Once cooking is complete, do a quick pressure release. Carefully open the lid. Remove from the basket to a plate and serve.

Mushroom Polenta Rounds

Prep time: 3 minutes | Cook time: 10 minutes | Makes 16 rounds

1 (18 ounce / 510 g) package precooked polenta
Cooking spray, for coating
1 ounce (28 g) dried porcini or dried mixed mushrooms (about 1 cup dry)
Water, to cover
8 ounce (227 g) fresh cremini mushrooms, halved

4 cloves garlic, minced
4 sprigs fresh thyme
⅛ teaspoon sea salt
Freshly ground black pepper, to taste
Truffle salt (optional), for finishing
¼ cup freshly chopped flat-leaf parsley or basil

Preheat the oven to 425ºF (220ºC). Coat a baking sheet with cooking spray. Cut the polenta crosswise into ½-inch (1.25 cm) rounds and place on the baking sheet. Coat the rounds with cooking spray. Bake for 15 minutes, flipping halfway. Meanwhile, to rehydrate the dried mushrooms, add them to the inner pot and cover with 1 inch (2.5cm) of water. Lock the lid and ensure the steam release valve is set to the sealing position. Select Pressure Cook (Low), and set the cook time for 10 minutes. Once the cook time is complete, immediately quick release the pressure. Drain the rehydrated mushrooms through a fine-mesh sieve over a bowl to reserve the cooking liquid—this is an excellent mushroom broth to use later. Roughly chop the mushrooms. Add the cremini mushroom halves and rehydrated mushrooms back into the pot. Add ½ cup mushroom broth. Top with the garlic, thyme, salt, and pepper. Lock the lid and ensure the steam release valve is set to the sealing position. Select Pressure Cook (High), and set the cook time for 3 minutes. Once the cook time is complete, immediately quick release the pressure. Select Sauté (Medium), and reduce the liquid for 2 minutes. Remove the thyme stems. Place the polenta rounds on a serving dish and spoon the mushroom mixture on top. Sprinkle with truffle salt, if using. Garnish with fresh parsley or basil. Enjoy warm.

Mushroom Stuffed Tomatoes

Prep time: 20 minutes | Cook time: 10 minutes | Serves 4

4 tomatoes
1 tablespoon ghee
2 tablespoons celery, chopped
1 yellow onion, chopped
½ cup mushrooms, chopped
1 tablespoon parsley, chopped
1 cup cottage cheese
Salt and black pepper, to taste
¼ teaspoon caraway seeds
½ cup water

On a clean work surface, remove the tops of each tomato about 1 inch, then scoop the tomato pulp out and reserve in a small bowl. Set aside. Set the Instant Pot on Sauté mode. Add the ghee and heat until melted. Add the celery and onion. Sauté for 3 minutes or until softened. Add the mushrooms, tomato pulp, parsley, cheese, salt, pepper, and caraway seeds, then stir well. Sauté for 3 minutes more. Stuff the hollowed tomatoes with the mixture. Pour the water in the Instant Pot, then arrange the steamer basket in the pot. Place the stuffed tomatoes inside. Seal the Instant Pot lid and set to the Manual mode. Set the cooking time for 4 minutes on High Pressure. Once cooking is complete, perform a quick pressure release. Carefully open the lid. Arrange the stuffed tomatoes on a platter and serve immediately.

Port Wined Short Ribs

Prep time: 20 minutes | Cook time: 1 hour 45 minutes | Serves 4

½ tablespoon lard
1 pound (454 g) short ribs
¼ cup port wine
1 tablespoon rice vinegar
1 tablespoon molasses
1 thyme sprig
1 rosemary sprig
1 garlic clove
½ cup beef bone broth
½ teaspoon cayenne pepper
Sea salt and ground black pepper, to season

Press the Sauté button and melt the lard in the Instant Pot. Add the short ribs and cook for 4 to 5 minutes, flipping periodically to ensure even cooking. Add the remaining ingredients and stir to mix well. Secure the lid. Choose the Manual mode and set the cooking time for 90 minutes at High pressure. Once cooking is complete, perform a natural pressure release for 30 minutes, then release any remaining pressure. Carefully open the lid. Transfer the short ribs into the broiler and broil for 10 minutes or until crispy. Transfer the ribs to a platter and serve immediately.

Queso Fundido

Prep time: 15 minutes | Cook time: 6 minutes | Serves 4 to 6

1 pound (454 g) chorizo sausage, chopped
½ cup tomato salsa
1 red onion, chopped
1 cup cream cheese
1 teaspoon Mexican oregano
½ teaspoon cayenne pepper
½ cup water
¼ teaspoon ground black pepper
1 teaspoon coriander
1 cup Cotija cheese

Combine the sausage, tomato salsa, red onion, cream cheese, oregano, cayenne pepper, water, black pepper, and coriander in the Instant Pot. Secure the lid. Choose the Manual mode and set the cooking time for 6 minutes at High Pressure. Once cooking is complete, perform a natural pressure release for 5 minutes, then release any remaining pressure. Carefully open the lid. Add the Cotija cheese and press the Sauté button. Sauté until heated through. Serve warm.

Roasted Nuts, Chickpeas, and Seeds

Prep time: 10 minutes | Cook time: 11 minutes | Serves 2 to 4

2 tablespoons pecans halves
¼ cup canned chickpeas
2 tablespoons almonds
1 tablespoon pumpkin seeds
1 tablespoon sunflower seeds
¼ teaspoon grated nutmeg
¼ teaspoon ground ginger
2 tablespoons maple syrup
1 tablespoon butter
¼ teaspoon kosher salt
¼ cup Sultanas

Place all ingredients, except for the Sultanas, in the Instant Pot. Stir to combine well. Press the Sauté button and sauté for 1 minute until the butter melts and the nuts are well coated. Secure the lid. Choose the Manual mode and set the cooking time for 10 minutes at High pressure. Once cooking is complete, perform a quick pressure release. Carefully open the lid. Transfer them on a baking pan and bake in the preheated oven at 375°F (190°C) for about 8 minutes. Remove the pan from the oven. Add the Sultanas and stir to combine. Serve immediately.

Super Pickles Deviled Eggs

Prep time: 15 minutes | Cook time: 4 minutes | Makes 12 deviled eggs

1 cup water
6 large eggs
1 teaspoon finely diced dill pickles
½ teaspoon dill pickle juice
1 teaspoon yellow mustard
3 tablespoons mayonnaise
⅛ teaspoon smoked paprika
⅛ teaspoon salt
⅛ teaspoon ground black pepper
½ cup crushed dill pickle flavored potato chips

Add water to the Instant Pot and insert a steamer basket. Place the eggs in the basket. Lock the lid. Press the Manual button and set the cook time for 4 minutes on High Pressure. When timer beeps, quick release pressure, and then unlock the lid. Transfer the eggs in a large bowl of ice water. Peel the eggs under the water. Slice each egg in half lengthwise and place yolks in a small bowl. Place egg white halves on a serving tray. Add the diced pickles, pickle juice, mustard, mayonnaise, smoked paprika, salt, and pepper to the small bowl with yolks. Stir until smooth. Spoon the yolk mixture into egg white halves. Sprinkle with crushed chips. Serve immediately.

Simple Broiled Baby Carrots

Prep time: 10 minutes | Cook time: 2 minutes | Serves 4

½ pound (227 g) baby carrots, trimmed and scrubbed
1 tablespoon raisins
¼ cup orange juice
1 tablespoon red wine vinegar
½ tablespoon soy sauce
½ teaspoon mustard powder
¼ teaspoon cumin seeds
½ teaspoon shallot powder
½ teaspoon garlic powder
1 teaspoon butter, at room temperature
½ cup water
1 tablespoon sesame seeds, toasted

Place all ingredients, except for the sesame seeds, in the Instant Pot. Stir to mix well. Secure the lid. Choose the Manual mode and set the cooking time for 2 minutes at High pressure. Once cooking is complete, perform a quick pressure release. Carefully open the lid. Transfer them into a large bowl, sprinkle the sesame seeds over and serve.

Simple Cinnamon Popcorn

Prep time: 5 minutes | Cook time: 1 minute | Serves 2

1 tablespoon coconut oil
¼ cup popcorn kernels
½ tablespoon ground

cinnamon
3 tablespoons icing sugar

Press the Sauté button and melt the coconut oil in the Instant Pot. Stir in the popcorn kernels and stir to cover. Cook for about a minute or until the popping slows down. Transfer the popped corn to a large bowl and toss with cinnamon and icing sugar to coat well. Serve immediately.

Simple Prosciutto Wrapped Asparagus

Prep time: 10 minutes | Cook time: 4 minutes | Serves 4

8 asparagus spears
8 ounces (227 g) prosciutto
slices

2 cups water
Salt, to taste

Wrap the asparagus spears into prosciutto slices and arrange them on a cutting board. Pour the water to the Instant Pot and sprinkle with a pinch of salt. Set a steamer basket in the Instant Pot and place the asparagus inside. Seal the Instant Pot lid and set to the Manual mode. Set the cooking time for 4 minutes on High Pressure. Once cooking is complete, perform a quick pressure release. Carefully open the lid. Arrange the asparagus on a platter and serve.

Shrimp and Blue Cheese on Sticks

Prep time: 10 minutes | Cook time: 1 minute | Serves 6

1 pound (454 g) shrimp,
shelled and deveined
¼ cup rice wine vinegar
¾ cup water
4 ounces (113 g) blue cheese,
cubed
1 celery stalk, diced
½ cup olives, pitted
Special Equipment:
6 cocktail sticks

2 bell peppers, sliced
1 cup cherry tomatoes
1 tablespoon olive oil
½ teaspoon cayenne pepper
Sea salt and ground black
pepper, to taste
½ teaspoon paprika

Place the shrimp, rice wine vinegar, and water in the Instant Pot. Secure the lid. Choose the Manual mode and set the cooking time for 1 minute at Low Pressure. Once cooking is complete, perform a quick pressure release. Carefully open the lid. Thread the shrimp, blue cheese, celery, olives, peppers, and cherry tomatoes onto the cocktail sticks. Drizzle olive oil over and sprinkle with cayenne pepper, salt, black pepper, and paprika. Arrange the skewers on a serving platter and serve.

Turkey and Pork Meatballs in Tomato

Prep time: 15 minutes | Cook time: 8 minutes | Serves 6

½ pound (227 g) ground turkey
½ pound (227 g) ground pork
⅓ cup almond flour
2 eggs
1 cup Romano cheese, grated
¼ cup minced fresh mint, plus
more for garnish
1 teaspoon dried basil

2 garlic cloves, minced
½ teaspoon dried thyme
Sea salt and ground black
pepper, to taste
½ cup puréed tomatoes
½ cup beef bone broth
2 tablespoons scallions

Combine all ingredients, except for tomatoes, broth, and scallions in a large bowl. Shape the mixture into 2-inch meatballs. Set aside. Add the tomatoes, beef bone broth, and scallions to the Instant Pot. Arrange the meatballs in this liquid. Secure the lid. Choose the Manual mode. Set the cooking time for 8 minutes at High Pressure. Once cooking is complete, perform a quick pressure release. Carefully open the lid. Serve immediately.

Simple Spiced Nuts

Prep time: 5 minutes | Cook time: 2 to 3 hours | Serves 10 to 14

1 large egg white
1 tablespoon water
1 teaspoon salt
3 cups whole unblanched
almonds, cashews, pecans, or
walnuts

¼ cup sugar
2 teaspoons ground cinnamon
1 teaspoon ground ginger
1 teaspoon ground coriander
Vegetable oil spray

Lightly coat Instant Pot with vegetable oil spray. Whisk egg white, water, and salt together in a large bowl. Add almonds and toss to coat, then drain thoroughly in a fine-mesh strainer. Combine sugar, cinnamon, ginger, and coriander in a separate large bowl. Add almonds and toss to coat. Transfer almond mixture to prepared Instant Pot, cover, and and press the Slow Cook button, and cook on high for 2 to 3 hours or until almonds are toasted and fragrant, stirring every 30 minutes. (Press Slow Cook again to toggle between Low and High cooking temperatures.) Transfer almond mixture to a rimmed baking sheet and spread into an even layer. Let cool to room temperature, about 20 minutes. Serve immediately. (Almonds can be stored at room temperature for up to 1 week.)

Crostini with Garlic

Prep time: 2 minutes | Cook time: 5 minutes | Serves 6

1 cup water
2 heads garlic
2 teaspoons extra virgin olive
oil, divided
Optional Toppings:
Baby arugula
Fresh basil
Roasted red peppers
Sun dried tomatoes

Sea salt, to taste
1 small loaf crusty bread, such
as ciabatta, cut into 6 slices

Halved cherry tomatoes
Grilled asparagus, eggplant, or
zucchini

Fit the inner pot with the trivet or steam rack and add 1 cup water. Cut about ¼ inch (0.5cm) off the top of the garlic heads. Drizzle with 1 teaspoon oil and sprinkle with a pinch of salt. Place the garlic cut-side up onto the trivet. Lock the lid and ensure the steam release valve is set to the sealing position. Select Pressure Cook (High), and set the cook time for 5 minutes. Once the cook time is complete, allow the pressure to release naturally. Carefully remove the lid. Preheat the broiler. Use tongs to transfer the steamed garlic bulbs to a baking sheet. Place the bread slices on the baking sheet, as well. Drizzle the garlic with the remaining 1 teaspoon oil. Transfer the sheet to the oven and broil until the tops of the garlic have browned and the bread is toasted, watching closely to ensure it doesn't burn. The toast may be done before the garlic. Serve the "roasted" garlic bulbs on a platter with the toast and any additional toppings. To make the crostini, remove the garlic from the skin and spread 1 to 2 cloves of the soft garlic on the crostini. Sprinkle with a pinch of salt and top with any additional toppings. Enjoy warm or at room temperature.

Cabbage and Mushroom Potstickers

Prep time: 15 minutes | Cook time: 3 minutes | Serves 15

2 tablespoons sesame or coconut oil, divided
½ small yellow onion, finely diced
1½ cups finely diced mushrooms
1 cup shredded carrots
2 cups shredded cabbage
2 tablespoons freshly minced ginger
2 cloves garlic, minced

¼ cup chopped chives
2 tablespoons soy sauce
1 package gyoza dumpling wrappers
1 cup water
1 teaspoon toasted sesame seeds
The Dipping Sauce:
⅓ cup soy sauce
2 tablespoons rice vinegar
1 tablespoon chives

To make the filling, Select Sauté (Medium), and heat 1 tablespoon oil in the inner pot. Add the onion and mushrooms and sauté until the onion is softened and golden, 3 to 5 minutes. Add the carrots, cabbage, ginger, garlic, and chives, and sauté until all the vegetables are tender and most of the liquid has evaporated, about 5 minutes. Add the soy sauce and simmer for 1 to 2 minutes more to reduce the liquid. To make each potsticker, place a tablespoon-sized mound of the filling onto the center of a gyoza wrapper. Moisten the edges of the wrapper with water. Bring both sides up and pinch together over the center of the filling. Pinch all along the edge, creating pleats to seal. Set aside and continue until all of the filling has been used up. If you used the inner pot to sauté, rinse and dry it, and place it back into the Instant Pot. Fit with the trivet or steam rack and fill with 1 cup water. Place a sheet of parchment paper, roughly the same size as the pot, over the rack to hold the potstickers. Place the potstickers on the parchment. If more room is needed, place a second piece of parchment on top, then add another layer of potstickers. Lock the lid and ensure the steam release valve is set to the sealing position. Select Steam (High), and set the cook time for 3 minutes. Once the cook time is complete, immediately quick release the pressure. Carefully remove the lid and the potstickers. Select Sauté (Medium), and heat the remaining 1 tablespoon oil in the inner pot until hot, or use a skillet on the stovetop over medium high heat. (Using the skillet is easiest, but both methods work.) Brown the potstickers on one or all sides. Transfer to a serving dish and immediately sprinkle with sesame seeds. Meanwhile, make the dipping sauce. In a small bowl, whisk together all ingredients. Serve the potstickers warm with the dipping sauce.

Syrupy Nuts

Prep time: 5 minutes | Cook time: 4 hours | Serves 2½ cups

1 tablespoon melted coconut oil, plus more to grease
⅓ cup pure maple syrup
1 tablespoon coconut sugar
1 teaspoon pure vanilla extract
1 teaspoon ground cinnamon

¼ teaspoon sea salt
Large pinch of nutmeg
⅛ teaspoon cayenne pepper
2½ cups raw nuts (any combination of almonds, walnuts, and cashews)

In a medium bowl, whisk together all ingredients except the nuts. Add the nuts and stir well to coat. Grease the bottom of the inner pot with coconut oil. Transfer the nut mixture to the pot and spread into an even layer. Select Slow Cook (Low), and set the cook time for 4 hours. Cover with a glass lid, if you have one, or the standard lid with the steam release valve set to the venting position. Stir halfway through. Once the cook time is complete, stir and transfer the nuts to a cookie sheet lined with parchment paper to cool for 1 hour. The nuts will crisp up as they cool. Store in an airtight glass container at room temperature for up to 3 weeks.

Popcorn with Cinnamon

Prep time: 1 minutes | Cook time: 4 minutes | Makes 6 cups

1½ tablespoons coconut oil
Optional For Seasoning:
Nutritional yeast and sea salt, to taste
Truffle salt, to taste
Dried rosemary and sea salt,

½ cup organic popping corn
to taste
Ground cinnamon and pure maple syrup

Select Sauté (High), and add the coconut oil to melt. Once the inner pot has reached maximum heat, add the popping corn and stir to coat well with the coconut oil. Cover with a vented glass lid. If you don't have a vented glass lid that fits the pot, you can use the standard lid set on top—but not locked—with the steam release valve set to the venting position. (This recipe will take longer when using the standard lid and result in fewer popped kernels, so using a glass lid is highly recommended.) Cook for about 4 minutes, without removing the lid, until the popping slows and most of the kernels have popped. Press Cancel. Immediately, while the popcorn is still hot, add your desired seasonings to taste. Stir to coat. Enjoy the popcorn warm or at room temperature.

Sweet and Spicy Peanuts

Prep time: 10 minutes | Cook time: 1½ hours | Makes 4 cups

3 cups salted peanuts
½ cup sugar
⅓ cup packed brown sugar
2 tablespoons hot water
2 tablespoons butter, melted

1 tablespoon Sriracha Asian hot chili sauce or hot pepper sauce
1 teaspoon chili powder

Place peanuts in a greased Instant Pot. In a small bowl, combine the sugars, water, butter, hot sauce, and chili powder. Pour over peanuts and stir to coat. Cover and press the Slow Cook button, and cook on high for 1½ hours. (Press Slow Cook again to toggle between Low and High cooking temperatures.), stirring once. Spread on waxed paper to cool. Serve warm.

Carrot Spread with Sesame

Prep time: 5 minutes | Cook time: 5 minutes | Makes 2½ cups

1 tablespoon sesame seeds
1 teaspoon ground toasted cumin
1 teaspoon grated fresh ginger
4 to 5 medium carrots, peeled and cut into 1-inch pieces (3 to 4 cups)
½ cup vegetable stock or water

2 tablespoons tahini
1 to 2 teaspoons rice vinegar, to taste
1 teaspoon ground ginger
¼ to ½ teaspoon salt
Freshly ground black pepper, to taste

Set the Instant Pot to Sauté. Add the sesame seeds and dry sauté for 2 minutes, until they smell toasty. Add the cumin and grated ginger, then stir. Add the carrots and stock. Lock on the lid. Bring to High Pressure; cook for 5 minutes. Let the pressure come down naturally. Carefully open the Instant Pot, tilting the lid away from you. Transfer the contents to a blender, carefully scraping in all the sesame seeds. Add the tahini, rice vinegar, ground ginger, and salt to taste. Blend for 1 to 2 minutes, until the mixture is smooth. Refrigerate for at least 1 hour before serving. The spread will keep in the refrigerator for up to 3 days or in the freezer for up to 1 month.

Pepper and Hummus with Tahini

Prep time: 5 minutes | Cook time: 40 minutes | Serves 2½ cups

1 cup dried chickpeas, rinsed
4 cups water
1 (12 ounces / 340g) jar roasted red bell peppers, drained and patted dry
¼ cup tahini
3 cloves garlic, roughly chopped
½ teaspoon sea salt
½ teaspoon smoked paprika
Pita bread, cut into triangles, for serving
Persian cucumbers, sliced, for serving

Add the chickpeas and 4 cups water to the inner pot. Lock the lid and ensure the steam release valve is set to the sealing position. Select Pressure Cook (High), and set the cook time for 40 minutes. Once the cook time is complete, allow the pressure to release naturally. Carefully remove the lid and drain the chickpeas over a bowl to reserve the cooking liquid. Transfer the drained chickpeas to the bowl of a food processor. (Blending while the chickpeas are still warm results in a creamier hummus.) Reserve a 1-inch (2.5 cm) piece of a red pepper for garnish, and add the rest of the red peppers to the food processor. Add the tahini, garlic, salt, and paprika. Lock the lid of the food processor and blend until combined. Add the reserved cooking liquid, also known as aquafaba, 1 tablespoon at a time through the tube to help blend. Continue blending and adding aquafaba as needed until very smooth and creamy. You may need up to ¾ cup aquafaba. Remove the lid and adjust the salt and paprika to taste. Transfer the hummus to a lidded container or serving bowl. Chop the remaining piece of roasted pepper and place on top for garnish. Refrigerate for at least 2 hours. Once chilled, serve the hummus with pita bread and cucumbers, or use as a sandwich spread. Store leftovers in an airtight container in the refrigerator for up to 5 days.

Cucumber and Carrot Sushi

Prep time: 20 minutes | Cook time: 3 minutes | Makes 4 rolls

2 cups dried sushi rice (such as Lundberg Family Farms Organic California Sushi Rice)
2 cups water
4 sheets sushi nori
1 large avocado, sliced
1 red bell pepper, deseeded
For Serving:
Soy sauce (or coconut aminos for gluten-free and soy-free)
and cut into thin strips
1 cup shredded carrot
2 Persian cucumbers, thinly sliced lengthwise
Sea salt (optional), to taste
2 tablespoons toasted sesame seeds

Prepared wasabi (optional)
Pickled ginger (optional)

Rinse the rice in several changes of water until the water is clear. Drain and add the rice to the inner pot along with 2 cups water. Lock the lid and ensure the steam release valve is set to the sealing position. Select Pressure Cook (High), and set the cook time for 3 minutes. Once the cook time is complete, allow the pressure to release naturally. Carefully remove the lid and stir the rice. Transfer to a bowl to cool. To make each sushi roll, lay one piece of nori on a bamboo sushi mat or on a piece of parchment paper slightly larger than the nori sheet. Cover the nori with a thin layer of rice (about 1 cup), leaving 1 inch (2.5cm) bare at the top and bottom. Place a line of veggies along the edge closest to you. Sprinkle with a pinch of salt, if desired. Wrap that edge of nori over the veggies and continue to roll as tightly as possible until you form a log—use the bamboo mat or parchment to help to roll the sushi tightly. Seal the roll by brushing a little water where the edge meets the other side of the roll. Use a very sharp chef's knife to cut the roll crosswise into 8 (1-inch; 2.5 cm) pieces. Sprinkle with sesame seeds.

Serve the sushi rolls immediately, or refrigerate until ready to eat. Serve with soy sauce or coconut aminos for dipping. Wasabi and pickled ginger add even more flavor for serving, but are optional.

Cashew Queso Dip with Potato

Prep time: 5 minutes | Cook time: 2 minutes | Serves 1½ cups

1⅓ cup water, divided
½ cup (1-inch; 2.5 cm cubes) peeled Yukon Gold potatoes
½ cup (1-inch; 2.5 slices) peeled carrots
½ cup raw cashews, soaked overnight or at least one hour
For Serving:
Homemade or store-bought salsa
Fresh cilantro, for garnish
1 bag tortilla chips (omit for oil-free)
in hot water
1 tablespoon garlic powder
1 to 2 jalapeños, deseeded
1 teaspoon tomato paste
1 teaspoon sea salt
¼ cup nutritional yeast
Hot sauce, to taste

2 carrots, peeled and cut into sticks
2 stalks celery, cut into sticks
1 red bell pepper, deseeded and cut into slices

Fit the inner pot with a steamer basket, and add 1 cup water. Place the potatoes and carrots in the steamer basket. Lock the lid and ensure the steam release valve is set to the sealing position. Select Pressure Cook (High), and set the cook time for 2 minutes. Once the cook time is complete, immediately quick release the pressure and carefully remove the lid. Check that the vegetables are tender. If they're not yet tender, lock the lid and pressure cook for 1 minute more. Transfer the steamed veggies to a blender. Drain the cashews and add to the blender. Add the garlic powder, 1 jalapeño, tomato paste, salt, nutritional yeast, and remaining ⅓ cup water. Blend until completely smooth. Taste and add another jalapeño or hot sauce for heat. Blend in more water as needed to thin. Use a rubber spatula to scoop the mixture into a small serving bowl. Top with ¼ cup salsa and a few cilantro leaves. Serve the queso dip warm on a platter with chips, carrots, celery, bell pepper, and a bowl of the remaining salsa.

Bean Bruschetta with Tomato

Prep time: 10 minutes | Cook time: 6 minutes | Serves 10

1 cup dry cannellini beans, soaked overnight
4 cups water
4 cloves garlic, minced
2 sprigs rosemary
4 sage leaves
3 tablespoons extra virgin olive oil, plus more to serve
Truffle salt (or sea salt), to
taste
Freshly ground black pepper, to taste
1 loaf crusty bread, such as baguette or ciabatta, sliced
2 cloves garlic, peeled and halved
2 Roma tomatoes, sliced
¼ cup chopped flat-leaf parsley

Add the beans, 4 cups water, minced garlic, rosemary, and sage to the inner pot. Lock the lid and ensure the steam release valve is set to the sealing position. Select Pressure Cook (High), and set the cook time for 6 minutes. Once the cook time is complete, allow the pressure to release naturally for 15 to 20 minutes. Carefully remove the lid and gently drain the beans in a colander. Transfer the beans to a bowl. Remove the rosemary stems. Dress with olive oil, salt, and pepper to taste. Toast the bread slices in the oven, on a grill, or in a grill pan. Rub the warm toast on one side with the raw garlic halves to impart garlic flavor. Top the toasted slices with tomato, then the beans. Top with a generous drizzle of olive oil, salt, and pepper. Garnish with chopped parsley. Enjoy warm or at room temperature.

Barbecue Sausage Bites

Prep time: 10 minutes | Cook time: 1 to 2 hours | Serves 8 to 10

1 cup ketchup
½ cup molasses
3 tablespoons cider vinegar
3 tablespoons Dijon mustard
1 tablespoon packed brown sugar

2 teaspoons chili powder
⅛ teaspoon cayenne pepper
3 pounds (1.4 kg) kielbasa sausage, sliced on bias ½ inch thick

Combine ketchup, molasses, vinegar, mustard, sugar, chili powder, and cayenne in the Instant Pot. Stir in kielbasa, cover, and press the Slow Cook button, and cook on low for 1 to 2 hours or until heated through and flavors meld. (Press Slow Cook again to toggle between Low and High cooking temperatures.) Serve. (Kielbasa can be held on warm or low setting for up to 2 hours. Adjust sauce consistency with hot water as needed, adding 2 tablespoons at a time.)

Beef and Green Olive Dip

Prep time: 15 minutes | Cook time: 3 to 4 hours | Makes 8 cups

1 pound (454 g) ground beef
1 medium sweet red pepper, chopped
1 small onion, chopped
1 (16-ounce / 454-g) can refried beans
1 (16-ounce / 454-g) jar mild salsa
2 cups (8 ounces / 227 g)

shredded part-skim Mozzarella cheese
2 cups (8 ounces / 227 g) shredded Cheddar cheese
1 (5¾-ounce / 163-g) jar sliced green olives with pimientos, drained
Tortilla chips, for serving

In a large skillet, cook the beef, pepper and onion over medium heat until meat is no longer pink, about 6 to 8 minutes. Drain. Transfer the beef mixture to a greased Instant Pot. Stir in the beans, salsa, cheeses and olives. Cover and press the Slow Cook button, and cook on low for 3 to 4 hours or until cheese is melted, stirring occasionally. (Press Slow Cook again to toggle between Low and High cooking temperatures.) Serve with chips.

Spinach and Artichoke Dip

Prep time: 10 minutes | Cook time: 20 minutes | Serves 6

1 cup raw cashews, soaked overnight or for 2 hours in hot water
1½ cups water, divided
⅛ cup nutritional yeast
1 teaspoon garlic powder
½ teaspoon sea salt
¼ teaspoon freshly ground black pepper
1 (16 ounce / 454g) bag frozen chopped spinach, thawed

2 (14 ounce / 397g) cans artichoke hearts in water, drained and patted dry
1 green onion, thinly sliced, for garnish
Options For Serving:
Seed crackers
Sliced and toasted baguette
Carrot sticks
Sliced hothouse cucumber

Drain the soaked cashews and transfer to a blender. Add ½ cup water, nutritional yeast, garlic powder, salt, and pepper. Blend until very smooth and creamy, about 2 minutes. Add up to another ¼ cup water if needed to blend. Cut the artichoke hearts into quarters and place in a medium bowl. Squeeze as much liquid as possible out of the thawed spinach. You can press it against a fine-mesh sieve or squeeze in a piece of cheesecloth or paper towel. Place the drained spinach into the bowl with the artichoke hearts. Pour the cashew cream over the artichokes and spinach, and stir to combine. Transfer the mixture to an oven-safe baking dish. Cover the dish with foil. Fit the inner pot with the trivet or steam rack, and add the remaining 1 cup water. Place the dish on the trivet. Lock the lid and ensure the steam release valve is in the sealing position. Select Pressure Cook (High), and set the cook time for 20 minutes. Once the cook time is complete, immediately quick release the pressure. Carefully remove the lid. Using potholders, remove the baking dish and foil. Garnish with green onion. Add a pinch more of sea salt and pepper to taste. Serve warm with the desired serving options.

Eggplant Caponata with Tomato

Prep time: 10 minutes | Cook time: 3 minutes | Serves 8

2 tablespoons extra virgin olive oil (optional)
1 small yellow onion, diced
2 cloves garlic, minced, divided
⅓ cup water
1 large eggplant (about 1 pound / 454 g), cut into 1-inch (2.5cm) cubes
2 stalks celery, diced
½ teaspoon sea salt

¼ teaspoon red pepper flakes
4 Roma tomatoes, deseeded and chopped
2 tablespoons tomato paste
⅓ cup pitted green olives, quartered
3 tablespoons capers, drained
1 tablespoon red wine vinegar
½ tablespoon organic sugar
¼ cup chopped flat-leaf parsley

Select Sauté (Medium), and heat the oil, if using, in the inner pot until hot. (Otherwise, you can dry sauté in the hot pot or add a bit of water in the bottom of the pot.) Add the onion and sauté until softened and golden, 3 to 5 minutes. Add half of the garlic and sauté 1 minute more. Add ⅓ cup water to deglaze the pan, scraping up any bits stuck to the bottom of the pot. Layer the eggplant, celery, salt, pepper, and tomatoes, in that order, and do not stir. Lock the lid and ensure the steam release valve is set to the sealing position. Select Pressure Cook (Low), and set the cook time for 3 minutes. Once the cook time is complete, immediately quick release the pressure. Carefully remove the lid and make sure eggplant is tender. If not, lock the lid and pressure cook for 1 minute more. Use a ladle to drain as much liquid as possible from the pot and discard. (You should be able to remove ½ to 1 cup of liquid.) Select Sauté (Medium), and simmer to cook off even more liquid for about 1 minute while stirring in the tomato paste. Stir in the remaining garlic, olives, capers, vinegar, and sugar. Transfer the caponata to a glass storage container or serving bowl and garnish with parsley. Enjoy warm or cold on top of pasta or scooped up with sliced and toasted baguette.

Eggplant Ganoush with Tahini

Prep time: 5 minutes | Cook time: 2 minutes | Makes 2 cups

4 cloves garlic, minced
1½ to 2 pounds (907 g) eggplant, peeled and diced
¼ cup vegetable stock
2 to 3 tablespoons tahini, to taste

1 to 2 tablespoons lemon juice, to taste
2 tablespoons chopped fresh flat-leaf parsley
Smoked or regular salt, optional

Set the Instant Pot to Sauté. Add most of the garlic and dry sauté for 30 seconds, adding a tablespoon of the stock if the garlic starts to stick. Add the eggplant and stock. Lock the lid. Bring to High Pressure; cook for 2 minutes. Quick release the pressure. Carefully open the Instant Pot, tilting the lid away from you. Check to be sure that the eggplant is cooked through. If it's not, bring back to pressure for 1 more minute and quick release. Transfer the cooked eggplant to a blender or food processor. Add the remaining garlic, lemon juice, tahini, and parsley. Pulse until almost smooth. Taste and add salt, if desired. Chill or serve at room temperature. Store for up to 5 days in the refrigerate or freeze for up to 1 month.

Pumpkin Pie Spice Pots De Crème
Prep time: 5 minutes | Cook time: 7 minutes | Serves 4

2 cups heavy cream (or full-fat coconut milk for dairy-free)
4 large egg yolks
¼ cup Swerve, or more to taste
2 teaspoons pumpkin pie spice
1 teaspoon vanilla or maple extract
Pinch of fine sea salt
1 cup cold water

Heat the cream in a pan over medium-high heat until hot, about 2 minutes. Place the remaining ingredients except the water in a medium bowl and stir until smooth. Slowly pour in the hot cream while stirring. Taste and adjust the sweetness to your liking. Scoop the mixture into four ramekins with a spatula. Cover the ramekins with aluminum foil. Place a trivet in the Instant Pot and pour in the water. Place the ramekins on the trivet. Lock the lid. Select the Manual mode and set the cooking time for 5 minutes at High Pressure. When the timer beeps, use a quick pressure release. Carefully remove the lid. Remove the foil and set the foil aside. Let the pots de crème cool for 15 minutes. Cover the ramekins with the foil again and place in the refrigerator to chill completely, about 2 hours. Serve.

Daikon and Almond Cake
Prep time: 10 minutes | Cook time: 45 minutes | Serves 12

5 eggs, beaten
½ cup heavy cream
1 cup almond flour
1 daikon, diced
1 teaspoon ground cinnamon
2 tablespoon erythritol
1 tablespoon butter, melted
1 cup water

In the mixing bowl, mix up eggs, heavy cream, almond flour, ground cinnamon, and erythritol. When the mixture is smooth, add daikon and stir it carefully with the help of the spatula. Pour the mixture in the cake pan. Then pour water and insert the trivet in the instant pot. Place the cake in the instant pot. Set the lid in place. Select the Manual mode and set the cooking time for 45 minutes on High Pressure. When the timer goes off, do a quick pressure release. Carefully open the lid. Serve immediately.

Almond Pie with Coconut
Prep time: 5 minutes | Cook time: 41 minutes | Serves 8

1 cup almond flour
½ cup coconut milk
1 teaspoon vanilla extract
2 tablespoons butter, softened
1 tablespoon Truvia
¼ cup shredded coconut
1 cup water

In the mixing bowl, mix up almond flour, coconut milk, vanilla extract, butter, Truvia, and shredded coconut. When the mixture is smooth, transfer it in the baking pan and flatten. Pour water and insert the trivet in the instant pot. Put the baking pan with cake on the trivet. Lock the lid. Select the Manual mode and set the cooking time for 41 minutes on High Pressure. Once the timer goes off, perform a natural pressure release for 10 minutes, then release any remaining pressure. Carefully open the lid. Serve immediately.

Chocolate Tortes
Prep time: 7 minutes | Cook time: 10 minutes | Serves 8

7 ounces (198 g) unsweetened baking chocolate, finely chopped
¾ cup plus 2 tablespoons unsalted butter (or butter-flavored coconut oil for dairy-free)
1¼ cups Swerve, or more to taste
5 large eggs
1 tablespoon coconut flour
2 teaspoons ground cinnamon
Seeds scraped from 1 vanilla bean (about 8 inches long), or 2 teaspoons vanilla extract
Pinch of fine sea salt

Grease 8 ramekins. Place the chocolate and butter in a pan over medium heat and stir until the chocolate is completely melted, about 3 minutes. Remove the pan from the heat, then add the remaining ingredients and stir until smooth. Taste and adjust the sweetness to your liking. Pour the batter into the greased ramekins. Place a trivet in the bottom of the Instant Pot and pour in 1 cup of cold water. Place four of the ramekins on the trivet. Lock the lid. Select the Manual mode and set the cooking time for 7 minutes at High Pressure. When the timer beeps, use a quick pressure release. Carefully remove the lid. Use tongs to remove the ramekins. Repeat with the remaining ramekins. Serve the tortes warm or chilled.

Apple and Pear Smoothie
Prep time: 2 minutes | Cook time: 4 minutes | Makes 3 cups

2 (1-pound / 454-g) large firm but ripe pears, peeled, quartered, and cored
2 (1-pound / 454-g) large
apples, peeled, quartered, and cored
¼ cup apple juice

Combine all the ingredients in the Instant Pot. Secure the lid. Select the Steam setting and set the cooking time for 4 minutes at low pressure. When timer beeps, let the pressure release naturally for 3 minutes, then release any remaining pressure. Open the pot. Use a hand mixer to break the pears and apples to make the smoothie. Serve immediately.

Raisin and Pecan Stuffed Apples
Prep time: 5 minutes | Cook time: 3 minutes | Serves 4

4 medium Honeycrisp apples
⅓ cup crushed pecans
½ cup raisins
⅓ cup coconut sugar
2 teaspoons ground cinnamon
Pinch of sea salt
4 tablespoons almond butter
¾ cup water

Core each apple from the top, removing most of the flesh, leaving about ¼ inch around the sides and at the bottom. In a medium bowl, mix the pecans, raisins, coconut sugar, cinnamon and salt. Fill each apple with the mixture. Top with almond butter. Pour the water into the Instant Pot. Place the apples in the pot. Secure the lid. Select Pressure Cook mode and set cooking time for 3 minutes on High Pressure. When timer beeps, use a quick pressure release, then open the lid and remove the apples. Serve hot.

Glazed Pumpkin Bundt Cake

Prep time: 7 minutes | Cook time: 35 minutes | Serves 12

Cake:
3 cups blanched almond flour	6 large eggs
1 teaspoon baking soda	2 cups pumpkin purée
½ teaspoon fine sea salt	1 cup Swerve
2 teaspoons ground cinnamon	¼ cup (½ stick) unsalted butter
1 teaspoon ground nutmeg	(or coconut oil for dairy-free),
1 teaspoon ginger powder	softened
¼ teaspoon ground cloves	

Glaze:
1 cup (2 sticks) unsalted butter	melted
(or coconut oil for dairy-free),	½ cup Swerve

In a large bowl, stir together the almond flour, baking soda, salt, and spices. In another large bowl, add the eggs, pumpkin, sweetener, and butter and stir until smooth. Pour the wet ingredients into the dry ingredients and stir well. Grease a 6-cup Bundt pan. Pour the batter into the prepared pan and cover with a paper towel and then with aluminum foil. Place a trivet in the bottom of the Instant Pot and pour in 2 cups of cold water. Place the Bundt pan on the trivet. Lock the lid. Select the Manual mode and set the cooking time for 35 minutes at High Pressure. When the timer beeps, use a natural pressure release for 10 minutes. Carefully remove the lid. Let the cake cool in the pot for 10 minutes before removing. While the cake is cooling, make the glaze: In a small bowl, mix the butter and sweetener together. Spoon the glaze over the warm cake. Allow to cool for 5 minutes before slicing and serving.

Mini Maple Bacon Upside-Down Cheesecakes

Prep time: 15 minutes | Cook time: 10 minutes | Serves 8

3 (8-ounce/ 227-g) packages	1 large egg
cream cheese, softened	4 slices bacon, chopped, for
⅔ cup Swerve	topping
½ cup unsweetened almond	Sweetened Whipped Cream:
milk (or hemp milk for nut free)	½ cup heavy cream
2 teaspoons maple extract	2 tablespoons Swerve, or more
¼ teaspoon fine sea salt	to taste

In the bowl of a stand mixer, add the cream cheese, sweetener, milk, maple extract, and salt and blitz until well blended. Add the egg and mix on low speed until very smooth. Pour the batter into 8 ramekins. Gently tap the ramekins against the counter to bring the air bubbles to the surface. Place a trivet in the bottom of the Instant Pot and pour in 1 cup of cold water. Stack the ramekins in two layers on top of the trivet. Cover the top layer of ramekins with 3 large pieces of paper towel to ensure that condensation doesn't leak onto the cheesecakes. Lock the lid. Select the Manual mode and set the cooking time for 6 minutes at High Pressure. When the timer beeps, use a natural pressure release for 10 minutes. Carefully remove the lid. Remove the ramekins with tongs. Place the cheesecakes in the fridge to chill completely, about 4 hours. Meanwhile, make the topping: Cook the bacon in a skillet over medium-high heat for 4 minutes until crisp and cooked through. Place the cooked bacon on a paper towel–lined plate to drain. Add the cream to a medium bowl and use a hand mixer on high speed to mix until soft peaks form. Fold in the sweetener and mix until well combined. Taste and adjust the sweetness to your liking. Drizzle with the sweetened whipped cream and place the bacon on top. Serve.

Maple-Glazed Zucchini Bundt Cake

Prep time: 7 minutes | Cook time: 40 minutes | Serves 8

Cake:
6 large eggs	2 teaspoons ground cinnamon
1 cup full-fat coconut milk	1 cup coconut flour
¾ cup (1½ sticks) unsalted	1 teaspoon fine sea salt
butter (or butter-flavored	1 teaspoon baking powder
coconut oil for dairy-free),	1 cup shredded zucchini
melted	3 teaspoons vanilla extract
½ cup Swerve	

Maple Glaze:
½ cup (1 stick) unsalted butter	(¼ cup) (or Kite Hill brand
(or butter-flavored coconut oil	cream cheese style spread for
for dairy-free)	dairy-free)
¼ cup Swerve	Chopped raw walnuts, for
2 ounces (57 g) cream cheese	garnish (omit for nut-free)

Whisk the eggs with a hand mixer until light and foamy in large bowl. Stir in the coconut milk, melted butter, sweetener, and cinnamon. In another large bowl, stir together the coconut flour, salt, and baking powder. Add the dry ingredients to the wet ingredients and stir well, then fold in the shredded zucchini and extract and stir again. Grease a 6-cup Bundt pan. Pour the batter into the prepared pan and cover the pan with a paper towel and then with aluminum foil. Place a trivet in the bottom of the Instant Pot and pour in 2 cups of cold water. Place the Bundt pan on the trivet. Lock the lid. Select the Manual mode and set the cooking time for 35 minutes at High Pressure. When the timer beeps, use a natural pressure release for 10 minutes. Carefully remove the lid. Let the cake cool in the pot for 10 minutes before removing. Chill the cake in the fridge or freezer before removing from the Bundt pan, about 1 hour. While the cake is cooling, make the glaze: Place the butter in a large pan over high heat and cook for about 5 minutes until brown, stirring occasionally. Remove from the heat. While stirring the browned butter, vigorously, add the sweetener. Carefully add the cream cheese and maple extract to the butter mixture. Allow the glaze to cool for a few minutes, or until it starts to thicken. Transfer the chilled cake to a serving plate and drizzle the glaze over the top. Sprinkle with the walnuts while the glaze is still wet. Place the cake in the fridge to chill completely for an additional 30 minutes before serving.

Creamy Pine Nut Mousse

Prep time: 5 minutes | Cook time: 35 minutes | Serves 8

1 tablespoon butter	1 cup Swerve, reserve 1
1¼ cups pine nuts	tablespoon
1¼ cups full-fat heavy cream	1 c water
2 large eggs	1 cup full-fat heavy whipping
1 teaspoon vanilla extract	cream

Butter the bottom and the side of a pie pan and set aside. In a food processor, blend the pine nuts and heavy cream. Add the eggs, vanilla extract and Swerve and pulse a few times to incorporate. Pour the batter into the pan and loosely cover with aluminum foil. Pour the water in the Instant Pot and place the trivet inside. Place the pan on top of the trivet. Close the lid. Select Manual mode and set the timer for 35 minutes on High pressure. In a small mixing bowl, whisk the heavy whipping cream and 1 tablespoon of Swerve until a soft peak forms. When timer beeps, use a natural pressure release for 15 minutes, then release any remaining pressure and open the lid. Serve immediately with whipped cream on top.

Almond Chocolate Fudge

Prep time: 5 minutes | Cook time: 5 minutes | Serves 30

2½ cups Swerve
1¾ cups unsweetened almond milk
1½ cups almond butter
8 ounces (227 g) unsweetened

baking chocolate, finely chopped
1 teaspoon almond or vanilla extract
¼ teaspoon fine sea salt

Line a baking dish with greased parchment paper. Place the sweetener, almond milk, almond butter, and chocolate in the Instant Pot. Stir well. Select the Sauté mode and cook for 2 minutes. Set the Instant Pot to Keep Warm for 3 minutes, or until the fudge mixture is completely melted and well mixed. Fold in the extract and salt and stir well. Pour the fudge mixture into the prepared baking dish, cover, and refrigerate until firm, about 4 hours. Cut the fudge into 30 equal-sized pieces and serve.

Espresso Cheesecake with Raspberries

Prep time: 5 minutes | Cook time: 35 minutes | Serves 8

1 cup blanched almond flour
½ cup plus 2 tablespoons Swerve
3 tablespoons espresso powder, divided
2 tablespoons butter
1 egg
½ cup full-fat heavy cream

16 ounces (454 g) cream cheese
1 cup water
6 ounces (170 g) dark chocolate (at least 80% cacao)
8 ounces (227 g) full-fat heavy whipping cream
2 cups raspberries

In a small mixing bowl, combine the almond flour, 2 tablespoons of Swerve, 1 tablespoon of espresso powder and the butter. Line the bottom of a springform pan with parchment paper. Press the almond flour dough flat on the bottom and about 1 inch on the sides. Set aside. In a food processor, mix the egg, heavy cream, cream cheese, remaining Swerve and remaining espresso powder until smooth. Pour the cream cheese mixture into the springform pan. Loosely cover with aluminum foil. Put the water in the Instant Pot and place the trivet inside. Close the lid. Select Manual button and set the timer for 35 minutes on High pressure. When timer beeps, use a natural pressure release for 15 minutes, then release any remaining pressure. Open the lid. Remove the springform pan and place it on a cooling rack for 2 to 3 hours or until it reaches room temperature. Refrigerate overnight. Melt the chocolate and heavy whipping cream in the double boiler. Cool for 15 minutes and drizzle on top of the cheesecake, allowing the chocolate to drip down the sides. Add the raspberries on top of the cheesecake before serving.

Coconut Whipping Cream

Prep time: 5 minutes | Cook time: 1 minute | Serves 5 to 6

1 (14-ounce / 397-g) can full-fat coconut milk, refrigerated
½ cup heavy whipping cream

½ teaspoon vanilla extract
⅓ cup Swerve

With a large spoon, carefully scoop out the cream portion of the coconut milk, discarding the remaining liquid. In a small bowl, mix the coconut milk with the heavy whipping cream, vanilla, and Swerve and stir until combined. Set the Instant Pot to Sauté mode and pour in the mixture. Melt together for 1 minute, stirring thoroughly. Remove cream mixture from the Instant Pot and whip with an electric mixer, until reaching desired consistency. Refrigerate until ready to serve.

Chocolate Molten Cake

Prep time: 5 minutes | Cook time: 5 minutes | Serves 2

1 large egg
4 tablespoons unsweetened raw cocoa powder
2 tablespoons blanched almond flour
2 tablespoons Swerve
2 tablespoons full-fat heavy cream

1 teaspoon vanilla extract
½ teaspoon baking powder
Pinch of sea salt
2 ounces (57 g) dark chocolate (at least 80% cacao), cut into chunks
½ cup water

In a small mixing bowl, beat the egg and add the cocoa powder, almond flour, Swerve, heavy cream, vanilla extract, baking powder and sea salt. Transfer half of the batter into a small oven-proof bowl, add the dark chocolate pieces and then the rest of the batter. Loosely cover with aluminum foil. Put the water in the Instant Pot and place the trivet inside. Place the bowl on the trivet. Close the lid. Select on Manual mode and set the timer for 5 minutes on High pressure. When timer beeps, use a natural pressure release for 5 minutes, then release any remaining pressure and open the lid. Remove the bowl, uncover, and serve immediately.

Lush Chocolate Cake

Prep time: 10 minutes | Cook time: 35 minutes | Serves 8

For Cake:

2 cups almond flour
⅓ cup unsweetened cocoa powder
1½ teaspoons baking powder
1 cup granulated erythritol
Pinch of salt
4 eggs

1 teaspoon vanilla extract
½ cup butter, melted and cooled
6 tablespoons strong coffee, cooled
½ cup water

For Frosting:

4 ounces (113 g) cream cheese, softened
½ cup butter, softened
¼ teaspoon vanilla extract

2½ tablespoons powdered erythritol
2 tablespoons unsweetened cocoa powder

To make the cake: In a large bowl, whisk together the almond flour, cocoa powder, baking powder, granulated erythritol, and salt. Whisk well to remove any lumps. Add the eggs and vanilla and mix with a hand mixer until combined. With the mixer still on low speed, slowly add the melted butter and mix until well combined. Add the coffee and mix on low speed until the batter is thoroughly combined. Scrape the sides and bottom of the bowl to make sure everything is well mixed. Spray the cake pan with cooking spray. Pour the batter into the pan. Cover tightly with aluminum foil. Add the water to the pot. Place the cake pan on the trivet and carefully lower then pan into the pot. Close the lid. Select Manual mode and set cooking time for 35 minutes on High Pressure. When timer beeps, use a quick pressure release and open the lid. Carefully remove the cake pan from the pot and place on a wire rack to cool. Flip the cake onto a plate once it is cool enough to touch. Cool completely before frosting. To make the frosting: In a medium bowl, use the mixer to whip the cream cheese, butter, and vanilla until light and fluffy, 1 to 2 minutes. With the mixer running, slowly add the powdered erythritol and cocoa powder. Mix until everything is well combined. Once the cake is completely cooled, spread the frosting on the top and down the sides.

Hearty Crème Brûlée

Prep time: 5 minutes | Cook time: 30 minutes | Serves 4

5 egg yolks
5 tablespoons powdered erythritol

1½ cups heavy cream
2 teaspoons vanilla extract
2 cups water

In a small bowl, use a fork to break up the egg yolks. Stir in the erythritol. Pour the cream into a small saucepan over medium-low heat and let it warm up for 3 to 4 minutes. Remove the saucepan from the heat. Temper the egg yolks by slowly adding a small spoonful of the warm cream, keep whisking. Do this three times to make sure the egg yolks are fully tempered. Slowly add the tempered eggs to the cream, whisking the whole time. Add the vanilla and whisk again. Pour the cream mixture into the ramekins. Each ramekin should have ½ cup liquid. Cover each with aluminum foil. Place the trivet inside the Instant Pot. Add the water. Carefully place the ramekins on top of the trivet. Close the lid. Select Manual mode and set cooking time for 11 minutes on High Pressure. When timer beeps, use a natural release for 15 minutes, then release any remaining pressure. Open the lid. Carefully remove a ramekin from the pot. Remove the foil and check for doneness. The custard should be mostly set with a slightly jiggly center. Place all the ramekins in the fridge for 2 hours to chill and set. Serve chilled.

Traditional Cheesecake

Prep time: 30 minutes | Cook time: 45 minutes | Serves 8

For Crust:

1½ cups almond flour
4 tablespoons butter, melted
1 tablespoon Swerve

1 tablespoon granulated erythritol
½ teaspoon ground cinnamon

For Filling:

16 ounces (454 g) cream cheese, softened
½ cup granulated erythritol
2 eggs

1 teaspoon vanilla extract
½ teaspoon lemon extract
1½ cups water

To make the crust: In a medium bowl, combine the almond flour, butter, Swerve, erythritol, and cinnamon. Use a fork to press it all together. When completed, the mixture should resemble wet sand. Spray the springform pan with cooking spray and line the bottom with parchment paper. Press the crust evenly into the pan. Work the crust up the sides of the pan, about halfway from the top, and make sure there are no bare spots on the bottom. Place the crust in the freezer for 20 minutes while you make the filling. To make the filling: In the bowl of a stand mixer using the whip attachment, combine the cream cheese and erythritol on medium speed until the cream cheese is light and fluffy, 2 to 3 minutes. Add the eggs, vanilla extract, and lemon extract. Mix until well combined. Remove the crust from the freezer and pour in the filling. Cover the pan tightly with aluminum foil and place it on the trivet. Add the water to the pot and carefully lower the trivet into the pot. Close the lid. Select Manual mode and set cooking time for 45 minutes on High Pressure. When timer beeps, use a quick pressure release and open the lid. Remove the trivet and cheesecake from the pot. Remove the foil from the pan. The center of the cheesecake should still be slightly jiggly. If the cheesecake is still very jiggly in the center, cook for an additional 5 minutes on High pressure until the appropriate doneness is reached. Let the cheesecake cool for 30 minutes on the counter before placing it in the refrigerator to set. Leave the cheesecake in the refrigerator for at least 6 hours before removing the sides of the pan, slicing, and serving.

Chocolate Chip Brownies

Prep time: 10 minutes | Cook time: 33 minutes | Serves 8

1½ cups almond flour
⅓ cup unsweetened cocoa powder
¾ cup granulated erythritol
1 teaspoon baking powder
2 eggs

1 tablespoon vanilla extract
5 tablespoons butter, melted
¼ cup sugar-free chocolate chips
½ cup water

In a large bowl, add the almond flour, cocoa powder, erythritol, and baking powder. Use a hand mixer on low speed to combine and smooth out any lumps. Add the eggs and vanilla and mix until well combined. Add the butter and mix on low speed until well combined. Scrape the bottom and sides of the bowl and mix again if needed. Fold in the chocolate chips. Grease a baking dish with cooking spray. Pour the batter into the dish and smooth with a spatula. Cover tightly with aluminum foil. Pour the water into the pot. Place the trivet in the pot and carefully lower the baking dish onto the trivet. Close the lid. Select Manual mode and set cooking time for 33 minutes on High Pressure. When timer beeps, use a quick pressure release and open the lid. Use the handles to carefully remove the trivet from the pot. Remove the foil from the dish. Let the brownies cool for 10 minutes before turning out onto a plate.

Caramelized Pumpkin Cheesecake

Prep time: 15 minutes | Cook time: 45 minutes | Serves 8

Crust:

1½ cups almond flour
4 tablespoons butter, melted
1 tablespoon Swerve
1 tablespoon granulated

erythritol
½ teaspoon ground cinnamon
Cooking spray

Filling:

16 ounces (454 g) cream cheese, softened
½ cup granulated erythritol
2 eggs
¼ cup pumpkin purée

3 tablespoons Swerve
1 teaspoon vanilla extract
¼ teaspoon pumpkin pie spice
1½ cups water

To make the crust: In a medium bowl, combine the almond flour, butter, Swerve, erythritol, and cinnamon. Use a fork to press it all together. Spray the pan with cooking spray and line the bottom with parchment paper. Press the crust evenly into the pan. Work the crust up the sides of the pan, about halfway from the top, and make sure there are no bare spots on the bottom. Place the crust in the freezer for 20 minutes while you make the filling. To make the filling: In a large bowl using a hand mixer on medium speed, combine the cream cheese and erythritol. Beat until the cream cheese is light and fluffy, 2 to 3 minutes. Add the eggs, pumpkin purée, Swerve, vanilla, and pumpkin pie spice. Beat until well combined. Remove the crust from the freezer and pour in the filling. Cover the pan with aluminum foil and place it on the trivet. Add the water to the pot and carefully lower the trivet into the pot. Set the lid in place. Select the Manual mode and set the cooking time for 45 minutes on High Pressure. When the timer goes off, do a quick pressure release. Carefully open the lid. Remove the trivet and cheesecake from the pot. Remove the foil from the pan. The center of the cheesecake should still be slightly jiggly. Let the cheesecake cool for 30 minutes on the counter before placing it in the refrigerator to set. Leave the cheesecake in the refrigerator for at least 6 hours before removing the sides and serving.

Southern Almond Pie

Prep time: 10 minutes | Cook time: 35 minutes | Serves 12

2 cups almond flour
1½ cups powdered erythritol
1 teaspoon baking powder
Pinch of salt
½ cup sour cream
4 tablespoons butter, melted
1 egg

1 teaspoon vanilla extract
Cooking spray
1½ teaspoons ground cinnamon
1½ teaspoons Swerve
1 cup water

In a large bowl, whisk together the almond flour, powdered erythritol, baking powder, and salt. Add the sour cream, butter, egg, and vanilla and whisk until well combined. The batter will be very thick, almost like cookie dough. Grease the baking dish with cooking spray. Line with parchment paper, if desired. Transfer the batter to the dish and level with an offset spatula. In a small bowl, combine the cinnamon and Swerve. Sprinkle over the top of the batter. Cover the dish tightly with aluminum foil. Add the water to the pot. Set the dish on the trivet and carefully lower it into the pot. Set the lid in place. Select the Manual mode and set the cooking time for 35 minutes on High Pressure. When the timer goes off, do a quick pressure release. Carefully open the lid. Remove the trivet and pie from the pot. Remove the foil from the pan. The pie should be set but soft, and the top should be slightly cracked. Cool completely before cutting.

Cannoli Chocolate Bites

Prep time: 5 minutes | Cook time: 20 minutes | Serves 5 to 6

3 tablespoons sugar-free chocolate chips
2 tablespoons coconut oil
1 egg
½ cup almond flour

½ teaspoon vanilla extract
½ cup Swerve
15 ounces (425 g) cream cheese

Pour 1 cup water into the inner pot of the Instant Pot, then insert the trivet. In a large bowl, combine the chocolate chips, coconut oil, egg, almond flour, vanilla, Swerve, and cheese. Mix thoroughly. Once mixed, evenly pour this mixture into 6 well-greased, Instant Pot-friendly ramekins. Place the ramekins on the trivet, and cover each loosely with aluminum foil. Lock the lid. Select the Manual mode and set the cooking time for 20 minutes on High Pressure. Once the timer goes off, perform a natural pressure release for 10 minutes, then release any remaining pressure. Carefully open the lid. Remove the ramekins. Place in the refrigerator for at least 20 minutes. Let cool, serve, and enjoy!

Chocolate Mousse

Prep time: 5 minutes | Cook time: 5 minutes | Serves 5 to 6

2 tablespoons grass-fed butter, softened
¼ cup sugar-free chocolate chips
1 cup full-fat cream cheese, softened

1 tablespoon raw cacao nibs
½ teaspoon vanilla extract
½ cup Swerve
⅓ cup unsweetened cocoa powder
½ cup heavy whipping cream

Set the Instant Pot to Sauté mode and melt the butter. Add the chocolate chips, cream cheese, cacao nibs, vanilla, Swerve, and cocoa powder to the Instant Pot. Stir continuously for 5 minutes. Remove the inner pot from the Instant Pot, and refrigerate for at least 20 minutes. Whisk to beat the heavy whipping cream, until stiff peaks form. Using a spatula, gently fold the whipped cream into the cooled chocolate mixture. Serve.

Coconut Cupcakes

Prep time: 5 minutes | Cook time: 10 minutes | Serves 6

4 eggs, beaten
4 tablespoons coconut milk
4 tablespoons coconut flour
½ teaspoon vanilla extract

2 tablespoons erythritol
1 teaspoon baking powder
1 cup water

In the mixing bowl, mix up eggs, coconut milk, coconut flour, vanilla extract, erythritol, and baking powder. Then pour the batter in the cupcake molds. Pour the water and insert the trivet in the instant pot. Place the cupcakes on the trivet. Lock the lid. Select the Manual mode and set the cooking time for 10 minutes on High Pressure. Once the timer goes off, perform a natural pressure release for 5 minutes, then release any remaining pressure. Carefully open the lid. Serve immediately.

Buttery Blueberry Muffins

Prep time: 5 minutes | Cook time: 14 minutes | Serves 3

¼ cup blueberries
¼ teaspoon baking powder
1 teaspoon apple cider vinegar
4 teaspoons butter, melted

2 eggs, beaten
1 cup coconut flour
2 tablespoons erythritol
1 cup water

In the mixing bowl, mix up baking powder, apple cider vinegar, butter, eggs, coconut flour, and erythritol. When the batter is smooth, add blueberries. Stir well. Put the muffin batter in the muffin molds. After this, pour water and insert the trivet in the instant pot. Then place the muffins on the trivet. Lock the lid. Select the Manual mode and set the cooking time for 14 minutes on High Pressure. Once the timer goes off, perform a natural pressure release for 6 minutes, then release any remaining pressure. Carefully open the lid. Serve immediately.

Chocolate and Peanut Butter Tart

Prep time: 20 minutes | Cook time: 25 minutes | Serves 4 to 6

5 tablespoons unsalted butter
1 cup granulated sugar
2 tablespoons peanut butter
1 tablespoon vegetable oil
¼ cup chocolate chips
½ cup peanut butter chips
⅓ cup cocoa powder
2 large eggs

1 cup all-purpose flour
1 teaspoon baking powder
2 teaspoons vanilla extract
½ teaspoon salt
2 tablespoons water
5 ounces (142 g) chocolate chip cookie dough, rolled into teaspoon-size balls

Combine the butter, sugar, and peanut butter in a microwave-safe bowl and microwave for a minute to melt and mix well. Add the vegetable oil to the bowl of butter mixture and whisk to combine. Whisk in the remaining ingredients, except for the cookie dough balls. Spritz a springform pan with cooking spray. Line the with parchment paper, then spritz with another layer of cooking spray. Pour the mixture into the pan and use a spatula to level the top. Arrange the cookie-dough balls and slightly push them into the mixture and they're still visible on the surface. Pour 2 cups of water in the Instant Pot, then fit in a trivet. Place the pan on the trivet. Secure the lid, and select the Pressure Cook mode and set the cooking time for 25 minutes. When cooking is complete, do a natural pressure release for 10 minutes, then release any remaining pressure. Open the lid. Carefully remove the pan and trivet from the Instant Pot and let cool for 30 minutes before slicing and serving.

Creamy Cheesecake

Prep time: 10 minutes | Cook time: 1½ to 2½ hours | Serves 8

6 whole graham crackers, broken into 1-inch pieces
2 tablespoons unsalted butter, melted
⅔ cup plus 1 tablespoon sugar, divided
½ teaspoon ground cinnamon
Salt, to taste
18 ounces (510 g) cream cheese, softened
1 teaspoon vanilla extract
¼ cup sour cream
2 large eggs

Pulse graham crackers in a food processor to fine crumbs, about 20 pulses. Add melted butter, 1 tablespoon sugar, cinnamon, and pinch salt and pulse to combine, about 4 pulses. Sprinkle crumbs into a springform pan and press into an even layer using the bottom of the dry measuring cup. Wipe out processor bowl. Process cream cheese, vanilla, ¼ teaspoon salt, and remaining ⅔ cup sugar in the processor until combined, about 15 seconds, scraping down sides of bowl as needed. Add sour cream and eggs and process until just incorporated, about 15 seconds; do not over mix. Pour filling into prepared pan and smooth top. Fill the Instant Pot with ½ inch water (about 2 cups) and place aluminum foil rack in bottom. Set pan on prepared rack, cover, and cook until cheesecake registers 150ºF (66ºC), press the Slow Cook button, and cook on high for 1½ to 2½ hours. (Press Slow Cook again to toggle between Low and High cooking temperatures.) Turn off Instant Pot and let cheesecake sit, covered, for 1 hour. Transfer cheesecake to a wire rack. Run a small knife around edge of cake and gently blot away condensation using paper towels. Let cheesecake cool in pan to room temperature, about 1 hour. Cover with plastic wrap and refrigerate until well chilled, at least for 3 hours or up to 3 days. About 30 minutes before serving, run a small knife around edge of cheesecake, then remove sides of pan. Invert cheesecake onto sheet of parchment paper, then turn cheesecake right side up onto a serving dish. Serve.

Lemon Mousse

Prep time: 5 minutes | Cook time: 10 minutes | Serves 4

2 tablespoons vegan butter, room temperature
⅓ cup beet sugar
½ cup plus ¼ cup plus ¼ cup plus ¼ cup coconut cream, whipped
2 lemons, zested and juiced
Pinch of salt
1 cup water
Extra lemon zest, for garnish

Whisk the vegan butter with the beet sugar with a hand mixer in a bowl. Beat in ½ cup of coconut cream, lemon zest and juice, and salt. Cover the bowl with aluminum foil. Pour the water into the Instant Pot and insert a trivet. Put the bowl on the trivet. Secure the lid. Select the Pressure Cook mode and set the cooking time for 10 minutes at High Pressure. Once cooking is complete, do a natural pressure release for 10 minutes, then release any remaining pressure. Carefully open the lid. Take out the bowl and remove the foil. The mixture will be curdy and clumpy, so whisk until smooth, and strain through a fine mesh into a bowl. Cover the mixture itself with plastic wrap, making sure to press onto the curd. Place in the refrigerator for 2 hours. When ready, remove the wrap and whisk the cream until stiff peak forms. Gently fold in the second portion (¼ cup) of coconut cream, then the third portion, and the last portion. Spoon the mousse into serving bowls. Garnish with the extra lemon zest and serve.

Classic Pumpkin Pie

Prep time: 4 hours 20 minutes | Cook time: 35 minutes Serves 6

½ cup crushed graham crackers (about 7 graham crackers)
2 tablespoons unsalted butter, melted
½ cup brown sugar
1 large egg
1½ cups canned pumpkin purée
1½ teaspoons pumpkin pie spice
½ teaspoon sea salt
½ cup evaporated milk
1 cup water

Make the crust: In a small bowl, combine the graham cracker crumbs and butter and mix until well combined. Press the mixture into the bottom and 1 inch up the sides of a springform pan. Set aside. In a large mixing bowl, whisk together the egg, pumpkin purée, pumpkin pie spice, sugar, salt, and milk. Pour the filling into the prepared crust. Cover the pan with aluminum foil. Place a trivet in the Instant Pot and pour in the water. Lower the pan onto the trivet. Lock the lid. Select the Manual mode. Set the time for 35 minutes on High Pressure. When timer beeps, let the pressure release naturally for 10 minutes, then release the remaining pressure. Unlock the lid. Remove the pan from the pot and then remove the foil. Allow the pie to cool. Cover with plastic wrap and refrigerate for at least 4 hours before serving.

Simple Vanilla Flan

Prep time: 10 minutes | Cook time: 10 minutes | Serves 4

4 egg whites
4 egg yolks
½ cup erythritol
7 ounces (198 g) heavy whipping cream
3 tablespoons water
1 tablespoon butter
½ teaspoon vanilla extract
1 cup water

In the saucepan, heat up erythritol and butter. When the mixture is smooth, leave it in a warm place. Meanwhile, mix up water, heavy cream, egg whites, and egg yolks. Whisk the mixture. Pour the erythritol mixture in the flan ramekins and then add heavy cream mixture over the sweet mixture. Pour water and insert the trivet in the instant pot. Place the ramekins with flan on the trivet. Lock the lid. Select the Manual mode and set the cooking time for 10 minutes on High Pressure. Once the timer goes off, perform a natural pressure release for 10 minutes, then release any remaining pressure. Carefully open the lid. Cool the cooked flan for 25 minutes. Serve.

Fast and Easy Custard

Prep time: 5 minutes | Cook time: 7 minutes | Serves 4

6 eggs, beaten
1 cup heavy cream
1 teaspoon vanilla extract
¼ teaspoon ground nutmeg
2 tablespoons erythritol
1 tablespoon coconut flour
1 cup water

Whisk the eggs and erythritol until smooth. Then add heavy cream, vanilla extract, ground nutmeg, and coconut flour. Whisk the mixture well again. Then pour it in the custard ramekins and cover with foil. Pour water and insert the trivet in the instant pot. Place the ramekins with custard on the trivet. Set the lid in place. Select the Manual mode and set the cooking time for 7 minutes on High Pressure. When the timer goes off, do a quick pressure release. Carefully open the lid. Serve immediately.

Traditional Kentucky Butter Cake

Prep time: 5 minutes | Cook time: 35 minutes | Serves 4

2 cups almond flour
¾ cup granulated erythritol
1½ teaspoons baking powder
4 eggs

1 tablespoon vanilla extract
½ cup butter, melted
Cooking spray
½ cup water

In a medium bowl, whisk together the almond flour, erythritol, and baking powder. Whisk well to remove any lumps. Add the eggs and vanilla and whisk until combined. Add the butter and whisk until the batter is mostly smooth and well combined. Grease the pan with cooking spray and pour in the batter. Cover tightly with aluminum foil. Add the water to the pot. Place the Bundt pan on the trivet and carefully lower it into the pot using. Set the lid in place. Select the Manual mode and set the cooking time for 35 minutes on High Pressure. When the timer goes off, do a quick pressure release. Carefully open the lid. Remove the pan from the pot. Let the cake cool in the pan before flipping out onto a plate.

Classic Lava Cake

Prep time: 5 minutes | Cook time: 4 minutes | Serves 4

1 teaspoon baking powder
1 tablespoon cocoa powder
1 cup coconut cream
⅓ cup coconut flour

1 tablespoon almond flour
2 teaspoons erythritol
1 tablespoon butter, melted
1 cup water

Whisk together baking powder, cocoa powder, coconut cream, coconut flour, almond flour, erythritol, and butter. Then pour the chocolate mixture in the baking cups. Pour the water in the instant pot. Insert the trivet. Place the cups with cake mixture on the trivet. Lock the lid. Select the Manual mode and set the cooking time for 4 minutes on High Pressure. Once the timer goes off, perform a natural pressure release for 5 minutes, then release any remaining pressure. Carefully open the lid. Serve immediately.

Coconut Chocolate Cake

Prep time: 10 minutes | Cook time: 40 minutes | Serves 5 to 6

3 tablespoons sugar-free chocolate chips
2 tablespoons grass-fed butter, softened
2 eggs
1⅓ cup almond flour
1 teaspoon baking powder
1 teaspoon pumpkin purée

½ cup Swerve
½ cup unsweetened coconut flakes
½ cup heavy whipping cream
½ teaspoon ground nutmeg
½ teaspoon ground cinnamon
½ teaspoon vanilla extract

In a large bowl, thoroughly mix together all ingredients, until a perfectly even mixture is obtained. Next, pour 1 cup filtered water into the Instant Pot and insert the trivet. Transfer the mixture from the bowl into a well-greased, Instant Pot-friendly pan. Using a sling, place the pan onto the trivet, and cover loosely with aluminum foil. Lock the lid. Select the Manual mode and set the cooking time for 40 minutes on High Pressure. Once the timer goes off, perform a natural pressure release for 10 minutes, then release any remaining pressure. Carefully open the lid. Remove the pan. Allow to cool completely before serving. Add any desired toppings on top of the finished dessert, serve, and enjoy!

Iced Cream Chocolate Bites

Prep time: 5 minutes | Cook time: 5 minutes | Serves 7

6 tablespoons sugar-free chocolate chips
4 ounces (113 g) full-fat cream cheese, softened

½ cup full-fat coconut milk
1 cup heavy whipping cream
½ cup Swerve
½ teaspoon vanilla extract

Pour 1 cup water into the inner pot of the Instant Pot, then insert the trivet. In a large bowl, combine the chocolate chips, cream cheese, coconut milk, whipping cream, Swerve, and vanilla. Mix thoroughly and transfer into well-greased egg bites molds. Place molds on top of the trivet, stacking on top of each other, if needed. Cover loosely with aluminum foil. Lock the lid. Select the Manual mode and set the cooking time for 5 minutes on High Pressure. Once the timer goes off, perform a natural pressure release for 10 minutes, then release any remaining pressure. Carefully open the lid. Remove the molds. Freeze for at least 1 hour, then serve. Keep uneaten bites stored in freezer.

Almond Chocolate Squares

Prep time: 10 minutes | Cook time: 40 minutes | Serves 8

1 cup almond flour
6 tablespoons sugar-free chocolate chips
¼ cup unsweetened cocoa powder
2 tablespoons coconut oil
2 eggs

2 tablespoons raw cacao nibs
1 cup chopped almonds
½ cup Swerve
¼ cup coconut milk
½ teaspoon vanilla extract
½ teaspoon salt

In a large bowl, mix together the chocolate chips, cocoa powder, coconut oil, eggs, cacao nibs, almonds, Swerve, coconut milk, vanilla, and salt. Combine them very thoroughly. Pour 1 cup water into the inner pot of the Instant Pot, and insert the trivet. Transfer the chocolate mixture from the bowl into a well-greased, Instant Pot–friendly dish. Place the dish onto the trivet, and cover loosely with aluminum foil. Lock the lid. Select the Manual mode and set the cooking time for 40 minutes on High Pressure. Once the timer goes off, perform a natural pressure release for 10 minutes, then release any remaining pressure. Carefully open the lid. Remove the dish. Refrigerate for at least 20 minutes. Once sufficiently firm, cut into 8 squares and serve.

Simple Coconut Balls

Prep time: 5 minutes | Cook time: 8 minutes | Serves 2

2 tablespoon coconut flakes
1 egg, whisked
2 tablespoons coconut flour
¾ teaspoon vanilla extract

1 teaspoon erythritol
1 tablespoon coconut oil
1 cup water

Combine together the whisked egg, coconut flour, coconut flakes, and vanilla extract. Add coconut oil. Add baking powder and erythritol. Make the balls from the coconut flour mixture. Pour the water in the instant pot. Insert the trivet inside and place the ramekin on it. Add coconut balls. Set the lid in place. Select the Manual mode and set the cooking time for 8 minutes on High Pressure. When the timer goes off, do a quick pressure release. Carefully open the lid. Chill the dessert for 5 to 10 minutes or until they are warm.

Crème Brulee

Prep time: 2 hours 40 minutes | Cook time: 10 minutes | Serves 4

2 cups graham crackers, crushed
3 tablespoons brown sugar
¼ cup butter, melted
Salt, to taste
2 (8-ounce / 227-g) cream cheese, softened
½ cup granulated sugar
2 large eggs
2 teaspoons vanilla extract
½ cup sour cream
2 tablespoons cornstarch
1 cup water
4 teaspoons white sugar

Make the crust: Mix the crushed graham crackers with brown sugar, butter, and salt in a medium bowl. Spoon the mixture into 4 medium ramekins. Place in refrigerator for 15 minutes to harden. In a bowl, stir the cream cheese and sugar until smooth. Whisk in eggs and vanilla until smooth. Fold in sour cream and cornstarch. Remove ramekins from the refrigerator, then pour in the cream cheese mixture, and cover with foil. Pour the water in the Instant Pot, then fit in a trivet, and place ramekins on top. Seal the lid, select the Pressure Cook mode and set the timer for 10 minutes at High Pressure. When cooking is complete, allow a natural pressure release for 10 minutes, then release any remaining pressure. Unlock the lid, carefully remove the ramekins and take off the foil. Allow to cool for 10 minutes and then chill further for 2 hours in the refrigerator. Remove the ramekins from the refrigerator and sprinkle 1 teaspoon of sugar on each ramekin. Use a torch to caramelize the sugar until browned in color. Serve immediately.

Banana Foster

Prep time: 15 minutes | Cook time: 2 minutes | Serves 4

¼ cup light rum
1 teaspoon cinnamon
1 cup brown sugar
8 tablespoons salted butter, cubed
¼ cup water
1 teaspoon vanilla extract
6 bananas, firm, peeled and sliced into 1-inch pieces
Vanilla ice cream, for serving

In the Instant Pot, combine the rum, cinnamon, brown sugar, butter, water, and vanilla. Stir to mix well until chunky. Add the bananas and stir gently to avoid breaking the bananas and coat them with the sauce. Secure the lid, and select the Pressure Cook mode and set the cooking time for 2 minutes. When cooking is complete, use a natural pressure release for 5 minutes, then release any remaining pressure. Carefully open the lid. Let cool for a few moments before serving over bowls of vanilla ice cream.

Mango and Rice Pudding

Prep time: 15 minutes | Cook time: 5 minutes | Serves 4

1 cup jasmine rice
1 mango, chopped into small bits
1 cup whole milk
1 teaspoon vanilla extract
½ teaspoon nutmeg powder
1 tablespoon unsalted butter
¼ cup granulated sugar
Salt, to taste
1 cup water

In the Instant Pot, combine all the ingredients. Stir to mix well. Seal the lid, set to the Pressure Cook mode and set the cooking time for 5 minutes on High Pressure. When cooking is complete, perform a natural pressure release for 10 minutes, then release any remaining pressure. Unlock the lid. Spoon the pudding into serving bowls. Serve warm.

Raisin and Oat Cookie

Prep time: 10 minutes | Cook time: 25 minutes | Serves 8

½ cup all-purpose flour
¼ teaspoon baking soda
½ cup sugar
¼ teaspoon fine sea salt
1 teaspoon ground cinnamon
1 egg
¼ cup melted butter
½ teaspoon pure vanilla extract
½ cup oats
½ cup raisins
1 cup water

Spritz a springform pan with cooking spray and line with parchment paper. In a large bowl, stir together the flour, baking soda, sugar, salt, and cinnamon. Whisk in the egg, butter, and vanilla and stir until smooth. Fold in the oats and raisins to make the batter thick and sticky. Transfer the batter to the prepared pan and use a spatula to smooth the top. Pour the water into the Instant Pot and fit in a trivet on the bottom. Place the pan on top of the trivet and cover it with an upside-down plate. Secure the lid. Select the Pressure Cook mode and set the cooking time for 25 minutes at High Pressure. When timer beeps, let the pressure naturally release for 10 minutes, then release any remaining pressure. Unlock the lid. Cut and serve.

Cinnamon Orange Toast

Prep time: 10 minutes | Cook time: 15 minutes | Serves 4

2 large eggs
1 cup milk
2 teaspoons vanilla extract
1 teaspoon ground cinnamon
Zest of 1 orange
6 bread slices, cubed
1 cup water
Maple syrup, for topping

Beat the eggs with the milk, vanilla extract, cinnamon and orange zest in a mixing bowl. Add the bread cubes and mix to coat. Pour the mixture into a greased baking pan and cover with aluminium foil. Pour the water into the Instant Pot and fit in a trivet. Place the covered pan on top. Seal the lid, select the Pressure Cook mode and set the cooking time for 15 minutes on High Pressure. When cooking is complete, perform a quick pressure release. Unlock the lid, remove the pan, and take off the foil. Let cool for 5 minutes. Drizzle with maple syrup to serve.

Chocolate Fudgy Brownies

Prep time: 10 minutes | Cook time: 5 minutes | Makes 3 brownies

2 cups water
3 ounces (85 g) dairy-free dark chocolate
1 tablespoon coconut oil
½ cup applesauce
2 tablespoons unrefined sugar
⅓ cup all-purpose flour
½ teaspoon baking powder
Salt, to taste

Pour the water into the Instant Pot and insert a trivet. Set your Instant Pot to Sauté. Stir together the chocolate and coconut oil in a large bowl. Place the bowl on the trivet. Stir occasionally until the chocolate is melted, then turn off the Instant Pot. Stir the applesauce and sugar into the chocolate mixture. Add the flour, baking powder, and salt and stir just until combined. Pour the batter into 3 ramekins. Cover each ramekin with aluminum foil. Using a foil sling or silicone helper handles, lower the ramekins onto the trivet. Lock the lid. Select the Pressure Cook mode and set the cooking time for 5 minutes at High Pressure. When the timer beeps, perform a quick pressure release. Carefully remove the lid. Cool for 5 to 10 minutes before serving.

Sweet Stuffed Apples

Prep time: 10 minutes | Cook time: 3 minutes | Serves 6

¼ cup toasted pecans, chopped
½ cup dates, chopped
¼ cup sultanas
1 tablespoon cinnamon powder
2 tablespoons brown sugar
4 tablespoons butter
6 red apples, whole and cored
4 tablespoons chocolate sauce, for topping

In a bowl, mix the pecans, dates, sultanas, cinnamon, brown sugar, and butter. Stuff apples with mixture. Pour 1 cup of water in Instant Pot and place stuffed apples in water. Seal the lid, select the Pressure Cook mode and set the timer for 3 minutes on Low Pressure. When cooking is complete, do a natural pressure release for 5 minutes, then release any remaining pressure. Open the lid. Carefully remove apples onto plates and drizzle with chocolate sauce.

Arrounce Con Leche

Prep time: 15 minutes | Cook time: 20 minutes | Serves 6

1 cup long-grain white rice, rinsed and drained
2 cups milk
1¼ cups water
2 tablespoons sugar
⅛ teaspoon sea salt
1 (10-ounce / 284-g) can condensed milk
1 teaspoon vanilla extract

Combine the rice, milk, water, sugar, and salt in the Instant Pot. Stir to mix well. Lock the lid. Select the Pressure Cook mode and set the cooking time for 20 minutes on High Pressure. When timer beeps, let the pressure release naturally for 10 minutes, then release the remaining pressure. Carefully open the lid. Stir in the sweetened condensed milk and vanilla. Serve warm.

Peanut Butter and Chocolate Tart

Prep time: 20 minutes | Cook time: 25 minutes | Serves 4 to 6

5 tablespoons unsalted butter
1 cup granulated sugar
2 tablespoons peanut butter
1 tablespoon vegetable oil
¼ cup chocolate chips
½ cup peanut butter chips
⅓ cup cocoa powder
2 large eggs
1 cup all-purpose flour
1 teaspoon baking powder
2 teaspoons vanilla extract
½ teaspoon salt
2 tablespoons water
5 ounces (142 g) chocolate chip cookie dough, rolled into teaspoon-size balls

Combine the butter, sugar, and peanut butter in a microwave-safe bowl and microwave for a minute to melt and mix well. Add the vegetable oil to the bowl of butter mixture and whisk to combine. Whisk in the remaining ingredients, except for the cookie dough balls. Spritz a springform pan with cooking spray. Line the with parchment paper, then spritz with another layer of cooking spray. Pour the mixture into the pan and use a spatula to level the top. Arrange the cookie-dough balls and slightly push them into the mixture and they're still visible on the surface. Pour 2 cups of water in the Instant Pot, then fit in a trivet. Place the pan on the trivet. Secure the lid, and select the Manual mode and set the cooking time for 25 minutes. When cooking is complete, do a natural pressure release for 10 minutes, then release any remaining pressure. Open the lid. Carefully remove the pan and trivet from the Instant Pot and let cool for 30 minutes before slicing and serving.

Lemon Pudding

Prep time: 1 hour 10 minutes | Cook time: 7 minutes | Serves 4

2½ cups whole milk
¼ cup cornstarch
Zest of 2 lemons
¼ teaspoon salt
1 cup granulated sugar
2 eggs
2 egg yolks
1 tablespoon butter, melted
¼ cup lemon juice
1 cup water

In a pot, combine the milk, cornstarch, lemon zest, salt, and sugar. Bring to a boil in a saucepan over medium heat for 2 minutes. Stir constantly. Turn off the heat. In a medium bowl, beat the eggs and egg yolks. Slowly whisk in the milk mixture until well combined. Mix in butter and lemon juice. Pour the mixture into 4 medium ramekins and cover with foil. Pour the water into Instant Pot, then fit in trivet and place ramekins on top. Seal the lid, select the Pressure Cook mode and set cooking time to 5 minutes on High Pressure. When cooking is complete, perform a quick pressure release. Unlock the lid, transfer the ramekin onto a flat surface, take off foil, and allow to cool. Chill in refrigerator for an hour before serving.

Lemon Custard Pie

Prep time: 10 minutes | Cook time: 15 minutes | Serves 6

½ cup coconut oil, melted, plus more for greasing the pan
¾ cup coconut flour
½ cup plus 2 tablespoons unrefined sugar, divided
1 (13.5-ounce / 383-g) can full-
fat coconut milk
½ cup freshly squeezed lemon juice (from 4 lemons)
¼ cup cornstarch or arrowroot powder
2 cups water

Grease a 6-inch springform pan or pie dish with melted coconut oil. Stir together ½ cup of coconut oil, coconut flour, and 2 tablespoons of sugar in a small bowl. Press the crust into the greased pan. In a medium bowl, whisk together the coconut milk, lemon juice, cornstarch, and remaining ½ cup of sugar until the starch is dissolved. Pour this mixture over the crust. Cover the pan with aluminum foil. Pour the water into the Instant Pot and insert a trivet. Using a foil sling or silicone helper handles, lower the pan onto the trivet. Lock the lid. Select the Pressure Cook mode and set the cooking time for 15 minutes at High Pressure. When the timer beeps, perform a quick pressure release. Carefully remove the lid. Serve at room temperature or chilled.

Cranberry and Pear Crisps

Prep time: 10 minutes | Cook time: 5 minutes | Serves 6

3 large pears, peeled, cored and diced
1 cup fresh cranberries
1 tablespoon granulated sugar
2 teaspoons ground cinnamon
½ teaspoon ground nutmeg
½ cup water
1 tablespoon pure maple syrup
6 tablespoons almond butter
1 cup old-fashioned rolled oats
⅓ cup dark brown sugar
¼ cup all-purpose flour
½ teaspoon sea salt
½ cup pecans, toasted

In the Instant Pot, combine the pears and cranberries and sprinkle with the granulated sugar. Let sit for a few minutes, then sprinkle with the cinnamon and nutmeg. Pour the water and maple syrup on top. In a medium bowl, stir together the almond butter, oats, brown sugar, flour and salt. Spoon the mixture on the fruit in the Instant Pot. Secure the lid. Select Pressure Cook mode, and set cooking time for 5 minutes on High Pressure. When timer beeps, use a quick pressure release. Open the lid. Spoon into bowls. Top with pecans and serve.

Cinnamon Cereal Mini Monkey Breads

Prep time: 10 minutes | Cook time: 20 minutes | Serves 4

1 (1-pound / 454-g) can buttermilk biscuits, cut into 6 pieces
⅓ cup granulated sugar
Salt, to taste
½ cup crushed cinnamon

crunch cereal, divided, plus more for sprinkling
¼ cup melted unsalted butter
1 cup water
1 cup maple syrup
2 tablespoons almond milk

In a bowl, combine the sugar, salt and half of the crushed cereal. Add the cut biscuit pieces to the bowl. Toss to evenly coat. Place 2 tablespoons of the coated biscuits, along with a spoonful of the cereal mixture, in each well of a silicone egg bite mold. Top each pile of coated dough with melted butter. Pour the water into the Instant Pot and insert a trivet. Place the filled mold on top of the trivet. Secure the lid. Press the Pressure Cook button and set cooking time for 20 minutes on High Pressure. When timer beeps, quick release the pressure. Remove the lid and take out the silicone mold. Let the monkey breads cool in the mold. Meanwhile, in a medium bowl, mix the milk and maple syrup until smooth. Remove the monkey breads from the mold. Drizzle each monkey bread with milk mixture. Top with a sprinkle of crushed cereal.

Tropical Coconut Crumble

Prep time: 10 minutes | Cook time: 6 minutes | Serves 6

3 cups chopped fresh mangoes
3 cups chopped fresh peaches
4 tablespoons unrefined sugar or pure maple syrup, divided
1 cup gluten-free rolled oats

½ cup shredded unsweetened coconut
2 tablespoons coconut oil
2 cups water

Toss together the mangoes, peaches, and 2 tablespoons of sugar in a baking dish. In a food processor, process the oats, coconut, coconut oil, and remaining 2 tablespoons of sugar until combined. Scatter the oat mixture over the fruit mixture. Cover the dish with aluminum foil. Pour the water into the Instant Pot and insert a trivet. Using a foil sling or silicone helper handles, lower the pan onto the trivet. Lock the lid. Select the Pressure Cook mode and set the cooking time for 6 minutes at High Pressure. When the timer beeps, perform a quick pressure release. Carefully remove the lid. Cool for 5 to 10 minutes before serving.

Mixed Berry Tarts

Prep time: 5 minutes | Cook time: 1 minute | Serves 6

2 cups blueberries, sliced strawberries, and raspberries
⅓ cup lemon juice
½ cup beet sugar
⅛ teaspoon salt
2 tablespoons cornstarch

2 tablespoons water
1½ tablespoons vegan butter
½ teaspoon vanilla extract
15 medium phyllo shells, thawed
1¼ cups coconut cream

Press the Sauté button on the Instant Pot. Add the berries, lemon juice, beet sugar, salt, cornstarch, and water to the Instant Pot and stir to combine. Bring the mixture to a boil while stirring occasionally and breaking the fruits. Cook for 1 minute, or until a stew forms with small chunks of fruits. Turn the pot off and stir in the butter and vanilla. Allow to rest for a few minutes until slightly cooled. Spoon 2 tablespoons into each phyllo shells and refrigerate for 2 hours. Remove the tarts and serve topped with the coconut cream.

Navy Bean and Walnuts Biscuits

Prep time: 10 minutes | Cook time: 12 minutes | Serves 8

6 ounces (170 g) navy beans, cooked
1 cup wheat flour
3 teaspoons brown sugar
2 tablespoons coconut oil
1 teaspoon vanilla extract

½ cup flax meal flour
¾ teaspoon salt
½ teaspoon ground cinnamon
¼ cup chopped walnuts
1 cup water

Mash the navy beans with a fork or blend them in a blender. Transfer the beans to a mixing bowl, along with the wheat flour, vanilla extract, brown sugar, coconut oil, flax meal flour, salt, and ground cinnamon. Stir the mixture with a spoon until you get a smooth dough. Fold in the chopped walnuts and knead the dough. Make the log from the dough and cut it into 8 even pieces. Make the balls from the dough pieces. Pour the water into the Instant Pot and insert a trivet. Line the trivet with parchment. Place dough balls on the trivet. Secure the lid. Select the Pressure Cook mode and set the cooking time for 12 minutes at High Pressure. Once cooking is complete, do a quick pressure release. Carefully open the lid. Let cool to room temperature and refrigerate until chilled before serving.

Peach Dumplings

Prep time: 5 minutes | Cook time: 10 minutes | Serves 2

1 (4-ounce / 113-g) can crescent rolls
¼ cup plus 1 tablespoon packed brown sugar
1 large peach, cut into 4 wedges

2 tablespoons vegan butter
½ teaspoon ground cinnamon
½ teaspoon vanilla extract
Pinch ground cardamom
½ cup white wine or rosé

Press the Sauté button to heat your Instant Pot. Remove the crescent rolls from the can and roll them out flat on a lightly floured surface. Sprinkle 1 tablespoon of brown sugar over the surface of the four triangles of dough. Roll each peach wedge up in a crescent roll. Add the butter to the pot and turn off the Instant Pot. Add the remaining ¼ cup of brown sugar, cinnamon, vanilla, and cardamom and stir until dissolved and mixed. Put the peach dumplings upright and side by side in the Instant Pot. Pour the wine around them. Lock the lid. Select the Pressure Cook mode and set the cooking time for 10 minutes at High Pressure. When the timer beeps, perform a natural pressure release for 10 minutes, then release any remaining pressure. Carefully remove the lid. Let the dumplings cool for 5 to 8 minutes, then transfer to serving bowls and serve.

Caramel Glazed Popcorns

Prep time: 5 minutes | Cook time: 7 minutes | Serves 4

4 tablespoons butter
1 cup sweet corn kernels

3 tablespoons brown sugar
¼ cup whole milk

Set the Instant Pot to Sauté mode, melt butter and mix in the corn kernels, heat for 1 minute or until the corn is popping. Cover the lid, and keep cooking for 3 more minutes or until the corn stops popping. Open the lid and transfer the popcorns to a bowl. Combine brown sugar and milk in the pot and cook for 3 minutes or until sugar dissolves. Stir constantly. Drizzle caramel sauce over corns and toss to coat thoroughly. Serve warm.

Classic Cheesecake

Prep time: 3 hours 40 minutes | Cook time: 40 minutes | Serves 4

2 cups graham crackers, crushed
3 tablespoons brown sugar
¼ cup butter, melted
2 (8 ounce / 227-g) cream cheese, softened
½ cup granulated sugar
2 tablespoons all-purpose flour
1 teaspoon vanilla extract
3 eggs
1 cup water
1 cup caramel sauce

Make the crust: Mix the crushed crackers with brown sugar and butter. Spread the mixture at the bottom of a springform pan and use a spoon to press to fit. Freeze in refrigerator for 10 minutes. In a bowl, whisk the cream cheese and sugar until smooth. Mix in the flour and vanilla. Whisk in the eggs. Remove the pan from refrigerator and pour mixture over crust. Cover the pan with foil. Pour the water in Instant Pot, then fit in a trivet and place the pan on top. Seal the lid, select the Manual mode and set the timer for 40 minutes on High Pressure. When cooking is complete, allow a natural pressure release for 10 minutes, then release any remaining pressure. Open the lid. Carefully remove the cake pan and take off the foil. Let cool for 10 minutes. Pour the caramel sauce over and refrigerate for 3 hours. Remove the pan from the refrigerator and invert the cheesecake on a plate. Slice and serve.

Coconut-Potato Pudding

Prep time: 5 minutes | Cook time: 10 minutes | Serves 4

1 cup water
1 large sweet potato (about 1 pound / 454 g), peeled and cut into 1-inch pieces
½ cup canned coconut milk
6 tablespoons pure maple syrup
1 teaspoon grated fresh ginger (about ½-inch knob)

Pour the water into the Instant Pot and fit in a steamer basket. Place the sweet potato pieces in the steamer basket and secure the lid. Select the Manual mode and set the cooking time for 10 minutes at High Pressure. When timer beeps, use a quick pressure release. Unlock the lid. Transfer the cooked potatoes to a large bowl. Add the coconut milk, maple syrup, and ginger. Use an immersion blender to purée the potatoes into a smooth pudding. Serve the pudding immediately or chill in the refrigerator for an hour before serving.

Carrot Kheer with Cardamom

Prep time: 10 minutes | Cook time: 15 minutes | Serves 6

3 carrots, peeled and cut into large chunks (about 1½ cups)
2 cups water
¾ cup cane sugar
3 whole cloves, crushed
2 cardamom seeds
1 cup full-fat coconut milk

Pressure cook the carrots. Place the carrots in the inner pot, and add the water. Lock the lid into place. Select Pressure Cook or Manual, and adjust the pressure to High and the time to 15 minutes. Make sure the steam release knob is in the sealed position. After cooking, naturally release the pressure. Purée the carrots. Unlock and remove the lid. Drain the carrots, reserving 1 cup of the water. Let the carrots cool for 10 minutes. In a blender, combine the carrots and reserved cooking water. Purée until smooth. Finish the kheer. Select Sauté. Once hot, add the carrot purée and sugar. Stir in the cloves and cardamom seeds, and simmer for 2 minutes or until the sugar has dissolved. Stir in the coconut milk, and simmer for another 3 minutes. Transfer to a serving bowl, and serve warm.

Oat and Raisin Cookie

Prep time: 10 minutes | Cook time: 25 minutes | Serves 8

½ cup all-purpose flour
¼ teaspoon baking soda
½ cup sugar
¼ teaspoon fine sea salt
1 teaspoon ground cinnamon
1 egg
¼ cup melted butter
½ teaspoon pure vanilla extract
½ cup oats
½ cup raisins
1 cup water

Spritz a springform pan with cooking spray and line with parchment paper. In a large bowl, stir together the flour, baking soda, sugar, salt, and cinnamon. Whisk in the egg, butter, and vanilla and stir until smooth. Fold in the oats and raisins to make the batter thick and sticky. Transfer the batter to the prepared pan and use a spatula to smooth the top. Pour the water into the Instant Pot and fit in a trivet on the bottom. Place the pan on top of the trivet and cover it with an upside-down plate. Secure the lid. Select the Manual mode and set the cooking time for 25 minutes at High Pressure. When timer beeps, let the pressure naturally release for 10 minutes, then release any remaining pressure. Unlock the lid. Cut and serve.

Easy Pecan Monkey Bread

Prep time: 15 minutes | Cook time: 25 minutes | Serves 6

1½ cinnamon powder
¼ cup brown sugar
¼ cup toasted pecans, chopped
1 pound (454 g) dinner rolls,
cut in half lengthwise
½ cup butter, melted
1 cup water
2 teaspoons whole milk
½ cup powdered sugar

Spritz a bundt pan with cooking spray. In a shallow plate, mix the cinnamon, brown sugar, and pecans. Coat the dinner rolls in the mixture, then in butter, and then place in bundt pan, making sure to build layers. Cover pan with foil and allow rising overnight. Pour the water into Instant Pot, then fit in a trivet and place bundt pan on top. Seal the lid, select the Manual mode and set the cooking time for 25 minutes at High Pressure. When cooking is complete, allow a natural release for 10 minutes, then release any remaining pressure. Unlock the lid, remove the pan from the pot, take off the foil, and allow to cool completely. In a bowl, whisk milk with sugar until smooth. Invert the bread on a serving platter and drizzle with sweetened milk. Slice and serve.

Easy Orange Cake

Prep time: 5 minutes | Cook time: 30 minutes | Serves 6

1½ cups orange soda
1 (15.25-ounce / 432-g) box orange cake mix
1 cup water
1 tablespoon caster sugar, for garnish

Spritz a bundt pan with cooking spray. In a bowl, mix orange soda and orange cake mix until well combined. Pour into bundt pan, cover with a foil. Pour the water in the Instant Pot, then fit in a trivet, and place the pan on top. Seal the lid, select the Manual mode and set the cooking time for 30 minutes at High Pressure. When cooking is complete, do a quick pressure release. Open the lid. Remove the pan from the pot and allow cooling. Turn over onto a platter, sprinkle with caster sugar. Slice and serve.

Flourless Chocolate Brownies

Prep time: 15 minutes | Cook time: 15 minutes | Makes 16 brownies

1 egg	¼ teaspoon fine sea salt
¾ cup almond butter	½ teaspoon pure vanilla extract
⅓ cup raw cacao powder	½ cup dark chocolate chips
¾ cup coconut sugar	1 cup water
½ teaspoon baking soda	

Line a springform pan with parchment paper. In a large bowl, whisk together the egg, almond butter, cacao powder, coconut sugar, baking soda, salt, and vanilla and stir well until it has a thick consistency. Transfer the batter to the prepared pan and level the batter with a spatula. Sprinkle with the chocolate chips. Pour 1 cup water into the Instant Pot and fit in a trivet. Place the pan on top of the trivet and cover it with an upside-down plate. Secure the lid. Select the Manual mode and set the cooking time for 15 minutes at High Pressure. When timer beeps, let the pressure naturally release for 10 minutes, then release any remaining pressure. Unlock the lid. Slice into 16 brownies and serve.

Creamy Banana Pudding

Prep time: 5 minutes | Cook time: 5 minutes | Serves 4

1 cup whole milk	2 tablespoons cold butter, cut
2 cups half-and-half	into 4 pieces
¾ cup plus 1 tablespoon	1 teaspoon vanilla extract
granulated sugar, divided	2 medium banana, peeled and
4 egg yolks	sliced
3 tablespoon cornstarch	1 cup heavy cream

Set the Instant Pot to Sauté mode. Mix the milk, half-and-half, and ½ cup of sugar in the pot. Heat for 3 minutes or until sugar dissolves. Stir constantly. Meanwhile, beat the egg yolks with ¼ cup of sugar in a medium bowl. Add cornstarch and mix well. Scoop ½ cup of milk mixture into egg mixture and whisk until smooth. Pour mixture into Instant Pot. Seal the lid, select the Manual mode and set the cooking time for 2 minutes on High Pressure. When cooking is complete, do a quick pressure release and unlock the lid. Stir in butter and vanilla. Lay banana pieces into 4 bowls and top with pudding. In a bowl, whisk heavy cream with remaining sugar; spoon mixture on top of pudding. Refrigerate for 1 hour before serving.

Chocolate Pudding

Prep time: 15 minutes | Cook time: 5 minutes | Serves 4

4 tablespoons cocoa powder	1½ tablespoons vanilla extract
3 medium eggs, cracked	¼ cup maple syrup
3¼ cups whole milk	1 tablespoon coconut oil
¼ cup collagen	1 cup water
1¼ teaspoons gelatin	

In a blender, combine all the ingredients, except for the water. Process until smooth. Pour the mixture into 4 ramekins and cover with aluminum foil. Pour the water in Instant Pot, fit in a trivet, and place the ramekins on top. Seal the lid, select the Manual mode and set cooking time to 5 minutes on High Pressure. When cooking is complete, allow a natural pressure release for 10 minutes, then release any remaining pressure. Unlock the lid. Refrigerate overnight and serve.

Classic New York Cheesecake

Prep time: 3 hours 45 minutes | Cook time: 40 minutes | Serves 4

12 graham crackers, crushed	2 eggs
2 tablespoons melted salted	½ cup sour cream
butter	2 tablespoons cornstarch
1½ tablespoons brown sugar	1 teaspoon vanilla extract
16 ounces (454 g) cream	¼ teaspoon salt
cheese, softened	1 cup water
1 cup granulated sugar	

Mix the crushed graham crackers with butter and brown sugar. Pour mixture into a springform pan and use a spoon to press to fit. Freeze for 15 minutes until firm. In a bowl, beat cream cheese and sugar until smooth. Whisk in the eggs, sour cream, cornstarch, vanilla, and salt. Remove the pan from refrigerator and pour cream cheese mixture on top. Spread evenly using a spatula and cover the pan with foil. Pour the water in Instant Pot, then fit in a trivet, and place cake pan on top. Seal the lid, select the Manual mode and set the cooking time for 40 minutes on High Pressure. When cooking is complete, do a natural pressure release for 10 minutes, then release any remaining pressure. Unlock the lid and carefully remove cake pan. Allow cooling for 10 minutes and chill in refrigerator for 3 hours. Remove from refrigerator, then slice and serve.

Jasmine Rice and Mango Pudding

Prep time: 15 minutes | Cook time: 5 minutes | Serves 4

1 cup jasmine rice	½ teaspoon nutmeg powder
1 mango, chopped into small	1 tablespoon unsalted butter
bits	¼ cup granulated sugar
1 cup whole milk	Salt, to taste
1 teaspoon vanilla extract	1 cup water

In the Instant Pot, combine all the ingredients. Stir to mix well. Seal the lid, set to the Manual mode and set the cooking time for 5 minutes on High Pressure. When cooking is complete, perform a natural pressure release for 10 minutes, then release any remaining pressure. Unlock the lid. Spoon the pudding into serving bowls. Serve warm.

Walnut Brown Bread

Prep time: 15 minutes | Cook time: 30 minutes | Serves 8

1 tablespoon vegetable oil,	1½ cups whole wheat flour
plus more for greasing the pan	½ cup cornmeal
1 large egg	½ cup chopped walnuts
1 cup buttermilk	¼ cup raisins
¼ cup molasses	2 teaspoons baking powder
¼ cup granulated sugar	1 teaspoon ground allspice

Generously grease a 6 cup Bundt pan with oil; set aside. In a large mixing bowl, whisk together the oil, egg, buttermilk, molasses, and sugar. Stir in the flour, cornmeal, walnuts, raisins, baking powder, and allspice. Pour the batter into the pan and cover with foil. Pour 1½ cups water into the pot. Place a trivet in the pot. Place the pan on the trivet. Secure the lid on the pot. Close the pressure-release valve. Select Manual and set the pot at High Pressure for 30 minutes. At the end of the cooking time, use a natural release to depressurize. Carefully remove the cake from the pot. Allow the cake to cool in the pan for 10 minutes. Run a knife around the edge of the pan, then unmold the cake onto a serving plate.

Pecan Bread Cream Pudding

Prep time: 10 minutes | Cook time: 35 minutes | Serves 6

1 cup heavy (whipping) cream
1 cup milk
½ cup sweetened condensed milk
2 tablespoons butter, melted, plus 1 tablespoon butter, at room temperature

1 teaspoon ground allspice
3 cups roughly chopped white bread
2 tablespoons raisins
10 pecans
2 cups water

Prepare the milk mixture. In a medium bowl, combine the cream, milk, and condensed milk. Add the melted butter and allspice, and mix thoroughly. Assemble the bread pudding. Grease a springform pan with the room-temperature butter. Evenly layer the bread cubes in the pan. Pour the milk mixture on top, and let rest for 5 minutes so the bread soaks up the liquid. Sprinkle the raisins and pecans over the bread, and tightly cover the pan with aluminum foil. Pressure cook the bread pudding. Pour the water into the inner pot, and place the trivet inside. Place the pan on top of the trivet, and lock the lid into place. Select Pressure Cook or Manual, and adjust the pressure to High and the time to 35 minutes. Make sure the steam release knob is in the sealed position. After cooking, naturally release the pressure. Unlock and remove the lid. Remove the pan, then carefully remove the foil. Let the pudding cool to the touch, then slice and serve it warm.

Raisin Rice Pudding

Prep time: 10 minutes | Cook time: 2 hours | Serves 6

2½ cups rice, cooked
1½ cups evaporated milk or scalded milk
⅔ cup brown or white sugar
1 tablespoon butter, softened

2 teaspoons vanilla
½ to 1 teaspoon nutmeg
1 eggs, beaten
½ to 1 cup raisins

Mix together all ingredients in a bowl. Pour into lightly greased Instant Pot. Cover and press the Slow Cook button, and cook on high for 2 hours or on low for 4 to 6 hours. (Press Slow Cook again to toggle between Low and High cooking temperatures.) Stir after first hour. Serve warm or cold.

Hearty Apricot Cobbler

Prep time: 20 minutes | Cook time: 25 minutes | Serves 4

4 cups sliced apricots
2 tablespoons plus ¾ cup all-purpose flour, divided
½ teaspoon cinnamon powder
¼ teaspoon nutmeg powder
1 teaspoon vanilla extract
½ cup plus ¼ cup brown sugar,

divided
1½ teaspoons salt, divided
1¼ cup water, divided
½ teaspoon baking powder
½ teaspoon baking soda
3 tablespoons butter, melted

In a baking pan, mix the apricots, 2 tablespoons of flour, cinnamon, nutmeg, vanilla, ½ cup of brown sugar, ½ teaspoon of salt, and ¼ cup of water; set aside. In another bowl, mix the remaining flour, salt and brown sugar, baking powder and soda, and butter. Spoon mixture over apricot mixture and spread to cover. Pour 1 cup of water in the pot, then fit in a trivet and place the pan on top. Seal the lid, select the Manual mode and set the timer for 25 minutes at High Pressure. When cooking is complete, perform a natural pressure release for 10 minutes, then release any remaining pressure. Carefully open the lid. Remove the pan and serve.

Cinnamon Applesauce

Prep time: 10 minutes | Cook time: 8 to 10 hours | Serves 8 to 10

8 apples, peeled, cored, and cut into chunks or slices (6 cups)

1 teaspoon cinnamon
½ cup water
½ to 1 cup sugar

Combine all ingredients in the Instant Pot. Cover and press the Slow Cook button, and cook on low for 8 to 10 hours or on high for 3 to 4 hours. (Press Slow Cook again to toggle between Low and High cooking temperatures.) Serve warm.

Chocolate Oreo Cookie Cake

Prep time: 8 hours 35 minutes | Cook time: 35 minutes Serves 6

12 Oreo cookies, smoothly crushed
2 tablespoons salted butter, melted
16 ounces (454 g) cream cheese, softened
½ cup granulated sugar
2 large eggs
1 tablespoon all-purpose flour

¼ cup heavy cream
2 teaspoons vanilla extract
16 whole Oreo cookies, coarsely crushed
1½ cups water
1 cup whipped cream
2 tablespoons chocolate sauce, for topping

Line a springform pan with foil, then spritz with cooking spray. Make the crust: In a bowl, combine smoothly crushed Oreo cookies with butter, then press into bottom of pan. Freeze for 15 minutes. In another bowl, add cream cheese, and beat until smooth. Add sugar to whisk until satiny. Beat in the eggs one by one until mixed. Whisk in flour, heavy cream, and vanilla. Fold in 8 coarsely crushed cookies and pour the mixture onto the crust in the springform pan. Cover pan tightly with foil. Pour the water in the Instant Pot and fit in a trivet. Place the pan on trivet. Seal the lid, set to the Manual mode and set the cooking time for 35 minutes at High Pressure. When cooking is complete, allow a natural pressure release for 10 minutes, then release any remaining pressure. Carefully open the lid. Remove the trivet with cake pan from the pot. Remove foil and transfer to a cooling rack to chill. Refrigerate for 8 hours. Top with whipped cream, remaining cookies, and chocolate sauce. Slice and serve.

Easy Bread Pudding

Prep time: 15 minutes | Cook time: 25 minutes | Serves 8

2 cups milk
5 large eggs
⅓ cup granulated sugar
1 teaspoon vanilla extract

5 cups (about ½ loaf) bread, slice into 2-inch cubes
2 tablespoons unsalted butter, cut into small pieces

In a medium bowl, whisk together the eggs, milk, sugar, and vanilla. Add the bread cubes and stir to coat well. Refrigerate for 1 hour. Spritz the Instant Pot with cooking spray. Pour in the bread mixture. Scatter with the butter pieces. Lock the lid. Select the Manual mode. Set the timer for 25 minutes on High Pressure. When timer beeps, let the pressure release naturally for 10 minutes, then release the remaining pressure. Unlock the lid. Serve the pudding immediately or chill in the refrigerator for an hour before serving.

Hearty Crème Brulee

Prep time: 2 hours 40 minutes | Cook time: 10 minutes
Serves 4

2 cups graham crackers, crushed	½ cup granulated sugar
3 tablespoons brown sugar	2 large eggs
¼ cup butter, melted	2 teaspoons vanilla extract
Salt, to taste	½ cup sour cream
2 (8-ounce / 227-g) cream cheese, softened	2 tablespoons cornstarch
	1 cup water
	4 teaspoons white sugar

Make the crust: Mix the crushed graham crackers with brown sugar, butter, and salt in a medium bowl. Spoon the mixture into 4 medium ramekins. Place in refrigerator for 15 minutes to harden. In a bowl, stir the cream cheese and sugar until smooth. Whisk in eggs and vanilla until smooth. Fold in sour cream and cornstarch. Remove ramekins from the refrigerator, then pour in the cream cheese mixture, and cover with foil. Pour the water in the Instant Pot, then fit in a trivet, and place ramekins on top. Seal the lid, select the Manual mode and set the timer for 10 minutes at High Pressure. When cooking is complete, allow a natural pressure release for 10 minutes, then release any remaining pressure. Unlock the lid, carefully remove the ramekins and take off the foil. Allow to cool for 10 minutes and then chill further for 2 hours in the refrigerator. Remove the ramekins from the refrigerator and sprinkle 1 teaspoon of sugar on each ramekin. Use a torch to caramelize the sugar until browned in color. Serve immediately.

Instant Pot Bananas Foster

Prep time: 15 minutes | Cook time: 2 minutes | Serves 4

¼ cup light rum	¼ cup water
1 teaspoon cinnamon	1 teaspoon vanilla extract
1 cup brown sugar	6 bananas, firm, peeled and sliced into 1-inch pieces
8 tablespoons salted butter, cubed	Vanilla ice cream, for serving

In the Instant Pot, combine the rum, cinnamon, brown sugar, butter, water, and vanilla. Stir to mix well until chunky. Add the bananas and stir gently to avoid breaking the bananas and coat them with the sauce. Secure the lid, and select the Manual mode and set the cooking time for 2 minutes. When cooking is complete, use a natural pressure release for 5 minutes, then release any remaining pressure. Carefully open the lid. Let cool for a few moments before serving over bowls of vanilla ice cream.

Orange Toast

Prep time: 10 minutes | Cook time: 15 minutes | Serves 4

2 large eggs	Zest of 1 orange
1 cup milk	6 bread slices, cubed
2 teaspoons vanilla extract	1 cup water
1 teaspoon ground cinnamon	Maple syrup, for topping

Beat the eggs with the milk, vanilla extract, cinnamon and orange zest in a mixing bowl. Add the bread cubes and mix to coat. Pour the mixture into a greased baking pan and cover with aluminium foil. Pour the water into the Instant Pot and fit in a trivet. Place the covered pan on top. Seal the lid, select the Manual mode and set the cooking time for 15 minutes on High Pressure. When cooking is complete, perform a quick pressure release. Unlock the lid, remove the pan, and take off the foil. Let cool for 5 minutes. Drizzle with maple syrup to serve.

Pecan, Date, Sultana Stuffed Apples

Prep time: 10 minutes | Cook time: 3 minutes | Serves 6

¼ cup toasted pecans, chopped	2 tablespoons brown sugar
½ cup dates, chopped	4 tablespoons butter
¼ cup sultanas	6 red apples, whole and cored
1 tablespoon cinnamon powder	4 tablespoons chocolate sauce, for topping

In a bowl, mix the pecans, dates, sultanas, cinnamon, brown sugar, and butter. Stuff apples with mixture. Pour 1 cup of water in Instant Pot and place stuffed apples in water. Seal the lid, select the Manual mode and set the timer for 3 minutes on Low Pressure. When cooking is complete, do a natural pressure release for 5 minutes, then release any remaining pressure. Open the lid. Carefully remove apples onto plates and drizzle with chocolate sauce.

Fruity Cake with Walnuts

Prep time: 10 minutes | Cook time: 3 to 5 hours | Serves 10 to 12

1 or 2 (21-ounce / 595-g) cans apple, blueberry, or peach pie filling	yellow cake mix
	1 stick (½ cup) butter, melted
1 (18¼-ounce / 517-g) package	⅓ cup chopped walnuts
	Nonstick cooking spray

Spray the insert of the Instant Pot with nonstick cooking spray. Place pie filling in the Instant Pot. In a mixing bowl, combine dry cake mix and butter. Spoon over filling. Drop walnuts over top. Cover and press the Slow Cook button, and cook on low for 3 to 5 hours or until a toothpick inserted into the center of topping comes out clean. (Press Slow Cook again to toggle between Low and High cooking temperatures.) Serve warm.

Banana Pecan Cake with Walnut

Prep time: 10 minutes | Cook time: 30 minutes | Serves 6

1½ cups all-purpose flour	grease the pan
1½ teaspoons baking powder	10 pecans, crushed, divided
½ teaspoon baking soda	10 walnuts, crushed, divided
2 medium very ripe bananas	2 cups water
½ cup sugar	1 cup vanilla cream cheese frosting
¼ cup milk	
¼ cup corn oil, plus more to	

Prepare the dry ingredients. In a large bowl, sift together the flour, baking powder, and baking soda. Purée the bananas. In a blender, purée the bananas until smooth. Set aside 1 cup of the purée. Prepare the wet ingredients. In a large bowl, mix together the sugar, banana purée, milk, and oil. Prepare the batter. Add the wet ingredients to the dry ingredients, and gently mix to form a smooth batter. Add 5 pecans and 5 walnuts to the batter, and gently fold them in. Grease a springform cake pan with some oil. Pour in the batter, and tap the pan twice on the counter to break any air pockets. Tightly cover the pan with aluminum foil. Pressure cook the cake. Pour the water into the inner pot, and place the trivet inside. Place the cake on the trivet, and lock the lid into place. Select Pressure Cook or Manual, and adjust the pressure to High and the time to 30 minutes. Make sure the steam release knob is in the sealed position. After cooking, naturally release the pressure. Decorate the cake. Unlock and remove the lid. Remove the cake pan and slowly remove the foil. Let the cake cool for at least 30 minutes. Release the cake from the springform pan. Frost the cake, and sprinkle the remaining pecans and walnuts on top. Slice and serve.

Apple Pie Oatmeal
Prep time: 10 minutes | Cook time: 4 to 5 hours | Serves 6

1 cup quick-cooking oats	3 eggs
½ cup all-purpose flour	1⅔ cups 2% milk, divided
⅓ cup packed brown sugar	1½ teaspoons vanilla extract
2 teaspoons baking powder	3 medium apples, peeled and
1½ teaspoons apple pie spice	finely chopped
¼ teaspoon salt	Vanilla ice cream (optional)

In a large bowl, whisk oats, flour, brown sugar, baking powder, pie spice and salt. In a small bowl, whisk eggs, 1 cup milk and vanilla until blended. Add to oat mixture, stirring just until moistened. Fold in apples. Transfer to a greased Instant Pot. Cover and press the Slow Cook button, and cook on low for 4 to 5 hours or until apples are tender and top is set. (Press Slow Cook again to toggle between Low and High cooking temperatures.) Stir in remaining milk. Serve warm or cold with ice cream if desired.

Coconut Bananas Foster
Prep time: 10 minutes | Cook time: 2 hours | Serves 5

5 medium firm bananas	½ teaspoon ground cinnamon
1 cup packed brown sugar	⅓ cup chopped walnuts
¼ cup butter, melted	⅓ cup flaked coconut
¼ cup rum	Vanilla ice cream or sliced
1 teaspoon vanilla extract	pound cake, for serving

Cut bananas in half lengthwise, then widthwise. Layer in the bottom of the Instant Pot. Combine the brown sugar, butter, rum, vanilla, and cinnamon, then pour over bananas. Cover and press the Slow Cook button, and cook on low for 1½ hours or until heated through. (Press Slow Cook again to toggle between Low and High cooking temperatures.) Sprinkle with walnuts and coconut and cook for 30 minutes longer. Serve with ice cream or pound cake.

Yogurt Brownies
Prep time: 10 minutes | Cook time: 35 minutes | Serves 6

1 cup all-purpose flour	½ cup milk
¼ cup cocoa powder	3 tablespoons plus 1 teaspoon
¾ cup confectioners' sugar	corn oil, divided
1 teaspoon baking powder	2 cups water
½ teaspoon baking soda	2 teaspoons sea salt
¼ cup plain Greek yogurt	

Prepare the dry ingredients. In a large bowl, sift together the flour, cocoa powder, and sugar. Add the baking powder and baking soda, and mix to combine. Prepare the wet ingredients. In a medium bowl, whisk together the yogurt, milk, and 3 tablespoons of oil. Prepare the batter. Little by little, add the wet ingredients to the dry ingredients, gently folding them together with each addition to form a smooth batter. Grease a spring-form pan with the remaining 1 teaspoon of oil. Pour the batter into the pan, and tightly cover with aluminum foil. Pressure cook the Brownies. Pour the water into the inner pot, and place the trivet inside. Place the pan on the trivet, and lock the lid into place. Select Pressure Cook or Manual, adjusting the pressure to High and the time to 35 minutes. Make sure the steam release knob is in the sealed position. After cooking, naturally release the pressure. Unlock and remove the lid. Remove the pan, and remove the foil. Sprinkle the brownies with the sea salt, and let cool for at least 30 minutes. Gently remove from the pan, slice, and serve.

Yogurt Custard
Prep time: 10 minutes | Cook time: 25 minutes | Serves 4

½ cup plain Greek yogurt	2 cups water
½ cup sweetened condensed	¼ cup chopped fruit or berries
milk	of your choice, for garnish
½ teaspoon ground cinnamon	

Prepare the custard. In a heatproof bowl that fits inside the Instant Pot, mix together the yogurt, condensed milk, and cinnamon. Tightly cover the bowl with aluminum foil. Pressure cook the custard. Pour the water into the inner pot, and place the trivet inside. Place the bowl on the trivet, and lock the lid into place. Select Pressure Cook or Manual, and adjust the pressure to High and the time to 25 minutes. Make sure the steam release knob is in the sealed position. After cooking, naturally release the pressure. Chill the custard. Unlock and remove the lid. Carefully remove the bowl. Let it cool at room temperature for 30 minutes, then refrigerate, covered, for 3 to 4 hours. Serve garnished with the fruits of your choice.

Mango Cheesecake
Prep time: 20 minutes | Cook time: 55 minutes | Serves 8

The Crust:

Cooking spray. for coating	pistachios
1¼ cups gingersnap or graham	3 tablespoons unsalted butter,
cracker crumbs or ground	melted

The Filling:

2 cups mango chunks (thawed	juice
if frozen)	½ teaspoon ground cardamom
2 (8-ounce / 227-g) packages	4 or 5 saffron threads
cream cheese, softened	½ cup granulated sugar
2 tablespoons fresh lemon	3 large eggs

The Topping:

2 tablespoons sour cream	1 ripe mango, peeled and
½ cup mango purée	sliced (optional)
2 teaspoons sugar	

Lightly spray a springform pan with cooking spray. Line the bottom of the pan with a circle of parchment paper. In a small bowl, mix together the crumbs and butter. Pat the mixture firmly into the bottom and about 1 inch up the sides of the pan. Place the pan in the freezer to allow the crust to set while you make the filling. In a blender or food processor, combine the mango chunks, lemon juice, cream cheese, cardamom, saffron, and sugar. Blend until smooth, scraping down the sides as needed. Add the eggs and blend until well incorporated and pourable, 10 to 15 seconds. Pour the mixture into the crust and cover with foil. Pour 1½ cups water into the Instant Pot. Place a trivet with handles in the pot, making sure the handles are in an upright position. Place the pan on the trivet. (If you do not have a trivet with handles, make a sling with foil and place it under the pan so you can easily lift it out of the pot.) Secure the lid on the pot. Close the pressure-release valve. Select Manual and set the pot at High Pressure for 55 minutes. At the end of the cooking time, allow the pot to sit undisturbed for 10 minutes, then quick-release any remaining pressure. (The sides of the cheesecake will be set, but the middle will still have a little jiggle. This will set as the cheesecake cools.) Use the handles on the trivet to carefully lift the pan out of the pot. Cool the cheesecake on a wire rack for 1 hour. In a medium bowl, stir together the sour cream, mango purée, and sugar. Spread the topping over the cheesecake. Chill in the refrigerator for at least 4 hours or overnight. Top the cheesecake with mango slices, if desired, and serve.

Lemon Blueberry Cornmeal Cake

Prep time: 10 minutes | Cook time: 2 to 3 hours | Serves 6

1 cup all-purpose flour
¼ cup cornmeal
½ teaspoon baking powder
½ teaspoon baking soda
Salt, to taste
½ cup plain yogurt
⅓ cup granulated sugar
1 large egg

2 teaspoons grated lemon zest plus 4 teaspoons juice
½ teaspoon vanilla extract
4 tablespoons unsalted butter, melted
5 ounces (142 g) blueberries
¾ cup confectioners' sugar
Cooking spray

Fill the Instant Pot with ½ inch water (about 2 cups) and place aluminum foil rack in bottom. Make foil sling for 8½ by 4½-inch loaf pan by folding 2 long sheets of foil; first sheet should be 8½ inches wide and second sheet should be 4½ inches wide. Lay sheets of foil in a pan perpendicular to each other, with extra foil hanging over edges of pan. Push foil into corners and up sides of pan, smoothing foil flush to pan. Lightly grease foil with cooking spray. Whisk flour, cornmeal, baking powder, baking soda, and ½ teaspoon of salt together in a bowl. In a large bowl, whisk yogurt, granulated sugar, egg, lemon zest, and vanilla until smooth, then slowly whisk in melted butter until well combined. Stir in flour mixture until just incorporated. Gently fold in blueberries. Scrape batter into prepared pan and smooth top. Gently tap pan on the counter to release air bubbles. Set pan on prepared rack, cover, and press the Slow Cook button, and cook on high for 2 to 3 hours. (Press Slow Cook again to toggle between Low and High cooking temperatures.) Cook until toothpick inserted in center comes out clean. Let cake cool in pan on wire rack for 10 minutes. Using foil overhang, lift cake out of pan and transfer to rack, discarding foil. Let cake cool completely, 1 to 2 hours. Whisk confectioners' sugar, pinch salt, and lemon juice in a small bowl until smooth. Flip cake over onto a serving dish. Drizzle top and sides with glaze and let glaze set before serving, about 25 minutes.

Egg Caramel Custard

Prep time: 20 minutes | Cook time: 22 minutes | Serves 6

¼ cup plus 5 tablespoons granulated sugar
2 tablespoons water
3 large eggs

2 cups whole milk
½ teaspoon vanilla extract
Fresh berries, for garnish (optional)

In a medium saucepan, heat 5 tablespoons of the sugar and the water over medium heat. Allow the sugar to caramelize without stirring (it will seize up if you stir it, especially once it's started boiling). Cook until it is a deep, rich color, but do not let it burn. Quickly—and very carefully—pour the liquid caramel into a 6-inch soufflé dish that fits inside the Instant Pot. In a medium bowl, whisk together the eggs, milk, remaining ¼ cup sugar, and vanilla. Pour over the top of the hardened caramel; cover the dish with foil. Pour 2 cups water into the pot. Place a trivet in the pot. Place the dish on the trivet. Secure the lid on the pot. Set the pressure-release valve to Venting. Select Sauté/Normal and set a kitchen timer for 22 minutes. At the end of the cooking time, insert a toothpick in the center of the custard to check for doneness. The center will be jiggly, but the toothpick should come out clean. Transfer the pan to the refrigerator to chill for 4 to 6 hours. When ready to serve, use a knife to loosen the edges, place a plate on top of the dish, and invert the custard onto the plate. Thump the bottom of the dish if necessary. Top with berries, if desired, and serve.

Butter Fudge Pudding Cake

Prep time: 15 minutes | Cook time: 20 minutes | Serves 6

½ cup (1 stick) unsalted butter, melted, plus room-temperature butter for greasing the pan
¾ cup all-purpose flour
1¼ cups packed dark brown sugar
½ cup whole milk
½ cup unsweetened cocoa

powder
2 large eggs
2 teaspoons baking powder
1 teaspoon vanilla extract
1¼ cups boiling water
Ice cream or sweetened whipped cream, for serving (optional)

Grease a round baking pan with softened butter; set aside. In a large mixing bowl, combine the melted butter, flour, ¾ cup of the brown sugar, milk, ¼ cup of the cocoa, eggs, baking powder, and vanilla. Using a hand mixer, beat until smooth. Pour the batter into the pan and sprinkle with the remaining ½ cup brown sugar and ¼ cup cocoa powder. Pour 1½ cups water into the Instant Pot. Place a trivet in the pot. Place the pan on the trivet. Carefully pour the boiling water on top of the batter. Do not stir. Secure the lid on the pot. Close the pressure-release valve. Select Manual and set the pot at High Pressure for 20 minutes. At the end of the cooking time, allow the pot to sit undisturbed for 10 minutes, then quick-release any remaining pressure. Serve warm with ice cream or whipped cream, if desired.

Mango Butter Cheesecake

Prep time: 20 minutes | Cook time: 50 minutes | Serves 8

½ cup unsalted butter, melted, plus 1 tablespoon unsalted butter, at room temperature
½ cup plus 2 tablespoons sugar, divided
2 cups plus 2 tablespoons water, divided
2 mangos, peeled and roughly

chopped, plus 1 mango, peeled and thinly sliced
16 ounces (454 g) cream cheese, at room temperature
1½ cups graham cracker crumbs
2 tablespoons cornstarch

Prepare the crust. In a medium bowl, mix together the graham cracker crumbs, melted butter, and 2 tablespoons of sugar. Reserve 2 tablespoons of the mixture to use as a garnish. Grease a springform pan with the room-temperature butter. Add the crumb mixture to the pan, and evenly press it down into the bottom. Place in the freezer for 15 minutes. Prepare the mango purée. Meanwhile, in a blender, combine the 2 chopped mangos and 2 tablespoons of water. Purée until smooth. This should make about 1 cup. Prepare the filling. In a large bowl, use a hand mixer to beat the cream cheese for 2 to 3 minutes or until light and fluffy. Add the remaining ½ cup of sugar, and mix until well combined. Add the cornstarch and mango purée. Using a spoon, gently fold the mixture until well combined. Remove the springform pan from the freezer, and pour the filling on top of the crust. Tightly cover the pan with aluminum foil. Pressure cook the cheesecake. Pour the remaining 2 cups of water into the inner pot, and place the trivet inside. Place the pan on top of the trivet, and lock the lid into place. Select Pressure Cook or Manual, and adjust the pressure to High and the time to 50 minutes. Make sure the steam release knob is in the sealed position. After cooking, naturally release the pressure. Finish the cheesecake. Unlock and remove the lid. Carefully remove the cake, then remove the foil. The center will be loose. Let it cool at room temperature for 1 hour, then cover the cheesecake again with foil and refrigerate for at least 6 hours. Before serving, sprinkle with the reserved crumb mixture and decorate with the sliced mangos.

Ginger and Pink Grapefruit Cheesecake

Prep time: 15 minutes | Cook time: 2 hours | Serves 6

¾ cup graham cracker crumbs
1 tablespoon plus ⅔ cup sugar, divided
1 teaspoon grated grapefruit peel
¼ teaspoon ground ginger
2½ tablespoons butter, melted

2 (8-ounce / 227-g) packages cream cheese, softened
½ cup sour cream
2 tablespoons pink grapefruit juice
2 eggs, lightly beaten

Place a greased springform pan on a double thickness of heavy-duty foil. Wrap foil securely around pan. Pour 1 inch water in the Instant Pot. Layer two 24-inch pieces of aluminum foil. Starting with a long side, fold up foil to create a 1-inch-wide strip; roll into a coil. Place in the Instant Pot to form a rack for the cheesecake. In a small bowl, mix cracker crumbs, 1 tablespoon sugar, peel, and ginger. Stir in butter. Press onto bottom and about 1 inch up sides of prepared pan. In a large bowl, beat cream cheese and remaining sugar until smooth. Beat in sour cream and grapefruit juice. Add eggs and beat on low speed just until combined. Pour into crust. Place springform pan on top of coil. Cover Instant Pot with a double layer of paper towels and place lid securely over towels. Cover and press the Slow Cook button, and cook on high for 2 hours. (Press Slow Cook again to toggle between Low and High cooking temperatures.) Do not remove lid. Turn off the Instant Pot and let cheesecake stand, covered, in Instant Pot for 1 hour. The center of the cheesecake will be just set and the top will appear dull. Remove springform pan from Instant Pot and remove foil from pan. Cool cheesecake on a wire rack for 1 hour before serving.

Fallen Chocolate Soufflé Cake

Prep time: 5 minutes | Cook time: 6 hours | Serves 10 to 12

1 (18¼-ounce / 517-g) package chocolate cake mix
½ cup vegetable oil
2 cups sour cream
4 eggs, beaten

1 (3-ounce / 85-g) box instant chocolate pudding mix
1 cup chocolate chips (optional)

Combine all ingredients in a greased Instant Pot. Cover and press the Slow Cook button, and cook on low for 6 hours. (Press Slow Cook again to toggle between Low and High cooking temperatures.) (Do not lift the lid until the end of the cooking time!) Insert a toothpick into the center of cake to see if it comes out clean. If it does, the soufflé is finished. If it doesn't, continue cooking for another 15 minutes. Check again. Repeat until it's finished cooking. Serve warm.

Simple Pineapple Tapioca

Prep time: 10 minutes | Cook time: 3 hours | Serves 4 to 6

2½ cups water
2½ cups pineapple juice
½ cup dry small pearl tapioca

¾ to 1 cup sugar
1 (15-ounce / 425-g) can crushed pineapple, undrained

Mix first four ingredients together in the Instant Pot. Cover and press the Slow Cook button, and cook on high for 3 hours. (Press Slow Cook again to toggle between Low and High cooking temperatures.) Stir in crushed pineapple. Chill for several hours before serving.

Strawberry Yogurt Cake

Prep time: 15 minutes | Cook time: 30 minutes | Serves 8

10 fresh strawberries, hulled, plus 10 fresh strawberries, hulled and halved
2 cups plus 1 tablespoon water, divided
1 cup sugar
½ cup plain Greek yogurt
½ teaspoon baking soda
1½ teaspoons baking powder

⅛ teaspoon kosher salt
1¼ cups all-purpose flour
2 tablespoons cocoa powder
½ cup corn oil
Nonstick cooking spray, for greasing
1 cup vanilla cream cheese frosting

Prepare the strawberry purée. In a blender, combine the whole strawberries and 1 tablespoon of water. Purée until smooth. This should make about ½ cup of purée. Prepare the yogurt mix. In a large bowl, whisk together the sugar and yogurt until the sugar is dissolved. Stir in the baking soda, baking powder, and salt. Let sit for about 5 minutes or until the mixture begins to bubble. Sift the flour. Meanwhile, in a medium bowl, sift the flour and cocoa powder together. Prepare the batter. Whisk the yogurt mixture again, then slowly whisk in the oil. Keep whisking until the oil is fully incorporated. Add the strawberry purée, and mix again. Add the flour-cocoa mixture, and gently mix to form a smooth batter. Bake the cake. Grease a springform pan with the cooking spray. Pour the batter into the pan, then tap the pan twice on the counter to break any air pockets. Tightly cover with aluminum foil. Pour the remaining 2 cups of water into the inner pot, and place the trivet inside. Place the pan on the trivet, and lock the lid into place. Select Pressure Cook or Manual, and adjust the pressure to High and the time to 30 minutes. Make sure the steam release knob is in the sealed position. After cooking, naturally release the pressure. Unlock and remove the lid. Remove the pan, and carefully remove the foil. Let cool for at least 30 minutes before removing the cake from the pan. Decorate the cake. Evenly spread the frosting over the cake. Place the fresh strawberry halves on top and serve.

Egg Sponge Cake

Prep time: 15 minutes | Cook time: 20 minutes | Serves 4

¼ cup vegetable oil, plus more for greasing the pan
4 large eggs
½ cup full-fat coconut milk or evaporated milk
½ teaspoon pandan or vanilla extract

1¼ cups all-purpose flour
¾ cup granulated sugar
2 teaspoons baking powder
Variations:
Substitute ½ teaspoon lemon, orange, or almond extract for the pandan extract.

Grease a 6 cup Bundt pan with oil; set aside. Using a hand mixer, blend the oil, eggs, and sugar until the sugar dissolves and the eggs are frothy. Add the evaporated milk and extract and continue blending. Add the flour and baking powder. Beat on low speed until the batter is smooth. Pour the batter into the pan and cover with foil. Pour 1½ cups water into the Instant Pot. Place a trivet in the pot. Place the pan on the trivet. Secure the lid on the pot. Close the pressure-release valve. Select Manual and set the pot at High Pressure for 20 minutes. At the end of the cooking time, allow the pot to sit undisturbed for 10 minutes, then quick-release any remaining pressure. Carefully remove the pan from the pot. Let the cake cool in the pan on a wire rack for 10 minutes. Release the springform pan ring and remove it. Allow the cake to cool completely before serving, about 20 minutes.

Butter Pie Custard

Prep time: 10 minutes | Cook time: 20 minutes | Serves 6

½ cup (1 stick) unsalted butter, melted, plus room-temperature butter for greasing the pan
½ cup granulated sugar
4 large eggs
⅓ cup evaporated milk
2 tablespoons cornmeal
1 tablespoon white vinegar
2 teaspoons vanilla extract

Grease a round baking pan with softened butter; set aside. In a large bowl, whisk together the melted butter and sugar until the sugar is mostly dissolved. Whisk in the eggs, evaporated milk, cornmeal, vinegar, and vanilla. Pour the mixture into the pan and cover with foil. Pour 1½ cups water into the Instant Pot. Place a trivet in the pot. Set the pan on the trivet. Secure the lid on the pot. Close the pressure-release valve. Select Manual and set the pot at High Pressure for 20 minutes. At the end of the cooking time, allow the pot to sit undisturbed for 10 minutes, then quick-release any remaining pressure. Cool the custard on a wire rack for about 15 minutes. Serve warm or transfer to the refrigerator to cool completely, then serve chilled.

Blueberry Cake

Prep time: 10 minutes | Cook time: 35 minutes | Serves 4

Vegetable oil, for greasing
1 cup blueberries
1 tablespoon granulated sugar, plus more for sprinkling
½ teaspoon ground nutmeg
1 (7-ounce / 198-g) package blueberry muffin mix
½ cup whole milk

Lightly grease a round baking pan with oil; set aside. In a small bowl, toss together the blueberries, sugar, and nutmeg. Spread the mixture over the bottom of the pan. Prepare the muffin mix according to the package directions, using the ½ cup milk for the liquid. Spread the batter on top of the blueberries; cover the pan with foil. Pour 2 cups water into the Instant Pot. Place a trivet in the pot. Place the pan on the trivet. Secure the lid on the pot. Close the pressure-release valve. Select Manual and set the pot at High Pressure for 35 minutes. At the end of the cooking time, use a natural release to depressurize. Preheat the broiler. Transfer the cake to a wire rack. Remove the foil. Let the cake cool for 5 to 10 minutes. Loosen the sides of the cake and invert onto a broiler-safe pan. Sprinkle the cake with a little sugar; broil until the sugar is melted and caramelized, 5 to 7 minutes. Let cool slightly before serving.

Rice Pudding with Raisins Cashews

Prep time: 10 minutes | Cook time: 20 minutes | Serves 4

¾ cup Arborio rice, rinsed and drained
1 (13.5-ounce / 383-g) can full-fat coconut milk
5 ounces (142 g) evaporated milk
½ cup granulated sugar
½ cup raisins
½ cup cashews
¼ teaspoon ground cardamom
3 or 4 saffron threads
½ cup water

In the Instant Pot, combine the rice, half the coconut milk, the evaporated milk, sugar, raisins, cashews, cardamom, saffron, and water. Secure the lid on the pot. Close the pressure-release valve. Select Manual and set the pot at High Pressure for 20 minutes. At the end of the cooking time, allow the pot to sit undisturbed for 10 minutes, then quick-release any remaining pressure. When you open the lid, there will be a little bit of curdling—don't worry about this. Stir to reincorporate all the ingredients. Add the remaining coconut milk and stir to combine. Serve warm or chilled.

Lemon Yogurt Cake

Prep time: 15 minutes | Cook time: 30 minutes | Serves 6

1 cup plain Greek yogurt
¾ cup sugar
½ teaspoon baking soda
1¼ teaspoons baking powder
½ teaspoon kosher salt
½ cup corn oil, plus more to grease the pan
1½ cups all-purpose flour
1 tablespoon plus ½ teaspoon freshly squeezed lemon juice, divided
1½ teaspoons grated lemon zest
2 cups water
¼ cup confectioners' sugar

Prepare the yogurt mix. In a large bowl, whisk together the yogurt and sugar until the sugar is well dissolved. Stir in the baking soda, baking powder, and salt. Set aside for 5 minutes or until the mixture begins to bubble. Sift the flour. Meanwhile, sift the flour into a medium bowl. Prepare the batter. Whisk the yogurt mixture, then slowly whisk in the oil until fully incorporated. Stir in ½ teaspoon of lemon juice and the lemon zest. Add the sifted flour, and gently mix to form a smooth batter. Grease a Bundt cake pan with corn oil, and pour in the batter. Tap the pan twice on the counter to break any air pockets, and tightly cover with aluminum foil. Pressure cook the cake. Pour the water into the inner pot, and place the trivet inside. Place the pan on the trivet, and lock the lid into place. Select Pressure Cook or Manual, and adjust the pressure to High and the time to 30 minutes. Make sure the steam release knob is in the sealed position. After cooking, naturally release the pressure. Assemble the cake. Unlock and remove the lid. Remove the pan, and slowly remove the foil. Let the cake cool for at least 30 minutes. Run the knife along the edge of the pan, and invert the cake onto a plate. In a small bowl, add the remaining 1 tablespoon of lemon juice to the confectioners' sugar and mix thoroughly. Drizzle the glaze on top of the cake and serve.

Dried Fruit Kesari with Saffron

Prep time: 10 minutes | Cook time: 10 minutes | Serves 4

½ cup farina (such as Cream of Wheat)
⅓ cup chopped mixed dried fruit
¼ cup granulated sugar
¼ cup ghee or vegetable oil

1 teaspoon ground cardamom
3 or 4 saffron threads, crushed
¾ cup water
Heavy cream and/or milk, for serving (optional)

In a round baking pan, mix together the farina, dried fruit, sugar, ghee, cardamom, saffron, and water. Pour 1½ cups water into the Instant Pot. Place a trivet in the pot. Place the pan on the trivet. Secure the lid on the pot. Close the pressure-release valve. Select Manual and set the pot at High Pressure for 10 minutes. At the end of the cooking time, allow the pot to sit undisturbed for 5 minutes, then quick-release any remaining pressure. Carefully remove the pan and stir the mixture until smooth. Serve hot or chilled. If desired, stir in some cream and/ or milk for a porridge-like texture.

Apple and Quinoa Porridge

Prep time: 10 minutes | Cook time: 5 minutes | Serves 6

1 cup quinoa, rinsed and drained
1 cup peeled diced apples
1 (12-ounce / 340-g) can evaporated milk
1 cup sweetened condensed

milk
1 teaspoon apple pie spice
¼ cup chopped walnuts (optional)
1 cup water

In the Instant Pot, combine the quinoa and water; stir to combine. Scatter the apples over the top (do not stir). Secure the lid on the pot. Close the pressure-release valve. Select Manual and set the pot at High Pressure for 1 minute. At the end of the cooking time, use a quick release to depressurize. Stir in the evaporated milk, condensed milk, and apple pie spice. Add the walnuts, if using. Serve hot immediately or chill and serve. (If you chill it, the porridge may thicken and you may need to add a little milk just before serving.)

Creamy Yogurt

Prep time: 20 minutes | Cook time: 8 minutes | Makes 6 cups

2 cups whole milk
½ cup heavy whipping cream
1½ teaspoons unflavored vegetarian gelatin
3 tablespoons Greek yogurt

½ teaspoon ground cardamom, ground cinnamon, or apple pie spice
¼ cup granulated sugar
1½ teaspoons honey (optional)

In a medium microwave-safe bowl, combine the milk and cream and heat on high in the microwave for 2 minutes. In a small bowl, combine ½ cup of the warm milk mixture and the gelatin. Stir until smooth, then add back to the rest of the milk mixture. Transfer to the Instant Pot. Add the yogurt and cardamom and stir until well combined. Secure the lid on the Instant Pot. Select YOGURT (the timer will show 8 hours by default). At the end of the incubation time, stir in the sugar and honey, if using. (Don't add the sweeteners before the yogurt is set, as they can interfere with setting.) Chill for at least 6 hours to allow the yogurt to firm up before serving. Cover and store in the refrigerator for up to one week.

Dulce De Leche with Almonds

Prep time: 5 minutes | Cook time: 45 minutes | Serves 4

1 (14-ounce / 397-g) can sweetened condensed milk
2 cups water
1 teaspoon sea salt

Chopped almonds, for topping (optional)
Chopped chocolate, for topping (optional)

Prepare the ramekins. Evenly divide the condensed milk among four ramekins, three inches in diameter. Tightly cover each with aluminum foil. Pressure cook the Dulce de Leche. Pour the water into the inner pot, and place the trivet inside. Place the ramekins on the trivet, stacking them if needed. Lock the lid into place. Select Pressure Cook or Manual, and adjust the pressure to High and the time to 45 minutes. Make sure the steam release knob is in the sealed position. After cooking, naturally release the pressure. Unlock and remove the lid. Carefully remove the ramekins. Remove the foil, and sprinkle with the sea salt. Let cool for 30 minutes before topping with chopped almonds and chocolate, if desired, and serving.

Chapter 13 Basics

Mushroom Chicken Stock
Prep time: 5 minutes | Cook time: 1 hour | Serves 8

2½ pounds (1.1 kg) chicken, bones only
1 cup diced cremini mushrooms
1 small onion, unpeeled and halved
1 leek, finely chopped
1 teaspoon dried bay leaf
1 teaspoon kosher salt
½ teaspoon white pepper
½ teaspoon whole black peppercorns
8 cups water

Place all the ingredients into the Instant Pot and stir well. Lock the lid. Select the Pressure Cook mode and set the cooking time for 1 hour at High Pressure. Once cooking is complete, do a natural pressure release for 10 minutes, then release any remaining pressure. Carefully open the lid. Strain the stock through a fine-mesh strainer and discard all the solids. Remove the layer of fat that forms on the top, if desired. Serve immediately or store in an airtight container in the refrigerator for 3 to 4 days or in the freezer for up to 6 months.

Corn and Mushroom Stock
Prep time: 10 minutes | Cook time: 15 minutes | Serves 8

4 large mushrooms, diced
2 cobs of corns
1 small onion, unpeeled and halved
1 celery stalk, chopped into thirds
1 teaspoon dried bay leaf
1 teaspoon grated ginger
1 sprig fresh parsley
1 teaspoon kosher salt
½ teaspoon ground turmeric
½ teaspoon whole black peppercorns
8 cups water

Place all the ingredients into the Instant Pot and stir well. Lock the lid. Press the Pressure Cook button on the Instant Pot and set the cooking time for 15 minutes at High Pressure. Once cooking is complete, do a natural pressure release for 10 minutes, then release any remaining pressure. Carefully open the lid. Strain the stock through a fine-mesh strainer and discard all the solids. Serve immediately or refrigerate in an airtight container for 3 to 4 days.

Posh Tomato Salsa
Prep time: 10 minutes | Cook time: 30 minutes | Serves 6

6 cups fresh tomatoes, diced, peeled, and deseeded
1½ (6-ounce / 170-g) cans tomato paste
1½ green bell peppers, diced
1 cup jalapeño peppers, deseeded and chopped
¼ cup vinegar
2 yellow onions, diced
½ tablespoon kosher salt
1½ tablespoons sugar
1 tablespoon cayenne pepper
1 tablespoon garlic powder

Place all the ingredients into the Instant Pot and stir to incorporate. Secure the lid. Select the Pressure Cook mode and set the cooking time for 30 minutes at High Pressure. Once cooking is complete, do a natural pressure release for 10 minutes, then release any remaining pressure. Carefully open the lid. Serve immediately or refrigerate in an airtight container for up to 5 days.

Beef Bone Broth
Prep time: 5 minutes | Cook time: 2 hours | Serves 8

8 cups water
4 pounds (1.8 kg) beef bones
5 cloves garlic, smashed
2 carrots, peeled and sliced in half
2 ribs celery, sliced in half
1 medium yellow onion, with skin-on, quartered
10 whole black peppercorns
1 tablespoon apple cider vinegar
1 teaspoon poultry seasoning
1 teaspoon kosher salt
2 sprigs rosemary
2 sprigs thyme
2 bay leaves

Add all the ingredients to the Instant Pot and stir to combine. Lock the lid. Press the Pressure Cook button on the Instant Pot and set the cooking time for 2 hours at High Pressure. When the timer beeps, perform a natural pressure release for 30 minutes, then release any remaining pressure. Carefully remove the lid. Let the broth cool for 15 minutes. Strain the broth through a fine-mesh strainer and discard all the solids. Serve immediately or store in a sealed container in the refrigerator for 1 week or in the freezer for up to 3 months.

Pork Bone Broth
Prep time: 5 minutes | Cook time: 1 hour | Serves 8

3 pounds (1.4 kg) pork bones
3 large carrots, cut into large chunks
3 large stalks celery, cut into large chunks
2 cloves garlic, sliced
1 bay leaf
1 tablespoon apple cider vinegar
8 cups water
1 teaspoon whole peppercorns
Salt, to taste

Place all the ingredients into the Instant Pot and stir to incorporate. Secure the lid. Select the Pressure Cook mode and set the cooking time for 1 hour at High Pressure. When the timer beeps, perform a natural pressure release for 10 minutes, then release any remaining pressure. Carefully remove the lid. Allow the broth to cool for 10 to 15 minutes. Strain the broth through a fine-mesh strainer and discard all the solids. Serve immediately or store in a sealed container in the refrigerator for 4 to 5 days or in the freezer for up to 6 months.

Mushroom and Bay Leaf Broth
Prep time: 5 minutes | Cook time: 15 minutes | Serves 8

4 ounces (113 g) dried mushrooms, soaked and rinsed
½ cup celery, chopped
½ cup carrots, chopped
4 cloves garlic, crushed
4 bay leaves
1 onion, quartered
8 cups water
Salt and ground black pepper, to taste.

Add all the ingredients except the salt and pepper to the Instant Pot and stir well. Lock the lid. Press the Pressure Cook button on the Instant Pot and set the cooking time for 15 minutes at High Pressure. Once cooking is complete, do a quick pressure release. Open the lid. Add the salt and pepper to taste. Over a large bowl, carefully strain the stock through a fine-mesh strainer. Discard all the solids. Serve immediately or store in a sealed container in the refrigerator for 4 to 5 days or in the freezer for up to 6 months.

Tabasco Hot Sauce

Prep time: 5 minutes | Cook time: 1 hour | Makes 2 cups

18 ounces (510 g) fresh hot peppers or any kind, stems removed and chopped

1¾ cups apple cider
3 teaspoons smoked or plain salt

Combine all the ingredients in the Instant Pot. Lock the lid. Press the Pressure Cook button on the Instant Pot and set the cooking time for 1 hour at High Pressure. Once cooking is complete, do a natural pressure release for 15 minutes, then release any remaining pressure. Carefully open the lid. Purée the mixture with an immersion blender until smooth. Serve immediately or refrigerate until ready to use.

Creamy Ancho Chili Sauce

Prep time: 5 minutes | Cook time: 8 minutes | Serves 4

4 medium-sized Ancho chili peppers, stems and seeds removed
2 teaspoons kosher salt
1½ teaspoons sugar
½ teaspoon ground dried oregano

½ teaspoon ground cumin
1½ cups water
2 cloves garlic, crushed
2 tablespoons heavy cream
2 tablespoons apple cider vinegar

On your cutting board, chop the peppers into small pieces. Place the pepper pieces into the Instant Pot along with the salt, sugar, oregano, and cumin. Pour in the water and stir to combine. Lock the lid. Press the Pressure Cook button on the Instant Pot and set the cooking time for 8 minutes at High Pressure. Once cooking is complete, do a natural pressure release for 10 minutes, then release any remaining pressure. Carefully open the lid. Transfer the mixture to a food processor. Add the garlic, heavy cream, and apple cider vinegar. Process until smooth and creamy. Serve chilled or at room temperature.

Cannellini Bean Dip

Prep time: 10 minutes | Cook time: 25 minutes | Makes 1 cup

8 ounces (227 g) dried cannellini beans, rinsed
2 tablespoons roasted garlic purée
2 tablespoons balsamic vinegar
1 tablespoon chopped fresh

sage
4 tablespoons extra-virgin olive oil, divided
1 teaspoon kosher salt
⅛ teaspoon freshly ground black pepper

In the Instant Pot, add the beans and fill the pot with enough water to cover beans by about 2 inches. Lock on the lid and set the timer for 25 minutes at High Pressure. When the timer goes off, natural release the pressure for 10 minutes, then quick release any remaining pressure and remove the lid. Drain the beans in a colander, reserving about ¼ cup of the cooking liquid. Transfer the beans to a food processor and pulse to begin puréeing the beans. Add the garlic, vinegar, 3 tablespoons of olive oil, sage, salt, and pepper. Continue puréeing until the dip is smooth and creamy. If the dip is too thick, add some of the reserved cooking liquid, 1 tablespoon at a time, as needed, to thin it out a bit. Transfer the dip to a serving dish and drizzle with the remaining 1 tablespoon of olive oil. The dip will keep, covered and refrigerated, for 3 to 5 days.

Eggplant Dip with Vinegar

Prep time: 10 minutes | Cook time: 4 minutes | Makes 2 cups

2 tablespoons extra-virgin olive oil, divided
2 medium eggplant, halved, and each piece cut crosswise into 3 pieces
2 tablespoons white wine vinegar
1 cup water
1 tablespoon prepared roasted

garlic
1 tablespoon freshly squeezed lemon juice
1 tablespoon tahini
½ teaspoon kosher salt, plus more as needed
½ teaspoon ground cayenne pepper

With the Instant Pot on the Sauté or brown setting, heat 1 tablespoon of olive oil until it shimmers. Working in batches, place the eggplant pieces, cut-side down, in the hot oil and sear until it has browned, about 5 minutes. Remove the eggplant and set aside. Add the vinegar to the pot and use a spatula or a wooden spoon to scrape up any browned bits on the bottom of the pot. Pour the water into the pot, then add the eggplant, stacking the pieces if necessary. Lock on the lid and set the timer for 4 minutes at High Pressure. When the timer goes off, quick release the pressure and remove the lid. Use tongs to remove the eggplant, and set the pieces aside until they are cool enough to handle. Scoop the flesh from the eggplant into a bowl and discard the eggplant skin. Stir in the garlic, lemon juice, tahini, remaining 1 tablespoon of olive oil, salt, and cayenne pepper. If you want a smoother dip texture, use an immersion blender to purée the mixture or process it in a food processor. Serve warm or at room temperature. The eggplant spread will keep, tightly covered and refrigerated, for up to 3 days.

Citrus Berry and Apple Sauce

Prep time: 5 minutes | Cook time: 5 minutes | Serves 6

1 pound (454 g) cranberries (fresh or frozen)
10 strawberries, chopped
1 apple, cored and chopped
Juice from 1 lemon
Juice from 1 orange

1 teaspoon grated lemon zest
1 teaspoon grated orange zest
1 cup sugar
¼ cup water
1 cinnamon stick

Combine all the ingredients in the Instant Pot. Secure the lid. Select the Pressure Cook mode and set the cooking time for 5 minutes at High Pressure. Once cooking is complete, do a natural pressure release for 10 minutes, then release any remaining pressure. Carefully open the lid. Serve immediately or refrigerate until ready to use.

Cauliflower Sauce

Prep time: 5 minutes | Cook time: 3 minutes | Serves 4

12 ounces (340 g) cauliflower florets
½ cup water

¼ teaspoon pepper
¼ teaspoon garlic salt
2 tablespoons almond milk

Except for the almond milk, combine all the ingredients in the Instant Pot. Secure the lid. Select the Pressure Cook mode and set the cooking time for 3 minutes at High Pressure. Once cooking is complete, do a quick pressure release. Remove the lid. Purée the mixture with an immersion blender until smooth. Pour in the almond milk and whisk to combine. Serve chilled or at room temperature.

Beef Stock

Prep time: 10 minutes | Cook time: 1 hour 30 minutes
Makes 4 cups

1 tablespoon oil
2 pounds (907 g) meaty beef bones

¼ teaspoon kosher salt (optional)
8 cups water

Press the Sauté button on the Instant Pot and heat the oil until shimmering. Working in batches, arrange the beef bones in a single layer and sear each side for 6 to 8 minutes. Season with salt (if desired). Add the water to the Instant Pot, making sure the bones are fully submerged. Lock the lid. Select the Manual mode and set the cooking time for 75 minutes at High Pressure. Once cooking is complete, do a natural pressure release for 15 minutes, then release any remaining pressure. Remove the lid. Carefully pour the stock through a fine-mesh strainer into a large bowl. Serve immediately or store in an airtight container in the refrigerator for up to 4 days or in the freezer for 6 to 12 months.

Fish Stock

Prep time: 5 minutes | Cook time: 50 minutes | Serves 10

1 tablespoon olive oil
2 salmon heads, cut into quarters, rinsed, and patted dry
2 cloves garlic, sliced
1 cup roughly chopped celery

1 cup roughly chopped carrots
2 lemongrass stalks, roughly chopped
8 cups water
Handful fresh thyme, including stems

Press the Sauté button on the Instant Pot and heat the oil. Add the salmon to the Instant Pot and lightly sear the fish on both sides, about 4 minutes. Add the remaining ingredients to the Instant Pot and stir to combine. Secure the lid. Select the Soup mode and set the cooking time for 45 minutes at High Pressure. Once cooking is complete, do a natural pressure release for 15 minutes, then release any remaining pressure. Remove the lid. Over a large bowl, carefully strain the stock through a fine-mesh strainer. Serve immediately or refrigerate until ready to use.

Carrot Broth with Apple

Prep time: 5 minutes | Cook time: 30 minutes | Serves 6

1 peach, quartered
2 apples, quartered
1 medium onion, quartered
4 cloves garlic, chopped (peel and all)
8 carrots, halved
6 stalks celery, halved
1 tomato, quartered
6 whole romaine lettuce leaves

1 teaspoon avocado oil (optional)
8 cups (2 L) water
½ teaspoon dried oregano
½ teaspoon dried sage
½ teaspoon dried sweet basil
½ teaspoon dried whole (rubbed) rosemary
1 teaspoon sea salt (optional)

Place all the ingredients in the Instant Pot. Stir to combine. Cover and bring to pressure. Cook at High Pressure for 15 to 30 minutes (for a richer broth, opt for 30 minutes). Remove from the heat and allow for a natural release. Remove the lid from the Instant Pot. Strain the broth through a fine-mesh strainer or cheesecloth. Use immediately or store in an airtight glass jar or container for up to 1 week; freeze in a heavy-duty freezer bag for 3 to 6 months.

Vegetable Stock

Prep time: 5 minutes | Cook time: 30 minutes | Serves 8

8 cups water
4 celery stalks, cut into chunks
4 carrots, cut into chunks
4 thyme sprigs
6 parsley sprigs

2 teaspoons chopped garlic
2 bay leaves
2 green onions, sliced
10 whole black peppercorns
1½ teaspoons salt

Except for the salt, add all the ingredients to the Instant Pot. Secure the lid. Select the Soup mode and set the cooking time for 30 minutes at High Pressure. Once cooking is complete, do a natural pressure release for 15 minutes, then release any remaining pressure. Remove the lid. Sprinkle with the salt and whisk well. Over a large bowl, carefully strain the stock through a fine-mesh strainer. Serve immediately or store in an airtight container in the refrigerator for 4 to 5 days or in the freezer for up to 3 months.

Seafood Stock

Prep time: 5 minutes | Cook time: 30 minutes | Serves 8

8 cups water
Shells and heads from ½ pound (227 g) prawns
3 cloves garlic, sliced
4 carrots, cut into chunks

4 onions, quartered
2 bay leaves
1 teaspoon whole black peppercorns

Place all the ingredients into the Instant Pot. Secure the lid. Select the Manual mode and set the cooking time for 30 minutes at High Pressure. Once cooking is complete, do a natural pressure release for 15 minutes, then release any remaining pressure. Remove the lid. Over a large bowl, carefully strain the stock through a fine-mesh strainer. Serve immediately or store in an airtight container in the refrigerator for 3 days or in the freezer for up to 3 months.

Cheeze Sauce with Potato

Prep time: 10 minutes | Cook time: 5 minutes | Makes 3 cups

1 medium sweet potato, peeled and chopped
1 cup water
1 cup raw cashews, soaked in water overnight, drained, and rinsed well
1 cup unsweetened nondairy milk (I like cashew)
¼ cup nutritional yeast

1 tablespoon apple cider vinegar
2 teaspoons salt
¼ teaspoon garlic powder
Pinch freshly ground black pepper
2 poblano peppers, roasted
Chili powder, to taste (optional)

In your Instant Pot, combine the sweet potato and water. Lock the lid and turn the steam release handle to Sealing. Using the Manual function, set the cooker to High Pressure for 5 minutes (4 minutes at sea level). When the cook time is complete, quick release the pressure. Carefully remove the lid and drain the water from the pot. In a high-speed blender or food processor, combine the cashews, milk, nutritional yeast, vinegar, salt, garlic powder, and pepper. Blend until completely smooth. Add the sweet potatoes and blend again. Finally, add the poblanos and pulse just until there are green specks throughout. Pour the blended mixture back into the Instant Pot. Using a rubber spatula, make sure you get as much as possible. Select Sauté Low. When the sauce is hot, turn off the Instant Pot. Taste and adjust the seasonings. If you want more heat, add chili powder to taste.

Butter Sauce with Vanilla

Prep time: 5 minutes | Cook time: 22 minutes | Makes 1¾ cups

1 (14-ounce / 397-g) can sweetened condensed milk
1 teaspoon vanilla extract
1 teaspoon ground cinnamon
8 cups water
2 tablespoons unsalted butter

Spoon the sweetened condensed milk into a 16-ounce glass jar with a lid, such as a canning jar. Stir in the vanilla and cinnamon. Place the lid on the jar so that it is screwed closed just until it catches but is not tightened, and place it in the Instant Pot. Add the water to the pot; it should come about halfway up the side of the jar. Lock the lid on the Instant Pot and set the timer for 22 minutes at High Pressure. When the timer goes off, turn off or unplug the Instant Pot and natural release the pressure. When the pressure has been completely released, quick release any remaining pressure and open the Instant Pot lid. Carefully remove the jar with an oven mitt, and let it cool slightly until it can be handled, 10 to 15 minutes. Open the lid and stir in the butter until the caramel is smooth and creamy. The caramel will keep for 2 weeks, covered and refrigerated.

Marinara Sauce

Prep time: 5 minutes | Cook time: 13 minutes | Makes 4 cups

1 medium onion, grated
3 garlic cloves, roughly chopped
1 (28-ounce / 794-g) can or carton whole or crushed tomatoes
1 teaspoon kosher salt, plus more as needed
2 tablespoons oil
Freshly ground black pepper, to taste
½ teaspoon dried oregano or 2 oregano sprigs
Pinch granulated or raw sugar (optional)

Press the Sauté button on the Instant Pot and heat the oil until it shimmers. Add the grated onion and sauté for 2 minutes until tender. Add the garlic and sauté for 1 minute. Fold in the tomatoes, salt, oregano, and pepper and stir well. Secure the lid. Select the Manual mode and set the cooking time for 10 minutes at High Pressure. Once cooking is complete, do a quick pressure release. Carefully open the lid. Taste and adjust the seasoning, if needed. Add the sugar to balance the acidity of the tomatoes, if desired. Store in an airtight container in the refrigerator for up to 4 days or freeze for up to 6 months.

Marinara Sauce with Onion

Prep time: 5 minutes | Cook time: 5 minutes | Serves 4

1 teaspoon extra-virgin olive oil
4 to 6 cloves garlic, minced
1 cup (160 g) diced onion
1 teaspoon dried basil
1 teaspoon dried oregano
1 teaspoon dried parsley
1 teaspoon dried thyme
½ teaspoon red pepper flakes
¼ teaspoon black pepper
1 can (28 ounces / 794 g) crushed tomatoes
½ cup (120 ml) vegetable broth
½ teaspoon sea salt
½ teaspoon sugar (optional)

In an uncovered Instant Pot, heat the oil on medium-high. Add the garlic and onion and sauté for 3 minutes, until the onion is soft. Add the seasonings, tomatoes, and broth. Stir to combine. Cover and bring to pressure. Cook at Low Pressure for 5 minutes. Allow for a natural release. Remove the lid, taste, and add salt and sugar as desired.

Garlic Red Sauce with Tomato

Prep time: 5 minutes | Cook time: 20 minutes | Makes 2½ to 2¾ cups

4 medium (about 1 pound / 454 g) tomatoes, quartered
1 small sweet onion, peeled and quartered
⅓ cup strong hearty wine (like a Cabernet Sauvignon or Merlot), plus more as needed
½ cup water, plus more as needed
4 ounces (113 g) tomato paste
4 or 5 garlic cloves, or to taste, peeled
1½ teaspoons dried oregano
1 teaspoon dried basil
1 teaspoon salt
¼ teaspoon baking soda
Pinch red pepper flakes

Drop the tomatoes and onion into the Instant Pot. Add the wine, water, and tomato paste. Cover the veggies with the garlic, oregano, basil, salt, baking soda, and red pepper flakes. There is no need to stir; it's better to have everything mostly on top of the tomatoes than at the bottom of the pot. Lock the lid and turn the steam release handle to Sealing. Using the Manual function, set the Instant Pot to High Pressure for 20 minutes (17 minutes at sea level). When the cook time is complete, turn off the Instant Pot and let the pressure release naturally for 15 minutes; quick release any remaining pressure. Carefully remove the lid. Using an immersion blender, create the red sauce of your dreams. Add a bit more water (or wine!) if you need to thin it.

Basic Quinoa

Prep time: 2 minutes | Cook time: 3 minutes | Serves 4

1 cup white quinoa
1¾ cups water
⅛ teaspoon kosher salt

Place the quinoa, water, and salt in the Instant Pot pot. Lock on the lid and set the timer for 3 minutes at High Pressure. When the timer goes off, natural release the pressure for 5 minutes. Quick release any remaining pressure and remove the lid. If water remains, cover the Instant Pot and let sit for 5 minutes until the water is absorbed. Fluff the quinoa with a fork. Serve hot. Or, to serve as a chilled salad, spread the cooked quinoa on a large plate or baking sheet to cool before using.

Hot Sauce with Mirin

Prep time: 5 minutes | Cook time: 15 minutes | Serves 2

½ cup brown rice syrup
½ cup rice vinegar
½ cup mirin
2 tablespoons red miso
¼ cup vegan chili paste (Thai
or Gochujang)
1 tablespoon tamari or soy sauce
1 tablespoon sesame seeds

Add 1 cup of water to an uncovered Instant Pot. Bring to a boil by using the Sauté function (adjust to more heat). Set a trivet over the water. Combine all the ingredients in glass or ceramic bowl that fits into the pot without touching the sides. Once the water is boiling, place the bowl on the trivet. Cover the pot, move the steam release handle to sealing, select Manual (High Pressure), and set to 15 minutes. Once done, allow for a natural release (release after 10 minutes). Transfer the hot sauce to a glass jar and cool at room temperature for 1 to 2 hours. Secure an airtight lid onto the jar before placing in the refrigerator. Use the sauce within 5 to 7 days.

Poached Eggs

Prep time: 2 minutes | Cook time: 3 minutes | Serves 2

1 cup water
Cooking spray, for coating
2 eggs

Pinch kosher salt
Pinch freshly ground black pepper

Place a rack in the Instant Pot and add the water to the Instant Pot. Spray the insides of two silicone egg poaching cups or heat-proof glass custard cups with cooking spray. Crack an egg into each cup and place the cups on the rack. Lock on the lid and set the timer for 3 minutes at Low Pressure. When the timer goes off, quick release the pressure and open the lid. If the eggs are not quite as set as you like, replace the lid and let them sit in the hot Instant Pot for an additional 1 to 2 minutes. Turn the eggs out onto a plate or on a piece of toasted bread or English muffin. Sprinkle with the salt and pepper. Serve immediately.

Hummus with Yogurt

Prep time: 15 minutes | Cook time: 45 minutes | Makes 2 cups

½ pound (227 g) dried chickpeas
1½ teaspoons kosher salt, divided
½ cup low-fat plain yogurt
1 garlic clove, minced
2 tablespoons freshly squeezed lemon juice

2 teaspoons extra-virgin olive oil
1 tablespoon dried thyme
1 tablespoon dried dill
1 teaspoon ground cumin
⅛ teaspoon ground cayenne pepper

Place the chickpeas in the Instant Pot pot and add enough water (about 6 cups) to cover them by about 2 inches. Stir in ½ teaspoon of salt. Lock on the lid and set the timer for 45 minutes at High Pressure. When the timer goes off, natural release the pressure for 10 minutes, then quick release any remaining pressure. Drain the chickpeas in a colander and let them cool. Transfer the chickpeas to the bowl of a food processor. Add the yogurt and garlic and process until creamy. Scrape down the sides of the bowl as needed to make sure everything gets well puréed. Add the lemon juice, olive oil, thyme, dill, cumin, cayenne pepper, and the remaining 1 teaspoon of salt, and pulse to mix. Continue to process until the mixture is smooth and creamy. It may take 2 or 3 minutes of processing to achieve the creamy texture. Transfer the hummus to a serving bowl and serve immediately or store, tightly covered and refrigerated, for 3 to 5 days.

Homemade Brown Rice

Prep time: 5 minutes | Cook time: 20 minutes | Serves 4

1 cup long-grain brown rice
1¼ cups water

¼ teaspoon kosher salt

In the pot of the pressure cooker or in a fine-mesh strainer, rinse the rice several times until the water seems less chalky. Drain well. Add the rice, water, and salt to the pressure cooker. Stir to combine and scrape down any loose grains of rice into the liquid. Lock on the lid and set the timer for 20 minutes at High Pressure. When the timer goes off, natural release for 10 minutes, then quick release any remaining pressure. Remove the lid and stir the rice with a fork to fluff. If any water remains, cover the cooker and let the rice sit for 5 minutes until the water is absorbed.

Tomato Sauce with Garlic

Prep time: 15 minutes | Cook time: 15 minutes | Serves 3½ cups

2 tablespoons extra-virgin olive oil
1 onion, diced
2 garlic cloves, minced
1 (28-ounce / 794-g) can whole or chopped tomatoes
2 tablespoons tomato paste

2 teaspoons dried oregano
1 teaspoon dried basil
½ teaspoon dried thyme
1 teaspoon kosher salt
⅛ teaspoon freshly ground black pepper

With the Instant Pot on the brown or Sauté setting, heat the oil until it shimmers. Add the onion and sauté, stirring frequently, until the onion is softened and translucent, about 5 minutes. Add the garlic and sauté, stirring constantly, for 1 minute. Add the chopped tomatoes, tomato paste, oregano, basil, thyme, salt, and pepper. Stir to combine. Lock on the lid and set the timer for 15 minutes at High Pressure. When the timer goes off, quick release the pressure. Stir the sauce and use or store.

Peanuts with Salt

Prep time: 5 minutes | Cook time: 1 hour | Serves 6 to 8

1 pound (454 g) raw (green) peanuts, in shells, rinsed

2 tablespoons vegetable oil
¼ cup kosher salt

Place the peanuts in the Instant Pot pot. Add water to the maximum fill line of the Instant Pot. Stir in the vegetable oil and salt. Lock on the lid and set the timer for 1 hour at High Pressure. When the timer goes off, natural release the pressure completely. Open the lid and use a slotted spoon to remove the peanuts from the cooking liquid. Serve hot or warm.

Pumpkin Butter with Apple Cider

Prep time: 10 minutes | Cook time: 12 minutes | Makes 1¾ cups

1 can pumpkin purée
½ cup apple cider
½ cup dark brown sugar

2 teaspoons pumpkin pie spice
⅛ teaspoon kosher salt

In the Instant Pot pot, stir together the pumpkin purée, cider, brown sugar, spice, and salt. Lock on the lid and set the timer for 12 minutes at High Pressure. When the timer goes off, quick release the pressure and stir the mixture, scraping it off the bottom of the pot with a spatula. It should be thick, with a jammy consistency. Transfer the mixture to an airtight container and keep, refrigerated, for up to 1 week.

Almond and Kale Pesto

Prep time: 15 minutes | Cook time: 0 minutes | Makes about 1 cup

2 cups chopped kale leaves, rinsed well and stemmed
½ cup toasted almonds
2 garlic cloves
3 tablespoons extra-virgin olive oil
2 teaspoons lemon zest

3 tablespoons freshly squeezed lemon juice
1 teaspoon salt
½ teaspoon freshly ground black pepper
¼ teaspoon red pepper flakes

Place all the ingredients in a food processor and pulse until smoothly puréed. It tastes great with the eggs, salads, soup, pasta, cracker, and sandwiches.

Mushroom Broth with Carrot
Prep time: 10 minutes | Cook time: 43 minutes | Makes 9 cups

2 ounces (57 g) dried mushrooms (shiitake, porcini, or a combination)
1 pound (454 g) fresh mushrooms (any variety), diced
1 large yellow onion, roughly chopped
2 carrots, unpeeled and roughly chopped
6 garlic cloves, smashed

1 cup dry red wine (such as Pinot Noir)
3 bay leaves
6 to 8 sprigs fresh thyme
1 teaspoon whole black peppercorns
¼ cup reduced-sodium tamari or soy sauce
8 cups water
¼ teaspoon kosher salt

Place the dried mushrooms in a large bowl and submerge in warm water. Soak while preparing the other ingredients (for about 20 minutes). Drain the mushrooms. Select the Sauté setting on the Instant Pot and after a few minutes, add the diced fresh mushrooms and onion. In order to prevent burning, stir frequently until the mushrooms begin releasing their liquid. Cook until the vegetables are softened and the mushrooms have reduced in size, 6 to 7 minutes. Add the carrots, garlic, and wine. Cook, stirring, occasionally, until the liquid has mostly evaporated and the smell of alcohol has dissipated, 4 to 6 minutes. Add the drained reconstituted mushrooms, bay leaves, thyme sprigs, peppercorns, tamari, water, and the salt. Stir to combine. Select the Cancel setting. Secure the lid and set the Pressure Release to Sealing. Select the Pressure Cook setting at High Pressure and set the cook time to 30 minutes. Once the 30 minute timer has completed and beeps, allow a natural pressure release for 15 minutes and then switch the Pressure Release knob from Sealing to Venting to release any remaining steam. Open the pot and, using oven mitts, remove the inner pot. Carefully strain the mushroom broth into a fine-mesh sieve set over a large bowl and discard the solids. Allow the mushroom broth to cool to room temperature. Store in the refrigerator for 3 to 4 days or in the freezer for 3 months.

Tomato Red Sauce with Basil
Prep time: 10 minutes | Cook time: 20 minutes | Makes 4 to 4½ cups

1 small butternut squash, peeled and cubed (2 to 3 cups)
2 medium or 3 small tomatoes, quartered
2 garlic cloves, peeled
¼ to ½ cup water (not necessary if your tomatoes are juicy)
4 ounces (113 g) tomato paste
1 bay leaf

1 teaspoon salt
½ teaspoon freshly ground black pepper
¼ teaspoon baking soda
Pinch red pepper flakes
½ cup fresh sweet basil leaves, torn
1 to 2 tablespoons fresh Italian parsley leaves

In your Instant Pot, combine the squash, tomatoes, garlic, and water (if using). Top with the tomato paste, bay leaf, salt, pepper, baking soda, and red pepper flakes. There is no need to stir. Lock the lid and turn the steam release handle to Sealing. Using the Manual function, set the Instant Pot to High Pressure for 20 minutes (17 minutes at sea level). When the cook time is complete, let the pressure release naturally for 10 to 15 minutes; quick release any remaining pressure. Carefully remove the lid. Let the sauce cool for a few minutes (use mitts or tongs to remove the inner pot). Discard the bay leaf, and add the basil and parsley. Using an immersion blender, blend the sauce until smooth.

Quick White Rice
Prep time: 5 minutes | Cook time: 3 minutes | Serves 4

1 cup long-grain white rice
1 cup water

¼ teaspoon kosher salt

In the pot of the pressure cooker or in a fine-mesh strainer, rinse the rice several times until the water seems less chalky. Drain well. Add the rice, water, and salt to the pressure cooker. Stir to combine and scrape down any loose grains of rice into the liquid. Lock on the lid and set the timer for 3 minutes at High Pressure. When the timer goes off, natural release for 10 minutes, then quick release any remaining pressure. Remove the lid and stir the rice with a fork to fluff. If any water remains, cover the cooker and let the rice sit for 5 minutes until the water is absorbed.

Lemon Sour Cream with Cashew
Prep time: 5 minutes | Cook time: 0 minutes | Serves 4 to 6

1 cup raw cashews, soaked in water overnight, drained, and rinsed well
Juice of 1 lemon, plus more as needed
1½ teaspoons apple cider

vinegar
¼ cup nondairy milk, plus more as needed
½ teaspoon salt, plus more as needed

In a blender, combine the cashews, lemon juice, milk, vinegar, and salt. Blend until completely smooth. Taste and add more salt or lemon juice as desired. If you want a thinner cream, add a little more milk. Keep refrigerated in an airtight container for 4 to 6 days.

Carrot Butter with Miso
Prep time: 5 minutes | Cook time: 6 minutes | Makes 2 cups

1 pound (454 g) carrots (about 6 carrots)
½ cup low-sodium vegetable broth
3½ tablespoons white or yellow miso paste
1½ tablespoons pure maple syrup

3½ tablespoons coconut oil, melted
½ teaspoon ground ginger or 1 teaspoon finely grated or minced fresh ginger
Freshly cracked black pepper to taste

Peel and dice the carrots into ½-inch pieces. You should end up with 3 to 3½ cups carrots. Place the carrots in the Instant Pot and add the vegetable broth. Secure the lid and set the Pressure Release to Sealing. Select the Steam setting at High Pressure and set the cook time to 3 minutes. Once the 3 minute timer has completed and beeps, perform a quick pressure release by carefully switching the Pressure Release knob from Sealing to Venting. Open the pot. There will be some vegetable broth remaining. Don't drain this liquid, as it will help bring the butter together. If you are using an immersion blender, leave the carrots and cooking liquid in the pot and add the miso, maple syrup, coconut oil, ground ginger, and pepper to taste. Blend all of the ingredients together until you have a smooth and spreadable texture. This process will take 2 to 3 minutes. If you are using a food processor, transfer the carrots and the cooking liquid to a food processor and add the miso, maple syrup, coconut oil, ginger, and pepper. Blend until you have a completely smooth puree. Store the miso butter in an airtight container in the fridge for up to 1 week.

Cashew Dipping Sauce

Prep time: 10 minutes | Cook time: 0 minutes | Makes 1 cup

¾ cup cashews, soaked in water for at least 4 hours and drained
Juice and zest of 1 lemon
¼ cup water

2 tablespoons chopped fresh dill
¼ teaspoon salt, plus additional as needed

Blend the cashew, lemon juice and zest, and water in a blender until smooth and creamy. Fold in the dill and salt and blend again. Taste and add additional salt as needed. Transfer to the refrigerator to chill for at least 1 hour to blend the flavors. This dip perfectly goes with the crackers or tacos. It also can be used as a sauce for roasted vegetables or a sandwich spread.

Dijon-Honey Vinaigrette

Prep time: 5 minutes | Cook time: 0 minutes | Makes about 6 tablespoons

¼ cup extra-virgin olive oil
1 garlic clove, minced
2 tablespoons freshly squeezed lemon juice

1 teaspoon Dijon mustard
½ teaspoon raw honey
¼ teaspoon salt
¼ teaspoon dried basil

Place all the ingredients in a mason jar. Cover and shake vigorously until thoroughly mixed and well emulsified. Serve chilled.

Lime-Peanut Dressing

Prep time: 5 minutes | Cook time: 0 minutes | Serves 8

1 cup lite coconut milk
¼ cup freshly squeezed lime juice
¼ cup creamy peanut butter
2 tablespoons low-sodium soy

sauce or tamari
3 garlic cloves, minced
1 tablespoon grated fresh ginger

Place all the ingredients in a food processor or blender and process until completely mixed and smooth. It's delicious served over grilled chicken or tossed with noodles and green onions.

Basil Cashew Pesto

Prep time: 10 minutes | Cook time: 0 minutes | Makes 1 cup

¼ cup raw cashews
Juice of 1 lemon
2 garlic cloves
⅓ red onion (about 2 ounces / 56 g in total)

1 tablespoon olive oil
4 cups basil leaves, packed
1 cup wheatgrass
¼ cup water
¼ teaspoon salt

Put the cashews in a heatproof bowl and add boiling water to cover. Soak for 5 minutes and then drain. Put all ingredients in a blender and blend for 2 to 3 minutes or until fully combined.

Appendix 1 Measurement Conversion Chart

VOLUME EQUIVALENTS(DRY)

US STANDARD	METRIC (APPROXIMATE)
1/8 teaspoon	0.5 mL
1/4 teaspoon	1 mL
1/2 teaspoon	2 mL
3/4 teaspoon	4 mL
1 teaspoon	5 mL
1 tablespoon	15 mL
1/4 cup	59 mL
1/2 cup	118 mL
3/4 cup	177 mL
1 cup	235 mL
2 cups	475 mL
3 cups	700 mL
4 cups	1 L

VOLUME EQUIVALENTS(LIQUID)

US STANDARD	US STANDARD (OUNCES)	METRIC (APPROXIMATE)
2 tablespoons	1 fl.oz.	30 mL
1/4 cup	2 fl.oz.	60 mL
1/2 cup	4 fl.oz.	120 mL
1 cup	8 fl.oz.	240 mL
1 1/2 cup	12 fl.oz.	355 mL
2 cups or 1 pint	16 fl.oz.	475 mL
4 cups or 1 quart	32 fl.oz.	1 L
1 gallon	128 fl.oz.	4 L

TEMPERATURES EQUIVALENTS

FAHRENHEIT(F)	CELSIUS(C) (APPROXIMATE)
225 °F	107 °C
250 °F	120 °C
275 °F	135 °C
300 °F	150 °C
325 °F	160 °C
350 °F	180 °C
375 °F	190 °C
400 °F	205 °C
425 °F	220 °C
450 °F	235 °C
475 °F	245 °C
500 °F	260 °C

WEIGHT EQUIVALENTS

US STANDARD	METRIC (APPROXIMATE)
1 ounce	28 g
2 ounces	57 g
5 ounces	142 g
10 ounces	284 g
15 ounces	425 g
16 ounces (1 pound)	455 g
1.5 pounds	680 g
2 pounds	907 g

Appendix 2 Instant Pot Cooking Timetable

Dried Beans, Legumes and Lentils		
Dried Beans and Legume	Dry (Minutes)	Soaked (Minutes)
Soy beans	25 – 30	20 – 25
Scarlet runner	20 – 25	10 – 15
Pinto beans	25 – 30	20 – 25
Peas	15 – 20	10 – 15
Navy beans	25 – 30	20 – 25
Lima beans	20 – 25	10 – 15
Lentils, split, yellow (moong dal)	15 – 18	N/A
Lentils, split, red	15 – 18	N/A
Lentils, mini, green (brown)	15 – 20	N/A
Lentils, French green	15 – 20	N/A
Kidney white beans	35 – 40	20 – 25
Kidney red beans	25 – 30	20 – 25
Great Northern beans	25 – 30	20 – 25
Pigeon peas	20 – 25	15 – 20
Chickpeas (garbanzo bean chickpeas)	35 – 40	20 – 25
Cannellini beans	35 – 40	20 – 25
Black-eyed peas	20 – 25	10 – 15
Black beans	20 – 25	10 – 15

Fish and Seafood		
Fish and Seafood	Fresh (minutes)	Frozen (minutes)
Shrimp or Prawn	1 to 2	2 to 3
Seafood soup or stock	6 to 7	7 to 9
Mussels	2 to 3	4 to 6
Lobster	3 to 4	4 to 6
Fish, whole (snapper, trout, etc.)	5 to 6	7 to 10
Fish steak	3 to 4	4 to 6
Fish fillet,	2 to 3	3 to 4
Crab	3 to 4	5 to 6

Fruits		
Fruits	Fresh (in Minutes)	Dried (in Minutes)
Raisins	N/A	4 to 5
Prunes	2 to 3	4 to 5
Pears, whole	3 to 4	4 to 6
Pears, slices or halves	2 to 3	4 to 5
Peaches	2 to 3	4 to 5
Apricots, whole or halves	2 to 3	3 to 4
Apples, whole	3 to 4	4 to 6
Apples, in slices or pieces	2 to 3	3 to 4

Meat			
Meat and Cuts	Cooking Time (minutes)	Meat and Cuts	Cooking Time (minutes)
Veal, roast	35 to 45	Duck, with bones, cut up	10 to 12
Veal, chops	5 to 8	Cornish Hen, whole	10 to 15
Turkey, drumsticks (leg)	15 to 20	Chicken, whole	20 to 25
Turkey, breast, whole, with bones	25 to 30	Chicken, legs, drumsticks, or thighs	10 to 15
Turkey, breast, boneless	15 to 20	Chicken, with bones, cut up	10 to 15
Quail, whole	8 to 10	Chicken, breasts	8 to 10
Pork, ribs	20 to 25	Beef, stew	15 to 20
Pork, loin roast	55 to 60	Beef, shanks	25 to 30
Pork, butt roast	45 to 50	Beef, ribs	25 to 30
Pheasant	20 to 25	Beef, steak, pot roast, round, rump, brisket or blade, small chunks, chuck,	25 to 30
Lamb, stew meat	10 to 15		
Lamb, leg	35 to 45	Beef, pot roast, steak, rump, round, chuck, blade or brisket, large	35 to 40
Lamb, cubes,	10 t0 15		
Ham slice	9 to 12	Beef, ox-tail	40 to 50
Ham picnic shoulder	25 to 30	Beef, meatball	10 to 15
Duck, whole	25 to 30	Beef, dressed	20 to 25

Vegetables (fresh/frozen)

Vegetable	Fresh (minutes)	Frozen (minutes)	Vegetable	Fresh (minutes)	Frozen (minutes)
Zucchini, slices or chunks	2 to 3	3 to 4	Mixed vegetables	2 to 3	3 to 4
Yam, whole, small	10 to 12	12 to 14	Leeks	2 to 4	3 to 5
Yam, whole, large	12 to 15	15 to 19	Greens (collards, beet greens, spinach,	3 to 6	4 to 7
Yam, in cubes	7 to 9	9 to 11	kale, turnip greens, swiss chard) chopped		
Turnip, chunks	2 to 4	4 to 6	Green beans, whole	2 to 3	3 to 4
Tomatoes, whole	3 to 5	5 to 7	Escarole, chopped	1 to 2	2 to 3
Tomatoes, in quarters	2 to 3	4 to 5	Endive	1 to 2	2 to 3
Sweet potato, whole, small	10 to 12	12 to 14	Eggplant, chunks or slices	2 to 3	3 to 4
Sweet potato, whole, large	12 to 15	15 to 19	Corn, on the cob	3 to 4	4 to 5
Sweet potato, in cubes	7 to 9	9 to 11	Corn, kernels	1 to 2	2 to 3
Sweet pepper, slices or chunks	1 to 3	2 to 4	Collard	4 to 5	5 to 6
Squash, butternut, slices or chunks	8 to 10	10 to 12	Celery, chunks	2 to 3	3 to 4
Squash, acorn, slices or chunks	6 to 7	8 to 9	Cauliflower flowerets	2 to 3	3 to 4
Spinach	1 to 2	3 to 4	Carrots, whole or chunked	2 to 3	3 to 4
Rutabaga, slices	3 to 5	4 to 6	Carrots, sliced or shredded	1 to 2	2 to 3
Rutabaga, chunks	4 to 6	6 to 8	Cabbage, red, purple or green, wedges	3 to 4	4 to 5
Pumpkin, small slices or chunks	4 to 5	6 to 7	Cabbage, red, purple or green, shredded	2 to 3	3 to 4
Pumpkin, large slices or chunks	8 to 10	10 to 14	Brussel sprouts, whole	3 to 4	4 to 5
Potatoes, whole, large	12 to 15	15 to 19	Broccoli, stalks	3 to 4	4 to 5
Potatoes, whole, baby	10 to 12	12 to 14	Broccoli, flowerets	2 to 3	3 to 4
Potatoes, in cubes	7 to 9	9 to 11	Beets, small roots, whole	11 to 13	13 to 15
Peas, in the pod	1 to 2	2 to 3	Beets, large roots, whole	20 to 25	25 to 30
Peas, green	1 to 2	2 to 3	Beans, green/yellow or wax,	1 to 2	2 to 3
Parsnips, sliced	1 to 2	2 to 3	whole, trim ends and strings		
Parsnips, chunks	2 to 4	4 to 6	Asparagus, whole or cut	1 to 2	2 to 3
Onions, sliced	2 to 3	3 to 4	Artichoke, whole, trimmed without leaves	9 to 11	11 to 13
Okra	2 to 3	3 to 4	Artichoke, hearts	4 to 5	5 to 6

Rice and Grains

Rice & Grain	Water Quantity (Grain: Water ratios)	Cooking Time (in Minutes)	Rice & Grain	Water Quantity (Grain: Water ratios)	Cooking Time (in Minutes)
Wheat berries	1:3	25 to 30	Oats, steel-cut	1:1	10
Spelt berries	1:3	15 to 20	Oats, quick cooking	1:1	6
Sorghum	1:3	20 to 25	Millet	1:1	10 to 12
Rice, wild	1:3	25 to 30	Kamut, whole	1:3	10 to 12
Rice, white	1:1.5	8	Couscous	1:2	5 to 8
Rice, Jasmine	1:1	4 to 10	Corn, dried, half	1:3	25 to 30
Rice, Brown	1:1.3	22 to 28	Congee, thin	1:6 ~ 1:7	15 to 20
Rice, Basmati	1:1.5	4 to 8	Congee, thick	1:4 ~ 1:5	15 to 20
Quinoa, quick cooking	1:2	8	Barley, pot	1:3 ~ 1:4	25 to 30
Porridge, thin	1:6 ~ 1:7	15 to 20	Barley, pearl	1:4	25 to 30

Appendix 3 Recipe Index

CPSIA information can be obtained
at www.ICGtesting.com
Printed in the USA
LVHW100329190321
681907LV00005B/131

9 781637 335420